Introducing the
New Sexuality Studies

Breaking new ground, both substantively and stylistically, the *Introducing the New Sexuality Studies, Second edition* offers students and academics an engaging thought-provoking introduction and overview of the social study of sexualities. Its central premise is to explore the social construction of sexuality, the role of social differences such as race or nationality in creating sexual variation, and the ways sex is entangled in relations of power and inequality. Through this approach the field of sexuality is considered in multicultural, global, and comparative terms, and from a truly social perspective.

The second edition of this definitive textbook consists of over seventy-five short, original essays on the key topics and themes in sexuality studies. It also includes interviews with fourteen leading scholars in the field, which convey some of the most innovative work currently being undertaken. Each contribution is original, presenting the latest thinking and research in clear and accessible terms, using engaging examples to illustrate key points.

Steven Seidman is a Professor of Sociology at the State University of New York at Albany. His books include *Romantic Longings: Love in America, 1830–1980* (Routledge, 1991), *Embattled Eros: Sexual Politics and Ethics in America* (Routledge, 1992), *Beyond the Closet* (Routledge, 2002), and *The Social Construction of Sexuality* (W. W. Norton & Co, 2003).

Nancy L. Fischer is an Associate Professor of Sociology, and the Director of Metro-Urban Studies at Augsburg College in Minneapolis, Minnesota. She is a former chair of the American Sociological Association's Section on Sexualities. She has written about incest, urban sustainability, and is currently working on a project on the social meaning of second hand and vintage clothing.

Chet Meeks was an Assistant Professor of Sociology at Georgia State University in Atlanta, Georgia. He was a queer theorist and taught courses in Sociology of Sexuality and Social Theory at Georgia State (and previously at Northern Illinois University). His published works include 'Civil Society and the Sexual Politics of Difference' published in *Sociological Theory* as well as the co-edited *Handbook of New Sexuality Studies* (Routledge, 2006). He passed away in 2008,

Introducing the New Sexuality Studies

Second Edition

Edited by *Steven Seidman, Nancy Fischer and Chet Meeks*

LONDON AND NEW YORK

First published 2011
by Routledge
2 Park Square, Milton Park, Abingdon, Oxon OX14 4RN

Simultaneously published in the USA and Canada
by Routledge
270 Madison Ave, New York, NY 10016

Routledge is an imprint of the Taylor & Francis Group, an informa business

British Library Cataloguing in Publication Data
A catalogue record for this book is available from the British Library

Library of Congress Cataloging in Publication Data
Introducing the new sexuality studies / edited by Steven Seidman, Nancy Fischer and Chet Meeks. – 2nd ed.
    p. cm.
    Previously published under title: New sexuality studies.
    1. Sex. 2. Sex–Social aspects. 3. Sexual orientation. 4. Sex and law. 5. Sexology. I. Seidman, Steven. II. Fischer, Nancy. III. Meeks, Chet. IV. New sexuality studies.
    HQ21.H3234 2011
    306.7–dc22

                    2010036791

ISBN 978-0-415-78125-1 (hbk)
ISBN 978-0-415-78156-8 (pbk)
ISBN 978-0-203-82983-7 (ebk)

Typeset in Bembo by
Taylor & Francis Books

This edition is dedicated to the memory of Chet Meeks,
our co-editor, co-contributor and dear friend.
We also dedicate this edition to the memory of Tamsin Wilton,
scholar, activist and contributor to this volume.
Their potential contributions to the study of sexualities is a true loss
to the field.

Contents

Contents

Contents

Contents

Acknowledgments

We would like to thank the authors who contributed to this volume for their commitment and the seriousness with which they approached their work. To be frank, we were overwhelmed by the positive response to this project and by the willingness of these authors to really work to get the right tone and theme. It has been deeply satisfying for each of us to work with authors who wrote thoughtful, very smart yet highly readable essays. We take this as a sign of the collective commitment to the idea of a new sexuality studies. A special thanks to Gerhard Boomgarden, our editor, for trusting our vision of a different kind of book.

General introduction

social constructionism

In the last few decades, there has been a revolution in the study of sexuality. Sex is today understood as fundamentally social. The aspects of sex that scholars – and ordinary folks – are most interested in, such as issues of desire, pleasure, identity, norms of sexual behavior, and intimate arrangements, are today recognized by the leading scholars in the field as social phenomena. This deep sociology of sexualities is what we call the new sexuality studies.

It wasn't too long ago that most Americans and Europeans viewed sexuality as natural. In America and Europe, scientists such as sexologists, psychologists, demographers, and medical researchers believed that sex was built into the body, into human genetics, hormones, into the very physiology of individuals. Humans were, it was assumed, born sexual. Just as nature programs humans to eat and sleep, humans were wired for sex. Humans were thought to be driven by a sexual instinct, a procreative gene, or a maternal drive to reproduce and rear children. While many of us still believe this to be true, the new social studies of sexuality have challenged the idea of sex as natural.

Initially, this new social perspective on sexuality was advanced by social activists. Feminists challenged a conventional wisdom that assumed a natural division between men and women that extended into their sexualities. It was widely assumed that men's sexuality is naturally genital-centered, pleasure-oriented, and aggressive in ways that express a masculine gender identity. By contrast, women's sexuality was said to be oriented to intimacy and relationship-building, diffusely erotic, and passive or other-directed in a way that reflected a feminine gender identity.

Against this naturalistic view of gender and sexuality, feminists argued that society, not nature, creates gender and sexual differences. In particular, feminists argued that women's sexuality is socially shaped in ways that sustain men's social and political dominance. For example, the view of women's sexuality as being oriented to pleasing men or driven by a maternal instinct reinforced the idea that women's appropriate social role should be that of wife and mother. In fact, as women have gained social and economic independence in the decades after the 1960s, they have also claimed control over their own bodies and sexualities. Today, as women have more choices, their sexualities are more openly varied. Some women still approach sexuality as a means to reproduction or as a way to gain intimacy, but other women look to sex for sensual pleasure, or want intimacy but not marriage or children. In short, women's sexuality, like men's, is not fixed by nature but shaped by social forces and circumstances, by factors such as economic independence, social values, peers, or family culture.

Alongside the women's movement, there developed a lesbian and gay movement. Lesbian and gay activists challenged a society that declared heterosexuality and heterosexuals to be natural and normal while homosexuality and homosexuals were stigmatized as unnatural and abnormal. This belief has had powerful social consequences. It contributed to making heterosexuality into a social norm and ideal, while often criminalizing and polluting homosexuality.

Individuals, who were labeled homosexual, were subject to discrimination, punishment, harassment, and sometimes violence and imprisonment.

Gay and lesbian activists not only protested against laws and practices of discrimination, but challenged the idea that nature produces two distinct human types or social identities: heterosexuals and homosexuals. Some activists argued that it is society that creates the idea of sexual identities or roles. Why? By stigmatizing and criminalizing homosexuality, heterosexuality is made into the only right way to be sexual and to organize families. Furthermore, some activists argued that a norm of heterosexuality reinforces a gender order that not only emphasizes gender difference but privileges men.

Historians and other scholars have since documented that, while there has always been heterosexual and homosexual behavior, there has not always been "heterosexuals" and "homosexuals" as human types or sexual identities. For example, in nineteenth-century America, homosexuality was viewed as a behavior, typically a criminal behavior punishable as an act of "sodomy." But sodomy included not only homosexual acts but a wide range of non-procreative, non-marital sexual acts such as fornication, oral genital sex, and bestiality. It was only in twentieth-century America that homosexuality was understood as indicating a social and sexual identity. It was, of course, initially constructed as a dangerous and abnormal identity, in contrast to a normal heterosexual identity. The point we want to underscore is this: it was only in the early decades of the twentieth century in America that sexuality became the basis of a social identity. This fact underscores the historical and social character of sexuality.

Feminists and gay and lesbian activists developed the beginnings of a social view of sexuality as part of their politics. But the activists were soon followed by the scholars. By the 1970s, sociologists were also beginning to view sex as social. Sociological researchers were studying the social patterns of heterosexuality, marriage, reproduction, and dating. Researchers highlighted the role of social forces such as gender, religion, occupation, and the role of peers in shaping variations in patterns of sexual behavior. And, some sociologists were fashioning labeling perspectives on homosexuality.

However, both activists and sociologists of the 1960s and 1970s had a limited view of the social character of sexuality. While they spotlighted the role of social forces in shaping patterns of sexual behavior and norms, their sociological analysis did not extend into the social making of sexual bodies, desires, acts, pleasures, and identities. These social researchers assumed an already sexualized body, assumed a natural landscape of sexual acts and pleasures.

The new sexuality studies raise questions that were not addressed, or even posed, earlier. For example, how is it that certain body parts become sexualized? In this regard, what social forces explain why the clitoris was not viewed as a sexual organ until the 1960s, at least in the United States and in many European societies? Or, what social changes help to explain the recent emergence of "anal sex" as a legitimate erotic pleasure? The new sexuality studies understand sexual identities as historically emergent. Homosexuality, as we've seen, was not always a sexual identity, and, even in societies where it serves as an identity, its meaning can vary and change. For example, "lesbian" may indicate a sexual orientation or identity, or a political standpoint against male dominance. Today, in the United States and the United Kingdom, "gay" may signal a master identity or a secondary identity or, as in many European nations, a behavior but not an identity. And new sexual identities may emerge, such as a bisexual or an S/M identity.

The new sexuality studies perspective does not deny the biological aspects of sexuality. There would be no sexuality without bodies. However, it is social forces which determine which organs and orifices become "sexual," how such organs and orifices may be used or expressed, their social and moral meaning, which desires and acts become the basis of identities, and what social norms regulate behavior and intimacies. It is this deep view of sex as social that we hope to convey in this volume.

Part 1
Sex as a social fact

Introduction

There have always been homosexuals. Just as nature produces heterosexuals, so it produces homosexuals. And homosexuals are different from heterosexuals – sexually, psychologically, and socially. In other words, heterosexuals and homosexuals are two different human or social types. *These statements are widely believed by many people across the globe.*

However, scholars have questioned these beliefs. True enough, there have always been individuals who desire individuals of the same sex. There are men who sexually prefer men and women who sexually prefer women. But these individuals may experience their sexuality very differently depending on the *meaning* and social *organization* of same-sex sexuality. If homosexuality is understood as a personal and social identity, especially a deviant identity, the experience of homosexuality will be very different than if it is understood as just a desire or behavior. In the former case, the individual may be viewed as a danger to society. This person might be stigmatized and driven to the margins of society or even forced to exit society. If homosexuality is viewed as a behavior, even a criminal behavior, the behavior, not the individual, will be punished. Homosexual behavior will be treated like any other legal violation such as drinking under age, adultery, or prostitution. In nineteenth century America, same-sex behavior was treated the same as fornication, adultery or bestiality – as a minor criminal violation.

In fact, we now know that the idea of a homosexual identity only appears late in history, and only in some societies. Even today, as the chapters on homosexuality in Denmark and the Netherlands show, being gay or lesbian is not an identity in those nations like it is in the US or the UK.

One of the pioneers of a social perspective on sexuality and homosexuality is the British sociologist Jeffrey Weeks. His research suggests that it was in the late nineteenth century in the US and Europe that the idea of homosexuality as an identity initially emerged. And this new identity was a creation of a new science of sexuality that was created by sexologists and psychologists who classified sexual behaviors into sexual types or identities. Weeks's research, along with the work of many others, made possible new studies in the history and sociology of all aspects of sexuality. While his research is historical, other sociologists have used interviews or surveys to examine the social patterns of sexuality. In one of the largest national surveys ever done in the United States, Edward Laumann and his colleagues charted the changing sexual

1

habits of Americans. One of the more interesting findings was how little change occurred in the last few decades. Differences between men's and women's sexuality remain strong, sexual dysfunction continues to plague Americans, and finding intimate happiness in marriage remains a compelling motivation. Yet there is a new frankness about sexual talk, especially about dysfunctions, and these researchers discovered a big divide between younger and older generations in terms of their sexual attitudes and behaviors. This generational divide suggests potentially significant change in the future.

Although sociologists have been innovators in the new sexuality studies, other social approaches have been equally important. For example, Marxists have underscored the role of the economy and class differences in shaping sexual desires, identities, and patterns of behavior. Marxists remind us that social class is expressed in intimate behaviors. As a simple illustration, we would expect lower divorce rates among blue-collar couples because of reduced financial flexibility. Similarly, feminists have pointed to the social role of gender in the dynamics of sexual patterns. They force us to confront the ways men and women differ in their sexual values, behaviors, and approaches to intimacy due to differences in their social roles. For example, sexual pleasure for women carries unique dangers associated with pregnancy and violence. In general, men, at least in contemporary America and in many European societies, rely heavily on their sexual prowess for their sense of gender identity. Women seem to value sex more as a building block of emotional intimacy. In addition to Marxist and feminist social approaches, recently there have developed perspectives that focus on the role of scientific knowledges, medical experts, and popular culture in shaping sexual meanings, norms and behaviors. So, in order for homosexuality to be viewed as a social identity, this idea has to be circulated throughout society by means of popular and scientific-medical culture.

In this part, you'll be introduced to different social perspectives on sexuality. These should not be seen as mutually exclusive; rather, they are conceptual resources that can help you to understand the complexities of sexual meanings and practices. You'll be treated to interviews with two leading researchers in the sociology of sexuality. You'll learn not only about their social research but something of the political and moral motivations of their sociology of sexuality.

Theoretical perspectives

Steven Seidman

STATE UNIVERSITY OF NEW YORK, ALBANY

What is the relationship between sex and society? Beginning with sexologists who propose a view of sex as fundamentally biological, I review various social approaches to understanding sexuality. I take for granted the belief that there is a biological basis for human impulses, drives, and desires. However, it is social forces that fashion a biological reality into "sexuality." Individuals and groups give meaning to bodily sensations and feelings, make erotic acts into sexual identities, and create norms distinguishing between acceptable and unacceptable sexualities.

Sexology: a natural order of sexuality

Why do many of us in America and Europe view sexuality as natural? One reason is the development of a science of sexuality. In the late nineteenth and early twentieth centuries, there developed a science aimed at discovering the laws of sexuality. This science has come to be called sexology.

Who are the sexologists? Among the more famous are Richard von Krafft-Ebing, Havelock Ellis, and Magnus Hirschfeld. While few of us today have heard of these nineteenth-century pioneers of sexology, many of us have heard of Alfred Kinsey or of Masters and Johnson. Sexologists have produced a body of knowledge that has influenced the way many of us think about sex, in part because their ideas have been stamped with the imprimatur of science.

What are the key ideas of sexology? First, sexology claims that humans are born with a sexual nature, and that sexuality is part of the biological makeup of all individuals. Second, sexology views sexuality as being at the core of what it means to be human: our sexual drive is no less basic than our need to eat or sleep. Sexuality is said to be basic to who we are. Third, sexuality is viewed as a powerful and driving force in our behavior. It influences all aspects of our lives, from the physical to the psychological. It motivates much of human behavior. Fourth, sexology states that the sexual instinct is, by nature, heterosexual. There is said to be a natural attraction between men and women. While few sexologists today believe that the chief purpose of sexuality is to procreate, they continue to think that heterosexuality is the natural and normal form of sexuality.

Sexologists aim to discover the laws of sexuality. Just as physics and biology distrust inherited ideas and test them in experiments, sexology has championed a vigorously scientific approach.

Facts, not beliefs, are to guide this science. The truth of sexuality is to be discovered by means of the "case study" method. Like physicians or psychiatrists, sexologists use intensive interviews and observation to uncover the true nature of sexuality. The details of human sexual desires, fantasies, and practices are recorded for the purpose of revealing the laws of the sexual instinct. Sexologists develop elaborate classifications of sexual types and detail the range of normal and abnormal forms of sexuality.

Sexology has always had a social purpose. In the nineteenth and early twentieth centuries, some sexologists sought to expand tolerance for different forms of human sexuality by emphasizing that sexuality is natural. Other sexologists saw their work as a way to contribute to creating a healthy, fit population. Often this meant that sexology was aligned to a belief in racial purity and improvement. Some sexologists even discouraged the sexual intermingling of races.

As racist ideas lost favor during the twentieth century, sexology has often been allied to a mission of strengthening the institutions of marriage and the family. Sexologists have argued that sex is at the core of love and marriage, and that a stable happy marriage requires a mutually satisfying sexual relationship. Individuals should not be burdened by guilt; they must be sexually knowledgeable and skilled. Sexology has aimed to make sexually enlightened and skillful citizens who would marry and stay married, in part because of a mutually satisfying sex life.

While their writings are sometimes technical and often tedious, sexologists have shaped Western sexual culture. Their ideas about the naturalness of sexuality have been popularized by an army of sex advice writers. Many of us believe in the idea of a natural sexuality because of the sexologists.

Freud: between biology and sociology

Alongside sexology, the discipline of psychology has been the source of many of our ideas about sex. In particular, Freud, the founder of psychoanalysis, has been probably the single most influential thinker in shaping Western sexual culture.

Freud aimed to uncover the roots of human psychology in our sex drives. Freud accepted many of the ideas of the sexologists. He believed in the biological basis of sexuality and insisted that sexuality is at the root of many of our feelings and actions. Freud also thought that there is a normal course of sexual development and there are abnormal or perverse forms of sexuality. The defining feature of sexual abnormality was deviation from genital-centered, intercourse-oriented heterosexuality based on love and monogamy.

But Freud also disagreed with the sexologists. Whereas sexologists defined the sexual instinct as reproductive and naturally heterosexual, Freud argued that the sexual instinct is oriented to pleasure. Moreover, humans get pleasure not only from sexual intercourse, but also from kissing, touching, caressing, looking, and sometimes dominating and being dominated. Freud argued that the body has many erotic areas and there are many ways of experiencing sexual satisfaction. Accordingly, he held that nongenital pleasures are not necessarily abnormal. It is normal, for example, to enjoy the range of pleasures that are today called foreplay.

Viewing the sexual instinct as a drive for pleasure blurs the line between normal and abnormal. To most sexologists, any sexual expression that deviated from a heterosexual reproductive aim was abnormal. However, Freud allows for a wide range of normal sexual expression beyond heterosexual reproduction. Pursuing nonprocreative pleasures is not in itself abnormal; sex drives become abnormal only when they are fixated on one specific sex act or pleasure. For example, it is normal for individuals to feel pleasure from looking at someone or from kissing and touching. It is abnormal, though, when these pleasures replace heterosexual intercourse.

Freud was convinced that sex is at the core of the self. It is, he thought, the drive for erotic pleasure that places the individual in conflict with social norms of respectability and self-control. Sexuality is then a major focus of psychological and social conflict. The psychological character of the individual rests on how the sex drive is managed. Too much sexual expression leads to psychological and social instability. Excessive social control results in psychosexual frustration that brings personal unhappiness.

Freud held to a much deeper social understanding of sexuality than the sexologists. If the sexual instinct is somewhat flexible in its purpose, it is society that shapes its form and meaning. In particular, the family is the formative social environment shaping our psyches and sexualities. Our psychological and sexual selves take shape as we struggle with the conflict between a drive for sexual pleasure and the social expectation to be productive, responsible citizens.

Marxism: the economics of sexuality

The ideas of the sexologists and psychologists have established important traditions in thinking about sex. However, they emphasize the natural, biological roots of sexuality. They have little to say about how social forces such as religion, the state, or the economy actually form biological impulses into sexual desires, create sexual identities, and establish rules and norms that regulate our sexual behavior.

In the twentieth century, *new social ways of thinking about sex* appeared. We will review some of the chief social theoretical perspectives that continue to influence the sociology of sexuality.

We begin with Karl Marx. Now, Marx himself had little to say about sex, but he was a great social thinker. One of his key insights was that human nature, including our sexuality, is shaped by society and changes historically.

Marxists argue that the economy is the most important social force shaping human behavior. Consider the way a capitalist economy shapes sexuality. Capitalism is oriented toward profit and economic growth. Marx believed that profit is based on exploiting labor, and growth occurs by reinvesting profits back into an enterprise. Marxists distinguish two phases of capitalist development in Europe and the United States. A market-based capitalism was dominant throughout the nineteenth century; since the early twentieth century, capitalism has been shaped by large corporations.

In the market phase, the chief challenge is to produce enough goods to meet the needs of the population. The answer: a disciplined labor force must be created. Individuals must adapt to the rhythms of a system of mass production that progressively strips work of individual imagination and skill. Ideally, capitalists would like to see laborers become machine-like. Anything that interferes with maximizing production, such as emotional or erotic feelings, is an impediment to efficient production. In other words, capitalists try to desexualize the work process and the body of laborers.

Business owners too must learn to avoid personal indulgence in order to remain competitive. While capitalists may flag their class status by acts of conspicuous consumption, their lives are fraught with anxiety. The market is unpredictable, and competitors threaten to take away their own and their family's livelihood. This drives capitalists to become economically and socially disciplined.

In a market economy, a repressed personality type is prominent. This kind of person is performance- and success-oriented and exercises tight internal controls over emotions and sensual desires. To this type of person, sexual impulses and desires are potentially disruptive of discipline; sexuality needs to be rigidly controlled. Accordingly, in market economies the pressures of industrial production and discipline shape a sexual culture that values self-control and the avoidance of sensual pleasure.

In the market economies of the nineteenth century, a sexual culture takes shape organized around procreation in marriage. Sex that is oriented to pleasure, sex outside marriage, autoerotic sex, sex in public, all nonheterosexual sex, and nongenital sex, were viewed as deviant. These sexualities were at odds with capitalism's need for disciplined, productive workers.

In the twentieth century, the corporation replaced the small business as the major economic institution. This development brought about changes in modern sexual culture. New technologies and a scientific approach to the labor process created a new problem: how to ensure that the vast sea of goods being produced would be consumed?

Many corporations looked to expand the domestic market. They brought commerce into areas of daily life such as leisure, recreation, and entertainment. For example, every aspect of sports, from clothes and equipment to games, has gradually been commercialized. Capitalists also tried to convince individuals to consume more goods. But how does this shift to consumption affect sexuality?

Marxists argue that the new consumer economy weakens the Victorian culture and its emphasis on privacy, self-control, and the desexualization of the body and intimacy. In the process of creating higher levels of consumption, advertising gains a new importance. Sex is used to sell commodities; the public realm is now filled with images and talk of sex.

The commercialization of sex challenged Victorian culture in another way: capitalism places a new value on sex as a source of pleasure. As sex is used to sell goods and sex businesses flourish (porn, sex toys, phone sex), sex is no longer just a procreative or loving act, but a form of pleasure and self-expression. From a Marxist perspective, business owners want one thing: to make money by selling their goods. If sex can be marketed as pleasure or as an authentic form of self-expression or identity, then sex becomes a valuable marketing resource.

Corporate capitalism promotes a view of sex as a basis of self-fulfillment. To most Marxists, however, this pleasure-oriented sexual culture does not promote real sexual freedom. A culture that celebrates a superficial drive for pleasure leads to an aimless, unhappy search for gratification. Moreover, with its focus on sexual performance, sex has come to resemble work; accordingly, it has lost much of its tender, intimate, and caring qualities. Finally, Marxists argue that, as we search for personal happiness, the gross inequalities between rich and poor go unchallenged. There can be no real sexual freedom until there is real individual freedom, which is impossible under capitalism.

Feminism: the gender of sexuality

Feminism offers an equally forceful social view of sexuality. Feminists challenge Marxists. They point out that all of us step into the world as men or women, regardless of the economic system. Our gender identity is not a superficial part of our lives, but shapes the personal and social aspects of our lives in important ways. Feminists view gender as a social identity and a set of norms that guide behavior. We are not born men or women but acquire these gender identities through a social process of learning and sometimes coercion. Feminists believe that our sexual desires, feelings, and preferences are imprinted by gender.

Feminists say that individuals acquire a sexual nature as they develop a gender identity. What exactly is the relationship between gender and sexuality?

In *The Reproduction of Mothering*, Nancy Chodorow argues that when women do the chief parenting work, gender patterns of sexual and individual development are different. For both boys and girls, the mother is often the primary source of love. However, girls sustain an intimacy with their mothers throughout their maturation; boys separate from their mothers at an early age in order to learn to be men. This difference shapes the psychosexual character of girls and boys.

The extended and intense intimacy between mothers and daughters results in girls developing a psyche that is relationship-oriented. Accordingly, girls tend to connect sex with intimacy and as a means of caring. They often approach sex more as a means of communication and intimacy than as a vehicle of erotic pleasure. Because boys typically break sharply from their mothers at an early age, and identify with their achievement-oriented fathers, they are more performance- and goal-oriented. Boys' sexuality tends to be more performance- and body-oriented. Boys can be intimate, but they will likely express sexual love in terms of the giving and receiving of erotic pleasure.

Chodorow's perspective is important because she holds that the family plays a crucial role in the making of the sexual self. Also, she says that boys and girls develop different sexual values and orientations.

Adrienne Rich also believes that gender dynamics creates sexual differences between men and women. She emphasizes the social creation of heterosexual men and women. In "Compulsive Heterosexuality and Lesbian Existence" she argues that we are all taught and coerced into adopting conventional gender identities. Why? Gender difference, Rich says, reinforces a society organized around the norm of heterosexuality. Shaping individuals into heterosexual men and women is a complex social process. Societies use positive inducements like economic rewards or a culture that romanticizes heterosexuality, but also resorts to ridicule, harassment, and violence to punish gender nonconformists and nonheterosexuals. The belief that heterosexuality is normal and natural plays a key role in creating heterosexual men and women. For example, many Europeans and Americans believe that there is a natural attraction between the sexes, that their bodies and minds "naturally" fit. Heterosexuality is then viewed as an extension of a natural order composed of two complementary sexes.

Catherine MacKinnon insists on the role of male dominance in shaping women's sexuality. She views sexuality as a product of men's power; sex is a means by which men control women. Indeed, it is the very basis of male domination. To the extent that men have the power to define what desires, feelings, and behaviors are sexual, they can define women's sexuality in a way that positions them as subordinate. For example, in male-dominated America, women's sexuality is supposed to be oriented to vaginal intercourse in marriage with the ultimate aim of procreation. This view defines women as heterosexual, or needing men, and as motivated to become wives and mothers, and therefore dependent on men.

Feminists like Rich and MacKinnon claim that the very essence of sexuality expresses men's wish for dominance. Every sexual desire and behavior in male-dominated societies is said to be related to gender dynamics, and either expresses men's dominance or women's resistance. From this perspective, feminists criticize the notion that women's sexual liberation is about claiming the right to pleasure or the freedom to do as one pleases, an approach that expresses men's view of sexual freedom. Instead, women's sexual liberation involves fashioning a sexual life that reflects their own needs, feelings, and desires. The point is not to liberate sexuality from social control, which could lead to more violence or unwanted pregnancy, but to claim the power to define one's own sexual desires and forge sexual-intimate lives.

Some feminists, like the anthropologist Gayle Rubin, have objected to the view that sexuality is a direct expression of gender politics. She argues that this perspective ignores considerable variation within women's and men's sexuality. Rubin believes that sexuality is connected to gender, yet also has its own dynamics.

In "Thinking Sex," Rubin makes the case that sex is fundamentally about erotic desires, fantasies, acts, identities, and politics – none of which are reducible to gender dynamics. She argues that all societies create sexual hierarchies that establish boundaries between good and bad or legitimate and illicit sexualities. Societies value specific desires, acts, and identities as normal, respectable, good, healthy, and moral; other forms of sexuality are classified as unhealthy, abnormal, sinful, and immoral. Society supports and privileges the "normal and good" forms of sexuality and aims to punish the "abnormal and bad" ones through law, violence, ridicule, or stigma. These sexual hierarchies create a series of outsider sexualites. This system of sexual regulation applies to both men and women. American society considers heterosexuality, monogamy, marriage, and reproductive sex to be considered good and normal; S/M (sadomasochism) and multiple-partner sex, commercial and public sex are defined and treated as bad. There are of course many sexualities that fall somewhere in between – for example, promiscuous heterosexuals or gays and lesbians in long-term monogamous relationships. It may be less socially acceptable for a woman to have multiple sex partners or to engage in S/M because of a gender order that associates femininity with purity and maternal feelings; still, these behaviors are disparaged by both men and women. Those who engage in such behaviors, regardless of gender, will be stigmatized and subject to a range of sanctions, from ridicule to criminalization. Rubin's point is simply that gender influences patterns of sexuality, but there is still a great deal about the organization and dynamics of sexuality that cannot be viewed solely through the lens of gender.

Sociology

Since the early decades of the twentieth century, sociologists have researched the role of religion, gender, class, race, and social values in shaping patterns of premarital, marital, and extramarital sex. In the 1960s and 1970s, Ira Reiss charted cultural and behavioral shifts among American youth as a sexual morality that associated sex exclusively with marriage transformed into one that permitted sex in a context of affection. Reiss believed that this cultural change was related to women's growing economic and social power. In this regard, he observed the decline of a double standard that permitted men to have sex outside of marriage, while labeling women who engaged in the same behavior as "bad girls."

Some sociologists urged a full-blown sociology of sexuality. John Gagnon and William Simon proposed a "script" theory of sexuality. Instead of understanding humans as born sexual, they argued that sexuality is socially learned. In the course of growing up, society teaches us what feelings and desires count as sexual and what the appropriate "scripts" for sexual behavior are. Sexual scripts tell us with whom we're supposed to have sex (based on age, race, or class), where, when, and what it means when we do. Gagnon and Simon were in effect saying that sexuality is not an inborn property, but a product of social labeling.

The British sociologist, Ken Plummer, developed a labeling perspective on sex. In *Sexual Stigma*, he argued that individuals aren't born homosexual, but learn to be homosexual. An individual may feel desire or attraction to people of the same sex, but he or she must learn that these feelings are sexual and that they indicate a homosexual identity. People learn this in the course of interacting with both the straight and gay world. For example, a high-school student hearing derogatory comments about "fags" and "dykes" begins to associate homosexuality with a stigmatized identity. This same individual may eventually be exposed to a gay subculture, which champions a view of homosexuality as natural and good.

One of the pioneers of a sociological approach to sexuality was the British sociologist Jeffrey Weeks. He introduced the ideas of essentialism and constructionism. Essentialism is the notion that sexuality is a basic and essential part of being human. Constructionism states that sexuality is a product of social forces. Weeks proposed a strong view of the social character of sexuality: "First, we can no longer set 'sex' against 'society' as if they were separate domains. Secondly, there is a widespread recognition of the social variability of sexual forms, beliefs, ideologies, and behavior. Sexuality has … many histories. … Thirdly, we must learn to see that sexuality is something which society produces in complex ways. It is a result of diverse social practices that give meaning to human activities, to struggles between those who have power to define and regulate, and those who resist. Sexuality is not given, it is a product of negotiation, struggle."

Gay and lesbian studies

Paralleling the rise of a gay movement, many advocates argued that some people are just born homosexual. If homosexuals have always existed, it is a natural status and therefore they should not be punished.

However, this view has been challenged by the new gay/lesbian studies. These new scholars assume that homosexual behavior is a natural part of the human condition, but the appearance of a homosexual identity is a rare historical event. When and why did a homosexual identity emerge, and how has the meaning of homosexuality changed historically?

Jonathan Katz argued that, between colonial times and the 1970s, homosexuality in the US changed from indicating a behavior (sodomy), to an abnormal personality (the homosexual), and finally to an affirmative social identity (gay/lesbian). Carroll Smith-Rosenberg showed that Victorian women, whose lives were organized around domestic tasks, often formed close ties with each other that at times blurred the line between friendship and romance. These intimate bonds sometimes developed into romantic relationships that were celebrated as complementary to marriage. These "romantic friendships" were often life-time romantic bonds. Similarly, Lillian Faderman wrote the first history of lesbianism in the United States, in which she documents changes in the meaning of same-sex behavior and in the social organization of lesbianism. Both Smith-Rosenberg and Faderman make the provocative argument that tolerance for intimacy between women diminished in the first decades of the twentieth century. As women started to attend college, work outside the home, and demand equal rights, their close ties to one another were often viewed as threatening. These women were stigmatized as lesbians.

Building on this growing body of historical scholarship on sexuality, John D'Emilio offered the first detailed analysis of the rise of a homosexual identity and community in the United States. He analyzed the social forces that shaped homosexuality into an identity, community, and social movement. For example, D'Emilio argued that the Second World War played a key role in shaping an awareness of homosexuality and homosexual bonds. During the war, many soldiers were, for the first time, exposed to individuals who thought of themselves as homosexual. Moreover, the intense closeness among the men and women in the military encouraged homosexual experimentation. After the war, many of these men and women with homosexual feelings settled in New York, Chicago, San Francisco, and Los Angeles. It was in these cities that the first major gay and lesbian political organizations initially took shape in the 1950s.

Historians have continued to refine their conceptions of the sexual past. One significant revision is in George Chauncey's *Gay New York*. Whereas historians and sociologists had come to believe that the modern homosexual emerged in the early twentieth century and was immediately stuffed into the closet, Chauncey argues that, in working-class New York, individuals were not classified as either homosexual or heterosexual, but as either "normal men" or "fairies." The former were masculine men, while the latter were effeminate. In other words, the homosexual indicated a type of gender deviance. If you were a masculine man who had sex with effeminate men, you were not necessarily considered a homosexual. Gender expression, not sexual preference, defined being a homosexual. Moreover, rather than being isolated and closeted, an open public gay life flourished in bars, taverns, speakeasies, restaurants, ballrooms, and parks.

Queer studies

The new gay/lesbian studies proposes a deeply social view of homosexuality. It helped to give rise to so-called "Queer studies." A queer perspective advances two key ideas. First, the idea of a natural human sexuality is a belief or cultural notion, not a biological truth. Second, this idea divides sexual behaviors and identities into those that are normal and healthy, and those that are abnormal and sick. Queer studies shifts the focus from homosexuality to sexuality and broadens our view of sexuality to see it also as a type of social control.

The ideas of Michel Foucault are central. He challenged the idea that sex was biological and natural. He proposed that it was the very idea or, in his terms, the discourse of sexuality that created what we know as sex. We are not born sexual, but learn to be sexual beings; this occurs only in societies that have created the idea of "sexuality."

But when did this idea of sexuality originate, and why? The birth of the science of sexuality in the nineteenth century was crucial. Scientists aimed to discover the hidden truth of human nature by uncovering the secrets of the sexual instinct. Sexologists charted the physiology and behavior of sexual desire, psychiatrists listened to their clients confess to a shadowy world of sexual fantasies, and demographers surveyed human fertility. But these researchers did not discover an uncharted territory of sex; they fashioned human pleasures, excitations, and acts into a new object of knowledge and social regulation: human sexuality. Foucault is not saying that the feelings and behaviors associated with the body were created by these discourses. Rather, these discourses compelled us to view these bodily experiences as expressions of human sexuality. The science of sexuality conceptualized our diverse somatic experiences into a coherent, organized subject called sexuality.

Why did a discourse of sexuality appear and what was its social importance? Foucault thought that the modern state and other social institutions had good reasons to want to control people's sexuality. Between the seventeenth and nineteenth centuries in many European nations there were massive migrations to cities, a growing need for mass literacy and schooling, intense economic competition between nations, and the growing dependence of national power on economic prosperity. These developments created a strong political interest in gaining detailed and useful information about human bodies – how they reproduce, stay healthy, react to different external stimulation, and can be made more productive, efficient, and cooperative. For example, as cities became social and economic centers, governments and other institutions responsible for keeping order and for the care of the indigent sought information about migration patterns, fertility rates, nutrition, and health. This growing need to know and control bodies helped to create the idea of sexuality. To control sex is to exercise great control over the individual and whole populations. Sexuality is at the center of a modern system of social control.

Did Foucault give up the notion of sexual freedom? He wrote during a period of sexual rebellion. Sexual liberationists of all types declared that today we are more enlightened; the present is pregnant with possibilities for sexual freedom. Sexual liberation had two aspects. The first was a negative freedom – freedom from unnecessary control. Liberation also had a positive aspect – the right to express one's true sexual nature and identity.

Foucault agreed that expanding individual choice is a good thing. He supported the fight for gay rights. But gay rights is not liberation. It does relieve individuals of horrific stigma and social discrimination. Also, the gay rights movement has reinforced a system that forces individuals to declare themselves either straight or gay, and reinforces the deviant status of bisexuality and other nonconventional sexualities. Moreover, a gay movement has its own ideal of how a gay person is supposed to look and act. In other words, the gay movement exercises control over its members, pressuring them to identify exclusively as gay and to act in ways that are recognized as gay.

If sexuality is today a system of social control, then ironically sexual liberation might involve freeing ourselves from the idea of sexuality. This would mean approaching our erotic desires and acts not as expressions of sexuality but as simply feelings and acts that give pleasure, create social ties, or are a source of cultural creativity. Foucault advocates a politics against sexuality – against a society that sexualizes selves, identities, and acts. Why would this be a good thing? By not assigning a moral meaning (either normal or abnormal) to adult, consensual sexual desires and behaviors, individuals would be subject to less social regulation. For example, instead of reversing the stigma of homosexuality by championing a normal gay identity, we could approach homosexuality as a desire and as a source of pleasure, new relationships and cultural expressions. Or, instead of celebrating the sexualization of the human body and all of its feelings and sensations, perhaps it is more liberating to desexualize pleasures, focus on nonsexual pleasures, learn to enjoy a wide range of sensual pleasures, and be free of controls that rely on notions of normality.

Foucault emphasized the role of discourses or networks of ideas in producing and regulating human sexuality. The philosopher Judith Butler has drawn from Foucault in order to offer a new social point of view on gender and sexuality.

Butler thinks that societies that believe in a natural gender order are also organized around the norm of heterosexuality. Heterosexuality is the basis of a culture of romance, marriage, and the family, and is enforced by our laws, government, churches, schools, and military. Viewing men and women as naturally complementary makes heterosexuality seem like the natural, normal, and right way of living.

A system of compulsory heterosexuality may help to explain why societies divide individuals into two gender types, but it does not explain how gender – and sexual – identities are sustained daily. Butler's ideas about gender identity have been very influential in the sociology of sexual identity.

Growing up in a society that classifies feelings, behaviors, and social roles as appropriate either for men or for women, we learn how to act in gender-correct ways. By means of a system of rewards and sanctions, we learn to present ourselves as either men or women. We come to know, almost without thinking, what gestures, styles of dress and grooming, and ways of walking and talking are considered "normal" for men and women. If a male acts "masculine," if his posture, talk, friends, dating, and job conform to masculine norms, his gender identity as a man will be taken for granted. If a male acts "feminine," he may not be considered a "normal" man.

Furthermore, Butler argues that, as we conform to gender norms, others will likely interpret our behavior as expressing a core gender identity. For example, most of us would probably assume that a male who looks and acts like a man (e.g. is aggressive, competitive, or decisive) *is* a man, and this status is at the core of his identity. In other words, his masculine actions are understood as expressing a deeply rooted male gender identity. However, Butler suggests that there is no core gender identity that drives our behavior. Rather than viewing our gender performances as expressing an inner gender identity, she says that these behaviors are modeled after images of what it means to be a woman or man that we take over from our families and our culture. The illusion of core feminine and masculine gender identities conceals the social and political forces that shape humans into gendered selves. Similarly, the ideology of a natural gender order conceals the role of gender in the perpetuation of heterosexual dominance.

Butler's ideas encourage us to view sexual identity as a process. We project a sexual identity by our actions. Accordingly, researchers would analyze the micro-dynamics of identity formation. For example, we would try to explain which behaviors and things (clothes, cars, homes, furniture, eyeglasses) come to be signs of sexual identity, and why. How do individuals acquire the skills to read each other's behaviors in terms of sex identity categories? A performative approach does not claim that sex identities are not real because they are produced through a performance. They are quite real as we experience them and in terms of their personal and social consequences. And, while they may be performances, they are hardly chosen; a system of compulsory heterosexuality exerts enormous social pressure on each of us to "perform" the appropriate gender and sexual identities. Deviance from gender or sexual norms carries serious dangers, from being denied respect to being the target of harassment or violence.

To summarize this chapter, there has been a revolution in the way scholars think about sexuality. Until recently, scholars believed that humans were born with a sexual nature; the natural order created a series of sexual types: heterosexuals, homosexuals, masochists, pedophiles, and so on. A science of sexuality would reveal the nature of the sexual instinct. The idea of sexual normality would serve as the standard to judge and regulate sexual behavior

Today, the leading edge of scholarship views sex as fundamentally social. We're born with bodies but it is society that determines which parts of the body and which pleasures and acts are sexual. And, the classification of sex acts into good and bad or acceptable and illicit is a product of social power; the dominant sexual norms express the dominant social groups. If we are supposed to grow up to be heterosexual, and if we are expected to link sex to love and marriage, this is because specific groups impose these social norms. Beliefs that there are natural and normal ways to be sexual are ideologies. How we come to have such beliefs, and their personal and social consequences, are important questions for the study of sexuality. Indeed, the question of who gets to define what is sexual and which institutions are responsible for regulating our sexualities are key sociological and political questions.

References

Judith Butler, *Gender Trouble: Feminism and the Subversion of Identity* (New York: Routledge, 1990).

George Chauncey, *Gay New York: Gender, Urban Culture, and the Making of the Gay Male World, 1890–1940* (New York: Basic Books, 1994).

Nancy Chodorow, *The Reproduction of Mothering: Psychoanalysis and the Sociology of Gender* (Berkeley: University of California Press, 1978).

John D'Emilio, *Sexual Politics, Sexual Communities: The Making of a Homosexual Minority in the United States, 1940–1970* (Chicago, IL: University of Chicago Press. 1983).

Lillian Faderman, *Odd Girls and Twilight Lovers: A History of Lesbian Life in Twentieth-Century America* (New York: Columbia University Press, 1991).

Michel Foucault, *The History of Sexuality. Vol 1: An Introduction* (New York: Vintage, 1980).

John Gagnon and William Simon, *Sexual Conduct: The Social Sources of Human Sexuality* (Chicago, IL: Aldine, 1973).

Jonathan Ned Katz, *Gay American History* (New York: Crowell, 1976) and *Gay/Lesbian Almanac* (New York: Harper & Row, 1983).

Catherine MacKinnon, *Towards a Feminist Theory of the State* (Cambridge, MA: Harvard University Press, 1989).

Ken Plummer, *Sexual Stigma: An Interactionist Account* (London: Routledge & Kegan Paul, 1975).

Ira Reiss, *Premarital Sexual Standards in America* (Glencoe, IL: Free Press, 1960) and *The Social Context of Premarital Sexual Permissiveness* (New York: Holt, Rinehart & Winston, 1967).

Adrienne Rich, "Compulsory Heterosexuality and Lesbian Existence," *Signs* 5 (1980).

Gayle Rubin, "Thinking Sex: Notes for a Radical Theory of the Politics of Sexuality," in *Pleasure and Danger: Exploring Female Sexuality*, ed. Carole Vance (Boston, MA: Routledge & Kegan Paul, 1984).

Carroll Smith-Rosenberg, "The Female World of Love and Ritual," *Signs* 1 (1975).

Jeffrey Weeks, *Sexuality* (London: Tavistock, 1986), p. 26.

2

The social construction of sexuality

Interview with Jeffrey Weeks

LONDON SOUTH BANK UNIVERSITY

Jeffrey Weeks is the author of numerous articles and some twenty books. These include *Coming Out* (1977), *Sex, Politics and Society* (1981), *Sexuality and its Discontents* (1985), *Sexuality* (1986/2003), *Between the Acts* (with Kevin Porter, 1990/1998), *Invented Moralities* (1995), *Making Sexual History* (2000), *Same Sex Intimacies* (with Brian Heaphy and Catherine Donovan, 2001), and *Sexualities and Society: A Reader* (edited with Janet Holland and Matthew Waites, 2003). He is Professor Emeritus at London's South Bank University, where he was executive dean of the Faculty of Arts and Human Sciences.

I understand that you were involved in the lesbian and gay movement in Britain in the 1970s. Could you talk about this?

I became involved in the Gay Liberation Front in London in November 1970, soon after it had started. Its first base was at the London School of Economics (LSE), and it so happened that I had started work at the School the previous month, in my first academic job as a researcher. So from the beginning my political involvement in the movement and my career were inextricably intertwined – certainly to the detriment of what passed for my career at first.

I had in fact been out for the previous three or four years, had flirted with the London scene, and had accumulated a small, tightly knit group of gay friends. I was also vaguely on the political left, but somewhat detached from its mainstream activities largely because I felt unwelcome because of my sexuality. There seemed to be two separate worlds, that of my still largely secret personal hopes and desires, and the public worlds of ideology and great events. My involvement in gay liberation changed that. For the first time I began to see how the private and the public, the sexual and the political, the everyday and grand historic processes could be brought together. It literally changed my life: I met new friends, I became involved with my first long-term lover, and I went through an ideological revolution which has marked me to this day. I became heavily involved in gay politics for the rest of the 1970s, especially as an editor of *Gay Left* which, in the late 1970s, became for a while a leading forum for gay theory and analysis. Edmund White, at the end of *The Beautiful Room is Empty*, talks about how Stonewall was "Our Bastille Day ... the turning point of our lives." That's what my immersion in gay liberation felt like to me.

How did your political involvement influence your academic work?

My involvement in the gay movement completely changed the direction of my academic work. When I got involved in GLF I had just moved to the LSE after a not very successful year teaching in a school. The school-teaching in turn had been a hurried escape from my first attempt at postgraduate work, where I had felt lonely and isolated. I went to the LSE in the hope that I would resume my studies in a more congenial atmosphere (and I did in fact complete my master's dissertation whilst I was there – a study of early-twentieth-century socialist and pluralist thought, themes which in a strange, roundabout way came to influence my later writings on sexuality). I soon, however, became heavily involved in the theoretical issues thrown up by gay liberation, especially the question of what was homosexuality, why was it so oppressed, what sort of politics were necessary to transform the situation, and so on. As a trained historian I naturally began exploring the historical context, and as someone who had already researched into the political and moral debates of the late nineteenth century I became very interested in the links between early (homo-) sexual politics in Britain – especially the work of people like Edward Carpenter, John Addingtom Symonds and the pioneering sexologist, Havelock Ellis – and broader radical politics. My first book was written with Sheila Rowbotham, and called *Socialism and the New Life: The Personal and Sexual Politics of Edward Carpenter and Havelock Ellis* (1977) – and I wrote the section on Ellis, who has continued to fascinate me ever since. He says somewhere that his strategy was to write about the most outrageously (for the time) controversial issues around sexuality in a calm, rational, matter-of-fact style, as if everything was straightforward and perfectly normal. I have found this a very useful tactic myself over the past thirty years or so.

Anyway, this little book contains the germs of much of what I was to write on sexuality into the mid-1980s: in *Coming Out, Sex, Politics and Society*, and *Sexuality and its Discontents* – what I later described as my "informal trilogy." The first traces the evolution of recognizably modern homosexual identities and ways of life from the nineteenth century; the second explores the wider social and political context of the regulation of sexuality in Britain; the third explores the ways in which sexuality became the object of would-be scientific attention, how sexology in particular can be said to have contributed to the "invention" of sexuality as a "continent of knowledge" – and how it was resisted through the emergence of grassroots knowledges.

In these brief descriptions you can see, I think, how my awareness of the significance of the new sexual movements (feminism as well as lesbian and gay politics) of the 1970s was influencing my thinking. My sense of the ways in which gay liberation had transformed the meanings of contemporary gay identities made me ask whether we could see similar shifts in meanings and identities in the past. My sense that you could not understand what was happening today with regard to homosexuality without putting it in the wider context of sexuality (and gender) led me to explore the changes over time. And my growing perception of the vital role of ideas and values pushed me into a study of the role of sexology as a science of desire.

Was it risky in the 1970s for an academic in Britain to study sexuality and homosexuality?

Writing about sex, Ken Plummer has written, makes you morally dubious, and it certainly felt like that for me in the 1970s and into the 1980s. I was gainfully employed at the LSE until 1977, but the job had nothing to do with sexuality – officially at least, though I had been able to do research on Havelock Ellis and for *Coming Out* during this period. Then I had a period of unemployment. This was followed by a year working with Ken Plummer and Mary McIntosh at the University of Essex, which had a liberal reputation, especially in the Sociology

Department, which was at the cutting edge of radical theory. This was an immensely creative period, where we collectively refined our ideas of what became known as "social constructionism" – the main collective product was *The Making of the Modern Homosexual*, edited by Ken Plummer, and published in 1981. Unfortunately that intellectual idyll soon came to an end: when the Conservative Party came to power in 1979 they cut the funding of the Social Science Research Council, which in turn cut my funding, and I was unemployed again. So you could certainly say that my career was pretty rocky in the 1970s, and my writing about homosexuality certainly did not help. In fact I did not get a permanent and senior academic appointment until 1990, when I got the chair in social relations at the University of the West of England. Three things helped me then. First, by then I had a long list of publications, not all on sexuality, and was clearly qualified. Second, I had spent four years in academic administration and policy-making in an accreditation body, and was almost respectable. And finally, by a tragic irony, writing about sexuality was itself less morally dubious now because of the AIDS crisis. Indeed, I found myself in demand as an expert on sexuality and was again able to obtain funding from the same research council that had truncated my earlier career.

Your book, Coming Out, *was important in creating a new kind of history and sociology of homosexuality. Can you talk about how your view of homosexuality was different?*

When I first conceived of *Coming Out* in the early 1970s I wanted, in a sense, to find precursors (*Ancestors*) for myself and my generation: I wanted to trace a history of oppression and resistance which would be *our* history. Unfortunately, once I began research I found that the task was not that easy. First of all the existing literature assumed there was a continuity of experience and feeling – but a cursory look showed that homosexual life was immensely varied throughout history, and even across the 200 years or so that I was limiting myself to. Second, I looked for traces of a common identity through history – and couldn't find it. There were many different homosexualities, not a unitary homosexuality. Third, I was interested in how homosexuality was a female as well as male phenomenon – but women were largely absent from existing histories. And fourth, I assumed that throughout history there would be a continuity of understandings of what homosexuality was – and there wasn't. On the contrary, the very idea of homosexuality as a distinct category did not exist until the late nineteenth century, and way into the twentieth century it was a very vague concept (alongside, it has to be said, the concept of heterosexuality). So I had to start again.

Luckily I had read Mary McIntosh's important essay on "The Homosexual Role," originally published in 1968, and this proved to be a revelation. She basically saw homosexuality as a social categorization that had a history worth exploring. She also demonstrated that this categorization was a specific historical pattern – based on the assumption that homosexuality was a characteristic of a certain type of person – that differed from other known patterns, where, for example, homosexuality might be seen as a gender inversion or as an aspect of the rites of passage of young boys. It wasn't even certain that the typical homosexual role that she described exhausted the ways we understood or lived homosexuality in our complex modern societies. Clearly the way we understood homosexuality – basically as the core of a particular type of identity that in the early 1970s was forcibly asserting itself through gay liberation – was a deeply historical phenomenon that had been, in a phrase that was subsequently to become notorious, "socially constructed." Here was a historical research agenda, and a theoretical debate, that I eagerly engaged with, and *Coming Out* was the first major product of my research.

Other people I got to know or know of at this time helped the evolution of my ideas: Ken Plummer, who was practically creating from scratch a sociology of sexuality in Britain by writing about sexual stigma; William Simon and John Gagnon who talked about the need that must have existed at an unspecified period to "invent" sexuality, and explained the importance of sexual scripts; Randolph Trumbach, who was exploring homosexuality in eighteenth-century London; Jonathan Ned Katz who was inventing gay American history single-handedly; Carroll Smith-Rosenberg, who was studying female friendship; Judith Walkowitz, who was exploring the categorization of the female prostitute in ways very similar to the way in which I was exploring the categorization of "the homosexual"; all these and others stimulated an intellectual excitement that I have rarely again encountered. And all this, I must note, came long before any of us encountered the work of Michel Foucault on sexuality. I had already completed *Coming Out* before I read the first volume of Foucault's *The History of Sexuality*. His work was certainly to influence mine, but my long-term preoccupations were already firmed up by the mid-1970s. And central to those preoccupations was, as I saw it, the need to develop a non-essentialist understanding of homosexuality (and indeed of sexuality generally), which tried to understand same-sex desires and practices in their real social and historical context; which saw all sexual identities (like indeed all identities) as historical contructs (even "fictions," as I subsequently argued); and which saw sexuality as a mobile field of power relation, shaped by a complex history and one in which we, the sexually marginalized, were increasingly becoming strategic actors. For the point of all this history, sociology, anthropology and theory was not simply to understand the world of sexuality, but to change it.

What do you mean by the idea that the homosexual came into existence some time in the late nineteenth century? And what social factors played a key role in creating this new sexual identity?

Mary McIntosh and Randolph Trumbach had argued that the early eighteenth century had been a key moment in the evolution of ideas of the homosexual as a distinct type of being. Whilst not disputing their evidence, I was more intrigued by what I saw happening in the late nineteenth century. This was the period when homosexually-inclined writers like Ulrichs, Kertbenny (who invented the term homosexuality), Symonds, and Carpenter began to try to describe the "turning," "invert," "homosexual," as a person with feelings, sensitivities, hopes and desires – as a real, living, breathing, loving person, not a sinner or pervert; when the new breed of sexologists, such as Krafft-Ebing, Ellis, Hirschfeld and later Freud, tried to make sense of this phenomenon, and began to theorize (inconclusively, it goes beyond saying) the causes of same-sex attraction, and the social consequences of accepting them; when complex subcultures, of women as well as men, in London, Paris, Berlin, New York, began to emerge in the public eye (not least through scandals, of which the agonies of Oscar Wilde became the most notorious); and also the period which saw the first dawnings of homophile groupings seeking to change the law and create a more tolerant climate. The work of Magnus Hirschfeld in Germany was the most internationally famous of these groupings but there were smaller echoes elsewhere, including in Britain and the USA (as myself and Jonathan Katz respectively were able to demonstrate).

In other words, by the late nineteenth century there was a distinctive categorization, set of identities, ways of life, and political responses that certainly built on what had gone before, since at least the eighteenth century, but which had distinctive elements that were to come to full flowering only in the course of the next hundred years. I think in those early years I probably overemphasized the extent of the changes of the 1880s and 1890s. The process was uneven and complex, and was far from being universal. Recent studies have shown that into the 1950s and 1960s distinctive homosexual identities were by no means universally accepted (if indeed they are today). But the crucial point is that the late nineteenth century was when all this really got going.

Why? I am averse to monocausal explanations, such as "the triumph of capitalism" or whatever. But we can point to key aspects. Urbanization in the nineteenth century created new spaces of both anonymity and intimacy, where alternative ways of life away from the home and the closed communities of rural life could be explored, mainly by men in the first instance, but increasingly too by women. New forms of communication allowed an easier transmission of ideas, concepts, and identities. The writings of the early sexologists clearly show the ways in which homosexual meanings were constructed in dialogue between the new social actors and the self-styled experts – in the clinics, the prisons, but also in the new text books. Self-identified "third sexers" did not passively imbibe the sexologists' ideas. They often gave the new concepts to the specialists and then saw them circulated and re-circulated as scientific definitions for all to borrow and amend. Perhaps overarching all these developments was the sharper institutionalization of heterosexuality within the family and culture generally, which in a real sense required the creation of "the pervert" as the execrated Other, the measure against which normality could be judged. But this in turn provoked a sense of self assertion and identity amongst this new "species," as Foucault put it, that was now emerging. The invention of the homosexual was not a deliberate act; it was classically over-determined in that there were many potential factors leading to the rise of the modern homosexual. And as I have said already, to talk about such a being does not exhaust the homosexual experience, then or now. But that something new happened in the nineteenth century still seems to me undeniable; just as something new happened in same-sex life in the 1970s.

What are the key changes in the meaning of homosexuality since the nineteenth century?

Sometime it's easy to forget when faced by continuing bigotry (not least from religions and some state forms) and even violent hate how far we have come since the nineteenth century, and especially since the 1970s. We no longer have to assert a precarious identity; we have a proliferation of possible subject positions we can identify with, including identity positions – for example as "queer" – which happily negate the very value of identity. In most Western societies toleration and acceptance have become the norm, even as it is frequently breached. Civil rights and equality under the law are largely institutionalized. Most European countries, and a number of other states (Canada, Australia and New Zealand) have recognized same-sex partnerships and even marriage, and increasingly this includes equal parenting and adoption rights. In Britain, so long a laggard on these issues, civil partnerships came into force in 2005 that are little different from marriage, even if the word "marriage" is not used: the only difference is that, unlike marriage, same-sex unions do not require sexual consummation to make them legal. Even in the United States, where same-sex marriage is most divisive and contested, the heat of the battle obscures the steady progress towards equality and acceptance of lesbian and gay life choices in everyday life. On a global scale there are huge variations in attitudes, beliefs, and behaviours. But there are increasing commonalities. Every major city of the world now has elaborate subcultures and varied sexual identities. Even as HIV/AIDS threatened to wipe out the gains of the past couple of generations, there has been a new social recognition of the role of lesbians and gay men in contemporary societies – what Dennis Altman called "legitimization through disaster."

So what is homosexuality today: a perversion, an inversion, a sickness, a natural anomaly, an orientation, a preference, a lifestyle, a performance, a universal potentiality, a minority experience, a genetic variation, a product of a particular gay brain? It is all and none of these things in an ever-changing sexual world because someone, somewhere, believes in one or more of these descriptions, and sometimes tries to act on that basis. For me, homosexuality is a range of possibilities, shadowed by the heterosexual assumptions which still govern much of our thought and social organization, but offering, as Foucault once said, the opportunities for creative life. The great achievement of the past thirty-five years since Stonewall is that so many people have seized those opportunities to make meaningful lives for themselves.

Do you see any major differences between the US and Britain with regard to the meaning and social status of homosexuality?

The USA has always been a model for many of us in Europe as the pioneer of modern gay politics and culture. It has had a vibrancy and creativity that has been enormously encouraging and has shown us what can be achieved in a pluralist culture. But looking back over the past few decades, it is hard now not to think that more has been achieved in Europe in terms of formal recognition of equal citizenship than in the USA. Just take the question of same-sex partnership rights as an example. Since Denmark pioneered the process in 1989, most European countries have passed legislation with relatively little fuss. Here in Britain the legislation went through with the support even of the opposition Conservative Party, which less than twenty years earlier had banned the "promotion of homosexuality." And the reason for that difference is quite simple: lesbian and gay rights have not been trapped here in the culture wars, and have not become a symbolic totem for religious battles. What amazes even the most sympathetic British observer of the United States is the power of religion, especially religion of an absolutist, morally conservative tinge. Here in old Britain, and old Europe generally, religion no longer has that determining force, despite the best efforts of various forms of fundamentalism. We have become largely secular cultures. Responses to sexuality are largely pragmatic. Homosexuality now arouses less drama in Britain than in the USA. The massive energy of the American gay world still entices and excites, but by and large we have found we can do things OK in our own ways.

Your work is credited with establishing a social constructionist perspective on sexuality. Can you discuss what this means, and does this mean that nature or biology has no role in shaping sexuality?

The social constructionist approach, quite simply, is about understanding the historical context which shapes the sexual. The starting point is the assumption that sexuality, far from being a force of nature external to society, is in fact always inevitably central to the social and cultural, and malleable by them. Sexuality is a highly social phenomenon, and as society changes so must sexuality. Does that mean that nature has nothing to do with it? Not quite. Sexuality builds on biological potentials, and is subject to psychosocial organization, so both biology and psychology can no doubt help us understand individual sexual development. But we must also recognize that sexuality, like everything else, attains meaning only in culture. We just cannot understand the subtleties and complexities of the sexual world if we try to reduce everything to the imperatives of Nature, or a particular type of brain or a special gene for this or that behaviour. The genetic revolution has had one undesirable consequence in that it reinforces attempts to understand sexuality in terms of the transmissions of genes over unimaginable time scales. To my mind attempts to understand contemporary sexual forms in terms of what our pre-historic ancestors did 500,000 years ago is a complete mystification, and an abandonment of what we should be doing as historians, sociologists, and anthropologists, which is to understand specific cultural configurations.

Even if there were a gay gene it could not possibly explain the varied historical patterning of homosexuality over time, or even within a single culture. And in a sense it removes responsibility from us as humans. As humans we have a degree of choice. I am not suggesting that we can by act of will change our sexual make-up. I do believe that that is to a large degree organized quite early in our individual development. But what we make of it is more in our hands, shaped of course all the time by what is culturally possible for us to do. To take an obvious example: there may be a large number of people in a particular culture who have homosexual desires, whatever the reasons for this. But how we live out those desires must depend on what means of expression exist. Are there possible identities open to us? What is the degree of acceptance or rejection of those identities? Are there spaces where like-minded people can meet, interact, have sex, love each other? A whole series of limiting factors come into play: religion, family and peer pressures, differences of status, class, race and ethnicity, age, etc. Individual sexual identities are the result of a constant negotiation between human possibilities and social and cultural opportunities. Social constructionism, at its simplest, is an attempt to understand the processes through which social and individual meanings and practices of the erotic are shaped and reshaped in an ever-changing history.

I want to ask you what is perhaps an impossible question. What is sexuality, or at least what would you include if you were forced to define sexuality?

Freud commented on the great difficulty on agreeing on the sexual nature of a process. Gagnon and Simon talked about the need that must once have existed to invent the importance of sexuality. Plummer once wrote that nothing is sexual, but naming makes it so. Yet Foucault famously complained that sex has become "the truth of our being." As the question suggests, there is no simple definition of sexuality, or explanation of its undoubted power. What complicates the issue is that "sexuality" as a concept operates on two levels. It refers to the bundle of social phenomena that shape erotic life: laws, religion, norms and values, beliefs and ideologies, the social organization of reproduction, family life, identities, domestic arrangements, diseases, violence and love – everything we evoke when we speak of the sexuality of a culture. And it also refers to the level of the individual – to the pleasures and pains that can shape our lives for good or ill. The two constantly interact, as I have suggested, shaping and reshaping the other. I do not believe, as Krafft-Ebing suggested, that sex is an all-powerful volcanic force that demands satisfaction. But I do believe that the erotic potentialities of the human body are immense, and tutored by human interaction they can become the focus of the most intense pleasures and pains. Which is why our culture can't quite let it go. It still fuels the personal and societal imagination.

3

Surveying sex

Interview with Edward Laumann

UNIVERSITY OF CHICAGO

Edward Laumann is the George Herbert Mead Distinguished Service Professor of Sociology at the University of Chicago. He is a co-author of *The Social Organization of Sexuality: Sexual Practices in the United States*. This volume is considered the most comprehensive survey of the sexual behavior of American adults since the work of Kinsey.

Much of your work as a sociologist has been in the area of urban and organizational studies. Why did you decide to study sexuality?

When I was serving as Dean of the Social Sciences Division at the University of Chicago in 1986, a medical faculty colleague, Dr. Mark Siegler, and I organized a joint Medical/Social Science faculty, year-long seminar series devoted to "AIDS and Society." Based on what I learned in this seminar, I became convinced that a properly designed survey of the US population that asked about their sexual practices was critical if we were to develop appropriate public health interventions to change people's sexual behavior toward safer sexual practices that would protect them from acquiring AIDS. Since at the time there was little prospect of an effective medical intervention being developed in the short term, such as a vaccine to prevent infection by HIV, our only hope of forestalling a massive epidemic was to devise effective behavioral interventions against the transmission of the disease. Robert Michael, who is an economic demographer, was then the director of the NORC on campus, one of the largest academically oriented survey organizations in the country. He and I decided to respond to the National Institutes of Health's call for proposals to design a national sex survey. We recruited John Gagnon, an internationally noted sex researcher, to help us do the study. We won the design competition in 1987 and immediately began developing the survey. Unfortunately, conservative political figures strongly opposed the idea of a government-funded sex survey and successfully prevented funding of the study for several years.

You and your colleagues did one of the largest surveys of sexuality ever done. Who funded the survey, and why did they fund it?

We have the dubious distinction of having had an act of Congress, the Senate voting 66 to 35 in September 1991 to deny funding the survey in favor of a "say no to sex" campaign favored by Senator Jesse Helms, passed in an attempt to stop the study. We were able to secure funding from a consortium of eight private philanthropic foundations because we could now convince them that the Federal government was not going to fund the survey in a timely way. We fielded the survey in 1992, just four months after the Senate vote. Unfortunately we had to cut the sample to one-fifth of the size we had originally recommended as being necessary to provide the detailed information we needed.

Can you describe your general sociological approach to understanding sexuality? Many sociologists focus on gender, cultural representations, economics, or state and the law to understand sexuality. What social factors do you think are the most important in trying to understand patterns of sexual behavior and attitudes?

We combined elements of three theoretical traditions in devising a general framework: (a) script theory, originally proposed by John Gagnon and William Simon, that distinguishes among cultural sexual scripts, interpersonal scripts, and intrapsychic scripts; (b) social network theory, with special focus on the organization of the sexual dyad and the larger social networks in which the sexual partners are embedded (this gives a powerful purchase on the epidemiology of disease spread); and (c) choice theory, which foregrounds how people engage in sexual decision-making. More fundamentally, we stress those aspects of sociological theory that feature how master statuses (such as age, gender, marital status, socioeconomic status, ethnicity/race, and religious preference); and master relationships – that is, we focus on four types of sexual partnerships, including marriage, cohabitation, dating (not living together), and casual sex (one-night stands), and socially organize the differential distribution of sexual practices, behavior, and attitudes. My special interest, flowing out of my earlier work on friendship formation, class, and status groups, was in the application of network theory to issues related to the spread of disease, the formation of enduring or more ephemeral sexual partnerships, and partner choice. We found that only three master statuses, age, marital status, and gender, do the lion's share of the work in organizing sexuality socially.

Your survey asks very personal and intimate questions about individuals' sexual and intimate practices. Why do you think people agreed to be interviewed and why you think they gave truthful answers?

People agreed to be surveyed because we convinced them that the information we sought was critical for informing public health interventions in the battle against AIDS. We had an exceptionally high completion rate: about 80 percent of the persons we had identified to be in our target sample agreed to be interviewed. Contrary to many expectations, the public at large does not in fact experience many problems in discussing sexual matters if they have good reasons to do so and they are asked in an appropriate and respectful manner. In the book that we published based on the survey, *The Social Organization of Sexuality* (1994), we provide several lengthy chapters evaluating the extent and nature of systematic distortions in responses to sexual questions. In general, we provide, I think, convincing evidence that these distortions are quite modest in degree and can be effectively taken into account when interpreting the results. There certainly were certain questions (e.g., about masturbation and family income) where we knew people were likely to be exaggerating or underestimating the behaviors, but these were generally very modest distortions. In fact, if we take "refused to answer the question" as an indicator of the sensitivity of the question, nearly all the questions directly asking about sexual things had refusal rates around 1 or 2 percent. In contrast, we had a 12 percent refusal rate about family income – far and away the most sensitive item in the interview.

21

What do you see as the main advantage of researching sexuality through surveys?

The main advantage of survey research is the cost-efficient capacity to ask about a wide range of topics with varying levels of detail across a representative sample of the adult population, so that one can estimate with known precision the prevalence and distribution of risky sexual practices and thus pinpoint points of intervention in the subpopulations at greatest risk for adverse health outcomes. We acquired an enormous amount of information on such topics as sexual practices, including oral and anal sex, vaginal intercourse, masturbation, and same-gender sex, subjective sexual preferences for different practices, the social factors influencing sexual partner choice, circumcision status, sexual dysfunctions (including erectile and lubrication problems, premature ejaculation, and difficulty having orgasm), sexually transmitted infections, general health and specific health conditions, the influence of social network composition on sexual expression, sexual attitudes and beliefs about appropriate sexual behavior, and extensive demographic and social characteristics of the respondent and his/her partners. With such information we are in an excellent position to map the distribution of various sexual practices across various population subgroups and to determine whether subpopulations are subject to different levels of risk of disease, happiness, and sexual health.

To convey something of the richness of your research, I would like to ask you about your findings on oral sex. In general, which Americans are practicing oral sex the most? Are there noteworthy social patterns to this sexual practice?

Roughly 75 percent of the men and women in the United States have had oral sex at some time in their lives. But only 1 in 4 engage in oral sex as a current sexual practice. Oral sex, then, is a technique with which most people have at least some familiarity, but it has in no sense become a defining feature of sex between women and men (as vaginal intercourse or, perhaps, kissing is). Somewhat less than 50 percent of men report oral sex as subjectively "very appealing," while only about half that percentage of women find it "very appealing." This should obviously translate into a relative reluctance on the part of women to engage in oral sex (when compared to men), but even among the men there is less than a majority who especially favor the practice. It is a practice that is likely to happen early on in a relationship, but does not remain a strong preference over the long haul of a relationship.

Did your survey find significant differences between men's and women's sexuality?

On practically every matter of sexual practice and preference, attitudes and beliefs, numbers of lifetime sex partners, reported levels of sexual fantasy and sexual interest and desire, there are marked differences in men's and women's modes of sexual expression. These gender differences are sometimes enhanced or moderated by marital status, educational level, socioeconomic status, religious group membership, or race/ethnicity. For example, there appears to be a greater gender gap between African-American men and women with respect to beliefs about appropriate sexual behavior than there is between white men and women. Men, in general, report a higher lifetime number of sexual partners (measured as a median) than do women. Older men (over 55) are substantially more likely to have an ongoing sexual partner than women will have. For example, 70 percent of women aged 70 will not have had a sex partner in the past year, compared to only 35 percent of men aged 70 who report that they lacked a partner in the past year. About 30 percent of women report that they lacked interest in sex for at least several months in the past year, when compared to only about 15 percent of the men.

Many Americans think of themselves as sexually enlightened and liberated. Does your survey support this view?

No, it most certainly does not. We asked a series of nine questions about people's beliefs about appropriate sexual behavior, including extramarital sex, abortion, homosexuality, the significance of religious beliefs in guiding sexual conduct, and premarital sex. There were huge differences of opinion on every one of these questions. We were able to group people on the basis of their shared beliefs into three broad categories that range from libertarian to "middle of the road" to conservative points of view. About 25 percent of the sample fell into a well-defined conservative camp and another 25 percent clustered around a strong pro-libertarian or "sexually liberated" point of view. The rest fell squarely in the middle, rejecting the more extreme views of either side. This split is not homogeneously distributed across the country but varies in important ways that greatly affect political debate in the various states. The east and west coasts tend to have more liberally oriented persons, while the south and midwest have substantially larger pluralities of sexually conservative believers. The correspondence with the "blue" and "red" voting patterns in the last Presidential election (2004) is striking.

What was the most surprising finding in your research?

There is widespread evidence throughout the survey for the notion that persons who are involved in ongoing, mutually monogamous sexual partnerships report substantially higher levels of physical and emotional satisfaction with their sexual partnerships than those who report being in concurrent or overlapping sexual partnerships. Sexual competition appears to interfere with the building of commitment and trust in the larger social relationship in which the sexual partnership is embedded, and this, in turn, seems to have consequences for the physical and emotional satisfaction with the partnership itself.

Based on your research, what are Americans' chief sexual frustrations and fears, and their chief sexual satisfactions?

Perhaps the most surprising finding of this research is the relatively high levels of sexual dysfunction being reported by both men and women at all phases of the life course. About 43 percent of the women and 31 percent of the men reported at least one episode of sexual dysfunction of several months' duration over the past year. Some 30 percent of women said they lacked sexual interest or desire for several months in the past year, while 30 percent of men complained about premature ejaculation as a problem. Nearly all these sexual difficulties could be shown to be associated with lowered levels of overall happiness and satisfaction with one's life. On the other hand, there was no simple relationship between the volume of sexual activity and general life satisfaction. Much more research needs to be done to clarify and elaborate on how people achieve positive sexual health, and its role in generating a good quality of life.

Part 2
Sexual meanings

Introduction

Sex, falling in love, the tingling excitement of sexual attraction, are often assumed to be part of being human. Throughout time, people have fallen in love and experienced sexual desire. But does that mean that falling in love has always *meant* the same thing? Or, that the meaning of what is sexually desirable is the same in Mexico as it is in the United States? While we may assume that all humans experience something like what we can call sexual feelings, the *meanings* of these sexual feelings will likely differ across cultures.

Well, what sort of meanings does sex have? If we look at history, and at different cultures today, we can distinguish a wide range of sexual meanings. Let's review some of these.

Sex can be a way to create a family. The link between sex and procreation seems to be universal. That is, all societies understand sex to be meaningful at least as an act of reproduction, which is typically linked to making a family. However, in many societies today, alternative insemination makes it possible to create a family without sexual intercourse. Moreover, the development of effective birth control has allowed us to think about sex in terms of pleasure; the meaning of sex is no longer limited to procreation.

In fact, heterosexual sex acts can be interpreted in various ways in different societies or even within the same society. For example, some researchers argue that American men and women differ in important ways in their experience of sexual pleasure. Men emphasize the erotic or sensual aspects of pleasure, whereas women have, historically, related pleasure to emotional connection or social bonding. And sexual pleasure can be understood as sinful, romantic, a validation of masculinity, or a type of individual adventure or play.

Also, while many of us think of sex as a very intimate romantic experience, it can also be about power and control. Some feminists view heterosexual sex as playing out a drama of men's dominance and women's subordination. Other feminists imagine sex as combining power with other meanings, such as intimacy or caring.

Sex can also be a way to express love. In many societies, sex is integral to romance and can serve as a standard to judge whether one is truly in love or not. And while "love" may be an emotion common to human experience, there are social rules that organize love. These social rules guide what it means to be "in love," what a romantic evening should look like and feel like, or what kinds of people are suitable to be in love with. And the very meaning of love is also dependent on social factors such as women's and men's gender roles, the regulation of marriage, and property rules. For example, in the past one married not for love but out of a sense of duty to one's family.

Sex is also associated with being a rite of passage from childhood to adulthood. In some societies, like the United States, the first sexual experience sometimes marks entry into adulthood. For lesbians and gay men, "coming out" is often a crucial rite of passage into becoming a self-accepting individual.

Sex, then, has many meanings attached to it. The chapters in this part discuss how meanings associated with sexual experiences – like sexual pleasure, coming out of the closet, marriage, falling in love, heterosexual sex, what is considered morally right and wrong – vary in different societies, and sometimes in the same society. These chapters also discuss how sexual meanings come to be constructed in particular ways.

4

Popular culture constructs sexuality

Interview with Joshua Gamson

UNIVERSITY OF SAN FRANCISCO

Joshua Gamson is a Professor of Sociology at the University of San Francisco. He is the author of *Claims to Fame: Celebrity in Contemporary America* (California, 1994), *Freaks Talk Back: Tabloid Talk Shows and Sexual Nonconformity* (Chicago, 1998), and *The Fabulous Sylvester: The Legend, The Music, The Seventies in San Francisco* (Henry Holt, 2005).

You wrote two books on popular culture. What is it about popular culture that fascinates you?

I'm first of all just interested in everyday life, and so much of everyday life gets its texture from popular culture – whether it's from commercial culture, or from more organic, self-created forms of culture. Pop culture is a common currency, and in this society there aren't that many things the whole population shares; the United States is so diverse, and just so huge, that commonalities are relatively rare, and mostly they come from pop culture. I also find thinking about popular culture challenging, because it so often combines social significance with tremendous superficiality. It's important almost by definition – it's the sea in which we swim, and to a large degree it sets the terms and boundaries of imagination; it is where discussions central to social life take place. But often the experience of pop culture, especially commercially produced culture, is thin, fleeting, and not that deeply felt or thought through. I find that combination intriguing. And finally, I'm interested in the politics of pop culture. There's this interesting tension between a sort of "top down" version of popular culture, in which people who control major cultural institutions create and manage what gets out there, and a "bottom up" version of popular culture, in which people at a more grassroots level make up their own stuff. I think those dynamics are important and interesting to understand.

In general, how do you see popular culture influencing or shaping sexuality?

There are a few ways this happens. Sexual statuses, populations, behaviors, and so on, all get processed through popular culture. Some become visible in it, others are rendered invisible; some are celebrated or treated as legitimate, others are denigrated or delegitimated. So popular culture affects who and what gets on the cultural map in the first place, and proposes ways of thinking about sexualities. (Some people think popular culture *determines* how people think about sexuality, but I don't think that's quite right.) So, for instance, for a long time there were just very few stories being told publicly about homosexuality, and those that were – in movies, in novels, and so forth – were mostly about the tragic lives of people presented as diseased. Obviously, gay people are now far from invisible in popular culture – right now there are at least two television shows with "queer" in their titles, advertising now explicitly targets lesbians and gay men, and I cannot possibly keep track any longer of all the films and books with gay content. Before that change in the popular culture, it was hard to make the argument for gay rights and respect, since people who don't exist don't get rights, and people who are sick are usually put away. Now, with the change in popular culture, we face a radically different environment with a different set of challenges: the conservative backlash against gay visibility; the commercialization and sanitizing of a lot of lesbian and gay life; the attempt to set off "good" gays (monogamous, gender-normative) from "bad" ones (promiscuous, gender-nonconforming).

Popular culture also is the main site of public discussion of sexualities, whether in the form of fictional or nonfictional representations – a "60 Minutes" report on same-sex marriage or an episode of "Will and Grace" – or in the sorts of public controversies that are a cultural constant. Pop culture is a kind of forum – a structured one, in which only some people get to speak, but a forum none the less. Ideas about sexuality are proposed, and people take those into everyday life. Even things like the exposure of Janet Jackson's breast at the 2004 Superbowl Halftime show, or the periodic complaints that this or that cartoon character is gay, silly as they are, are also significant moments when people are publicly debating whether and how sex should be publicly visible, battling out sexual norms. These discussions are also important for affecting what gets on the policymaking agenda around sexuality, and often also in how policy decisions are resolved. How sexuality is framed is especially crucial here, I think. So when African-Americans' sexuality is framed in popular culture as "out of control," for example, it is easier for policymakers to justify something like forced sterilization.

I also think popular culture is simply a central source of how people imagine themselves as sexual beings: they see images and hear stories about what sex can or should look like, what kinds of relationships are available to be had, and so on, and these become the source material for building their sexual identities and practices. For example, in recent years popular culture has involved much, much more open discussion of women's sexuality, and not just of women as passive servants to male sexual needs. It's one thing for a woman to grow up with the "happy home-maker pleasing her man" images and stories that dominated pop culture of earlier decades, and quite another for a woman to see hookups on "The Real World" and reruns of "Sex in the City" in which women discuss masturbation and orgasms, and are shown, literally, pursuing their own pleasure.

What do you think are some of the big changes in the way popular culture views sexuality over the last few decades?

It's been a strange few decades. On the one hand, there has been a massive opening up of pop-cultural images and discussions of sexuality, to the point where homosexuality – while still obviously controversial – is presented on television, for instance, in a diverse set of genres, with an increasingly diverse range of gay and lesbian characters, and in storylines or formats that are quite flattering to gay people. This is a hugely dramatic change, given that in the fifties and sixties homosexuality was barely visible in popular culture, and when it was, it was usually presented as a sad, sick, stigmatized existence. Homosexuality is out of the pop-culture closet, to the degree that we've got entire TV shows, and now even TV networks, built around gay life. Similarly, as I suggested earlier, while a few decades ago the idea that women could be sexual subjects rather than only objects, that women could be in control of their own sexuality, was not all that prevalent in popular culture, now, images of women making decisions about who and how to be, sexually, are common-place. On the other hand, the last few decades have also seen both a huge backlash – with consistent attempts to desexualize popular culture, to re-closet the ideas and images that have become part of pop culture – and a major expansion of exploitation of sexuality, especially women's sexuality, for selling.

You study daytime talk shows in Freaks Talk Back. *Why?*

Mainly because daytime talk shows were among the first significant sites of consistent discussion of lesbian, gay, bisexual, and transgender issues in popular culture, and also because they are places where people actually speak for themselves – sometimes edited, always constrained, often distorted, but at least speaking. I thought talk shows would be a great place to go to understand how stigmatized sexualities became visible in popular culture, what kinds of visibility were available and why, what happened to the sexuality discourse when the genre changed (becoming, in the case of talk shows, more "tabloid"), and just how public discussions and spectacles of sexuality operated.

Many people think that talk shows promote either degrading views of sexual minorities or portray them as exotic and bizarre. What did your research find?

I found that, although there was certainly plenty of degrading and exoticizing and stigmatizing content in the shows, that was neither the most significant nor the most interesting aspect of them. After just a little while into the research process, I began to take the exploitation of sexual and gender minorities as a starting premise. Of course, shows built on conflict, taboo subjects, sensationalizing, and so on, were using their guests for entertainment purposes. But one of the most interesting findings was that exploitation and voice were not mutually exclusive, and that the people presented on the shows as "freaks" were often given, and took, plenty of space to talk back, and they often got a lot of support from the studio audiences for doing so. In fact, in the earlier version of the genre, the more middle-class debate shows like "Donahue," people were invited to testify and demystify their sexual identities, and were treated as experts on their own experience. Even in the newer version of the genre, the louder, scrappier, nastier shows like "Springer," oftentimes the anti-gay bigots were the ones who really got raked over the coals. Another interesting finding was that the kind of gay, lesbian, bisexual, and transgender visibility on the more tabloid shows was much, much more diverse in terms of race and class than on the older, more staid shows, which were almost exclusively white and middle-class. Sexual minorities also became, oddly, more incidental, mixed into programming that was about something else. For instance, a show on "You stole my boyfriend!" would have a gay storyline thrown into the mix. Finally, I found that, when I looked more closely at just who was being degraded and treated as bizarre, it was really not sexual minorities in general, but people who departed from conventional gender norms or monogamy norms. None of this means we should celebrate talk shows as advocates for sexual minorities, but that the picture was much more complicated than degrading or bizarre portrayals.

Some researchers argue that the media today promotes stereotyped views of gay men and lesbians; others argue that the media champions images of gays and lesbians as normal or ordinary Americans. What view is supported by your research?

As I implied in my response about talk shows, it seems obviously to be both, and the important question – at the center of a lot of my research – has to do with the conditions and forces that drive in one direction or the other. You have to break it down, I think: how the stereotype vs. normalized process plays out has to do with which particular medium and industry and genre you're looking at. For instance, various wings of the media have clearly discovered that images of gays and lesbians can be profitable, for attracting both a gay niche audience and straight audiences. But there are different strategies for doing so. If you look at advertising images aimed directly at gays and lesbians, you see more "normal" images, partly because advertisers have an interest in seeing lesbians and gay men as normal and predictable consumers; if you look at films marketed to teenaged boys, you still see a fair amount of gratuitous and old-fashioned gay stereotyping, since that's familiar and comfortable to the market being pursued. Oftentimes, you get both normalization and stereotyping at once. For instance, "Queer Eye for the Straight Guy" has none of the sick-and-self-hating stereotypes, no interest whatsoever in the closet, and the gay men there are emulated by the straights they're in charge of transforming. Their sexuality itself is uncontroversial. But the show also promotes certain old stereotypes (gay men are more "cultured" than straight ones) and generates new ones (gay men are in charge of instructing straight men in how to be good consumers). The news coverage of gay marriage countered the stereotype of lesbians and gay men as "different," while also further stigmatizing those gays and lesbians who choose different relationship frameworks. All that complicated stuff aside, though, I think the overall trend has been towards images of certain gays and lesbians (gender-conforming ones, in particular) as normal, ordinary, even possibly boring.

What are your chief criticisms of the way the mass media presents sexuality, and especially sexual minorities?

My chief criticisms are just that the mass media have not yet made enough room for all kinds of sexualities to be visible and thoughtfully considered; that they still proceed, for the most part, from a heterosexist worldview, in which they speak to their audience as if everyone were heterosexual; and that the images of sexual and gender minorities currently available are still quite narrow racially and class-wise. The coverage still tends to center around sexual minorities as sources of controversy and conflict (always a good way to attract an audience, but not always so in touch with the actual experience being presented), or on "good gays" versus "bad gays."

Is there a TV show that comes close to what you would like to see in its presentations of sex and sexualities?

The one that comes closest, for me, is "Six Feet Under." Sex is complex and visible on that show, but not overly burdened with significance. It's an integrated part of the characters' lives – or when it's unintegrated, that's because sex has taken on some unusual role in their lives, as a way of acting out or testing boundaries or working through some emotional issue. There's a remarkable diversity of sexual practices and sexual persons on the show. The sex isn't always sexy, and it's only presented as "dirty" if the character is feeling shame. That's quite different from elsewhere on television, where sexuality seems to be simultaneously suppressed as something shameful and exposed as something titillating, which in both cases inflates the significance of sex.

As a researcher of television and sexuality, what is your response to recent government efforts to impose stricter regulations on sexual content?

I find it mostly misplaced and intensely hypocritical. Let's just say that my research suggests it is unlikely that Janet Jackson's exposed breast is a significant threat to Western civilization. I understand people not wanting their kids exposed to hypersexualized images early in life, and I think there is a lot of very irresponsible sexual content on television, especially sexualized images of girls; and I'm not against regulation. My objection is more that, in the context of other attempts to impose "traditional" sexual norms – in schools, for instance – the strict regulations on sexual content seem to be more about social control than about protection of kids. (I might see it differently were there similar attempts to regulate violent content.) Also, I'm just not convinced that such regulation is a very effective option, if the goal is to create a climate for people to think about sexuality and integrate it into their lives in the most satisfying and emotionally and physically healthy manner. I would like to see efforts to make sexual content more honest, humane, funny, and open, rather than efforts to shut people up or to generate shame. Rather than the current "morality"-based attempts to keep sexuality tightly reined in, I'd love to see more efforts to present sexuality as a natural aspect of human existence, and to present information about the various ways people use their bodies with each other for pleasure and how to do so without endangering oneself. Even if it's more messy, I think that would serve both children and adults much more effectively. I can dream, right?

5

Sexual pleasure

Kelly James

WINTHROP UNIVERSITY, SOUTH CAROLINA

Let's talk about pleasure. You want pleasure? A lot of pleasure is conditioned. It's anticipation. It's not in the skin. It's not in the genitalia. It's what it means that imbues it with that sense of joy. Otherwise, it's just like eating a peach in the summer. I mean, it's really nice, but it's not ecstatic – well, it depends on the peach, but it's usually not that ecstatic. It's the symbolic investment that makes sex ecstatic.

(Tiefer 2004: 97)

Making sexual pleasure does not read like a recipe for making a pie, complete with ingredients and instructions. The parts might be in place, the people in the correct combination, and the directions followed exactly, but after tasting your final product, you are left wanting a different piece. Pleasure is not guaranteed with the experience. You may order an interesting item from the restaurant menu, but after consuming the dish you find yourself displeased or unfulfilled. Money is not returned and substitutions are not provided. Society does not guarantee pleasure in its many entertainment forms. People have sex hoping for a good time, but only after the event takes place will they know if they succeeded. Just like the gambler rolling the dice, he or she wins based on statistical formulations. Having sex may bring sexual pleasure, but, for some, hitting the sexual jackpot is rare. Pleasurable sex requires many elements, including feelings of attraction, techniques used with skill, and positively labeled bodies that fit well together. Once these diverse factors align, pleasure results. I submit that sexual desire, interest in sex, and sexual behavior mix together to yield pleasure, but, depending on the formula used, produce different versions of pleasure. The answers to the "what," "how," and "who" questions determine the "how good" answer. Explaining sexual pleasure requires the disentangling of its components.

Social construction of sexuality

Understanding sexual pleasure requires unpacking sexual norms. Desire and sexuality are socially constructed through a multitude of social processes. From social folkways of flirting to laws prohibiting sexual acts between consenting adults, sex is a cultural product. Sexual meanings must be defined and shared for two people to mate pleasurably. From the first flush of physical sensation to the final analysis of successful pleasure, we learn the symbols, standards, and forms of acceptable sexuality. Human sexual practice may vary greatly from those societal meanings, but we share a cultural sexual lexicon dictating sexuality's parameters.

Cultural norms even shape what turns us on or off sexually. When a fragrance is marketed to men as enticing to women, or when bras sell because they enhance female breasts, the decisions made to create and sell these products indicate societal influence. Of the many fragrances found in nature, who decides what is masculine, sexy, or alluring? Female breasts remain a secondary sex characteristic, but the social practice of wrapping them in lace for sexual excitation is culturally produced. Interpreting sensory information requires understanding these normative constructs. For the stimuli to elicit sensation, the human identifies the cause and links it to the effect. As the curvy bottom swings by, or the muscular biceps flex, the person must realize on some level that those events were sexy. Although the "what is sexy committee" doesn't actually exist, sexiness is heavily mitigated by mainstream values. Each choice to act on all that exciting material comes embedded in a larger construction of sexual behavior. Through different time periods and with various social leaders, sexual pleasure is socially constructed. Consequently, our experience of sexual pleasure reflects those values, beliefs, and standards.

Sexual desire

Desire has many metaphors describing its manifestations and power. Whether it courses through veins, sends chills down spines, or hits like a ton of bricks, desire leaves the unsuspecting person breathless, enervated, and weak-kneed. The flood of feeling starts with catching a person's eye and exchanging glances, or hearing a sultry voice and finding its owner close by. Maybe desire starts with a whiff of a fragrance or a gentle hug, but the body responds to the various environmental stimuli and starts to tingle, flush, or swell, letting the owner know lust has arrived (Regan and Berscheid 1999). With multiple physiological changes taking place simultaneously, the person interprets the sensations and concludes "I'm turned on."

The steps resulting from excitement ultimately affect the amount of pleasure gained. The lust must be assigned to the object of desire who inspired the feelings, but sex might take place with someone else or not at all. After identifying the lucky recipient, calculations begin. Could you, should you, will you have sex with this person? If yes, what acts will you perform and how much fun will you have? You won't know those answers until later in the sexual process, but you plan for the best outcome and play to win. All the while, you are filtering each decision through your norm set. This male is acceptable, but the other one is too short. The red-headed female is stereotypically attractive, but her shoes are too cheap, her voice too loud. People make sexual choices from their contextual meanings derived from multiple media sources, peer group preferences, and familial socialization. One need only watch a single episode of "Elimidate" or eavesdrop on a mother–daughter conversation to grasp the impact of social influence on sexual.

Senses inform desire by providing data through what we see, touch, smell, hear, and taste, but the mind decides what happens next (Resnick 2002). The excited person must choose; is it time for sex or time to watch television? What is the better plan: invest your time, energy, and emotions into sex or some other fun activity? The individual's interest in sex predicts the answer. Desire and interest for sex overlap, but they are not the same. Sexual interest implies action, but all of that sensory data may not push a person beyond lust and on toward sexual behavior (Regan and Berscheid 1999). The mind analyzes the situation while flirting, conversing with potential partners, and looking for mutual interest signals. More data ensues and more interpretation takes place. Once a body is aroused, the person chooses the partner(s) and the sex acts that yield pleasure. Lust has flooded the body, causing the mind to form an action plan: play, or walk away. Get in the game, or move on.

Sex play as pleasure

The sexual process can be convoluted. The lusting person must be willing, the body and brain must be ready, and an appropriate object of desire must be available for pleasure to occur. Sexual energy inspires sexual choices, and sexual pleasure depends on those choices. Selecting a sex partner directly affects pleasure possibilities (Schwartz and Rutter 1998; Resnick 2002). Your body says "go for it," but your brain arranges for sex, sorts through the multitude of rules, and hopes for the best. Maybe your playmate has good skills, attractive parts, and the willingness to please, and that increases your pleasure odds. Or you choose a less exciting partner because he or she delivers emotional security, making sex gratifyingly safe. Pleasure occurs in both scenarios, but they show different versions of pleasure. With research, we can determine which path brings the most pleasure. The possibilities for mates and sexual pleasure are endless and constrained only by norms and opportunity (Goode 2000; Gagnon 2004).

Whether the partner is of the same sex or the opposite sex, people have multiple reasons for partnering with one person over another. Social opportunities provide endless potential partners; even if a person is already partnered, he or she may seek more or different partners to enhance pleasure or increase the likelihood of pleasure occurring. Sexual pleasure can indicate the quality of a relationship leading to partner choices (Seidman 1993). Bonds strengthen and intimacy grows with sexual pleasure over time, but people seek sex from others even when they have a steady supply at home (Rathus et al. 1998). Whether they are in good relationships or bad ones, adulterers get pleasure from having sex outside the marriage bed. Desiring the same partner fluctuates over time and people seek variety to end boredom and feel good (Rathus et al. 1998). By stepping out of the main relationship, sexual pleasure escalates.

Who is the lucky recipient of your choice after processing potential partners? Whether you walk on the wild side or the tame side, you get the most pleasure if you choose a hottie with all the right moves. Fortunately or unfortunately, defining "hottie" and "the right moves" complicates the process. Who has what you want and knows how to use it? Partner attractiveness greatly contributes to sexual pleasure. Beauty norms embed in human desire patterns and partner choice is not exempt from their influence (Rathus et al. 1998; Regan and Berscheid 1999; Goode 2000). People want sex with appealing people, and many characteristics affect the prettiness of the package. Race and ethnicity shape beauty standards, as well as clothing style, facial features, and body shape (Nagel 2003). Preferences for some traits dominate the social scene. and people learn from media and peers to favor some qualities over others (Schwartz and Rutter 1998; Regan and Berscheid 1999; Nagel 2003). Good looks increase sexual pleasure and positive attitudes toward some features, skin colors, and body types over others shape our sexual decisions. Negative stereotypes about different races or ethnicities can make us want some people more than others. We may choose a sex partner because of his or her forbidden status, or may reject anyone dissimilar from us, finding pleasure in the sameness of our mates.

People choose sex partners in a few seconds or after much thought. Describing the partner choice process takes longer, in some instances, than actually choosing one. Men may be looking for brief sexual encounters or looking to plant their seeds in fertile wombs, while women may be seeking life-mates and casual hook ups are the last thing on their minds (Rathus et al. 1998). College kids are more likely to "hook up," or have short-term sex encounters with peers, but casual sex is not limited to the young (Regan and Berscheid 1999). Society provides many venues for choosing sex partners, from bars to college residence halls to nationally televised dating shows. Leisure time often involves seeking attractive and willing people for sex. At the game, the party, or the club, you scan the crowd for the right look, the best body, or the most attractive package. Does he or she look back? Respond positively to your advances? Accept your offer of sexual pleasure? After this negotiation, many more will follow. You have moved on to the "having sex" stage of the process, and, consequently, face many more behavior choices.

The body as pleasure

Sexual pleasure requires many systems to filter information and provide sensations, including our emotional, psychological, and physical ones (Rathus *et al.* 1998; Regan and Berscheid 1999; Resnick 2002). The brain's limbic system dictates how we experience pleasure. Our bodies have erogenous zones that send information to the brain for interpretation. Our genitalia respond to touch, but there are many other sensitive body parts like our lips, tongues, neck, ears, and the backs of our knees. The shorter list is one of parts not related to sexual pleasure and that don't respond to sexual touch. From our skin to our brain, we experience sexual pleasure when our bodies are touched in the right ways, but finding a good combination of parts and moves fulfills our desires and pleases us more. We experiment with various behaviors and learn what combination increases our pleasure. The formula may change with knowledge and experience, because many paths lead to pleasure (Rathus *et al.* 1998). As we try various combinations, we do so with cultural approval or disapproval. Sex acts are not equally utilized or supported.

Sexual scripts inform people about normative constraints and influence personal choices regarding sexual behavior (Gagnon 2004). Body parts are embedded in a larger social context of good and bad, clean and dirty, sexualized and chaste. Penile penetration of the vagina, commonly known as sexual intercourse, remains the most important indicator of lost virginity, even as the young explore oral sex earlier (Rathus *et al.* 1998; Schwartz and Rutter 1998). Genital–anal contact may be common behavior among consenting adults, but this act doesn't get the same normative support as does vaginal penetration. Socialization tells us what these acts mean, and we learn fairly early that some behavior is labeled normal and some is considered deviant (Goode 2000; Gagnon 2004). The negative connotations are inescapable, but we may enact them despite their bad press – one of sexual pleasure's conundrums. Why do we enjoy sex acts deemed less desirable in our society? Even when rules are enforced and punishments doled out, we enjoy having sex in deviant ways. The level of kinkiness in sex acts can even increase pleasure for the lusting partners (Goode 2000).

Body parts are scripted as well (Schwartz and Rutter 1998; Regan and Berscheid 1999; Gagnon 2004). Breasts are acceptable for kissing, but toes are taboo. Male nipples are less primary to the sex act than female ones. We associate sexiness and desirability with attractive bodies, but beauty standards vary throughout cultures and time periods. Determining the sexiest shape for a breast requires mass media's power and relates directly to societal norms. Women's magazines and underwear catalogs bombard the public with acceptable breasts which may vary greatly from those breasts actually encountered by the readers. Movie stars pose and exhibit stereotypically attractive bodies, and we watch them, calculating their beauty levels and determining the pleasure they will bring to us should we have them. Drop by your local sundries store, notice the number of celebrity posters for sale and see who buys them. Even the young learn lust through watching famous bodies. Calculating how much hair on a man's chest will attract the most mates, inspire the most desire, and bring the most pleasure, depends on what magazines and movies show. Committees don't meet to determine the amount of hair necessary, but people proffer standards that influence our answer to that question. Sexual scripts are omnipresent and inescapable, but do not exclusively dictate behavior (Gagnon 2004). People experiment, choose non-normative partners, and act outside their own comfort zones, despite strong cultural edicts.

Sexual acts

Acts are interpreted and labeled in a similar fashion. Religious authority may reign more powerfully over this social construction, but we learn meanings of acts, and these affect both our behavioral choices and our enjoyment (Resnick 2002). Pleasure comes from having positive interpretations or enjoying the naughtiness of a sex act (Seidman 1993; Goode 2000). To fully understand this pleasure principle, imagine enjoyment as a range starting with pleasure deriving from deviant status to pleasure stemming from acceptability. The other side of the continuum ranges from the lack of pleasure despite acceptability to missing pleasure because of unacceptability. Pleasure may increase specifically due to the taboo status of a sex act. Conversely, pleasure may decrease due to a sex act's acceptability. Through deviant acts, people experience more pleasure than if they engaged in conforming sex. Risks occurring with dangerous partners or acts can enhance pleasure for people (Seidman 1993). Whether the sex acts and partners are new, unusual, or fantasy fulfilling, we experience sexual pleasure when we explore beyond the norms. Perhaps the omnipresence of sex stimulus and opportunity fuels our search for alternative pleasure. The sex industry produces sexual possibilities in many forms, from talking sex on the phone to looking at nude prints and film images. The internet enhances the industry's wares in ways ranging from viewing live sex acts to offering personal ads for fringe sex seekers.

Boys will be boys and girls will be girls

Pleasure occurs when sex takes place, but the amount of pleasure obtained depends on many of the factors outlined above. One additional factor that impinges upon the sexual pleasure-seeking process relates to gender identity (Kimmel 2005). Sex roles and rules vary according to gender norms and the sexual social process. Lessons we learn about who should do what to whom affect our interpretation of sex acts and, ultimately, pleasure (Schwartz and Rutter 1998). Expression of sexual interest and response to sexual interest are different parts of the gender dance, and can increase or decrease desire for the dancers. Resistance or capitulation to sexual advances may have some bearing on pleasure, and these roles are gendered by design (Kimmel 2005; Schwartz and Rutter 1998). The initiator expects to receive pleasure after requesting attention, but the gatekeeper may deny that claim.

Double standards change meanings for sex partners regarding desire, acts, thoughts, and partners. If a girl is labeled a slut, her relationship to pleasure may change. Her sexual life may be stigmatized by others, altering her ability to feel pleasure during the act. The stud label may pressure young men to seek sexual activity before they are ready, or to have sex with partners they don't enjoy. Although the stud label more likely enhances a male's reputation, men experience gender constraints as well. Normative constraints can change male and female experiences of sex acts.

Sexual pleasure derives from a multiple sensory experience, and is contingent on many factors including those described in this chapter, as well as beyond its scope. Emotional meanings derived from sex shape pleasure. The skills our partners possess expand our enjoyment. Having good sex with someone you care about increases satisfaction, as does connecting briefly with a stranger. Both options, although different in composition, bring pleasure. I unwound and disentangled the components of sexual pleasure by explicating desire, interest, and behavior. The delights experienced through sexual relations are endless, socially constructed, and individually obtained. The pleasure formula is widely discussed and explored, but not universally defined and explained. People are left to their own devices, armed with the little or great knowledge they have discovered along the way.

References

Gagnon, John. 2004. *An Interpretation of Desire: Essays in the Study of Sexuality*. Chicago, IL: University of Chicago Press.

Goode, Erich. 2000. *Deviant Behavior*. Upper Saddle River, NJ: Prentice-Hall.

Kimmel, Michael. 2005. "Gendering Desire." In *The Gender of Desire: Essays on Male Sexuality*, ed. Michael Kimmel. Albany, New York: SUNY Press.

Nagel, Joane. 2003. *Race, Ethnicity, and Sexuality: Intimate Intersections, Forbidden Frontiers*. New York: Oxford University Press.

Rathus, Spencer, Jeffrey Nevid, and Lois Fischner-Rathus. 1998. *Essentials of Human Sexuality*. Boston, MA: Allyn & Bacon.

Regan, Pamela C. and Ellen Berscheid. 1999. *Lust: What We Know about Human Sexual Desire*. Thousand Oaks, CA: Sage.

Resnick, Stella. 2002. "Sexual Pleasure: the Next Frontier in the Study of Sexuality." *SIECUS Report*, V30: 6–12.

Schwartz, Pepper, and Virginia Rutter. 1998. *The Gender of Sexuality: Exploring Sexual Possibilities*. Lanham, MD: AltaMira Press.

Seidman, Steven. 1993. *Romantic Longings: Love in America, 1830–1980*. London: Routledge.

Tiefer, Leonore. 2004. *Sex is Not a Natural Act and other Essays*. Boulder, CO: Westview Press.

6

Purity and pollution

Sex as a moral discourse

Nancy L. Fischer

AUGSBURG COLLEGE, MINNEAPOLIS, MINNESOTA

If you read the newspaper or internet news headlines regularly, you're likely to come across ones that express fear that our culture is becoming morally corrupt. This moral corruption is often linked to sex. The media is a common target as the cause of corruption for exhibiting sexual content – like Janet Jackson's nipple during the Superbowl – or for featuring shows that consist of explicit sex talk and innuendo like *Desperate Housewives* or *Sex in the City*. Nor is the media the only institution allegedly corrupting youth through exposure to sex. Educational institutions are also under fire. In many school districts parents have protested against sex education that gives students birth-control information as part of the curriculum. The opinion of these protesting parents is that exposing students to this knowledge will "give them ideas" and lead them down the path to premature sexual relationships and unwanted pregnancies.

All this talk about sexual morality raises some questions. Where have our current ideas about sexual immorality come from? What is morality all about? Who labels others as immoral? Who gets labeled? And who is seen as vulnerable to the dangers of sexual corruption? In this chapter, I will show how what is considered right and wrong – sexually speaking – is not fixed and absolute, but has changed over time. Moreover, I will discuss how past ways of thinking about sexuality have influenced what we think about sexual morality today, and how moral rhetoric often reveals deeper cultural tendencies and meanings.

The arbitrariness of sexual immorality

One thing to keep in mind when thinking about how we talk about sexual immorality is that sexual acts have no meaning in and of themselves – it is only the surrounding culture which gives sexual practices or the people who engage in them particular meanings. Thus, in one sense, we could say that what gets defined as moral or immoral in a culture is arbitrary. Throughout the world, there is no universal agreement as to what constitutes sexually immoral behavior. For example, in the United States a woman baring her breasts at the beach is considered morally questionable, but not so in France, while in some parts of Afghanistan baring even her calves would be considered scandalous.

Moreover, what gets defined as moral or immoral is arbitrary in a historical sense as well. Two hundred years ago, any sex act undertaken in other than the missionary position was considered sodomy, and thus sinful. At this time, it was specific *sexual acts* such as oral sex or masturbation that were considered morally corrupt. Today, sexual immorality is not necessarily evaluated according to specific acts, but instead is often judged according to *who* engages in that behavior. In American culture, it is usually only married couples who are safe from having their sex acts associated with moral corruption. Even for devout Christians, it seems that any sex act between married people is considered potentially acceptable. For example, the 2003 Colorado Statement on Biblical Sexual Morality states that "[s]exual behavior is only moral within the institution of heterosexual, monogamous marriage". Notice that the emphasis in this statement is on *who* is practicing the sexual behavior, not on the type of sexual behavior itself. This reflects an important historical shift that took place in the 1800s when Western society became more concerned with conceptualizing deviance in terms of *identities* rather than acts (Foucault 1990). Sexual behavior came to be seen as indicative of some deep truth about the individual's character rather than as a sinful act for which one could repent and be forgiven by one's community. This had enormous implications, in that individuals who engaged in immoral acts were no longer considered as displaying a mere aberration in their behavior. They were considered fundamentally different types of people than those who were "normal." In the words of Michel Foucault, "[t]he sodomite had been a temporary aberration; the homosexual was now a species" (Foucault 1990: 43). Calling someone a "slut" or a "pervert" reflects this logic – it suggests that sexual immorality is part of the person's character rather than a behavior that arose out of a specific situation.

The implications of these cross-cultural and historical differences in what is considered morally corrupt are that we should be suspicious of any group's claims that a particular type of person or a sexual practice has always been regarded as immoral. Moreover, we should keep in mind that sexual practices that might be considered as being within the confines of acceptable moral behavior today could be construed to be morally corrupt in the future.

What is morality about?

So what is morality all about? Why do people judge others as morally corrupt, particularly in cases between mutually consenting partners? Activist Michael Warner argues that "most people cannot quite rid themselves of the sense that controlling the sex of others ... is where morality begins"; thus, in Warner's viewpoint, sexual morality is about controlling *someone else's* sex life (Warner 1999: 1). From a sociological point of view, there is some truth to this statement, though morality is also more complex. Sociologists who have studied how individuals and communities defend their moral values have observed that, on one level, morality can be about communicating to others that they are not fitting into the shared values of the group. People may use what we call "informal social control" – gossip, shunning, giving people nasty looks, calling them names – to communicate that they are not following the norms of their social milieu and that they had better step in line and conform if they want others' acceptance and friendship. In this sense, sexual morality *is* about trying to control others' sex lives.

But there is more to morality, even if we stay at this most basic level of thinking about it in terms of small-group dynamics and interpersonal relations. Think about the last time you heard an acquaintance refer to someone as "nasty" or "dirty," or as a "slut" or a "pervert." The speaker is trying to say something about *themselves* and *their own sexual morality* as much as they are saying something about someone else. The implication of calling someone else immoral is the unsaid statement, "*I* would never do that." Social psychologists refer to this type of statement as "downward comparison," where an individual tries to raise their own self-image by putting down someone else. Expressions of morality on an interpersonal level often involve this social psychological dynamic. And in this sense, sexual morality is not just about trying to control someone else's sex life. It is about claiming a morally superior position for oneself through stigmatizing others. This dynamic is often visible when people or groups make claims about morality, whether at the interpersonal level or at the level of the larger society.

Frameworks for conceiving of sexual immorality: purity and pollution

Some sociologists who study morality say that how a culture labels moral and immoral behavior reveals deeper cultural patterns. American culture is often described as a "dualistic" culture in terms of how members are taught to make sense of physical and social reality. Dualistic cultures conceptualize the world through mutually exclusive, opposing values: right and wrong; black and white; male and female; good and bad; sacred and profane. People who are strongly socialized to think in a dualistic manner tend to make judgments in either/or terms: either someone is right or wrong, good or bad, black or white, male or female; there is no in-between. Such people are often uncomfortable with categories that could potentially fall in the middle of the polarities. Discomfort with the in-between means that people feel ill at ease with anything or anyone that falls in the "liminal" zone – the realm of the in-between – and they would rather categorize something or someone as belonging on one side of the polarity or the other. For example, in the United States, many people are not comfortable with "morally gray issues," with people who claim "interracial" identity (rather than claiming to be black or white), or with intersexuals (people whose bodies are neither wholly male nor female).

Dualistic thinking affects how we think about sexual morality. Sociologist Eviatar Zerubavel (1991) suggests that one reason many Americans seem to find sex morally repugnant is because the bodily fluids associated with sex – saliva and semen – are sticky, a liminal category between solid and liquid. He also argues that many people feel uncomfortable with sex because it is associated with the breakdown of boundaries between two people – literally the opening and merging of bodies, and perhaps even a merging of consciousness.

One of the most important dualistic metaphors that cultures use to organize social reality along moral lines is purity and pollution. In her classic work *Purity and Danger* (1966), anthropologist Mary Douglas argues that cultures try to impose order and meaning on a chaotic, meaningless world through classifying some things as "dirty," "polluted," "dangerous," or "taboo" while other things are labeled as "clean," "pure,"and "safe."

Things that get placed into the "polluted" side of the equation – such as dirt, mold or bodily fluids – are often metaphorically associated with disease, and thus are thought to contaminate whatever they come into contact with. Things designated as "polluted" are thought to be dirty and dangerous. For example, one is not supposed to eat food that has fallen on the floor because that is where dirt accumulates, which will pollute the food. The expression "One rotten apple spoils the whole barrel" is based on the idea that mold or rot is something that spreads, ruining what it touches. By contrast, that which is categorized as "pure" is thought to be clean. Those who study morality argue that the purity and pollution metaphor serves as an organizing system in a culture. This has implications for how moral arguments are made and what the underlying meanings associated with such moral arguments are. What this means is that when we call someone "nasty" or "dirty" we are invoking the pollution metaphor and all that goes with it. That is, we are implying that someone is potentially dangerous and that they are likely to contaminate others.

It is easy to see how the pollution metaphor operates in the ways that people talk about sexuality. For example, in the late 1800s, white upper-class parents often spoke about their own moral purity in sexual matters. They saw themselves as morally superior to members of the working class, African-Americans and new immigrants to the United States. Their illusions of grandeur concerning their own moral purity led the white upper class to become consumed by fears that their own sons and daughters would be sexually corrupted by the "degenerate" lower classes and people from different ethnic backgrounds (Beisel 1989). Rumors and urban legends spread that black servants and other people of low social standing were constantly seeking to expose upper-class children in boarding schools to sexually prurient materials like photos of naked women, people engaged in sex acts, or "purple prose" (writing that contained explicit sexual content).

One need not look back to the 1800s to witness metaphors of pollution and contamination being applied to sex. Currently, activists who challenge gay rights have tried to uphold existing laws or pass new laws which allow employers to discriminate against gay men or lesbians as schoolteachers because parents argue that they will corrupt their children. Similarly, the contamination argument is used by those who argue that same-sex marriage must be banned because it will damage heterosexual marriage. This is a clear case where we can see the contamination logic operating. Logically speaking, allowing same-sex couples to marry should not induce heterosexual individuals to suddenly seek same-sex lovers; nor should it cause them to avoid marrying or suddenly break off an existing relationship. However, the pollution metaphor helps make sense of this type of moral corruption argument. It is not rational logic but *metaphorical* logic of contamination that is operating. Understanding this metaphorical logic of pollution can help us understand why many people do not have a "live and let live" or a "to each his own" attitude when it comes to judging others' sexual morality. In many people's minds, sex and anything associated with sexuality is placed on the pollution side of the pure/polluted dualism. Therefore, sexual "immorality" becomes rhetorically associated with danger, rot and disease. Because of this metaphorical logic, at some level, people believe that those whose behavior they find distasteful will contaminate and corrupt others.

It is important to keep in mind that these distinctions between what a culture considers pure/polluted or sexually moral/immoral are socially constructed. The metaphorical logic only reflects social reality to the degree that these metaphors become self-fulfilling prophecies. There are no sexual practices that are universally condemned across cultures or throughout history. Even incest – long thought to be *the* universal taboo – shows variation cross-culturally in terms of which relatives are and are not forbidden to join in sexual relations. Those practices that a culture defines as impure or morally corrupt tell us more about the society that created the categories than the individuals who are labeled as immoral.

Who labels others as morally corrupt?

The purity/pollution dualism is invoked by cultures in order to draw symbolic boundaries around groups. Symbolic boundaries describe how communities either include or exclude people based upon certain criteria. Moral boundaries are one type of symbolic boundary. People within a community will try to claim that someone doesn't "belong" because their behaviors supposedly don't match up to the community's moral standards. Moral boundaries mark a group's borders in much the same way that countries arbitrarily decide that a river or a line drawn on a map marks a national boundary. Those inside the line are citizens who deserve certain rights and privileges; those on the other side of the line are not. With moral boundaries, people claim that members of their own group (like Christians, or upper-class whites) are morally superior, while those outside the group are morally suspect.

Sexuality is a key axis along which groups draw moral boundaries. For example, in high school, girls in the popular cliques may exclude other girls by calling them "sluts," inferring that their sexual morality is not up to snuff. In her book *Slut!* (2000) Leora Tanenbaum found that calling someone a slut had little to do with a girl's actual sexual behavior, such as whether or not she was "promiscuous," but the label was used as a weapon in social conflicts between girls. Who labels whom as morally corrupt reflects *power relations* – the relationships between dominant and subordinate groups. In the example above, Tanenbaum found it was often the more dominant, popular girls doing the name-calling. It is their more powerful position that allows this group of girls to portray others as promiscuous and make the label stick.

Likewise, at the societal level, groups that have more power are able to label others as sexually immoral in ways where the stereotype is likely to persist. For example, claims that someone is morally corrupt are often used by those who have power compared to minority groups. The labeling of subordinate groups (such as the lower class, different ethnic and racial groups, gay and lesbian individuals) as sexually immoral has been used to justify personal insults, systematic discrimination and even violence against members of a subordinate group. Unfortunately, there are numerous examples of this in US history. In the example above where white upper-class Americans made claims about their own moral superiority, they did so by labeling black servants, immigrants and working-class people as sources of moral corruption.

Claims of immorality often reflect societal tensions between the upper and lower classes, the native-born and the foreign-born, and between black and white (Beisel 1989). History is rife with examples of whites making claims that black people are sexually immoral in order to rationalize violence and racial oppression. During slavery, white slave owners justified raping black slave women by claiming that they were promiscuous and thus were "asking for it." Similarly, after the Civil War, the lynching of black men by white mobs was almost always justified by whites claiming that black men were "hypersexual" and that they were driven to rape white women. Whites were not just maintaining a moral boundary, but were using charges of sexual immorality to maintain a racial boundary as well.

If we look at who labels whom as morally corrupt today, power relations between dominant and subordinate groups are frequently apparent. African-American men and women are still targets for being labeled as sexually immoral. For example, this can be seen in white middle-class criticisms of rap music that narrowly characterize it as about sex, ignoring how the music developed as an artform of political struggle. The power of majority populations to suppress minorities through sexual scapegoating can also be seen in moralistic rhetoric which stereotypes low-income African-American women as "welfare queens" who supposedly become pregnant in order to receive welfare checks. Likewise, the sexual double standard, by which women who have sex with numerous partners are considered "sluts" while men are considered "players," shows the power relations between these two groups. In this sense, drawing lines between who is considered sexually pure and who is impure is not a simple matter of a culture going through some "natural" process of determining its own particular norms and sorting out who follows the rules and who breaks them, but is one more way that dominant groups demonstrate their power against minorities.

Who gets corrupted?

According to our culture's dualistic logic, in order to become polluted one must first be pure; corruptibility only makes sense in relation to innocence. Which groups of people can be portrayed as symbols of sexual purity? Who can be socially constructed as innocent in a society? Sexual innocence is not symbolically available to everyone in society. For example, adult men are almost never thought of as sexually innocent.

There has been some change in who historically has been constructed as innocent. Victorian upper-class white women were once symbols of moral purity. In Victorian society, there were dichotomized public and private spheres for upper-class men and women which carried moral implications. The public sphere was the place where competition and the desire to get the upper hand meant that "anything goes" in terms of moral behavior. Bourgeois men braved this dangerous public world and those they thought were its seedy constituents – working-class men and foreigners. Many an upper-class man used this notion of a sullied, prurient, seedy public sphere to excuse their own immoralities as they sought sexual relationships with working-class women and men (D'Emilio and Freedman 1998). Meanwhile, upper-class wives were safely tucked away in the private sphere of blissful domesticity, nurturing and watching over their children. They were supposed to be the moral pillars of Victorian society. This meant that they were responsible for controlling sexual relations within marital relationships, making sure that conjugal relations were more about procreation than recreation (Smith-Rosenberg 1978). Sex between married partners was to be viewed by wives as a necessary evil, or part of one's "wifely duties," and was not necessarily something to be enjoyed. This lack of sexual desire helped define mothers as innocent and made them the pinnacles of morality in Victorian society. But not all women in Victorian times could be constructed as innocent. The working-class woman who had to work for her living – either in the factory or on the street – was at the bottom of the moral hierarchy and was often characterized as a "fallen woman."

However, women – even Victorian mothers – could not remain the symbols of moral purity in the twentieth century. Women began to recognize the constraints of this virgin–whore stereotype, seeing how it limited their roles to childcare and ensured their financial dependence upon men. It also left them out of the important political decisions of the day. Women began to protest by demanding the vote. Additionally, many women argued for new ways of organizing society on a sexual basis. Women played strong roles in movements for birth control and were vocal advocates for free-love societies (communities that believed in sexual relationships without marriage) (D'Emilio and Freedman 1998). In the wake of these sexualized protests, women could not remain the symbols of moral purity in American society.

According to Estelle Freedman (1987), children took women's place as symbols of moral purity. At one time, children were thought to be inherently evil; they were born into sin, and the devil must be beaten out of them. The phrase "Spare the rod and spoil the child" reflects this ethos. But by the turn of the twentieth century they were instead constructed as innocent and free from sin until they became enveloped in the adult world of moral corruption. In the realm of sexuality, children were considered blank slates – unaware of adult desires and lust. In the late 1800s, fears arose about children becoming the victims of adult sexual corruption. Sexual knowledge was thought to ruin children morally. For example, here are the thoughts of Anthony Comstock, a moral crusader who succeeded in passing "The Comstock Laws" which forbid sending "obscene" materials through the US mail:

> The boy's mind becomes a sink of corruption and he is a loathing unto himself. In his better moments he wrestles and cries out against this foe, but all in vain. ... Despair takes possession of his soul as he finds himself losing strength of will – becoming nervous and infirm; he suffers unutterable agony during the hours of the night, and awakes only to carry a burdened heart through all the day.
>
> *(Quoted in Beisel 1989: 110)*

Not surprisingly, the dominant ideology became one where people believed that children must be protected from sexual knowledge and experiences at all costs. This belief, that can be traced to the late 1800s, has remained with us today.

Today, most adults equate sexual innocence with the assumption that children should be ignorant of all sexual matters. To that end, they actively try to shield them from sexual knowledge in terms of talking about sex or allowing them to see sexual imagery. One of the most notable ways we can observe that children are shielded from sexual knowledge today is in the push for abstinence-only sex education in schools. Abstinence-only sex education avoids discussion of birth-control options or ways for teens to have safe sex, and instead recommends that the only way to prevent unwanted pregnancies and sexually transmitted infections is to avoid all sexual contact. Politicians and parents who promote abstinence-only education claim that regular sexual education programming which includes instruction on birth control will put ideas into children's heads and lead them to sex and unwanted pregnancies. However, the price of shielding children from more comprehensive sexual education programming seems to be more sexual violence and coercion in teenage relationships, higher rates of sexually transmitted illnesses and more teenage pregnancies than in France and The Netherlands, where sexual education is incorporated throughout the entire school curriculum (Levine 2002).

Conclusion

If we consider current discourse about sexual corruption in US newspaper headlines, in politicians' speeches or in battles of words between activists, it seems apparent that, in the United States at least, most people do not have a libertarian view when it comes to sexual morality. A libertarian view could be described as having a "live and let live" attitude, where other people's sexuality is not a concern as long as they do not harm anyone else. In this chapter, I have provided some historical and cultural context that helps explain why this is the case. Sexual morality is a loaded issue in US culture in the sense that we can unpack deeper cultural meanings and long historical trends that influence how people understand sexuality. Whenever we talk about how people express themselves sexually, we invoke deeper cultural meanings about purity and pollution, innocence and guilt, acts and identities, and power relations between dominant and subordinate groups.

References

Beisel, Nicola. 1989. "Constructing a Shifting Moral Boundary: Literature and Obscenity in Nineteenth-Century America" in *Cultivating Differences: Symbolic Boundaries and the Making of Inequality*, M. Lamont and M. Fournier (eds). Chicago, IL: University of Chicago Press.

Council on Biblical Sexual Ethics. 2004. "Colorado Statement on Biblical Sexual Morality" available online at http://www.pureintimacy.org/gr/theology/a0000108.cfm (accessed 9 March 2006). Copyright held by Focus on the Family.

D'Emilio, John and Estelle Freedman. 1998. *Intimate Matters*. Chicago, IL: University of Chicago Press.

Douglas, Mary. 1966. *Purity and Danger*. London: Routledge & Kegan Paul.

Foucault, Michel. 1990 [1978]. *The History of Sexuality: Volume I*. New York: Random House.

Freedman, Estelle. 1987. "'Uncontrolled Desires': The Response to the Sexual Psychopath, 1920–1960." *Journal of American History* 74: 83–106.

Levine, Judith. 2002. *Harmful to Minors*. Minneapolis, MN: University of Minnesota Press.

Smith-Rosenberg, Carroll. 1978. "Sex as Symbol in Victorian Purity." *American Journal of Sociology*. 84 Supplement.

Tanenbaum, Leora. 2000. *Slut! Growing Up Female With a Bad Reputation*. New York: Harper.

Warner, Michael. 1999. *The Trouble with Normal*. Cambridge, MA: Harvard University Press.

Zerubavel, Eviatar. 1991. *The Fine Line: Making Distinctions in Everyday Life*. Chicago, IL: University of Chicago Press.

7

Sex and power

Kristen Barber

UNIVERSITY OF SOUTHERN CALIFORNIA

Many of us do not question the popular ideology that views sex as natural. Yet, for the purpose of this chapter, I ask that the reader temporarily put aside the assumption of sex as natural and view sex rather as a social construct in order to explore sex as it relates to social power. In this chapter, I discuss the way some feminists have thought about the link between gender, sexuality, and power.

Heterosexuality and power

In the 1980s, Andrea Dworkin and Catherine MacKinnon argued that hetero-sex is a mechanism by which men dominate women. MacKinnon (1989) argues that, in order to understand the subordination of women in the United States, one *must* analyze the practice of heterosexuality. Dworkin and MacKinnon assert that, in America and elsewhere, sex is about male dominance and female subordination. In *Intercourse* (1987), Dworkin asks whether sex is a loving, intimate act between two mutually consenting people, or if it is the display of male social, political, psychological, and economic dominance over women.

Dworkin and MacKinnon argue that the expression of masculine traits such as aggression, power, and violence during sex shapes the meaning of sexuality for both men and women. In America, men define what sex is, and they have defined it in terms of men's dominance and women's submission. Dworkin and MacKinnon claim that women then come to understand their role within hetero-sex as passive and accommodating. Dworkin claims that women are expected to say "yes" to sex because they are expected to be compliant and to fulfill the man's "implicit right" to get laid regardless of the woman's desires. She suggests that women learn to view sex in a way that reflects men's desires and wishes.

There are, however, feminist critics. Pat Califia (1994) agrees that we live in a society where power and privilege lie within the hands of men. She also feels that patriarchy controls women and limits their freedom. However, she does not believe that heterosexual sex is only about power and women's lack of it. This perspective reinforces an image of women solely as victims. Califia argues that under conditions of male dominance women's sexuality is limited. Women may have less freedom to explore, discover, and play with their own desires and pleasures, but they are not completely powerless.

Instead of viewing sex as dangerous for women, as just another area where men control them, Califia affirms sex as necessary for women's sexual liberation. She argues that women need to explore their own desires and sexualities and fully embrace sexual variety, so long as it is between adults and consensual.

In this regard, Califia defends sadomasochistic sex, which involves eroticizing power in a consensual sexual exchange. For Dworkin, women who participate in masochism are traitors, self-haters, who are socialized into wanting to be helpless and assaulted. Califia argues that sadomasochism is usually understood, among those involved, as an intimate act between two mutually consenting people who come together to experience intense sexual pleasure. "Vanilla people send flowers, poetry, or candy, or they exchange rings. An S/M person does all that and may also lick boots, wear a locked collar, or build her loved one a rack in the basement" (Califia 1994: 177).

Califia argues that sadomasochism is not about dominance, but rather about using power for sexual pleasure. She says that this is because the relationship between the individual who plays the dominant role and the one who plays the submissive role is freely chosen by the individuals depending on their erotic preferences. The roles are negotiated and the power is understood as play, enacted through role playing. "Hardly instruments of the sexual repression of women, fetish costumes [including leather, rubber, and spiked heels] can provide women who wear them with sexual pleasure and power" (Califia 1994: 176).

Pornography: gender domination or sexual liberation?

Pornography has also spurred much debate among feminists. Some feminists reject pornography because they feel that it is an expression of men's power over women; other feminists find in porn a potential avenue by which women may learn to be more sexually open and assertive.

Dworkin (1981) criticizes pornography because she believes it teaches men and women "gender appropriate" sex which reinforces women's oppression. She claims that male power is the chief theme throughout pornography. She defines pornographic sex as women being humiliated, beaten, hung, having objects shoved up their vaginas, killed; all of which are supposed to illicit sexual arousal from the male consumer. Dworkin asserts that the force depicted in pornography is real because it is used against women. She argues that men form their understanding of sexuality and of women through their consumption of pornography. Pornography may depict a woman smiling as she is being raped. Thus, as feminist Susan Cole (1995) points out, men learn that women have uncontrollable sexual urges and enjoy being dominated and humiliated.

Critics of Dworkin do not deny that some porn is hateful toward women. However, they argue that much pornography offers images that encourage women to explore and enhance their sexuality and erotic freedom. Another feminist, Drucilla Cornell (2000), agrees that women need both to view images of sexually active women and to explore their bodies and desires. She suggests that pornography has the potential to prompt women to play with sex and can create an image of a healthy, unconstrained female sexuality.

Cornell refers to the pornography-producer Candida Royalle as creating a form of feminism that encourages women to explore their sexuality. Royalle (2000), traditional porn actress turned feminist porn-producer, produces films that are not sexist and are meant to be enjoyed by women and couples alike. She aims to create pornography that is enriching. Royalle claims that anti-porn feminists tend to associate good sex for women with romantic or vanilla sex. She argues that this keeps women from exploring and expressing their sense of sexual and sensual power. Royalle argues against the assumption that women want delicate sex. Instead, she contends that her pornography creates a safe place for women to play with power and erotic variety. She says that women have power if they are able and encouraged to control their own fantasies, even if their fantasies are of rape and being dominated.

Royalle is critical of much pornography to the extent that it is defined by genital sex and cum shots. Rather, she expands pornography for women to encompass the entire body as an erogenous zone. She encourages women and couples to sexually explore their entire bodies, expanding their understanding of what is sexy.

Califia criticizes some feminists for being prudish and uptight about sex. She is especially critical of anti-porn activists such as Women Against Violence in Pornography and Media (WAVPM) who have tried to censor pornography. Censoring sexual material, Califia argues, hurts women and all sexual minorities such as lesbians. By censoring sexual material, it will become more difficult to talk about issues such as birth control, safe sex, and pregnancy. Further, censorship laws will make it possible to remove educational materials that encourage women to get in touch with their bodies, selves, and desires. In short, Califia believes that stigmatizing pornography reinforces the ambivalent and negative feelings many women already have about sex.

Rape and state-sponsored sexual terrorism

While hetero-sex and pornography may be morally and politically debatable because they involve both power and consent, sexual violence such as rape stands in stark contrast. Even further removed is rape as state-sponsored sexual terrorism. Unlike an individual man having sex or consuming pornography, soldiers are not acting as individuals. Rather, they are agents of the state who participate in sex acts that are not consensual, but coerced and violent.

R. W. Connell (1995) suggests that sexual violence is part of what it means to be a "real" man in Western society. Men are believed to be uncontrollably aggressive and sexual. Society therefore has a tendency to understand rape as a natural consequence of men's uncontrollable sexual desires and natural tendency toward violence.

In any event, many sociologists have shown that men, as the dominant gender, use violence as a means to obtain and sustain power over women, and sometimes over other men. Men also sustain their dominance by using sex to intimidate women. This can include anything from cat-calls on the street to rape. Given the social privilege of masculinity, such sexual abusers feel that it is their right to exercise power over women, because they are "authorized by an ideology of supremacy" (Connell 1995: 83).

In *Race, Ethnicity, and Sexuality: Intimate Intersections, Forbidden Frontiers* (2003), Joane Nagel explores rape as an important aspect of war. She argues that sexual assault is a means of obtaining power and a way to humiliate and victimize the enemy. The use of sex as power is especially prominent during wars between ethnic groups. Military men often use sex in order to exercise power over men of an opposing ethnicity. For example, in the former Yugoslavia in the 1990s, the Serbs exercised power over Croatian and Bosnian men by having them castrated.

However, it is women who are typically the focus of sexual violence during wars of ethnic conflicts. Militaries often set up camps that they fill with local enemy women whom they refer to as "comfort" women. These women are at the disposal of the soldiers as sexual servants. During war, women are involuntarily rounded up and given to soldiers as rewards. They become sex slaves. Nagel states that the sexual worth of the women is based on their class and ethnicity. For example, the Japanese, during World War Two, forced 200,000 women into camps. Most of these women were of the lower class. The Korean and other Asian women were given to low-ranking soldiers. The Japanese and European women (often Dutch), however, were reserved for the high-ranking Japanese officers.

Nagel points out that, in times of war, it is not power over the *woman* that is the ultimate goal of rape. Rather, ethnically different enemy women are raped and sexually assaulted in order for *men* to exercise power and dominance over one another. She argues that, ultimately, the raping of the enemy's women is used to intimidate, humiliate, and dominate the enemy men.

Rape as a war tactic can further be understood as psychologically degrading the enemy. Since women often stand as a symbol of nationality (take the Statue of Liberty, for example), Nagel posits that sexually assaulting a woman pollutes not only her and her family, but also her entire nation.

> The logic of rape in war is always the same: rapes are committed by both sides for the familiar time-honored reasons … to terrorize and humiliate the enemy, and as a means of creating solidarity and protection through mutual guilt among small groups of soldiers.
>
> *(Nagel 2003: 153)*

Nagel goes on to say that raping the enemy women also serves as a technique of ethnic cleansing. For example, Serbian men raped Croatian women in order to impregnate them so that the women would give birth to Serbian babies. Often these women were gang-raped. In order to ensure that these women would not have an abortion, the Serbian military set up concentration camps in which they would imprison women until they gave birth to the next generation of Serbs.

I want to underscore a key point here. Some governments breed and train their soldiers to be sexually violent and aggressive. The widespread social belief that men are aggressive, especially sexually aggressive, justifies and conceals the role of the government in promoting sexual violence. In fact, the government is in effect teaching soldiers that they should, as a matter of national loyalty, sexually violate enemy women.

References

Califia, Pat. 1994. *Public Sex: The Culture of Radical Sex*. San Francisco, CA: Cleis Press.

Cole, Susan G. 1995. *Power Surge: Sex Violence & Pornography*. Toronto: Second Story Press.

Connell, R. W. 1995. *Masculinities*. Berkeley: University of California Press.

Cornell, Drucilla. 2000. "Pornography's Temptation." In D. Cornell (ed.), *Feminism and Pornography*. New York: Oxford University Press.

Dworkin, Andrea. 1981. *Pornography: Men Possessing Women*. London: The Women's Press.

Dworkin, Andrea. 1987. *Intercourse*. New York: Free Press Paperbacks.

MacKinnon, Catherine A. 1989. *Toward a Feminist Theory of the State*. Harvard, MA: Harvard University Press.

Nagel, Joane. 2003. *Race, Ethnicity, and Sexuality: Intimate Intersections, Forbidden Frontiers*. New York: Oxford University Press.

Royalle, Candida. 2000. "Porn in the USA." In D. Cornell (ed.), *Feminism and Pornography*. New York: Oxford University Press.

8

Sexual politics in intimate relationships

Sexual coercion and harassment

Lisa K. Waldner

UNIVERSITY OF ST. THOMAS, ST. PAUL, MINNESOTA

Todd meets Jan at a party and flirts while playing a drinking game. He is feeling the effects of too much alcohol and lies down in an adjacent bedroom. Jan enters and begins kissing him and taking off his clothes. Todd does not want to have sex with Jan. Besides feeling sick, he has a steady girlfriend. However, he lets Jan unzip his pants and has sex with her because he can hear his friends cheering him on from the living room. To leave without having sex would have meant losing face with his friends and enduring taunts of "pussy" and "fag."

Linda is taking a sociology class at a local community college. One of her female classmates frequently asks her out and makes sexually suggestive comments in front of the other students. This made Linda uncomfortable but she hoped that ignoring Tammy would encourage her to stop. The last straw was when Tammy followed Linda into the women's restroom, pushed her up against a stall, and grabbed her breasts. Linda dropped the class.

Nancy and Tom are engaged but have not had sex because Nancy wants to wait until her wedding day. This annoys Tom because he thinks he has waited long enough. One evening, after too many drinks, Tom initiated sex but after Nancy refused his advances Tom became angry and physically forced her to have sexual intercourse. Tom told her afterwards that he wanted to make sure they were sexually compatible and not to worry because she was "great." Nancy was devastated that someone she loved and trusted violated her. While she has broken off the engagement, she was too ashamed to call the police.

Labels such as date rape, sexual harassment, and sexual coercion may be applied to some of the situations described above, yet there are important distinctions along dimensions of power, sexual meaning, and behavior. Unlike sexual harassment, rape, and date rape, sexual coercion is less widely reported by the media. The first three have become part of the American lexicon due to widespread news coverage of events such as the Anita Hill/Clarence Thomas hearings and more recent Kobe Bryant's legal troubles. Yet most of us have probably experienced some form of sexual coercion at one time or another. Social scientists have been studying aspects of sexual coercion between intimates since the 1950s, yet it has only been within the last twenty years that the multidimensional nature of this concept has been actively explored. By comparing sexual coercion to the more well-known concept of sexual harassment, we can better understand the common denominator of power.

Rape, sexual coercion, and sexual harassment all have in common the use or abuse of power. "Imposing one's own will, even against opposition" (Weber, in Runciman 1978: 38) is a classic sociological definition of power and an example of what feminists term "power over." Sexual coercion, which encompasses rape as well as a continuum of milder behaviors, is a type of interpersonal power grab similar to sexual harassment. What differentiates harassment from coercion is that labeling an incident as harassment requires neither evidence of forced sexual behavior, nor a sexual interest in the victim.

Types of sexual harassment

Any setting where interaction is guided by professional rules of conduct, whether written or unwritten, such as the workplace, university classroom or a physician's office, needs to prevent both "quid pro quo" and "hostile environment" sexual harassment. These types of harassment differ in terms of the behaviors experienced and the social position of the harasser. All share in common the misuse of power to sexually degrade and humiliate.

We more often think of sexual harassment as something done *by* persons with power *to* their subordinates. Different kinds of socially superior positions have in common the requirement to exercise power over others. We expect professors to assign homework, physicians to prescribe medical treatment, and bosses to give orders to their employees. We understand that, if we refuse to comply, there may be serious consequences such as being fired or failing a class. We may not like it, but rarely do we question the "right" of persons in these positions to dictate our behavior, so long as what we are told is within the boundaries of what is socially considered acceptable. Max Weber terms the legitimate exercise of power "authority," in order to distinguish it from illegitimate power exercised through brute physical force or other types of coercion.

Pressurizing or forcing a subordinate into sexual interaction in exchange for promotion, more favorable work assignments, or keeping a job, is inappropriate and is an example of "quid pro quo" sexual harassment. If Linda's professor rather than her classmate had insisted on a date or sexual contact in exchange for a better grade, not failing, or staying in the class, this would also constitute quid pro quo harassment. Note that quid pro quo in this context usually involves two persons in an unequal power exchange. Professors, employers, doctors, and ministers, by virtue of their professional roles, have power and influence over their students, employees, patients, and parishioners.

In the example of Linda and Tammy, both are presumably in equal student roles. Tammy does not have the means to engage in quid pro quo harassment, as she does not determine Linda's grade. However, Tammy's persistent requests for a date and inappropriate sexual banter is an example of "hostile environment" harassment or creating an uncomfortable setting through off-color jokes, sexual innuendoes, or other sexually charged behavior aimed at degrading the intended target. Tammy is using her influence among her classmates to informally exercise power through her sexual degradation and humiliation of Linda.

Hostile environment harassment can also be used by those occupying formal positions of power. In fact, professors, employers, and the like usually have more control over the environment than their subordinates. My geology professor would pull down the video screen to show slides, and act surprised to find a *Playboy* centerfold taped to it. When this continued to happen we realized it was intentional. Some students thought it was funny and told their offended classmates to "lighten up." This type of harassment is often disguised as humor where the offended often find themselves on the defensive for being "too" sensitive, serious, unsophisticated, sexually repressed, or other (insert character flaw here). This "turn the tables" strategy of defending inappropriate behavior enables harassers to avoid acknowledging their degradation of others.

Finally, subordinates may create a hostile environment as a means of destabilizing or reversing a power imbalance deemed inappropriate based on cultural expectations of who *should* be dominant. For example, a male student who intentionally writes inappropriate sexual comments in an essay for his female professor is also creating a hostile environment. While it is possible for a female student to make a male professor uncomfortable by engaging in similar behavior, this strategy is more commonly used by those who expect to be in control by virtue of being male, white, or heterosexual, but find they are subordinate to a female, person of color, or homosexual (or perhaps someone who is all three). Although a female boss or professor has more formal power, being male gives these subordinates more cultural power and thus is an example of what is called *contrapower harassment* (Graverholz 1989, cited in Gratch 1996).

In quid pro quo sexual harassment there is pressure on the subordinate to be sexually or romantically intimate with a superior. Documenting a hostile environment does not require providing evidence that the harasser has a sexual interest in the victim. As a result, same-sex harassment is possible even if the parties differ in sexual orientation. In other words, a heterosexual man or woman can sexually harass a gay man or lesbian and vice versa (according to the US Equal Employment Opportunity Commission: http://www.eeoc.gov/). While we assume Tammy had a sexual interest in Linda because of her persistent requests for a date, her unprofessional behavior rather than her sexual interest is the key determinant. In contrast, sexual coercion involves someone with a sexual interest in a more resistant partner.

Defining sexual coercion

Depending upon the type of sexual harassment, exercising "power over" someone may come from formal or more informal power sources. While no one occupies a formal position of power within a romantic or sexual dyad, American culture historically has supported the "right" of husbands to force sex on their wives. For the unmarried, including gays and lesbians, exercising "power over" someone through sexual coercion is likely to be based on informal power.

Stranger rape is an example of extreme sexual coercion, but the focus here is on the activity that takes place between two people who know each other more or less, and who have been interacting with each other in a romantic or sexual way. Sexual coercion occurs whenever one partner pressures or forces the other to engage in any sexual behavior, ranging from kissing to various types of intercourse (oral, anal, vaginal). Because pressure or force is used, the outcome is unwanted by the resisting partner. Rape, or physically forcing sexual intercourse, is the most severe form of sexual coercion; unwanted kissing achieved through verbal and/or emotional manipulation is at the milder end of the continuum. The introductory scenario including Tom and Nancy would usually be recognized as an example of rape, because Tom physically forced Nancy to have sexual intercourse. What becomes more difficult to determine is the boundary between milder versions of sexual coercion and acceptable seduction strategies.

Because the milder pressure used by partners is similar to socially acceptable seduction strategies, the line between coercion and seduction can be blurry. In American culture, candlelight, wine, and music are all thought to enhance the mood and render sexual activity more likely. Indeed many of us have planned the perfect "romantic evening" for a special partner, hoping that the night would end in physical intimacy even if just a prolonged kiss. However, someone who sneaks a shot of vodka into his date's drink with the intent to take sexual advantage has crossed the line. Where does gentle persuasion end and coercion begin?

Clarifying this boundary are three factors that must all be present to label an experience as sexual coercion: (i) a sexual outcome, (ii) an active agent, and (iii) a victim perception of the experience as unwanted. The range of potential sexual outcomes and coercion strategies will be discussed subsequently, but note that this definition only includes situations when pressure is directly attributed to the actions of an aggressive partner. There are situations when a person feels pressure or has subsequent regrets but sexual coercion, as currently defined, did not occur.

An initial query is, when was the sexual outcome defined as unwanted? Everyone has experienced second thoughts or buyer's remorse: "I wish I had not made out with the blonde at the party." Even if the "blonde at the party" initiated the saliva exchange, it is not sexual coercion if both parties desired physical contact at the time. An exception to this rule is in situations when the initiator deliberately lies to or otherwise manipulates the partner. Lying about being in love in order to have sex is coercion, because some individuals would only choose to be sexual within the context of a loving relationship. Because the facts were mis-represented, the sexual outcome was potentially unwanted. In this latest example, the third criterion, an active agent or individual who misled the partner is also present. Unwanted sex does not require an active agent, but coercive sex does.

In the opening scenario including Todd and Jan, only two of the three conditions for sexual coercion were met: a sexual outcome and Todd's perception of unwanted sex. While it is true that Todd did not want to be sexual with Jan, there is no active agent because neither party was pressuring or coercing the other. While Jan initiated sex, she did not deliberately get him drunk, use physical force, or employ any coercion technique. She never calls him "pussy" or "fag." What compels him to have sex despite being uninterested is his fear of what he perceives his friends *might* do or say. Furthermore, there is no evidence that Todd communicated in any manner his reservations to Jan. Todd's unwanted sexual experience was more the result of sharing his friends' definition of masculinity, including pursuing every available sexual opportunity. Women defining femininity as taking care of their partner's sexual needs, even when they do not coincide with their own, may also find themselves feeling pressure. Neither of these situations are examples of sexual coercion. Although the sexual outcome was unwanted, there was no deliberate manipulation or pressure from a partner. To label Todd's situation as sexual coercion would necessitate Jan taking responsibility for Todd's beliefs on masculinity and her inability to read his mind.

While Todd's situation is not sexual coercion, this is not to say that we should be uncon-cerned with external influences such as cultural values. Given the potential negative con-sequences of unwanted sex, situations where individuals feel societal pressure to be sexually intimate because of gender roles, homophobia, concerns about popularity, or perceptions of peer pressure, are problematic yet fall outside the scope of interpersonal sexual coercion. However, partners that actively use cultural ideologies as a coercion tool do fall within the current definition. Examples in American culture include questioning someone's masculinity, femininity, or sexual identity for turning down heterosexual sex. If Jan had threatened to tell Todd's friends that he turned her down, questioned his masculinity or sexual identity by name-calling, or questioned his ability to perform sexually, she would have been guilty of using verbal sexual coercion strategies. While the verbal attacks can be gender-specific (accusing a man of being impotent, or calling a woman cold), the motivation for both is similar, wanting sexual interaction from a resistant partner.

Coercion strategies and sexual outcomes

Sexual coercion has two dimensions, the target sexual outcome and the tactic used by the aggressor. Women have reported being coerced into a variety of outcomes (kissing, fondling, and various forms of intercourse) by male perpetrators using a range of tactics including verbal-emotional and physical strategies (Christopher 1988). Verbal strategies may or may not contain some aspect of emotional pressure or manipulation. Common strategies include: telling lies ("I love you"); making false promises ("we'll get engaged"); blackmail (threatening to disclose negative information that may or may not be true); and saying things to make a partner feel guilty ("If you really loved me, you would"). Rape is the most severe form of coercion because the more extreme sexual outcome of intercourse is obtained through the use of physical force or threat of force.

Not all physical strategies include the use of force associated with rape. For example, persistent physical attempts by continual touching or being "handsy" is also a form of refusing to take no for an answer. Other physical strategies include encouraging partners to drink excessively or use drugs, physical detainment (blocking a car door, not letting someone leave), physically holding someone down, threatening to use force, using physical force (slapping and hitting), or physical force with a weapon. Even with physical strategies there is a continuum, with physical detainment and persistent touching being less aggressive than holding someone down or using physical force. Encouraging someone to drink too much is less aggressive than spiking a drink with vodka or Rohypnol (a date-rape drug). This is not to say that we should ignore milder forms of coercion, but we must acknowledge that tactics can differ by the degree of force or pressure applied. Furthermore, situations are complicated and any coercion incident might include several different tactics.

Because women usually lack the physical capacity to force sex on men, coercive women rely more on verbal-emotional strategies. Threats of disclosing real or imagined problems with sexual functioning have long been associated with things said to women ("What's the matter; are you frigid?"), but men too are vulnerable to verbal attacks that question masculine ("Can't you get it up?") and heterosexual ("You must be gay") identities. Social scientists know very little about the content of the "parting shots" that men and women fire at each other to humiliate, degrade, and verbally pressure partners into sexual activity. We do know that the lies men tell women to manipulate and deceive tend to revolve around feelings about caring, and promise of commitment (DeGue and DiLillo 2004).

Current findings on sexual coercion

A basic question is, how much sexual coercion is occurring between intimate partners? Sociologists often use surveys to answer this question. Reported rates from surveys differ because of how coercion is defined, the wording of questions, and the time period under study. For example, surveys that focus only on instances of coerced intercourse will report lower rates than those that include questions measuring instances of unwanted kissing and fondling. Additionally, physical force may be the only tactic studied, or one of several including verbal strategies. Asking individuals if they have experienced sexual coercion without some sort of behavioral checklist that defines what we mean by targeted outcomes (intercourse, kissing, fondling) and tactics (intoxication, physical force, verbal pressure, etc.) is likely to yield a smaller number of affirmative responses. The target time period may also have an impact on reported rates. Sometimes we want to know "lifetime prevalence rates" by asking individuals "have you ever experienced" some form of sexual coercion, while in other studies we focus on a narrower time period, such as within the last twelve months. Because of these differences, rates for heterosexual women with a coercive male partner range from 83 percent (Waldner-Haugrud and Magruder 1995) to 27.5 percent (Larimer *et al.* 1999). These same studies suggest the proportion of heterosexual males with a coercive female partner ranges between 73 percent and 20.7 percent.

For both heterosexual men and women, unwanted kissing or fondling happens more often than does intercourse (this is not true for gays and lesbians). Physically aggressive tactics such as force or holding someone down are reported less often than less aggressive methods such as making false promises or telling lies. Tactics commonly reported by both heterosexual male and female victims include intoxication, persistent touching, and lies.

Although both heterosexual men and women report sexual coercion, these experiences are not equivalent. Numerically, there are more women than men who report being pressured or forced into sexual interaction. The context of the experience also differs between men and women in two important respects. First, women are much more likely than men to report the use of physical force (Struckman-Johnson 1988; Waldner-Haugrud and Magruder 1995; Larimer et al. 1999). Second, men are much more likely to report stopping the coercion at kissing or fondling. In contrast, women are more likely than men to report sexual intercourse as the eventual outcome (Waldner-Haugrud and Magruder 1995).

Same-sex sexual coercion

Compared to heterosexuals, we know a great deal less about the lives of gays and lesbians, and sexual coercion is no exception. Prevalence rates for gay men and lesbians vary for the same reasons previously discussed. Currently, it appears that lesbians (30–50 percent) are more likely than gay males (12–29 percent) to have a sexually coercive partner (Waldner-Haugrud 1999). Yet, compared to heterosexual women, lesbians are less likely to experience sexual coercion. Recall that heterosexuals are more likely to experience coerced kissing and fondling than intercourse. In contrast, both lesbians and gay men are more likely to report penetration (oral, anal, vaginal) rather than kissing or fondling as the eventual sexual outcome (Waldner-Haugrud and Gratch 1997). The reason for this difference is unknown, but possibly fear of pregnancy may inhibit heterosexuals who would otherwise pressure their partners into intercourse. Similar to heterosexuals, gays and lesbians report that milder coercion strategies (lies, persistent touching) are more frequently used against them than being held down or other types of physical force.

Risk factors

More attention has been paid to describing outcomes and tactics than identifying what types of characteristics or situations increase the likelihood of being involved in sexual coercion. What is known is the connection to alcohol. Gay or straight, male or female, victim or aggressor, those who drink excessively are more likely to report being victimized or perpetrating unwanted sexual contact even when other tactics besides intoxication are used. What constitutes excessive drinking is somewhat subjective, as some individuals can tolerate higher levels of alcohol consumption than others, but the definition of binge drinking can serve as a useful benchmark. Binge drinkers are women who consume four drinks or more per drinking occasion and men who consume five or more drinks. Individuals who engage in binge drinking are at a higher risk for coercion than those who abstain or consume less.

The attitudes and beliefs of rapists have been compared to those of men who are not sexually aggressive. Rapists tend to have more negative attitudes towards women and more traditional ideas about gender, including the meaning of masculinity and the role of women. For example, they are more likely to agree that men should be the ones to initiate sex, and that women who drink and flirt are "asking for it." This latter belief is called a rape myth, or a false belief used to justify rape. Widespread acceptance of rape myths gives men more cultural power over women.

Men who are not rapists but use verbal methods of sexual coercion are also different from non-aggressive men. Coercive men have less empathy for women, more experiences with child abuse, a stronger adherence to rape myths, a higher level of acceptance for relationship violence, and a greater level of distrust and anger towards women. None of these factors necessarily causes sexual coercion but may help us better to understand both the social (cultural attitudes towards women, rape myths, male dominance, homophobia, gender ideologies), familial (history of child abuse, experiences with relationship violence), and interpersonal (lack of empathy, distrust and anger towards women) conditions that foster sexual coercion.

Not crossing the line

We can reduce but not completely eliminate our chances of becoming a victim of sexual harassment or coercion. What is completely within our own power is the choice to live a sexually ethical life by choosing not to use harassment or coercive strategies in our interpersonal interactions. While avoiding more blatant violations such as quid pro quo sexual harassment and rape seems clear, milder sexual coercion strategies and sexual banter (that may or may not be labeled as hostile environment harassment) are less clear. What further complicates matters in the case of sexual harassment is that both the workplace and the classroom are often a meeting place for marriage and dating partners. The key to distinguishing whether or not something is sexual harassment or harmless sexual banter is how *wanted* the behavior is perceived by the recipient (Gratch 1996). Asking a co-worker or classmate out on a date is not going to be labeled as sexual harassment if the one asked was hoping for such an opportunity. Neither is someone apt to label their partner sexually coercive if they wanted to be kissed or to have sex. This ambiguity between actual wants and what others perceive creates the potential for conflict, because some of us are better at correctly interpreting situational cues than others. However, all of us need to be truly committed to listening to those we interact with and not using historically acceptable excuses to justify offensive behavior. This doesn't mean that we should never ask colleagues out on dates, refrain from sexual banter, or avoid making sexual advances.

Putting aside the question of Linda's sexual orientation, Tammy's request for a date need not have been an example of sexual harassment. It was Tammy's *persistent* requests despite Linda's lack of interest, communicated by ignoring Tammy, that constituted harassment. Sexual banter in the workplace need not be sexual harassment if the parties involved are comfortable interacting with each other in this way. Linda's ignoring of Tammy should have been a signal that her sexual comments were unwelcome. The same rules also apply for sexual coercion. Resistance should always be taken as a sign that a sexual invitation is not wanted unless the parties involved have negotiated a different understanding. This is more practical than the approach of requiring parties to receive verbal consent at every level of sexual intimacy, because people communicate in both verbal and non-verbal ways. Making a sexual pass at someone and being turned down is not sexual coercion unless the initiator refuses "to get it" by *persistently* making sexual overtures or resorting to name-calling and other sorts of bullying behavior.

Max Weber defines "life chances" as the likelihood of experiencing a phenomenon connected to one's position within the social hierarchy. The likelihood of experiencing sexual harassment or sexual coercion is always higher for those with low social power. Yet power is not always connected to a formal position. Understanding the different avenues for acquiring and exercising power allows for a fuller, more complicated picture of social reality that defies easy categorizations or simplistic solutions.

Lisa K. Waldner

References

Christopher, F. S. 1988. "An Initial Investigation into a Continuum of Premarital Sexual Pressure." *Journal of Sex Research* 25: 255–66.

DeGue, Sarah and David DiLillo. 2004. "Understanding Perpetrators of Nonphysical Sexual Coercion: Characteristics of Those who Cross the Line." *Violence and Victims* 19: 673–88.

Gratch, Linda Vaden. 1996. "Recognizing Sexual Harassment: Problems Caused by Labeling Difficulties." In Bernice R. Sandler and Robert J. Shoop (eds), *Sexual Harassment in the University*. Boston, MA: Allyn & Bacon.

Larimer, M. E., A. R. Lydum, B. A. Anderson, and A. P. Turner. 1999. "Male and Female Recipients of Unwanted Sexual Contact in a College Student Sample: Prevalence Rates, Alcohol Use, and Depression Symptoms." *Sex Roles* 40: 295–304.

Runciman, W. G. 1978. *Weber: Selections in Translation*. Cambridge, MA: Cambridge University Press.

Struckman-Johnson, Cindy. 1988. "Forced Sex on Dates: It Happens to Men Too." *Journal of Sex Research* 24: 234–40.

Waldner-Haugrud, Lisa K. 1999. "Sexual Coercion in Lesbian and Gay Relationships: A Review and Critique." *Aggression and Violent Behavior* 4: 139–49.

Waldner-Haugrud, Lisa K. and Brian Magruder. 1995. "Male and Female Victimization in Dating Relationships: Gender Differences in Coercion Techniques and Outcomes." *Violence and Victims* 10: 203–15.

Waldner-Haugrud, Lisa K. and Linda Vaden Gratch. 1997. "Sexual Coercion in Gay/Lesbian Relationships: Descriptives and Gender Differences." *Violence and Victims* 12: 87–98.

United States Equal Employment Opportunity Commission. 2004. "Discriminatory Practices." Available online at http://www.eeoc.gov/abouteeo/overview_practices.html (accessed 22 March 2006).

9

Gay and straight rites of passage

Chet Meeks (1973–2008)

GEORGIA STATE UNIVERSITY

Probably no area of social life is more commonly thought of in terms of nature and individual psychology than sexuality. When people talk about sexuality, they frequently use terms like "instinct," "biology," "hormones," and so on. It is certainly true that sexuality is an important feature of most individuals' lives and psyches, and it is also true that, when we're in the realm of sexuality, we often feel in the grip of something emotionally volatile and beyond our own control, and hence part of nature or some other force outside of us and outside of man made, social things. Could it be, though, that the "outside" force that infuses sexuality with such emotional, bodily, and sensual volatility, is society itself?

In this chapter, I discuss *rites of passage* as they relate to sexuality. I discuss the rite of passage that, in the gay and lesbian community, is referred to as "coming out." Then, I discuss the phenomenon of the temple marriage in the Church of Jesus Christ of Latter Day Saints ("the Mormons"). I have chosen these two examples of rites of passage not because they are extraordinary, unusual, or exotic, but precisely because they are so typical. These rites shed light on sexual meanings that apply to us all, gay or straight, Mormon or otherwise. They show us quite clearly that an area of life we commonly think of as instinctual – sexuality – must in fact be learned and enacted through complicated social processes.

Before I discuss coming out and temple weddings, though, let's look more closely at what a rite of passage is, exactly.

The rite of passage

Think of your favorite book. That book is composed of long and short sentences that turn into paragraphs, paragraphs into pages, pages into chapters, and so on. Now, imagine what it would be like if someone suddenly removed all of the punctuation in this book of yours. All of the periods and semi-colons, all of the dashes and commas, indeed even the separation of one paragraph from another – all of this is gone, and what you are left with is one, long, run-on sentence. You could probably read this book, but chances are it would not make much sense, and eventually you would give up. In other words, it is the punctuation that gives the book meaning. The pause that is indicated by a comma, for example, actually gives the sentences you read a meaning that might otherwise escape your attention. Punctuation tells us how to read a sentence, when to accentuate certain words or phrases, even what emotions to convey while reading.

Rites of passage are the punctuation of social life. They are conveyers of meanings that, due to the nature of rites of passage, come to be felt deeply by individuals who participate in them. For our discussion here, rites of passage have several important characteristics, many of which were originally formulated by the anthropologist Arnold van Gennep (1960). I want to summarize some of those features here in order to help us understand both coming out and Mormon temple weddings as sexual rites of passage.

First, rites of passage involve the removal of the individual from the everyday world. This removal can be real or imaginary, partial or total, but some separation of the individual from the usual world he or she inhabits must occur. Rites involve the invention of an alternative space where the rituals associated with the rite of passage unfold. The isolation of the individual from his or her typical, everyday life is essential, because it helps to focus his or her attention on the features of identity, self-hood, community values, and symbolic meanings that the rite of passage conveys. Hence, baptisms are held in churches, inductions into secret clubs and sororities in dark basements, and so on. Separation tells the initiate that he or she is about to participate in something extremely important and sacred.

Second, once the individual is isolated, he or she undergoes a significant and intense process of re-learning. Rites of passage affirm for initiates very specific communal values and norms, ethical codes of conduct, and bonds of solidarity. Rites always involve some refashioning of the self and identity. An individual who passes through a rite is a different person once he or she finishes; their identity, sense of self-hood, and sense of social obligation changes. Sometimes the change in consciousness that occurs with the rite is minimal – for example, when college seniors go through a graduation ceremony. Other times, though, features of the self and identity are either drastically amplified, or erased entirely, and the change in selfhood and consciousness is far more radical – such as when draftees are trained to serve in the military. But all rites, in the end, always involve a transformation and refashioning of the initiate's sense of self.

Third, rites of passage involve the reshaping of symbolic boundaries and meanings. They confirm for the initiate his or her membership in a group and, in doing so, often change his or her relationship to the broader social groups of which he was once a member. Once a rite is completed, and the initiate re-enters his or her everyday world, that world can appear very different. Initiates can perceive some or even all of their typical social relationships with members who are not a part of their new community in very different terms; individuals who were once friends and intimates can suddenly appear to be strangers. The things that once passed as common sense can suddenly seem bizarre. The rite of passage can thus convey for the initiate a sense of being different from his or her peers, because the symbolic boundaries that regulate the initiate's social life have changed.

This brings us to a final characteristic of rites of passage. Because the transformation of self-hood is so central to their purpose, rites of passage tend to be fairly emotional events for their participants. If you think about rites of passage you have been through – a baptism, perhaps, a graduation ceremony, or induction into a special club – you'll probably remember that these rites tend to invoke fairly strong feelings. You might have felt a slight tingling in your neck when your classmates threw their graduation caps into the air, or an equally emotional feeling when learning a special hand-shake. You might have wept. Emile Durkheim (1915) referred to this feature of rites of passage as "collective effervescence." The rite of passage is often infused with intense feeling, and this emotional volatility makes the impact of the rite profound for the initiate. Durkheim believed that rites evoke such strong emotions because the initiate experiences a fusing of his or her own identity with the identity and consciousness of the group.

During the rite, an individual's sense of themselves as separate fades as their membership in a broader collective takes over. Rites are emotional events because, when we participate in them, we are participating in a drama that transcends our own particularity as individuals.

Let's now look at two examples of sexual rites of passage – coming out, and Mormon temple weddings. Because these rites of passage convey meanings – just like the punctuation in a book – it is through them that both gay and heterosexual identity become meaningful.

Coming out – a lesbian and gay rite of passage

Because we live in a society where heterosexual identity is most often presumed, it becomes necessary for individuals who are not heterosexual to disclose their sexual identity. By now, the phrase "coming out" is fairly common, at least in American culture. This phrase commonly refers to the disclosure of homosexual identity by gay and lesbian people – to themselves, to friends, family and loved ones, and even to bosses, co-workers, physicians, and other people they encounter in their day-to-day lives. Such disclosures can seem like intensely personal, private, and individual matters. But coming out is also social. Coming out also often refers to becoming a part of a more or less visible lesbian and gay community and culture. Coming out is a rite of passage and, as such, has features that are common to most individuals who come out. Coming out, because it is a rite of passage, does not mean simply revealing a gay or lesbian identity that was already there; it means that, by coming out, individuals' sense of self is altered. They *become* gay.

The phrase "to come out" or "coming out of the closet" dates back to the 1970s and gay liberationist politics. Gay liberationists encouraged other gay and lesbian people to "come out of the closets and into the streets." By coming out, the liberationists did not only mean telling oneself and others about one's homosexuality, although this was part of the process. Rather, coming out meant changing one's consciousness. Coming out meant becoming aware of the way society demeans and denigrates any form of sexual expression that is not heterosexual. Coming out, as one liberationist put it, requires "rejecting the society within us" and attaining a "gay consciousness" ("Murray" 1973). Coming out, liberationists realized, might entail risks – of being rejected by family, or fired from a job, for example – but liberationists encouraged gay and lesbian people to "reject the values of the system" and to think of their homosexual desires in positive, prideful terms, rather than negative, homophobic terms.

Coming out, then, for liberationists, was about far more than simply disclosing one's sexual identity to others. It was about a change in consciousness, a shift in the way one perceived and viewed the world. It was also about espousing new values. For example, gay liberationists encouraged gay people to be less materialistic. They believed that American materialism – the intense focus on making money, having the best job, buying the nicest house, etc. – was responsible for sexual alienation. They believed Americans were so busy making money and being materialistic that they did not have time to have fulfilling personal lives. And when an entire culture is unhappy and unfulfilled, they often look for others to blame, demonize, and ostracize – like homosexuals. For this reason, coming out entailed espousing more non-materialist values, being less individualistic, more community minded, and trying to be less alienated from one's own sexual expressive capacities. Coming out, in other words, was about far more than just saying "I'm gay."

Gay liberationism did not last very long in the world of lesbian and gay politics, but the notion of coming out and coming into a lesbian and gay community certainly did. About thirty years after the emergence of gay liberationism, an anthropologist named Gilbert Herdt (1992) did an ethnographic study of coming out amongst gay teenagers in Chicago, Illinois. Herdt studied the interactions amongst teenagers at "Horizon," a gay and lesbian youth center. He argued that, while coming out is often understood in psychological terms, it is actually social and cultural – a rite of passage.

The teenagers in Herdt's study experienced Horizon as an alternative space, an "inside" place set apart from the "outside" world of their everyday lives. Thus they were, as we would expect, isolated from their typical worlds while at Horizon. This provided them with a sense of safety from homophobia, a place where they could "be themselves," but Herdt also argues that this safe place also worked to focus their attention on the significance of same-sex desire in their sense of self and identity. The gay teenagers in Herdt's study viewed the door to Horizon as "a porthole into a 'magical circle' … [they] expressed wild and fantastic ideas about what they imagined awaited inside" (1992: 39). The way in which Horizon was experienced by Herdt's subjects gave them a sense that what was discussed there was extremely important, both personally and socially.

The teenagers Herdt studied also experienced coming out at Horizon as a significant process of re-learning. Horizon was not simply a place where they would disclose their identities; it was a place where their identities were made. They *became* gay and lesbian at Horizon. And this meant becoming part of a gay and lesbian community that espouses different values than the broader, "straight" world. For example, the teenagers had to re-learn the meaning of homosexuality. In the outside world, they learned that homosexuality was sick, abnormal, and disgusting. But at Horizon they learned more positive definitions of homosexuality. In addition to re-learning the meaning of homosexuality, the teenagers in Herdt's study learned a different set of communal values. The rule at Horizon was to always be non-judgmental, to not discriminate on the basis of race, class, or gender, and to accept those who dress, act, or speak differently than oneself. The teenagers at Horizon believed equality of this sort was very important, because it set them apart from the outside world, and it ensured that they would not commit the same injustices as their straight counterparts on the "outside." Thus, coming out at Horizon entailed far more than just disclosing their lesbian and gay desires and identities to each other; it required a refashioning of their individual consciousness, their subservience to a ritual process, to ethical codes, solidarities, and collective values that transcended them as individuals.

Coming out, then, is a sexual rite of passage. It is through coming out that gay and lesbian people become gay. All of the features of the rite of passage I discussed above are present in coming out. Individuals are isolated from their everyday lives, even if just minimally. They must undergo a process of re-learning, where they reject negative definitions of homosexuality and adopt a more positive, affirmative view. Coming out entails a shift in consciousness, where individuals come to view others outside of their new group very differently than they did before, and where individuals suddenly feel very different as they move about the world outside of their new community. And, as one can imagine, coming out is intensely emotional, not only because it is personal, but because individuals who come out are participating in a drama that transcends them and that binds them to a community and that community's values.

Of course, homosexuality is a marker of difference in our society, and one might be tempted to think that rites of passage only apply to those who are "different," but as the next section makes clear, heterosexuality is no more instinctual. Heterosexuality has to be achieved and enacted through rites of passage, too.

The Mormon temple wedding – a heterosexual rite

Heterosexuality in American culture is normative. This means that the basic idea that heterosexuality is "normal" and "natural" is so taken for granted, being heterosexual usually doesn't even need to be stated directly. We might be led to believe that only gays and lesbians have rites of passage, since their sexuality is marginalized. But, in fact, heterosexuality too involves complicated rites of passage through which the meaning of heterosexuality, and the values it rests upon, are conveyed. We might believe that heterosexuality is just a matter of instinct, but we'd be wrong. It has to be learned, just as the gays and lesbians in Herdt's study had to "learn" gay identity through their rites. We do not often think of there being a "heterosexual community," but there is one, and like gays and lesbians, heterosexuals must engage in certain rites of passage in order to become full members of this community. And, like gays and lesbians who come out, participation in rites of passage changes the consciousness of heterosexual participants. Heterosexuality, it turns out, has to be achieved through a rather complicated ceremony: the wedding.

The Church of Jesus Christ of Latter Day Saints, or "The Mormon Church," was founded in 1830 by Joseph Smith. Smith claimed that he had been visited by one of God's angels, Moroni, and that this angel had revealed to him the story of Christ's gospel on the American continent before the arrival of the European colonists and pilgrims. Most historians believe that Christianity only arrived on this continent with the arrival of the Europeans, but Smith argued that a lost Israeli tribe had traveled to the Americas long, long before Columbus or other Europeans. This tribe, the Nephites, brought the gospel of Christ with them. Smith wrote this revelation, and hundreds of others, down in what is now known as *The Book of Mormon*, the central text of the Mormon faith.

Like all religions, Mormonism is replete with rites of passage, symbols, and rituals which are used to stylize the Mormon belief system and to solidify Mormon communality. The Mormon temple marriage is *the most important* rite of passage in Mormon life. Little can be known directly about this rite since only the most devout Mormons are ever allowed inside a Mormon temple. Those who wish to marry there must pass a strict interview with their Bishop in order to receive a "temple recommend." And what goes on inside a temple is guarded with the utmost secrecy — secrecy which adds to the emotional intensity and significance of the marital rite. Nevertheless, a few ex-Mormons have written about their experiences.

In the overlap from these accounts, we can glean a partial understanding of how this secret rite of passage works, as well as how it is connected to very specific heterosexual meanings. Two books that give very similar accounts are *Leaving the Saints* by Martha Beck (2005), and *Secret Ceremonies* by Deborah Laake (1993).

Both Beck and Laake write about their temple wedding as the most important day of their life, and as the day they had looked forward to since their youth. As Mormons, they had been taught by their parents and church leaders that there are three levels of heavenly existence. Only Mormons who are married in a temple ceremony can ever be permitted to the highest, "celestial kingdom" of heavenly after-life, where they will become Gods themselves and rule over their own earth-like planets. And, importantly, when Mormons are married in the temple, they are "sealed" to each other and to each other's families for eternity. Individuals who do not marry in the temple will not make it into the celestial kingdom, but will instead be relegated to one of the lower levels of heaven and, quite importantly, will not be sealed to their families — which means that they will be alone *for eternity*.

The temple ceremony itself, as described by Beck and Laake, is highly ritualized. Upon entering the temple, bride, groom, and their respective immediate families must shower and remove all of the "earthly" impurities from their bodies. All individuals who work in the temple wear white, and only white. Unlike most heterosexual weddings, Mormons who marry in the temple often marry in groups, so the ceremonies are less centered around the happy young couples than on the very important lessons the ceremonies convey to them. Importantly, bride and groom prepare for the wedding ceremony separately. In fact, all of the rituals except for the last one are sex-segregated. Many of the rituals are targeted toward women, since men undergo extensive temple rites when embarking on the two-year-long Mission nearly all college-aged Mormon men participate in.

After showering, women undergo an "anointing." Special oils are rubbed on specific areas of her body, including her genitals, and prayers for her "fruitfulness" are said by the female temple attendants who anoint her. When she is finished being anointed, she is presented with her "temple garments" (men must wear these, too). Temple garments are underclothes which Mormons believe protect them from Satan. Temple workers instruct initiates that these garments can only be removed when showering and that, when they are worn out, they must cut off the insignia (signs on the garments that are thought to have derived from the insignia of the Masonic Temple, of which Joseph Smith was a member) before throwing the garments away. After men and women receive their temple garments, they are told something very important: their name in the afterlife. Mormons believe that, after death, the devout become Gods in their own heavenly kingdoms, and the learning of one's afterlife name is an essential part of this rite of passage. After learning their names, bride and groom finally put on their wedding clothes. These look much like the same clothes one wears at any wedding, except that men wear a small hat, and both bride and groom wear small green aprons that are meant to symbolize the fig leaves worn by Adam and Eve (who Mormons believe were the first heterosexuals).

The actual wedding ceremony begins in "The Creation Room," a spacious chapel with murals depicting the creation of the world by God. Upon entering this room, brides sit on one side of the chapel, grooms on the other. Then, the couples and their families watch a movie. This movie depicts the creation of the earth by God, Jesus Christ, and the archangel Michael (Adam). This movie (which, before the age of the DVD, was enacted live by temple workers) instructs the couples about the central place marriage between men and women occupies in the creation, not just of the earth, but of the entire universe. It is while watching this movie that the couples recite their vows to each other including, for the women, a vow to abide by The Law of Obedience, in which they promise to obey their husbands so long as their husbands are obedient to God. After reciting this and other vows, initiates learn a special handshake which Mormons call "The First Token of the Aaronic Priesthood" (probably also borrowed by Joseph Smith from Masonic rituals). This and many other gestures are ritualistically performed during this ceremony, including one gesture which involves the simulation of cutting one's own throat, a penalty for revealing temple rituals to anyone.

The wedding culminates when couples enter "The Celestial Room," which is ornately decorated with beautiful murals depicting heaven, and crystal chandeliers. It is here that the most important ritual in this rite of passage unfolds. Bride and groom are divided from each other by a sheet which hangs from the ceiling. This sheet represents the "veil" separating earthly from heavenly life. With men on one side, and women on the other, couples are instructed to meet each other at the "five points of fellowship": foot to foot, knee to knee, breast to breast, hand to back, and mouth to ear. The sheet has a large slit cut through it so that couples can embrace in this fashion. Once embraced through the "veil," couples practice the various handshakes and gestures they have been learning throughout the wedding ceremony. Then, with her mouth pressed close to her new husband's ear, the bride whispers her afterlife name and the groom, in turn, pulls his bride through "the veil." This action symbolizes the Mormon belief that, in order for a woman to enter heaven, she must remember the secret and sacred gestures, and be pulled through the veil by her husband. Importantly, the bride never learns her husband's afterlife name.

Like coming out, the temple marriage bears all of the marks of a rite of passage. Individuals are isolated from their everyday lives; they undergo significant re-learning and self-transformation;

the rite of passage shifts symbolic boundaries and meanings for them; and, as many would surely report, the wedding is characterized by the kind of "collective effervescence" we discussed earlier. Many of you probably find the details of this particular rite of passage quite strange. Indeed, in America and elsewhere, Mormons have often been persecuted for their religious beliefs and for the secrecy which surrounds temple rituals. Like homosexuals, Jews, and Catholics, Mormons have historically been thought of as "different" in America.

But, are Mormons really *that* different? Through this rite of passage, Mormons adopt two identities, one fairly obvious, but the other less so. In an obvious way, it is through the wedding that young Mormons finally *become* true Mormons. Their beliefs and social bonding to the rest of the Mormon community are solidified. And this identity certainly sets them apart from the rest of Judeo-Christian America. But less obvious is the fact that through this wedding young Mormons *become* heterosexual. Through the Creation movie, Mormons learn that hetero-sexuality is central to the universe and that marriage is an institution created by God, not man. Through the movie and the anointing, Mormons learn that procreation is a heavenly duty, and that children are God's gift to humanity through marriage and marriage alone. Procreation and child rearing are such sacred heterosexual duties, bride and groom learn that they will continue procreating after death, when they will become Gods themselves (the men, at least) and create souls to populate the earthly planets they will someday rule over. Heterosexuality links them to the divine origin of the universe, and makes them eligible for Godly status in afterlife. And, finally, through the Five Points of Fellowship ceremony, Mormons learn that heterosexuality does not simply involve procreative sexual relations between men and women, but absolute obedience and subservience of women to men. Their salvation after death depends on it! A Mormon woman who does not remain devoted to her church and husband will not be pulled through the veil.

Is this version of heterosexuality Mormons learn different than the one most heterosexuals undergo? My guess would be: no. When those of you who are heterosexual get married, you will likely exchange rings, signifying your joint ownership over each other. And this ownership will not be an equal one, since most of you who are women will take the last name of your new husbands, signifying the superior status of men. At most of your weddings, the person who marries you will recite lessons about the importance of having children and a real "family." You will all say prayers that convey the message that your weddings are special, and sacred, and that being heterosexual makes you closer to God and "his" laws. No matter how strange you might think the temple wedding is, most of you will go to elaborate detail in planning your own weddings, including the expensive gowns and tuxedos, the high-end caterers, and the fantasy honeymoon in Hawaii, the Greek Isles, or Las Vegas. According to the sociologist Chrys Ingraham, heterosexuals spend about $32 billion a year on these rites of passage. They do so in order to claim membership in a very important community, one they believe was created by God, and one that entitles them to certain God-given rights and privileges. Many heterosexuals wouldn't view heterosexuality as a "community," and they also wouldn't view heterosexuality as something that has to be ritualistically enacted and performed, but they are a part of a com-munity, and as the Mormon temple wedding illustrates, heterosexuality can only be achieved through very complicated performances and rites. Heterosexuality is not instinctual – it requires a lot of work, a lot of learning, and a lot of money.

Conclusion

Rites of passage are the punctuation of social life. They convey meaning and tell us what is important, sacred, and valuable. They solidify communal bonds. They give us ethical codes to live by. And they change our sense of ourselves, oftentimes quite dramatically. Through coming out, gays and lesbians *become* gay. Coming out is not only about disclosing one's homosexuality to others, but usually also involves seeing oneself as gay in a new, more positive way, as well as solidifying one's bonds with others in the gay community. As Herdt showed, coming out often involves adopting very specific values – such as the value of tolerating differences. Marriage – for Mormons and others – is the key rite of passage through which heterosexuals *become* heterosexual. It is through the marital rite that women learn to be obedient to men, that both partners learn the Godly pricelessness of procreation, babies, and families, and it is through this rite that heterosexuals internalize the belief that their sexuality is connected to God, the origins of the universe, and the continuity of time. Without these rites, neither heterosexuality nor homosexuality – at least as we know them – would exist.

References

Beck, Martha. 2005. *Leaving the Saints*. New York: Crown Press.

Durkheim, Emile. 1915. *The Elementary Forms of Religious Life*. New York: Free Press.

Herdt, Gilbert. 1992. "Coming Out as a Rite of Passage: A Chicago Study," in G. Herdt, ed., *Gay Culture in America*. Boston, MA: Beacon Press.

Ingraham, Chrys. 1999. *White Weddings*. New York: Routledge.

Laake, Deborah. 1993. *Secret Ceremonies*. New York: William Morrow & Co.

"Murray". 1973. "Out of the Closets, Into the Streets." *The Berkeley Barb*, 19.

van Gennep, Arnold. 1960. *The Rites of Passage*. London: Routledge & Kegan Paul.

Part 3
Sexual bodies and behaviours

Introduction

Most people think of certain body parts as either sexual or not. We think of penises and breasts as sexual, for example, but probably think of feet as not sexual. Most of the time, we think that sexual body parts are sexual for natural or biological reasons. But in this part of the book we will be exploring the way that body parts *become* sexual through a variety of social forces. What counts as sex depends on how the body is defined or viewed.

You might say that in all societies there is a hierarchy of sexual bodies and behaviors. In America, this hierarchy has two important features. First, the penis is widely considered to be the most important sexual body part. The penis has been socially constructed to be the "actor" in the sex act. The erect penis is associated with virility, power, and masculinity. The body of the heterosexual, white, young, able-bodied male, poised and ready with his erection, is at the top of the social hierarchy of bodies in our society. Second, heterosexual coitus (the penetration of the vagina with the penis) is thought to be the most normal and natural sexual behavior. Everything from the education about sex we receive in high school to the way medical authorities talk about sex tells us that there is a natural "fit" between the penis and vagina.

Body parts other than the penis, and sexual behaviors other than heterosexual coitus, are socially judged to be less natural, less normal, and less sexual. The vagina, for example, is thought of as a sexual organ, but a passive, receptive one – with nowhere near the sense of virility and power of the penis. Anal sex violates the social norm that tells us that heterosexual coitus is the only natural way to have sex. In doing so, it has been constructed as dirty, unclean, and unnatural. Even heterosexual activities other than coitus are thought of as less important or sexual. Foreplay, for example, is constructed as something one does *on the way to* coitus, but not as a sexual end in itself.

So, in America, heterosexual men and their bodies are at the top. But not all heterosexual men. Some heterosexual men very definitely do not come to be thought of as sexual, much less virile, powerful, and masculine. Asian men, for example, have long been constructed in popular culture as effeminate, slight, and dainty – far less sexual and far less powerful compared to their white American, hypermasculine counterparts. Older men and men who have lost their ability to achieve an erection are constructed by the medical community and culture at large as having a "dysfunction." The medical community has created a "Viagra culture" to restore to these men what our society deems most important: the erection. So even heterosexual men can have their bodies marginalized and constructed as asexual by social authorities.

The hierarchy of bodies and behaviors we will talk about in this part is always open to challenge. Anal sex was once almost uniformly only associated with gay men and moral pollution, but has increasingly become an act that some heterosexuals participate in, too. Gay pornography that features anal sex sometimes challenges the idea that the penetrator or "top" is the most powerful partner in the sex act. Women, too, have challenged the idea that they are simply passive participants in the sex act. Not long ago, the vagina was considered the primary female sexual body part. But the women's movement of the 1960s and 1970s challenged this notion, and women have increasingly come to understand the clitoris as central to sexual behavior and pleasure. Feminists also encouraged women to "be responsible for your own orgasm," in order to challenge the notion that men do sexual things and women passively participate.

Sometimes the way we challenge the hierarchy of sexual bodies and behaviors ends up re-affirming the dominant norms. Many Asian men and gay men resist the depiction of themselves as effeminate and slight by going to the gym, "beefing up," in order to better fit into the dominant American mold of what a man should look like. But other times, challenges to this hierarchy appear where you might least expect them. The very Viagra culture that re-affirms the notion that the erection is all-important has also opened a door for older women to talk about their sex lives. Older women have long been thought of as asexual, and "dried up." But the cultural buzz surrounding Viagra has made possible new discussions about sex among the elderly, and especially the sexuality of older women.

So, taken together, these essays do what a sociology of sexuality should do: they show us how certain body parts have *become* sexual through a variety of interesting social processes. What is considered a sexual body part changes over time. What is considered a legitimate sexual act is not related to nature as much as to social forces. As you'll learn, even something as seemingly simple as an orgasm changes over time and is experienced in remarkably different ways in different cultures.

10

Medicine and the making of a sexual body

Celia Roberts

LANCASTER UNIVERSITY, UNITED KINGDOM

Sex and sexuality are inextricably bound up with medicine in the West today. Sexual desires, sexual health, and sexual identities are both subjects for medical practice and objects of extensive scientific study. This is evident in multiple ways. As a discipline, medicine has developed a detailed language to describe and discuss sexual issues, and has established numerous professional journals and societies to support the scientific and medical study of sex. The medical knowledge produced in these journals and relevant textbooks and clinical guidelines understands some sexual behaviors and identities as illnesses and produces treatments to address these. These treatments, including pharmaceutical and behavioral interventions, are offered to patients presenting with sexual problems in general practitioners' offices and specialized clinics. In public health campaigns around sexually transmitted diseases, members of the general population and specific targeted groups are given medical information and encouraged to change their sexual behaviors in order to protect their physical health. In all of these cases, particular versions of sex and sexuality are produced or performed in interactions amongst medical professionals, scientists, patients, and members of populations. Sex and sexuality, in other words, are not "natural" objects worked on or taken up by medicine, but are produced in these interactions in particular ways.

This combination of sex and medicine is a historically specific phenomenon, but one that has become very normal to most of us in the West today. It is also a model that is increasingly distributed within non-Western societies, particularly through sexual health education campaigns and medical products and services. In these countries, Western scientific understandings of sex and sexuality interact and intersect with indigenous understandings in complex ways. The development of medical and scientific knowledge about sex has had profound global implications for how we experience our bodies and our sexual relationships, and indeed how many aspects of different societies operate.

Whilst historically there have been many societies in which religion or morality was the most important knowledge framework for understanding sex and sexuality, in the West today this is no longer the case. When someone demonstrates unusual or socially unacceptable sexual desires or behaviors today we are much more likely to consider them sick than merely morally corrupt. Although we may well punish them criminally, and even expect them to repent morally, we seek explanations of their behaviors and feelings from medicine and psychiatry, and may well provide them with medical treatments as well as legal punishments. On a more everyday level, those experiencing difficulties with sexuality are very likely to seek medical help – in the advice columns of popular magazines and health books, in doctors' surgeries, or in sexual health clinics – and to expect medical solutions to their problems. This provision of medical treatments in turn provides a profitable market for the pharmaceutical industry. The case of so-called "sexual dysfunction" is a case in point. Rather than being understood as stemming from a mix of psychological, biological and cultural factors and managed accordingly, the erectile problems of older men are commonly treated with Viagra™, a medication that increases blood flow to the penis. Providing a simple medical "solution" to a complex problem, Viagra™ is a sign of our sexual times, one whose popularity produces significant profits for its manufacturer.

This chapter discusses the nature of these multiple and deep connections between sex and medicine. Its aim is not to simply critique medicine, or to suggest that these connections are necessarily negative. Rather, the chapter explores the culturally and historically specific development of connections between medicine and sex and asks questions about the implications of these for the everyday lives of people in the West and across the globe.

Histories of sex

This strong association between sex and medicine developed in the West over the last two-and-a-half centuries was dependent on the growth of modern science. As Michel Foucault (1987) has argued in his important book, *The History of Sexuality: An Introduction*, the development of European modern science established sex as something central to our identity, our "core" or "essential" being. Rather than being only a set of activities or actions, from the nineteenth century sexual behaviors and feelings have become something that tells us about who we "really" are (see also Garton 2004; Weeks 1981). As such, they become subjects for scientific analysis and research. In the late nineteenth century, Foucault demonstrates, medicine and science established norms of sex and sexuality and began to measure individuals and groups against them. This happened at the level of biological bodies, at the level of sexual desires, and in relation to what have come to be known as sexual identities. Through these processes of medical classification, measurement, and discussion, individuals and groups came to recognize themselves as particular types of sexual subjects, and framed their experiences in culturally valorized ways (Garton 2004: 18). In turn this produced populations of people understood to need (and sometimes also desiring) medical treatment of what had come to be understood as sexual pathologies. These processes, as historian Jeffrey Weeks (1981) has shown, also produced forms of resistance against medicine and its practices of pathologization. Some sexual identities, such as homosexuality, were formed in part in resistance to Western medicine's insistence on the pathological nature of certain desires and behaviors (a pathologization that was also linked to criminalization in the case of homosexuality) (Garton 2004: 214). The categories of sexual pathology created by medicine, then, were always received by "passive victims" of pathologized subjects, but were developed in relation to active contestation and the formation of new socio-sexual ways of being (see also Terry 1999).

Sexual desire and sexual identities

Social theorists argue that contemporary sexualities have been formed in relation to the production of medical and scientific knowledge. Even the very "basic" categories that we associate with sexuality today ("heterosexuality," "homosexuality," "libido," for example) are words and concepts developed within specialist medical fields. This argument has been made most strongly in the case of homosexuality, but is also valid in relation to the more normative case of heterosexuality.

The medical study of sexuality has long been interwoven with the social sciences. This is evident in the field of sexology, the scientific study of sex and sexual behavior. Historian Janice Irvine (1990) has documented the development of this field in her book *Disorders of Desire* (see also Garton 2004; Foucault 1987; Weeks 1981; Terry 1999). The term "sexology" was coined in 1907 by German physician Iwan Bloch to name a growing field established in Europe in the late nineteenth century, in particular by Austrian Richard von Krafft-Ebing and Englishman Havelock Ellis. The aim of this new science was to study the sexual life of the individual within the context of medicine and the social sciences (Irvine 1990: 5). Perhaps the most important role of sexology in the late nineteenth and early twentieth centuries was its painstaking cataloging of the known variety of sexual behaviors and desires. This work produced a population of subjects and patients for doctors and scientists to study and treat.

Irvine argues that early European sexologists "were a disparate group with conflicting professional and political agendas" (Irvine 1990: 6). Some wanted to use sexology to change society; others thought sexology should be a pure and nonpolitical science. Irvine suggests that the tensions between social and biological sciences in sexology have always been a problem – gradually sexology leaned more and more towards biology and medicine in an attempt to legitimate the field as a science. Accordingly, modern sexology (which after the Second World War was based in America rather than Europe) became highly biological and scientific, studying physical measurements such as hormonal levels and neurological patterns in connection with sexual behaviors and identities. The groundbreaking survey work of American Alfred Kinsey in the mid-twentieth century is a key example of this emphasis on the scientific study of sex. In more contemporary times, reliance on "objective" measures of biological factors such as hormone levels establishes sexology's difference from both "nonscientific" sex therapies and humanities or purely social science–based sexuality research (Irvine 1990).

In the realm of treatments also, sexology has come to rely more and more on the biological and medical sciences. This tendency existed in the early twentieth century, when sexologists and doctors used sex hormones to try to change the sexual desires and drives of homosexual men. In some instances, these men were understood to have too much "female" hormones (estrogens) which were understood to be feminizing, and so were given "male" hormones (androgens) in an attempt to "normalize" them. In other cases, homosexuality was seen as best treated by dampening sexual drive through the administration of "female" sex hormones. Both methods were unsuccessful in changing homosexual men's desires and behavior. Later, in the mid-twentieth century, even more severe methods were used, including the administration of electric shocks. All of these "treatments" assumed that homosexuality was a pathology or illness. It was not until 1973 that activists were able to pressure psychiatrists and doctors to remove homosexuality from the official list of psychological pathologies (the Diagnostic and Statistical Manual of psychiatric disorders) and to stop attempting to change the sexual desire and behaviors of homosexual men and women.

In other arenas, however, sexologists and general practitioners continued to use hormonal and other pharmacological products to treat problems of desire and sexual behavior. The advent of Viagra™ in the 1990s is the most well-known example of this. This highly commercially successful medication assists men who have problems achieving or sustaining erections, providing increased blood flow to sustain an erection that makes intercourse possible. Hailed as a "wonder drug" in popular culture, and well regarded in medical circles, this medication plays a key role today in maintaining a narrow understanding of sex as sexual intercourse. Rather than assisting aging men to come to terms with bodily changes or to explore forms of sexual practice other than intercourse, argues sociologist Barbara Marshall (2002), Viagra™ provides a short-term and narrowly focused "quick fix." One direct-to-consumer advertisement for Viagra™

broadcast on American television, for example, shows a middle-aged man brimming with confidence on returning to work after an evening of satisfying sex. Puzzled work colleagues ask if it is a new haircut, exercise regime, or suit that has made all the difference, but viewers understand that it is the pharmaceutical product that has turned this man's life around. Such advertisements reinforce connections between sexual drive, work-related performance and masculinity, clearly suggesting that Viagra™ can solve a multitude of life problems through making sexual intercourse possible.

Hormone replacement therapies (HRT) have also been used to treat sexuality-related problems encountered by older people since the 1960s, in women and more recently also in men. Medical and scientific discourses and pharmaceutical advertisements describe HRT as maintaining youthful sexual drive and desire and suggest that HRT can be a kind of elixir of youth (Roberts 2002). Pharmaceutical advertisements for HRT show unhappy, bad-tempered women being changed into smiling and receptive beings, and depict men taking androgens as strong and potent god-like creatures. Maintaining sexual drive is described in the medical literature as essential to healthy aging, something that should be biochemically managed and supported. Like those around Viagra™, discourses around HRT reproduce narrow ideas of sex, sexuality, and gender relations, reinforcing culturally prevalent connections between sex, happiness, and success, and suggesting that medication can concretize or make real these connections for aging people. Such concretization, of course, also establishes a profitable and ever-growing market, as the proportion of older people in Western populations increases.

Sexual pathologies and biologies

The use of medical products to treat sexual problems relies on an understanding of sexuality and sexual drive as a biological, rather than social, force. Discourses around HRT, for example, assume that sexual drive comes from hormonal levels in the body: when these change as a person ages, the logical way to treat problems, according to contemporary medicine, is to supplement the body so that it has the hormonal profile of a younger person.

This biologistic way of thinking is also linked to understandings of sexual behaviors deemed pathological by medical discourse. Although, as discussed above, hormonal treatments of homosexuals are no longer acceptable in Western countries, some scientists continue to search for biological determinants of homosexuality (Irvine 1990: 246–52), and even in the late twentieth century some researchers, for example Gunter Dörner of Germany, have proposed hormonal interventions for pregnant women in order to avoid the birth of homosexual babies (Irvine 1990: 19). Male sex offenders – rapists and pedophiles, for example – are sometimes treated with anti-androgens and other hormones as well as being incarcerated. In all of these cases, sexuality is understood, at least in part, as a biological force that can be changed by the administration of pharmaceuticals. The assumptions here are that sexuality and sexual desire arise from the biological body, and that they can, in many cases at least, be medically altered.

The biological origin of sexual desire and drive is one that has troubled medicine and science since the nineteenth century. This question has always been linked with questions of sex and gender. Since the mid-eighteenth century, scientists and doctors have worked with a notion of sex that understands men and women as complementary opposites. Since the twentieth century, genes and hormones have been figured as the main biological causes of the physical (and in many cases also the psychological) differences between men and women. In human fetuses, the so-called "male" sex hormones (androgens) are understood to cause maleness, whilst the absence of significant amounts of these is seen to produce femaleness. At puberty, "male" hormones begin to produce a sexually mature man, and "female" hormones produce sexually mature women. This understanding of humans as having two "opposite" sexes underlies scientific and medical understandings of sexuality. Heterosexuality, which is seen as fundamentally linked to sexual reproduction, demonstrates that the two opposite sexes are also "complementary." The two sexes, in other words, are understood to be designed to come together for the purposes of reproduction and to "naturally" find each other attractive, so that the species will continue to reproduce and survive.

This model of sex and (hetero)sexuality is much troubled by the existence of individuals and groups who do not fit it. At the level of biological bodies, the model of two opposite sexes has been challenged at least since the 1930s, when it was discovered that male horses (and male humans) have "female" sex hormones in their bloodstreams. Although this famous finding contradicted an early idea that each sex has its "own" hormone only, it has since been incorporated by reference to relative amounts of hormones. Human males (and other male mammals) have "female" hormones as well as "male" ones, but they have less than females do. The model of the two "opposite" sexes has also been long disrupted by the existence of people born with what is known as "indeterminate sex," that is, whose genitals, genes or hormonal levels do not correlate clearly to either maleness or femaleness. These individuals, who are today referred to as "intersexed," have long been regarded as biological anomalies, with their bodies seen medically as faulty or pathological. Despite there being no medical need to intervene, most babies born intersexed in the West today receive hormonal and/or surgical treatment in an attempt to fit them into a "normal" male or female category (Fausto-Sterling 2000). Critics of this medical approach, such as biologist Anne Fausto-Sterling, have argued that decisions about which sex the baby should be "made into" are based on narrow ideas about heterosexual sex. The decisions to operate on a baby's genitals and to use hormonal medication are made according to whether doctors feel that, as an adult, the person would be capable of penetrating a vagina with his/her penis. If it is not felt that the penis would ever be large enough, it is "reduced" and a vagina constructed, if one is not present (Fausto-Sterling 2000). It is never considered that the baby may grow up to be homosexual, or indeed that s/he might want to have sex in other ways. This example demonstrates the deeply assumed link between biological sex (maleness and femaleness) and (hetero)sexual practice prevalent in medicine. If born not clearly male or female, a person is understood as in need of medical assistance, and this assistance is justified on the basis of imagined future heterosexual identity and behaviors. Unsurprisingly, in recent years there has been much political resistance to this kind of medical treatment, as documented in the work of Fausto-Sterling, amongst others. As in the earlier case of homosexuality, this resistance to medical practices and discourses is intimately intertwined with the development of a socio-sexual identity (intersexuality).

Biological theories about sex and sexuality also have a complex historical connection to ideas of racial differences. In his *History of Sexuality: An Introduction*, Foucault (1987) argues that modern racism was born alongside modern sexuality. Ideas about heterosexual reproduction are important here in different ways. In the late nineteenth and early twentieth centuries, many scientists and social theorists argued that reproduction should be controlled by the state, with some individuals encouraged to reproduce whilst others were discouraged or even prevented. These ideas were linked to understandings of evolution and to Darwin's notion of "the survival of the fittest," in which species' survival was related to the reproduction of characteristics best fitted to the organism's environment. Coming out of a period of massive Western expansion into non-Western countries, and the colonization of vast areas of Africa, Asia and South America, scientists in the eighteenth and nineteenth centuries had produced theories of racial hierarchy in which white men and women were figured as superior to non-whites. With the development of the early-twentieth-century science of eugenics, these theories gained new medical weight. Given that this was also the time at which modern birth-control methods were beginning to be developed, this new medical attention to issues of race and reproduction was highly consequential. As is well known, this connection was taken to its most brutal extreme in Nazi Germany, where many individuals were sterilized and millions of others killed in order, supposedly, to promote the reproductive purity of the Aryan "race."

The connections between sex, race, and reproduction have remained important to Western medicine and science since the Second World War, despite global horror regarding Nazi atrocities. Evidence shows, for example, that women in the developing world continue to be exposed to more invasive and potentially dangerous forms of medical contraceptive technologies (such as implants and long-lasting injections) in the hope that the population of developing countries will be kept in a particular proportion to that of developed countries. Women of color in the United States and other Western countries have also experienced significantly different forms of reproduction-related healthcare than their white compatriots. Access to new reproductive technologies for infertile couples is also highly unevenly distributed across the globe and within individual countries.

Sex and reproduction

Since the 1970s, second-wave feminists have hoped that medicine might disentangle historical and seemingly oppressive connections between sex and reproduction, through the development of the contraceptive pill, for example, and to a certain extent this has happened. Many women in the West and across the world are now able to use one or more of a range of medical contraceptive technologies to have non-reproductive heterosexual sex and to engage in "family planning." The development of medical technologies of safe abortion and the morning-after pill have also helped in this regard. Many millions of women in the world do not have access to these technologies, or are exposed involuntarily to more dangerous versions of them.

Alongside this increasing control over reproduction, medicine has also developed a significant discourse and set of practices around infertility. It is now claimed that one in seven couples in the West will struggle to become pregnant when they stop using contraception. These problems have been linked to the use of hormonal contraception, to increasing levels of chemicals in our environment, and to social changes, such as couples wanting to have children at later ages. The solutions developed to address this problem have been chiefly medical. They involve new reproductive technologies, such as *in-vitro* fertilization, interuterine insemination, ovarian stimulation and intracytoplasmic sperm injection. These scientific techniques move reproduction from the intimate sexual sphere and place it within a medical, technical realm, promising a level of control that is not actually matched with pregnancy outcomes. Most of these technologies involve extensive failure and entail significant physical and psychological risks for women patients, as well as currently unknowable lifetime risks for the babies born through these procedures. Like the drugs discussed above, however, they are immensely popular and currently provide ever-increasingly profitable markets in medical services and pharmaceutical products.

More recently, new genetic technologies have been developed to assist couples whose fertility problems are linked with genetic disease, or who are at serious risk of giving birth to children who will suffer from severe genetic disease. These techniques can provide genetic testing of embryos made using IVF or of fetuses *in utero*, and are linked in the latter case to abortion technologies (women can decide to terminate fetuses that will develop certain genetic conditions). In the West today, it is standard for women over the age of thirty-five to be given prenatal testing for chromosomal conditions such as Down's Syndrome as part of normal medical care. American anthropologist Rayna Rapp (1999) has studied the social impact of this development, arguing that women are given a historically unique role in deciding which babies should be born today. She calls pregnant women undergoing this type of testing (known as amniocentesis) "moral pioneers" (Rapp 1999: 306). In everyday life, then, pregnant women are making moral decisions about continuing with pregnancies or not according to information produced by medicine, thus demonstrating the depth to which medical knowledge now penetrates the intimate, daily life of "ordinary" people and the very constitution of society (who will be born and who will not).

In all of these examples, medicine and reproductive sex are deeply intertwined: medical interventions take over, replace or become substitutes for more "traditional" practices of impregnation and abortion. This is not to argue that processes of reproduction (impregnation, pregnancy, birth) were previously "natural," but rather that, in the West today (and increasingly, but in different ways, in non-Western countries as well), they have moved into the realm of medicine and become inextricably enmeshed with medical understandings of sex and biology.

Sex and disease

Medicine is also deeply intertwined with sex in the areas of disease and sexual health. The advent of the global HIV/AIDS epidemic in the mid-1980s is the most significant example of this in the current epoch. As many commentators have argued, HIV/AIDS has provided an enormous and enduring stimulus to medical and scientific work on sex and sexuality, fostering ever-deeper relations between these two fields of human life (see, e.g., Epstein 1996).

Faced with an initially untreatable, fatal disease that was transmitted via body fluids during sex (as well as by needle-sharing), social scientists, activists and policymakers argued that it was important to learn more about contemporary sexual practices and how body fluids were actually shared. Research in both Western and non-Western countries since the 1980s have studied a full range of sexual practices amongst a wide variety of groups, asking who does what, when, and with whom. This work led to the development of what has come to be known as "safe" or "safer" sex, forms of sexual practice that minimize the risk of the transmission of the HIV virus that causes AIDS. These practices are widely promoted today, both in medical settings (doctors' offices, waiting rooms, sexual health clinics and hospitals) and in other public arenas (television, magazines, public transport, etc.). In many Western and non-Western countries today, these campaigns are linked to other sexually transmitted diseases, rates of which are rising even as HIV infection rates decrease (syphilis, chlamydia, and herpes, for example). In all of this work, medical research on the spread of disease within particular social groups and geographical areas, and on how specific diseases are transmitted, is linked with social scientific work on sexual behavior. Through the dissemination of public health advice on safe sex, then, medicine enters the most intimate spaces of our lives, as people take up (or fail, or refuse, to take up) this advice when they have sex.

Conclusion

Medicine and science have had profound consequences for how we experience sex today. In many ways, medicine has contributed to making sex safer and more pleasurable for many people. The possibility of treating sexually transmitted diseases and sexual dysfunctions, of preventing unwanted pregnancies and of diagnosing and treating reproductive problems and the genetic profile of future children, have arguably improved the lives of many who have come into contact with medicine. The development of medical categories for sexual desires and identities is perhaps a more mixed blessing: some social theorists have argued that categories;

such as homosexuality and heterosexuality, maleness and femaleness, have produced severe limitations on sexual expression and the unnecessary pathologization of biological and social diversity, thus contributing to the production of societies characterized by intolerance of those who do not fit well into established categories. For many people, then, the combination of sex and medicine has produced spaces of fear, suffering, and unnecessary and painful "treatment."

However ambivalent, the connection between sex and medicine is profound and enduring. It is also constantly reinforced by the production of new pharmaceutical products to treat sexual problems; through the continued research on sexual biologies, behaviors, and desires; and through the development of medical treatments for sexually transmitted diseases. The social sciences have an important role to play in all of this: to describe and analyze what is happening in medicine and in broader society, and to continue to describe the diversity of human sexualities in order to promote better ways of living with this diversity. Medicine cannot take on sex and sexuality without the social sciences – it does not have the skills and resources to provide adequate accounts of the complexity of human behavior – so the uneasy relationship between medicine and social science will continue into the foreseeable future.

References

Epstein, Steven (1996) *Impure Science: AIDS, Activism and the Politics of Knowledge*, Berkeley: University of California Press.

Fausto-Sterling, Anne (2000) *Sexing the Body: Gender, Politics and the Construction of Sexuality*, New York: Basic Books.

Foucault, Michel (1987) *The History of Sexuality: An Introduction*, Robert Hurley (trans.), London: Penguin Books.

Garton, Stephen (2004) *Histories of Sexuality: Antiquity to Sexual Revolution*, London: Equinox Press.

Irvine, Janice M. (1990) *Disorders of Desire: Sex and Gender in Modern American Sexology*, Philadelphia, PA: Temple University Press.

Marshall, Barbara (2002) "Hard Science: Gendered constructions of sexual dysfunction", *Sexualities* 5(2), 131–58.

Rapp, Rayna (1999) *Testing Women, Testing the Fetus: The Social Impact of Amniocentesis in America*, Durham NC: Duke University Press.

Roberts, Celia (2002) "Successful aging with hormone replacement therapy: it may be sexist, but what if it works?", *Science as Culture* 11(1), 39–59.

Terry, Jennifer (1999) *An American Obsession: Science, Medicine and Homosexuality in Modern Society*, Chicago, IL: University of Chicago Press.

Weeks, Jeffrey (1981) *Regulation of Sexuality since 1800*, London: Longman.

1. Chapter 1 - Theoretical Perspectives; Chapter 2 - The social construction of sexuality; Chapter 4 - Popular Culture Constructs Sexuality

2. Part 2 Introduction; Chapter 8 - Sexual Politics in intimate relationships?

3. For Wednesday Sept 25/2013 read Chapter 10 Medicine and the making of a sexual body; Chapter 11 - The body, disability ...

11

The body, disability, and sexuality

Thomas J. Gerschick

ILLINOIS STATE UNIVERSITY

We do not express or even show our wishes, because we have learned that in our condition of disablement or disfigurement, no one could (or should) find us sexually attractive.

(Zola 1982: 215)

People with disabilities face formidable challenges in establishing self-satisfactory sexualities; yet despite these challenges, they are increasingly doing so. This chapter conveys a range of scholarship from advocates, researchers, and other interested parties regarding the relationship among the body, disability, and sexuality. I begin with a brief contextualization of disability and then turn my attention to the role of the body in social life using the experiences of people with disabilities to highlight key social dynamics. Subsequently, I provide an overview of the challenges that people with disabilities face in determining self-satisfactory sexualities and conclude with a discussion of their active responses to those challenges.

Disabled bodies

Those who are characterized as disabled experience a wide range of medically defined conditions, some readily visible, others much less so. These conditions are conceptualized in a variety of ways by doctors and scholars, but generally they are grouped under physical and psychological conditions. Examples include deafness, blindness, spinal cord injury, multiple sclerosis, muscular dystrophy, developmental disabilities, bipolar disorder, and mental illness. These definitions serve to distinguish people with disabilities from the temporarily able-bodied in society. I intentionally utilize the term temporarily able-bodied to highlight the fact that aging is disabling and many of us will live long enough to develop a disability during our lifetime. Such language highlights the fact that human variation reflects a continuum, rather than a dichotomy of being disabled or not.

As many scholars have noted, it is exceedingly difficult to determine the size of the population of people with disabilities globally due to lack of consensus regarding definitions of disability and differential abilities within countries and regions to count their populations. One well-informed researcher, Gary Albrecht (2004), placed the number at approximately 500 million worldwide, the vast majority of whom live in the developing world. Reflecting our limited understanding of the scope of the population, there is much we do not know regarding the circumstances, conditions and treatment of people with disabilities. As a consequence of this, the bulk of this chapter will focus on the existing scholarship which largely attends to the West, especially the United States. Furthermore, given the relatively new attention to disability and sexuality, not much attention has been paid to the intersection of these with other social factors such as race, class, gender, sexual orientation, and ethnicity. Wherever possible, I include available understandings of these intersections.

The importance of the body in social life

The body is central in social life. People are privileged by the degree to which they approximate the cultural ideal. Bodies physically exist along a continuum. Given the large amount of human variation across time and culture and the array of expectations and standards, the body must be framed in terms of degrees of normativity: from more normative to less (Gerschick 2005). There are many ways in which a body can be less normative. Characteristics such as race, ethnicity, class, age, physique, weight, height, ability, disability, appearance, and skin color predominate. People can be less normative by being too light, too dark, too fat, too skinny, too poor, too young, too old, too tall, too short, too awkward, and/or too uncoordinated. Scholars have noted that the degree to which one is bodily-normative matters considerably because it helps place one in the stratification order. The degree to which bodily variation has been accepted has also varied across time and culture. The societal treatment one experiences, then, depends on the degree of normativeness, one's resources, and the particular historical, cultural, and structural contexts in which one lives (Gerschick 2005). For example, consider the resources available to the late actor, Christopher Reeve, following his injury in 1995, due to his celebrity and wealth. Although his injury was severe, he received the highest quality of care possible and became a cultural icon for his work on behalf of others with spinal cord injuries. Many other people with disabilities, lacking Reeve's status and resources, are treated much more poorly. Their opportunities are also much more limited.

The negative treatment experienced by most people with disabilities can be understood by considering how bodies are symbolic. One's body serves as a type of social currency that signifies one's worth. Consequently, people with less-normative bodies, such as people with disabilities, are vulnerable to being denied social recognition and validation. People respond to one another's bodies, which initiates social processes such as validation and the assignment of status. Summarizing the research, Patzer (1985: 1) observes:

> Physical attractiveness is the most visible and most easily accessible trait of a person. Physical attractiveness is also a constantly and frequently used informational cue … Generally, the more physically attractive an individual is, the more positively the person is perceived, the more favorably the person is responded to, and the more successful is the person's personal and professional life.

Thus, researchers maintain that to have a less-normative body, such as having a disability which is perceived by most to be unattractive, is not so much a physical condition as it is a social and stigmatized one.

This stigma is embodied in the popular stereotypes of people whose bodies are less normative. People with disabilities, for instance, are perceived to be weak, passive, and dependent. The English language exemplifies this stigmatization; people with disabilities are de-formed, dis-eased, dis-abled, dis-ordered, ab-normal, and in-valid (Zola 1982: 206). Having a disability can also become a primary identity that overshadows almost all other aspects of one's identity.

This stigma is embedded in daily interactions among people. People are evaluated in terms of normative expectations and, because of their bodies, are frequently found wanting. As demonstrated by the social responses to people with disabilities, people with less-normative bodies are avoided, ignored, and marginalized. They experience a range of reactions from subtle indignities and slights to overt hostility and outright cruelty (Gerschick 2005, 1998). This treatment creates subtle but formidable physical, economic, psychological, architectural, and social obstacles to their participation in all aspects of social life.

A hierarchy of bodies exists in any particular historical, cultural, structural, and global context. The degree to which one's body is devalued is also affected by other social characteristics including social class, sexual orientation, age, and race and ethnicity. The type of disability – its visibility, the severity of it, whether it is physical or mental in origin, and the contexts – mediate the degree to which a person with a less-normative body is socially compromised (Gerschick 2005, 1998). For instance, a severe case of Chronic Fatigue Syndrome can disable someone, thereby creating a less-normative body; however, typically the condition is not readily apparent and as a consequence does not automatically trigger stigmatization and devaluation. Conversely, having quadriplegia and utilizing a wheelchair for mobility is highly visual, is perceived to be severe, and frequently elicits invalidation. One of the challenges facing researchers is to develop a systematic theory to address the degrees of non-normativity and the circumstances that lead to different levels of stigmatization and marginalization and how these differ for different groups of people based on their gender, race, ethnicity, social class, sexual orientation and origin (Gerschick 2005).

People with less-normative bodies, such as people with disabilities, are engaged in an asymmetrical power relationship with their more-normative bodied counterparts, who have the power to validate their bodies and their identities (Gerschick 2005, 1998). An example comes from Jerry, aged sixteen at the time of his interview, who lived with Juvenile Rheumatoid Arthritis:

> I think [others' conception of what defines a man] is very important because if they don't think of you as one, it is hard to think of yourself as one or it doesn't really matter if you think of yourself as one if no one else does.
>
> *(Gerschick and Miller 1994: 50)*

In order to be validated, each person in a social situation needs to be recognized by others as appropriately meeting the situated expectations. Those with whom we interact continuously assess our performance and determine the degree to which we are meeting those expectations. Our "audience" or interaction partners then hold us accountable and sanction us in a variety of ways in order to encourage compliance. Our need for social approval and validation further encourages conformity. Much is at stake in this process because one's sense of self rests precariously upon the audience's decision to validate or reject one's performance. Successful enactment bestows status and acceptance; failure invites embarrassment and humiliation (West and Zimmerman 1987). This point is illustrated by Kit, one of researchers Shakespeare, Gillespie-Sells and Davies's informants:

> I actually think my being a disabled lesbian is a very … it's a struggle, I don't mean that it's a struggle in that I don't want to be a disabled lesbian, it's a struggle in that you are completely, you are completely insignificant and denied any identity or importance.
>
> *(Shakespeare, Gillespie-Sells and Davies 1996: 154)*

It is challenging to maintain one's dignity and sense of self under such circumstances.

Challenges to sexual satisfaction

Before turning my attention to the ways in which people with disabilities seek sexual self-determination, I want to focus on five particular challenges to developing self-satisfactory sexualities: the medicalization of disability, the attitudes of the temporarily able-bodied, internalized oppression, fetishists, and physical and sexual abuse.

The medicalization model of people with disabilities

Historically, disability has been defined in part in medical terms. It has been perceived as an individual, physical problem requiring a medical or mechanical solution. Scholars point out that the emphasis in this model is on deficiency, pathology, tragedy and loss that can, with medical intervention, be remedied. This mindset locates the problem solely in the individual, not in society. As such it is apolitical. The person with a disability is defined as passive, dependent and infant-like, one who needs others to care for them. It reinforces the power of others, especially care professionals, to define people with disabilities and their circumstances. While there is no doubt that medical attention has significantly improved the lives of people with disabilities over the last several decades, the attendant mindset has also undermined disabled people's ability to self-determine their lives, including their sexuality.

Associated with this is the view that people with disabilities are asexual. As a consequence, scholars maintain that medical practitioners tend not to provide information to people with disabilities about sexual functioning or sexual healthcare. In denying them information about sexual pleasure, medical practitioners send a tacit but powerful message about how people with disabilities are perceived as sexual beings. They are, apparently, not entitled to this kind of pleasure, as explained by then 53-year-old essayist, Nancy Mairs:

> … the general assumption, even among those who might be expected to know better, is that people with disabilities are out of the sexual running. Not one of my doctors, for example, has ever asked me about my sex life. Most people, in fact, deal with the discomfort and even distaste that a misshapen body arouses by disassociating that body from sexuality in reverie and practice. "They" can't possibly do it, the thinking goes; therefore, "they" mustn't even want it; and that is *that*. The matter is closed before a word is uttered. People with disabilities can grow so used to unstated messages of consent and prohibition that they no longer "hear" them as coming from the outside, any more than the messengers know they are "speaking" them. This vast conspiracy of silence surrounding the sexuality of the disabled consigns countless numbers to sexual uncertainty and disappointment.
>
> *(Mairs 1996: 51–2)*

One can easily imagine, then, how debilitating this mindset can be in cultures that emphasize sex and sexuality.

Attitudes of people with disabilities as sexual partners

Successfully creating and maintaining self-satisfactory sexualities and identities under these challenging social circumstances is an almost Sisyphean task. Consequently, sexuality is threatened when corporeal appearance and performance are discordant with cultural expectations, such as in the case of having a disability (Gerschick 1998). Depending on the degree of their difference, people with disabilities contravene many of the beliefs and expectations associated with being desirable and sexual. For instance, in the contemporary West, to be perceived as physically attractive is to be socially and sexually desirable. Due to their invalidated condition, however, women and men with disabilities are constrained in their opportunities to nurture and to be nurtured, to be lovers and to love, and to become parents if they so desire (Gerschick 1998). These dynamics are particularly acute in subcultures where a premium is placed on bodily appearance. Poet Kenny Fries, in his memoir, discusses what it is like to be a man with a disability within a gay culture that idealizes bodies:

> ... in bars I would plant myself at a table or on a stool at the bar and stay in one place as long as possible. When I saw someone I would like to get to know, I would stay put. And even when I had to go to the bathroom I would put it off for as long as I could to avoid making my disability noticeable by standing up and walking. By deciding to remain stationary, I rarely met the men I wanted to meet, the men I was attracted to. Those I met would have to come over to me, or I would meet them by chance when they happened to take an empty seat near where I sat at a table or at the bar.
>
> *(Fries 1997: 131)*

Thus people with disabilities, many with few social resources, face deeply entrenched prejudice and stereotypes when seeking to establish self-satisfactory sexualities. They rarely have the power to challenge the dominant discourse which infantilizes them and perceives them to be asexual (Shakespeare, Gillespie-Sells and Davies 1996).

Internalized oppression

Sexuality and a sense of oneself as a sexual being are not created in a vacuum. Frequently people with disabilities internalize societal negative stereotypes and act on them as if they were true. In the following quote, writer and filmmaker Billy Golfus, who was disabled due to a motorcycle accident, illustrates the insidiousness of internalizing asexual stereotypes about people with disabilities when he discusses a woman for a potential relationship:

> Even though she is attractive, I don't really think about her that way partly because the [wheel]chair makes me not even see her and because after so many years of being disabled you quit thinking about it as an option.
>
> *(Golfus 1997: 420)*

The woman in this illustration was as invisible to him as his own sexuality was. This example reveals how deeply some people with disabilities internalize societal standards of desirability and sexuality, which then makes them complicit in their sexual oppression (Gerschick 1998).

Similarly, people with disabilities internalize the belief that their degree of function, attractiveness and desirability determines their self worth. Author and cartoonist John Callahan explained:

> I can remember looking at my body with loathing and thinking, Boy, if I ever get to heaven, I'm not going to ask for a new pair of legs like the average quad does. I'm going to ask for a dick I can feel. The idea promoted in rehab of the socially well-adjusted, happily married quad made me sick. This was the cruelest thing of all. Always, I felt humiliated. Surely a man with any self respect would pull the plug on himself.
>
> *(Callahan 1990: 121)*

The lack of self-esteem in this crucial human arena leads people with physical disabilities to limit themselves at times, as Nancy Mairs (1996: 52) describes:

> ... my wheelchair seals my chastity. Men may look at me with pity, with affection, with amusement, with admiration, but never with lust. To be truthful, I have so internalized the social proscription of libido in my kind that if a man did come on to me, I'd probably distrust him as at least a little peculiar in his erotic tastes.

As the following section demonstrates, Mairs has reason to be concerned.

Fetishists

One of the paradoxical issues facing people with disabilities are devotees: temporarily able-bodied people who are attracted to them because of their disabilities. Because most devotees are heterosexual males pursuing women with disabilities, especially women amputees, this section focuses on them.

There are many websites and magazines devoted to community, companionship, relationships, and picture and DVD exchange and sale between temporarily able-bodied men and women with disabilities. These forums provide locales where women with disabilities can meet and interact with their followers. They can run, or respond to, personal ads and arrange to meet potential suitors in person. Many of these forums are controlled by women with disabilities (Kafer 2000).

The social meanings and ramifications of these sites, communities, and behaviors are difficult to discern. In a society which does not value emotional, mental, or physical difference, relationships between people with disabilities and their devotees are created in an environment of vast power differentials. However, many of the women involved in these communities experience their participation as empowering. Additionally, if we define the attraction of devotee men as deviant, what does that say about the social desirability of women with disabilities? Is it problematic to find women with disabilities attractive? If we define these relationships in this way, are we defining women with disabilities as victims in need of protection, thereby further infantilizing them (Kafer 2000)?

Read another way, these communities challenge the dominant cultural stereotype of women with disabilities as being unattractive and asexual. Some women with disabilities report enhanced self-esteem, self-confidence, and comfort with their bodies since joining devotee communities. These communities and associated social gatherings can be a source of revenue as well, since they provide a market for women with disabilities to sell photos and DVDs of themselves. Supporters claim that this phenomenon allows women with disabilities more power to define and control their sexuality (Kafer 2000).

While some women with disabilities experience a positive effect, these communities simultaneously sexually objectify women with disabilities. The degree to which devotee communities challenge or alter the social structure is highly debated (Kafer 2000). This is especially true regarding power relations between people with disabilities and the temporarily able-bodied. As of now, these communities are relatively small and have had little apparent effect on the perceptions or actions of the temporarily able-bodied. Furthermore, one cannot ignore that devotees are almost entirely temporarily able-bodied men, most of whom are heterosexual, some of whom are gay. There are very few women devotees seeking men or women with disabilities (Kafer 2000). This raises further concerns about power differentials. For instance, these relationships cannot be understood outside of a patriarchal culture which empowers men at the expense of women. Thus, it would be difficult to create an egalitarian relationship when male devotees have cultural and structural power as men while women with disabilities are devalued.

Although women and men with disabilities share similar experiences of devaluation, isolation, marginalization, and discrimination, their fortunes diverge in important ways. One of these ways is in terms of the violence they face.

Physical and sexual abuse

Although there is much that we do not know regarding the extent of violence that people with disabilities experience, research suggests that children with disabilities are 70 percent more likely to be physically or sexually abused than their able-bodied counterparts (Crosse, Kaye, and Ratnofsky 1993). Researchers report that this abuse is more likely to be chronic than episodic and perpetuated by someone the victim knows, such as a family member or personal attendant. Furthermore, this abuse is gendered; females with disabilities are more likely to be sexually assaulted, whereas males with disabilities are more likely to experience physical abuse (Sobsey, Randall, and Parrila 1997). Thus, having a disability exacerbates one of the worst elements of oppression and does untold amounts of damage to disabled people's sense of and experience of their sexuality (Gerschick 2000).

Claiming their own sexualities

As the preceding pages have demonstrated, people with disabilities face formidable challenges to creating self-satisfactory sexual experiences and identities. However, we would be making a grave mistake if we did not simultaneously highlight the agency of people with disabilities to fight the beliefs and social dynamics that hinder the development and expression of their sexualities (Shakespeare *et al.* 1996).

Scholars point out that the Disability Rights Movement, while slow to address issues of sexuality, has for several decades championed a sociopolitical understanding of people with disabilities as a minority group with all the attendant human rights. Movement members have fought for the access and employment rights of people with disabilities. As a result, they have created a social space for activists and scholars to address sexuality by publishing books, educating, and advocating. Key to these efforts is reframing issues of bodily difference as problems with societal definitions, accommodations, and expectations, rather than with people with disabilities themselves. As a consequence, prejudice and discrimination towards people with disabilities are likened to other forms of political, cultural, and social oppression such as racism, sexism, and heterosexism. Thus, the emphasis in the Disability Rights approach is on the cultural, attitudinal, and structural barriers that people with disabilities face rather than on their physical differences. Physical differences, such as disabilities, are only limitations to the degree that society makes them so.

Activists' and scholars' work takes place on multiple levels. On the individual level, they are facilitating people with disabilities' redefinition of their bodies and their relationship with them. They encourage them to embrace their bodily differences and increase self-esteem about them. In so doing, they create positive images and role models that acknowledge, nurture, and promote self-esteem and sexuality for other people with disabilities. This redefinition is clearly illustrated by Penny, one of Shakespeare *et al.*'s informants:

> For me, sex is about pleasure, humour and respect. It is with these factors in mind that I approach any seeming "difficulty" my impairments present me. Of course there are

techniques and positions I will never manage to do. But I know this is true of most people, along that huge scale of human variety that in reality exists in human beings. Some activities I choose not to do, because I have no taste for them. This is as it should be. But I also know my open attitude to my sexuality, arising because I am a disabled person, often defines sex for me as a much more celebratory and explorative experience than for many non-disabled people.

(Shakespeare et al. 1996: 205)

On an individual and societal level, scholars and activists challenge the limited definition of what constitutes sexuality and sexual behavior, especially the emphasis on heterosexual intercourse. People without genital sensation, from a spinal cord injury for instance, can have orgasms through the stimulation of other parts of their bodies. It is well known that the skin and the brain are two of the largest sources of sexual pleasure.

On a societal level, activists and scholars recognize that the formation of their own culture is key to developing their sexual freedom, for it is in this culture that they can develop their own images, beliefs, and standards, and from this social space they can challenge those of the dominant culture. They emphasize that the pursuit of sexuality and sexual happiness regardless of the condition of one's body is a fundamental human right. They argue that people with disabilities must have the power to define sexuality for themselves. Movement members also seek to shatter the stereotypes associated with people with disabilities, including that they are infantile and asexual. Finally, they are strong advocates for reproductive freedom and contraception for people with disabilities.

Conclusion

Disability has a profound effect on people's sexuality. The barriers are great, but so is the agency challenging them. Yet there is still much we do not know about this process. For instance, we have scant information regarding how disability intersects with other social characteristics like sexual orientation, race, class, ethnicity and gender, to shape sexualities. Furthermore, we know little about global variations. As a consequence, there are many opportunities for scholars to add to our understanding. I close this chapter with encouragement to take up these issues, so that we may better understand the social factors and dynamics that shape the sexualities of people with disabilities today, and so that we may eradicate the social, cultural, and political barriers to their sexual self-definition and self-satisfaction.

References

Albrecht, Gary L. 2004. "Disability as a Global Issue", in George Ritzer (ed.), *Handbook of Social Problems: A Comparative International Perspective*. Thousand Oaks, CA: Sage.

Callahan, John. 1990. *Don't Worry, He Won't Get Far on Foot*, New York: Vintage.

Crosse, Scott B., Elyse Kaye, and Alexander C. Ratnofsky. 1993. *A Report on the Maltreatment of Children with Disabilities*. Washington, DC: National Center on Child Abuse and Neglect.

Fries, Kenny. 1997. *Body, Remember: A Memoir*. New York: Dutton.

Gerschick, Thomas J. 2005. "Masculinity and Degrees of Bodily Normativity in Western Culture," in Michael S. Kimmel, Jeff Hearn and R. W. Connell (eds), *Handbook of Studies on Men and Masculinities*. Thousand Oaks, CA: Sage.

——2000. "Toward A Theory of Disability and Gender," *Signs*, 25 (4): 1263–8.

——1998. "Sisyphus in a Wheelchair: Men with Physical Disabilities Confront Gender Domination", in Judith Howard and Jodi O'Brien (eds), *Everyday Inequalities: Critical Inquiries*. New York: Basil Blackwell.

Gerschick, Thomas J. and Adam S. Miller. 1994. "Gender Identities at the Crossroads of Masculinity and Physical Disability", *Masculinities* 2 (1): 34–55.

Golfus, Billy. 1997. "Sex and the Single Gimp", in Lennard J. Davis (ed.), *The Disability Studies Reader*. New York: Routledge.

Kafer, Alison. 2000. "Amputated Desire, Resistant Desire: Female Amputees in the Devotee Community". Paper presented at the Society for Disability Studies Conference, Chicago Sheraton, June 29–July 2.

Mairs, Nancy. 1996. *Waist-High in the World: A Life among the Nondisabled*. Boston, MA: Beacon Press.

Patzer, Gordon L. 1985. *The Physical Attractiveness Phenomena*. New York: Plenum.

Shakespeare, Tom, Kath Gillespie-Sells, and Dominic Davies. 1996. *The Sexual Politics of Disability: Untold Desires*, London: Cassell.

Sobsey, Dick, W. Randall, and Rauno K Parrila. 1997. "Gender Differences in Abused Children with and without Disabilities." *Child Abuse and Neglect* 21 (8): 707–20.

West, Candace and Don Zimmerman. 1987. "Doing Gender", *Gender and Society* 1 (2): 125–51.

Zola, Irving. 1982. *Missing Pieces: A Chronicle of Living with a Disability*. Philadelphia, PA: Temple University Press.

12

Sexualizing Asian male bodies

Travis S. K. Kong

UNIVERSITY OF HONG KONG

What comes to your mind when you think about Asian men? The Kung Fu masters Bruce Lee and Jackie Chan, famous for their martial art skills? Or those who excel professionally such as Yo Yo Ma (a cello player), Michael Chang (a tennis player) and Yao Ming (a basketball player)? What about Mickey Rooney in *Breakfast at Tiffany's* who plays the grumpy, almost hysterical Japanese landlord who constantly shouts at Audrey Hepburn? Or William Hung, the infantile and non-threatening (sexually and physically) Chinese boy who jumps and sings with "no regrets" in *American Idol*?

More likely, when you think of Asian males, you will have pop into your head the image of a pragmatic and money-driven Asian man working in a laundry or restaurant in Chinatown, or of an intelligent, hardworking, nerdy-looking professional wearing (thick) glasses!

Sex and Asian men? Hard to imagine these two things could go together. But if you look at Leslie Cheung in *Farewell My Concubine* (a sad love story which depicts a Beijing Opera gay actor who always played the feminine role on stage and fell in love with his lifelong stage partner who was a straight man), or John Lone in *Madame Butterfly* (a true story which tells of a French diplomat who "mistakenly" fell in love with an opera singer who was actually a Chinese spy and a *man*), these two actors might have gained some "sexual currency" for Asian males. They were praised for dragging-up as women, as they "passed" the test of behaving like women with their elegant performance and delicate sensitivity.

From the above examples, you can see that Asian male bodies, hard or soft, whether their owners are Kung Fu masters, talented professionals, Chinamen or nerds, are almost always sexually neutered or asexual unless these men behave like a woman or a gay man. If we consider that an Asian female body always embodies excessive sexuality (for example, Lucy Liu in *Charlie's Angels* and Sandra Oh in *Sideways*), then we could say that an Asian male body is always devoid of sexuality.

Why are there such limited representations of Asian male bodies? Do these representations reflect social reality? To what extent is the male body shaped by nature or social forces? For example, are Asian male bodies genetically smaller than Western ones? Do Asian males learn to behave like white men? And regardless of the genetic or social construct, why does a smaller male body occupy an inferior position? Why is the Asian male body always aligned with femininity (and thus passivity) and/or homosexuality? Even inside the gay world, why does a specific Asian gay image ("feminine and smooth-skinned") seem to predominate?

The hierarchy of male bodies

The male body is central to the formation of men's masculine identity. The notion of masculinity is based on a rigid gender system of two sexes (male and female), in which masculinity is defined as opposed to femininity. Gendered identities (man and woman) with "appropriate" attributes are derived from this gender regime. For example, the alleged masculine attributes of men are physical prowess, virility, independence, aggressiveness, competitiveness, objectivity, rationality and emotional controllability. In contrast, the alleged feminine attributes of women are passivity, fragility, non-aggressiveness, non-competitiveness, sensitivity, nurturance, intuitiveness and emotional liability. Also, the dominant notion of masculinity assumes that the "normal" sexual orientation and identity are heterosexuality. To be a "man" is to be a heterosexual man. The common-sense logic of homosexuality is thus simple: being gay means lacking masculinity. If someone is attracted to masculinity, that person must be feminine, if not in body (the biological explanation), then somehow in the mind (the psychological explanation).

Biology – genes, genitalia, hormones, instincts, or even the mysterious workings of the dynamic unconscious – is important to determine the *potential* of our body and identity. However, culture and social forces play a crucial role in shaping our desires, emotions, and identities. Think about how difficult it will be to understand the complexity and richness of food by merely reducing it to a simple desire of hunger! Gender and sex socialization begin as soon as an infant is born. Children are taught to conform to their feminine or masculine roles, including exhibiting heterosexual desires, by meeting the expectations attached to these roles. There are of course negative sanctions or forms of disapproval and punishment for those who deviate. Our body, gender, and sexuality is shaped or even created through a continuous interplay of biological and social forces (Gerschick 2005).

However, no matter whether the body is genetically and/or socially constructed, we tend to be forced to conform to a cultural definition of being men/women, masculine/feminine, heterosexual/homosexual, that appears to be "natural." This cultural definition seems to create rigid psychological and social boundaries that inevitably give rise to systems of dominance and hierarchical organization (Butler 1990; Seidman 1996). In most societies, people are rewarded if they can approximate cultural ideals of masculinity/femininity, or punished if they fail to do so. In Western culture, career orientation, activeness, athleticism, sexual desirability and virility, independence and self-reliance seem to be exalted as white masculine attributes and a strong and hard body as the desired white masculine body form (Connell 1995; Kimmel 1994). One's masculinity is threatened if one's physical appearance and cognitive achievement fail to perform these ideal attributes. Subordinate forms of masculinity or "devalued" bodies vary according to many factors, such as physical capability (disabled men as "weak"), body size (timid body as "passive" or smooth body as "feminine"), age (old men as "dependent"), race and ethnicity (Asian men as "asexual," black men as "hypersexual"), sexual orientation (homosexual as "feminine"), and so on and so forth. This creates a hierarchy which privileges certain bodies and stigmatizes others. No matter how unrealistic it might be, both men and women use these standards to judge other men. However, it should be noted that these hegemonic ideas of body and gender can change over time. And people respond to them in different ways – some conform, accommodate, or challenge these ideas and norms.

These ideas of the body, gender, and sexuality are the lens through which we can understand how an Asian male body – small, smooth and hairless – is being structured in a white-dominated society as "the other," "the feminine," "the homosexual," or "the asexual."

The struggle over the sexualization of Asian male bodies

The US treatment of Chinese men could serve as an example. The depiction of Chinese men, or "Chinamen," was characterized in the mid-nineteenth century by their inability to speak perfect English. Due to their perseverance, their independence from whites, and their willingness to help each other, they established their own shops, laundries and restaurants. They were then depicted as economic competitors against whom a series of immigration laws was enacted to restrict and limit their rights. However, these "Chinamen" were also described as "bachelors," even though most of them were married in their homelands. The term "bachelor" not only had the connotation of viewing these Chinese men as "boys" (and thus "infantile") but also carried the hidden meaning of homosexuality. The implication seemed to suggest that their sexuality was always "repressed." So these Chinese men seemed to be a potential threat (both economically and sexually) to white society. Although the situation is different now, the image of Chinamen in contemporary Western mass culture still shifts between a workaholic figure and a Kung Fu master. They are "sometimes dangerous, sometimes friendly, but almost always characterized by a desexualized asceticism" (Fung 1996: 183).

Second or third generation Asian-Americans tend to reject these stigmatized images of Asian masculinity. Many contemporary American men try to act masculine. A large number of Asian-American men have a daily workout routine. Bodybuilding or even body modification can be considered as a political act to reject the derogatory stereotype of the "timid, infantile, yellow body" which is always assigned to Asian men living in a white society.

Conforming to the Western, hard-pumping body (and thus reinforcing the Kung Fu master at the expense of a timid body) might be one option. Another way Asian men challenge the stereotypical Asian male image is to reassert the *wen* ideal of Chinese masculinity without equating muscle with masculinity. Chinese masculinity has been constructed around two intertwining ideals – the *wen* ideal ("cultured behavior, refinement and mastery of scholarly work") and the *wu* ideal ("martial prowess, strength, and mastery of physical arts"). The *wu* ideal has always been devalued because Confucian culture devalues physical power. An ideal man is one who has a strong personality with high moral standards – a result of harmony and unity between human nature and knowledge. A strong man is never a man with superior physical strength but one with an excellent moral personality (Brownel and Wasserstrom 2002). Think about the new modern martial arts classic movie *Crouching Tiger, Hidden Dragon*. The legendary sword-master Li Mu Bai (played by Chow Yun Fat) is glorified not because of his martial arts power but his moral personality (though he also has a suppressed sexuality).

A third way Asian men challenge stigmatized images is to sexualize their Asian-ness. Movies have begun to picture Asian men as sexual beings. For example, set in colonial Vietnam in 1929, the French film *The Lover* tells a story of a white French teenage girl who befriended a rich Chinese man so as to escape her lonely experience in boarding school. The Chinese man, played by Tony Leung Kar Fai, was portrayed in such a sensual and sexual way that the Asian male body became an object of erotic desire and fantasy. Moreover, a number of artists (such as Troy Philips, Ken Chu, and Michael Joo) have examined the complicated relationship between sexuality and race. Through their artwork (e.g., photography, installations, painting), these artists criticize the desexualized Asian men and the myths that equate Asian men with femininity, homosexuality, asexuality, or passivity (Kee 1998).

When golden boy meets white men

The historicity of gay images in Western societies has changed from "camp," to "gay," to "super-macho." It is argued that masculinity has been claimed, asserted, or re-appropriated by male homosexuals: "a moustached 'clone,' the tattooed 'leather man' or 'biker,' and more recently the all-American 'jock'" (Forrest 1994: 97). This super-macho look seems to focus entirely on the body, in which the male athletic masculine body is being glorified. Of course, this super-macho look is more pronounced among those gay men who are young, in-the-scene and in large cities.

Gay culture in most urban cities, like society at large, is stratified along the lines of gender, class, race, age and body. Generally speaking, the commercial gay scene is highly class-specific, youth-oriented, and fashion conscious. The ideal for gay men is to be young, fit and muscular, and have money to spend on clothes, travel, and home decoration. The hyper-feminine body, the elderly body, the disabled body, the poor body and many others are all regarded as subordinate gay variants, or as "failing bodies" (Kong 2004).

In terms of race, it is common to see a mixed crowd of white and Asian men in most local gay bars. You might hear terms such as "rice queen" (a Western or Caucasian man who is predominantly sexually interested in Asian men) or "potato queen" (an Asian man who is predominantly sexually interested in Western or Caucasian men). In terms of the hegemonic gay masculine ideal, the term "golden boy" seems to be the best euphemism to characterize the potato queen in this inter-racial gay culture. "Golden boy" in traditional Chinese literature signifies a young virgin boy who is innocent, infantile, feminized and even androgynous. The golden boy – infantilized (age), feminized (gender), and golden (race) – signifies a representation of Chinese (and also Asian) gay men which seems to appear in many different disguised forms. For example, one scholar argues that Asian men are always designed to play the passive part (i.e., the role of "bottom," "houseboy," or "servant") in gay pornography (Fung 1996).

Some Asian gay men use their "exotic" attributes as a survival strategy to help them gain entry to the Western world. They consciously control their bodies and benefit from the white fetishism of colored bodies (Kong 2002). There is nothing wrong with "passivity" or the image of "servitude" *per se*. The problem seems to lie in the fact that whenever the "East" meets the "West," the "East" always adopts the role of servant. The absence of other possible scenarios seems to suggest that the uniformity reflects real social hierarchy, economic inequality and political domination. The gay community can be a place of sexual freedom and comfort, but is also "a site of racial, cultural, and sexual alienation sometimes more pronounced than that in a straight society" (Fung 1996: 190).

The problems facing Asian gay men living in Western countries have not gone unnoticed or passively accepted. Many young Asian gay men, especially from the middle class and the second or third generation of immigrants, reject the "houseboy" scenario as the only way of entering the Western homosexual world. Some of these men work hard at the gym to refute the "timid yellow body" myth, while others deliberately eroticize Asian male bodies. Many artists and writers have challenged Asian male gay stereotypes, while advancing more positive and diverse images of being gay and Asian (for independent films and videos, see *The Queen's Cantonese Conversational Course*, Wayne Yung, Canada 1998; *China Dolls*, Tony Ayres, Australia, 1997; *Forever Bottom*, Nguyen Tan Hoang, USA, 1999; and *Yellow Fever*, Raymond Yeung, UK, 1998; for academic studies, see Leong 1996; Eng and Hom 1998).

Conclusion

Although biology sets the potential for how we can act, social forces play a significant role in shaping the meaning of our bodies, emotions, and identities. The male body, as the cornerstone of male identity, is governed by social expectations and pressures to be masculine and to be heterosexual. To be a "man" is to exhibit a cluster of attitudes, forms of self-presentation and behavior that are different from women and convey an emphatic sense of heterosexuality. Our society constructs a hierarchy of male bodies which privileges certain bodies (e.g., white, middle-class, able, young, heterosexual, etc.) while often stigmatizing others (e.g., Asian or colored, disabled, aged, homosexual, etc.). However, the attitudes and behaviors that are associated with masculinity can and do change. We have the ability to challenge masculine norms and ideals. Although Asian male bodies are alleged to be effeminate, asexual or even homosexual, a newly-emerging Asian masculinity is evident in societies like the UK, US, Australia and elsewhere. Some Asian men conform to the Western masculine ideal by working out. Some redefine masculinity without equating it with muscle, while some sexualize Asian male bodies.

The gay world, like the straight world, also operates according to a hierarchy of gay bodies in which colored, disabled, aging or hyper-feminine bodies are less valued. In terms of race, the "silent golden boy" seems to be a dominant image for Asian gay men in a white-dominated gay world, and is sometimes embraced by Asian men as a way to gain entry into the white-dominated gay world of Western societies. However, more diverse representations are being created by Asians, which view Asian gay men as full sexual and social agents who can be desiring as well as objects of desire.

In the still-dominant culture of Western societies, white men seem to express the norm and the ideal of "masculinity," the point of origin and reference for what it means to be a man. Asian or other nonwhite men always seem inferior – poor imitations or undesireable deviations. How can such race logic be reversed? What could Asian men tell us about men in New York, London, or Paris, rather than vice versa? Without viewing Asian men as "other" or as inferior, how can we describe their uniqueness and simply think of them as men in their own right? Instead of questioning how Asian men fall short of "normal" masculinity, what can Asian men tell us about our assumptions of masculinity in general? How can Asian men offer us new positive ways of being men? Maybe this is the time when we should take sexuality and race (among other factors such as class, age, gender) seriously and be more sensitive to the hierarchy of bodies, identities, and genders in both the gay and the straight worlds.

References

Brownel, S. and J. N. Wasserstrom (eds) 2002. *Chinese Femininities and Chinese Masculinities: A Reader*. Berkeley: University of California Press.

Butler, J. 1990. *Gender Trouble: Feminism and the Subversion of Identity*. London: Routledge.

Connell, R. W. 1995. *Masculinities*. Cambridge: Polity Press.

Eng, D. L., and A. Y. Hom (eds) 1998. *Q & A: Queer in Asian America*. Philadelphia, PA: Temple University Press.

Forrest, D. 1994. "We're Here, We're Queer, and We're Not Going Shopping", in A. Cornwall and N. Lindisfarne (eds), *Dislocating Masculinity: Comparative Ethnographies*. London: Routledge.

Fung, R. 1996. "Looking for My Penis: The Eroticised Asian in Gay Video Porn", in R. Leong (ed.), *Asian American Sexualities*. London: Routledge.

Gerschick, T. J. 2005. "Masculinity and Degree of Bodily Normativity in Western Culture", in M. S. Kimmel, J. Hearn, and R.W. Connell (eds), *Handbook of Studies on Men and Masculinities*. London: Sage.

Kee, J. 1998. "(Re)sexualizing the Desexualized Asian Male in the Works of Ken Chu and Michael Joo", available online at http://social.chass.ncsu.edu/jouvert/v2i1/Kee.htm (accessed 10.3.2006).

Kimmel, M. S. 1994. "Consuming Manhood: The Femininization of American Culture and the Recreation of the Male Body, 1832-1990", in L. Goldstein (ed.), *The Male Body*. Ann Arbor, MI: University of Michigan Press.

Kong, T. S. K. 2002. "The Seduction of the Golden Boy: The Sexual Politics of Hong Kong Gay Men", *Body & Society* 8 (1): 29-48.

——(2004) "Queer At Your Own Risk: Marginality, Community and Hong Kong Gay Male Bodies", *Sexualities* 7(1): 5-30.

Leong, R. (ed.) 1996. *Asian American Sexualities*. London: Routledge.

Seidman, S. 1996. *Queer Theory/Sociology*. Oxford: Basil Blackwell.

13

Sex and the senior woman

Meika Loe

COLGATE UNIVERSITY, NEW YORK

On a warm summer evening, a women's discussion group was underway at a senior community center in northern California. At this particular meeting, one longtime participant, Jerry, a short, white-haired woman in her seventies, made an announcement to the group. "After years of work, I just sent off my book manuscript ... it is about my sexual relationship with a younger man, and the importance of society recognizing senior women and our sensuality." The room erupted in cheers. Afterwards, several women approached Jerry, wanting to share stories about their own sexual experiences and to hear more about hers.

As this story reveals, now more than ever seniors are expressing themselves as sexual beings. In the Viagra era, sexual desire and performance is more visible and more valued than ever – for men of a broad range of ages and ethnicities. Think about recent Viagra endorsers Bob Dole, Raphael Palmiero, and Pele. None the less, despite new public attention to the sexualized senior man, the stereotype of the asexual senior woman continues to prevail. Even in the Viagra era, nobody seems to be talking about women's sexualities, or asking senior women about their sexual desires. However, in the context of my research on Viagra, I found senior women who were eager to talk about how they view health, sexuality, and culture in the Viagra era.

I met senior women through two senior citizen organizations in Southern California: a singles social club and a seniors-only summer school. Agnes, Annette, Bette, Doris, Hilda, Nora, Pauline, and Sally are the focus of this chapter. At the time of their interviews, they ranged in age from sixty-seven to eighty-six years of age. Most were living either in Florida or Southern California, approximately half were Jewish, and all were white, heterosexual, middle- or upper-middle-class American citizens. They all had differing relationships to Viagra: four had partners who tried Viagra, others had friends who used the product, and a couple only knew of Viagra through news reporting or conversations with friends. Importantly, all but Bette, who was divorced, were widows. At the time of our conversations, Bette and Doris were actively dating, while the others were not. All names were changed to protect my informants. All interviews took place over the phone in October and November 2000. All were conducted by the author and tape-recorded.

Research on sex and senior women

Before interviewing senior women, I looked for existing research on sexuality and senior women. Unfortunately, the assumption that sexuality declines and disappears with age has led to gaps and silences in the few landmark national sexuality studies that have been conducted. Research by Kinsey in the 1950s and Masters and Johnson in the late 1960s are examples of such negligence, as there is little to be learned in these studies about senior sex. Such assumptions about lack of sex may have even informed the latest *Sex in America* survey (1994) which included only those aged eighteen to fifty-nine. One notable exception came in 1976 with Shere Hite's *The Hite Report on Female Sexuality* that received questionnaire responses from women aged fourteen to seventy-eight. According to Hite, one of the major findings was that age is not a factor in female sexuality, or in other words: "Older women are NOT less sexual than younger women – and they are often more sexual."

Bob Dole's erectile dysfunction was not the only senior Viagra story that existed for the women I interviewed. Indeed, for many, the public chatter created by the Viagra phenomenon marked an opportunity for women to weigh in on the larger social discourse on health, aging, and medicine, and the construction of their own sexual selves. In the pages that follow, senior women fill in the gaps left by centuries of sex research and Viagra promoters, by sharing their desires and viewpoints, and, in the process, revealing how social sex really is.

Senior women's views on sexual pleasure and partners

It is no surprise that, for most seniors, Viagra is viewed in the context of health and aging. For many, Viagra may represent the elusive pursuit of youth, reminiscent of the ways in which male consumers of the drug can construct Viagra as a fountain-of-youth pill, enabling them to "feel eighteen again." However, few of the women I spoke with longed to return to the sexuality associated with their teenage years. Instead, sexuality represented a means to feeling healthy and vital. For example, Bette, age sixty-nine, told me that she views sexuality as a "really good calorie burner." Another volunteered: "[Viagra] has allowed us to enjoy sex again – makes us mentally feel younger." In addition, Pauline, age eighty-one, was one of several women who volunteered that her "sexual prime" was post-menopause:

> Well, menopause made sex less risky for me, and I didn't have to put a diaphragm in every night or interrupt sex for that. The risks were much less, which made it more enjoyable.

As opposed to accounts calling sexuality "risky" for the elderly, Pauline found sex less risky when she didn't have to worry about pregnancy. Just as Pauline declared sex enjoyable later in life, several of her peers, some of whom were widows, confided to me that they had been feeling sexual desire in recent years. However, their stories reveal that such desires may not be acted upon in the context of social constraints.

For example, 74-year-old Nora's "sexual urges" were mitigated by concerns about appearing "oversexed" or disrespectful in the context of widowhood, or by frustration over finding a willing and able sexual partner in one's age group.

> I was appalled that, 6 weeks after my husband died, somebody would want to kiss me or I might want to respond, because I don't think truthfully that I was what I would call an oversexed woman. I had sexual urges but I never initiated lovemaking too much.

For senior women like Nora, acting on sexual desire may have been seen as risky or fruitless for a number of reasons. First, as Nora noted, expressions of desire fed into stereotypes about appearing "oversexed" as a senior woman of her generation. Second, Nora had to confront life expectancy patterns that result in a "partner gap," leaving four out of five women of seventy-five and older without male partners. Finally, a number of social factors including the idealization of youth may lead older men in Nora's age bracket to want to date younger women..

Doris, a witty, practical, sexually active 86-year-old, was similarly vocal about her sexual desires as well as her concerns about the lack of potential sexual partners in her age group. For Doris, men are not necessarily in short supply, but *healthy* male sexual partners are. In her comments below, Doris described her desire to have a sexual relationship at her age, as opposed to the platonic arrangements she saw her friends having.

> Bear in mind that I am eighty-six years old, and I am interested in sex under certain conditions. Clean bill of health is my number-1 priority. Protection is right up there with number-1, and I don't care if it does sound clinical ... that's the world I live in. And I have to say that most of the men I have met have been inadequate in performance, so my conditions didn't either enhance or hinder the act ... I have about given up on the whole thing ... not worth the effort ... at least at the moment. I am satisfied to have someone for company at movies, restaurants, concerts, short trips, etc. I find that the older I get, the less sex has to do with my happiness. And since I am financially independent, I really do not need anyone living with me, I can manage my daily life very well, and doing "wifely" things is not something I would care to do. If things get to be desperate, there is always a vibrator, which is ready to "go," providing the batteries are new. Who could ask for more?

Doris's pursuit of pleasure was thwarted by male partners she perceived as unhealthy, who do not use protection, or those that could not "perform." As a result, Doris considered giving up on finding a sexual partner, and turning instead to her vibrator for pleasure.

Perhaps these comments of sexual dissatisfaction are one reason we never heard from the likes of Elizabeth Dole and the other sexually frustrated partners of senior men. This is the side of the story that Pfizer (the manufacturer of Viagra) doesn't talk about – some women's desire for sex and men's inability to respond positively to these desires. These comments show the other side of impotency; that is, the sexual frustration for women. Again contrary to the ideas about sex that we are used to hearing, these women appear to be the sexual initiators in these relationships. Senior women like Doris remind us that sexual pleasure exists in the context of social rules and relationships. Rather than pleasure and desire being static and natural, Doris reveals how sexuality is socially contingent and fluid.

While several senior women confided in me that they turn to vibrators in place of sexual partners, other women, like 80-year-old Hilda, like the idea of a female Viagra, or a future pill for women's sexual pleasure.

ML: What would be your ideal drug?

H: I'd want to experience what I've read about. The ecstasy.

ML: Do you mean libido? Orgasm?

H: Yes. I have two friends who make reference to the fact that they have had wonderful sex lives. They are both widows. And both very unusual for my generation since they've had more than one partner. One told me that she never experienced with her husband what she had with another man. So maybe some guys do it better than others. I wouldn't know – I've only had one. And this is the way I'm going to finish.

Hilda's comments illustrate the role that social networks, or peers, play in the construction of sexual desires. Like most of us, Hilda based her sexual knowledge and ideals in relation to the experiences of friends. In the process, she highlighted one of the key differences between men's and women's desire for a Viagra-like drug. Generally, while men of Hilda's generation may need the drug to help them continue to pursue sexual pleasure, senior women of her generation may want a drug to discover sexual pleasure for the first time.

Clearly, Pauline, Nora, Doris and Hilda do not fit the "asexual" stereotype associated with generations of senior women. For them, like the rest of us, sexuality is complex, fluid, and social. Their sexual desires and pursuit of viable partners are mediated by perceived health and social risks, sanctions, and ideals. As individuals, then, these senior women reveal the role society plays in shaping their sexual identities and behaviors. In the next section, senior women directly confront the role that culture may play in constructing and reinforcing pressures to be sexual beings.

Senior women's concerns about sexualized culture

While some senior women are curious about a mythic "pink Viagra" that can enhance pleasure, others see both pink and blue Viagra pills as representative of a problematic quick-fix pill culture, and an increasingly sexualized culture. For example, senior women like 81-year-old Annette believe that sex is more often used to demonstrate physicality and efficiency, rather than romance and feelings.

> All of that preparation an hour in advance, it makes sex not grow out of a loving feeling. It becomes planned and purely physical. And I just don't like that. The whole idea of sex has become so physical. Such gymnastics involved! And while I'm not opposed to experimentation and variety – not at all – it's become only that. The love is missing. The affection!

For Annette and others, Viagra marketing was the instigator of, or the scapegoat for, changing sexual norms. Nora linked this cultural change to a generational shift in sexual discourse, which is "too open" today, leaving no sexual mystique. Concurrently, the marketing of Viagra-like drugs is to blame for an increasingly sexualized culture that promotes promiscuity. Nora commented, "It would be hard to be celibate today. Sex is idealized on the TV and in movies as perfect and acceptable and it's just not that way in real life." For women like Nora, a culture dangerously focused on the sexual fix is perceived not only as over-sexed, but also masculine, leading women to act "too much like men and ignore romance, intimacy, and emotions." A move toward goal-oriented, or masculine sexual ideals in the Viagra era was also implied by 67-year-old Agnes:

> What is important to me is being in love. I wouldn't be with someone just for the sex. This is a woman's point of view. That love and affection are more important than sex. A man would say the opposite. That sex is most important.

Together, Agnes, Annette, and Nora blame Viagra-like drugs for promoting new problematic cultural expectations and pressures related to sexuality. They construct women's sexuality as emotional, mysterious, and romantic, as opposed to male sexuality which is non-emotional and physical. In sum, these senior women claim that masculine sexuality has set new and dangerous standards for women and society.

Despite the cultural shift toward masculine ideals and sexual pressures, Sally, age seventy-five, and then Hilda, age eighty, also convey a sense of being "caught" in a pill culture that both promotes and benefits from people's limited tolerance for personal discomfort, as well as a culture that excludes people who cannot afford these solutions.

> I think the price is going to leave even the middle-classes behind. The insurance companies may not want to pay for some of these high-priced wonders. But I do think that the rich will have a greater advantage in all of these things.
>
> People's tolerance levels are really low. If it hurts, go get a pill. I'm not like that. I figure you should fight it. Like here at the pool, I tell people with arthritis to go in the pool, because water is good for it. But they'd rather take a pill. I wouldn't. It's too easy to take a pill. Even a diet pill. They'd rather take a diet pill than go to a gym.

Senior women such as Agnes, Annette, Sally and Hilda point to problems they see as exacerbated by the marketing of Viagra-like drugs, including the promotion of exaggerated sexual norms and expectations, prohibitively expensive prescriptions, a quick-fix ethic, and an underemphasis on romance and emotions. In response, some actively resist such cultural pressures, choosing to associate sex with romance and to avoid quick-fixes.

What do senior women want?

In the Viagra era, particularly as pharmaceutical companies race to produce and market a potential blockbuster "female Viagra," senior women are slowly being acknowledged as sexual agents. But senior women's sexual lives are nothing new. As Agnes put it:

> These days, seniors are still falling in love and feeling young and sexually active again. Is this new? Probably not. It has probably been the case for some time now, but people didn't talk about it.

What do senior women want? At the very least they deserve to be included in public discussions on sexuality. In my interviews with medical practitioners I was troubled to hear some describe their "horror" as elderly patients began to ask for Viagra-like products. They were not used to imagining their parents or their patients as sexual beings.

Rather than dismiss or ignore senior women, I suggest that we learn from them. Talking to these women really opened my eyes. I knew that women had responses to the Viagra phenomenon, but I never imagined how rich, varied, and self-aware these responses might be, particularly from a group of women largely without sexual partners. Like all of us, between stories these women wanted to know if they were normal for having desires, fears, and doubts related to sexuality. At the same time, not having current sexual partners seemed to free them up to be able to reflect on their sexual lives, and even to make plans for the future.

Their stories reveal complex sexual identities and desires. These stories convey how sexuality can be mitigated and enabled by social expectations and constraints. They remind us that, just as everyone is a product of this culture, all of us have complex and conflicting ideas and feelings about sexuality in the Viagra era. Senior women, like all of us, are caught up in the social realities of our time, including medicalization, gendered and sexual oppression, and increased commercialization, perhaps even to a larger degree than men. At the same time, their lives also reflect vast generational changes in the social construction of gender, sexuality, medicine, and health. Most importantly, they remind us that, whether by taking a pill or talking about our desires, all of us are sexual agents, actively defining sexuality for ourselves and one another. In sum, they remind us of the "messy" social side of sex and sexuality that, as sociologists, we should care deeply about.

References

Hite, Shere. 1994. *Women as Revolutionary Agents of Change: The Hite Reports and Beyond*. Madison: University of Wisconsin Press.

Levy, Judith A. 1994. "Sex and Sexuality in Later Life Stages," in *Sexuality Across the Life Course*. Alice S. Rossi (ed.). Chicago, IL: University of Chicago Press.

14

Polishing the pearl

Discoveries of the clitoris

Lisa Jean Moore

STATE UNIVERSITY OF NEW YORK, PURCHASE COLLEGE

In the early 1990s, I worked on a national sex information switchboard for a couple of years. Much to my surprise, a majority of the callers were men, and their two most common questions were: "What is the normal penis size?" and "Where is the clitoris?" Trained to provide anonymous, non-judgmental, and accurate information to callers, I would respond that most penises when erect were between 5 and 7 inches long. I could almost feel the relief as these callers thanked me, quickly hanging up the phone to get on with their days, secure in the validation that they (and their penises) were "okay."

As for the clitoris question, I instructed callers to place their hands in a praying position, bend their knuckles slightly and imagine this as the vagina. If the area between the thumbs was the vagina opening, the clitoris was roughly located in the place above the tips of their thumbs, in the triangular area. I never felt as if this answer was quite as successful. Many callers fumbled or dropped the phone while trying to follow my instructions. Some callers were clearly confused by the model as they asked, "So it's a hole?" or "But what does the vagina really look like?" Furthermore, I was increasingly alarmed by the steady stream of female callers who asked for instructions on how to find their own clitorises or wanted suggestions on how to experience orgasms exclusively through vaginal penetration. "Is there something wrong with me?" they inquired when discussing how dissatisfying penis–vagina sex was, oftentimes explaining that they had never experienced an orgasm during sex. (Tellingly, decorating the office wall was a hand-drawn cartoon of a vagina that said "The clitoris. If you can't find it, you can't come.") Clearly there is something baffling and mysterious about the clitoris. According to a small sample of people calling a sex information line, even though size doesn't matter, location and purpose do. Where is it? What does it do?

And finding and exploring the clitoris is not just an intimate affair. Simultaneous to these personal concerns about one's own and others' sexual bodies, the management of the clitoris also figures prominently in international human rights, through debates about female genital cutting (FGC, sometimes also referred to as clitoridectomy, or female genital mutilation, FGM). According to the United Nations, "FGC/FGM refers to all procedures involving partial or total removal of the external female genitalia or other injury to the female genital organs for cultural or other non-medical reasons." Generally presented as a practice that is exclusively performed by "other" cultures,

[F]emale circumcision has been practiced in the United States since at least the nineteenth century. Cases of its use in the late nineteenth through the early twentieth century were for the treatment of masturbation (by both women and girls) and nymphomania – a term used interchangeably with masturbation and with what was regarded as excessive amounts of sex.

(Webber 2003: 65)

According to the Center for Reproductive Rights, it is estimated that, worldwide, 130 million women have experienced female genital cutting.

When one attempts to define the clitoris, it becomes increasingly apparent that the definitions are constrained by social and political forces. In other words, there is no universal or stable definition of the clitoris, and many of the definitions reveal anxieties about women's bodies and sexualities. How is it, then, that this piece of flesh has inspired such personal and cultural anxiety? Taking a look at some of the Western "experts" who have produced images of female bodies and sexualities, it is clear that the clitoris is a very elusive, dangerous, and complicated invention. Referring to the clitoris as an "invention" means that the definition and representation of this piece of flesh is something that changes through time and depending on who is defining it.

Histories of the clitoris

Anatomists, psychoanalysts, sexologists, and pornographers have all established their professional reputations by claiming expertise about the clitoris. "Anatomies of private parts are perhaps the most intently and minutely examined as they often provide us with some of the earliest available, 'most scientific,' and supposedly, therefore, neutral knowledge of body parts least visually accessible in contemporary Western daily life" (Moore and Clarke 1995: 256). Different male anatomical explorers dispute the "scientific" discovery of the clitoris. In 1559, Realdo Colombo wrote of discovering the clitoris, "the seat of women's delight," and he called it "so pretty and useful a thing" in his *De re anatomica*. But bio-colonizers Kasper Bartholin, Gabriel Fallopius and Ambroise Pare were also making claims to parts of women's bodies and challenged the crediting of Colombo with the clitoris. According to historian Thomas Laqueur (1990), prior to the mid-eighteenth century, scientific explanations of men's and women's genitalia were based on a one-sex model whereby women's genital anatomy was an inversion of men's. The clitoris and the uterus were internal, or inverted, versions of the penis and scrotum.

In the biomedical textbooks of the 1900s through the 1950s, the clitoris is depicted and described as homologous to the penis – that is, it is formed from the same evolutionary structure – but is also considered inferior to the penis. In 1905, Sigmund Freud, the father of psychoanalysis, published essays that argued for a differentiation between clitoral and vaginal orgasms. Clitoral orgasms were considered immature and, as women became properly socialized into their adult sexual orientation of heterosexuality, they would experience the "mature" orgasm in their vagina. Sexologists of the 1930s and 1940s, notably Havelock Ellis and Robert Latou Dickinson, read female genital physiology as evidence of their sexual experiences, often citing an enlarged clitoris as proof of prostitution or lesbianism. "Whether she chose under examination to reveal her 'sins' verbally or not, a woman's genitalia revealed her confession to the sexologist, her confessor. Her sex practices alone or with others, with men or women, in a normal or abnormal manner, thus entered the realm of the scientifically knowable. On the examining table, literally wide open under his scrutiny, Dickinson's subject could not hide her sexual secrets from him" (Miller 2000: 80). In this context, the clitoris can reveal a woman's transgression against patriarchal sexual norms. And the control of women's sexual expression and "perverted desires" is evident in other academic disciplines. During the 1930s, art criticism of Georgia O'Keeffe's flower paintings pejoratively labeled her a woman first and an artist second, generally dismissed her artistic contribution and wrongly described her paintings as male genitalia – a male critic wrote: "much of her earlier work showed a womanly preoccupation with sex, an uneasy selection of phallic symbols in her flowers, a delight in their nascent qualities" (cited in Mitchell 1978: 682).

In 1953, Alfred Kinsey published *Sexual Behavior in the Human Female*, which was comprised of 5,940 interviews with women. Kinsey and his colleagues interpreted this data to define the clitoris as the locus of female sexual sensation and orgasm. Despite this scientific evidence culled from women's own voices, the practice of labeling and describing the function of the clitoris was abandoned in anatomical textbooks during the 1950s–1970s. Importantly, a survey of lay and medical dictionaries found that definitions of the clitoris refer to the male body as a template or norm from which the female body is somehow derived (Braun and Kitzinger 2001). This definition process often implies that the clitoris is inferior to the penis. If one's knowledge were based on historical anatomical rendering and dictionary definitions alone, it would be possible to believe that the clitoris is small, purposeless, and subaltern to the penis.

Pornography is another realm where individuals get information about human genitalia that contributes to the confusion and mystique about the clitoris. In an issue of *Men's Health* magazine (2000), an article called "Sex Tricks from Skin Flicks" provides advice for readers from forty X-rated films. For example: "You know her clitoris needs attention, especially as she nears climax. But it's hard to find such a tiny target when both your bodies are moving. Use the flat of your palm to make broad, quick circular motions around the front of her vaginal opening. That way, you're sure to hit the spot." Clearly, some men and women are viewing pornography as an instructional aid in their genital and sexual exploration.

Whether it is in print, film, or online media, the clitoris (or "clit," as it is referred to almost exclusively in porn) has been depicted with great attention to detail and celebration of diversity of shape, size and color. That is not to say all renderings of the clitoris are intentionally feminist or particularly instructive. In 1972, in the most profitable movie in film history, *Deep Throat*, directed by Gerard Damiano, the actress Linda Lovelace's clitoris is nine inches down her throat. The only way for her to experience orgasm is to have her throat stimulated with a long, erect penis. Contemporary films feature the clitoris, such as director Jack Remy's *Pleasure Spot* (1986) plotted around a clitoral transplant, and *Papi Chulo Facesitting* (2005) presenting the main character "Luv" positioning her clitoris over the nose of Tom. Pornographic series such as *Tales from the Clit*, *Terrors from the Clit*, and *Pussy Fingers* each offer a variety of shots of the clitoris as part of female genital anatomy and female sexual expression.

Feminist insurgencies

During the 1970s, consciousness-raising groups of women equipped with plastic vaginal speculums, mirrors and flashlights taught one another how to explore their sexual and reproductive organs. These groups of women fueled the Feminist Self-Help Health Movement and created fertile ground for feminist reformation of anatomical texts. These self-examinations and group meetings revolutionized existing descriptions and renderings of the clitoris (Federation of Feminist Women's Health Centers 1981). "From minor homologue it is transfigured into the raison d'être of other organs. Deliberate, self conscious effort is made to present the clitoris as a 'functioning integrate unit'" (Moore and Clarke 1995: 280). The Hite Report on Female Sexuality published in 1976 was based on data drawn from 1844 of 3,000 anonymous questionnaires distributed to American women aged between fourteen and seventy-eight. Although many questioned the methodological rigor of this study, the project amassed significant and compelling data about the importance of clitoral stimulation for female orgasm.

But these feminist insurgencies were met with great resistance from mainstream anatomical practices. Throughout the 1980s and 1990s, the backlash to feminism in anatomy reasserted women's sexual response as linked exclusively to reproduction, not sexual pleasure. For example, in *Human Anatomy and Physiology*, the author argues that "With the current emphasis on sexual pleasure and the controversy over the role of women (and men) as sex objects, it is easy to lose sight of the fact that a large part of woman's body is adapted specifically for functions of conceiving, bearing and nurturing children" (Silverstein 1988: 740). Certain anatomical texts of this time seem to purposefully render the clitoris as useless or unnecessary (Moore and Clarke 2001).

Throughout the 2000s, video, CD-ROM, and web-based anatomies emerge as modes of viewing genital anatomy. These new ways of accessing images and descriptions of the clitoris do not necessarily change the definition of the clitoris., "Continuities with previous textual anatomies abound in new visual and cyber forms such as the heterosexual requirement, the female body as reproductive not sexual, and the biomedical expert as the proper and dominant mediator between humans and their own bodies" (Moore and Clarke 2001: 87). Notably, feminists still participate in research on women's genital anatomy. For example, Rebecca Chalker (2002), a pioneer of the Self-Help Health Movement, has established that the clitoris is made up of eighteen distinct and interrelated structures. Biometric analysis of a diverse sample of female genitals has "proven" that there is a great range of variation in women's genital dimensions, including clitoral size, labial length and color (Lloyd *et al.* 2005).

In sum

Mapping, representing and defining the clitoris is a political act. As a result, the clitoris has many competing and contradictory narratives that vary depending upon personal, cultural, political, and historical circumstances. So, based on who is defining the clitoris, it can be classified as an inverted and diminutive penis, a small erectile sex organ of the female, a love button, an unhygienic appendage to be removed, a site of immature female sexual expression, a key piece of evidence of sexual perversion, or a vibrant subject of pornographic mediations. These different definitions of the clitoris are constrained by the political and cultural context, including who is representing the clitoris, for what purposes, and under what conditions.

References

Braun, Virginia and Celia Kitzinger. 2001. "Telling it Straight? Dictionary Definitions of Women's Genitals", *Journal of Sociolinguistics* 5, 2: 214–33.

Chalker, Rebecca. 2002. *The Clitoral Truth: The Secret World at Your Fingertips*, New York: Seven Stories Press.

Colombo, Realdo. 1559. *De Re Anatomica*.

Federation of Feminist Women's Health Centers. 1981. A *New View of the Woman's Body*, New York: Simon Schuster.

Freud, Sigmund. 1905. *Three Essays on the Theory of Sexuality*, Standard Edition, London: Hogarth Press.

Hite, Shere. 1976. *The Hite Report: A Nationwide Study on Female Sexuality*, New York: Macmillan.

Kinsey, Alfred C. *et al.* 1953. *Sexual Behavior in the Human Female*. Philadelphia, PA: W. B. Saunders.

Laqueur, Thomas. 1990. *Making Sex: Body and Gender from the Greeks to Freud*, Cambridge, MA: Harvard University Press.

Lloyd, Jillian, Naomi Crouch, Catherine Minto, Lih-Mei Liao, and Sarah Crieghton. 2005. "Female Genital Appearance: 'Normality' unfolds", *British Journal of Obstetrics and Gynaecology* 112, 5: 643.

Men's Health. 2000. "Sex Tricks from Skin Flicks", 15, 7: 54.

Miller, Heather Lee. 2000. "Sexologists Examine Lesbians and Prostitutes in the United States, 1840–1940", *NWSA Journal*, 12, 3: 67–91.

Mitchell, Marilyn Hall. 1978. "Sexist Art Criticism: Georgia O'Keeffe, A Case Study", *Signs* 3, 3: 681–7.

Moore, Lisa Jean and Adele E. Clarke. 1995. "Clitoral Conventions and Transgressions: Graphic Representations of Female Genital Anatomy, c1900–1991", *Feminist Studies* 21(2): 255–301.

——2001. "The Traffic in Cyberanatomies: Sex/Gender/Sexualities in Local and Global Formations", *Body and Society* 7(1): 57–96.

Silverstein, Alvin. 1988. *Human Anatomy and Physiology*, New York: John Wiley and Sons.

Webber, Sara. 2003. "Cutting History, Cutting Culture: Female Circumcision in the United States", *The American Journal of Bioethics* 3, 2: 65–6.

15
Orgasm

Juliet Richters

UNIVERSITY OF NEW SOUTH WALES, AUSTRALIA

Orgasm can be defined from a physiological point of view as a reaction to sexual stimulation in both males and females. It consists of a series of muscular contractions in the pelvic muscles around the anus and sexual organs. It is preceded by increasing muscular tension and involves high blood pressure and rapid breathing and a visible red flush of the skin. In men, it is usually accompanied by ejaculation of semen.

This physiological description does not tell us much about what orgasm feels like. Orgasm is usually experienced as the climax, or high point, of a sexual event (either partnered sex or masturbation). It is preceded by an intensely pleasurable feeling of growing excitement and is usually followed by a feeling of delicious relaxation. However, these are generalizations. Rather than feeling calm immediately afterwards, people sometimes feel excited, elated or weepy, and orgasm need not signal the end of the sexual event. Erection of the penis and fullness of the vaginal area may disappear slowly or rapidly after orgasm. People vary in how soon after an orgasm they are ready to resume sexual activity: some people like to continue immediately or start again within minutes, and others may lose interest in sex for days or even longer. Some people may experience repeated orgasm or waves of orgasmic tension and pleasure without an apparent peak and collapse. "At best, an organ-moving cataclysm: my ovaries, uterus, breasts, and brain become one singing dark pulsating sea of the most exquisite feeling" (Hite 1976: 129).

Orgasm in social context

Describing orgasm as a physiological reaction makes it sound as though it is something that happens to humans everywhere, like digestion or sneezing. But this is not the case. The experience of orgasm varies greatly in different cultures and at different times in history. In all cultures it is usual for men to ejaculate during sex, and sex usually includes vaginal intercourse. None the less, it is possible for men to ejaculate after minimal stimulation – especially in a stressful situation – without feeling much or any orgasmic pleasure.

> Having orgasms is the most pleasant physical experience in my life, bar none, and as far as having sex without them, how can there be sex without orgasms? An orgasm is the logical culmination of sex, and the two, orgasm and sex, cannot be differentiated.
>
> *(Hite 1982: 468)*

Female orgasm is more variable. There have even been some cultures in which orgasm for women was virtually unheard of, generally ones with very restrictive sexual mores. A study of the sexual culture of mid-twentieth-century Inis Beag, an island off the west of Ireland, reported that the islanders had the view (shared with many Western peoples) that men were by nature far more interested in sex than women (Messenger 1971). Women were taught by the clergy and at home that sex with their husbands was a duty which must be endured, because it was sinful to refuse intercourse (Messenger 1971: 39). Inis Beag people were very shy about (even partial) nudity, about urination and defecation, and about heterosexual social interaction. They lacked a tradition of "dirty jokes," and even the men felt that intercourse would use up their energy or harm their health ("a common belief in primitive and folk societies," says Messenger). Although it was hard for the researchers to get details about people's sexual habits, they concluded that "intercourse takes place with underclothes not removed; and orgasm, for the man, is achieved quickly, almost immediately after which he falls asleep" (Messenger 1971: 41). Female orgasm appeared to be unknown. Other physiological processes such as menstruation and menopause were traumatic for women because local traditions had no explanation for them.

More sexually liberal cultures assume that women take at least as much pleasure in sex as men, and regard orgasms for men and women as a "natural" part of sexual interactions. We should not make the mistake of thinking that this is only a result of contemporary scientific knowledge and post-feminist liberalism in developed countries. In the *Kama Sutra*, a Sanskrit treatise on love-making that dates from about the fourth century CE (Vatsyayana 1963), the author does not refer to orgasm by a distinct name, but it is clear from the discussion that he regards women and men as deriving pleasure and satisfaction from sex.

> At the first time of sexual union the passion of the male is intense, and his time is short, but in subsequent unions on the same day the reverse of this is the case. With the female, however, it is the contrary, for at the first time her passion is weak, and then her time long, but on subsequent occasions in the same day, her passion is intense and her time short, until her passion is satisfied.
>
> *(Vatsyayana 1963: 122)*

People learn what to feel in sex as much as they learn what to do. For people to understand a bodily sensation as sexual, it needs to have a place in a script that labels and organizes it. As Gagnon and Simon put it in *Sexual Conduct*, "Without the proper elements of a script that defines the situation, names the actors, and plots the behavior, nothing sexual is likely to happen." In sexually repressive cultures it is even possible for people to masturbate to orgasm (defined physiologically), or have spontaneous orgasm while asleep or awake, without experiencing what is happening as sexual – they may experience it as emotional or religious passion, or some kind of fit or weird feeling. This can also happen to children before they know about sex. Even in recent years parents have taken small children to the doctor because of "fits" or "attacks," only to have the behaviour explained as masturbatory orgasm. Orgasm as a purely physiological event can occur without the person having any awareness of it *as sexual*. There is no direct correlation between physiological events and social ones – and sexual events are deeply social, even those that happen when we are alone.

A social constructionist view of sex places it firmly within the realm of culture. As anthropologist Carole Vance (1991) put it: "The physiology of orgasm and penile erection no more explains a culture's sexual schema than the auditory range of the human ear explains its music." By sexual schema she meant the patterns of sexual understandings and behaviour within which sex in that culture is organized. This shows us that a physiological definition of orgasm cannot tell us about the meaning of orgasm in people's lives. Sexual arousal or orgasm experienced by a person in a social situation is not equivalent to a single measurable physiological response. Physiology concerns itself with bundles of biochemical mechanisms that do not have meaning in themselves. We are unconscious of many of them. Only through our interpretation of sensations and their meanings do they become connected with sex in the social sense.

Having and not having orgasms

In medical circles orgasm is no longer seen as weakening or damaging to one's health, as it was by some experts up to the nineteenth century. However, many clinicians and researchers see variations of sexual practice or experience as dysfunctions. One could cynically observe that, if something is a medical dysfunction or problem, a therapist or drug manufacturer can make money out of fixing it. Yet most sexual "dysfunctions" are not due to illness or the failure of some part of the body to work properly (erectile dysfunction due to diabetes is an obvious exception). Rather, they are social failures to perform sex in a way that is socially acceptable (Morrow 1994). Many writers refer to orgasmic dysfunction (the inability to reach orgasm) or coital orgasmic dysfunction (the inability to reach orgasm through vaginal intercourse). This medicalization of sexual problems has been widely criticized (Kaschak and Tiefer 2001; Tiefer 2004; Potts *et al.* 2004).

Another way of interpreting this notion of dysfunction would be to say that what is seen as a problem reflects social expectations. The existence of "difficulty reaching orgasm" as a sexual problem tells us that, in contemporary Western sexual mores, each partner is generally expected to reach orgasm at least once in a sexual encounter. Thus a person may feel inadequate if they do not reach orgasm, and may even pretend that they have done so, rather than admit that they cannot. A person may also feel inadequate if the partner does not reach orgasm. This is another reason why someone may fake orgasm, to save the partner's feelings, perhaps fearing to cause offence by making them feel sexually unattractive or inept in technique. It is more often men who feel a duty to make the partner reach orgasm, as it is more often women who miss out on orgasm in heterosexual partnered sex. "My partner thinks I do when I show signs, like special hard breathing and body movements. But I never have orgasms – *never*" (Hite 1976: 156).

Experts have argued over whether repeated sexual stimulation and excitement not relieved by orgasm is harmful to health. Certainly many people find it irritating and disappointing, and a sense of frustration or of being used can lead people to avoid sexual arousal altogether. How they feel may depend largely on their perception of the meaning of the sexual acts which caused the excitement and the social context in which they occur. "I think orgasms are overrated. When I masturbate, it is to achieve orgasm, but with my lover I really don't care if I do or not. I just want to feel warm and close" (Hite 1976: 136).

People are less likely to have an orgasm during sex when they are young and inexperienced and when they are with a new, unfamiliar partner. It is statistically common for men in regular relationships to reach orgasm during sex while women often do not. Studies show that women who have frequent orgasms tend to enjoy sex more, have sex more often and report that they are satisfied with their sex lives (de Visser *et al.* 2003; Laumann *et al.* 1994; Haavio-Mannila and Kontula 1997).

In the past some writers have argued that upbringing, attitudes, religion, relationship issues, anxiety, previous traumatic experiences or even the woman's relationship with her father determined whether she would reach orgasm during sex (Andersen and Cyranowski 1995; Fisher 1973). Men's orgasms have rarely been seen as problematic in this way. A recent large survey in Australia showed that the likelihood of a man reaching orgasm at the last encounter he reported with an opposite-sex partner was high (over 95 percent) as long as the encounter included vaginal intercourse. This is an effective way for most men to reach orgasm, and it is widely regarded as the standard and expected sexual act that should be included in every sexual episode. Nearly 70 percent of women overall had an orgasm in the last encounter they reported with a male partner. However, the likelihood of having an orgasm varied considerably depending what sexual practices they engaged in. Women were more likely to reach orgasm (86 percent) in encounters that included both manual stimulation and cunnilingus. (Women were also more likely to have had an orgasm – 76 percent – at the last encounter they reported if their partner was a woman.) This is supported by earlier research showing that the change women wanted most in their sex lives was "more foreplay" (Davidson and Darling 1989).

For women, difficulty in reaching orgasm is a commonly reported sexual problem. Men rarely suffer from this problem. But it is not necessarily a great advantage for men that they have more and faster orgasms. Many men struggle during sex to avoid ejaculation that occurs too early, before they have had much chance to enjoy themselves. Women often complain, however, that men are too goal-oriented in sex and see it as a rush towards the reward of orgasm rather than enjoying the sensual pleasures of extended arousal.

More men than women report reaching orgasm "too early" – though we do not know whether men who say this in surveys actually reach orgasm faster than men who do not. It is possible that men who feel they come too fast are just more aware of a social expectation or requirement for them to "last longer." Women who reach orgasm rapidly are more likely to be praised for responsiveness; it is rarely seen as a problem. This highlights the difference in socially acceptable behaviour during sex. When a woman reaches orgasm during sex, it would be unusual behaviour if she were to immediately turn over and fall asleep, assuming the encounter to be over, even if the man had not had an orgasm.

The sexual politics of orgasm

What goes on in sex is therefore not neutrally negotiated between two equal parties. It is no accident that the dominant or most widely accepted sexual practice, vaginal intercourse, is one that reliably delivers sexual pleasure and orgasm to men but less reliably to women. In other chapters of this volume, we see that sexual practice is shaped by dominant discourses. Men and women bring to sexual encounters their enculturation as masculine and feminine, the injunctions of parents, school, the media, and wider society. Young men are more likely than young women to have experience of masturbation, and to be more familiar with what stimulation effectively brings about orgasm for themselves, and to be more confident that it is acceptable for them to openly seek orgasmic gratification in an encounter. Sex therapists and counsellors have tended to accept social norms and to enforce rather than challenge the idea that it is normal and preferable to experience orgasm through intercourse rather than through other forms of stimulation. This emphasis on intercourse is not "natural" or politically neutral: it is a way in which women have been required to serve or service men over the centuries. There are signs that this may be changing, however. Oral sex is becoming more acceptable and more widespread, and young people with access to explicit sexual information in magazines and on the internet may be less bound by the "coital imperative" than their parents were.

Unlike many heterosexuals, gay men do not assume that each sexual encounter will include penetrative intercourse; this usually has to be negotiated, and often does not occur. Even during anal intercourse, they do not assume that it will lead to orgasm for the insertive partner – they often stop and do something else, or stop after the receptive partner has had an orgasm. Without the traditional heterosexual script for practice, assumptions that are seen by many men as "natural" desires of the body – such as the need to reach orgasm during penetration – are shown to be socially variable.

Orgasmic variations

Humans rarely have sex with the primary or conscious intention of causing a pregnancy. Thus variations of practice in search of intense or extended sexual pleasure need not necessarily include ejaculation in the vagina.

One variation of practice is for the man to avoid orgasm so as to prolong intercourse and avoid pregnancy. This is technically called *coitus reservatus*. In the Oneida Community, a socially experimental commune in nineteenth-century United States, every man was regarded as the "husband" of every woman but reproduction was strictly limited. The men had to learn to have intercourse without ejaculating, and were said to be able to do so for an hour or more. The community believed that the "spilling" of semen led to the loss of men's energy or strength, so they presumably disapproved of men reaching orgasm by other means than intercourse. Men were supposed to lose their erections gradually after intercourse without having an orgasm.

One could regard any intercourse in which the man does not simply head for orgasm as soon as possible as a form of *coitus reservatus*. Extended intercourse may give a female partner more time and more chance of reaching orgasm. As in the Oneida Community, a man's control over when he ejaculates can also be used as a form of contraception, if he takes care to ejaculate well away from the vagina (and has the good fortune not to "leak" semen beforehand). Ejaculation may occur during some other sexual practice (such as oral sex or masturbation) or by withdrawing from the vagina just before ejaculation, which is technically called *coitus interruptus*. It is a less reliable form of contraception than modern methods such as the pill, but can be useful in cases where other methods are not available.

Some strands of Tantrism (a group of Indian mystic sects dating from the sixth century CE or earlier) include ritual sex in which the man is similarly required to avoid ejaculating while the woman is encouraged to have orgasms.

There is a great deal of debate about the definition and nature of the "multiple orgasm." It can be hard to distinguish mini-peaks in protracted high-level sexual arousal from multiple orgasms. Some experts define several orgasms separated by refractory periods (when sexual stimulation is unwanted or ineffective) in one sexual session as "repeated" rather than "multiple," while "multiple orgasms" are not separated by refractory periods. Although women are more likely than men to have trouble having orgasms at all, women who do easily have orgasms seem to have a better chance of having multiple ones, though even women for whom this is possible may only experience it occasionally. Men who want to experience several orgasms in a single sexual session of sex need to have a quick recovery period so that they can reach orgasm and regain their erection several times – this is easier for young men. Alternatively they may be able to train themselves to have multiple orgasms. This involves learning to have an orgasm without ejaculation. This sounds crazy to many men who equate the two, but it is possible for some men to learn to inhibit the ejaculatory reflex so that they can have a "dry" orgasm. (A man who has had an "accidental" ejaculation without the sensation of orgasm may be aware that the two do not necessarily go together.) Men can also train themselves to maintain a level of high arousal just before the moment when ejaculation becomes inevitable, to experience waves of orgasmic-level pleasure (Brauer and Brauer 1990).

There have been arguments over the years about whether women also ejaculate or release fluid at orgasm. In earlier centuries discussion of this topic was confused by lack of knowledge of the physiology of reproduction. In some cultures, the woman's vaginal moisture was thought to combine with the man's semen to bring about conception; thus an unaroused woman was assumed to be infertile. Once the ovum and sperm (as distinct from seminal fluid) were discovered and seen under the microscope, it became clear that conception depended on women's ovulation, not on their sexual fluids. The idea that women sometimes ejaculated – released whitish or clear fluid in spurts at orgasm or during high arousal – was ignored in sexual medicine, though it survived in pornography through the eighteenth and nineteenth centuries. Twentieth-century research showed that some women do ejaculate, and this fluid is different from urine as it contains high levels of a chemical that occurs also in male prostatic fluid (one of the components of semen) (Zaviacic *et al.* 1988). When the ejaculate is thin and copious it presumably contains urine as well, though the mechanism by which this occurs in someone who otherwise has perfectly good control of urination is not well understood. Indeed, some women who ejaculate have tried to stop themselves having orgasms so that they did not wet the bed. Some have been treated surgically for incontinence, as their sexual response was seen as a dysfunction. It is probably simpler to put a towel on the bed.

All these variations make it clear that human orgasm is a highly variable phenomenon, both in whether it occurs at all, and how it is experienced. People can live their whole lives without it, while others will risk their lives to achieve it.

References

Andersen, Barbara L. and Jill M. Cyranowski 1995. "Women's Sexuality: Behaviors, Responses, and Individual Differences", *Journal of Consulting and Clinical Psychology* 63: 891–906.

Brauer, Alan P. and Donna J. Brauer 1990. *The ESO Ecstasy Program: Better, Safer Sexual Intimacy and Extended Orgasmic Response*. New York: Warner.

Davidson, J. Kenneth, Sr and Carol A. Darling 1989. "Self-Perceived Differences in the Female Orgasmic Response", *Family Practice Research Journal* 8: 75–84.

de Visser, Richard O., Anthony M. A. Smith, Chris E. Rissel, Juliet Richters and Andrew E. Grulich 2003. "Sex in Australia: Heterosexual Experience and Recent Heterosexual Encounters among a Representative Sample of Adults", *Australian and New Zealand Journal of Public Health* 27: 146–54.

Fisher, Seymour 1973. *Understanding the Female Orgasm*. Harmondsworth, Middx: Penguin.

Gagnon, J.H. and Simon, W. 1973. *Sexual Conduct: The Social Sources of Human Sexuality*. Chicago, IL: Aldine Publishing Company.

Haavio-Mannila, E. and O. Kontula 1997. "Correlates of Increased Sexual Satisfaction", *Archives of Sexual Behavior* 26: 399–419.

Hite, Shere 1976. *The Hite Report: A Nationwide Study of Female Sexuality*. New York: Dell.

——1982. *The Hite Report on Male Sexuality*. New York: Ballantine.

Kaschak, Ellyn and Leonore Tiefer (eds) 2001. *A New View of Women's Sexual Problems*. Binghamton, NY: Haworth Press.

Laumann, Edward O., John H. Gagnon, Robert T. Michael and Stuart Michaels 1994. *The Social Organization of Sexuality: Sexual Practices in the United States*. Chicago and London: University of Chicago Press.

Messenger, John C. 1971. "Sex and Repression in an Irish Folk Community", in D. S. Marshall and R. C. Suggs (eds), *Human Sexual Behavior*. New York: Basic Books.

Morrow, Ross 1994. "The Sexological Construction of Sexual Dysfunction", *Australian and New Zealand Journal of Sociology* 30: 20–35.

Potts, Annie, Victoria Grace, Nicola Gavey and Tiina Vares 2004. "'Viagra Stories': Challenging 'Erectile Dysfunction'", *Social Science and Medicine* 59: 489–99.

Richters, Juliet, Richard O. de Visser, Chris E. Rissel and Anthony M. A. Smith in press. "Sexual Practices at Last Heterosexual Encounter and Occurrence of Orgasm in a National Survey", *Journal of Sex Research*.

Tiefer, Leonore 2004. *Sex Is Not A Natural Act and Other Essays*. Boulder, CO: Westview Press.

Vance, Carole S. 1991. "Anthropology Discovers Sexuality: A Theoretical Perspective", *Social Science and Medicine* 33: 875–84.

Vatsyayana 1963. *The Kama Sutra of Vatsyayana*. Trans. Sir Richard Burton and F. F. Arbuthnot. London: William Kimber & Co.

Zaviacic, M., A. Zaviacicová, I. K. Holomác and J. Molcan 1988. "Female Urethral Expulsions Evoked by Local Digital Stimulation of the G-spot: Differences in the Response Patterns", *Journal of Sex Research* 24: 311–18.

16

Anal sex

Phallic and other meanings

Simon Hardy

WORCESTER UNIVERSITY, MASSACHUSETTS

It hits me like an iron fist in the chest that in this global communications village somehow, in some way, my father's going to see me getting a butt-fuck I didn't actually get. I hate the idea of having anal sex; as a woman it's a negation of your femininity. Most of all I hate being a fake. My family. The boys at the uni, some of the bitter, immature little nothings I've knocked back, all wanking off at the image in their bedsits. Others, thinking they know all about me, all about my sexuality from that image. McClymont, once his wife goes to bed, will sit with the handset and a Scotch pulling his wire at the image of me getting it up the arse.

(Irvine Welsh, Porno*)*

Welsh's novel of Scottish lowlife raises some important themes concerning the murkier aspects of contemporary experience rarely addressed by sociologists. However, the characterization of the female protagonist, Nikki, soon takes us far beyond what is likely in reality. She is more assertive, more in control and more "feminist" than it is possible for most female performers to be in the porn industry. This is evident in that she refuses to do anal sex, which is the very trademark of the do-it-yourself, Gonzo pornography being described, and she even objects to a video edit that makes it appear as if she has. What arises here is not simply a question about the meaning of anal sex in modern culture, of why a woman might object to it, but also the issue of sexual truth, of personal identity and the role of sexuality and of sexual representation in its formation and authentication. Sexuality and pornography have become a means of existential assertion for modern-day men and women: "Look at me, see my body, see me fucking, see what I am, who I am, *that* I am."

This chapter will consider contemporary cultural constructions of anal sex. This may strike the reader as an unprepossessing theme for academic attention but it is a fact, and an increasingly common fact, of everyday social experience and conduct, which deserves our attention as much as any other. In fact it is arguable that anal sex represents the "final frontier" for many of the key themes that have defined modern sexual culture. These include the struggle for equality of gender and sexual orientation; the relationship between sexuality and self-identity; and the clash between a phallic model of sexuality, which is both normative and patriarchal, and a more diverse range of "perverse" sexualities.

It is important to be clear from the outset what we mean when speaking of "phallic sexuality." This is really shorthand for the dominant way of doing and thinking about sexuality in modern Western culture. It is a form of sexuality that centres around the penis and its penetrative role in coital intercourse, between a heterosexual, and traditionally married, couple. It is normative in that it is widely accepted as the normal and, perhaps, natural form that sexuality should take. It is also patriarchal because the act of intercourse is understood in terms of an anatomical dichotomy in which the penis is seen as "active" and the vagina as "passive," and therefore, at least implicitly, the male partner as superior and the female as inferior. The sources of this view of sexuality will be discussed further.

To a great extent our understanding of penetrative anal sex has been subsumed into this phallic model, with the anus becoming interchangable, in the "passive" position, with the vagina. In such a case, of course, a male may take on the symbolically "inferior" role in the act, although phallic sexuality always accords the "superior" role to the owner of a penis. Certainly most academic commentaries on either male–female or male–male anal sex, whether in a contemporary or historical context, seem automatically to assume that it is an act of phallic domination by the inserting partner over the receptive partner. Yet, as we shall see, even if the phallic interpretation remains the most common, it is only one of a range of different ways of understanding the act. In fact, anal sex is an especially interesting case to consider on this point because the naturalizing discourse that underpins phallic sexuality cannot be so easily extended to the supposedly "unnatural" act of anal penetration.

Let us consider, then, the wider range of present-day constructions of anal sex, as we find them discussed in sociological, psychological and medical literature. We encounter anal sex in a variety of guises: as a method of contraception, as a health risk, as a heterosexual substitute, as a perversion, as a routine variation of sexual repertoire, as a special/ultimate intimacy, as a fashionable theme of cultural representation, as an obligatory pornographic number, and, yes, as an act of phallic domination.

A method of contraception

It is quite possible that in global terms the majority of instances of anal intercourse have no particular erotic meaning distinct from those already associated with genital intercourse. In many cases anal sex is practiced as a pragmatic method of contraception by heterosexual couples for whom genital–anal intercourse offers a direct substitute for vaginal intercourse, where other forms of contraception are unavailable or unacceptable. Such circumstances may not often apply in the USA but the practice has, for instance, been cited by public health agencies as a possible contributing factor in the rapid spread of HIV infection in parts of Africa.

A health risk

This leads us to a theme about which we have heard a good deal in recent years: anal sex as health risk. Anal intercourse is associated with a number of health issues, but it is above all the potential for the sexual transmission of HIV infection (especially from the inserting to the receptive partner) that has led to its being cited as a risk behavior by health educators.

Yet the medical profession no longer monopolizes the concept of risk, which has recently hopped from medical to erotic discourse. Sociological studies, such as D.T. Ridge's (2004) research on young gay men in Melbourne, Australia, show that the element of risk now associated with unprotected anal intercourse may sometimes heighten its erotic appeal. In this context the practice of "barebacking," as it is called, is often experienced as a daring and adventurous form of transgression that provides the individual with a sense of being carried away by an overwhelming male sex-drive, and thus provides a powerful affirmation of masculine identity.

A heterosexual substitute

In some institutional settings anal, male-to-male penetration can substitute for vaginal penetration, not, in this case, for the purposes of contraception but because of the absence of women. John Gagnon and William Simon's (1973) classic study of sexual conduct in prison shows that "homosexual" acts take place between "straight" men, not so much to release sexual tension but to affirm masculine identity. A large part of the prison population, they argue, is drawn from sections of society for whom the body and its performance of sex acts is the principal means of demonstrating a powerful, commanding masculinity. In prison this depends not on the sex of one's partner but on one's role in the act. Masculinity is affirmed by anally penetrating, or receiving fellatio from, a feminized male in scenarios that are frequently cohesive but always defined as "heterosexual."

A perversion

The status of anal sex as a perversion has a complex history, as the work of scholars such as Katz (1995) has shown. The Puritan settlers of seventeenth-century New England considered sodomy the most serious of a range of sexual sins. But the perversity of sodomy lay, like the other sins, in being a pleasure that wasted procreative potential in the context of communities that were struggling to survive and grow. Nor was sodomy seen as the proclivity of a specific, separately defined minority; anyone might succumb to any form of temptation, including sodomy with either sex.

The notion that the act of anal intercourse was a behavioral manifestation of a particular "type" of person, who was characterized by a perverted sexual nature, was the invention of nineteenth-century medical discourse. This tradition culminated in the psychology of Sigmund Freud (1977), who elaborated a developmental model of psychosexual identity. For Freud, the monogamous heterosexual whose sexual drive is directed to genital intercourse was the *normal* outcome of a process of individual development that involved an interaction of innate drives and social experience. However, getting to that stage was always a precarious process with, more often than not, a less-than-perfect outcome. Along the way, many individuals acquired a degree of perverse deviation from the straight and narrow course of normal development.

Freud made a distinction between sexual objects and sexual aims. Those who experience desire for a person-object of the opposite sex were classified as the "heterosexual" type, and those who experience desire for a person-object of the same sex were classified as the "homosexual" type. Thus the sexual feelings of the individual came to be a clue to his or her nature and identity. At the same time, Freud delineated a series of sexual aims that arise from the successive stimulation of the erogenous zones of the body through early development. The oral phase corresponds to breast-feeding; the anal phase to the acquisition of control over holding and releasing feces; and the genital phase to the subsequent discovery of genitalia and sexual difference. Adult interest or preoccupation with oral or anal themes therefore represented a throwback or "fixation" with immature sexual aims. Moreover, all aims had both "active" and "passive" variants, the former to stimulate or penetrate, and the latter to be stimulated or penetrated. The qualities of active and passive were associated respectively with masculinity and femininity and seen to inhere in the anatomy of sexual difference itself: penises and clitorises were active, and vaginas and anuses passive. Thus Freudian psychology helped to establish many of the hallmarks of *our* way of seeing sex acts. These include the idea that anal sex is a developmental perversion, largely but not exclusively associated with male homosexuality; and the idea that sex acts are inherently divided into active-masculine and passive-feminine roles, and that they express the inner essence of the individual.

A routine variation

The view of anal sex as perversion provides the background for another, more contemporary, meaning of this activity: anal sex as a routine variation of sexual repertoire. While Freud may have defined anal intercourse as "abnormal," in so doing he also said that its roots lie in universal processes of psychosexual development and acknowledged that it had behind it the same libidinal energy as "normal" sex. The effect of this was to, as it were, open the back door to its partial normalization. As a partially redeemed perversion, anal sex brings the erotic force of norm violation to bear as a routine variation of sexual repertoire, especially in the context of long-term relationships. Gagnon and Simon's (1973) research on heterosexual couples showed that sexual encounters early in a relationship followed a fairly strict "menu" of kissing, petting, oral sex and coitus, but that as relationships became more established anal intercourse was one of a number of variations that could be gradually integrated: typically by the male partner's suggestive use of his fingers followed by increasingly insistent attempts to penetrate, with the passivity of his female partner taken as assent.

There is strong evidence that this "routine variation" is increasingly widely practiced within the general and predominantly heterosexual community. A particularly authoritative survey of sexual behavior is *The National Survey of Sexual Attitudes and Lifestyles*, carried out for the United Kingdom government, which found that the proportion of men to have experienced anal sex in the past year had risen from 7 percent in 1990 to 12.3 percent in 2000, while the proportion for women had increased from 6.5 percent to 11.3 percent over the same period. It should be noted that the report's authors caution that part of this change may arise because people are more willing to admit to such behavior in an increasingly permissive social environment. Yet the suggestion that the cultural climate has changed is also of interest.

A fashionable theme

Even allowing for the above figures, it is likely that anal sex fits into that category of those items in the collective imagination that are talked about far more than they are actually done. Anal sex, and the butt more generally, have become fashionable themes of cultural representation and sex talk, from "chick lit" to teenage banter. At the cinema we see Bridget Jones grin sheepishly as her lover tells her what they have just done is still illegal in many American states. At home we hear our teenage sons and daughters, sisters or brothers declare that anal is the only kind of sex anyone *they* know is interested in. The former porn actress Georgina Spelvin once said that boys in the part of America where she grew up had two great ambitions: first, to own a gun so they can kill Pepsi bottles; second, to get a blow-job. That was the 1970s; today we can be forgiven for thinking that the scope of teenage sexual fashion and fantasy has moved on. It would seem that anal sex has finally emerged from its closet into the cultural mainstream. Yet at the same time its current popularity depends precisely upon the last vestiges of taboo. The ass, long the locus of shame in the Freudian psyche, has become the symbol for a new cult of voluptuous sensuality. This trend is evident from Hip Pop videos to TV commercials, such as the advertisement for the Renault Megane, an automobile with a heavily built up boot(y), set to the Groove Armada lyric "I see you baby, shaking that ass."

A porno number

The form of popular culture most directly responsible for the current obsession with the anus is surely pornography. In her study *Hardcore*, Linda Williams (1989) notes that, in the 1970s heyday of pornographic cinema, anal sex was cited as one of eight generic numbers that a successful pornographic film would need to provide for the heterosexual market. Yet at that time the defining image of hardcore porno was the so-called "money-shot" of a man ejaculating onto the face or body of the female performer. This was crucial to the genre because it proved the authenticity of the moment, the truthfulness of at least the male performer's arousal, and it provided a sense that what the viewer was seeing was *real*. The task that pornography set itself was to uncover the truth of sex, to explore and document it in vivid detail; including, crucially, those aspects that Freud and others had proscribed as perverse. The pornographic lens sought out the secrets of the body, of sexuality, of orgasm and ejaculation. Porno became an expression of the modern *will to knowledge*; the desire to discover the "truth" about sexuality and, inevitably therefore, an important part of the truth about ourselves.

Today pornography is no longer made on film or distributed through cinemas, but its role as a means of discovering and defining sexual truth has been extended by new media technologies, such as video, the internet, webcams, email links and so on. Cheap, accessible and, especially, interactive media have enabled many more people to produce as well as to consume pornography. If engaging in sexual activity has long been an important way to prove our authenticity and identity as human beings, seeing ourselves represented in televisual media is another way to validate our existence. The burgeoning world of amateur porno has provided many people with the opportunity to combine the sexual and representational means of self-authentication by selling or exchanging images of themselves having sex. Even the – still large – proportion of pornography that circulates with a clear division between producers and consumers exhibits the rough and ready realism of the gonzo format in order to achieve the vital sense of authenticity.

At the same time one of the key features of this modern pornography is surely the obsession with anal sex. Although the "money-shot" is clearly still crucial, it has increasingly been joined at the top of the list of porno numbers by the "meat-shot" of anal penetration. This too is an expression of pornography's revelatory mission, whereby each "perversion" must be documented and recorded in live action; each orifice penetrated and explored in turn. Within this scheme anal penetration seems to have become the *coup de grâce* of the endlessly repeated "menu" of pornographic scenes: the phallic hunt of a man, or group of men, through the body of a woman: mouth, vagina, and anus; the last of these being penetrated repeatedly until it gapes wide open, while the camera zooms in to inspect the raw dark hole. The camera may not be able to capture female orgasm, to prove the truth of a woman's pleasure, which Williams (1989) argues was the ultimate goal of pornographers in the 1970s and 1980s. But modern pornographers have found that their camera can do something else instead: it can witness the impact of the phallus on the body of a woman, in the form of the temporary and extreme dilatation of her anal passage. If modern pornography has a defining moment or image, this is now it. It is as if, with the retreat of feminism, the dream of documenting female sexual pleasure has been abandoned in favour of the most brutal objectification. Recently we have had the still more extreme spectacle of double penile penetration of the female performer's anus, without regard to the limitations of bodily anatomy or the recent HIV/AIDS crisis in the Californian porno industry.

An act of phallic domination

For all the desire of pornography to break though conventional barriers and taboos, it has never really challenged those of gender hierarchy. It is notable that, in mainstream, heterosexual porn, amid all the prodding and probing of female orifices, the anuses of the men remain strictly off-limits.

While we have seen something of the variety of different ways of thinking about anal sex, pornography shows that the predominant meaning associated with the act remains that of phallic domination, in which the *one* individual asserts himself through the subordination of the other (*zero*). Yet it is important to avoid giving the impression that pornography should be seen as having created this conception rather than simply amplifying an idea that was already current. In a sense pornographic discourse reproduces, in simplified and literal form, the phallic interpretation of sex acts provided by the more authoritative discourse of post-Freudian psychology, which made them into a window on the soul, or the nature of the self, whilst dividing them into rigidly dichotomized relations of active and passive roles.

A special, ultimate intimacy

Since the sexual revolution of the 1960s there have been more or less conscious attempts to re-imagine the erotic connotations of anal sex. The idea of anal sex as the ultimate intimacy between a loving couple has appeared particularly as a theme in relationships between gay men.

One study (Sik and Kat 2000) of Chinese gay men in Hong Kong found that, since the period of de-colonization (1984–97), their relationships with British or other "European" men had become more equal. In many cases this included the adoption of the practice, common to gay men elsewhere, of reciprocating roles in anal sex, which was widely seen as the ultimate expression of gay love. Although these roles were still interpreted in terms of "top–bottom" or "zero–one," they became negotiable and interchangeable. A similar tension around issues of power and intimacy appears in an Australian study (Kippax and Smith 2001). Here, some gay men saw the receptive role as feminizing and submissive, and they therefore needed to reassure themselves by role swapping, while others felt that the power relations involved in the most intimate of acts were much more complex and less one-sided than is usually assumed. A Norwegian study (Middelthon 2002) found that most young gay men interviewed expressed anxieties about a loss of manhood that they associated with the receptive role. Some expressed the view that, while a woman can play the receptive part in the act of genital intercourse with the grace ordained by nature or tradition, this did not extend to men playing the receptive role in anal intercourse, which was seen as potentially humiliating. Sex acts, and the part played in them by the individual, were experienced as playing a crucial role in defining self and identity. Yet these anxieties could be counteracted provided some or all of the following conditions were met: that the act was erotically satisfying, reciprocal, face-to-face, and above all with a caring partner or preferably the love of one's life.

Conclusion

We have completed this brief overview with a glimpse of some pioneering attempts to re-imagine anal sex. The gay practice of reciprocal anal penetration has been seen as de-centering the phallus, which, since Freud, has been at the heart of normative sexuality. But it seems that as yet, for all the cultural veneer of newness and excitement, in the heterosexual, mainstream erotic imagination anal sex remains much as Gagnon and Simon (1973) found it over thirty years ago: an act generally understood in terms of a symbolic power relation. We have seen that, although there are many possible meanings for anal sex, the fashion for it in heterosexual pornography and practice, far from diminishing the power of the phallus, actually reasserts it with new emphasis through a motif of anal conquest. The multiple meanings and subversive potentials of anal "perversion" resolve themselves into the all-too-familiar male-dominant phallic form, featuring the same old symbolic dichotomy of active-masculine and passive-feminine. At a time when we have begun, at last, to get over the idea that a woman's receptive contribution to the act of genital intercourse makes her in any way inferior, the switch in emphasis from penetration of the vagina to anus seems to constitute a symbolic reaffirmation of phallic power. Maybe that is why the fictional porn actress Nikki, in Welsh's novel, would have refused anal sex as a negation of her femininity.

References

Freud, S. 1977. 7. *On Sexuality: Three Essays on the Theory of Sexuality and Other Works*. London: Penguin.

Gagnon, J. H. and Simon, W. 1973. *Sexual Conduct: The Social Sources of Human Sexuality*. Chicago, IL: Aldine Publishing Company.

Katz, J. N. (1995) *The Invention of Heterosexuality*. New York: Dutton.

Kippax, S. and Smith, G. 2001. "Anal Intercourse and Power in Sex Between Men", *Sexualities* 4(4): 413–34.

Middelthon, A.-L. 2002. "Being Anally Penetrated: Erotic Inhibitions, Improvisations and Transformations", *Sexualities* 5(2): 181–200.

Ridge, D. T. 2004. " 'It was an Incredible Thrill': The Social Meanings and Dynamics of Younger Gay Men's Experiences of Barebacking in Melbourne", *Sexualities* 7(3): 259–79.

Sik Ying Ho, P. and Kat Tat Tsang, A. 2000. "Negotiated Anal Intercourse in Inter-Racial Gay Relationships in Hong Kong", *Sexualities* 3(3): 299–332.

Williams, L. 1989. *Hardcore: Power, Pleasure and the "Frenzy of the Visible"*. Los Angeles: University of California Press.

17

Sexual intercourse

Kerwin Kaye

NEW YORK UNIVERSITY

Intercourse is often imagined to be an entirely "natural" act, the central biological function which links humans with non-human animals. And of course, in some sense this is true: if at least some humans had not been engaging in heterosexual, reproductive intercourse throughout history, our species would never have survived. But an acknowledgement of this basic truth should not draw attention away from the multitude of ways in which intercourse is a profoundly social affair, starting with the fact that the act inherently involves more than one person. While intercourse is often so taken-for-granted that it becomes the proverbial *it* in "doing it" – as if we all knew what that meant with no further explanation – the ideas and practices which surround and constitute intercourse have varied enormously across both cultural and historical contexts. Indeed, the very idea that intercourse is primarily or exclusively "about" reproduction is a recent one, and it is worth turning a critical eye toward the assumptions that this narrow focus upon reproduction carries with it.

Almost everyone will acknowledge that moral assessments of intercourse are social. Even those who believe that such evaluations ultimately derive from God, or those who take physical or psychological "health" as an ethical standard, accept that people learn such norms through their interactions with others. But much more than this is involved in the social construction of intercourse. As the anthropologist of sexuality Niels Teunis has observed, anyone who thinks back upon their own ineptitude the first time they had sex will realize just how much they still had to learn about it, and none of this social learning would be needed if intercourse were a purely "natural" event. A sampling of "thought questions" about the precise conduct of intercourse might better give an indication as to just how fabricated it really is:

- What other sex acts are associated with intercourse? To what extent is intercourse governed by a larger script, for example one which begins with "foreplay" and culminates in "going all the way"? Does *every* "proper" sex act end in intercourse? How is this decided, and by whom?
- Are one's eyes open during intercourse? Are the lights on? What difference does the visibility of intercourse make? To what extent is one "supposed to" focus upon the other senses (taste, smell, touch, hearing) during intercourse?
- Does one talk during intercourse? If so, what types of things is it appropriate to say?
- Are certain types of clothing, or stages of undress and nakedness, particularly apt for intercourse?

- Are specific positions mandated or preferable for intercourse?
- Which rooms within a house, and which pieces of furniture, are most suitable for intercourse? If intercourse occurs outside of these spaces, what does it mean about the people involved? Are such people "wild," "slutty," "fun," or "perverse"? Does it matter if we are evaluating a woman or a man? If the person is young or old?
- What type of relationship must exist between two people in order for intercourse to be proper and legitimate? Must people be married? Coupled? Monogamous? In love? Is it preferable for partners to be of the same race? Or of the same social class? Or within the same general age group? Must people be of a different sex?
- What constitutes "good" versus "bad" intercourse?

In raising these questions, I hope to highlight the many ways in which social meaning shapes both the practice and the experience of sexual intercourse. The idea that intercourse is a social rather than a natural act carries with it three important propositions: (1) it varies between different societies and within a single society; (2) it changes over time; and (3) it can be a site of political conflict.

Defining intercourse

The social nature of intercourse thus extends much further than is typically recognized. Even the very question as to what exactly constitutes "intercourse" is socially determined. Historically, for example, Western Christianity has spoken of "coitus" rather than of "intercourse." "Coitus" implies that a woman and a man have penetrative vaginal–penile intercourse *and continue to do so until the man achieves orgasm*; to stop prior to this moment would constitute *"coitus interruptus"* (which was sharply condemned for centuries, along with other forms of contraception). Today, the word "intercourse" is primarily used in medical contexts and includes situations which stop short of *coitus* as such. On the other hand, a remnant of the older idea of *coitus* seems to still be operative within the concept of intercourse; to say that one "had intercourse" three times, for example, would commonly refer to the fact that a man ejaculated three times, and implies nothing about the experience of the female partner.

While *coitus* necessarily refers to intercourse between a woman and a man, the more recent term "anal intercourse" has extended the definition of intercourse to sex acts which might occur between men. "Strap-on sex" – in which a woman penetrates her partner with a dildo (either vaginally or anally) – might also be considered "intercourse." Whatever one's exact definition, *intercourse* is generally defined in a more narrow manner than *sex*, and typically excludes "oral sex" and other forms of contact that would nevertheless be considered "sexual." The point is not to find the single "correct" definition, but rather to see that the meanings associated with these terms shift over time and are inherently susceptible to social conflict.

The sociology of intercourse

Sociological study has revealed that ideas and practices associated with intercourse vary across social groupings. In his studies conducted during the 1940s and 1950s, Alfred Kinsey discovered that men with higher educational levels practiced masturbation and "petting" techniques more regularly than their less educated peers, while men with less education engaged in more homosexuality and had more intercourse (whether with friends, prostitutes, or unmarried lovers) than their college-educated peers (Kinsey *et al.* 1948: 378). Although Kinsey found less variation by educational level among women, women's sexual behavior varied by decade of birth, with younger women engaging in more "petting" and more intercourse both inside and outside of marriage (Kinsey *et al.* 1953: 685).

Laumann *et al.*'s more recent survey of US sexual preferences and practices found that more educated persons more strongly enjoyed masturbation, oral sex, and anal sex than their less educated peers (1994: 152–5), but also found that homosexuality was more prevalent among the people with greater education (1994: 303–5). Again in contrast to Kinsey, Laumann *et al.* found that these differences correlated to educational level among both women and men. Although the two studies yield somewhat different findings, neither set of data necessarily contradicts the other; the historical patterns simply may have shifted over time. What both studies show, however, is that the ideas and practices that a given person has concerning intercourse are shaped by social considerations such as social class, race, gender, and so on.

The history of sexual intercourse

Large-scale social transformations have produced epochal shifts in how we think of these issues. The very word "sexuality," for example, was first coined only in 1879. Prior to the idea of "sexuality," philosophers and theologians had spoken of "carnality" and the sins of "the flesh." Drawing on remarks made by the French historian Michel Foucault, Arnold Davidson has written about the precise nature of the shift (Davidson 1987). *Sexuality*, says Davidson, is an idea that focuses attention upon one's personal feelings, fantasies, and desires as much as it is upon anything that one actually does. It is not, in other words, limited to the body (as the saying goes, the brain is the most sexual organ we have). The idea of *carnality*, on the other hand, presumed that sexual impulses rose *directly from the flesh*, imposing themselves within the psyche like an unwanted visitor.

The difference between these two conceptions may seem subtle but its consequences are quite profound for the ways in which sexual intercourse was understood. When sexual impulses are seen as originating in "the flesh," those desires are perceived as having nothing to do with one's personality. When one has a "deviant" desire, therefore, it is not because one's "inner nature" inclined in that direction. In fact, early Christian theologians presumed that all manner of sins were pleasurable and that "the flesh" was inclined toward all of them. *Anyone* – not just "homosexuals" – might enjoy same-sex contact, for example. The idea that some people were unlike others – that some people had an inner inclination to be "heterosexual" while others were innately "homosexual" – simply did not arise. "Sodomy" was known, and roundly condemned, but anyone might become a sodomite. (The term "sodomy," incidentally, was sometimes used to refer to anal intercourse, and sometimes to refer to any non-procreative sex act; in the latter case, women might be "sodomites" as well.) With the rise of a new focus on the constellation of "sexuality," however, various "types" of people came to be named. For the first time, one could be a "masochist," a "fetishist," a "heterosexual," or a "homosexual." Not surprisingly, those who believed in "the flesh" felt little need to carefully examine the nature of their sexual longings; the key was simply to control one's desires, whatever they might be. Those who sought to pigeonhole people into distinct sexual categories, on the other hand, felt compelled to engage in a great deal of self-scrutiny; every single passing thought might be a sign of a "disorder" which emanated from one's innermost personality.

One important consequence of this deep change in meaning was apparently a more intense concentration upon intercourse within sex. The historian Randy Trumbach argues that the new sexual regime placed heightened requirements upon men in particular to prove they were exclusively interested in women, lest they be considered not just sinful, but "queer" (1998: 69). Whereas the older system of carnality had presumed that any instance of sin – such as visiting a prostitute – might lead to further transgressions such as sodomy, the new system of sexual types presumed that one's "heterosexuality" was not threatened by such behavior. Having intercourse with a woman, whether licitly or illicitly, "proved" that men did not belong to the newly formed category of homosexuality. The pressure to achieve "normality" thus produced new pressures beyond those entailed by the category of "sinfulness" alone.

The Dutch historian Theo van der Meer has explored this epochal shift from a slightly different perspective. Van der Meer notes that early theologians presumed that a sexual sin might follow from other types of sin, such as swearing or gambling. This idea made sense because bodies were understood to be inclined toward *all manner* of sin; one's willpower kept these bodily desires in check in all ways or in none. Those who began to swear, therefore, might lose some of their willpower and begin to gamble; gambling would then lead to a further loss of self-control and the possible commission of still more grievous sins, such as heterosexual adultery, and eventually this slippery slope might lead to rape, thievery, bestiality, sodomy, murder, and whatever other sort of sin one can imagine (1993: 182–3). This chain of events tends to sound rather peculiar to our modern ears. Sexual acts are associated with sexual thoughts and sexual feelings, not with a "non-sexual" activity such as swearing, and someone is not seen as being more likely to commence engaging in homosexual acts simply because they have engaged in heterosexual adultery. The sharp difference between these ways of thinking illustrates how very differently we might understand the ideas which give meaning to the experience of intercourse.

The politics of sexual intercourse

The profoundly social nature of sexual intercourse has led some thinkers to examine it as political. Feminists, in particular, have carried on a sometimes heated debate concerning the political nature of intercourse. Some feminists criticized conventional intercourse for furthering male dominance. A compelling analysis of the subject was undertaken by Andrea Dworkin in her 1987 book entitled, straightforwardly enough, *Intercourse*. Dworkin argues that intercourse has been defined in terms of a penetrator and a penetrated, and that the act carries with it a strong sense of social domination or inequality. As she puts it: "Intercourse is commonly written about and comprehended as a form of possession or an act of possession … He has her, or, when he is done, he has had her. … The normal fuck by a normal man is taken to be an act of invasion and ownership undertaken in a mode of predation" (1987: 63). Dworkin goes on to argue that in the United States one becomes a "true man" only by successfully subordinating a woman through intercourse.

Some feminist critics of Dworkin have acknowledged that, while intercourse can involve a dynamic of male dominance/female subordination, it also involves sensual and emotional pleasures as well. Rather than avoiding intercourse, these critics suggest that women must balance "pleasure" and "danger" in their sexual decision-making (Vance 1984). Others question how Dworkin's insights might apply in situations where partners (whether of the same sex or differently sexed) take turns in penetrating one another. Lastly, Dworkin's perspective has been criticized for ironically reinforcing a sexual double standard: whereas the usual double standard says that women who enjoy intercourse "too much" or with "too many people" are "sluts," Dworkin argues that women who enjoy intercourse are "collaborators, more base in their collaboration than other collaborators have ever been" (1987: 143). To many, this seems merely to duplicate an older set of sexist messages.

Scholars of masculinity have noted that the social criteria which define conventional intercourse affect men in powerful ways as well (Kaye 2000; Kimmel 2005; Segal 1990). While the act of heterosexual intercourse can be associated with losing power for women, for men it often involves demands to be powerful and in command. Any performance which fails to meet this standard – which comes up limp, so to speak – can be taken as an instance of male failure. Despite the fact that a wide array of sexual pleasures are available to men with non-erect penises, one's "manhood" may be placed in jeopardy if intercourse somehow fails. Men's feelings of insecurity and inferiority about this issue, in other words, derive precisely from the fact that they are expected to be "potent," powerful, and in charge.

Given the difficulties associated with the conventional definition of intercourse, some sex and gender activists have moved to shift the focus of sexual relations away from this one, limited act and toward a wider variety of erotic activities. As the authors Cathy Winks and Anne Semans argue:

> An emphasis on the primacy of penis–vagina intercourse devalues not just the experience of gay and lesbian couples, but the experience of bisexual and heterosexual couples who have learned that there's more to sex than sticking the proverbial plug in a socket. The negative results of this single-minded approach to sex are manifold: If the pleasures of "outercourse" were openly acknowledged, surely we'd see a decrease in the rate of teenage pregnancies, the spread of sexually transmitted diseases and the number of preorgasmic women.
>
> *(Winks and Semans 1997: 123)*

By shifting sex away from a narrative whose plot moves rather predictably along from "foreplay" to "climax during intercourse," Winks and Semans hope to turn intercourse into just one item on a much more varied menu. While Sigmund Freud suggested that any person who derived sexual pleasure from activities that did not ultimately lead to intercourse suffered from a neurotic "fetish," this alternative approach explicitly works to open up such "kinky" possibilities in an effort to create a less restrictive sexual encounter.

References

Davidson, Arnold. 1987. "Sex and the Emergence of Sexuality," *Critical Inquiry 14* (Autumn).

——2001. *The Emergence of Sexuality: Historical Epistemology and the Formation of Concepts.* Cambridge, MA: Harvard University Press.

Dworkin, Andrea. 1987. *Intercourse.* New York: The Free Press/Macmillan.

Kaye, Kerwin (ed.). 2000. *Male Lust: Pleasure, Power, and Transformation.* Binghamton, NY: Haworth Press.

Kimmel, Michael. 2005. *The Gender of Desire: Essays on Male Sexuality.* Albany, NY: State University of New York Press.

Kinsey, Alfred, Wardell Pomeroy, and Clyde Martin. 1948. *Sexual Behavior in the Human Male.* Philadelphia, PA: W.B. Saunders Company.

Kinsey, Alfred and the Staff of the Institute for Sex Research. 1953. *Sexual Behavior in the Human Female.* Philadelphia, PA: W. B. Saunders Company.

Laumann, Edward, John Gagnon, Robert Michael, and Stuart Michaels. 1994. *The Social Organization of Sexuality: Sexual Practices in the United States.* Chicago, IL: University of Chicago Press.

McPhillips, Kathryn, Virginia Braun, and Nicola Gavey. 2001. "Defining (Hetero)Sex: How Imperative is the 'Coital Imperative'?" *Women's Studies International Forum* 24, 2, 229–40.

Segal, Lynne. 1990. *Slow Motion: Changing Masculinities, Changing Men.* New Brunswick, NJ: Rutgers University Press.

Tiefer, Leonore. 1995. *Sex is not a Natural Act and Other Essays.* Boulder, CO: Westview Press.

Trumbach, Randolph. 1998. *Sex and the Gender Revolution: Heterosexuality and the Third Gender in Enlightenment London,* vol. 1. Chicago, IL: University of Chicago Press.

van der Meer, Theo. 1993. "Sodomy and the Pursuit of a Third Sex in the Early Modern Period", in Gilbert Herdt (ed.), *Third Sex/Third Gender. Beyond Sexual Dimorphism in Culture and History*. New York: Zone Books.

Vance, Carole (ed.). 1984. *Pleasure and Danger: Exploring Female Sexuality*. New York: Routledge & Kegan Paul.

Winks, Cathy and Anne, Semans. 1997. *The New Good Vibrations Guide to Sex*, 2nd edition. San Francisco, CA: Cleis Press.

18

Viagra and the coital imperative

Nicola Gavey

UNIVERSITY OF AUCKLAND, NEW ZEALAND

Anyone encountering Viagra for the first time through direct-to-consumer promotions of the drug could be forgiven for thinking they had stumbled onto a miraculous new elixir of relational health and wellbeing. Viagra, according to drug company advertisements, will generate not only sex, but also the restoration of closeness, romance, love and intimacy. It will, in fact, protect against the very breakup of relationships threatened by "distance" – a distance born, it is implied, of the ailing self-esteem and crumbling masculinity caused by "failure to admit" and therefore to overcome the condition of "erectile dysfunction" (see Gavey 2005). And what is the route to such happiness and harmony? It is the biotechnological production of a penile erection with all the qualities – of firmness and duration – required for vaginal penetration and "successful" intercourse.

As critics have pointed out, the promotion of Viagra as a magic-bullet remedy to this host of personal and relational troubles relies on a whole array of contemporary assumptions about sex and gender. So too, of course, does the construction of the very problem (erectile dysfunction) it is designed to fix. Most blatantly, the whole phenomenon of Viagra relies on a hard-core "coital imperative" (Jackson 1984). This is the widely shared presumption that heterosexual sex *is* penis–vagina intercourse; and that anything else is either a preliminary to – or an optional extra beyond – real sex.

In magazine advertisements targeted at potential consumers, notions like "satisfactory sexual activity" and "making love" are premised on the requirement of a penis erect enough for penetration that lasts (see Gavey 2005). (Hetero)sex, within the Viagra promotion industry, *is* penetration – of the vagina by the penis. And the penetrating penis must be capable of reliable and durable action to avoid pathologization. According to a "sexual health inventory" on the drug company's website, even the man who reports he is able to maintain an erection that is firm enough and lasts long enough for "satisfactory" intercourse "most times" and reports "high" confidence in his ability to "get and keep an erection" scores the advice that he "may be showing signs of erection problems" (see Gavey 2005). The possibility that sexual activity or making love could happen without penile penetration of the vagina – which conceivably might be an option that some heterosexual men with erectile changes (as well as some without), and their partners, might otherwise consider – is completely obscured within the promotional advice.

Of course drug companies did not invent the coital imperative. Contemporary culture is thoroughly saturated with the commonsense assumption that (hetero)sex is coitus. In fact, to question that mature heterosexual sex could be otherwise – that it might not require intercourse – is likely to generate bemused and/or dismissive responses emphasizing the power of *nature* to determine the proper form of sexual practices and desires. From this perspective, the coital imperative might be seen as simply the way things are; as a taken-for-granted feature of human nature. However, in this chapter I argue not only that the coital *imperative* in its current form is highly problematic, but also that it is neither simply natural nor immutable.

The dangers of the coital imperative

Feminists have long debated the symbolic meaning of intercourse. Some have portrayed it as a key site of women's oppression (e.g., Dworkin 1987), while others have sought to resurrect it as a viable sexual practice for heterosexual feminists (e.g., Segal 1994). However, despite these exchanges about the politics of coitus, the coital *imperative* which casts intercourse as an *essential* part of heterosexual sex, unquestionably has a downside – for women in particular. Heterosexual intercourse is a sexual practice that has life-changing implications, in particular pregnancy and the transmission of sexual infections (some of which have lasting complications and/or are life-threatening). While a myriad of techniques and technologies exist for circumventing potential consequences like an unwanted pregnancy or an STI, they are widely perceived and/or experienced as difficult or adverse in their own right. For example, the most technically effective methods of birth control, such as oral contraceptives and IUDs (intrauterine devices), are well known for their "dangerous or troubling side effects" that lead many women to discontinue use (e.g., Petchesky 1990: 189). Also, while many women report enjoying intercourse (see Segal 1994), others go through with it in the absence of their own desire or pleasure (e.g., Gavey 2005) because of the assumption it is normal and, therefore, required. Some women continue to have intercourse even despite routinely experiencing outright pain and discomfort. One 51-year-old woman, for instance, said she was sometimes unable to "disguise how much discomfort" she experienced during intercourse due to her own advanced illness; yet she persisted because of her belief that it was not good for men to go without regular intercourse (e.g., Potts *et al.* 2003: 706).

Given the potential for intercourse to have serious adverse consequences for (particularly women's) health and wellbeing, it would be reasonable to assume that it might be better regarded as a choice within sex rather than as a taken-for-granted act if "sex" is to occur. However, by and large this is not the case. Elsewhere I have discussed the poignant case of Romanian women who continued to engage in coital sex with their husbands, in the absence of their own pleasure, and despite the painful consequences associated with unwanted pregnancies, which were difficult if not impossible to avoid during the extreme pronatalist regime under Ceausescu. One woman, who had had seven illegal abortions, said: "When I was asked by my husband to make love with him I began to feel pains in my stomach because of fear" (cited in Gavey 2005: 123). Despite the especially harsh social conditions these women were living under, which exacerbated the stakes of engaging in unwanted intercourse, the fantasy of sexual and reproductive choice does not necessarily play out fully even in neo-liberal societies in which the notion of choice seems to be fetishized above all else. Girls and women commonly report having sexual intercourse even when they don't want it and/or gain no pleasure from it (e.g., Gavey 2005). Intercourse, it would seem, is part and parcel of sex; not an item that can freely be chosen *or* discarded from the (hetero)sexual menu. Sanders and Reinisch (1999), for instance, found that while virtually everyone in their study regarded penile–vaginal intercourse as constituting having "had sex," 60 percent were of the view that oral–genital contact (if it was "the most intimate behavior" they engaged in) would not.

The coital imperative is not natural

One of the interesting insights gained from historical studies of sex is the finding that some of the assumptions that currently operate as taken-for-granted truths about (hetero)sexuality are not in fact historically constant. For instance, historians write of a "sexual revolution" in the eighteenth century during which the whole nature of what heterosexual sex *was* changed radically. According to Tim Hitchcock (2002), drawing on data from England and Western Europe, it became increasingly phallocentric at this time, moving away from a set of practices that encompassed mutual masturbation, kissing and fondling, mutual touching, and so on. Instead, "putting a penis in a vagina became the dominant sexual activity" (Hitchcock 2002: 191). By the nineteenth century, "proper" marital sex in the United States not only centered on the act of coitus, but reference to noncoital sex was rare in publications of the era, and when it was mentioned it was always associated with prohibitions (Seidman 1991). Perceptions of women's sexuality also changed markedly over this period. From being seen as sexually aggressive (Hitchcock 2002), women came to be seen as sexually passive. Their pleasure during sex, and their orgasm in particular, became increasingly less important (see also Laqueur 1990). More recent changes over the twentieth century include the shift away from seeing (hetero)sex in primarily procreative terms. Through the "sexual revolution" of the mid- to late twentieth century, women's sexual pleasure has come back onto the agenda – at least in theory.

It seems ironic, then, that at a time when the procreative function of sex has perhaps never been less important, the sexual act "designed for" procreation has not only persisted as the defining feature of hetero(sex); but, with the Viagra moment, it is increasingly being stretched across the lifespan. Most men using Viagra and similar products are beyond a procreating stage of life. Yet, while the reproductive function of coitus is no longer valorized, the particular heterosexual act for reproduction is. Apparently, in the nineteenth-century United States when the reproductive function of sex was still of primary importance (D'Emilio and Freedman 1988), and sex was based even more narrowly around the procreative act of coitus than it is today, it was assumed that sex between a husband and wife would generally diminish over the course of their marriage (Seidman 1991). By the age of fifty, it was thought, men's sexual life would be over: the "sex drive" being "either absent by that age or enfeebled to a point where it would have little significance in the marriage" (Seidman 1991: 25). Today, when men's bodies give up on producing the kind of rigid penile arousal required for "successful" intercourse, it is considered to be a sexual dysfunction (even though to some extent statistically normal, as the drug company promotions like to reassure people). Such trends might have been predicted by Jeffrey Weeks's (1985) diagnosis of the colonization of sex by capitalism since the beginning of the twentieth century. As part of a more general "commoditisation and commercialisation of social life," Weeks (1985: 22, 23, 24) pointed to an "expansion of perceived sexual needs, particularly among men." This was fertile ground for the "proliferation of new desires as the pursuit of pleasure became an end in itself." Not only the pursuit of pleasure; for sex has become increasingly entangled with all sorts of "higher" psychological and relational meanings, such as intimacy and identity (e.g., Seidman 1989). Intercourse is practiced not simply as a (possible) means to physical pleasure, but as an expression and/or confirmation of love and closeness (e.g., Gavey *et al.* 1999).

The coital imperative is not immutable

Attention to the historical antecedents of our contemporary sexual norms, as we have seen, suggests that there are no single cultural or biological determinants of human sexual behavior that are rigidly prescriptive over time and place. Further support for this contention exists in contemporary evidence that (at least) some people do act otherwise, to embody alternative forms of (hetero)sexuality (not to mention those who escape the strict confines of hetero-normativity through lesbian, gay, or other forms of queer sexuality). One example of this comes from the accounts of women and men who have faced erectile difficulties only to find that it enhanced their sexual relationships (Potts *et al.* 2004: 497). As one man who did not have erections commented:

> Matter of fact … in some ways our sex life has been, in a *different* way, better since … It was a matter of adapting to suit the occasion rather than giving all away, which I sup-pose … some people give it all away, but we were determined not to … And she can get me to a climax and sort of keep me going, you know, far more than I used to before … so in that way the sex is … different and arguably better than what it was before.

Stories such as this – and there were more – disrupt the pharmaceutical company's uni-dimensional hype about the devastation that erectile difficulties (necessarily) cause for heterosexual relationships, as well as for sex itself.

Viagra's intervention

As part of the increasing medicalization (e.g., Tiefer 1995) and commercialization of sexuality, "Viagra" is a cultural phenomenon rather than simply a (set of) biotechnological products; a phenomenon that relies on, reinforces, and extends existing sociocultural norms. The impact of Viagra can be felt at several different levels, from the intimate lives of individual women and men to the broader public domain of popular culture. Given that the promotion, and pre-sumably the appeal, of Viagra trades on the coital imperative, it is not surprising that it can intervene within people's private sexual lives in ways that directly (re)assert this imperative. For instance, a 48-year-old woman described how Viagra enforced the coital imperative within her sexual relationship, with the unwelcome extinction of noncoital sexual activities (Potts *et al.* 2003: 704–5):

> [Viagra use began] during a time when I was trying to impress upon him that foreplay would be a nice thing. After twenty-odd years of marriage, foreplay is one of those things that goes by the way; however, I was trying to maintain that this was, you know, quite an important part of making love, so when Viagra came along the whole foreplay thing just *vanished*, I mean it wasn't even a suggestion, it was: "OK, I've taken the pill, we've got about an hour, I expect you in that time to be acquiescent."

Not only does Viagra intervene in men's bodies, minds, and sexuality (and, therefore, in women's experience of heterosex and in relationships between men and women), but the Viagra phenomenon intervenes in culture itself. This phenomenon is more than just the che-mical compound sildenafil citrate. It is the potent mix of the drug itself (as well as newer similar drugs) and their promotion within drug company marketing, professional endorsements, and various popular cultural representations. The promotion of Viagra as a biotechnological miracle for restoring men's potency, and with it personal and relational happiness, plays with culture. It shifts the meanings of intercourse – not by inventing new meanings, but by reinforcing and intensifying existing ones in ways that move to squeeze out any comfortable spaces for alternative meanings around having or not having intercourse. At the same time, it prescribes new norms for coitus by extending normative expectations for its place in the lives of aging men, and those with health conditions that threaten erectile reliability. In these ways the Viagra phenomenon shifts the cultural conditions of possibility for (hetero)sex, in ways that are both prescriptive and restrictive.

Some of the interviewees in Potts *et al.*'s research observed that the cultural phenomenon of Viagra involved the *construction* of a problem. That is, it represented the invitation to understand erectile changes as pathology rather than simply a natural change or as an expression of acceptable corporeal and sexual diversity. For example, as one 60-year-old woman explained (Potts *et al.* 2003: 712):

> Yes, it would definitely be different for everybody, I guess, but I think you'd probably find that … a large percentage of women in my age group would say that … the desire decreases as you get older and … Possibly, if I think about it, it'll come up *because* Viagra has been brought up, right? Because I think Viagra has made a lot of people feel inadequate … everybody's on the defensive about how often they have sex and so on, in the older age group.

Even for women and men who already do see erectile changes as a problem to be fixed, Viagra delivers one solution (pharmaceutically restoring the erectile capacity) with such force that other potential "solutions" are either obscured or devalued. In the case of men for whom Viagra poses a serious health risk (e.g., those taking nitrates in medication prescribed for angina or those using recreational drugs that contain nitrates), this fixation with an erect penis and coitus *as* sex is potentially fatal. In these ways, we can see how the Viagra phenomenon works both prescriptively, to install new needs for intercourse, and at the same time restrictively, to close down other legitimate possibilities for sexuality.

In this chapter I have argued that the Viagra phenomenon reinforces and hardens the coital imperative. Not only does it potently work to re-naturalize and re-normalize the centrality of intercourse to heterosexual sex, but it extends its reach to areas of society that previously were able to slip it by (that is, men and women beyond middle age, and those with certain health conditions). And, on the way, it pathologizes bodies and people who cannot, or prefer not to, engage in sexual intercourse on every, or even any, sexual occasion.

In the midst of a Western cultural moment that is arguably open to all sorts of possibility for progressive social change around sexuality, the Viagra phenomenon is profoundly *disappointing*. Social constructionist perspectives (e.g., Foucault 1981; Tiefer 1995) which draw attention to the shifting and contextual nature of human behavior and experience have become highly influential within sexuality studies. Moreover, even recent trends within biology emphasize the co-constitution of organisms and their environments (see Gavey 2005). The convergence of these constructionist perspectives from biology, social science and history permits a cautious optimism that the plasticity of human sexuality might allow for shifting and less rigid norms that promote increased tolerance and an ethic attentive to difference and power. It is just possible that these trends within the academy, as well as within the queer margins of culture, might have signalled broader movements towards new cultural understandings and practices. Were such an ethic brought to bear on questions relating to health, wellbeing, and equality, the coital imperative would surely be due for some wider critical scrutiny. Instead, such potentially radical cultural shifts have arguably been stalled by the escalating medicalization of sexuality within the corporate thrust of pharmaceutical companies hungry for new markets in which to expand profit. Through their prominent co-option of the coital imperative, which is strategically necessary in order to create a new market for a costly erectile fix, the disappointing spin-off is that many men and women are likely to be deprived of the cultural conditions for realizing diverse sexual and reproductive choices that might have enhanced their health and wellbeing.

References

D'Emilio, John and Estelle B. Freedman. 1988. *Intimate matters: A history of sexuality in America*. New York: Harper & Row.

Dworkin, Andrea. 1987. *Intercourse*. New York: The Free Press.

Foucault, Michel. 1981. *The history of sexuality (Volume 1: An Introduction)* (R. Hurley, trans.). Harmondsworth, Middlesex: Penguin.

Gavey, Nicola. 2005. *Just sex? The cultural scaffolding of rape*. New York and London: Routledge.

Gavey, Nicola, Kathryn McPhillips, and Virginia Braun. 1999. "*Interruptus coitus*: Heterosexuals accounting for intercourse", *Sexualities* 2 (1): 35–68.

Hitchcock, Tim. 2002. "Redefining sex in eighteenth-century England." In Kim M. Phillips and Barry Reay (eds), *Sexualities in history: A reader*. New York and London: Routledge.

Jackson, Margaret. 1984. "Sex research and the construction of sexuality: A tool of male supremacy?" *Women's Studies International Forum* 7:43–51.

Laqueur, Thomas. 1990. *Making sex: Body and gender from the Greeks to Freud*. Cambridge, MA and London: Harvard University Press.

Petchesky, Rosalind P. 1990. *Abortion and woman's choice: The state, sexuality, and reproductive freedom (Revised Edition)*. Boston, MA: Northeastern University Press.

Potts, Annie, Nicola Gavey, Victoria Grace, and Tiina Vares. 2003. "The downside of Viagra: Women's experiences and concerns", *Sociology of Health and Illness* 25 (7): 697–719.

Potts, Annie, Victoria Grace, Nicola Gavey, and Tiina Vares. 2004. "'Viagra stories': Challenging 'erectile dysfunction'", *Social Science and Medicine* 59: 489–99.

Sanders, Stephanie A. and June M. Reinisch. 1999. "Would you say you 'had sex' if … ?" *Journal of the American Medical Association* 281 (3): 275–77.

Segal, Lynne. 1994. *Straight sex: Rethinking the politics of pleasure*. Berkeley and Los Angeles: University of California Press.

Seidman, Steven. 1989. "Constructing sex as a domain of pleasure and self-expression: Sexual ideology in the sixties", *Theory, Culture & Society* 6: 293–315.

——1991. *Romantic longings: Love in America, 1830–1980*. London and New York: Routledge.

Tiefer, Leonore. 1995. *Sex is not a natural act and other essays*. Boulder, CO: Westview Press.

Weeks, Jeffrey. 1985. *Sexuality and its discontents: Meanings, myths and modern sexualities*. London and New York: Routledge & Kegan Paul.

Part 4
Gender and sexuality

Introduction

Feminists have changed the way we think about ourselves and our social world. Statements such as "we are just individuals" or "the social world is made up of individuals who are essentially the same" have been challenged. Such seemingly self-evident statements of truth are now suspect as feminists have argued that we are almost always thinking, feeling, desiring, and acting in gendered ways, as either men or women or against these gender statuses. In other words, being a man or woman is a significant part of us, a status we cannot easily, if at all, shake off.

Feminists have also taught us that our gendered status is social. We are not born men or women but acquire these gender identities beginning with our social designation as male or female. Our families, schools, popular culture and government help to produce gendered selves. Gender status, at least as its lived in many parts of the contemporary world, fashions our bodies and psyches to fit into the rigid boxes of male/female and man/woman.

Finally, feminists have taught us that the relationship between men and women is, in part, oppositional and hierarchical. In other words, the traits that define being a man are the opposite of those defining women. If women are expected to exhibit caregiving, nurturing, and accommodating behaviors, men are either expected to either minimize these behaviors or give them a very different meaning. So, if women's caregiving is supposed to be expressed in tender communicative acts, men's nurturing takes the form of doing tasks such as making money or mowing the lawn.

Social roles are distributed based on these normative gender traits. For example, women are expected to be the primary parent and to do the lion's share of the housework. Furthermore, conventional gender roles, men in masculine and women in feminine roles, position men and women as unequal. In virtually every institutional sector in the United States and the world, from churches to schools and the government, men are disproportionately in positions of power, are paid better, and occupy positions of higher status than women. These patterns of gender difference and inequality are, feminists claim, socially created and reproduced; they are not dictated by nature but produced by history.

Does the social influence of gender stop at the door of sexuality? Clearly not. Sexuality is gendered as much as our work life. There is a considerable body of research and scholarship that shows the gender patterning of the meaning and social organization of sexuality and intimacies. For example, while both men and women look for sex and love in romantic relationships, men in general tend to value sexuality for its performative and erotic aspects while women emphasize its communicative, emotionally bonding aspects. Similarly, whereas women express love through tender, nurturing behavior, men will often speak of what they do for their partners, e.g. earn money or provide security. More dramatically, violence in intimate relationships is a decidedly masculine behavior. Somewhere between 20–30 percent of young women report incidents of coercion or violence by men, often by their romantic partners.

Of course, gender is not only about men and women. In the last decade or so, we have seen the rise of new gender styles that reject rigid binary gender norms and roles. From metrosexuals to queer straights and transgendered persons, gender is increasingly approached as a flexible aspect of identity and behavior. Many individuals are today struggling to step outside the gender binary, to rewrite the dynamics of intimacy in post-gender ways. In particular, young people are struggling to find ways to express themselves and to forge intimacies beyond the binary models of gender and sexual identity. But make no mistake. These new currents of self and intimate invention are occurring in social contexts still very much rooted in gender-binary norms.

19

Unruly bodies

Intersex variations of sex development

Sharon E. Preves

HAMLINE UNIVERSITY, SAINT PAUL, MINNESOTA

> In any human culture, a body is never a body unto itself, and bodies that openly challenge significant boundaries are particularly prone to being caught in struggles over those boundaries.
> Doubtful Sex: Cases and Concepts of Hermaphroditism in France and Britain, 1868–1915
>
> *(Dreger 1995: 34)*

Distinctions between sex, gender, and sexuality

Let's begin with what we know to be true. There are two and only two sexes, right? And you know with certainty which one of the two you are, I'm sure. Have you ever stopped to consider *how you know* what sex you are? It sounds pretty simple; just a quick check of the genitalia is all it takes. It's actually not so easy to draw a binary distinction between the sexes, despite common belief, given that so much variation in genital and other sexual anatomy occurs with great regularity. If that is the case, in this era of many states altering their constitutions to permit only women and men to marry one another, then we must have means to unambiguously define someone as a woman or a man. Most often, as noted above, we consider external genitalia to be the unequivocal sign of anatomical sex. In fact, a cursory examination of the genitalia is typically how sex assignment occurs at birth.

What happens if the genitalia aren't typically female or male in their appearance, as occurs in roughly 1 of 2,000 births (Blackless et al. 2000)? Should we then turn to an examination of the sex chromosomes, gonads, or hormones? The state supreme courts of Texas and Kansas both recently ruled that sex is chromosomal; we know someone is a man if he has XY chromosomes and we know someone is a woman if she has XX chromosomes (Lum 2002). In Texas, this chromosomal definition of sex has permitted a lesbian couple to be legally married in a state that doesn't allow same-sex marriage, because one of the women is a male-to-female transsexual and has XY chromosomes (Koidin 2000).

Getting back to the sense of confidence you have about your own physical sex, do you know whether you have XX or XY sex chromosomes (or some other variation, such as XXY or XO)? What about your gonads? Are you certain that you have ovaries, testes, or some combination of the two? Moreover, have you ever had your levels of estrogen or testosterone assessed to see if you are producing these hormones at typically female or male levels? Those of us who don't know the answers to these questions because we've never had reason to really ponder them experience a gender privilege that is akin to the racial privilege of being Caucasian and relatively unaware of the ways in which racial categorization shapes one's existence. That is, while most of us are sexed as female or male at birth and gendered as feminine or masculine in later life, to do so without pause or difficulty is indeed a privilege, as is the ease with which many people enter and exit women's or men's lavatories, locker rooms, and the countless other gendered spaces we inhabit on a daily basis.

Some readers may find it surprising to know that babies are born with external genitalia that look neither clearly female nor male with great regularity. As noted above, conservative estimates suggest that children are born with intersexed genitalia in 1 or 2 of every 2,000 births (Blackless et al. 2000) – the same rate at which Down syndrome and cystic fibrosis occur (Desai 1997; Dreger 1998; Roberts et al. 1998). I would venture to guess that most readers know of someone who has Down syndrome or cystic fibrosis. If that is the case, then based on frequency data alone, most readers also know someone who is intersexed (or hermaphroditic). Many readers may be dubious about this, as they are not aware that they know someone who has intersexed anatomy. Given the stigma and secrecy that frequently accompany variations of sex, gender, and sexuality, the lack of education and awareness about the continuum of sexual anatomy is understandable.

Why is there such a shroud of secrecy with regard to variations of sex development? Put simply, exceptions to the rule of two clearly distinct sexes (female and male) disrupt the very foundation of our social structure, thus creating a breach in social order. Not only are there predominant social expectations regarding two clearly distinct physical sexes, there is also a social expectation for one's anatomical sex (e.g. female or male) to be congruent with one's gender identity and role – as a clearly feminine or masculine person. Moreover, there is a social expectation for one's sexual identity to be attracted to the anatomy and gender "opposite" one's own. Thus, normalcy with regard to sex, gender, and sexuality is reliant upon having clear, causal, and linear connections between anatomical sex, gender identity and role, and sexuality (Butler 1990, 1993). Following this model, if a person's sexual anatomy is ambiguous, it will be difficult to know their gender, as a woman or a man, and nearly impossible to ascribe their sexual orientation within a framework that assumes binary sex. That is, if a person's genitalia, chromosomes, gonads, or hormones are not typically female or male, how can that person identify as hetero-, bi-, or homosexual, given that these categories presume female and male anatomies that are clearly distinct from one another?

Social expectations of sex, gender and sexuality

Binary sex and gender expectations surround us; everything from restrooms to clothing to identification cards to religious rites of passage and sporting events relies on a sex/gender binary. When the shared social expectation of this sex/gender binary is disrupted via anatomical sex or gender role variation, the social response typically revolves around attempts to decrease the uncertainty and proclaim the person in question as unequivocally female or male. Take the recent heart-wrenching investigation of the 18-year-old South African runner Caster Semenya's sex by the International Association of Athletics Federation (IAAF), the worldwide governing body for track and field. When Semenya won the 800 meter race at the World Championships in Berlin in August 2009, finishing nearly two and a half seconds before her closest competition, her record-breaking win was overshadowed by rumors that the IAAF had required her to undergo sex verification testing before the race (Levy 2009). Sure, Semenya's physical build and voice are more masculine than many women's, but it was her tremendous speed that drew speculation among her competitors and the IAAF that her sex may be in question.

Caster Semenya's eligibility to compete against women was challenged just six months before U.S. figure skater Johnny Weir's flamboyant behavior both on and off the ice at the 2010 Winter Olympics in Vancouver had two Canadian broadcasters suggesting that he should be subjected to sex verification testing (McKnight 2010) – something that has never been required of male athletes. Indeed, in an attempt to level the playing field, the International Olympic Committee (IOC) has used various means of weeding out "sex imposters" among female athletes since 1966 to disqualify genetic males from competing as women (Fausto-Sterling 2000a). After nearly a decade of protest from athletes, the IOC suspended mandatory sex verification of female athletes for the 2000 Olympic Games on a provisional basis (Newman 2001). As of this writing, Semenya's future as a competitive runner remains uncertain. The IAAF has yet to rule on whether they consider her "female enough" to continue the tremendously promising career that she only just began. That decision could be issued soon, as members of the IAAF and the IOC met in January 2010 with medical experts in "disorders of sex development" (DSDs) at a two-day private gender symposium to discuss recommendations for female athletes whose sex may be deemed questionable by medical standards (e.g. genitalia, chromosomes, hormones, and/or gonads that are not female-typical or congruent with one another). The IOC left this meeting with a recommendation to further medicalize variations of sex development by establishing world-renowned centers for excellence in the diagnosis and treatment of disorders of sex development, and requiring female athletes whose sex may be in question to seek hormonal, surgical, and/or psychological treatment from one of these medical facilities in order to be eligible to compete (O'Reilly 2010).

Cultural and historical variations on sex, gender and sexuality

This discussion of Semenya brings us back to a critical exploration of how sex, gender, and sexual normalcy are socially constructed. As the following examples illustrate, social expectations with regard to sex, gender, and sexuality are culturally dependent and vary significantly throughout history and across regions. Take homosexuality as an illustration. Being sexually attracted to others of the same sex or gender was considered a psychiatric disorder by the American Psychiatric Association until it was removed from the conditions listed in the *Diagnostic and Statistical Manual* in 1973 (Conrad and Schneider 1992). Claims of equality and human rights, spurred by the Civil Rights Movement, gave birth to the lesbian, gay, bisexual, and transgender (LGBT) movements that have flourished throughout the Western world in the last 40 years (Preves 2003, 2004). In contrast, institutionalized homophobia reigns supreme in some parts of the world. In Uganda, where homosexuality is already considered criminal behavior, punishable by up to 14 years in prison, legislation proposed in October 2009 aims to punish those convicted of homosexual behavior by death. This bill has been condemned by the United States, Britain, and the European Union, with concern that such legislation could set in motion a trend for similar legislation throughout Africa, where many countries already outlaw homosexuality (Ryu 2010).

Across the Indian Ocean on the South Pacific island of Papua New Guinea, behavior that would be considered homosexual (and criminal) throughout much of Africa is a mere right of passage for preadolescent boys. For the Sambia of Papua New Guinea, one of the country's 850 recognized tribes, men's ability to be fertile and develop male typical secondary sex characteristics, such as facial and body hair, a deep voice, fertility, and physical strength, is attributed to the ingestion of semen. Sambian belief holds that semen is not produced internally, but rather must be introduced externally through the ingestion of semen during fellatio rituals carried out as a standard rite of passage between men and boys (Herdt 1997). Behavior that would be condemned as illegal homosexuality throughout much of Africa or as criminal child abuse in the United States is socially constructed as not only normal but as necessary among this Papua New Guinean tribe.

Closer to home, we could reflect upon the variability in our own constructions of gender normalcy. Take, for example, the highly gendered colors of pink and blue. It might seem impossible to imagine either color being gender neutral, let alone associate the color blue with girls or the color pink with boys. However, a look into our rather recent history reveals the fickle (and social) nature of defining such colors as strictly gendered. It seems that pink was the preferred color for boys until after World War II, as it was considered a derivative of the color red, which was thought to be a fierce color. Similarly, the color blue was seen as a softer, gentler color, and thus associated with girls (Frassanito and Pettorini 2008). As evidence, *The Sunday Sentinel* advised Americans in 1914 "If you like the color note on the little one's garments, use pink for the boy and blue for the girl, if you are a follower of convention" (Frassanito and Pettorini 2008:881). In the same vein, in 1918, the *Ladies Home Journal* told its readership: "There has been a great diversity of opinion on the subject, but the generally accepted rule is pink for the boy and blue for the girl. The reason is that pink being a more decided and stronger color is more suitable for the boy, while blue, which is more delicate and dainty, is prettier for the girl" (Frassanito and Pettorini 2008:881).

Now that we have established distinctions between the terms sex, gender, and sexuality, illustrated social expectations about the binary and linear connections that socially link these terms to one another, as well as cross-cultural and historical variations in social norms regarding gender and sexuality, it is time to return to the discussion of variations of sex development, with which this chapter began.

Societal reactions to ambiguous sexual anatomy

Just as views about homosexuality vary considerably across time and space, so do social responses to sexual anatomy that is deemed difficult to label as distinctly female or male. In societies where childbirth is medicalized, such as throughout much of Europe and North America, the response to a child whose genitalia seem ambiguous is a medical one. Despite the fact that the vast majority of infants born with variations of sex development exhibit no medical concerns (Diamond and Sigmundson 1997), most newborns with ambiguous genitalia are responded to as though a variation in sex development is a medical emergency. The American Academy of Pediatrics made this sentiment clear in their position statement on this topic:

> The birth of a child with ambiguous genitalia constitutes a social emergency. Abnormal appearance can be corrected and the child raised as a boy or a girl as appropriate. Parents should be encouraged not to name the child or register the birth, if possible, until the sex of rearing is established. Infants raised as girls will usually require clitoral reduction which, with current techniques, will result not only in a normal-looking vulva but preservation of a functional clitoris. [These children's] diagnosis and prompt treatment require urgent medical attention.
>
> *(American Academy of Pediatrics 2000: 138)*

The treatment protocol to make a child appear unambiguously female or male was created in the United States as recently as the 1950s. This model of surgically and hormonally "sexing" intersexed children is most closely associated with the late psychologist John Money and usually entails early surgery and hormonal intervention. The rationale for early intervention to decrease outward sexual ambiguity is to help children form gender and sexual identities that are congruent and to preclude intersexed children from experiencing stigma (Preves 2003; Karkazis 2008). Both motives are logical, given the overwhelming social expectation for sex, gender, and sexual normalcy.

To further the attempt to prevent or decrease stigma that might accompany variations of sex development, this treatment model not only attempts to physically erase the evidence of genital ambiguity, but to conduct "social surgery" as well, by encouraging parents and loved ones to keep the child's ambiguous anatomy a secret from the child her/himself. In short, the theory goes, a child's gender and sexual identity may develop problematically if s/he were to know about or suspect anatomical sex features which are incongruent with a binary female or male role. By intervening early and erasing visible sexually ambiguous features, both parents and child will respond to the "clarified" genitalia as the essential sign of gender and develop a healthy bond and normal gender and sexual identity in the future.

This model, while rooted in benevolence, has been widely criticized as creating rather than preventing feelings of stigma and shame. In the 1990s an alternative patients–rights model emerged via the mobilization of the first generation of adults who as children underwent sex "clarification" procedures. The most vocal and visible of these critics was Cheryl Chase, founder and executive director of the now defunct Intersex Society of North America (ISNA). In their early activism, Chase and "Hermaphrodites with Attitude" (the activist branch of the Intersex Society of North America) resorted to picketing at medical conventions to have their voices heard. Such was the case at the 1996 meeting of the Academy of Pediatrics in Boston after the group was denied a place on the meeting's agenda (Beck 1997/1998). Largely due to the effectiveness of her advocacy, just four years later Chase delivered a keynote address at the Lawson Wilkins Pediatric Endocrine Society's annual meeting in 2000, giving "the grand finale to a four-hour symposium on the treatment of [sexual] ambiguity in newborns" (Fausto-Sterling 2000b). That same year, Chase was invited to the table with the most prominent clinicians in the field to serve as a member of the North American Task Force on Intersex. This promising work group dissolved scarcely more than a year later due to heated disagreements about treatment options and research proposals (Preves 2003; Karkazis 2008).

A dramatic turn of events in the advocacy and treatment of intersex came in 2005, when a group of medical experts and intersex activists, including Chase, convened to attempt to overcome their seemingly insurmountable differences in how best to respond to physical sexual ambiguity. One of the main outcomes of this historic meeting was a change in the language used to refer to physical sexual ambiguity. More specifically,

> terms should be as precise as possibly and should reflect the genetic etiology when available ... The new nomenclature should be understandable by patients and families and should be psychologically sensitive. In particular, gender labeling in the diagnosis should be avoided, and use of the words "hermaphrodite," "pseudohermaphrodite," and "intersex" should be abandoned, as they either are confusing or have a negative social connotation that may be perceived as harmful by some patients and parents. The term "disorders of sex development" (DSD) was proposed and was defined as "congenital conditions in which development of chromosomal, gonadal, or anatomic sex is atypical."
>
> *(Vilain et al. 2007: 66)*

Shortly thereafter, this group published the 2006 "Consensus Statement on Management of Intersex Disorders" (Hughes et al. 2006).

Reaction to the shift in terminology from "intersex" to "disorders of sex development" has been mixed. Clinicians and parents largely seem to embrace the new DSD term, as it offers a welcoming distance from the highly politicized and sexualized terms "intersex" and "hermaphrodite." Some activists, however, are not so pleased. Many see the use of the word "disorder" as a giant step backward in their work toward destigmatizing variations of sex development. Perhaps the most outspoken faction against the term DSD is the international activist group Organization Intersex International (OII) that operates the "We are Not a Disorder" blog. In sharp contrast, Cheryl Chase, founder of the Intersex Society of North America and former "hermaphrodite with attitude", closed down operation of the Intersex Society of North America and started a new disorders of sex development non-profit called Accord Alliance, to work more closely with clinicians in her efforts to destigmatize variations of sex development. ISNA says on its the homepage of its (now archival) website about this change:

> In 2007, ISNA sponsored and convened a national group of health care and advocacy professionals to establish a nonprofit organization charged with making sure the new ideas about appropriate care are known and implemented across the country.
>
> This organization, Accord Alliance, opened its doors in March, 2008, and will continue to lead national efforts to improve DSD-related health care and outcomes. Accord Alliance believes that improving the way health care is made available and delivered is essential to ensure that people receive the services and support they need to lead healthy, happy lives.
>
> With Accord Alliance in place, ISNA can close its doors with the comfort and knowledge that its work will continue to have an impact. Archives of our historical documents and accomplishments will be preserved at the Kinsey Institute at Indiana University.
>
> This website will remain up as a historical artifact.
>
> *(www.isna.org)*

Activists and clinicians haven't been the only ones caught up in the struggle over nomenclature. Biologist Milton Diamond has argued against the word "disorders" and has proposed that the word "differences" be used in its place, to retain the acronym DSD, to mean differences, rather than disorders, of sex development (Diamond 2009). Others scholars have proposed VSDs rather than DSDs: "variations of sex development" (Tamar-Mattis and Diamond 2007). Throughout this essay and in its title, I have used the terminology with which I am most comfortable: "intersex" and "variations of sex development".

The case of intersex, and particularly a cross-cultural and cross-historical examination in the variations of its "treatment", brings to the fore the social processes of defining what is normal and what is deviant. The politicization of the terminology that surrounds intersex variations of sex development is merely a new twist to the enduring cultural battles to control and predict sex, gender, and sexuality. With surety, conflicts about how best to corral and respond to those deemed sex, gender, or sexual deviants will continue in perpetuity.

Further information

For an interactive overview of how some variations of sex development occur, see the website: www.aboutkidshealth.ca/HowTheBodyWorks/Sex-Development-An-Overview.aspx?article ID=7671& categoryID = XS

Readers may learn more about Organization Intersex International by visiting their website: www.intersexualite.org/

Readers can visit www.isna.org and www.accordalliance.org to learn more about both organizations.

References

American Academy of Pediatrics, Committee on Genetics. 2000. "Evaluation of the Newborn with Developmental Anomalies of the External Genitalia." *Pediatrics* 106(1): 138–42.

Beck, Max. 1997/1998. "Hermaphrodites with Attitude Take to the Streets." *Chrysalis: The Journal of Transgressive Gender Identities* 2(5) (Fall/Winter): 45–46; 50.

Blackless, Melanie, Anthony Charuvastra, Amanda Derryck, Anne Fausto-Sterling, Karl Lauzanne, and Ellen Lee. 2000. "How Sexually Dimorphic Are We?" *American Journal of Human Biology* 12(2): 151–66.

Butler, Judith. 1990. *Gender Trouble: Feminism and the Subversion of Identity*. New York: Routledge.

——. 1993. *Bodies That Matter: On the Discursive Limits of "Sex."* New York: Routledge.

Conrad, Peter, and Joseph W. Schneider. 1992. *Deviance and Medicalization: From Badness to Sickness*. 2nd edition. Philadelphia, PA: Temple University Press.

Desai, Sindoor S. 1997. "Down Syndrome: A Review of the Literature." *Oral Surgery, Oral Medicine, Oral Pathology, Oral Radiology, and Endodontics* 84(3): 279–85.

Diamond, Milton. 2009. "Human Intersexuality: Difference or Disorder?" *Archives of Sexual Behavior* 38: 172.

Diamond, Milton and Keith Sigmundson. 1997. "Management of Intersexuality: Guidelines for Dealing with Persons with Ambiguous Genitalia." *Archives of Pediatric Adolescent Medicine* 151(October): 1046–50.

Dreger, Alice Domurat. 1995. *Doubtful Sex: Cases and Concepts of Hermaphroditism in France and Britain, 1868–1915*. Ph.D. dissertation, Indiana University.

——. 1998. *Hermaphrodites and the Medical Invention of Sex*. Cambridge, MA: Harvard University Press.

Fausto-Sterling, Anne. 2000a. *Sexing the Body: Gender Politics and the Construction of Sexuality*. New York: Basic Books.

——. 2000b. "The Five Sexes, Revisited." *The Sciences* 40(4): 18–23.

Frassanito, Paolo and Benedetta Pettorini. 2008. "Pink and Blue: The Color of Gender." *Child's Nervous System* 24(8): 881–82.

Herdt, Gilbert H. 1997. *Same Sex, Different Cultures: Exploring Gay and Lesbian Lives*. Boulder, CO: Westview Press.

Hughes, I. A., C. Houk, S. F. Ahmed, P. A. Lee and LWPES/ESPE Consensus Group. 2006. "Consensus Statement on Management of Intersex Disorders." *Archives of Disease in Childhood* 91: 554–63.

Karkazis, Katrina. 2008. *Fixing Sex: Intersex, Medical Authority, and Lived Experience*. Durham, NC: Duke University Press.

Koidin, Michelle. 2000. "Texas Ruling Allows 'Same Sex' Marriage." *Chicago Sun Times*, September 7.

Levy, Ariel. 2009. "Either/Or: Sports, Sex, and the Case of Caster Semenya." *New Yorker*, November 30: 46–59.

Lum, Matt. 2002. "'Slap in the Face': Christie Lee Littleton's Historic Texas Court Ruling Crosses State Lines to Deny Equality." *Texas Triangle*, March 22: 20.

McKnight, Peter. 2010. "Here's the Rule: Men are Men and Women are Ladies: Figure Skaters are Expected to Adhere to Strict Gender Roles, but that Doesn't Work for Everyone." *Vancouver Sun*, February 27.

Newman, Judith. 2001. "How Sexism and Bad Science Have Teamed Up Against Athletes." *SportsJones*. August 24.

O'Reilly, Ian. 2010. "Gender Testing in Sport: A Case for Treatment?" *BBC News*, February 15.

Preves, Sharon E. 2003. *Intersex and Identity: The Contested Self*. New Brunswick, NJ: Rutgers University Press.

——. 2004. "Out of the O.R. and into the Streets: Exploring the Impact of Intersex Media Activism." *Research in Political Sociology* 13: 179–223.

Roberts, Helen E., Janet D. Cragan, Joanne Cono, Muin J. Khoury, Mark R. Weatherly, and Cynthia A. Moore. 1998. "Increased Frequency of Cystic Fibrosis among Infants with Jejunoileal Atresia." *American Journal of Medical Genetics* 78:446–49.

Ryu, Alisha. 2010. "Petition against Anti-Gay Bill Delivered to Ugandan Parliament." *Voice of America News*, March 1.

Tamar-Mattis, Anne and Milton Diamond. 2007. "Managing Variations in Sex Development." *Journal of Pediatric Endocrinology and Metabolism* 20: 552–53.

Vilain, Eric, John C. Achermann, Erica A. Eugster, Vincent R. Harley, Yves Morel, Jean D. Wilson, and Olaf Hiort. 2007. "We Used to Call Them Hermaphrodites." *Genetics in Medicine* 9(2): 65–66.

20

Transgendering

Challenging the "normal"

Kimberly Tauches

STATE UNIVERSITY OF NEW YORK AT ALBANY

This chapter examines the problems transgendered individuals in America face as they challenge a certain idea of a normal order of sex, gender, and sexuality. I will consider the kinds of discrimination faced by these individuals in their everyday lives, and point to public policies which might address these concerns.

I begin by looking at the way the relationship between sex, gender, and sexuality is socially constructed in American culture. I then introduce a critical discussion of this idea of a normal sex, gender, and sexuality order. Finally, there is a description of transgendering, and some of the challenges transgendered individuals confront in their lives.

Let's first define the terms of this discussion. Sex refers to a biological categorization based upon examination of the genitals, chromosomes, and/or hormones. Gender is the social traits and behaviors that are expected to be on display depending on your biological sex. Sexuality can be either an identity or an act. As an identity, it is based on an individual's object of sexual desire. As an act, it is based on sexual acts performed, whether for pleasure or reproduction. Transgender is an umbrella term that is used to describe a diverse group of people who intentionally "mismatch" their sex and their gender identity or behavior.

Sex

Sex is understood as a biological concept. The assumption is that biology creates two distinct sexes: females and males. In America, they are mutually exclusive. That is, only two categories exist and a person cannot exist in both of those categories at once. Several different biological factors go into determining the sex of an individual. Typically, a doctor will look at a newborn child and determine its sex based on its genitalia. If the genitals of the infant cannot be determined, other factors may be used to determine the sex of the child, such as the chromosomes and hormones of the child.

In the US, male and female are the only sex categories recognized. Sex is seen to have two and only two mutually exclusive possibilities, and every person is thought to fit into one of those categories. One consequence of viewing sex this way is that those who are born neither male nor female, according to their genitalia, chromosomes, and/or hormones, are forced into one or the other category, typically through surgical intervention at a young age. Those born with ambiguous genitals are called Intersexed (Kessler 1998: 5). Another consequence is that it places emphasis on being one or the other sex.

The ways in which sex is determined or constructed by doctors point to the ways in which sex is not necessarily natural. While most people do fit into the categories of male and female, those who do not are frequently forced to be altered surgically, which shows how even the notion of "sex" may be socially constructed. Doctors determine, in many cases, whether a person's genitals need to be "fixed" to appear within medical definitions of normality. Doctors will surgically alter the bodies of those who do not fit into either sex when they are born. This is done for two reasons. First, there are only two recognizable genders, so a child who is not surgically altered to fit an idea of a normal sex and gender would have to choose one gender or the other. Second, the doctors believe intersexed children will face social problems if they are not surgically altered, because their bodies do not fit within the boundaries of normal.

Gender

Gender is a social construction that arises from biological sex. It consists of socially defined behaviors and traits that are considered normal for each sex. Gender varies over time and space, so that what might be considered appropriate for a woman in the United States in 2006 might not have been considered appropriate for a woman in the United States in the 1950s. For example, the definition of what is considered feminine has changed. White middle-class women are now able to work outside the home without having their femininity questioned, whereas in the 1950s such women would have been considered non-feminine.

Because gender is thought to be based on sex, there are only two genders, masculine and feminine. Due to the binary categories, a person is seen as fitting into one and only one gender, masculine or feminine, but never both masculine and feminine. This is because they are seen as mutually exclusive – the masculine is defined as not feminine and the feminine is defined as not masculine.

Gender operates at a personal, interactional, and institutional level. At the personal level, society dictates what is considered normal for a person in terms of their gender identity; individuals use hair-style, clothing, mannerisms, and ways of talking to express the appropriate gender. At the interpersonal level, gender is performed so that others can easily tell a person's sex and gender. When two people interact, appearance, behavior, and social norms will all come together to create gender attribution. Each person involved in the interaction is placed into one of the gender categories by the other (Bornstein 1995: 26). After the gender of a person has been established by him or herself and others, his or her behavior is expected to conform to that gender identity.

Gender also exists at the institutional level. Gender is organized in a hierarchy; men and their masculine traits are valued more than women and their femininity. Gender affects all institutions, such as the economy, politics, and the family. For example, in the healthcare field, men are expected to be doctors while women should be nurses. This is not dictated by nature, but by social or gender norms. This gender order has serious consequences. Doctors are held in higher esteem than nurses. Doctors are paid higher than nurses. Doctors have authority over nurses. In short, men dominate women in the healthcare field. Furthermore, a man who wishes to be a nurse might be seen as effeminate, since nursing is considered work that women do. In addition, the political system is affected by gender. For example, women are grossly under-represented in Congress and the judiciary. And why, in over two hundred years, has there not been a woman President or Vice President? The family is also affected by gendered ideas of who is appropriate to perform what roles. Despite some changes, housework is still viewed as primarily a woman's role. These are all examples of institutions and situations in which gender operates. These institutions have a major effect on people's lives. The result is that a gender order means men and women often live different lives. And men have more status, power, and wealth than women.

Sexuality

Sexuality is also a social construction, in that what is deemed sexual very much depends on the social environment. For example, society tells us what is sexual and what is not, including what is considered a sexual body part, and what are appropriate sexual acts and objects of affection. This varies across time and space, so that what was desirable during one period of time might be less desirable at another time. For example, different breast sizes are preferred by men according to the economy, so that men prefer larger breasts during times when the economy is doing well and smaller breasts when the economy is doing badly (Kimmel 2000). A social constructionist view of sexuality is distinguished from essentialist notions of sexuality. The latter views sexuality as natural. Such naturalistic views have often served to justify reproductive heterosexuality as the highest form of sexuality. Non-heterosexual forms of sexuality are seen as inferior.

Heteronormativity, or the view that heterosexuality is the only acceptable form of sexuality, figures prominently in American sexual culture. Heterosexual is seen as the only right or normal way a person can be. This is seen in everyday life through the assumptions that everyone is heterosexual. Heteronormativity also creates a stigma for homosexuality. Like sex and gender categories, we have two more categories that are mutually exclusive and oppositional. People are seen to be either heterosexual or homosexual, but not both. Moreover, normality is associated with the former, abnormality with the latter. Bisexuality falls within the heterosexual/homosexual binary because sexual acts are categorized based on the gender of the sex partner. Yet, bisexuality challenges the sexual binary of homosexuality and heterosexuality because a bisexual person falls into both sexual identity categories.

Social institutions regulate sexuality, in particular political institutions, the family, religion, media, and the medical community. Political institutions regulate sexuality through laws which deem who can have sex with whom and where. In addition, laws regulate who can have sex in terms of age, through age of consent laws. Furthermore, laws serve as a legitimating factor in sexual relations, through, for example, marriage. The family also regulates sexuality in this way, through the view of a family as an institution consisting of a married man and woman and their children. Religion produces sexual morals and rules which regulate who is supposed to have sex with whom, where, and for what reasons, as can be seen through the religious condemnation of homosexuality and abortion. The media produces images of what is considered right and wrong sexuality. The medical community can shape sexuality through, for example, technologies such as birth control.

Interrelations of sex, gender, and sexuality

An exploration of these interrelations is necessary in order to understand the ways in which transgendered individuals transgress not only gender, but also sex and sexuality.

Sex and gender intersect through the ways in which gender is seen to be based on what is considered appropriate for the sex of an individual. While we frequently cannot see a person's genitals, chromosomes, or hormones, in everyday public life, secondary sex characteristics come to represent the sex of a person. Secondary sex characteristics could include facial hair and breasts, but when they are absent or hidden, then gender becomes increasingly important for gender attribution. Through interaction, gender attribution occurs, which serves to place a person in an interaction into one sex category or the other, even though the actual sex of a person has not necessarily been determined. In addition, Kessler (1998) shows that gender forms the basis for sex, as doctors look to social norms of gender to dictate what is considered normal for the appearance of genitals. Sex also intersects with sexuality due to the use of body parts in sexual acts. However, researchers have shown that, in different times and places, different body parts are seen as "sexual" and sexually desirable.

Gender and sexuality are also related to each other. Gender in the US and many other nations is viewed in binary ways, leading to different gender norms for men and women. For example, there are different hair and clothing styles for women and for men. These differences are important because it allows a person easily to see what the sex of another person is, which enables them to tell whether that person is an appropriate object of desire. This is directly related to heterosexuality and homosexuality. Since sex is seen as a binary, and male and female genitals are necessary for heterosexuality, gender differentiation is seen as desirable. If there was no way to distinguish between men and women, then it would be nearly impossible to tell whether a person is engaged in heterosexual or homosexual relations.

Gender and heterosexuality seem tightly related. Our ideas of what it means to be a real man or a real woman are based on heteronormativity. So, a woman is only a woman if she is heterosexual, otherwise her femininity is called into question. But also, if a woman departs too far from feminine gender roles, she may be called a dyke. This woman may be heterosexual or homosexual; however, the notion that she violated gender norms may call into question her femininity by calling into question her heterosexuality.

Transgendering

Transgendered is an umbrella term that is used to describe many groups of people, such as transsexuals, cross-dressers, and transgendered individuals. The characteristic that these otherwise diverse groups of people have in common is that their gender does not match the sex category they were placed into at birth. Transsexuals are people who seek to change their sex. Cross-dressers are those who either occasionally or frequently dress in the clothes of the opposite sex. In addition, there are those who identify as transgendered, meaning that their sex and gender do not "fit" in accordance with social norms.

Transgendering disrupts the ways in which sex, gender, and sexuality intersect with each other. Here, gender is based on how an individual wishes to express himself/herself, regardless of "sex." As a result, gender attribution is also disrupted because a person cannot be placed easily into the appropriate sex category. Transgendering frequently results in gender attribution that is correct, but sex categorization that is incorrect.

In addition, though the gender binary of masculinity and femininity is seen as mutually exclusive, transgendering can highlight the ways in which these two genders can be combined in order to produce a gender that is neither one nor the other, but one that falls outside of the gender binary. Indeed, other cultures have provided social spaces for more than two genders: for example, some Native American Tribes (Herdt 1993). One example of a culture that has a specific space for transgendered individuals is India, in which Hijra, or male-to-female transgendered individuals, perform in birth ceremonies.

Transgendering can also disturb our ideas about the relationship of gender and sexuality. To the extent that sexual identity refers to the way in which people are categorized as homosexual or heterosexual according to the sex of their partner, transgendering suggests a person might be attracted to the gender of the individual, not the sex. For example, a heterosexual woman might be attracted to the masculinity of a biological female, but one who is presented as a socially masculine transgendered individual. The heterosexual woman might not realize the actual sex of the transgendered individual given the assumption that a person who is masculine is male.

The heterosexual–homosexual distinction assumes that everyone falls into one category of sexual identity. Transgendering, however, could result in "passing," in which a person is seen as having the sex other than that with which they were born. This would result in an unrecognizable mismatch (between sex and gender), and therefore could be seen as disrupting the link between gender and sexuality. For example, the "butch lesbian" is female but masculine in "her" gender presentation. And, what about "her" sexual identity? Is the butch lesbian desire for feminine women a heterosexual or homosexual desire?

Implications of transgendering in everyday life

Because transgendering disrupts our ideas of a normal and correct relationship between sex, gender, and sexuality, it is hardly surprising that transgendered individuals encounter challenges on a daily basis. Let's briefly consider how such individuals deal with public spaces, language, official identification, sexuality, and the medical world.

Public spaces that are considered ordinary and uneventful for most people could pose serious challenges for transgendered individuals. Halberstam (1998) identifies the bathroom as a site in which transgendered individuals face potential problems (Halberstam 1998: 20). Though bathrooms in the United States are usually clearly differentiated according to sex, there becomes a necessity to maintain that differentiation through a policing of the space. So, for example, when a masculine female walks into a ladies' room, other women in the bathroom may object, or even call security.

Language is another place in which the disjuncture between sex and gender becomes challenging for transgendered individuals. The use of pronouns is one place in which this occurs. He/she, him/her, his/hers assume people are either male or female, men or women. This may force transgendered individuals to choose one pronoun or another, even though each is misleading. Or, such individuals may feel they have to challenge this binary, which itself can cause tension and conflict. Those who write about transgendered individuals in the media or in schools frequently fail to acknowledge the ways in which their use of pronouns fails adequately to portray the transgendered individual in ways consistent with how they lead their life (Scott 2005; Halberstam 2005).

Documentation of identity is a third area in which transgendered individuals face problems. Sex becomes a primary marker for identification, but if we consider the issue of a transgendered individual with a picture identity card, the picture would show one gender, while the identification would state that the individual falls into a different sex category. This could lead to confusion in bars, stores, police situations, or at customs agencies. For example, a driver's license may convey a conventional male name and picture, but an individual's self presentation may blur masculinity and femininity.

Sexuality and gender form another intersection that creates problems for transgendered individuals. For example, many of us would likely view transgendering as related to homosexuality. Yet transgendered individuals are not necessarily homosexual and, indeed, being transgendered is a gender, not a sexual identity. A transgendered individual could desire a man, a woman, or another transgendered individual. Again, how should we describe a male who is presented as transgendered with a clear feminine aspect who desires a butch man or a butch woman?

The uncertain relationship between transgendering and homosexuality points to problem of politics. Although transgendering has recently found a place in the sexual politics of the gay and lesbian movement, many transgendered individuals do not feel represented in this movement. The notion that transgendered individuals are covered under the antidiscrimination laws based on sex and sexual orientation fails to acknowledge the unique gender issues mentioned above, which pertain mainly to transgendered individuals. Many transgendered individuals would prefer to forge their own movement around gender politics.

Finally, transgendered individuals also face the problem of a medical world that is not always friendly. For example, the fields of psychology and medicine have often promoted negative, stereotyped views of transgendered individuals. Many in the field of psychology still view transgendered individuals as mentally ill, diagnosing those who seek help as having "gender dysphoria" or a gender identity disorder. Some psychologists and physicians recommend sex change through sex reassignment surgery as the main way to "fix" transgendered individuals, to realign sex and gender in a "normal" order.

Conclusion

In American society, sex, gender, and sexuality are understood in binary terms. The only sex categories available are male and female, the only gender categories are masculine and feminine, and the sexual categories are chiefly heterosexual and homosexual. Moreover, it's been assumed that there is a logical order between sex, gender, and sexuality. For example, a normal female will become a woman whose femininity will express itself in a heterosexual identity. Most Americans understand these binaries and this logical order as natural. The recent visibility of transgendered individuals challenges the presumed naturalness of these binaries. Transgendering allows for varied relationships between sex, gender, and sexuality. It challenges the binaries and a presumed natural order between sex, gender, and sexuality. This is precisely why transgendered individuals face hostility and many challenges in their daily lives, as I have shown. They refuse to conform to ideas of normal gender and sexuality. But America, as it is currently organized, cannot easily accommodate individuals who are not either male or female, men or women, or heterosexual or homosexual.

In the face of this hostility and challenges, transgendered individuals have rallied around a gender identity or expression movement. They aim to gain rights to free gender expression, rights that would prohibit bullying and harassment based on gender. The struggle for freedom of gender identity/expression will benefit not only those who are now differently gendered, but those who are normatively gendered but feel constrained by such "normality." My own view is that the queer movement, women's movement, men's movement, and transgendered movement need to work together in order to ensure freedom of gender and sexuality. Failure to do so produces incomplete protection for all.

References

Bornstein, Kate. 1995. *Gender Outlaw*. New York: Vintage Press.
Halberstam, Judith. 1998. *Female Masculinity*. Durham, NC: Duke University Press.
——2005. *In a Queer Time and Place: Transgender Bodies, Subcultural Lives*. New York: New York University Press.
Herdt, Gilbert. 1993. *Third Sex, Third Gender*. New York: Zone Books.
Kessler, Suzanne J. 1998. *Lessons From the Intersexed*. New Brunswick, NJ: Rutgers University Press.
Kimmel, Michael. 2000. *The Gendered Society*. Oxford: Oxford University Press.
Scott, Gunner. 2005. "Introduction". In Toni Amato and Mary Davis (eds), *Pinned Down by Pronouns*. Jamaica Plains, MA: Conviction Books.

21

Transsexual, transgender, and queer

Interview with Viviane Namaste

CONCORDIA UNIVERSITY, MONTREAL, CANADA

Professor Namaste teaches at the Simone de Beauvoir Institute, Concordia University, Montréal. She is the author of *Sex Change, Social Change: Reflections on Identity, Institutions and Imperialism* (Toronto: Women's Press, 2005), *C'était du spectacle! L'histoire des artistes transsexuelles à Montréal, 1955–1985* (Montréal: McGill-Queen's University Press, 2005) and *Invisible Lives: The Erasure of Transsexual and Transgendered People* (Chicago: University of Chicago Press, 2000). She has also been active in establishing community-based health services for transsexuals in Montréal.

Can you briefly describe the terms "sex," "gender," "transsexual" and "transgender"?

In sociology, the term "sex" is generally used to indicate the biological body with which an individual is born. Commonly, people understand there to be two sexes – males and females. Sex is further defined in terms of *genitals* – so males have penises, for example. Sex is also commonly understood as a function of *hormones* – the prevalence of testosterone in males and estrogen in females. Hormones produce secondary sex characteristics – the presence of facial hair in men, for example. Sex is also often understood as a function of *chromosomes*: XX chromosones for females, and XY chromosomes for males.

However, there is a great deal of evidence to indicate that the world is not as simple as it may appear. With regard to hormones, everyone produces both testosterone and estrogen. Concerning chromosomes, many individuals have a chromosomal make-up that differs from "the norm" – for example, individuals who are born male, who live as men, but who have an XXY chromosome pattern. With regard to genitals, many individuals are born with genitals that cannot easily be classified as male or female – a genital organ may be too short to be considered a penis, yet too long to be characterized as a clitoris. These individuals are known as intersexed. So the notion of "sex" itself is quite complicated.

If "sex" refers to the biological body, the physical form in which one is located, sociologists use the term "gender" to indicate specific social relations and social meanings. Gender includes both the role that people are expected to occupy – for instance, that women are responsible for taking care of others – as well as the meanings that can be associated with a particular role – for instance, the idea that women are nurturing.

The term "transsexual" refers to individuals who are born in one sex – male or female – but who identify as members of the "opposite" sex. They may take hormones and undergo surgical intervention, usually including remodeling the genitals, to live as members of their chosen sex. Transsexuals are both male-to-female and female-to-male.

The term "transgender" is really popular in Anglo-American communities, and is used as an umbrella term to include all kinds of people who do not fit into normative relations between sex and gender. This would include, for instance, transsexuals, drag queens (men who perform as women on stage only, usually in a gay male club or social environment), intersexed individuals (people who are born with genitals that cannot be easily classified as "male" or "female"), drag kings (females who perform as men on the stage in lesbian cultural spaces), transvestites (heterosexual males who cross-dress in "women's" clothes and who receive sexual gratification from this act), as well as people who do not identify with either the category "male" or "female."

While the term "transgender" is currently one of the most popular, it needs to be pointed out at this point in history that, increasingly, transsexuals object to being included under the catch-all phrase of "transgender." They argue that the healthcare and social service needs of transsexuals are quite specific, and that this specificity is lost when people use a vague "transgender." Furthermore, the popularity of the term "transgender" emerges from the Anglo-American lesbian and gay community. While this discourse may have meaning for some transsexuals who understand their lives in these terms, it does not speak to the transsexuals who do not make sense of their lives, and their political struggles, within the confines of a lesbian/gay framework. It is important to point this out, because most of the Anglo-American writers and self-designated activists on "transgendered" issues come out of the lesbian/gay community and express themselves in those terms. My empirical research contradicts this underlying assumption, since most of the transsexuals I have interviewed do not articulate their needs according to a lesbian/gay framework.

All of this is to say that questions of language are deeply political!

What are some of the types of discrimination that transsexual and transgendered people face?

There are a variety of forms of discrimination. Access to services is one of the major barriers: detoxification programs especially, state funding for surgery, access to hormones in prison, access to emergency shelter. For example, some women's shelters do not accept male-to-female transsexuals as clients, arguing that they are not women. Much of transsexuals' access is dependent on the individual attitudes of service providers. So when someone is uneducated about transsexuals and transvestites, they may refuse access to services based on misinformation or prejudice. Another type of discrimination comes out of a total lack of institutional policies for transsexuals. This is especially true for female-to-male transsexuals. In these instances, some people cannot get services because bureaucrats do not have a clear written directive. Some of the empirical research I conducted in Québec illustrates this situation well. In 1997 and 1998, for example, the Québec government office responsible for issuing a change-of-name certificate for transsexuals (the Office of Civil Status) would not provide clear indication of the administrative procedure to be followed in the case of female-to-male transsexuals. At that time, for example, the Office of Civil Status clearly stated that a male-to-female transsexual must undergo a vaginoplasty, the construction of a vagina, in order to change her name and sex. Yet in the case of female-to-male transsexuals, the Office invoked a rather vague criterion of structurally changing the genital organs. They did not say if this meant a phalloplasty (the construction of a penis), or if it referred to the removal of the uterus and the ovaries alongside a double mastectomy and taking male hormones. Simply put, the interpretation of the law was contradictory and arbitrary. My research indicates that at certain times there is no standardized procedure in this area. (Since that time, however, this situation has been rectified and the Office has a clear policy with regard to female-to-male transsexuals.) Obviously, living with a bureaucratic context in which things are unclear and arbitrary is a form of discrimination: it does not provide people with the information they need to access institutions, and thus pushes them to the margins of society. In practical terms, the transsexuals I interviewed spoke about the consequences of living without identity papers that corresponded to their bodies: they did not enroll in school, could not find paid employment, and were refused access to health services.

Access to the media is a whole other form of institutional discrimination. Transsexuals are required to give their autobiography on demand: how long have you known? Are you operated? How did your family take the news? These kinds of personal questions can provide some insight into the lives of transsexuals, but they are also, in a sense, quite invasive and rude. It is astounding to me that within fifteen seconds of knowing an individual is transsexual, some people feel comfortable enough to ask them to describe the physical appearance and sexual function of their genitals. How is it that cultural taboos regarding speaking openly about sexuality and genitalia with people you do not know well go out the window when it comes to transsexuals? One of the effects of this demand is that it is difficult for transsexuals to address the real issues: cops who harass street prostitutes and escorts, access to healthcare and social services, changing one's name and sex. The other thing with respect to access to the media is the whole affiliation with lesbian/gay and feminist communities. As I mentioned earlier, most of the self-designated activists emerge from lesbian/gay and/or feminist communities, and they frame the issues in these terms. This means that transsexuals who do not make sense of their lives according to lesbian/gay discourse have no voice. And I reiterate here that, based on my empirical research and observations within the milieu for more than 10 years, the majority of transsexuals do not make sense of their lives in lesbian/gay terms. Yet we never hear these voices. And even though we have some empirical research which challenges an equation amongst transsexuals and lesbians/gays – I refer here to my research as well as that of Henry Rubin, whose book on female-to-male transsexuals, *Self-Made Men*, was published by Vanderbilt University Press in 2003 – our observations are ignored both by critics in queer theory and by transgendered activists who align themselves with queer politics. So, institutionally, transsexuals experience discrimination to the extent that they cannot express themselves in their own terms.

The last institutional barrier I want to cite is that of consultation. So often, the government develops policies without consulting transsexuals at all. Or in certain cases, consultation happens with middle-class non-prostitute transsexuals, who represent their unique interests without ensuring that the broader needs of transsexuals are addressed.

What is the focus of transsexual and transgender politics?

This is a difficult question to answer, in part because of the vast differences among transsexual and transgendered individuals. To begin to answer this question, it is necessary to underline that there is not one broad "transsexual or transgendered community," but rather many different networks of people. Some of the most prominent and visible networks include prostitutes, female-to-male transsexuals and transgendered people who come from a university background, and older transsexuals. There are, of course, many other different kinds of networks of transvestites and transsexuals.

What gets established as a political priority for transsexuals differs depending on the network one is discussing. In the Canadian context, the history of transsexual activism is one intimately bound up with matters related to prostitution, drugs and addiction, and prison. The services that were developed for transsexuals in the mid-to-late 1990s all emerged from these worlds, with local community leaders taking a central role. Individuals like Sandra Laframboise in Vancouver, Diane Gobeil in Montréal and Mirha-Soleil Ross in Toronto all worked to integrate transsexuals into the healthcare/social service network. In practical terms, the priorities were not exclusively focused on transsexuality or gender identity – issues such as access to methadone in prison, or social housing, were understood as important and relevant to transsexual health more broadly.

If one considers a different network of transsexual individuals, however, the political priorities change. A consideration of transsexual politics from the United States, and more specifically from locations closely linked to the university, emphasize questions of identity much more strongly than in the example I have just cited. There is a movement, for instance, to depathologize gender identity disorder from the institution of psychiatry. (Currently, individuals who wish to change their sex require the authorization of psychiatric, psychological and/or sexological personnel.) In a related manner, this network of transsexual people often invokes more abstract discussions about gender and identity: how many genders are there? Why do people only think there are two genders? How can one move beyond a gender binary? These questions are centrally concerned with identity. They are different questions, and different political priorities, than those put forward by prostitutes, prisoners, and drug users.

Let me provide another example to make this point, this time from an international perspective. In May of 2005 I participated in a Day of Citizenship and Rights for Trans People at the City Hall of Paris. There were different speakers from around the world, outlining the situation of trans people in their respective countries. The symposium included representatives from Colombia, France, Algeria and the Magreb, Ecuador, Brazil, Ethiopia, and many other countries. The forum was organized by Dr. Camille Cabral of PASTT (Prevention Action Santé Travesti et Transsexuel), a non-governmental organization in Paris that offers resources, education and services to transsexuals and that has strong links to transsexual prostitutes. And what was so remarkable that day was to listen to the issues identified as important by transsexual women from around the world: matters of citizenship, immigration, drugs, prisons, and the regulation of prostitution. These are the elements of transsexual politics for activists around the world. And they differ greatly from the kinds of political priorities identified by many university-affiliated transsexuals in the United States who only speak English. Such a tremendous gap – in terms of nation, language, and politics – is instructive in and of itself in a reflection on social movements.

What do you see as the sexual political significance of transsexuals?

For me, transsexual politics are integrally related to those of prostitution and poverty. The history of transsexual organizing in Canada and internationally is a history of understanding and challenging the laws that are used to regulate prostitutes. So one of the most important contributions transsexuals make to sexual politics, in my opinion, concerns understanding and challenging how sexuality itself is criminalized.

How do transsexuals and transgendered people challenge the gender binary?

This question is one that comes up again and again on the left. I am happy to have the opportunity to answer it, in a sense to undo this question, because it helps to illustrate some of the issues that I have raised in my previous answers.

Let me begin by briefly summarizing some of the underlying assumptions of this question. The question follows a line advanced by some self-designated transgendered activists and repeated over and over again by queer theorists in the university. It argues that the binary sex/gender system, the exclusive division of the world into "men" and "women," is oppressive. And this argument further contends that this is oppressive not only to transsexuals, but indeed to men and women who consider themselves "properly" sexed and gendered. And having made this critique of the binary sex/gender system, this position then goes on to state that social change can happen through some kind of disruption or displacement of the sex/gender system. That's where transgendered people come in, located within this framework as those who successfully challenge the status quo and point out a new way of going forward.

Now, having given a brief overview of what I see as some of the underlying assumptions of the question, let me return to the division I made earlier between "transsexuals" and "transgendered." I said that, more and more, a lot of transsexuals take a critical distance from the term "transgendered." And this question allows us an opportunity to think through why. The question assumes that "transgendered" people will see their bodies, identities, and lives as part of a broader process of social change, of disrupting the sex/gender binary. Now many transgendered people make such an argument: you can read it in the works of Leslie Feinberg, Riki Ann Wilchins, or Kate Bornstein. But many transsexuals do not see themselves in these terms. They would situate themselves as "men" and as "women," not as "gender radicals" or "gender revolutionaries," or as "boyzzz" or "grrrrrrls."

Most transsexuals I know, and most I have interviewed, describe themselves as men or women. And there is a sense in which this position cannot be understood in relation to the question posed, "what is the significance of the challenge to the two-gendered dichotomous system that transsexual/transgendered people raise?" Because transsexuals seek to have a different embodied position within that system. I hope it is clear here what I am trying to do – I hope to show how asking the question in this way forces transsexuals to speak a language that is foreign to us. And while it may have meaning and relevance for *transgendered* people, it has very little to do with the everyday lives of *transsexuals*.

Now it is usually assumed, in the university and even in progressive movements for social change, that people who adopt "essentialist" positions are not politically progressive. But, you know, I think that the interest in social constructionism in the Anglo-American university is in danger of blinding people to the very good political work that one can do from an essentialist position. And I will go out on a limb here – because to be a good thinker and activist and teacher means taking some risks – and I will say that in the case of transsexuals, essentialism has such a bad name!

Let me cite an example to help illustrate my case. It is so often assumed, as the question posed to me does, that in disrupting a binary sex/gender system, transgendered people are in the forefront of social change. I cited the works of Leslie Feinberg and Riki Ann Wilchins earlier. Both of these writers are located within this framework: they advocate a "transgendered" revolution. Now, this is supposed to be a position that is so much more sophisticated than that of those terrible essentialist transsexuals. And the position advocated by Feinberg and Wilchins is the one cited by critics in queer theory. These are the authors who make it onto the course outlines of university studies. And it is all done by well-intentioned, well-meaning teachers who would situate themselves as allies of transsexuals.

But let us examine in more depth some of the political work of Feinberg and Wilchins. Wilchins has been not only active, but instrumental, in lobbying for the de-listing of gender identity disorder from the manual of psychiatrists, the Diagnostic and Statistical Manual IV. And Leslie Feinberg also supports such a position, notably in publishing the "International Bill of Gender Rights" in her book. This Bill also contends that gender identity disorder has no place in the psychiatric diagnostic manual. If such a lobby is successful, it will mean that it will be impossible to pay for sex reassignment surgery either through a private insurance company or through state/provincial health insurance. In this light, the activism of Wilchins and Feinberg supports the privatization of healthcare. (Feinberg represents herself as a Marxist activist, which is the biggest irony of all!) So here we have a case of some transgendered activists, influenced by social constructionist theory, who argue that they are the cutting edge of social change. Yet they are involved in political work which is deeply conservative.

Now let us contrast this with the work of some transsexuals like Margaret O'Hartigan, who has been instrumental in ensuring that sex reassignment surgery is paid for through state health insurance in Minnesota, and who has offered a trenchant critique of the funding of healthcare services in Oregon, including services for transsexuals. Now, O'Hartigan is an essentialist: she is not making any claims to disrupting the sex/gender binary, she is not hailing herself as the new vanguard of third-wave feminism. What she is doing is the highly unglamorous work of research, lobbying, and activism to ensure that all transsexuals can have access to healthcare, regardless of their economic or financial resources. So here we have an example of an essentialist (gasp!) who is, in my opinion, doing some excellent political work.

Yet I want to go even further. In certain discussions in a university context, there is an acknowledgement that essentialism can be useful politically. Judith Butler, for example, recognizes that while her theoretical work interrogates the idea of "woman," it is at times necessary to invoke the category "woman" in order to make political gains. This argument, of course, could easily be extended to the case of transsexuality: that one needs an identity of "transsexual" in order to advance things politically. I can accept the terms of this argument. However, what I am saying today also goes far beyond this idea. I think that academics and activists set a very dangerous precedent if we maintain that people's identities are acceptable only if and when they can prove that they are politically useful. Who gets to decide what constitutes "politically useful" anyway? To my mind, this still reinforces a dynamic in which transsexuals have to prove themselves: you see, we're really all right because we use our transsexual identity for some good law reform. I refuse to accept these terms. I cited the case of Margaret O'Hartigan earlier, arguing that she was involved in some critical healthcare activism. Now, in very specific and practical terms, she and other activists in Portland, Oregon, engaged in a very detailed reading of the kinds of state coverage offered to its citizens. And they found significant gender differences with respect to the ranking of different procedures for reimbursement. So, for instance, state coverage paid for testicular implants in the case of a male who has lost his testicles, but did not allow for breast implants in the case of a woman who loses her breasts. This kind of activism, then, shows a clear gender bias in social policy. And in point of fact the activism is not particularly premised on any kind of transsexual identity. So my earlier statement that this was good work being done by an essentialist is a bit unfair. The work is good, period. And whether or not O'Hartigan is an essentialist is irrelevant. So that is one of the points I am happy to make here today. In many university and activist contexts, essentialist identities can only be accepted to the extent that they clearly satisfy some unspecified political agenda. And I am saying something quite different, albeit perhaps unpopular in social constructionist circles. Accepting transsexuality means accepting that people live and identify as men and women, although they were not born in male or female bodies. And that this needs to be kept separate from political work. Some transsexuals situate themselves on the left, and do their political work from this perspective. Others are moderate, or deeply conservative politically. I want to say that, if we accept transsexuality in and of itself, then we don't need to make it conditional on a particular political agenda.

So I hope it is clear, then, how the question posed to me contains all kinds of assumptions that I do not accept. And so one of the things I hope to do is to encourage people to be deeply critical of the kinds of information and knowledge available on transsexuals, perhaps especially the knowledge advocated by "transgendered" people. In practical terms, this means reading more than Leslie Feinberg, Riki Ann Wilchins, Kate Bornstein, or Judith Butler.

What is the relationship between queer politics and transsexuals?

In English-speaking contexts, it is now generally assumed that there is a relationship, affinity, and even "natural" coalition among transsexuals and a "broader" lesbian and gay community. This can be witnessed most notably in the names of organizations, which often follow the model LGBT – lesbian, gay, bisexual and transgender. While this is certainly one model that is available, it is not the only way of thinking about this relationship. In my empirical research on the history of transsexual artists here in Québec, for example, the women I interviewed told me that they worked and socialized in heterosexual establishments. They had virtually no affiliation to or identification with a lesbian/gay milieu. Yet, interestingly, one rarely hears this perspective articulated. This raises the important issue of what sociologists call *generalizability*: can one take information from a particular sample of people interviewed, and be confident that it can be extended to the population more broadly? The question I am raising here is that much of the information and research about transsexuals is produced by people who advocate an alignment with queer communities. Yet this political program is disconnected from the viewpoints and realities of many transsexual people. So while people may commonly assume that there is some kind of affinity between transsexuals and queers, I do not see this to be so. For me, transsexual worlds are primarily those of the street, of prostitutes, of drugs. So, in terms of language, culture, community, and politics, I believe that transsexuals are much more closely aligned to prostitutes, migrants, people without identity papers, the poor, drug users and prisoners, than with queer activists.

What role can research play in improving the lives of transsexuals?

This is an important question. If we examine the history of much of the research on transsexuals, it is necessary to be quite critical and skeptical of the effects of this research. There exist all kinds of studies and theories which invoke transsexuals to make a broader point about sex/gender relations. Examples of such research can be found in the discipline of sociology, but also in history, criminology, law, political science and women's studies. Yet in most of these studies, transsexuals are positioned exclusively as objects of an investigation. The research question is one determined by a university-based researcher with little or no knowledge of the needs of transsexuals. And so what happens, in the long run, is that the knowledge produced has little relevance for the actual people about whom one is speaking. The knowledge satisfies the requirements of the university – publications and conference papers – but it remains disconnected from everyday people and their problems. Now, this general situation provides good evidence of the need to be critical of research on transsexuals in general.

Yet if research can have a function that is objectivist, that reduces transsexuals to a mere pawn of academic knowledge, it can also play an important part in transforming social relations in which transsexuals are marginalized. Solid empirical documentation of the problems that transsexuals experience can inform the development of social policy, law, and the delivery of social service programs. Moreover, if transsexuals find themselves shut out and excluded from the everyday world and its institutions, then a process of conducting research which gives voice to transsexuals themselves – which allows them to provide *their* analysis of the problems, issues and political priorities – can help facilitate a broader process in which transsexuals enter the institutional world. Such an accomplishment cannot be underestimated. So to return explicitly to the question posed, research can play a fundamental role in improving the lives of transsexuals. But not any kind of research will do: there is a need for research which involves transsexuals themselves in a process of knowledge production. And to go back to some of the issues I outlined earlier about different networks of transsexual people, it is important to evaluate critically the kinds of information that is produced on and even *by* transsexuals. Is the knowledge relevant to the worlds and lives of immigrant prostitutes, or of prisoners? Or does it reflect a more limited scope? Was the study conducted only in English, even though many participants did not have English as a mother tongue? Does the research begin with questions related to poverty, and integrate transsexuality within this framework? Or does the research put the accent on gender identity? These are some of the questions that a critical activist transsexual agenda must ask.

22

Gender and heterosexism in rock-and-roll

Interview with Mimi Schippers

TULANE UNIVERSITY, LOUISIANA

Mimi Schippers is Associate Professor of Sociology and Women's Studies at Tulane University. Her research focuses on how gender and sexual inequalities are produced, sustained, and challenged through face-to-face interaction and cultural practice. She is author of the book, *Rockin' Out of Box:Gender Maneuvering in Alternative Hard Rock* (Rutgers University Press, 2002).

What do you mean by the heterosexism of mainstream rock and roll culture?

When I talk about the heterosexism of mainstream rock and roll culture, I'm not talking about the attitudes of individuals who play or listen to rock. While there are, no doubt, individuals who are heterosexist in rock, I'm more interested in how rock culture encourages people to assume and go along with heterosexism even if they don't hold negative beliefs or attitudes towards queer sexuality or queer people.

Rock culture is not only produced through the lyrical and video content of rock music; it also exists in the way musicians and fans talk about and do rock culture. For instance, picture the quintessential rock musician. My guess is, you pictured a man. This is not only because the majority of rock musicians have been men; it is also because rock culture defines the ideal rock musician as masculine. Now imagine something about this quintessential rock musician's sexuality. Does the word "groupie" come to mind? Now picture the groupie. Why did you picture a woman? All of the lyrical, video, and interview content of rock culture compels you to think that groupies are women. In other words, the erotic complement to the masculine rock musician is the female groupie. Isn't "getting chicks" what being a rock musician is all about? Thus, the taken-for-granted relationship between the rock musician and the groupie, as a key part of rock culture, is a heterosexual relationship.

In contrast to the groupie, the *real fan* of rock is not interested in the sexual availability of the rock musician, but in the music and the musical competence of rock musicians. Moreover, real fans aspire to *be* the rock musician, not *do* the rock musician. And one of the main perks to being a rock musician, as defined through rock culture, is access to women. Groupies are defined as those who musicians fuck and real fans are defined as those who listen to and aspire to play the music so they too can fuck groupies. In other words, those who have sex with musicians are not real fans and real fans don't have sex with musicians.

What we never see as a feature of rock culture is an eroticized relationship between men rock musicians and male fans. Also, we do not see women musicians fucking boy fans. In fact, a woman musician often becomes the object of desire for male fans, not the musician to be envied for her musical abilities or for her access to sex with fans. Even more telling, a woman who is a real fan quickly loses that status if she expresses any erotic desire for musicians or pursues a sexual relationship with her favorite musician purely on the basis of his musician status. The prominence of the contrast between the groupie and the real fan in rock culture means that homoeroticism is viewed as outside rock culture. The erotic in rock music is the relationship between the male musician and the female groupie, and in this way rock reproduces heterosexuality as a social institution. In this way, rock culture reflects and reproduces heterosexuality as natural, normal, and inevitable, even if individuals are not heterosexual or are not homophobic.

In what ways do alternative rockers aim to challenge this heterosexist order?

Alternative hard rockers work together to redefine the meaning of being a musician, groupie, and fan, and by doing so, challenge the heterosexual structure of rock culture. The main way in which they do this is by collapsing the distinction between groupie fans and real fans. Both women and men express their appreciation for the musical abilities of musicians and their sexual attraction to musicians. In fact, the competence of musicians is itself eroticized by women and men. When people in the subculture talk about their favorite musicians, women and men are acting like both groupie fans and real fans, as defined in mainstream rock culture. Once sexual attraction becomes part of the definition of a real fan, gender is no longer a criterion for drawing distinctions between kinds of fans. More importantly, however, men and women in the subculture eroticize all musicians, regardless of gender. In other words, there is not a consistent heterosexual or homosexual orientation to the expression of sexual desire by alternative hard rockers. Instead, the orientation of the desire shifts depending on the gender of the fan and the gender of the musician. Any individual might at one moment express his sexual attraction to a woman musician, but as the conversation shifts to a man, he might be as likely to express both musical appreciation for and sexual attraction to the male musician. *The eroticization of the relationship between musicians and fans is no longer limited to men musicians and women fans, but is open to everybody*. In this way, the relationship between the musician and rock fan is eroticized, but it is not always hetero-sexualized.

Alternative rock culture is viewed by some as gender bending while others see this culture as reproducing mainstream gender norms, including gender norms of sexuality. What did your research find?

The phrase "gender bending," especially in the context of rock music culture, most often refers to the way in which people express masculinity or femininity through their clothing or body comportment. I think this is one of the reasons people often see alternative hard rock as reproducing gender norms. Unlike the glam rockers of the eighties who wore make-up, big hair, and spandex, men in alternative hard rock look very masculine. No make up, no spandex, and though they wear their hair long, they do not use hair spray for extra volume.

Instead of "gender bending" in their embodied performance of masculinity, I found that the men disrupt gender, including gender norms for sexuality, in the way they act as rock musicians. Unlike glam rockers, alternative hard rock musicians do not talk about their sexual access to fans. That is simply not part of their understanding of what it means to be a rock musician.

While they look masculine, they do not establish a public, heterosexual identity by talking about fucking women. In fact, the musicians sometimes express erotic desire for men on stage. To the extent that masculinity, especially in rock culture, is defined as a hyper-heterosexuality, these guys definitely disrupt gender norms.

Further, many of the men in alternative hard rock express a political commitment to feminism. If we think of gender bending as more about practices and less about clothing, male rock musicians publicly expressing an interest and commitment to feminist sensibilities is certainly gender bending. In fact, I would argue that the combination of a very masculine appearance and a public expression of both homoerotic desire and a commitment to feminism challenge gender norms far more than the glam rockers' spandex, make-up, and big hair.

I found that women in alternative hard rock were also gender benders. They do not so much reject femininity as they reject the feminine roles of mainstream rock. Alternative rock women may dress in conventionally feminine ways, but they are rocking as hard and harder than the boys. So, the distinction between competent rock musician and sexy woman is collapsed. And remember, the fans themselves are eroticizing the boys and the girls, not so much for their physical attractiveness, but for their musical competence. So, what we have is very sexy women on stage, but instead of being reduced to sexual objects, we have musicians who are "hot" because of their competence as musicians *combined with* their presentation of a free-wheeling sexuality.

The public often thinks of the rock culture as sexually liberated, but is it?

I think that when people refer to rock culture as being sexually liberated, they are talking about the public promiscuity of rock musicians. In many ways, rock emerged as a rebellion against the dominant sexual norms of the 1950s that defined sexuality as private and limited to heterosexual, marital relationships. Rock made sexuality public, and the musician/groupie relationship certainly dislodges sexuality from marriage.

Real sexual liberation, I would argue, is the elimination of inequality on the basis of gender and sexuality. As I described earlier, though rock musicians wear their promiscuity like a badge and claim to be giving the finger to conventional sexual norms, they still celebrate a sexuality that reproduces sexism and heterosexism. No matter how often or how publicly the men in mainstream rock talk about the pleasure and power derived from fucking nameless, faceless women, they are reproducing a relationship between masculine and feminine sexuality that makes femininity inferior and homosexuality invisible. *In fact, rather than being sexually liberated, I would argue that mainstream rock culture is no less conventional than other aspects of mainstream culture.* And the claim that, because it is public and promiscuous, it is liberated and anti-establishment only masks the ways in which mainstream rock sexuality reproduces hegemonic gender and sexuality.

There is a stereotype of the alternative rock culture as sexually loose, nonconventional and experimental with regard to sexual practices. What did your research show?

Being sexually promiscuous and public about sex and desire is a central part of all rock culture. Alternative hard rock is rock culture, and therefore people in the subculture embrace a rebel stance toward conventional sexuality. However, as with "gender bending," they turn the sexual rebelliousness of mainstream rock on its head. Rather than constructing a public, hyper-heterosexuality through lyrics, videos, and interviews, alternative hard rockers make sexuality public by embracing an overtly political stance against homophobia and heterosexism. Musicians and fans never miss an opportunity, whether on stage, in an interview, or in casual conversations to chastise any form of gay bashing. This is, one feature of the subculture, along with publicly rejecting racism and sexism, that alternative hard rockers use to define their subcultural boundaries and distance themselves from mainstream rock.

Interestingly, none of the alternative hard rockers I interviewed or with whom I spent time talked about sexuality outside of the context of rejecting sexism and heterosexism. Unlike mainstream rockers who constantly talk about their own sexual exploits, alternative hard rockers avoid talking about their own sexualities and sexual experiences. In the clubs or in interviews, talk about sexuality is not about the backstage groupie thing; it is about the social problems of heterosexism and homophobia.

Though they don't talk about it, alternative hard rock shows are saturated with sexuality. Kissing, grinding, simulated sexual acts are all part of the rock experience on and off the stage, and importantly, there is both inter-gender and intra-gender erotic contact. Fans talk about not only wanting to fuck particular musicians across and within gender, but also a desire to fuck the music itself. In other words, *the rock show is highly eroticized, but the sexuality is never straightforwardly hetero or homo, but is more diffuse and fluid*. The overt and public heterosexism and sexism of mainstream rock is replaced with a public queer sexuality. And the sexuality of alternative hard rock is not found in the lyrics, video content, or interviews with musicians as it is in mainstream rock. It's found in the club, in the practices of people as they do rock music. That is not to say that musicians and fans don't have sex with each other; it is to say that *talking about it as a way to do rock culture* is not part of this scene. In other words, sexuality is less a backstage phenomenon between men musicians and women fans, and more an eroticization of the rock club by everybody through the on-stage performance of musicians and the reactions of the audience.

Are there "out" lesbian and gay rockers, and, if so, how are they received in this culture?

This is one of the more interesting findings in my research. Despite being overtly anti-homophobic and engaging in quite a bit of homo-erotic activity at the rock show, not one alternative hard rocker that I interviewed or spent time with publicly identifies as gay or lesbian. For the most part, gay men and lesbians are defined as people outside of the subculture who are deserving of all the rights and privileges that come with heterosexuality. This was one way in which the subculture does reproduce hegemonic sexuality and is heterosexist. *By defining gay men and lesbians as people outside the subculture, alternative hard rockers establish an unspoken heterosexuality for those in the subculture.* Gay men and lesbians, in other words, are the "Other," not "Us."

This illustrates how heterosexism is not only maintained by individual homophobic attitudes or actions. Alternative hard rockers are explicitly anti-homophobic and engage in quite a bit of homo-erotic behavior. However, they assume a sense of subcultural boundaries that leaves gays and lesbians on the outside.

These findings also point to the importance of distinguishing between talk and practices. If I had distributed a survey, I am certain that the people in this subculture would have checked a box for sexual orientation, and most of them would have chosen "heterosexual." If I had only talked with the people in this subculture, I never would have recognized "queer" forms of sexual rebellion in alternative hard rock. In the club, categories of sexual identity seem to fade into the background; sexual desire and contact become more fluid, opening space for inter- and intra-gender eroticism. Further, if I had distributed a survey to identify the sexual attitudes of alternative hard rockers, I would have concluded that there are no negative attitudes toward homosexuality, and thus that the subculture is not heterosexist. However, by listening to how alternative hard rockers talked about homosexuals as outsiders, I could identify an aspect of heterosexism that is not about individual attitudes.

I wonder if you could say a little about the sexual meanings in the music and lyrics of alternative rock.

I didn't do an in-depth analysis of the lyrics in alternative hard rock because I was more interested in the lived cultural experiences of rockers. However, I can say that there really isn't a whole lot of sex in the lyrics of alternative hard rock. In fact, some of the men I interviewed said that they specifically avoid explicit sexual content because, as men, it's difficult to not come across as just a typical rock guy.

I would say, then, without having done a content analysis of lyrics, that alternative hard rockers challenge conventional heterosexual and gender norms *in the context of rock music culture* by writing songs about things other than sex and relationships. By not including straightforward sexual content in their lyrics, they avoid situating themselves in romantic or sexual relationships. In a subculture where heterosexuality is presumed, not singing about sex and relationships is one way to avoid both heterosexism and sexism.

23

Adolescent girls' sexuality

The more it changes, the more it stays the same

Deborah L. Tolman

SAN FRANCISCO STATE UNIVERSITY

Army girls gone wild!
Lesbian girls gone wild!
Girls gone wild in Dallas!
Barely legal sorority girls gone wild!
Korean Girls gone wild!
Anime girls gone wild!

Results of a Google search on girls and sexuality (March 8, 2010)

At the last half of the twentieth century, not long after adolescence itself was invented, adolescent girls' sexuality was under heavy surveillance, and the root source of plenty of panic. An epidemic of teen pregnancy among African-American girls (not true); an epidemic of White middle-class girls giving boys oral sex in empty houses, in hallways and under table cloths (not true); an epidemic of teens rejecting relationships in favor of hooking up (not true). I suggest that one of the reasons these ostensible "epidemics" are grabbed, spun (and in essence created) by the media into the latest catastrophe is that they harbor possibilities of adolescent girls' sexual desire.

Good girls and bad girls

As we enter the next decade of the twenty-first century, the tightrope that girls walk separating good girls from bad has not been taken down but has in fact gotten tighter (Valenti 2008). Adolescent girls' sexuality is a fulcrum of contradictions: Girls want relationships, boys want sex, but everybody is just hooking up – no strings attached. "Virgins" can be reborn, but "sluts" can never shake the moniker that they still get. To be popular, with girls and with boys, girls are told to wear less and less to be more and more sexy, but girls who dress in skimpy clothes look like prostitutes. Girls are sexually aggressive, no longer sexual objects, but the coolest shirts are stamped with phrases like "Rub These for Luck" and "Who Needs Brains When You Have These?" "Sexting" is the latest supposed craze to incite panic among parents – and it's girls sending naked pictures of themselves to boys, never the other way around – but girls who "sext" are pathetic, not normal.

So what is it? Are girls now just as into sex, just as sexually assertive as boys or does the double standard still rule? Do girls (finally) just want to have fun? While the media saturates us with the fantasy or fear that deep down, girls are into being like porn stars, they are still as vulnerable as ever to being labeled and scorned for evidencing real sexual feelings and more than ever under pressure to appear – but not to actually be – sex kittens. Adolescent girls' sexuality is still not their own. And the landscape of what is normal sexuality for teenage girls, what "everyone" does or feels, is more confusing than ever.

The fundamental organizing principle of girls' sexuality remains firmly in place: if girls want to be considered good, nice or even normal, adolescent girls are not (really) supposed to have sexual feelings of their own. And there is much inequity for girls embedded in this division of teen girls into "good" and "bad." Stereotypes about African-American girls being hypersexual, Asian-American girls unlocking secret doors to male pleasure, Latina girls being hot, hot, hot make it very difficult (if they are middle-class or elite) and virtually impossible (if they are working-class or poor) for girls of color even to get on the "good girl" pedestal, and they bear the constant risk of being knocked off (American Psychological Association 2007).

Girls' sexuality development

This contradiction continues to obscure what is normal for girls' sexuality and its development. In fact, we know very little about how sexuality develops in adolescence. We do know that as the female body matures, sex hormones are released (Halpern et al. 1993). In addition to sexual development – i.e. getting breasts, hips, pubic and armpit hair – it is, on average, normative for girls to start to have sexual feelings in early adolescence. The new twist is that, as they go from early to middle to late adolescence, what they are actually supposed to do is *to seem to have them* – to "perform" sexual assertiveness, and not so much for their own curiosity or satisfaction, but as especially "good" objects of others' sexual desire. In other words they incite desire rather than express it.

The irony is that in fact, most girls do experience sexual feelings in their own bodies – embodied sexual desire. These feelings may surface when a girl sees someone to whom she is attracted or while she is kissing someone she loves – or not. Learning how to become a sexual person – what sexual desire feels like, how to think about making decisions about sex, who is sexually attractive – is a normative part of adolescent development for both girls and boys. This process, called sexual socialization, includes learning to find the "right" people desirable, the contexts in which it is "appropriate" – or not – to have or express sexual feelings, and what are acceptable "sexual scripts." These norms are conveyed by family, by peers, and by media. Girls continue to be sexually socialized into being sexy rather than being sexual, which results in girls and women learning not only that they are the object of another's desire, that they are to be looked at, but that they also come to experience their own bodies in this fashion. An object has no feelings of her own. This message stands in stark contrast to other domains of young women's lives, where they learn that they can be and do "anything," producing yet another confusing contradiction anchoring female adolescence.

Girls' sexual desire and the double standard

Given the escalation of the overt and in-your-face presence of sexuality in our social landscape, what's the big deal? Why is even the possibility that girls might have and act on their own sexual feelings such a problem? In fact, by the age of 19, the majority of girls have had sexual intercourse, more than half of girls have performed oral sex, and an increasing percentage have had anal sex (Advocates for Youth 2010). Some of these sexual encounters were protected, some of them were coerced; the little we know about young women's experiences of their own sexuality suggests that most of these encounters were not about young women's sexual desire or their sexual pleasure (Fine and McClelland 2007; Levy 2005; Tolman 2002, 2010). Why isn't *this* the problem?

Even as demands on teenage girls to be sexy have intensified and the sexualization of younger girls is now standard fare (APA 2007), young women's sexual desire is still not considered an anchor of young women's sexuality; dressed in heels, thongs and short skirts, in the end, it is desire for relationships that is (still) what girls are "supposed" to have (Bogle 2008). In fact, in order to keep boys – who are said to have uncontrollable sexual urges for which they cannot be held accountable – in check, the suppression of girls' sexual desire is required. If girls had or acted on their sexual feelings, the entire system would be in chaos – or so the panic goes. The norms and beliefs that sustain this conception, this construction of what normal and appropriate male and female sexuality are in adolescence, are institutionalized by the double standard. Without understanding or acceptance that girls too have and are entitled to sexual feelings, the double standard has not and will not budge. The interplay between these ideas is mutually reconstituting and reinforcing.

Resisting the double standard: sexual subjectivity

The good news is that in recent years, there has been some important and potent resistance to these constraining and unfair conceptions and norms. And some teenage girls refuse to be controlled by the regulating image of "the slut." That is, some girls claim their entitlement to their own sexual feelings, whatever they are. While few and far between, these resistant girls offer the outline of potential alternative stories of how young women might claim their own sexuality, and how social norms may be shifted. They are on the Web, writing zines, launching protests against being sexualized and objectified, creating communities where they can rant against this injustice, talk about how denying desire diminishes sexual and reproductive health, and gain courage and strength from knowing they are not alone. In unprecedented ways, teenage girls can take action not only in their personal relationships but in changing the "way things are." Bucking the system is hard work, and potentially socially and materially costly for many girls. But they have shown us that it can be done. They enact what researchers call "sexual subjectivity."

The concept of "sexual subjectivity" has recently been developed in relation to adolescent women's sexuality and its development (Horne and Zimmer-Gembeck 2006; Tolman 2002). Sexual subjectivity means having a sense of oneself as a sexual person who is entitled to have sexual feelings and to make active decisions about sexual behavior. It is the opposite of "it just happened," which is how many adolescent girls describe their sexual experiences, and has been identified as one of the only "stories" girls can tell about their sexual behavior (Tolman 2002). The phrase "It just happened" is passive rather than active; it literally has no people in it, no one who is responsible or accountable. Being a sexual subject is the opposite of being a sexual object – rather than solely being the target of someone else's desire, a sexual subject has agency, that is, she has her own desire as a compass in actively negotiating her sexuality. Sexual subjectivity offers an alternative to, and denaturalizes the idea that it is normal for girls not to be only sexy but also to acknowledge and be acknowledged as legitimately sexual beings. This dissociation from one's sexual feelings remains a key part of how young women are socialized into their sexuality. Resisting this message is hard to do, but some girls do in fact do so. These girls have a sense of entitlement to their sexuality and also an awareness of the consequences of being a girl who has and acts on her sexual desire. These girls have figured out that if they do not let being labeled a "slut" affect them – that if they reject it as a viable way to think about girls' sexuality – the label will lose its power over them, at least psychologically. These girls may have a hard road to plow socially, but the resilience that can come with this choice can also enable these young women to lead the charge to resist dividing girls into good and bad, the very heart of what keeps desire so dangerous.

Another tension that is developing is around sexual identity or orientation. The "good girl" is assumed to be straight – not lesbian, bisexual or not sure – if she is attracted to women. The fact that desiring girls is another "violation" is no accident. Heteronormativity – becoming a *heterosexual* person – has been considered what is normal and right. It is depicted on television as "the way things are" between young men and women, with a clear script for how everyone is supposed to behave (Kim et al. 2007). Many young women are rejecting this belief and claiming sexual identities that are not heterosexual, including having no label at all. Recently, both research and social changes have shown that having and acting on same-sex sexual desires is not uncommon for anyone, and for some people is the organizing principle of their sexuality (Russell 2005). Sexual fluidity – shifts and changes in whom women are sexually attracted to and/or with whom they have sexual experiences – has been documented in the last decade as a feature of female sexuality (Diamond 2009).

Wild girls?

The latest and most confusing notion about young women's sexuality appears constantly in the media, which is that all young women and teenage girls are sexually aggressive and want to go out and get sex just like guys do (Levy 2005; Zurbriggen and Roberts, in press). This portrayal – and what is wrong with it – is best exemplified in the wildly successful *Girls Gone Wild* franchise. Primarily on location at spring break from college extravaganzas on beaches, this television series has created a spectacle of real young women performing male sexual fantasies – kissing other girls, having a threesome, masturbating for the camera, making it seem that young women are doing what they really want to do. In fact, young women will often say they want to bare it all and do it all, but a contradictory, ironic and very problematic slippage has actually occurred.

It is not an accident that virtually all of these young women are drunk when they take the dare to engage in a variety of sexual behaviors and exhibition of themselves. Many feel guilt and regret afterwards; virtually none of them describe these experiences as pleasurable or about their own sexual desire. It is about the desire to look and be seen as sexy. This is a desire that has been stirred, teased and aroused by the recent intensification of using sex – and sexualized girls' and women's bodies – to sell products. In fact, more than ever, sex has become something to give, to get, to trade and less about expressing emotions, a sense of connection to another person, or an embodied experience. It is not cool to want relationships – even when teenage girls (and boys) actually do. Perhaps this notion that relationships are toxic, risky or to be avoided is an unintended consequence of abstinence-until-marriage sex education, or the sensationalism of celebrity break-ups and heartbreaks which make relationships seem not worth the costs. Relationships require two authentic and complete people, which sexual objectification makes difficult. Constant exposure to images of girls and women who are portrayed only as sex objects is taking its toll on young women's sexuality development (Tolman 2010).

Reinforcing girls' sexual well-being

Why is it that the more things seem to change, the more they in fact stay the same? Having listened to many teen girls and also boys talk about their experiences with sexuality and relationships, I can hear it loud and clear. Teen boys are under pressure to embrace and "perform" ideas about masculinity that include being dominant *over* (and especially not dominated *by*) girls, wanting and trying to "get" sex (whether they actually want to or not) and showing that they are not gay (Tolman et al. 2003; Pascoe 2007). Girls are still split into two groups by adults, peers, the media, and social institutions into good and bad. This division is predicated on sexual restraint of themselves and of boys and being successful but being feminine at the same time. While there is a large and growing movement to demand and secure sexual rights for LGBT people (and teens), there is no social movement for girls' sexual rights – the right to be a sexual person, to have resources to make safe, healthy and fulfilling decisions, and to be safe from violence. Danger still trumps pleasure for women and girls (Vance 1994). Interestingly, in developing countries, such demands have taken hold, fueled by community groups and alliances of girls with others in their communities to demand these rights (Tolman and Costa 2010). In the United States, we can learn from the successes that have been achieved to begin to change how we think, talk about and thus experience and negotiate adolescent girls' sexuality.

Rather than focusing on risk reduction, we can start thinking about the development of sexual well-being as a part of our humanity that we do, can and should begin to develop in adolescence and then foster across our lifetimes. Sexual well-being includes: sexual and reproductive health (and access to required resources); comfort with one's own body and emotions; pursuing one's desires (barring harm to others); and being aware of and having the freedom to act (without threat of violence, material or social consequences) upon our sexual desires. Sexual well-being also includes the ability to identify risk, to make choices that diminish risk when possible, and to feel comfortable, happy and empowered in one's own body. The idea that all girls have a right to sexual well-being is predicated in part on sexual subjectivity, on resisting a system of dividing girls into categories of good and bad and pitting them against one another, and on recognizing, resisting and reframing the ongoing gender inequities that still characterize young people's sexual lives. Tackling demands for masculinity in boys that have harmful consequences for girls as well, refusing to tolerate homophobia, and enabling young women to be comfortable with their own sexual feelings, will be part of the task of articulating and securing sexual rights for teenage girls.

References

Advocates for Youth, accessed March 8, 2010. www.advocatesforyouth.org/index.php?option=com_cont ent& task = view& id = 30& Itemid = 59.

American Psychological Association (APA). 2007. *Task force on sexualization of girls report*. Washington, DC: APA.

Bogle, K. (2008). *Hooking up: Sex, dating and relationships on campus*. New York: New York University Press.

Diamond, L. (2009). *Sexual fluidity: Understanding women's love and desire*. Cambridge, MA. Harvard University Press.

Fine, M. and McClelland, S. (2007). "The politics of teen women's sexuality: Public policy and the adolescent female body." *Emory Law Journal*, pp. 993–1038.

Halpern, C., Udry, J., and Suchindran, C. (1997). "Testosterone predicts initiation of coitus in adolescent females." *Psychosomatic Medicine*, 59(2), 161–71.

Horne, S., and Zimmer-Gembeck, M. (2006). "The female sexual subjectivity inventory: Development and validation of a multidimensional instrument for late adolescents and emerging adults." *Psychology of Women Quarterly*, 30(2), 125–38.

Kim, J., Sorsoli, C., Collins, K., Zylbergold, B., Schooler, D., and Tolman, D. (2007). "From sex to sexuality: Exposing the heterosexual script on primetime network television." *Journal of Sex Research*, 44 (2), 145–57.

Levy, A. (2005). *Female chauvinist pigs: Women and the rise of raunch culture.* New York: Free Press.

Pascoe, C. J. (2007). *Dude, you're a fag: Masculinity and sexuality in high school.* Berkeley: University of California Press.

Russell, S. (2005). "Introduction to positive perspectives on adolescent sexuality: Part 2." *Sexuality Research and Social Policy: A Journal of the NSRC*, 2(4): 1–3.

Tolman, D. (2002). *Dilemmas of desire: Teenage girls talk about sexuality.* Cambridge, MA: Harvard University Press.

—— (2010). "It's bad for all of us: The impact of the sexualization of girls on boys', women's and men's sexuality." In E. Zurbriggen and T. A. Roberts (Eds), *The sexualization of girls and girlhood.* New York: Oxford University Press.

Tolman, D. and Costa, S. (2010). "Sexual rights for young women: Lessons from developing countries." In R. Parker and P. Aggleton (Eds), *Routledge Handbook of Sexuality, Health and Rights.* London: Routledge.

Tolman, D., Spencer, R., Rosen-Reynoso, M. and Porche, M. (2003). "Sowing the seeds of violence in heterosexual relationships: Early adolescents narrate compulsory heterosexuality." *Journal of Social Issues*, 59(1): 159–78.

Valenti, J. (2008). *He's a stud, she's a slut and 49 other things women should know about the double standard.* Seattle, WA: Seal Press.

Vance, C. (Ed.). (1994). *Pleasure and danger: Exploring women's sexuality.* New York: Routledge.

Zurbriggen, E. and Roberts, T. A. (in press). *The sexualization of girls and girlhood.* New York: Oxford University Press.

24

Not "straight," but still a "man"

Negotiating non-heterosexual masculinities in Beirut

Ghassan Moussawi

AMERICAN UNIVERSITY OF BEIRUT, LEBANON

Despite persisting cultural taboos and silence that covers the topics of sexuality and sexual non-conformity in the Arab Middle East, there has been a recent upsurge in studying sexualities and non-heterosexual identities in the Arab World (Whitaker, 2006; Khalaf and Gagnon, 2006; Habib, 2007). Still, there has been virtually no research on the ways that the normative status of heterosexuality creates gender and sexual divisions in the Arab World.

In this chapter, I will be looking at the ways that 10 self-identified non-heterosexual Lebanese men understand and negotiate their masculinities. I will argue that even though almost all the informants reject notions of "hegemonic masculinity," they also reject what they perceive as feminine men. I rely on my respondents' perceptions of what constitutes masculinity rather than imposing my own definition. Nonetheless, I assume that masculinity has varied meanings and that it is always defined in relation to a complex field consisting of varied ideas of femininities and masculinities. In addition, I assume that masculinity should be looked at as a performance; that is, masculinity "is more linked to something that one does, rather than what one is" (Whitehead and Barrett, 2001; 28).

It is important to note that even though all societies have ideas about gender, they do not all share a concept of masculinity. According to Connell, in many societies masculinity is understood as indicating a type of person rather than a type of behavior (Connell, 1995: 30). Based on my research, I believe that men and women in Lebanon are seen as quite different and are often regarded as polar character types. In addition, masculinity and manhood are highly regarded and often idealized in Lebanese culture.

Hegemonic masculinity in Lebanon assumes that homosexuality is the negation of masculinity. It is important then to look at the ways that these non-heterosexual men construct their masculinities. Homosexuality is officially criminalized and punishable by up to one year imprisonment. Thus, a public affirmation of a homosexual identity is quite risky and so I assume that these men would be more likely to highlight other aspects of their personal identity. Also, since being a man brings social privileges, I would expect these men to embrace masculinity and engage in what is considered normative masculine behaviour.

As I see it, any discussion of sexuality should consider gender to be central. In this regard, I argue that in Lebanon compulsory heterosexuality is enforced through enforcing dichotomous gender norms and roles. So, how do non-heterosexual men approach gender so as to affirm their masculinity?

For this research, I interviewed 10 men between 18 and 30 years old who were either currently enrolled in a university or had recently graduated. I chose this sample due to its convenience, since I relied on personal social networks and a snowball sampling, i.e. friends of those I interviewed. My interviews ranged between one and a half to two and a half hours and were conducted between September 2007 and April 2008. Almost all of them belonged to the middle or upper middle class of Beirut. Four out of the ten had their own apartments in Beirut and all were living in Beirut at the time except for one who had moved to the United States but was in Beirut for a vacation. Finally, almost all my interviews were conducted in both English and Arabic. Almost all of my respondents found it easier to talk in English when it came to discussing their sexuality. This preference is understandable since the Arabic "neutral" term for homosexuality, *mithli*, is rarely used.

I chose the term "non-heterosexual," rather than gay, because not all the men I interviewed identified as gay. The term non-heterosexual is an effort to keep in mind the complexity of sexuality. I also thought that using this term might capture a wider spectrum of individuals, including men who are not necessarily "out" or exclusively gay-identified. However, I do use the term "gay" in this essay when it is used by my informants. Finally, I am interested in the way that these men understand their sexuality and gender, rather than trying to impose categories of gay, straight or bisexual upon them.

Masculinities among non-heterosexual men in Beirut

In this section, I will consider the accounts these men give of their gender identity and ways that they conceive and define "Lebanese masculinities." I will attempt to look at how these men define and position their masculinities against the dominant notion which assumes that masculinity is an attribute of heterosexual men and which assumes that homosexuality is indicative of a feminine man. For example, in many television shows in Lebanon non-heterosexual characters are depicted and often mocked as extremely feminine, and overtly sexual.

Even though my informants had slightly differing conceptions of Lebanese masculinity, almost all of them claimed that Lebanese masculinity is characterized by the image of the *rijjal*; this is a man who is physically strong, well groomed, loud and proud of his sexual prowess. This type of man tells stories about women as sexual conquests and this is considered a way to demonstrate a sense of prideful manhood. These notions of masculinity were brought up on several occasions, especially when my respondents talked about strategies for "passing" as heterosexual in some situations.

Raed, a 23-year-old graphic designer, claimed that a Lebanese masculine man is always ready to pick a fight, highly interested in sports and cars, and publicly boasts about his sexual escapades with women. When it came to defining his own masculinity, Raed claimed that he does not believe in the concepts of masculinity and femininity, and that he does not think of himself in these terms. By contrast, Talal, a 22-year-old graduate student, asserted that a masculine man is someone who is responsible, "a man of his words" and someone that can handle stress and difficult situations. "Men are more adept at handling stress than women," he said. However, he also made it a point to distinguish between his own conception of masculinity and the "typical" Lebanese man. According to him, the stereotype of the Lebanese masculine man pretends to know everyone and everything, projects self-confidence, is very social, and goes out with many women. And, not least, "real" men are thought to be always strong, decisive and opinionated. Talal believed in a different notion of masculinity, one that emphasized respectability and responsibility. When asked whether he consider himself masculine, Talal claimed that indeed he is a man. "I am just naturally masculine. I don't do it on purpose." According to him, being masculine also means that he is not feminine. This is demonstrated when he further claims that "I don't walk or talk like a woman. Thus I am considered to be masculine."

Wael, a college student in his early twenties, made a distinction between two types of Lebanese men. One type of a masculine Lebanese man is muscular, has sharp facial features, and is always well groomed. The other type is considered "regular"; he keeps to himself in matters of the heart. Interestingly, Wael was somewhat critical of straight men. "Heterosexual Lebanese men," he asserted, "are very dull." This illustrates one of the ways by which non-heterosexual men can distance themselves from heterosexual masculinity by looking at it as more "rigid" than the masculinities of many non-heterosexual men. In this regard, Wael does not consider himself masculine in the rigid sense, but also he does not see himself as feminine.

Another young man I interviewed, Joe, also criticized straight Lebanese men as loud, too confident, and as making up stories about sexual adventures with women. "In Lebanon, masculinity is all about talking," he said. In particular, straight men boast about their sexual prowess in order to prove they are real men. Even though Joe claimed that he displays some feminine mannerisms, he insisted that he is not feminine. "I get angry when I see a feminine guy, I don't know why. I would never be with a feminine man," he added.

Khaled, who recently moved to New York City to pursue his graduate studies, described Lebanese masculine men as pride-oriented and a bit swaggering in the way they talk, walk and act. He told me that Lebanese men must always project strength, a sense of being decisive and dominant. Khaled was the only one who made a distinction between conceptions of masculinity in the Arab world and the "West." After having lived in NYC for a couple of months, Khaled felt more comfortable because he could express himself much more openly. In addition, he claimed that he is considered more masculine in NYC than he is in Beirut because in the latter city conceptions of appropriate masculinity are more rigid. In Lebanon, one has to know when to act "hyper-masculine" and when not to. This is less true in New York. Khaled does not consider himself masculine but also claimed that he doesn't really care about his gender presentation. He does think, however, that some people can tell he is gay by his body language.

Most of my interviewees shared similar notions of what were normative notions of masculinity in Lebanon. I found it interesting that when asked whether they consider themselves masculine, those who said no, also insisted that they are not feminine either (even though I didn't ask. Most define their masculinity in terms of not being "typically Lebanese," but also not being feminine. They reject both the extreme ideal of masculinity and the "shameful" status as a feminine man. The hegemonic Lebanese man was seen as unnatural and rigid and boring. However, almost all the men were equally critical of "feminine" men. This prompted me to probe deeper into the ways that these men viewed gender non-conformity and their strategies to distance themselves from it.

Perceptions of femininity and gender non-conformity

Almost all my informants considered themselves broadly masculine, if not hypermasculine. They also expressed a decidedly negative view of feminine men, even those who identified with the "gay" community. These men seemed to be trying to negotiate a type of masculinity that was neither stereotypical masculine nor feminine. I want to focus a bit more on the notion of gender non-conformity. I use the term "gender non-conformity" to refer to any mannerism, ways of talking, dressing or presenting oneself that does not necessarily conform to the gender ideals of a specific culture. In my interviews, gender non-conformity was often understood as men acting in a "feminine" way, but it also meant men departing from hegemonic norms of masculinity. In addition, extreme gender non-conformity is often understood in Beirut as indicating some form of sexual deviance. In a word, feminine men and masculine women are often perceived to be non-heterosexual. Interestingly enough, it was striking how most of my respondents embraced the conventional view that gender non-conformity expresses sexual non-conformity. Even though almost all of the men I interviewed claimed that they are gender non-conforming in their rejection of hegemonic masculinity, they expressed discomfort and even ridiculed feminine-acting men, including those who were gay-identified. The reasons stated for this discomfort was that these feminine men drew public attention to non-heterosexual men.

For instance, when I asked Tarek whether he considers himself to be masculine, he wondered whether I could tell he was gay. Tarek, like many other men relied on his masculine demeanour to pass as "straight." On more than one occasion, many of my informants ridiculed feminine gay men in Beirut. "It is funny how gay men make fun of other gays in the community," Tarek stated. "Everyone is a tante." The labelling of feminine acting men as *tante*, the French term for auntie, illustrates this point. *Tante* is used among many Lebanese to refer to non-heterosexual men who are both feminine acting and who are generally interested in gossip (as explained to me by one of the informants).

Tarek was quite uncomfortable with effeminate men and claimed that he believes gay men should not be feminine. "If you want to be a woman," he said, "then be one." According to him, a guy's mannerisms are quite important and he considered it quite central for a man, whether gay or straight, to maintain gender conformity. He added that he does not have any feminine gay friends and that all of his gay friends are "straight acting." "I wouldn't be comfortable with a guy who is very feminine, especially in ordinary places" (i.e. places that are not "gay friendly"). Tarek expressed discomfort in "being seen" with feminine acting men, in routine social situations. Being seen with feminine men might make people suspect that he is non-heterosexual. Even though he believes that most Lebanese society view people who are gender non-conforming to be non-heterosexual, he himself does not believe that.

Salim also ridiculed feminine gay men on more than one occasion during the interview. Even though he said he doesn't mind feminine men, he still made a point of saying that he isn't sexually or emotionally aroused by them. He repeatedly used *tante* in reference to feminine gay men. Salim brought up an interesting point when he said that feminine gay men, whom he referred to as "queens," do harm to the gay community in Lebanon. Interestingly, he drew a parallel between the way "feminine gay men" project a negative image of the gay community and the way "hypermasculine" men project a bad image of straight men. The harm is linked to the fact that they present a stereotypical image of a gay man as lacking valued "masculine traits." "They are not doing well for the community and for its public image as a whole," he said. It is important to keep in mind, that it is the performance of gender by men that is evaluated as appropriately masculine or inappropriately feminine.

Joe's approach to gender was interesting because of his perception of his own gender difference. At the outset, Joe expressed outrage at the closeted gay men and extremely flamboyant men. Yet, he was aware that he displays some feminine attributes, most apparent in the way he walks and the way he gestures with his hands. He related that men, even after having sex with them, have distanced themselves from him in public. They apparently don't want to be seen with him because of his gender non-conforming behavioural traits. He related the following to me:

> I will be walking with a man on the streets after having been with him for the night, and he will constantly tell me how to act and how not to act. For example, he would give me comments on the way I move and walk by telling me to stop moving my hands or stop

walking the way I do. So what if I moved a little bit feminine? Some men also walk in front of me or behind me, and refuse to walk next to me on the streets.

Joe added that even his sister used to get angry because of his effeminate mannerisms when, for example, they went out to nightclubs. At the same time, Joe said that even though he does not consider himself to be hegemonically masculine, he does not see himself as feminine either. In fact, he rejects feminine men. "Even though I am gay, I get pissed off and angry when I see a feminine guy. I don't know why. I just don't want to be with a feminine guy." When I inquired more into his perception of feminine men, Joe claimed that these are men who wear makeup and refer to each other in the feminine of *kifik*, for example ("How are you?" in Arabic). He believes that some people view him as gay not because he is feminine but because he is gentle (*na'im*). Still, even some of his fellow students at the university make fun of him and call him the "biggest fag" because of his gender non-conformity. He says that it never bothers him.

Almost all the men I interviewed agreed that there exists discrimination against feminine acting men in Beirut. Karim claimed that there is a lot of discrimination against feminine men even within the gay community. "They are not very welcomed," he said, "because, if you're seen with someone who is feminine, you are directly associated with or thought of as gay. It makes many people uncomfortable." In fact, Karim thought that things are getting worse for feminine men in Beirut because today men are obsessed with their body image, and with being muscular and fit. "Part of it is reaffirming their masculinity. The image is very important. There's an obsession with being fit and looking good and being viewed as 'ordinary' (heterosexual)." Karim acknowledged that he too was once quite uncomfortable with feminine gay men, but that this attitude changed. "If I want people to accept me for who I am then I have to accept the other guys for who they are."

Raed and Wael also talked about how feminine men are excluded in the gay community. Wael terms this exclusion "sissyphobia." Of course it's even worse in the broader culture. Wael recalled being ridiculed at school for not being "typically" masculine. He was called names in high school, such as *tobje* ("fag"), even though he had not thought of himself as gay or non-heterosexual at that time. Finally, and most strikingly, Talal seemed to summarise the views of many of those I interviewed:

> In Lebanon, if you're gay, you're no longer considered a man. It is the closed-minded and illiterate people who think that. You're not considered a man, even if you are very masculine, as long as you are gay. It doesn't matter. There might be some exceptions, but generally this is the rule. If you're straight and feminine, you also have a problem.

Talal's fear of being viewed as "less of a man" is felt as real and widely shared by my respondents. Talal has known a few gay-identified feminine men, but his fear has meant that he is not close to them. "I don't mind them, but I don't understand why do they have to be so obvious or why they act that way. I am sure they're not doing it on purpose, but I still don't understand why." Despite knowing how Lebanese culture excludes feminine men, Talal himself avoids hanging out with them in public. When I asked him to describe a feminine guy, he said that it was a man who "acts like a woman, uses hand gestures, and body language, [and] is interested in makeup and shopping." So anxious is Talal of being exposed and rejected as not straight that he spoke of feeling very self-conscious when he is out in public. The fear of being "found out" as gay may be linked to the fact that he has only quite recently acknowledged his non-heterosexuality. He feels that straight people will respect him less if they found out. Khaled was the only one who claimed that he doesn't mind feminine-acting men. "I completely understand where they're coming from. They are very courageous. They have a lot of guts to do what their instincts tell them to do." Still, Khaled also used the derogatory term *tante* to refer to feminine-acting men.

Homophobia and anti-femininity

As I've argued, maintaining a masculine demeanour was deemed important by almost all of my respondents. In part, gender conformity concealed non-heterosexuality and conferred social privileges on these men. But a culture of masculinity and heterosexuality in Beirut was also sustained by a culture of homophobia. The anthropologist Sofian Merabet (2004) documented the way homophobia works in Beirut. For example, as non-heterosexual men began to gain a certain visibility, the police intervened by closing down businesses friendly to non-heterosexuals. Also, public homophobic behaviour almost always targets "overtly feminine men." Such homo-phobic behaviour is tolerated in part because feminine men are considered undesirable by both heterosexual and non-heterosexual individuals.

Recently, the controversial status of feminine men among Beirut's non-heterosexual com-munity surfaced online. The controversy revolved around one of the few gay-identified bear bars in Beirut ("bear" is a term used to refer to hairy and masculine men in the gay commu-nity.) A blog post in the Gay Middle East Blog titled "Beirut's Anti-Gay Gay Bar," described an incident where a man was barred from entering the bar because of his feminine demeanour. According to the blog, the owner of the bar admitted to having instructed the bouncer to turn away "overtly feminine" men, presumably to safeguard the desired "bear ambiance" of the bar (GayMiddleEastBlog, 2006). The author of the blog commented: "I will no longer frequent [this bar]. It's reprehensible for some gay men to reject others based on vague notions of mas-culinity. As gay men, we are all rejected by the larger society, and further segregation serves no positive purpose."

The sense of outrage that the author expresses is not necessarily widely shared by other men in the community. From my interviews, it is clear that feminine gay men have been routinely stigmatized and rejected within this small, fragmented "community," and by the larger Lebanese society. It is these feminine men, whatever their sexuality, that perhaps suffer the most in a culture that enforces a seamless norm of hegemonic masculinity and heterosexuality.

Conclusion

I attempted to look at how 10 non-heterosexual men define their own masculinity. As we've seen, these men resisted being associated with what they perceived as the stereotypical image of Lebanese masculinity. They also resisted being perceived as "feminine." All of the informants spoke of multiple masculinities and defined their own masculinity as neither a version of hegemonic masculinity nor male femininity.

By way of a conclusion, I want to briefly return to the link between sexuality and gender. Even though all of the men I interviewed embraced their same-sex desires or claimed that they seek other men for emotional and sexual relations, a majority resisted defining themselves as "gay." For most of my respondents, the label "gay" was associated with having one's sexual identity as a core or defining identity. Although most of these men acknowledged that their sexuality was central to them, they refused to primarily define themselves as gay. This can be explained by the fact that in Lebanon there is currently no local positive conception of a gay identity. At the same time, as previously mentioned, the lack of commonly used neutral Arabic terms that refer to both heterosexual and non-heterosexual identities makes it harder for these men to talk about their sexuality.

However, it is interesting that most of my informants did not hesitate to refer to other non-heterosexuals in the community as "gay." My sense is that many of these men used this term because of its positive resonance, but we should not assume that its meaning is the same as in an American context. In order to comprehend the meanings people attribute to gender and sexuality the specific cultural contexts and local understandings must be taken into account.

Finally, throughout my interviews it was apparent that the performance of gender-conforming behavior was a central way in which the institutionalization of heterosexuality functions at the level of everyday life. Almost all of my informants were concerned with being regarded as "real men." I would argue that in projecting a conventional masculine self my respondents were also enforcing a norm of "compulsory heterosexuality." The latter is sustained not only by enforcing a norm of heterosexuality but by not tolerating gender non-conformity. By distancing themselves from the feminine man, these men were reinforcing the institution of heterosexuality. As long as heterosexuality is enforced though "the policing and shaming of gender and the damning of gay men as failed men and lesbians as not proper women," men and women will tend to reject the fluid and variable possibilities of gender (Jackson, 1999: 175).

References

Connell, R. W. 1995. *Masculinities*. London: Allen and Unwin.

GayMiddleEastBlog. 2006. http://gaymiddleeast.blogspot.com/2006/04/beiruts-anti-gay-gay-bar.html, retrieved April 2006.

Habib, Samar. 2007. *Female Homosexuality in the Middle East: Histories and Representations*. New York and London: Routledge.

Jackson, Stevi. 1999. *Heterosexuality in Question*. London: Sage Publications.

Khalaf, Samir and Gagnon, John (Eds). 2006. *Sexuality in the Arab World*. London: Saqi Books.

Merabet, Sofian. 2004. "Disavowed Homosexualities in Beirut". *Middle East Report* 23: Spring.

Whitaker, Brian. 2006. *Unspeakable Love: Gay and Lesbian Life in the Middle East*. London: Saqi Books.

Whitehead, Stephen. 2006. *Men and Masculinities*. New York: Routledge.

Whitehead, Stephen M. and Frank J. Barrett (Eds). 2001. *The Masculinities Reader*. Cambridge: Polity Press.

25

How not to talk about Muslim women

Patriarchy, Islam and the sexual regulation of Pakistani women

Saadia Toor

CITY UNIVERSITY OF NEW YORK, STATEN ISLAND

In recent years, the status of the Muslim woman – often coded in the image of a veiled female figure – has become a major preoccupation of the mainstream media in the West, where it is framed as an issue of "Islam and gender." Regardless of whether the tone of the commentary is critical or sympathetic, the organizing logic is the same – that something called "Islam" exists and that it can explain all aspects of Muslim society. Note that the terms – "Islam," "Muslim society," "Muslim culture," etc. – circulating in this discourse are all in the singular, implying that there is one essential, monolithic thing called "Islam" which remains consistent across time and space, and that all Muslims are somehow essentially identical regardless of where they may come from geographically and culturally. The overwhelming conclusion of this discourse is that there is something uniquely sexist – even misogynist – about Islam, "the Muslim world," and thereby all Muslims, which in turn explains the low status of Muslim women.

The main thrust of this chapter is to show that this mainstream Western discourse on Islam is misleading insofar as it is premised on an essentialized and monolithic "Islam" emptied of history, diversity, complexity and dissent. I will show that, far from "unveiling" the insidious workings of an actually existing "thing" called "Islam," this discourse actually actively *constructs* it. Not only that, it does so in order to legitimize certain political projects. In other words, this discourse is deeply ideological.

In order to understand what I mean, let's turn first to the discourse and its history. In *Orientalism*, Edward Said (1978) argued that Western discourse on "the Orient" provided the ideological justification for European colonialism in Asia and in the "Islamic world" from the eighteenth century onwards. This justification included the idea that colonialism was, first and foremost, a "civilizing mission" rather than an exercise in the occupation of non-European lands and the exploitation of non-European peoples and their resources. It is also important to note that the concept of the "civilizing mission" came out of the ideology of liberalism which was on the ascendance in Europe at this time. Postcolonial scholars – particularly postcolonial feminists – extended this initial work on the ideological roots of European colonialism to emphasize the centrality of gender and sexuality to the colonial enterprise. Their scholarship has highlighted how non-Western women became cast in colonial discourse as victims of their oppressive culture(s) and tradition(s), in a way that allowed colonialism to emerge as their *savior*. The post-colonial feminist scholar Gayatri Spivak (1988) has captured this logic in her pithy reformulation of the colonial civilizing mission as "white men saving brown women from brown men."

Of course, white *women* also played an important role in the colonial enterprise. For example, many of the early British suffragettes were fervent supporters of imperialism and uncritically accepted their government's claims that the British imperial project was actually about protecting and furthering the rights of "native" women. This was paradoxical, given the fact that they were facing opposition from the same government with regard to their demands for the rights of British women. In fact, the discourse in Britain around the plight of native women served to undermine feminist claims domestically, since it allowed critics to argue that British women were much better off than women elsewhere in the world; therefore, they had no cause for complaint and no reason to demand greater rights. This support of imperialism in the name of native women's rights has come to be known as "imperial feminism."

A contemporary version of "imperial feminism" surfaced in the West in the immediate aftermath of 9/11, when George and Laura Bush – notoriously anti-feminist in their political and cultural agenda – invoked the very real plight of Afghan women under the Taliban to justify the attack on, and subsequent occupation of, Afghanistan. In this they were enthusiastically supported by well-known feminist organizations such as the Feminist Majority. The most familiar media image during this period became the *burqa*-clad Afghan (read: Muslim) woman; in fact the *burqa* itself became a symbol of Islam's attitude towards women.

Once more, white men – and women – were exhorted to save brown women from brown men. This was an ideological move designed to secure the consent of the American public for an unprecedented act of international aggression. Notably, after the initial rapturous accounts of newly liberated Afghan women shedding the *burqa*, wearing make-up and learning how to be beauticians, these women disappeared from the view of the American public.[1] So did the Revolutionary Association of the Women of Afghanistan (RAWA), an organization which had been ubiquitous in the American press during the key period before the attack on Afghanistan, and whose reputation as an authentic and fearless feminist organization was used to authorize the mainstream account of Afghan women's plight. After the occupation, however, RAWA was no longer useful for the United States' political agenda. In fact, it became downright *inconvenient*, since its bulletins make it clear that life for Afghan women not only did not improve under the new US-approved administration, but actually worsened.

What we had instead was an outpouring of "expert commentary" and "analysis" on women and Islam which argued that Afghan women's troubles under the Taliban were part of a broader problem of Islam's essential and unique misogyny. This is now an accepted part of popular Western discourse on Islam. One of the problems with this discourse, as Said (1981) argued in *Covering Islam*, is that it constructs a flattened and monolithic idea of Islam which is then used to explain the behavior of all Muslims regardless of their varied cultural, social and political contexts.

> "Islam" as it is used today seems to mean one simple thing but in fact is part fiction, part ideological label, part minimal designation of a religion called Islam. In no really significant way is there a direct correspondence between the "Islam" in common Western usage and the enormously varied life that goes on within the world of Islam, with its more than 800,000,000 people, its millions of square miles of territory principally in Africa and Asia, its dozens of societies, states, histories, geographies, cultures.

> *(Introduction, x)*

Said goes on to question the notion that this thing called "Islam" can explain complex behaviors, at the individual as well as the collective level:

> Is there such a thing as Islamic behavior? What connects Islam at the level of everyday life to Islam at the level of doctrine in the various Islamic societies? How really useful is "Islam" as a concept for understanding Morocco *and* Saudi Arabia *and* Syria *and* Indonesia?
>
> *(Said 1981: xv)*

Unfortunately, in the 30 years since Said penned his original critique of Orientalism, things have only gotten worse as far as the mainstream Western understanding of, and discourse on, Islam is concerned. Perhaps this is not surprising, given that Western – specifically US – political investment in parts of the world that are predominantly Muslim has also intensified during precisely this period. This neo-colonial project requires an ideological framework to legitimate it just as the earlier colonial project did. As before, this ideological discourse features a civilizing mission focused on the status of "native" women and on rescuing them from "their" men and "their" culture.

What are we talking about when we talk about "Islam"?

As the above quotes from Said indicate, there are serious problems with trying to use "Islam" to explain too much of the personal and social life of Muslims. In fact, any attempt to deploy the category in a meaningful or systematic way immediately reveals its fuzziness. When we use the term "Islam," do we mean the textual sources of Islamic tradition, namely the *Quran* and *Sunnah*? Do we mean the *shariah*, or system of Islamic jurisprudence, which is itself not a unitary thing? Do we mean the ways in which various political groups – and often the state – in Muslim societies deploy Islam? Or do we mean Islam as it is popularly understood and practiced, which changes every 50 miles or so?

These issues are not specific to Islam, obviously. Sociologically speaking, culture and religion are difficult, if not impossible, to separate in any context – even in the "secular" West. However, and ironically, Islam *does* pose a unique problem because of its decentralized nature. Unlike Christianity (and especially Catholicism) there is no single religious authority, and no institutionalized clerical hierarchy. Even Islamic law – the *shariah* that is so often invoked in the mainstream discourse as if it were one monolithic body of religious law – is interpreted differently by different Muslim communities depending on which *fiqh* – or school of jurisprudence – they tend to favor. Interestingly, Muslims can switch back and forth between different schools of jurisprudence depending on which orientation they prefer at any given time. This is a far cry from the idea of a unitary "Islamic law" popularized by the mainstream Western press.

Scholars have argued that instead of invoking Islam to explain behavior in "the Muslim World" we should look at historical as well as contemporary social conditions, relations and conflicts. In order to understand what this sort of analysis might look like, and what sorts of insights it might yield, let us turn to a specific Muslim country – Pakistan. Pakistan provides us with a crucial lens through which to examine the issues we are trying to grapple with here. It is a Muslim-majority country which officially designates itself an "Islamic Republic" and it has often been the subject of media attention in the West – not only for its role in the nine-year-old war in neighboring Afghanistan, but also because of the declining status of its women.

For our purposes here, I will focus on three important cases from Pakistan: first, the "Saima Love-Marriage Case"; second, the increase in the practice of "honor killings" in the 1990s; and last, the situation of women who are in state custody because they have been accused of *zina* (or illegitimate sex) by their families. Each of these will help us understand just how impossible it is to think of "Islam" as being the source of Muslim women's problems, and how complex the reality actually is. What I seek to demonstrate through these cases is that Islam is invoked very selectively even in so-called "Islamic societies," and even when the issue is the control of women's sexuality. In fact, sometimes the rights granted to women under Islamic law become inconvenient for the purposes of patriarchal control, in which case "Islam" is all too easily tossed aside in favor of "custom" and "tradition." This is an aspect of what I call "patriarchal opportunism," whereby patriarchal structures from families to nation-states strategically select elements from an ideological "toolbox" in their attempt to gain support for the sexual regulation of women.

Let us begin with what the Pakistani media referred to as the "Saima Love-Marriage Case." The pertinent details of the case were as follows: In February 1996, 22-year-old Saima Waheed married against the wishes of her parents, leading to a contentious legal battle which gripped the country. Saima was the college-educated daughter of an economically and politically influential family. Arshad Ahmad, the man she chose to marry, was a teacher at a government college in a small town. To give a sense of the class divide here, Ahmad supplemented his income of Rs5,000 a month (less than $60) by giving private lessons, while Saima's pocket money alone – which she received as a director of her father's company – was double that.

Saima informed her parents of her desire to marry Arshad, and his parents (following prescribed social norms) formally requested her hand for their son. However, when it became clear that her family had no intention of accepting the proposal, Saima took decisive action and married Arshad. She expected that her family would eventually accept the marriage. Instead, she was severely punished and then imprisoned in her parents' home. Saima finally managed to escape and to engage the services of Asma Jahangir, a prominent women's and human rights lawyer, in order to defend her right to marry without the consent of a *wali*, or legal (male) guardian.

Legally, the issue seemed fairly straightforward. A precedent-setting case had already established that an adult Muslim woman in Pakistan had the religious and legal right to contract marriage on her own behalf, without the intercession of a *wali*. Moreover, such "runaway marriages" are hardly news even – or perhaps especially – in socially conservative societies such as Pakistan where they are often the only means for young men and women to assert some modicum of control over their lives. However, in the legal discourse around the case, Saima's exercise of a right granted to her both by secular and religious law was still understood as a source of shame, both for her family and "the nation."

Ultimately, the Lahore High Court did validate her marriage on legal grounds. However, what is important to note is that Saima's case was argued, and ultimately judged, not within the terms of existing Muslim family law in the Pakistan Penal Code, or *shariah* law – both of which were unambiguous in their understanding of the rights of adult Muslim women with regard to marriage – but on the *general undesirability of filial disobedience*. In fact, both the judge who decreed the marriage legal under Muslim law, and the judge who wrote the dissenting opinion, expressed the wish that parental authority could be juridically enforceable.

Any close look at this case highlights the fact that despite ubiquitous references to "Islam," the *shariah* and even to Pakistan as the "Islamic Republic," it was in fact patriarchal control that was at issue here. Despite the conservative nature of her family, Saima was hardly a stereotypically oppressed or even a "traditional" young woman by Pakistani standards. She was active in intercollegiate (and therefore non-segregated) events; she first met Arshad at one such event. Her father was aware of her attendance at such events, and by all accounts he took intense pride in her achievements. She owned a car and a cell phone, both symbols of mobility and autonomy as well as wealth and social status. She and her female cousins were also not denied access to activities such as swimming and riding, both associated with the Westernized upper classes. Their dress code was also unconventional – they wore jeans and T-shirts at home and, even when outside, continued to wear them under the *hijab*. This is rather different from what we have learnt to expect of conservative Muslims, and shows in fact how important class is to any analysis of purportedly Muslim societies.

However, these accoutrements of capitalist modernity were given to Saima to enhance her *father's* social status, in particular by making her a more desirable item on the marriage market. Given that marriages in Pakistan are still very much about cementing relations between families, Saima's father expected to leverage his daughter's desirability to his strategic advantage. His anger, therefore, was not the result of a religious injunction – as we saw, religious (Islamic) law was squarely on Saima's side – it was anger at being deprived of a patriarchal privilege. Thus the minute she challenged his authority, all *her* privileges were summarily taken away.

What should be clear from our discussion of this case is that it is impossible – even in a country that calls itself an "Islamic Republic," where *shariah* law is institutionalized to some degree and when the issue is women's sexual agency – to claim that "Islam" is somehow the explanatory variable. If anything, the Saima case shows us that often the rights granted to women by Islamic law become *inconvenient* for local patriarchies. In such cases, any existing "Islamic" provisions are either "reinterpreted," finessed, tactfully ignored or even explicitly superseded by "custom" or "tradition." "Islam" should thus be understood as one out of several available tools in the ideological toolbox of patriarchies in Muslim societies.

The issue of "honor killings" in Pakistan provides a second illustration of "patriarchal opportunism." Contrary to the mainstream discourse in the West, honor killings are not "Islamic" either in the sense of being sanctioned by Islamic law or being popularly understood as such by ordinary people. Moreover, as a practice it is neither limited to Muslim communities – being prevalent in parts of the world as disparate as Latin America, South Asia and parts of North Africa – nor is it remotely universal *across* the Muslim world. Pakistan is one Muslim society where honor killings do exist; in fact, they have become more visible since the 1990s, prior to which they were limited to certain areas of rural Pakistan. The earlier version of the practice differs from its contemporary urban cousin in significant ways. For example, the older version was a highly ritualized and regulated mechanism by which specific communities policed the sexual behavior of its members, and the punishment for the transgression of sexual norms extended to both the man and the woman. By contrast, in the contemporary version, the victim is always a woman and the practice is increasingly "privatized" and "unregulated." One of the main reasons behind the rise of honor killings in Pakistan is the impunity with which the state allows family members – from parents to husbands and brothers – to get away with what is clearly understood as murder within both the Pakistan Penal Code and *shariah* law. This is the result of the increasing power of landed and tribal elites. In 1999, after a particularly high-profile case of "honor killing" which had shaken the country, a special session of the Pakistani Senate was called to address the issue. However, a resolution condemning the growing incidence of this practice was rejected under pressure from these elites in the Senate, who defended it as an essential part of their "culture" and "tradition." "Islam" thus has very little to do with the motive or justification of honor killings in Pakistan and is conspicuously absent from the discourse around them.

Lastly, I wish to turn to the issue of women who have been incarcerated under the *zina* laws in Pakistan. These laws are part of the Hudood Ordinances, promulgated by the military dictator General Zia ul-Haq as the cornerstone of his project of "Islamizing" the Pakistani state and society in the 1980s. The Zina Ordinance laid out various categories of sex crimes, from rape to adultery and fornication (pre-marital sex) which were all to be treated as crimes against the state. In order to entertain the charge of *zina* against an individual or individuals, however, the law required the testimony of "four adult male Muslim witnesses of good moral character" who had actually witnessed the act of penetration. The purported idea behind setting the bar for eyewitness this high was to prevent the abuse of this law through spurious accusations, and thereby protect the reputations of innocent men and women. On the surface, both men and women fell equally under the purview of the part of the law pertaining to adultery, and the law on rape appeared designed to protect women from sexual violence. However, the case of Safia Bibi soon made it clear that this law against sex crimes had serious implications for Pakistani women.

Safia Bibi was a blind teenaged girl in domestic service who charged her employer with rape; she had become pregnant as a result. Unsurprisingly, she couldn't round up the required witnesses to the crime. However, instead of simply dismissing the case for lack of evidence, the *shariat* court charged Safia Bibi with fornication because she was pregnant despite being unmarried.[2] This case galvanized a public outcry against the Zina Ordinance, led by the newly formed feminist group, the Women's Action Forum, which was joined by other secular pro-democracy groups as well as some Muslim clerics who publicly supported the defendant. The charge against Safia Bibi was ultimately struck down by the Supreme Court of Pakistan which makes it clear that *shariah* did not trump secular law in Pakistan even under the very martial law regime which had forcibly institutionalized this parallel legal system.

The high courts and the Supreme Court have continued to overturn the decisions of the appellate *shariat* courts in *zina* cases.[3] However, despite the efforts of Pakistani feminists, the Zina Ordinance remains on the books, and women continue to be its major victims. In fact, the majority of women incarcerated in Pakistani jails are there because they have been accused of *zina* by their families. In her critical ethnographic work with these women, Shahnaz Khan (2007) shows that far from being an expression of religious piety at the familial or state level, the *zina* laws are wielded as a potent weapon of control and extortion by families of "disobedient" women. The women are almost entirely from the lower classes. Men, who may also be charged with *zina*, rarely end up in jail since they are better able to negotiate a financial settlement with their accusers. It is clear then that, in its impact, this law is classed as well as gendered.

One of Khan's most surprising findings was that incarceration is actually seen by these poor women as a form of "protective custody" and thereby an *escape* from their families. The role of the state, Khan finds, is complicated in these cases – sometimes it sides with family, and sometimes with the woman, and Khan can unearth no discernible pattern to the variation. Complicating matters even further, Khan finds that the women themselves invoke the moral authority of Islam – and specifically what they understand as the rights it grants them – *against* their families. Islam also becomes a source of solace for them during this difficult period.

These facts disrupt the manner in which the mainstream media in the West constructs the role of Islam in the lives of Muslim women, and highlight the pitfalls of not distinguishing between the different forms and contexts within which "Islam" is invoked, and by whom. Among other things, a distinction must always be made between what I call "Islamization from below," within which we can slot the rise of (voluntary) public piety among Muslims such as the adoption of particular styles of facial hair by men and of various forms of *hijab* by women, and "Islamization from above," which refers to the ways in which structures of power – from families to states – deploy "Islam" in order to control women (and men) (Toor 2007). State policies imposing particular dress codes and enforcing gender segregation in public would be examples of the latter. However, the adoption of the veil by female university students in Cairo in the late 1970s as a protest against the state would be an example of the former. There is, of necessity, a relationship between the two levels of Islamization, but it is complicated and certainly does not lend itself to easy generalizations. Moreover, ignoring this distinction and collapsing all forms of "Islamization" results in a serious misunderstanding of the social processes at work.

Khan's (2007) research on incarcerated women leads her to conclude that poverty is an important causal factor in the imprisonment of women under the charge of *zina* in Pakistan. She follows other Pakistani scholars in linking this poverty to the structural adjustment policies imposed on Pakistan by the World Bank and IMF from the 1980s on. The importance of this observation cannot be understated because feminist scholarship on structural adjustment across the world has shown a strong link between the deprivations created by these policies and a rise in violence against women. Khan's research thus allows us to connect something that appears to be a result of "Islamic law" (the incarceration of women under *zina* laws in Pakistan) to similar developments in other places, which are in turn the result of larger global political and economic processes. Needless to say, issues such as class and international political economy are never part of the explanatory framework when it comes to discussions around Muslim women in the West, since they do not fit into a framework in which everything to do with Muslims is explained by "Islam."

Structural adjustment is one aspect of globalization – defined as the increasing interconnectedness of different parts of the world at the economic, political and cultural levels – which has resulted in an intensification in the dynamics of social change across the developing or postcolonial world. Such rapid and intense social change produces anxieties in the societies and communities experiencing this change; anxieties which feminist scholars have shown to result in greater regulation of women. This was just as true of Europe during the period of capitalist modernization in the eighteenth and nineteenth centuries, and of colonized and decolonizing societies in the mid-twentieth century.

Issues related to women and gender in contemporary Muslim societies must be understood within the same framework. What passes for the victimization of women by "Islam" is all too often part and parcel of a more global phenomenon – an increase in the moral and sexual regulation of women by communities and kin-networks as a response to political, social and cultural anxieties; such anxieties have intensified under economic and cultural globalization. The regulation of women and their sexuality is, after all, a common feature of all patriarchal societies, traditional or modern, and certainly not simply Muslim ones. It is the discourse of Islamic exceptionalism – in essence the form of Orientalism operative today, which is defined by an exclusive focus on Islam – which prevents us from seeing the "family resemblances" between honor killings in the Pakistani or Jordanian Muslim communities and honor killings in Hindu and Sikh communities in India, between the violent protests against the celebration of Valentine's Day in Pakistan and India (led by the goon squads of the Muslim and Hindu religious right respectively), and between the attempts at the regulation of women by "Islamists" and the Christian Right in the United States alike.

The three cases from Pakistan discussed above illustrate just how difficult it is to understand the role played by Islam even in a single country. "Islam" can be, and often is, simultaneously a convenient ideological tool in the hands of the powerful, a source of spiritual succor for the powerless, and part of an identitarian response to the anxieties and ravages of an increasingly globalized world. Thus, instead of assuming that we already know what "Islam" means when we see it invoked in a particular context, we should actually always ask *how* it is being invoked, by *whom*, and for *what purpose*. We should also refrain from assuming that "Islam" is the only or even the best explanatory variable when it comes to understanding Muslim cultures, societies and individuals.

Conclusion

I have shown here that, unlike what mainstream discourse would have us believe, "Islam" is not the engine which explains all aspects of "Muslim" societies. When they prove inconvenient, even codified Islamic laws are summarily sidelined, ignored or glossed over. An obsessive focus on "Islam" alone misses the actual threats faced by women across the world. In postcolonial states – of which Muslim states are a sub-set – these range from local custom to colonial "family" and "sodomy" laws to policies promoted by international agencies which impoverish people (especially women) and make them more vulnerable to local (patriarchal) elites. We must also recognize that the conservative backlash that we see in the "Muslim" world and in the postcolonial world more generally can also be observed in the United States. Here, too, this backlash is articulated within a religious framework, and we can see a revitalized Christian movement gaining ground on issues such as a woman's right to choose and gay marriage.

Nuanced and thoughtful research on Muslim societies indicates that Islam itself should be understood as a deeply contested terrain. Like all ideologies, much of the form of its expression depends on the class or confluence of classes which wields it, and the historical context in which this expression happens.

In the absence of appropriate historical and sociological context it is impossible to come away with anything but a superficial and often incorrect understanding of the role Islam plays with regard to women. We should reject the idea that something stable and immutable called "Islam" exists anywhere. For example, the fact that Muslims in Pakistan, as elsewhere, invoke Islam in everyday discourse doesn't tell us anything about what they mean when they invoke it. The "Islam" invoked by the women imprisoned under the *zina* law and interviewed by Khan is not the same Islam featured in the discourse of Islamic political parties. We must therefore keep clear the distinction between Islamization-from-above and Islamization from-below, and acknowledge Muslim women's agency even if it seems to contradict what we understand as "feminist" goals or politics and even if we understand this agency to be exercised within structural constraints. This is, after all, true of all agency, anywhere – there simply is no such thing as a "pure" freedom of choice unconstrained by social norms.

Thus, the concept of "Islam," whether deployed by state or private actors, needs to be something the researcher must unpack rather than assume a priori. The "Islam connection," when it is there, is complex and there is simply no shortcut around historically and sociologically nuanced analyses. And, finally, in the current geopolitical context in which the United States is at war with several Muslim countries, and where Islamophobia and racial profiling of Muslims across the world are growing concerns, the need for such methodological deliberateness becomes even more acute.

Notes

1 This equating of make-up with liberation is very common in mainstream discourse on Muslim women, as is evidenced by the titles of contemporary books and films such as *Lipstick Jihad* and *Kabul Beauty School*.
2 *Shariat* is the Urdu word for *shariah*; Urdu is the national language of Pakistan.
3 Many Islamic jurists and scholars at the time pointed out that the practice of using the juridical requirement to entrap and punish women (and women alone) for sexual transgression violated its intent, and was against the spirit of Islamic law. However, the fact that the law still stands, even if no other individual has since been found guilty under it, is a testimony to the ways in which Islam is opportunistically deployed in Pakistani politics.

References

Hussain, Neelam. 1997. "The Narrative Appropriation of Saima: Coercion and Consent in Muslim Pakistan." In Neelam Hussain, S. Mumtaz, and R. Saigol (Eds), *Engendering the Nation-State*. Vol. I. Lahore: Simorgh Publications.

Khan, Shahnaz. 2007. *Zina, Transnational Feminism and the Moral Regulation of Pakistani Women*. British Columbia, Canada: University of British Columbia Press.

Said, Edward. 1978. *Orientalism*. New York: Pantheon Books.

———. 1981. *Covering Islam: How the Media and the Experts Determine How We See the Rest of the World*. New York: Pantheon Books.

Spivak, Gayatri. 1988. "Can the Subaltern Speak?" In Cary Nelson and Lawrence Grossberg (Eds), *Marxism and the Interpretation of Culture*. Champaign: University of Illinois Press.

Toor, Saadia. 2007. "Moral Regulation in a Postcolonial Nation-State: Gender and the Politics of Islamization in Pakistan." Special issue of *Interventions: International Journal of Postcolonial Studies* 9(2): July.

26

"Guys are just homophobic"

Rethinking adolescent homophobia and heterosexuality

C. J. Pascoe

COLORADO COLLEGE, COLORADO SPRINGS

Teenage masculinity

Kevin, a high school student in suburban San Francisco, sits at an IHOP, short of money for dinner. His friend, Craig, agrees to lend him money, but only on the following condition – that Kevin repeat a series of confessional phrases which Craig can videotape and place on YouTube. Kevin buries his head in his hands asking, "You're going to take a video of this and post it on YouTube aren't you?!" Craig ignores Kevin's plea saying, "Anyway, repeat after me. I Kevin James Wong."

KEVIN: I, Kevin James Wong.
CRAIG: 17 years old.
KEVIN (WHO AT THIS POINT STARTS TO GIGGLE EMBARRASSEDLY):   17 years old.
CRAIG: Senior at Valley High School.
KEVIN: Senior at Valley High School.
CRAIG: In Santa Clarita.
KEVIN: In Santa Clarita.
CRAIG: Am now confessing.
KEVIN: Am now confessing.
CRAIG: That I, Kevin Wong.
KEVIN: That I, Kevin Wong.
CRAIG: Am a homosexual male.
KEVIN: Am a homosexual male.

They dissolve into laughter as their friend Jesse jumps into the frame behind Kevin. Craig posted the video on YouTube and eagerly showed it to me as I interviewed him in a local Starbucks. He and his friends giggled as they continued to show me other YouTube videos, one of which featured them imitating men engaging in anal intercourse and then bursting into fits of laughter.

About two years before I watched Craig's video in that Santa Clarita coffee shop I found myself two hours away, at a high school in Riverton California, where a group of fifth graders had been bussed in for the day to participate in the local high school's performing arts day. As I looked around the outdoor quads decorated with student artwork and filled with choirs singing and bands playing, a student from River High, Brian, ran past me to the rear quad yelling to a group of the elementary school boys. He hollered at them, pointing frantically, "There's a faggot over there! There's a faggot over there! Come look!" The group of boys dashed after Brian as he ran down the hallway, towards the presumed "faggot." Peering down the hallway I saw Brian's friend, Dan, waiting for the boys. As the boys came into his view, Dan pursed his lips and began sashaying towards them. He swung his hips exaggeratedly and wildly waved his arms on the end of which his hands hung from limp wrists. To the boys Brian yelled, referring to Dan, "Look at the faggot! Watch out! He'll get you!" In response, the 10-year-olds screamed in terror and raced back down the hallway. I watched Brian and Dan repeat this drama about the predatory faggot, each time with a new group of young boys.

Kevin, Craig, Brian and Dan enacted similar scenes containing similar messages: men or boys who do not conform to normative understandings of masculinity and sexuality should be mocked, humiliated and possibly feared. I have spent the better part of the last decade interviewing teens about and observing their behavior around definitions of masculinity and sexuality. Across a variety of geographic settings, boys from a range of class and racial/ethnic groups report sentiments much like those expressed by Kevin, Craig, Brian and Dan. Conversations with and observations of these boys indicate that homophobic taunts, jokes, teasing and harassment are central to the ways in which contemporary American boys come to think of themselves as men.

The homophobia articulated by Kevin, Craig, Brian and Dan seems representative of many American youth. Nationally, 93 percent of youth hear homophobic comments at least occasionally and 51 percent on a daily basis (National Mental Health Association 2002). Interestingly, in one state, 80 percent of youth who have been targeted with anti-gay harassment identify as heterosexual (Youth Risk Behavior Survey – Washington 1995). While this harassment is primarily directed at boys, girls suffer from sexualized harassment as well. The American Association of University Women (2001) documents that 83 percent of girls have been sexually harassed at school. These cursory statistics point to an educational experience in adolescence characterized in part by sexualized and gendered aggression directed from boys at other boys *and* at girls.

This type of joking and teasing can have dire consequences. Ninety percent of random school shootings have involved straight-identified boys who have been relentlessly humiliated with homophobic remarks (Kimmel 2003). For instance, Michael Carneal and Andy Williams, both involved in rampage school shootings, had been harassed for being gay (Kimmel 2003; Newman et al. 2004). Michael Carneal's school newspaper actually published a report outing him as gay (though he did not self-identify as such) (Newman et al. 2004). Eric Mohat, a 17-year-old high school student in Ohio who enjoyed theater and playing music, shot himself in 2007 after hearing homophobic taunts. Similarly, Carl Joseph Walker Hoover, an 11-year-old middle school student in Massachusetts, suffered homophobic harassment from his classmates for performing well academically. He hung himself as a desperate response to the teasing. Lawrence King, having been bullied relentlessly since third grade for his non-traditional gender presentation, was shot and killed by a fellow student in 2008 whom he had asked to be his Valentine.

While certainly the sort of joking and minor humiliation exhibited in the two opening stories does not match the level of violence in these examples, a problematic intersection of gender and sexuality undergirds all of them. Practices that seem to reflect basic homophobia –

imitating same sex eroticism, calling someone queer or mincing about with limp wrists – are also about policing gendered identities and practices. Through making homophobic jokes, calling other boys gay and imitating effeminate men boys attempt to assure themselves and others of their masculinity. For contemporary American boys, the definition of masculinity entails displaying power, competence, a lack of emotions, heterosexuality and dominance. Says Kevin, for instance, to be masculine is to be "tough." The ideal man is "strong" and he "can't be too emotional" adds Erik. Maleness does not confer masculinity upon a given boy. Rather masculinity is the repeated signaling to self and others that one is powerful, competent, unemotional, heterosexual and dominant.

This signaling appears in two ways, through practices of repudiation and confirmation. Repudiatory practices take the form of a "fag discourse," consisting of homophobic jokes, taunts, and imitations through which boys publicly signal their rejection of that which is considered unmasculine. Boys confirm masculine selves through public enactments of compulsive heterosexuality which include practices of "getting girls," physically confining girls under the guise of flirtation and sex talk. For many contemporary American boys masculinity must be repeatedly proven, as one's identity as masculine is never fully secured. This essay unpacks adolescent boys' public enactments of homophobia and heterosexuality, examining them as sexualized as well as gendered processes which have ramifications for all teenagers – male, female, straight and gay.

The fag discourse

Boys repeatedly tell me that "fag" was the ultimate insult for a boy. Darnell stated, "Since you were little boys you've been told, 'hey, don't be a little faggot.'" Jeremy emphasized that this insult literally reduced a boy to nothing, "To call someone gay or fag is like the lowest thing you can call someone. Because that's like saying that you're nothing." Indeed, much like the boys terrorized by Brian and Craig, boys often learn long before adolescence that a "fag" is the worst thing a guy could be. Thus boys' daily lives often consist of interactions in which they frantically lob these epithets at one another and try to deflect them from themselves.

Many boys explained their frequent use of insults like queer, gay and fag by asserting that, as Keith put it, "guys are just homophobic." However, analyzing boys' homophobic practices as a "fag discourse" shows that their behavior reflects not just a fear of same sex desire, but a specific fear of *men's* same sex desire. Many told me that homophobic insults applied primarily to boys, not to girls. While Jake told me that he didn't like gay people, he quickly added, "Lesbians, okay, that's good!" Now lesbians are not "good" because of some enlightened approach to sexuality, but because, as Ray, said, "To see two hot chicks banging bodies in a bed, that's like every guy's fantasy right there. It's the truth. I've heard it so many times." So their support of lesbians is more about heterosexual fantasy than about a progressive attitude (Jenefsky and Miller 1998).

Furthermore, several boys argued that fag, queer and gay had little to do with actual sexual practices or desires. Darnell told me "It doesn't have anything to do with being gay." Adding to this sentiment, J. L. said, "Fag, seriously, it has nothing to do with sexual preference at all. You could just be calling somebody an idiot, you know?" As David explained, "Being gay is just a lifestyle. It's someone you choose to sleep with. You can still throw a football around and be gay." David's final statement clarifies the distinction between popular understandings of these insults and teens' actual use of them. That is, that they have to do with men's same sex eroticism, but at their core discipline gendered practices and identities (such as the ability, or lack thereof, to throw a football). In asserting the primacy of gender to the definition of these seemingly homophobic insults, boys reflect what Riki Wilchins (2003) calls the Eminem

Exception, in which Eminem explains that he doesn't call people "faggot" because of their sexual orientation, but because they are weak and unmanly. While it is not necessarily acceptable to be gay, if a man were gay *and* masculine, as in David's portrait of the football-throwing gay man, he does not deserve the insult.

What renders a boy vulnerable to homophobic epithets often depends on local definitions of masculinity. Boys frequently cited exhibiting stupidity, femininity, incompetence, emotionality or same sex physicality as notoriously non-masculine practices. Chad, for instance, said that boys might be called a fag if they seemed "too happy or something" while another boy expounded on the dangers of being "too smiley." Ironically, these insults are pitched at boys who engage in seemingly heterosexual activities. Kevin, when describing his ideal girlfriend said, "I have to imagine myself singing, like serenading her. Okay, say we got in a fight and we broke up. I have to imagine myself as a make-up gift to her singing to her out of her window." Kevin laughed as he said that when he shares this scenario with his friends "the guys are like, 'dude you're gay!'"

Because so many activities could render a boy vulnerable to these insults, perhaps it is little surprise that Ben asserted that one could be labeled for "anything, literally anything. Like you were trying to turn a wrench the wrong way, 'dude you're a fag.' Even if a piece of meat drops out of your sandwich, 'you fag!'" While my research shows that there are particular set of behaviors that could get a boy called the slur, it is no wonder that Ben felt a boy could be called it for "anything." In that statement he reveals the intensity and extent of the policing boys must do of their behaviors in order to avoid the epithet.

The sort of homophobic harassment detailed above has as much to do definitions of masculinity as it does with actual fear of other gay men (Corbett 2001; Kimmel 2001). Being subject to homophobic harassment has as much to do with failing at masculine tasks of competence, heterosexual prowess or in any way revealing weakness as it does with a sexual identity. Homophobic epithets such as fag have gender meanings *and* sexual meanings. The insult is levied against boys who are not masculine, even momentarily, and boys who identify (or are identified by others) as gay. This sets up a very complicated daily ordeal in which boys continually strive to avoid being subject to the epithet, but are simultaneously constantly vulnerable to it.

This sort of homophobia appears frequently in boys' joking relationships. Sociologists have pointed out that joking is central to men's relationships in general (Kehily and Nayak 1997; Lyman 1998). Through aggressive joking boys cement friendship bonds with one another. Boys often draw laughs though imitating effeminate men or men's same sex desire. Emir frequently imitated effeminate men who presumably sexually desired other men to draw laughs from students in his introductory drama class. One day his teacher, disturbed by noise outside the classroom, turned to close the door saying, "We'll shut this unless anyone really wants to watch sweaty boys playing basketball." Emir lisped, "I wanna watch the boys play!" The rest of the class cracked up at his imitation. No one in the class actually thought Emir was gay, as he purposefully mocked both same-sex sexual desire and an effeminate gender identity. This sort of ritual reminded other youth that masculine men didn't desire other men, nor did they lisp or behave in other feminine manners. It also reminded them that men who behaved in these ways were worthy of laughter and derision.

These everyday joking interchanges, however, were more than "just jokes." For some boys, such as Lawrence King, the intolerance for gender differences espoused by these joking rituals has serious, if not deadly, consequences. Ray and Peter underscore this in their conversation. Ray asserted "I can't stand fags. Like I've met a couple. I don't know. The way they rub you. Gay people I don't care. They do their thing in their bedroom and that's fine. Feminine guys bother me." Peter, his friend, continued "If they try to get up on you. I'll kill you." Ray and

Peter illuminated the teenage boys' different responses to gay and effeminate men as Ray espouses tolerance for the presumably gender normative former and Peter threatens violence against the latter. In this sense the discourse runs a continuum from joking to quite violent harassment. While boys said that the "fag" insult was more about failing at masculinity, than about actually being gay, it seemed that a gay and unmasculine boy suffered the most under this "gender regime" (Connell 1987).

As a talented dancer who frequently sported multicolored hair extensions, mascara and wore baggy pants, fitted tank tops and sometimes a skirt, Ricky violated norms of gender *and* sexuality. He told me that harassment started early, in elementary school. "I'm talking like sixth grade, I started being called a fag. Fifth grade I was called a fag. Third grade I was called a fag." Though he moved schools every two years or so, this sort of harassment continued and intensified as he moved into high school. At his school's homecoming game (for which Ricky had choreographed the half time show) he was harassed until he left after hearing things like "there's that fucking fag" and "What the fuck is that fag doing here? That fag has no right to be here." When watching him dance with the school's all female dance team other boys reacted in revulsion. Nils said, "It's like a car wreck, you just can't look away." J. R., the captain of the football team, shook his head and muttered under his breath, "That guy dancing, it's just disgusting, Disgusting!" shaking his head and stomping off. Even though dancing is the most important thing in his life, Ricky didn't attend school dances because he didn't like to "watch my back" the whole time. He had good reason for this fear. Brad said of prom, "I heard Ricky is going in a skirt, it's a hella short one." Sean responded with "I wouldn't even go if he's there." Topping Sean's response Brad claimed, "I'd probably beat him up outside."

The harassment suffered by Ricky featured none of the joking or laughter exhibited in other interchanges. Very real threats of violence undergirded boys' comments about him. Ricky told me that he walked with his eyes downcast in order to avoid guys' eye contact, fearing that they'd see such eye contact as a challenge. Similarly he varied his route home from school each day and carried a rock in his hand to protect himself. For many boys, in order to maintain a sense of themselves as masculine, they felt they had to directly attack Ricky, a symbol of what they feared most, of unmasculine nothingness.

Compulsive heterosexuality

If daily life for many boys entails running a gauntlet of homophobic insults, how do they avoid being permanently labeled as Ricky was? Boys defend against homophobic teasing and harassment by assuring others of their heterosexuality. By engaging in a number of cross-gender rituals, a boy can relatively successfully defend himself against ending up in Ricky's position, the object of harassment, derision and violence. In the same way that boys' homophobia is not specifically about a sexual identity, compulsive heterosexuality[1] is not only about expressing love, desire and intimacy, but about showing a sexualized dominance over girls' bodies. The sort of gendered teasing in which boys engage in takes a toll on girls as well as other boys. In my research I found three components of compulsive heterosexuality: rituals of getting girls, rituals of touch, and sex talk.

Perhaps the most obvious example of "getting girls" is having a girlfriend. Having a girlfriend seems a normal teen behavior. For boys who are identified as feminine and teased for unmasculine practices, having a girlfriend functions as some sort of protection against homophobic harassment. Justin told me that some boys have girlfriends "so they look like they're not losers or they're not gay." David told me that a lot of the kids at his high school think that he is gay because of his preppy clothing choices and his lisp such that for him "it's better to have a girlfriend ... because people think I'm gay. I get that all the time." In order to defend against teasing and harassment boys like David need to establish a sort of baseline heterosexuality by proving they can "get a girl." Because of the difficulty in avoiding all of the behaviors that might render one vulnerable to teasing, having a girlfriend helps to inure one to accusations of the "fag discourse."

Similarly, cross-gender touching rituals establish a given boy's heterosexuality. These physical interchanges may first appear as harmless flirtation, but upon closer inspection actually reinforce boys' dominance over girls' bodies. The use of touch maintains a social hierarchy (Henley 1977). Superiors touch subordinates, invade their space and interrupt them in a way subordinates do not do to superiors and these superior–inferior relationships are often gendered ones. Boys and girls often touch each other as part of daily interaction, communication and flirtation. In many instances cross-sex touching was lightly flirtatious and reciprocal. But these touching rituals ranged from playfully flirtations to assault-like interactions. Boys might physically constrain girls under the guise of flirtation. One time in a school hallway a boy wrapped his arms around a girl and started to "freak" her, or grind his pelvis into hers as she struggled to get away. This sort of behavior happened more often in primarily male spaces. One day for instance, in a school weight room, Monte wrapped his arms around a girl's neck as if to put her in a headlock and held her there while Reggie punched her in the stomach, albeit lightly, and she squealed. A more dramatic example of this was during a passing period in which Keith rhythmically jabbed a girl in the crotch with his drumstick, while he yelled "Get raped!" These examples show how the constraint and touching of female bodies gets translated as masculinity, embedding sexualized meanings in which heterosexual flirting is coded as female helplessness and male bodily dominance.

While people jokingly refer to boys' sex talk as "boys will be boys" or "locker room" talk, this sex talk plays a serious role in defending against acquiring an identity like Ricky's. Boys enact and naturalize their heterosexuality by asserting "guys are horndogs" or by claiming that it is "kind of impossible for a guy" to not "think of sex every two minutes" as Chad does. Thinking about boys' sexual performance in terms of compulsive heterosexuality shows that asserting that one is a horndog and cannot help but think about sex is actually a gendered performance. Boys' sex talk often takes the form of "mythic story telling" in which they tell larger than life tales about their sexual adventures, their bodies and girls' bodies that do not reflect love, desire or sensuality, but rather dominance over girls' bodies. Pedro, for instance, laughed and acted out having sex with his girlfriend by leaning back up against the wall, legs and arms spread and head turning back and forth as he continued to say proudly "I did her so hard when I was done she was bleeding. I tore her walls!" The boys surrounding him cheered and oohed and aahed in amazement. Violence frequently frames these stories. Much like the touching rituals in which boys establish dominance over girls' bodies, these stories show what boys can make girls bodies do. Rich, after finishing lifting weights in his school's weight room, sat on a weight bench and five boys gathered around him as he told a story, after much urging, about sex with his now ex-girlfriend. He explained that they were having sex and "she said it started to hurt. I said we can stop and she said no. Then she said it again and she started crying. I told her to get off! Told her to get off! Finally I took her off," making a motion like he was lifting her off of him. He continued, "There was blood all over me! Blood all over her! Popped her wall! She had to have stitches." Boys start cracking up and moaning. Not to be outdone, other boys in the circle begin to chime in about their sexual exploits. Even those who don't have stories about themselves, asserted their knowledge of sex through vicarious experiences. Troy joined the discussion with a story about his brother, a professional basketball player for a nearby city. He "brought home a 24 year old drunk chick! She *farted* the whole time they were doing it in the other room! It was *hella* gross!" All the boys crack up again. Adam, not to be outdone, claimed "My friend had sex with a drunk chick. He did her in the butt! She s★★★ all over the place!" The boys all crack up again and yell out things like "Hella gross!" or "That's disgusting!" These graphic, quite violent stories detail what boys can make girls bodies do – rip, bleed, fart and poop.

To understand the role of sexuality in maintaining gender inequality it is important to look at sexuality, and specifically heterosexuality, not as a set of desires, identities or dispositions, but as an institution. Adrienne Rich (1986) does this when she argues that heterosexuality is an institution that systematically disempowers women. Similarly, compulsive heterosexuality is a set of practices through which boys reinforce linkages between sexuality, dominance and violence. This heterosexuality is a defensive heterosexuality, not necessarily a reflection of an internal set of emotions.

Conclusion

Many boys' school-based lives involve running a daily gauntlet of sexualized insults, as they simultaneously try to lob homophobic epithets at others and defend themselves from said epithets. In this sense masculinity becomes the daily interactional work of repudiating the labels of fag, queer or gay. Unpacking the definition of what appears to be homophobia clarifies the gender policing at the heart of boys' harassment of one another and of girls. Homophobic epithets may or may not have explicitly sexual meanings, but they always have gendered meanings. Many boys are clearly terrified of being permanently labeled as gay, fag or queer, since to them such a label effectively negates their humanness. As a part of boys' defensive strategy, girls' bodies become masculinity resources deployed in order to stave off these labels.

The practices of compulsive heterosexuality indicate that control over girls' bodies and their sexuality is central to definitions of adolescent masculinity. If masculinity is, as boys told me, about competence, heterosexuality, being unemotional, and dominance, then girls' bodies provide boys the opportunity to ward off the fag discourse by demonstrating mastery and control over them. Engaging in compulsive heterosexuality also allows boys to display a lack of emotions by refusing to engage the empathy that might mitigate against such a use of girls and their bodies. It is important to note that many of these boys are not unrepentant sexists or homophobes. In private and in one-on-one conversations, many spoke of sexual equality and of tender feelings for girls. For the most part these were social behaviors that boys engaged in when around other boys, precisely because they are less reflections of internal homophobic and sexist dispositions and more about constituting a masculine identity, something that is accomplished interactionally.

This gendered homophobia, as well as sexualized and gendered defenses against it, comprises contemporary adolescent masculinity. Fear of any sort of same sex intimacy (platonic or not) polices boys' friendships with one another. The need to repudiate that which is not considered masculine leads to a very public renunciation of same sex desire. Heterosexual flirtation becomes entwined with gendered dominance. What this means is that the public face of adolescent sexuality is rife with reproduction of gender inequality, through processes of the fag discourse and compulsive heterosexuality.

Note

1 This concept draws upon Adrienne Rich's (1986) influential concept of "compulsory heterosexuality" as well as Michael Kimmel's (1987) notion of "compulsive masculinity."

References

A.A.U.W. 2001. *Hostile Hallways*. Washington, DC: American Association of University Women.

Connell, R. W. 1987. *Gender and Power*. Stanford, CA: Stanford University Press.

Corbett, Ken. 2001. "Faggot = Loser." *Studies in Gender and Sexuality* 2(1): 3–28.

Henley, Nancy. 1977. *Body Politics: Power, Sex, and Nonverbal Communication*. Englewood Cliffs, NJ: Prentice-Hall.

Jenefsky, Cindy and Diane H. Miller. 1998. "Phallic Intrusion: Girl-Girl Sex in Penthouse." *Women's Studies International Forum* 21(4): 375–85.

Kehily, Mary J. and Anoop Nayak. 1997. "'Lads and Laughter': Humour and the Production of Heterosexual Masculinities." *Gender and Education* 9(1): 69–87.

Kimmel, Michael. 2001. "Masculinity as Homophobia: Fear, Shame, and Silence in the Construction of Gender Identity." Pp. 266–87 in *The Masculinities Reader*, ed. S. Whitehead and F. Barrett. Cambridge: Polity Press.

——. 1987. "The Cult of Masculinity: American Social Character and the Legacy of the Cowboy." Pp. 235–49 in *Beyond Patriarchy: Essays by Men on Pleasure, Power and Change*, ed. M. Kaufman. New York: Oxford University Press.

Kimmel, Michael S. 2003. "Adolescent Masculinity, Homophobia, and Violence: Random School Shootings, 1982–2001." *American Behavioral Scientist* 46(10): 1439–58.

Lyman, Peter. 1998. "The Fraternal Bond as a Joking Relationship: A Case Study of the Role of Sexist Jokes in Male Group Bonding." Pp. 171–93 in *Men's Lives* … , Fourth ed., ed. M. Kimmel and M. Messner. Boston, MA: Allyn and Bacon.

National Mental Health Association. 2002. *What Does Gay Mean? Teen Survey Executive Summary*.

Newman, Katherine, Cybelle Fox, David J. L. Harding, Jal Mehta and Wendy Roth. 2004. *Rampage: The Social Roots of School Shootings*. New York: Basic Books.

Rich, Adrienne. 1986. "Compulsory Heterosexuality and Lesbian Existence." Pp. 23–74 in *Blood, Bread and Poetry*. New York: W.W. Norton.

Wilchins, Riki. 2003. "Do You Believe in Fairies?" *The Advocate*, February 4, pp. 72.

Youth Risk Behavior Survey – Washington. 1995. Washington, DC: NYRBS.

27

Mis-conceptions about unintended pregnancy

Considering context in sexual and reproductive decision-making

Jennifer A. Reich

UNIVERSITY OF DENVER, COLORADO

Half of all pregnancies in the United States are unplanned.

A college student who used a condom that broke. A 40-year-old woman who thought she couldn't get pregnant. A new mother who is breastfeeding and assumed that would prevent pregnancy. A married couple who are debating whether they are really done having children. A teenager who thought you couldn't become pregnant the first time. Break-up sex or make-up sex. Some who feel lucky, others who feel unlucky.

It is impossible to discuss reproduction without considering the social meanings of sexuality and gender that are always layered over it. For example, when I ask students to think of what kind of woman becomes pregnant without intending to be, students often visualize a woman who has multiple partners, routinely has unprotected sex, is generally irresponsible, or is ignorant of how to prevent pregnancy. The more generous ones sometimes explain that she is someone with low self-esteem or argue how schools should do more to institute comprehensive sex education with accurate information into their curricula. None think of these stories as funny; rarely do they condemn the men who also have sex that results in unintended pregnancy, though they might think of them as unlucky, even as they are suspicious of such women.

Yet when I ask those same students if there are any family stories of the "Drunk-on-New-Year's-Eve-Oops-Baby" or the other family legends of the unplanned but much loved child, most laugh and share such tales. Some have a sibling much younger than they – and sometimes they volunteer, "That story is me!" These stories are not embarrassing or perceived as stigmatizing, and no one condemns these drunken women for having unprotected sex. When women are married, unintended pregnancies are not viewed in the same light, and married women are spared the suspicion or contempt we so freely serve up to single women.

In fact, half of all pregnancies in the United States are unplanned. But as the above examples illustrate, the meanings of sexuality and reproduction shape perceptions and outcomes of these unintended pregnancies. In this essay, I describe the context in which unintended pregnancies occur, what sexually active people do to avoid pregnancy, and what we know about their choices about pregnancy outcomes. I do not devote space to considering the myriad ways reproduction also occurs that might not result from intercourse, or the challenges and choices faced by those who wish to become pregnant and experience difficulties in doing so. This in no way suggests that these experiences and decisions are less important. Rather, I have chosen to focus more specifically on reproductive decisions that arise from heterosexual intercourse – and that have remained controversial in US public policy.

Becoming sexual, avoiding pregnancy

Much of the concern about unintended pregnancy flows from a misguided belief that young people are becoming sexually active at younger ages. In fact, young people are waiting longer to have sex than in past years. In a survey of teens between the ages of 15 and 19, about 13 percent of never-married females and 15 percent of never-married males reported that they had had sex before age 15 in 2002, compared with 19 percent and 21 percent, respectively, in 1995 (Abma *et al.* 2004). When having sex, more than three-quarters of teen females report that their first sexual experience was with a steady boyfriend, a fiancé, a husband or a cohabiting partner.

This does not mean that all sex is welcome or freely chosen. When teens were asked how much they wanted their first intercourse to happen at the time it did, 13 percent of females and 6 percent of males really didn't want it to happen at the time, and 52 percent of females and 31 percent of males had mixed feelings about it. Ten percent of young women aged 18–24 who have had sex before age 20 report that their first sex was involuntary. The younger they were at first intercourse, the higher the proportion (Abma *et al.* 2004). Knowing the meanings of sex, the ability to plan for it, and the ability to feel secure in the choice, alters efforts to prevent pregnancy.

Today, most young people have sex for the first time at about age 17, but don't marry until their middle or late twenties. If we assume that these young people want to avoid pregnancy until marriage, this means that they are at risk of unwanted pregnancy (and sexually transmitted infections) for nearly a decade (AGI 2010). Even after marriage, challenges in pregnancy prevention remain. The average woman in the United States aims to have two children. To achieve this goal, she will have to use birth control for approximately 30 years of her life. As a result, estimates are that "virtually all women (98 percent) aged 15–44 who have ever had intercourse have used at least one contraceptive method" (AGI 2008a). Given that there are more than 62 million women of reproductive age, this represents a sizable need (Mosher *et al.* 2004).

Contraception in context

While birth control is common, so are controversies surrounding its use. For example, controversies surround questions of whether birth control should be paid for by insurance companies, whether teens should be able to access contraceptive services without parental consent, how the safety and efficacy of new methods should be reviewed and evaluated, and whether and how potential users learn about pregnancy prevention. Each of the policies and controversies around birth control has its own fascinating history and is worthy of further research and reading, beyond what I can provide here.

All these controversies reflect concerns about the appropriate role of sex more generally: broad support for easy access to birth control is seen by some as communicating that sex is primarily non-procreative, that is, not limited to efforts to have children, and occurs commonly outside of marriage. For some, this contradicts many assumptions about gender, marriage, and morality, which are often built around views of women's sexuality.

Although we often talk about the importance of pregnancy prevention, it is worth acknowledging that birth control is difficult to use consistently and effectively all the time. The effectiveness of birth control hinges in part on how much a user has to do and how motivated they are to avoid pregnancy. Approximately 5 percent of unintended pregnancies result from method failure. The rest are the result of inconsistent or incorrect use of contraceptives, or failure to use any birth control. When users have to do something every day or every time they have sex, they are less likely to do so successfully than those who use methods that require little effort on the part of the user. Successful use also seems to reflect how much women have to lose by becoming pregnant, and other changing needs. Although we think of women who become pregnant as careless or not trying to prevent pregnancy, about half of women who faced an unintended pregnancy report using birth control in the month prior to becoming pregnant (Finer and Henshaw 2006). As such, we can ask better questions about why women have gaps in usage. Women who have gaps in birth control use attribute these to lack of access, unpleasant side effects, infrequent sexual activity, or life transitions, like the beginning or ending of a relationship, changing jobs, or moving (AGI 2008c; Frost and Darroch 2008). Thus, birth control and pregnancy prevention rise and fall in priority based on what else is going on in women's lives, the context of their relationships, and their own understanding of risk.

The outcome of these transitions, choices, and challenges can be seen in Table 27.1, which shows the failure rates of theoretically perfect use of birth control next to the failure rate of actual use. Next to that is the frequency of use of that contraceptive method.

Women from all backgrounds experience unintended pregnancy, but some women are more affected than are others. Women between the ages of 18 and 24, women from low income backgrounds, women who live with their partners, and women from minority backgrounds, particularly Black women, are most affected. Education also seems to matter a great deal. Women without a high school diploma were about three times more likely to face an

Table 27.1 First-year contraceptive failure rates

Method	Percentage of women experiencing an unintended pregnancy and popularity of method			
	Perfect use	Typical use	Number of users (000s)	% of users
Pill (combined)	0.3	8.7	11,661	30.6
Tubal sterilization	0.5	0.7	10,282	27.0
Male condom	2.0	17.4	6,841	18.0
Vasectomy	0.1	0.2	3,517	9.2
3-month injectable	0.3	6.7	2,024	5.3
Withdrawal	4.0	18.4	1,513	4.0
Periodic abstinence		25.3	583	2.4
IUD (all)			774	2
Copper-T	0.6	1.0		
Mirena	0.1	0.1		
1-month injectable	0.05	3.0		
Patch	0.3	8.0		
Diaphragm	6.0	16.0	99	0.3
No method	85.0	85.0		

Source: Taken from AGI 2008a.

unintended pregnancy than were college graduates and were less likely to terminate that pregnancy. As a result, women without a high school diploma had about four times as many births from unintended pregnancies as did college graduates (Finer and Henshaw 2006). This likely underscores the importance of future goals in providing a reason to prioritize pregnancy prevention, and illustrates how the perceived risks unintended pregnancy presents shape sexual and contraceptive decisions.

Social location, including age, education, and income, also affects the kind of contraception you might use. For women younger than 30, the pill is the leading method. However, by the time women are 35, sterilization (tubal ligation) becomes the leading method. Use of sterilization is not evenly distributed; sterilization is the leading method among Black women and Hispanic women and for women with less than a college education, while the pill is the leading method for White women (Mosher et al. 2004). This may reflect delayed childbearing for women who complete college, but it also might suggest that low income women and women of color are offered different contraceptive services by healthcare providers than are White women who are disproportionately more likely to be seen by a privately funded healthcare provider (rather than by a publicly funded healthcare or family planning clinic).

Most data we have about unintended pregnancy come from health or survey data collected from women. As such, we know less about boys' and men's reproductive lives. What we do know is that young men (15–19-year-olds) are waiting longer than in previous years to have sex (meaning vaginal intercourse), but that three-fourths of men report becoming sexually active by the age of 20, with 96 percent having sex prior to marriage (AGI 2008b).

Seventy-one percent of 15–19-year-old men report using a condom the first time they had sex. However, fewer than half of sexually active young men aged 15–19 reported using condoms 100 percent of the time during the previous year (48 percent in 2002) (Mosher et al. 2004). Interestingly, condom use seems to decline with age. For example, in 2007, 76 percent of sexually active ninth grade boys used condoms at last sexual intercourse, compared with 60 percent of twelfth graders. At the same time, older male students were more likely to report that their partner used the pill at last sex (8 percent of ninth graders vs. 21 percent of twelfth graders) (AGI 2008b). Thus, it appears that over time, contraceptive responsibility shifts to women. Although most teens use contraception at least some of the time, teens who do not use contraception have a 90 percent chance of becoming pregnant.

In thinking about successful pregnancy prevention, we should consider where individuals receive accurate information and access to contraceptive technologies. One clear place is from healthcare providers. Nationally, 15.4 percent of Americans have no health insurance (about 46 million people) (DeNavas-Walt et al. 2009). While this is a significant barrier to reproductive healthcare, there is evidence that the picture is even worse for young men who are much more likely to be uninsured. Adult males aged 19–29 were the fastest growing age group among the uninsured between 2000 and 2004; 31 percent were uninsured in 2004, compared with 12 percent aged 18 and younger (Kaiser Family Foundation 2005). Lack of access to healthcare also serves as a barrier to access to information, contraceptive services, and treatment for sexually transmitted infections that might affect their future fertility or that of their partners.

Even when men do access healthcare, it is not clear they are offered reproductive health services. One government report found that although two out of three young men (aged 15–19) had a physical exam in the past year, fewer than 20 percent received counseling or advice from a healthcare provider about birth control, sexually transmitted infections, or HIV (Martinez et al. 2006). For older men, the data are similar. About one-half (55 percent) of all men 15–44 years of age received a health service in the twelve months before the survey, but only 11 percent of men received birth control counseling, 10 percent received advice about

STIs, and 12 percent received advice about HIV in that same time period (Martinez et al. 2006). This suggests that as we aim to communicate greater need for men to share responsibility for pregnancy prevention and family planning, integrating opportunities to discuss and access contraception is important.

Unintended pregnancy and abortion

Even with perfect contraceptive use, abortion will always be a necessary option, as there is no method that can successfully prevent pregnancy 100 percent of the time. As mentioned, about half of all pregnancies are unintended and 40 percent of these (or 22 percent of all pregnancies) end in abortion. Estimates are that almost one in three women will have an abortion in her lifetime. However, because abortion is highly stigmatized, few of us know who those women are. Some celebrity women have come forth to share their experiences – for example, Whoopi Goldberg, Margot Kidder, Ani diFranco, Lil' Kim, Gloria Steinem, Ursula LeGuin, and Margaret Cho – but when women talk to other women, or when men listen to the women they know, we find that we all know someone who has chosen to terminate a pregnancy.

Pregnancy is calculated from the first day of a woman's last menstrual period and lasts about 40 weeks. Although conception occurs when a sperm and egg join and begin cell division (forming a pre-embryo or zygote), pregnancy does not occur physically until that zygote has implanted into the wall of the uterus. At that point, women often experience hormonal changes and associated physical changes.[1] Abortions in the first 12 weeks – when 90 percent of abortions occur – are exceedingly safe and have virtually no long-term negative effects on fertility or pregnancy complications.

All kinds of women seek abortions, but there are some trends. Of women who choose to terminate pregnancies, 56 percent are in their twenties; 61 percent already have one or more children; 67 percent have never married; 57 percent are economically disadvantaged; and 78 percent report a religious affiliation. When faced with an unintended pregnancy, women's reasons for choosing to terminate a pregnancy vary, but are also highly patterned. Most commonly, women expressed fear that having a child would interfere with their education, work or ability to care for dependents (74 percent). About 73 percent of women said they could not afford a baby now. Almost half of women (48 percent) expressed a desire to avoid becoming a single mother, or were "having relationship problems." Almost 40 percent of women terminated a pregnancy because they had completed their child-bearing. About one-third said they were not ready to have a child (Finer et al. 2005).

Focusing specifically on the 61 percent of women who already have children, one study found that women chose to terminate their pregnancies precisely because they aimed to be good mothers, and "believed that children were entitled to a stable and loving family, financial security, and a high level of care and attention" (Jones et al. 2008:79). This is a good reminder that the desire to be a good parent – to the children we already have or might have in the future – significantly drives reproductive decision-making.

We know less about men's roles in abortion. It is clear that some men never know about the abortion of a fetus they co-conceived or learned about it after the pregnancy was terminated. One study found that only about 22–25 percent of women who had abortions left the clinic with the man by whom they had become pregnant (Beenhakker et al. 2004). Although we cannot know how many of the absent men knew of the pregnancy or supported the decision to terminate the pregnancy, we can assume this suggests that there are some points of disconnect between men and women around abortion.

For men who were involved in the abortion experience, we see some patterns. In general, young men perceive unintended pregnancy to be negative and interfere with their activities, schooling, and future goals. In my own research, I looked at how men account for the decision to terminate a pregnancy of a fetus they co-conceived. Men often explained the decision to end a pregnancy in terms of their relative desire to reproduce themselves, whether they felt ready to take on the responsibilities of being financially supportive or a family man, or whether they felt they could have a traditional family and be a good father, as they defined it (Reich 2008). Men are bombarded with information about "taking responsibility." Some research suggests that adolescent and adult males identify responsibility as central to definitions of masculinity, and that the abortion experience may be an expression of responsibility.

In comparing research on men and women, both groups speak of their future goals and ambitions and their desire to feel better prepared to become parents, or to do a good job parenting children they already have. Women seem to speak more specifically of the challenges of day-to-day care of children or access to healthcare or childcare, while men tend to discuss more abstract concepts of how to become someone who plays catch or can meet their children's needs. In both cases, those facing unintended pregnancy voice a desire to feel prepared to parent.

Abortion is a highly divisive arena of public opinion. It is worth acknowledging how our assumptions about those who choose to terminate unintended pregnancies may be wrong. As the statistics show, almost 80 percent of women who seek abortions identify with a religious faith or tradition. Many women who object to abortion in the abstract seek out abortion services when it is their own pregnancies that cause a sense of crisis. Many women who support the right to safe, legal abortion services choose to continue unintended pregnancies. We also sometimes imagine that there are two kinds of women: those who have abortions and those who have babies. In fact, these are the same women, at different points in their lives.

Thinking about our family planning futures

Most of us have long reproductive lives. Although we may move in and out of relationships, become more or less sexually active, or change our goals for our future families as our lives change, we are all engaged in deliberate efforts to control, manage, and plan our procreative selves. How we feel about these processes reflects our cultural understandings of gender, sexuality, relationships, responsibility, morality, risk, and chance.

Even as this is an individual process, we see from research that there are also patterns. As we make choices, we do so from our social location and in interaction with the structures and resources that surround us. It is clear that education, age, ethnicity, and relationship status all matter in making decisions about reproduction and encountering unintended pregnancies.

In thinking about this as a near-universalizing experience that is experienced entirely differently by different men and women, I found the following statistic: by age 45, half of all women have experienced an unplanned pregnancy (AGI 2008c). This figure is so large that it is difficult to fully understand what it means. Yet what it does ask us to consider is, what do we mean when we talk about unintended or unplanned pregnancy? We should also understand that there are times women are not intending to become pregnant, but may not be actively working to avoid it. They may view intent, not just in terms of the presence or absence of contraception, but also in terms of the choices and statuses of their relationships (Barrett and Wellings 2002). Returning to our story of the "oops-baby" at the beginning, that baby is by definition unintended. But how does that pregnancy get discussed? How do women think of their own pregnancies? How do they define intent and accidents? How do they redefine those meanings throughout pregnancy? And how do those around them view their reproduction or sexuality: as normative or problematic? We should also remember that unplanned does not necessarily mean unwelcome or unwanted.

Finally, in thinking about the ways our reproductive desires change over time, we should also think of how our political and interpersonal discourse can be more respectful of each other's reproductive goals and experiences. Although there is political will to reduce rates of unintended pregnancy, there has been decreased support for access to comprehensive education on family planning in schools, a movement away from minors' abilities to access contraceptive and abortion services on their own (without parental consent), and laws in several states that ban the use of public and private insurance funding for abortion services. We also have inadequate support for women and men who choose to continue unintended pregnancies. Funding for children's health insurance, prenatal care, parental leave from paid employment, or affordable childcare have not been broadly supported and have in fact faced cuts across the country. As we work toward respecting each other's struggles around reproduction, we should also ask how we can support ways to help people make their reproductive plans and desires their reality.

Note

1 Estimates are that about 30 percent of conceptions or early pregnancies are lost before a woman knows she could be pregnant. Davidoff, Frank. 2006. "Sex, Politics, Morality at the FDA." *The Hastings Center Report* 36:20–25.

References

Abma, J. C., G. M. Martinez, W. D. Mosher, and B. S. Dawson. 2004. "Teenagers in the United States: Sexual activity, contraceptive use, and childbearing, 2002." National Center for Health Statistics, Washington, DC.

AGI. 2008a. "Facts on Contraceptive Use." edited by A. G. Institute. Washington, DC: Alan Guttmacher Institute.

——. 2008b. "Facts on Young Men's Sexual and Reproductive Health." edited by A. G. Institute. Washington, DC: Guttmacher Institute.

——. 2008c. "Improving Contraceptive Use in the United States." Washington, DC: Guttmacher Institute.

——. 2010. "Facts on American Teens' Sexual and Reproductive Health.." Pp. on-line. Washington, DC: Alan Guttmacher Institute.

Barrett, Geraldine and Kaye Wellings. 2002. "What Is a 'Planned' Pregnancy? Empirical Data from a British Study." *Social Science and Medicine* 55: 545–57.

Beenhakker, B., S. Becker, S. Hires, N. Molano Di Targiana, P. Blumenthal, and G. Huggins. 2004. "Are Partners Available for Post-Abortion Contraceptive Counseling? A Pilot Study in a Baltimore City Clinic." *Contraception* 69:419–23.

DeNavas-Walt, Carmen, Bernadette D. Proctor, and Jessica C. Smith. 2009. "Income, Poverty, and Health Insurance Coverage in the United States: 2008." U.S. Census Bureau, Washington, DC.

Finer, Lawrence B., Lori F. Frohwirth, Lindsay A. Dauphinee, Susheela Singh, and Ann M. Moore. 2005. "Reasons U.S. Women Have Abortions: Quantitative and Qualitative Perspectives." *Perspectives on Sexual and Reproductive Health* 37: 110–18.

Finer, Lawrence B. and Stanley K. Henshaw. 2006. "Disparities in Rates of Unintended Pregnancy In the United States, 1994 and 2001." *Perspectives on Sexual and Reproductive Health* 38: 90–96.

Frost, Jennifer and Jacqueline E. Darroch. 2008. "Factors Associated with Contraceptive Choice and Inconsistent Method Use, United States, 2004." *Perspectives on Sexual and Reproductive Health* 40: 94–104.

Jones, Rachel K., Lori F. Frohwirth, and Ann M. Moore. 2008. "'I Would Want to Give My Child, Like, Everything in the World'." *Journal of Family Issues* 29: 79–99.

Kaiser Family Foundation. 2005. "Health Insurance Coverage in America: 2004 Data Update Report." Henry J. Kaiser Family Foundation, Menlo Park, CA.

Martinez, G. M., A. Chandra, J. C. Abma, J. Jones, and W. D. Mosher. 2006. "Fertility, Contraception, and Fatherhood: Data on Men and Women from Cycle 6 (2002) of the 2002 National Survey of Family Growth." Washington, DC: National Center for Health Statistics.

Mosher, William D., Gladys M. Martinez, Anjani Chandra, Joyce C. Abma, and Stephanie J. Willson. 2004. "Use of Contraception and Use of Family Planning Services in the United States: 1982–2002." Centers for Disease Control and Prevention, Atlanta, GA.

Reich, Jennifer A. 2008. "Not Ready to Fill His Father's Shoes: A Masculinist Discourse of Abortion." *Men and Masculinities* 11: 3–21.

Part 5
Intimacies

Introduction

If we could transport ourselves to America or England in 1900, we would likely find ourselves in both a familiar and foreign environment. Familiar because most Americans or Brits, then and now, were married, had children, and lived in their own households independent of their family of origin. The link of intimacy and marriage was tight and celebrated by rituals of engagement and weddings, just as we often do today. Also, some of these marriages ended in separation and divorce, and some of these divorcees would remarry. All this would feel familiar and perhaps comforting to us.

Our time traveler would, however, feel like a stranger, even a foreigner, in some important ways. In Victorian America or England, the different aspects of intimacy were all bundled into the institution of marriage. That is, sexuality (meaning heterosexuality), love, companionship, and parenthood, were expected to occur entirely within the institution of marriage. There may have been sex outside of marriage, or same-sex intimacies, or even children born out of wedlock, but all of these practices would have been stigmatized and likely resulted in scandal or worse. The institution of marriage was the only legitimate, respectable social context for romantic intimacy for our Victorian ancestors.

In the last 100 years, however, these different dimensions of sexual intimacy are no longer necessarily bundled together. Today, in most Western nations, individuals, especially the young, have choices about whether and how to combine the different aspects of intimacy. You can choose to marry but you can also cohabit with your partner without ever marrying; while most Americans marry after a period of cohabitation, many West Europeans are in fact choosing to not marry. The same Americans and Europeans may today choose a non-heterosexual intimacy, for example, same-sex intimacy or a romantic bond between two trans persons. While same-sex couples cannot marry in America, they can in many European nations. Today, marriage may or may not involve children, while same-sex couples may decide to adopt or to have children through alternative forms of insemination. And while love remains the center of romantic intimacy, as it did for our Victorian ancestors, its meaning has changed. Sexual compatibility, a deep sense of soulful connection, and the dense intertwining of personal and social lives are central to romantic love today. In Victorian times, love was expected to develop after marriage, and it had more to do with fulfilling gender roles and maintaining mutual respect than self-realization and communicative solidarity.

In short, individuals today, at least in America and across much of Europe, have a wide range of intimate choices available to them. We can choose whether or not we want to forge an intimate relationship, with whom, whether to marry, have children, be monogamous, and even whether we want to live together. And, of course, we can choose to dissolve our intimate bonds when we are no longer happy or satisfied. The sphere of romantic love has become for many of us a primary site of freedom and self-fulfillment through forging a transformative intimacy with our soul mate.

As a result, intimacies exhibit a diversity of forms and meanings, flexibility and openness, that is unique to our present age. Some critics may assail this intimate diversity for weakening the institution of marriage and the family, or for tolerating too much individual choice, but there is no going back to our Victorian ancestors. Our challenge today is to figure out how to balance our desire for choice and self-fulfillment with our equal need for intimate security and solidarity. This challenge will almost certainly mean that the sphere of romantic intimacy will continue to be a site of enormous hope, promise, and conflict for decades to come.

28

Romantic love

Interview with Eva Illouz

HEBREW UNIVERSITY OF JERUSALEM, ISRAEL

Eva Illouz was born in Morocco and moved to France when she was ten. She went on to get a PhD in Communications at the Annenberg School of Communications at the University of Pennsylvania. Since 1991 she has lived in Israel, where she teaches at the Hebrew University of Jerusalem. She is the author of four books, *Consuming the Romantic Utopia* (University of California Press, 1997), *The Culture of Capitalism* (Israel University Broadcast), *Oprah Winfrey and the Glamour of Misery* (Columbia University Press, 2003), and *Befuhle im Kapitalismus* (Suhrkamp Verlag, forthcoming).

Is romantic love a natural feeling or is it a product of social and cultural life?

When sociology and anthropology took up the subject of emotions – some twenty years ago – they rejected *en bloc* the psychological and biological view that emotions are pre-cultural, individual, and not subject to historical forces. In short they rejected what we may call an essentialist view of emotions, the view that emotions are things that exist in themselves and are permanent. My own work is very much influenced by the opposite view, the constructivist view, which holds that the experience of emotions is shaped by language and that the rules governing their expression and exchange are essentially social.

But if it is now well established that ideas pertaining to God or to sexuality are subject to cultural and historical variations, we are less inclined to think that emotions can and do change and that they are subject to the influence of culture. Like anger, love is often thought to be a universal emotion. To make things more difficult for us, there seems to be evidence that falling in love takes similar characteristics in different periods of time and in different cultures. For example, in many cultures, sight plays an important role in the activation of emotion (many languages have an equivalent of the expression "love at first sight"); the feeling of falling in love is sudden and is experienced as a disruption of one's routine and daily life; it is overwhelming and often takes an obsessive character; finally, the emotion of falling in love is experienced as overpowering the person's will. All of these characteristics can be found in the sixth-century Arabic legend of Majnoun and Leyla, in the thirteenth-century German epic by Gottfried von Strassburg "Tristan und Isolde," or the early thirteenth-century French fable "Aucassin et Nicolette," in William Shakespeare's sixtenth-century *Romeo and Juliet*, as well as in contemporary

Hollywood cinema. And to top it all, contemporary research in neuro-psychology seems to confirm the existence of specific brain regions which are activated when falling in love, which would in turn suggest that falling in love is grounded in biology, not culture, and therefore likely to be universal rather than bound by culture and language.

Contrary to some of my colleagues, I think it is unproductive to engage in a head-on collision with the biological research paradigm. Instead of arguing about the biological versus contextual nature of emotions, we should try to understand exactly just which aspects of the life of emotions, each paradigm – biological or constructivist – can or cannot account for. The question which I have thus tried to address in my work is: what can constructivists, like me, account for in love which the essentialists can't? I think that the biological approach to emotions cannot say anything about the social rules which activate emotional experiences and the fine-grained meanings contained in them.

The emotion of romantic love cannot be separated from social rules pertaining to the control of women's and men's sexuality, the regulation of marriage, and the ways in which property is transmitted. Without knowing something about these topics, we cannot understand which mental scripts fill people's heads when they say they are in love, nor can we understand whether and how love is encouraged or prohibited in a given society. For example, I would argue that falling in love is an importantly different experience whether women's virginity is defined as a condition for marriage or whether sexual experimentation before marriage is encouraged. When women's sexuality is closely regulated and limited to marriage, as was the case, say, in nineteenth-century America, romantic love takes the form of an all-encompassing narrative engulfing the self, expressing an absolute emotion and total commitment. Because sexual love was to be entrusted to one person only, such a conception of love emphasized the irreplaceable uniqueness of the love object. When, after the 1960s, women's sexuality became more a matter of individual desire and choice, romantic love took the form of a narrative of self-exploration; the link between sex, love, and marriage was weakened.

Let me take another example. In Ancient Greece, the supreme form of love was that between a mature man and a young boy. What preoccupied Greek culture was not to formulate a life-long commitment or to translate love into the institution of marriage, but rather, who penetrated whom. The older man had to be the one to penetrate, not be penetrated. He was to be active because the love between them was an affection between the mature man and the younger man in which the mature man was to guide the younger man and be a sort of substitute father to him. All this is done at the same time that the older man is married, has a legitimate wife, and children.

So we see in these examples that the biological approach to emotions cannot account for the social rules that guide the expression and social organization of emotions, and more importantly, biological views cannot explain the changing meanings of emotions and love.

Many of us think of the world of romantic love and the world of the marketplace as different and antagonistic. Is this a mistaken view?

Let me answer this question with a literary, but historically accurate, example. In his memoirs, Casanova, the eighteenth-century adventurer and seducer of a large number of women, recounts how, on being introduced to a lady of quality, a countess, he is taken by her beauty and charm. The day after meeting her, he goes to call on her in her house. He finds himself in a sitting room furnished with "four rickety chairs and a dirty old table." This sad and surprising spectacle is not improved by the countess's appearance, for, when she arrives, Casanova is struck by the misery and uncleanliness of her *déshabillé*. Understanding his dismay, she appeals to his pity and explains that, although of noble extraction, her father receives only a very small salary which he must share with his nine children. Casanova's immediate and unapologetic reaction deserves to be quoted: "I was not rich myself, and, as I was no longer in love, I only heaved a deep sigh, and remained as cold as ice."

Casanova, the reckless adventurer and charming seducer, turns out to have the soul of a cold-blooded accountant. His ardent love evaporates as soon as he is confronted with the countess's shabby economic situation. In the thoughts and feelings Casanova lets his reader take a peek at, economic interest breathes naturally through sentiments. Contrary to what a modern reader would think today, Casanova's thoughts were far from immoral. Quite the opposite; in a pre-capitalist world, to be moral implied one knew to choose an object of desire by taking into account his or her social standing. In an economy with restricted labor markets and circulation of commodities, property and inheritance were crucial to one's social standing, and property could be maintained or increased mostly through marriage. In a pre-capitalist world, the conduct of private life was thus subservient to economic strategies, interests, and modes of evaluation. If in non- or pre-capitalist societies, economic decisions were based on moral meanings (for example, who could work where on the basis of their religious membership; who could engage in banking activities, etc.), by the same token, sentimental or emotional decisions were always colored by economic considerations.

In contrast, and contrary to conventional wisdom and even contrary to some strands in sociological thought, I would claim that capitalism has been a great separator of sentiments and economic calculations.

By taking economic production out of the household, by making people less dependent on inherited property, and by making the family into an emotional – rather than an economic – unit, capitalism made marriage out of love entirely legitimate and even commendable, affirmed the sovereignty of individuals' emotional choices, and radically separated sentiments from interests. In capitalism, people could sell their labor on an open market, and thus became less dependent on inheritance for their economic survival, making them better able to choose according to their inclination. Moreover, by taking economic activity out of the household, capitalism made the family specialized in emotions, rather than in economic production.

Engels, Marx's famous collaborator, thought that in bourgeois marriage the desire to preserve or transmit private property was simply too strong to override disinterested love and sentiments, but Engels was wrong, for in many ways the reverse has happened: because capitalism made economy into a specialized activity – independent of sexual reproduction and marriage – it also made the family into a non-economic unit, an emotional hothouse in which men and women would become increasingly preoccupied with their mutual love, sexuality, individual self-development and parental affection. The norm of love that has been made possible by the capitalist economy has disturbed the rules by which people came to choose a partner and which governed what they could expect from marriage.

Thus, I am saying that capitalism has instituted a divide between interests and emotions, channeling each of them into a distinctive institutional sphere. The ironical conclusion of this is that the market and the social organization of capitalism are intricately intertwined with the fact that love became defined as a strictly disinterested emotion, that is, one without an a priori consideration of the partner's economic assets and social standing. So there is a paradox here, for it is the market society which has made possible the separation between interests and intimate relationships.

What are some of the social forces that create a culture of romantic love?

First, let us establish what a culture of romantic love means. It is a culture whereby the definition of the good life includes finding a person able to generate long-lasting and yet exciting feelings, and being able to extend the experience of love throughout one's life. In other words, a culture of love is a culture where the experience of love plays a central role in the definition of self and in which actors engage in a wide variety of symbolic practices to create, experience and maintain the emotion of love. Moreover, this love is not just any kind of love: it is heterosexual but not necessarily oriented toward child-bearing and child-rearing; it is connected to marriage, but can very well thrive without it; it privileges intensity and excitement, yet aims or claims to be long-lasting; finally, it is individualistic both in the sense that it gives expression to the innermost unique and authentic aspects of the self and in the sense that it is closely associated with the idea of self-realization.

Contrary to a naive view of modernity as a heartless and bureaucratized era, I would say that modernity has made love into our categorical imperative, the experience without which we do not feel fully accomplished human beings.

A number of factors have contributed to creating such culture: the most important is the public/private divide I mentioned earlier. Without the creation of an institutional and cultural divide between the public and private self and a massive cultural shift making the private self the sole repository of authenticity, meaning, and commitment, a culture of love as I defined it would not be possible.

Moreover, love flourishes in individualistic cultures. Individualism is the social transformation without which we cannot understand the rise of a culture of love. Individualism has many institutional sites (legal, economic, moral, etc.). But in the twentieth century it was the culture of consumption which shaped most significantly the individualist search for love. It is the individualism promoted by consumption which has perhaps most contributed to institutionalize a culture of romance. Contrary to conventional wisdom, I would say that consumer culture is not a materialist culture, but rather a deeply emotional one. Consumer culture caters to and elicits some deeply rooted emotions – as love or the need for security – through scenarios of the good life and models of self-realization. Consumer culture has used extensively the image of the couple in love to promote its goods (a man and a woman engaged either explicitly or implicitly in a romantic interaction is probably the most widespread image in advertising culture). Moreover, at the end of the nineteenth century, the leisure industries, avid to expand their economic and social reach, catered to men's and women's search for intimacy. Thus what we call dating implies both that the couple meet outside the home and that they purchase together a leisure good: to go to a movie, to a bar, or to a restaurant – which have all become normal arenas for romantic meetings – is to engage in a consumer activity which gives expression to an individual's inner self and search for pleasure and happiness.

For these different forces to coalesce into a coherent cultural model which can in turn guide the self, experience must be organized in a cultural form which expresses and gives shape to a new way of feeling. If, during much of the eighteenth and nineteenth centuries, it was the novel which offered to the self a narrative model of love (especially to its female readers), in the twentieth century this role was assumed (and even amplified) by the movie. In this way Hollywood transformed the culture of love in a few significant ways: if, until then, love had been connected to the rhetoric of religious devotion, it now became more radically secular and a project for its own sake; whereas the nineteenth-century novel contained sexuality in a euphemized and implicit way, Hollywood, using the obvious characteristics of the visual medium, abundantly depicted romantic kisses, embraces, and petting, and explicitly alluded to sexual interactions and naturalized the association of love and sexuality. More than any other cultural medium, the movies defined romantic interactions in visual terms: a romantic moment would now be defined not only by culturally explicit scenarios of sexual interactions, but also by a certain kind of "atmosphere" containing specific props (for example, a romantic dinner or the proximity of the sea). Finally, contrary to literary strands which had preceded it, Hollywood built a strong association and equivalence between love, marriage, and happiness. Thanks to the movies, love became a powerful motive in the modern cultural imagination.

What do you mean by the idea of romantic love as a kind of utopia?

A utopia is a narrative through which societies think out loud about and formulate their preferred social arrangements. This is why utopias typically erase contradictions: to dream that the lamb and the wolf will coexist (as the Book of the Prophets envisioned), negates nature and the state of scarcity to which the human condition has often been submitted to. The romantic utopia describes how self-fulfillment, authenticity, meaning and happiness are reached in the experience of heterosexual love. Similar to other utopias, it negates a number of contradictions particularly rife in modern societies, such as the contradiction between marriage and the non- or anti-institutional love that is implied by the traditional ideal of love. But this does not mean that utopias are a form of false thinking. On the contrary: utopias must be distinguished from ideology – even if this distinction is tenuous and open to argument. Utopias make us dream about a better world, about alternative arrangements, and even if those dreams often degenerate in control and manipulation, we still must account for the hope and creativity they contain and often generate. Utopias inspire change.

Moreover, utopias shape our thoughts or dreams through specific means of expression and communication. The romantic utopia is essentially a visual one, combining ideals of beauty, models of masculinity and femininity, visual scenarios of romantic scenery, with models of sexual manners and courtship.

What I find particularly interesting in the romantic utopia is that it reproduces ideals of masculinity and femininity, yet it is simultaneously a genderless ideal. Historically, we observe that the greater the injunction to love inside marriage, the higher the status of women. But the romantic utopia went one step further, in that it "femininized" men, that is it drew them inside the purview of domesticity, and offered to merge men and women in a genderless model of intimacy. Through the ideal of intimacy, men and women are enjoined to foreground similar selves centered around the verbal expression and sharing of their emotional inner self. In fact, the tension which haunts modern couplehood can be understood precisely as a tension between genderless ideals and the persistence of gender differences and inequalities.

You argue that the idea of dating didn't become widespread until the 1930s. What do you see as the significance of dating for the development of romantic love?

At the end of the nineteenth century, dating was a word reserved for the working class because it implied that the couple would meet outside the confines of the domestic sphere. By and large, members of the middle class met inside the home, and commercial amusements were not considered as appropriate venues to meet. Dating was inappropriate because, let us remember, it implied two different things: one is an interaction that has a potentially romantic character in a public space, not guarded or defined by middle-class values; the second is that this interaction takes place in the sphere of commercial entertainment. Dating could become widespread and common when leisure consumption became generalized – reaching all social classes – and institutionalized. For example, going to a fancy restaurant or on a vacation in a faraway location becomes the privileged site for the experience of romance. Thus we may say that dating is the outcome of a romanticization of commodities (the refrigerator becomes romantic when associated with a couple dining by the light of candles) and a commodification of romance (experiencing romance becomes increasingly connected to being able to purchase leisure goods). Dating is an outstanding example of how the interaction between a new technology, images, gender definitions, and economic changes converge to create a new social form, in the Simmelian sense of that word.

But what exactly does this entail? Many would argue that this entails a severe degradation of the romantic bond. I am not convinced that commodities and consumption as such debase human relationships. In fact, meeting in such consumption-oriented places as restaurants, or going on a weekend in a luxurious resort, often end up generating (or regenerating) intense feelings. Commodities have the power to ritualize interactions by making clearer their spatial and temporal boundaries, that is by making them mark off the conduct and objects of daily life.

Moreover, in the culture of dating the idiom of pleasure becomes dominant and the anonymity afforded by public spaces entails a perceived greater freedom, which in turn leads to one of the processes Seidman and Giddens have described, namely a progressive disconnection of romance from marriage. So, if from the eighteenth century onward we see a close association of marriage and love, in the twentieth century we see a progressive separation of these two modes of conduct.

Between the nineteenth century and World War Two the meaning of love changed from spiritual edification to personal happiness. Have there been any significant changes in the meaning of romantic love since World War Two?

I don't think the changes have been as dramatic as those we observe in the passage from the nineteenth century to World War Two. Still, they are important changes which are related to the transformations undergone by sexuality. I am going to set aside the question of the transformation of sexuality during that period. Seidman's work explores this question thoroughly and I have very little to add to it. I think that two cultural persuasions have massively altered the meaning of love: one is psychologism – the broad cultural worldview and language derived from various schools of clinical psychology, especially dynamic psychology; the other is feminism – the view inspired by political liberalism, a view which calls on granting men and women equal rights and status inside the private and public spheres. How have these two formations altered the romantic bond?

Both contributed to what we may call with Max Weber a disenchantment of the romantic bond. By this I mean a new ironic detachment from the idea of love and a reflexive attitude *vis-à-vis* its psychological and sociological underpinnings. Psychology, for one, put forward the idea that love is never quite what it looks like. For psychoanalysis, the psyche is deeply ambivalent, and thus love turns out to be a close cousin of its opposite, hatred. Moreover, the culture of psychology invites us to doubt how seriously we should take our feelings. Where the romantic tradition suggested that love was an inexplicable recognition of a unique person destined to us, psychology explains love as the need to reenact losses and painful aspects of our past relationships with caring characters.

Feminism also has put love under the microscope.[1] Contrary to popular mythology, radical feminists argue, love is not the source of transcendence, happiness, and self-realization. Rather, romantic love is one of the main causes of the divide between men and women, as well as one of the cultural practices through which women are made to accept (and "love") their submission to men. For, when in love, men and women continue to perform the deep divisions that characterize their respective identities: in Simone de Beauvoir's famous words, even in love men retain their sovereignty, while women aim to abandon themselves. Or, in her *Dialectic of Sex*, Shulamit Firestone argues that the source of men's social power and energy is the love women have provided and continue to provide for men, thus suggesting that love is the cement with which the edifice of male domination has been built. Romantic love not only hides a sex segregation, but in fact it makes it possible.

I think that the two cultural persuasions of feminism and psychology have thus made us deeply suspicious of love, or at least ironic *vis-à-vis* its most conventional aspects.

In the popular media, romantic love is viewed as something we all experience in more or less the same way. But is romantic love truly experienced in a classless way and is it the same between men and women?

Well, yes and no. If romance and love are such powerful utopias, it is precisely because they are genderless and classless. In a way, this is why romantic love has been a transgressive social force, precisely because it often disturbed class boundaries and mechanisms of transmission of property: for a prince to fall in love with a poor shepherdess means to relinquish a great source of power. In our popular representations, love makes men leave the competitive realm of power, and draws them in the emotion-filled female sphere of care and nurturance. It is true that capitalism was responsible for locking men and women in separate gender spheres – relegating women to what Hannah Arendt has dubbed "the shadowy realm of the interior," and throwing men into the harsh and competitive arena of the market – but in making romantic love an intrinsic component of bourgeois marriage it also increased the status of women and in fact slowly eroded male supremacy inside the household. It is also true that modern marriages are not as far from arranged marriages as one would like to think (statistics show we often end up marrying somebody socially and economically compatible with us). Yet, the norm of love has changed importantly how people choose a partner and what they expect from marriage.

In that sense, romantic love has been an anti-institutional force, if not destroying then at least disturbing class and gender divisions. The connection of consumer culture and love in a way only reinforced this "oecumenical" appeal of the romantic utopia.

Yet, things are not that simple. Let's take the gender dimension. Past the stage of courtship, women tend to be the ones who monitor the relationship and who bear the burden of doing "emotional work." Or, take the class dimension: in many subtle and not-so-subtle ways, people's cultural tastes and ways of talking – which are deeply connected to one's education and socioeconomic level – affect how they express their emotions, how they are able to draw other people into their emotional life, and whether they are able to create moments of intense bonding, those precise moments where you forget another's socioeconomic status. Quite often, in order to be able to do that – that is, to create moments of pure bonding – two people need to be in harmony together, but such harmony of the hearts is quite often a social harmony, predicated on common cultural and social references. Finally, I would say that romance has been and continues to be an upper-middle-class way of life because it presupposes a not inconsiderable amount of resources in time and money.

So Lady Chatterley might be attracted for a while to the raw sexuality of her working-class lover, but when she needs expressions of love and emotions, she will most likely be flustered by the social and economic gap that normally separates them.

In American culture, the first date often involves going out to a restaurant. Are there sociological reasons for this?

The restaurant is the quintessential consumer space: it is both public and private, in that it caters to a large number of people, yet it also enables two people to isolate themselves and feel thoroughly individualized in their experience. Moreover the restaurant mobilizes a vast array of artifacts (food, light, tablecloth, music, general design); this is why it is able to ritualize the meeting, by which I mean, following Durkheim, that it enables two people to withdraw from daily conduct and to (re)generate intense feelings. What enables a couple to do that is the fact that a restaurant makes the activity of eating into a formal and aesthetic one (food, clothes, light, music, all conspire to make the meeting stylized), sharply distinct from daily life. The typical imagery of a romantic restaurant involves soft light (candles), langorous music, exotic and luxurious food presented in beautiful dishes, and an elegant décor. All of this creates an esthetic experience which de-familiarizes and enhances daily life. The restaurant thus enables a ritualization of the romantic bond. Moreover, given that a restaurant represents a small expenditure in the income of middle- or upper-middle-class people, the experience can be renewed frequently. The restaurant is thus the perfect meeting between consumer and romantic culture, whereby pleasure of the gustatory and olfactory senses and a wide variety of artifacts combine to create privacy, intimacy, and novelty, easily purchasable and renewable.

(By the way, in the era of internet dating, the restaurant is no longer likely to be the place where people meet on their first date.)

There is a trend in the United States for individuals to experience romantic love but remain single or cohabit. Why do you think this is happening, and will this trend continue?

Capitalism produces contradictions. I think that one of the most salient and less discussed contradictions is between the idea that forming long-lasting intimate bonds is of the utmost importance for the self, and the idea that the individual must strive for self-affirmation, autonomy, self-reliance, and self-realization. The culture of individuality from which romantic love emerged and in which it flourished has produced a culture in which men and women are increasingly self-reliant, take their own self as the object and center of their life narrative and life goals, and are thus less willing to engage in the kind of Other-oriented (what some view as self-sacrificing) practices demanded by family and marriage. This is especially true of women, who are less inclined to want to face the sometimes difficult tasks of having to combine work and children. Also, marriage has been and to a certain extent still is a primarily economic institution. Given that many women do not feel the need to marry for their economic survival, the necessity of marriage also fades.

But again, things are not simple, because even if marriage as such is on the decline, the norm of monogamy – which has been historically enforced as the prerogative of married people – seems to pervade heterosexual (nonmarried) relationships as if one of the main characteristics of marriage had been thoroughly internalized.

Note

1 This chapter deals with heterosexual love. Unless otherwise specified, use of the term "love" should be understood in this sense.

29

Gender and the organization of heterosexual intimacy

Daniel Santore

STATE UNIVERSITY OF NEW YORK AT ALBANY

Popular images of romance tend to suggest an idyllic bond between partners; intimacy, as portrayed in movies, television, books and other media, is a spontaneous, mutually fulfilling experience. Yet few of us would dispute that romantic intimate relationships can be more complicated than that. It is difficult for individuals to agree about what a "good relationship" entails, and who should be responsible for which kinds of duties. For all the carefree pop-culture imagery, the fact remains that intimacy is not free of conflict and involves tough decisions.

Sociology seeks out social explanations for the ways couples resolve disagreements and negotiate intimate life. Research on heterosexual intimate relations has found that *gender* is one resource upon which people rely when arranging their relationships. Cultural ideas about gender roles, as well as the different social positions occupied by women and men, are key social forces shaping our intimate relationships. This chapter explores how gender organizes heterosexual intimacy. Attention is paid throughout to power dynamics and inequalities between women and men in intimate relationships.

The claim of gender difference

Why is gender an important concept in understanding intimate relationships between women and men? One explanation, often associated with feminist perspectives, is that there are funda-mental differences between women and men. These differences are of the utmost importance in patterning all of our social experiences, including intimate relationships. Throughout the 1970s and 1980s, feminist social science and theory was rich with accounts of the salience of "gender difference" (Connell 1987). Gender-difference arguments posited essential differences between women and men based not on biological, but on *social* conditions. For example, one strand of gender-difference argument claims that women and men have different social experiences by virtue of living within a patriarchal capitalist system. Historically, capitalism has placed women in the private sphere (the home), and men in the public sphere (the workplace). The fact that women and men occupy systematically different social positions means that they experience social life in different ways. This arrangement has implications for heterosexual intimate life. A man oriented around his role as a capitalist worker assumes a practical, unemotional disposition toward intimacy that corresponds with the structural and cultural demands of such a role. A woman, on the other hand, placed in charge of maintaining the emotional well-being of the private realm of home and family, is expected to function primarily as a caring supporter of the man/worker. These different dispositions, then, rooted in the structure of capitalist society, are relevant to the intimate lives of women and men; the images of the emotionally closed-off man and the emotionally driven woman speak to the different social roles of men and women.

To continue with our example, these opposed gender roles (that is, the worldly, active man and the domestic woman), so prevalent in industrial capitalism, also structure sexual scripts for women and men. The man is expected to be the more aggressive initiator of sexual activity, while the more passive woman, whose own interests in or demands for sex are considered "bad form," merely supports (sexually) one more of the man's needs. Note that the differentiated experiences conditioned by capitalism are not *merely* differences; relations between women and men are characterized by inequality or relations of dominance and subordination. Gender inequality in intimacy is in this way bound up with the social structure of capitalist society.

Gender-difference arguments have been challenged on a number of grounds. For example, asserting essential *social* differences between women and men may be as damaging as assuming essential *natural* or *biological* differences. Why might that be so? The attempt to homogenize women's experience – according to any characteristic – leads to uniform accounts of women's lives, inattentive to differences among women. To assume broad similarities across so wide-ranging a group inevitably privileges certain characteristics and obscures others, none of which are representative of all women. The lives of women with variable sexual identities, of women of color, and of other marginalized women are obscured in a "capital-W" concept of woman. Moreover, many of the characteristics attributed to women (and men) in gender-difference arguments are not so easily spread around (Kimmel 2004). Warmth and sensitivity, perennial "feminine traits," are not the exclusive province of women, any more than assertiveness is the province of men. To the extent that gender-difference arguments assume a socially produced gender dichotomy, women and men alike are pigeonholed. Differences between the genders are highlighted, while differences within are ignored.

Is gender disappearing?

The idea that different, "gendered" experiences shape intimate relationships relies in part on an understanding of the social conditions that exist alongside gender. What does this mean? It means that, to understand the way ideas about gender develop, attention must be paid to the broader social context that shapes the lives of women and men. This idea can be illustrated by looking briefly at two periods in American heterosexual intimacy. We can think of America in the early 1800s as a setting in which intimate relationships between women and men were approached in a practical manner, as material needs weighed heavily upon the intimate relationship. Far from being barred from productive labor, women during this period often had an important if limited role in economic production. Not only men but women too had a hand in producing subsistence for the family, through farming, crafts, and other labor. Material survival during this period demanded that everyone pitch in, women and men alike.

In the late 1800s and early 1900s, at least in the middle classes, only the man was needed as a producer of material subsistence for the family. Women's roles shifted. To be sure, women's roles retained some responsibilities such as household maintenance, care-giving, reproducing healthy workers, etc. Yet women's participation in explicitly economic production (for example, making goods to be sold) was reduced. Along with these material changes, cultural ideas about gender also changed. In the early 1800s, when women and men performed similar labor, an ideology that women were unsuited for "real work" was less defensible. Yet such an ideology flourished during the end of the nineteenth century, when women were relieved (forced out) of many sectors of the labor market; it is in this period that American cultural ideas about "women's place is in the home" really became prominent. A new ideology declared that women's appropriate place was in the private sphere of the household, while men's was in the public world of work and government. This was justified by the idea that men were seen as decision-makers and leaders whereas women were viewed as caring and submissive. The point here is that the interaction of gender, culture, and economic structure is complicated and undergoes change.

Today we can observe new social shifts. It appears that major social changes in Western capitalist countries have profoundly affected the contemporary landscape of heterosexual intimacy. There is lessened dependence by women on men's wages, as more women attend college and go out to work. As a result, women have a reduced material need to be involved in intimate relationships. What people expect out of intimacy also changes. Intimate relationships become more romantically based, rather than based on survival; intimate desires can expand to include emotional and spiritual fulfillment. Finally, it is no longer only men who are encouraged to strike out and live a personally fulfilling life. Women too are increasingly advised not to feel forced to decide between emotional fulfillment through intimacy, or a fulfilling career. Women are encouraged to blaze their own path, much more so than they were before the 1960s.

These changes potentially mean real improvements for heterosexual intimacy. In particular, they promise to place women and men on more equal footing in their intimate relationships. This is the spirit in which Anthony Giddens (1991) has articulated the idea of the "pure relationship." To Giddens, intimacy between women and men in contemporary society points to a more democratized, mutually fulfilling relationship. As women's and men's lives and goals begin to look more similar, and women's right to a personally fulfilling intimate life is given equal weight, the chance emerges for an "intimacy of equals." Pure relationships leave behind many of the patterned gender differences that created inequality in relationships; now, women and men can openly discuss their needs and desires, and assess their relationship in terms of their personal fulfillment.

Gender, intimacy and (in)equality

There is a rich body of sociological work that indicates the jury is still out regarding the reality of egalitarian relationships. Even if cultural ideas about gender are changing, and ideals of intimacy emphasize equality, it does not necessarily mean real equality. For example, a culture of egalitarianism may lead men and women to agree to openness about communicating their needs and wants. But if there are still persisting *structural* gender inequalities, if men make more money and if their careers are more highly valued, men may still have more power in intimate decision-making.

So, what does the empirical record indicate about the status of gender equality in heterosexual intimacy? A lot of research has been done on heterosexual marriage. While married men do more housework than they did during the 1950s and 1960s, they still don't do nearly as much as their wives. Survey research conducted during the late 1980s found that married women perform almost 80 percent of all housework duties (Berardo et al. 1987). And even as gender disparities in *amounts* of housework shrink somewhat, the *types* of tasks performed by wives and husbands remain gender-role specific. Men tend to perform physical tasks like mowing the lawn, but not "administrative" tasks like arranging the family holiday dinner. The gender roles extend further, into the more "personal" realm of physical intimacy between women and men. Before marriage, young men in America typically enjoy freedom of sexual activity; monogamy is an expectation that comes along only *with* marriage. Women have not traditionally enjoyed such liberation. Indeed, it is only recently that women's bachelorette parties – a symbol of relinquishing sexual privileges – have sprung up, indicating a measure of women's own sexual freedom (Montemurro 2003).

Inequality in intimate relationships can have less obvious negative consequences for women. To the extent that women come to expect equality in intimacy, the failure to actually achieve this can lead, unsurprisingly, to frustration. Women may feel that they have to at least present their married lives – their divisions of housework, depth of emotional connection, and ideas of what's fair – in a manner consistent with popular expectations. This promises tension for women whose intimate lives fall far short of equality. For example, interviews with married women found that it can be a daily effort to construct a narrative of an egalitarian intimate life when actual practice is otherwise (Dryden 1999). When actual relationships do not measure up to what is expected, married women may engage in a complicated string of justifications and denials in order to fashion their "square-peg" intimate relationship into the "round-hole" ideal. Of course, this should not be interpreted as a reason why women should alter their expectations! Rather, it should be viewed as one more reason to redouble efforts to engage the deeper roots of gender inequality and male dominance in intimate relationships. If women are frustrated in their desires for equality in intimate life, it is not the expectations but the cultural and material causes of inequality that need fixing.

It is important to note that ideals of equality do exist in relationships – commitments to equality are no myth. Difficult though it is to shed gender when we step into an intimate relationship, there are heterosexual couples who consciously strive to do just that. Couples who actively reject gender as a resource in decision-making processes have succeeded to some extent, if only in small numbers (Risman and Johnson-Sumerford 1998). These couples commit to an ideal that women and men need not relinquish careers, hobbies, and friendships, simply because they enter into a romantic bond. For women this promises to be a liberating condition, as this privilege has not always been so readily extended to them. Moreover, this egalitarian ideal holds that the couple should strive for a fair division of jobs and responsibilities, and try to not use gender to determine who does what. Finally, these couples stress deep communication, a commitment to be attentive to each other's personal histories (often negatively referred to as "baggage") and to each other's individual aspirations and goals.

While an egalitarian ideal of intimacy may be widespread in American society, research suggests that the couples who are most likely actively to try to arrange their lives in this fashion tend to be dually employed, often professionals, and possess high levels of education. This means that many couples who do not have these economic and cultural resources will be at a structural disadvantage in trying to pursue and realize an egalitarian ideal.

The research suggests that this egalitarian ideal is elusive even for women in the most advantageous position. Even in couples where each person holds a high-status occupation, women may still defer to men's interests and wishes. For example, women employed as university faculty members have been shown to live within gendered patterns when it comes to decisions about professional and leisure activities. This is the case in part because the professional couples are more likely to live in "long-distance" relationships. Along with distant relationships come a number of issues to be addressed (for example, who goes to see whom; how often; how does each party make use of their valuable free time?). Research indicates that more often than not women visit men, not the other way around, putting aside work at their own jobs (Holmes 2004). And to the extent that women in distant relationships tend to spend more time at their male partners' residence/community than do men at women's, men need not cope, as women surely must, with the lack of friends and acquaintances associated with traveling in unfamiliar circles.

Conclusions

Intimate relationships between women and men change. Intimacy today looks different than it did 50 years ago, and looked different then than it did 50 years before that. There are cultural and structural reasons (for example, changes in economic production, and in gender roles and expectations) why relationships between women and men look the way they do at any given period. For all the large changes, however, we have durable, persistent themes on which to focus our analyses of intimate life. Gender, inequality, and power are core topics in any discussion of heterosexual intimacy, and have been since relationships between women and men were first considered by social science.

Whether we have moved to a place where intimacy between women and men is an "intimacy of equals" is a complicated question, Anthony Giddens's portrait of the pure relationship is neither accurate nor inaccurate. It is clear that women are a larger presence in the male-dominated public sphere; it is also clear that women's personal goals are often held to be as important as men's, and many relationships provide space for the pursuit of those goals. As a result, in many relationships women's needs and desires are more diverse, and are taken more seriously, than ever before. Yet gender inequalities persist within intimate relationships. It seems that the "gender revolution" – in heterosexual intimacy and myriad other areas – still has its work cut out, as has been the case since its beginnings.

Contrary to popular culture representations, romance between women and men does not guarantee equality; love, it turns out, does not conquer all. Even men and women's best intentions (for example, dividing chores, stressing emotional engagement, sharing child rearing) to erase a gender-ordered relationship are likely to remain incomplete fixes in the struggle for equality, *so long as institutional obstacles remain in place*. As many sociologists have noted, personal solutions alone are not enough to combat structural inequalities. Gender disparities in wages, lack of child-care, and sex-segregated labor markets, all pose problems for equality in heterosexual intimacy. A culture of equality in intimacy gets us part of the way; naming and fixing social-structural disadvantages for women are necessary for fuller equality.

References

Berardo, Donna Hodgkins, Constance L. Shehan, and Gerald R. Leslie. 1987. "A Residue of Tradition: Jobs, Careers, and Spouses' Time in Housework." *Journal of Marriage and the Family* 49(2): 381–90.

Connell, R. W. 1987. *Gender and Power*. Stanford, CA: Stanford University Press.

Dryden, Caroline. 1999. *Being Married, Doing Gender: A Critical Analysis of Gender Relationships in Marriage*. London: Routledge.

Giddens, Anthony. 1991. *Modernity and Self-Identity: Self and Society in the Late Modern Age*. Cambridge: Polity Press.

Holmes, M. (2004) "An Equal Distance? Individualization, Gender and Intimacy in Distance Relationships." *The Sociological Review* 52(2): 180–200.

Kimmel, Michael S. 2004. *The Gendered Society*. Oxford: Oxford University Press.

Montemurro, Beth. 2003. "Sex Symbols: The Bachelorette Party as a Window to Change in Women's Sexual Expression" *Sexuality & Culture* 7(2): 3–29.

Risman, Barbara J. and Dannette Johnson-Sumerford. 1998. "Doing it Fairly: A Study of Postgender Marriages." *Journal of Marriage and the Family* 60(1): 23–40.

30

Shopping for love

Online dating and the making of a cyber culture of romance[1]

Sophia DeMasi

MONTGOMERY COUNTY COMMUNITY COLLEGE, PENNSYLVANIA

Ten years ago, a reader of any mainstream national publication or local weekly could not have helped but notice the ubiquitous personal advertisements that saturated their back pages. Today, these same personal advertisements have migrated to the virtual pages of the World Wide Web. A casual glance at the content of online personal advertisements suggests that their writers solicit readers for a variety of reasons, including friendship, a long-term relationship, and casual sex; however, dating dominates the virtual landscape. The vast majority of online personal ads are written by people who want to date as a prelude to a satisfying long-term relationship (Brym and Lenton 2001). With an estimated 2,500 dating websites in operation entertaining approximately 40 million visitors each month (Sullivan 2002), internet dating is now a popular and vital part of the process by which people seek and find intimate partners.

Until recently, the use of personal advertisements to locate intimate partners was understood as a deviant activity resorted to only by "losers" left out of the marriage market, or "perverts" seeking illicit sexual encounters. In addition, the stigma attached to users of personal ads made many reluctant to reveal the activity to others (Darden and Koski 1988; Rajecki and Rasmussen 1992). Those days are gone. Now it is quite common for people to publicly reveal their experiences with online dating. It is not at all unusual to hear coworkers, friends, and acquaintances shamelessly boast about a successful date or to confess to a dating fiasco that began with an online personal advertisement. In offices, classrooms, and living rooms across the country, online daters boldly relate the latest update to their online profile and how many "hits" it got.

Another sign of the astonishing popularity of online dating is its visiblity in popular culture. Currently available are over thirty self-help books that instruct users of dating websites in the finer points of creating an effective online profile. Book titles like *E Dating Secrets: How to Surf for your Perfect Love Match on the Internet, Everything you Need to Know about Romance and the Internet, 50+ and Looking for Love Online*, and *Worldwide Search: The Savvy Christian's Guide to Online Dating* indicate that online dating now has mass appeal across sexual orientation, race, age and religious groups. The popular press has also put internet dating in the spotlight by publishing the revelations of ordinary people who found their companions through online personals

(Foston 2003; Wilkinson 2005). Self-help books and the public testimony of online daters help put to rest the belief that online dating is something resorted to only by desperate people.

The tremendous expansion of online personals, along with the public pronouncements of the people who use them, suggests that technologically mediated dating is now a socially acceptable method for finding intimate partners. Stigma and shame are no longer associated with people who seek to connect with others through personal advertisements. How has the formerly "deviant" activity of using print personal ads to seek and find partners given way to the apparently routine practice of seeking and finding companions through online personal advertisements? Moreover, what consequences might this change in medium have on the process of finding romantic and/or sexual partners?

Recent technological innovations and demographic changes are part of the reason why online dating has become such a common practice in the first decade of the twenty-first century. More significant, however, are the deliberate marketing strategies used to increase the appeal of online dating. Together, these factors work to expand possibilities for finding partners and establishing intimate relationships. But, paradoxically, online dating also limits the possibilities for creating relationships, particularly those that exist outside the narrow confines of relationship ideals historically identified with heterosexual intimacy. To attract a large number of participants, dating websites rely primarily on a particular construction of intimate relationships that emphasizes love, romance, and monogamy; they rarely mention sex for pleasure and the desire for physical intimacy. Moreover, embedded in the structure of online dating websites are existing gender and sexual identity categories that preclude explorations of novel identity constructions. Consequently, online dating ensures homogeneity in the types of relationships that are sought and found online.

"Anyone can do it": the normalization of internet dating

It is impossible to understand how online dating has become mainstream without mentioning the rise of internet technology. Access to the internet rose steadily throughout the 1990s. In 1995, only 9 percent of adults in the United States were online. This figure increased to 56 percent by 1999 and to 67 percent by 2003 (Harris Poll 2003). Along with increased access to the internet, its ease of use has increased as low-cost, high-speed connections have become available to more people. Also significant is the demographics of internet users. Initially, the use of internet technology was limited to the young, affluent, and highly educated. Though these groups are still slightly more likely than older, poorer, and less educated groups to use internet technology, a recent Harris Poll (2003) reveals that the internet population is beginning to look more like the general US population in terms of education, income, and age. As internet use expands to include more people, it provides the mass audience needed for internet dating.

When internet technology was first made available to the general public in the mid-1990s, it was enthusiastically hailed as an innovation that would fundamentally alter the way individuals accomplish the routine tasks of life. Today, the internet is used to do practically everything from reading the newspaper, paying bills, buying a home, searching for a job, taking educational courses, and purchasing consumer items. Finding a partner through the internet represents just one more of the many activities that the technology enables.

In addition to technological innovation, demographic changes have contributed to the growth of internet dating. According to social historian Barbara Dafoe Whitehead (2003), in the last three decades there has been a tremendous increase in the pool of people seeking mates. Thirty years ago, the dating pool was limited to young people who had never married. Today, it includes never-married men and women across a much wider age range, because both men and women marry at much later ages. In addition, the high divorce rate has created a large number of people who are looking for second and even third relationships. As well, older people who are living longer are also seeking companionship. Finally, the rise in the legitimacy of gay and lesbian relationships has propelled these individuals into the open market for relationships. Gays and lesbians are now able to seek partners through more conventional channels than they did thirty years ago, when they suffered greater public condemnation of their relationships. A large audience of actual and potential online daters has been created by these cultural changes.

While technological and demographic changes are part of the explanation for the rise of internet dating, they are not sufficient to explain why it has become such an enormously popular and commonplace activity. Equally significant is the purposeful effort by marketers to construct online dating as a legitimate way for ordinary people to meet partners. In order to increase revenues through paid customer subscriptions, marketers of online dating sites have deployed strategies to increase their mass appeal (Sullivan 2002). One approach has been to promote online dating websites as places where romantic relationships are easily acquired by all participants, a strategy evident in print advertisements and on network and cable television.

Typically, advertisements for online dating services promise quickly to transform unhappy, lonely, single people into blissful, content couples, if they just take the initiative to join and post a personal profile. For example, the advertising copy of a recent television ad campaign by Match.com, an online dating site that claims to have the largest number of personal profiles, asks potential members: "Will you ever find the person who will change your life?" This rhetorical question is, of course, followed by an emphatic "Yes!" By using the free guide from Match.com entitled "How to find the right person in 90 days," the ad implies that finding a partner online is so easy that *anyone* can do it. Advertisements such as these present online dating as an efficient and utterly conventional activity. Moreover, they help convince the public that internet dating is a viable way to meet a partner.

The legitimacy and appeal of online dating is further enhanced by the prominent suggestion that it is fundamentally about realizing the relationship goals of romance, love, and monogamous coupling. Regardless of whether online dating services are intended for heterosexual, gay, or lesbian users, they are typically constructed as places where conventionally established ideals of intimacy can be attained. For example, a visitor to the home page of EHarmony, a popular website for heterosexuals, is told that it is the website to use "when you are ready to find the love of your life." Similarly, Match.com proclaims itself to be "the world's number 1 place for love." Almost identical declarations are made on dating websites intended exclusively for lesbians and gays. Visitors to Planet Out will immediately notice the advertising copy that reads: "Find your Mr. or Ms. Right now!" Just underneath the bold headline is a link to the personal ads that reads: "Find Love." Although the home page of GayFriendFinder, an online dating site for gay men, carefully alludes to the possibility of a purely sexual relationship, it too makes love and romance a central part of its purpose. Its banner exclaims: "Find sexy single men for dating, romance, and *more*" [italics mine]. For additional emphasis, the headlines plastered across the home pages of heterosexual and gay and lesbian dating websites are routinely accompanied by visual graphics that conspicuously display stereotypical images of love and romance. Pictures that accompany print banners typically show two people holding hands, locked in a warm embrace, or gazing into each other's eyes over a candlelit dinner.

The inclusion of gays and lesbians within the rubric of love, romance, and monogamy is ironic precisely because gays and lesbians have historically been seen as incapable of achieving the relationship ideals typically linked to heterosexuality. Indeed, the idea that gays and lesbians are so far outside the boundaries of intimate convention that they cannot sustain intimate relationships based on love and monogamous commitment is an argument made by gay marriage opponents today. Of course, gay and lesbian patterns of intimacy do not necessarily preclude love, romance, and monogamy, but these options are not always the fundamental criteria around which lesbians and gays construct their relationships. A variety of historically unique types of intimate relationship characterize gay and lesbian subcultures: serial monogamy among lesbians, gay male subcultures based on sex, lesbian "Boston marriages" where physical intimacy is apparently absent, and butch–femme relationships that play on a heightened awareness of gender. Dating websites ignore these complex relationships in favor of assimilating gay and lesbian intimacy into a framework modeled on heterosexual standards of intimacy.

Indeed, most dating websites follow a similarly generic formula that includes the relentless depiction of words and images associated with heterosexual romance and a calculated muting of the sexual possibilities that might inspire or follow online encounters. Certainly, many online services exist primarily to link people who desire to meet others only for sexual activity, but websites whose business is limited to dating intentionally desexualize their content. The specific rules many dating sites have for creating profiles illustrate this point. For instance, Match.com expressly prohibits "overt solicitation for sex or descriptions of sexual activity, anatomy, etc." Similarly, YahooPersonals.com warns prospective ad writers not to "post detailed descriptions of physical characteristics or the types of sexual activities that interest you [*sic* them]" and forbids any video greetings that contain nudity or sexual language. Many dating sites also preempt the potential for any relationship that might develop outside the boundaries of monogamous coupling by forbidding the "solicitation of multiple or additional partners." In addition, some online dating sites seek to ensure that subscribers who deviate from the normative standards of heterosexual coupling are excluded from participation. People who are married, partnered, incarcerated, or under age 18 are generally not permitted to post profiles.

Also significant is the absence of questions about sex on the lengthy questionnaires that prospective members of dating websites must fill out before they make their profiles available to other members. Most dating websites require the completion of a comprehensive questionnaire that covers minute details regarding the social, recreational, and relational interests of the applicant and those attributes sought in a partner. The questionnaires typically include inquiries about the kinds of sports activities members enjoy, the type of pets they have or would like to have (or not), the foods they eat, their sense of humor, their political views, and even their astrological sign. Questionnaires on dating sites exclusively targeted at gays and lesbians generally contain additional questions about identity disclosure (that is, how "out" the person is, questions about a person's membership in established lesbian and gay subcultures, for example "butch–femme," "lipstick lesbian," "leather," etc.). Each of these categories is usually covered in extensive detail. For example, the question on the Match.com questionnaire that asks "What kind of sport and exercise do you enjoy?" lists twenty-two activities ranging from aerobics to yoga. But curiously absent from the questionnaires are any questions about the type of erotic and sexual practices users enjoy and/or are seeking.

It would seem that people interested in finding someone to connect with, on an intimate level, might want to know something about the sexual desires, interests, and experiences of their prospective partner. Yet questionnaires on both heterosexual and gay and lesbian dating sites are entirely devoid of questions about prospective partners' definition of sex, the kind of sex members expect to have, the sexual experiences they have had, where they like to have sex, how often they like to have sex, or whether they even want to have sex. A few dating sites that serve gay men do ask whether the prospective member is specifically looking for sex, but remarkably the questionnaires on these sites also fail to ask any detailed questions about sexual practice preferences. The exclusion of explicit questions about sex on gay male questionnaires is particularly surprising in light of the fact that gay men have established subcultures of intimacy that are based entirely on sex. The omission of inquiries about sexual desires and interests serves to normalize the practice of online dating by cleansing it of the taint of sexual perversion.

Almost without exception, internet dating sites are marketed to mass audiences as user-friendly venues where heterosexual, lesbian, and gay participants can secure the relationship goals historically associated with idealized heterosexuality: namely, a long-term, monogamous, and preferably connubial relationship between two people. This vision is reinforced by the "success" stories regularly found on the homepages of dating websites. Couples who have realized a committed and exclusive relationship, or become engaged or married as a result of "meeting" through a particular online dating service, are counted among the website's success stories. To reinforce this point, online dating websites routinely publish the sometimes lengthy testimonials – along with photos of course – of members who have secured their relationship through the site. Typical are narratives that make reference to the esteemed status of couplehood or that invoke the idealized concepts of "romance" and "soul-mate":

> Gay FriendFinder helped me find my soul mate. I work hard and don't really have time or energy to go out to bars and clubs to meet people. I tried Gay FriendFinder mostly out of curiosity and met Jeff – he's too good to be true! Thank you, thank you, thank you.
>
> *(BizGal28)*

> I just wanted to tell you that I have found that special someone and also wanted to say thanks. If it hadn't been for your site [curiouslove.com], I would probably be single and very miserable. Just wanted to say that your site is very awesome …
>
> As Ryan walked me to my car we kissed again. And he invited me to spend the following day wandering in San Francisco. I had really planned to spend the day getting a bunch of errands done, but his talk of sipping tea at the Japanese Tea Garden and a romantic picnic in Golden Gate Park was too much to pass up. We decided to meet the next morning. For the first time in years I've found a man that I can have a real relationship with.
>
> *(Julie; perfectmatch.com)*

On heterosexual dating websites, testimonial narratives are often supplemented by statistics on how many marriages have been produced through the site. An illustration of this common practice can be seen on EHarmony's home page. Here, a selection of smiling, apparently happy, hand-holding couples is continuously flashed on the background of the page along with the prominent display of the date of their first meeting and the date of their subsequent engagement or marriage. With the exception of marriage, the definition of "success" in online dating does not appear to vary by sexual orientation. A successful online dater is one who has secured the ideal type of pairing historically linked to heterosexuality – a monogamously committed coupling of two people who are thereafter forever linked through romance and love.

The visual images and advertising copy displayed by online dating services make it clear to potential subscribers that these are not venues in which to find casual sexual encounters, non-monogamous relationships, or experiment with new gender or sexual identities. They are places where one can safely seek and find intimate relationships that embody the ideals of love and romance. Consistent reinforcement of the idea that romance, love, and long-term monogamous coupling can be realized through online dating eases the public's fear that sexual deviants are lurking behind the online profiles. Moreover, it induces confidence in the belief that placing or responding to an advertisement online is not a stigmatized activity undertaken by sexual deviants and losers, but an activity that anyone can easily and safely engage in.

Technological and demographic changes, along with deliberate marketing strategies that link internet dating with conventional relationship goals, have helped make the process of seeking and finding partners through online personal advertisements attractive to a mass audience. Today, people who, in the past, may have hesitated to meet someone in a virtual space eagerly participate in placing and reading online personal profiles. Indeed, Whitehead suggests that internet dating is "likely to be as influential in shaping the patterns of mating in the early 21st century as the internal combustion engine was in shaping patterns of youthful dating in the early 20th century" (2003: 175). If her analogy is accurate, it is useful to consider some of the possible consequences of online dating.

Expressway to romance: the increased efficiencies of online dating

One of the more obvious effects of online dating is that it increases temporal efficiency in the search for a partner. Traditional methods of finding a partner require intense investments in time. One must first find a compatible mate through workplace, school, or family networks, and then spend time with the prospective person to discover whether there is potential for pursuing the relationship. But online dating allows users to establish the specific qualities they are seeking in a partner prior to meeting him/her. To ensure that a prospective partner has the desired characteristics, users of online dating websites may select the age, race, and sexual orientation of the person they are looking for; read the biographical profile of a prospective partner; scan photos; and, if available, watch a video or listen to a voice greeting. In short, the online dater can ensure that a prospective date meets all of the requirements for a relationship prior to any actual contact with the person. Online dating effectively functions as a labor-saving device in the search for a partner.

Facilitating the efficiency of online personals are new and increasingly sophisticated software programs that allow users to select partners who are likely to have compatible personality traits. Several online dating websites have hired social scientists to develop tests that purport to measure the personality and character traits of their members. Though the validity of these tests is suspect, they are used to increase the likelihood that people will find a well-suited match. For example, EHarmony boasts that its "personality profile" measures twenty-nine dimensions of personality that are scientifically proven to predict long-lasting relationships. Perfect Match offers a similar test that measures a member's character traits and value orientation to better fit him/her with someone who shares a common "relationship style." Presumably, these tests make the process of partner-seeking more efficient because they eliminate the possibility of subjective "error" in selection.

Online dating not only increases the efficiency of partner selection, but also expands opportunities for people to find partners. Because they draw from a national (and even a global) pool of applicants, online dating sites provide a far larger pool of potential eligible partners than conventional social networks typically allow (Whitehead 2003). As such, online dating is particularly useful for members of sexual and/or racial/ethnic minorities who are typically limited in their search by a small pool of eligible partners. Simply stated, online dating websites that serve specific identity groups make it easier to locate partners. The many dating websites hosted in the United States intended specifically for Blacks, Latinos, Asians, transgendered, and gay people, allow them to reach an audience outside the confines of their geographically limited social networks.

In theory, online dating should also expand opportunities to create new forms of relationships, courtship patterns, and identity expressions. In the online environment, relationships can take place entirely in virtual space. Contact between a reader and the originator of an online profile may begin in a public chatroom and then proceed to private emails and perhaps Instant Messages, but need never be realized in a face-to-face encounter. In this sense, online dating provides the potential to go beyond existing categories of gender, sexuality, and even race, because relationships that take place entirely online are not mediated by voices, bodies, smells, or – in the case where pictures are unavailable – faces. New forms of sexual relationships may also be defined because online sexual partnerships can and do develop without physical sexual contact. As well, traditional patterns of courtship where men have historically been the initiators may also give way to greater freedom for women to initiate romantic and sexual encounters and exercise control over the process and content of their interactions. But the realization of these possibilities is incomplete, largely because online dating websites construct intimate relationships along the constricted confines of romance, love and monogamy, and rely on existing categories of sexuality and gender to make the sale.

Consuming love: the commercialization of intimacy

Online dating transforms the search for intimate partners into a consumer activity. The process can be likened to a retail shopping experience that provides patrons with expansive options in partner selection. Each dating website resembles a store that stocks an enormous variety of "products." Shoppers who visit an online dating website browse among the many items available and, like their counterparts in the mall, specify the size, color, and overall quality of the one they are seeking. If buyers don't like what is offered, they can easily move on to the next store until they find exactly what they are interested in. Moreover, if the product does not perform as promised, shoppers may return to the store for a replacement model. Similar to consumer protection agencies that police conventional retail shops, websites like Truedater.com allow online daters to "turn in" writers of advertisements who are less than candid about their appearance, or marital, or financial status. Indeed, online dating transforms people into rational consumers who scrutinize the marketplace for the "best available deal" on intimate relationships.

A consumer market model may provide the greatest number of choices for people who are looking for a date, but it simultaneously reproduces the boundaries of existing gender and sexual identity categories and, therefore, may actually limit the relationship choices people have. Like their more conventional retail counterparts, online dating websites categorize the products they sell in a way that makes them easy to find. As such, they structure the options shoppers may select along the lines of established identity categories that consumers easily recognize. When shoppers search for partners online, they make their initial selection on the basis of gender, sexual orientation, race, and age. Already embedded in the software are the categories "man," "woman," "gay," "straight," "white" and "black." Online daters decide on the prescribed criteria for the "product" they want and then the computerized sorting mechanism returns only profiles of those people who represent the specific categories selected. The online format does not permit people to consider or define alternatives to the categories already given.

Gender, sexual orientation, race, and age are invisible in virtual space; therefore, online dating contains the potential to create relationships that are modeled outside the boundaries of these established identities. Online dating websites could, for example, allow users to define searches around specific personal character traits, shared interests, or life goals. To be sure, these criteria are often used in the secondary aspects of a partner search, but the primary step in the selection process involves choosing candidates by gender, sexual orientation, age, and race. The paradox here is that the very efficiencies of online dating that expand the possibilities of finding partners also confine the parameters of the search and, therefore, limit the prospects of expanding conventional constructions of intimate relationships.

The potential for online dating to transcend established identity categories is further constrained by the fact that, as mentioned earlier, online dating sites are increasingly targeted toward particular sexual orientation, racial/ethnic, social class, religious, and age groups. Inarguably, the separation of dating websites by specific identity categories makes it easier to find someone who meets one's desires. After all, gay people don't ordinarily yearn to date heterosexuals. But the construction of online dating sites by narrowly-bounded definitions of gender and sexuality compels the users of online websites to express their allegiance to a set of fixed identities prior to engaging in the activity of searching for an intimate partner. Online dating websites do not encourage users to explore the space in between categories, nor do they promote the possibility of creating new ones beyond existing constructs.

Because online dating websites compel users to identify with established gender and sexual categories, they may also encourage writers of personal profiles to rearticulate rather than transform the boundaries of gender. Though social scientists have yet to produce a systematic study that explores gender expression in online advertisements, a casual overview of online profiles suggests that writers typically adhere to established social meanings around masculinity and femininity. For instance, the online profiles of heterosexual and lesbian females routinely make references to a desire for love and romance. In contrast, both gay and straight male profiles tend to describe the physical attributes of the partner(s) they are interested in. If online personal profiles solidify rather than expand conventionally understood meanings of gender, they too are unlikely to offer possibilities for creating relationships outside of conventionally established frameworks.

Online dating represents a spectacular change in the process of finding partners, and provides more efficient ways for people to meet their relationship needs, but it has yet to transform prevailing ideas about intimate relationships. Just as internet users shop the net for retail items, they can search the global marketplace for intimacy. Indeed, finding relationships in virtual space now has mass appeal. But online dating websites sustain their mass appeal through the insistent and ever-present reliance on a particular relationship model that embodies the characteristics historically tied to heterosexual couplings. Online dating websites construct ideal relationships within the boundaries of convention. The trilogy of romance, love, and monogamy dominates the online dating scene, while alternative models of intimacy and the sexual possibilities of intimate relationships are de-emphasized. Moreover, online dating websites provide few opportunities to contest socially imposed boundaries around sexuality and gender because these recognized identity categories are embedded in the very structure of the websites themselves. As a result, internet dating strengthens rather than expands the boundaries of the categories through which people imagine their intimate relationships and, therefore, limits ideas about alternative forms they might take.

Note

1 The writer thanks Susan Bass and Anne Colvin for helpful comments on earlier versions of this essay.

References

Brym, R. and R. Lenton. 2001. *Love Online: A Report on Digital Dating in Canada*. Available online at http://www.nelson.com/nelson/harcourt/sociology/newsociety3e/loveonline.pdf (accessed March 15 2006).
Darden, D. and P. Koski. 1988. "Using the Personal Ads: A Deviant Activity", *Deviant Behavior* 9: 383–400.
Foston, N. 2003 "I met my husband online!", *Ebony*, April.
Harris Poll 2003. *Those With Internet Access Continue to Grow But at a Slower Rate*, February 5th. Available online at http://www.harrisinteractive.com/harris_poll/index.asp?PID = 356 (accessed March 15 2006).
Rajecki, D. W. and J. L. Rasmussen. 1992. "Personal ads as deviant and unsatisfactory: Support for evolutionary hypothesis", *Behavioral and Brain Sciences* 15: 107.

Sullivan, B. 2002. *Online Dating: Everyone's doing it: A dot-com business that actually makes a profit*, September 19. Available online at http://msnbc.msn.com/id/3078729 (accessed March 15 2006).

Weaver, J. 2004. *Personals, Sex Sites Changing the Rules of Love*, May 19th. Available online at http://msnbc.msn.com/id/4917480 (accessed March 15 2006).

Whitehead, B. Dafoe. 2003. *Why There are No Good Men Left*. New York: Broadway Books.

Wilkinson, D. 2005. "Online: A Search for Act II", *New York Times*, April 12th, p. 12.

31

Covenant marriage

Reflexivity and retrenchment in the politics of intimacy

Dwight Fee

UNIVERSITY OF VERMONT

In recent years, sociologists have pointed to many transformations in personal life. We have heard quite a bit about the "questioning of tradition," the "redefinition of gender," the "reworking of relationships," or the "transformation of intimacy" and so on. Some sociologists have understood changes in private life in terms of an increase in "reflexivity" (see Giddens 1991, 1992; Beck and Beck-Gernsheim 1995; Swidler 2001; Weeks 1995; Weeks, Heaphy and Donovan 2001). Generally speaking, reflexivity means that, in a time of change and heightened social diversity, people no longer are able unconsciously to rely on traditions and customs to determine how they live. Applied to intimacy and sexuality, people are thrown back upon themselves to define their relationships and their identities within them. Crudely put, we must make decisions for ourselves once ingrained institutions and traditions are questioned, or once it becomes harder to say, "That's just the way the world is."

Therefore, once traditions are questioned, conventional intimate arrangements assume the status of mere *choices* that exist among many other competing ones. Not everyone has the same choices or can act on them as easily as others, but nevertheless, most of the time choice rules. Of course, tradition "hangs around" among all the options – but that hardly sounds like a tradition.

The travails of reflexivity

Being thrown back upon oneself when figuring out relationships and sexuality is surely challenging. For example, it would stand to reason that "commitment" itself would have to be debated and defined within each relationship, rather than simply assumed across all of them. And because we can't assume much cultural uniformity about such things, how do we establish trust in our relationships? Perhaps more than anything else, *risk* comes to paint the entire landscape of intimate life.

Despite all of the problems and ambiguities, however, most of those researching the growing uncertainty surrounding intimacy are encouraged. After all, people have to talk more, figure things out together, "be open." Consider Beck and Beck-Gernsheim's (1995: 5) view of the situation:

[I]t is no longer possible to pronounce in some binding way what family, marriage, parenthood, sexuality, or love mean, or what they should or could be; rather, these vary in substance, exceptions, norms and morality from individual to individual and from relationship to relationship. The answers to the questions above must be worked out, negotiated, arranged and justified in all the details of how, what, why or why not, even if this might unleash the conflicts and devils that lie slumbering among the details and were assumed to be tamed. Increasingly, the individuals who want to live together are, or more precisely becoming, the legislators of their own way of life, the judges of their own transgressions, the priests who absolve their own sins, and the therapists who loosen the bonds of their own past … Love is becoming a blank that the lovers must fill in themselves, across the widening trenches of biography …

If these authors are right, even when we pick up the pieces of the old system we are patterning new relational forms, if only subtly. It may be that in many cases this reflexive work is opening up new avenues for autonomy in relationships, making our lives more "our own" and authentic, and, perhaps most crucially, making equality in relationships more possible. We might say that it is our historical lot to endure these struggles. Nardi (1999) and others have already shown that, in many same-sex relationships, equality and reciprocity are pretty much assumed.

Giddens (1992) calls this mode of relationality the "pure relationship." By calling it "pure" Giddens is suggesting that the viability of this type of relationship depends only on the people involved. The participants are the ones in charge; in this way it is "internally self-referential" through mutual disclosure. Reflexivity "disarms" those forming and moving through relationships. All that there is is that other person, and you – "free floating" as Giddens (1992) puts it. For some, it sounds a lot less romantic; for others, it is the beginning of possibility. For still others, as we will soon see, it reflects a moral decline, as relationships are seen as increasingly whimsical and self-serving.

The fact is that the moral and political meaning of a changing culture of intimacy is unclear or varied. For example, many conservatives who embrace a tradition-based approach to intimacy cite the recent advocacy of gay marriage as illustrating the danger of an individualistic reflexive culture. In fact, some conservatives see the very foundation of human relationships at stake in the gay marriage debate. On the other hand, many "liberal" individuals believe that introducing more reflexivity and choice into intimacy opens this field to progressive change; for example, with regard to gender roles or equality in marriage. Yet we are beginning to see many ironies here, as conservative forces realize it takes a lot of work to establish that things are in fact "set in stone." There is now a lot of effort going into retooling institutions, public policy, and individuals themselves so as to ensure that the right choices are made.

Covenant marriage: "super-sizing" matrimony?

On Valentine's Day 2005, Governor Mike Huckabee (Republican-Arkansas) and his wife entered into a covenant marriage in front of about 6,400 onlookers. Already married for thirty years, the Huckabees took a new kind of plunge, one that was established to "inspire confidence" in marriage, and one usually discussed by proponents as important counter-strategies to the high divorce rate and to the "changing social values" that "threaten marriage." According to an Associated Press article in the *New York Times* (February 15 2005), the governor announced to the crowd: "There is a crisis in America. The crisis is divorce. It is easier to get out of a marriage than [to get out of a] contract to buy a used car." After the Huckabees renewed their vows, the governor instructed the couples in the audience to do the same – to face each other and to repeat the vows of the Governor and First Lady. Many couples followed suit, crying, and then kissing after their spontaneous recitations.

Originally emerging from conservative Protestant churches in the late 1980s and early 1990s, the covenant marriage movement began as a response to a declared "divorce culture" and a "crisis of the family" in the US. Religious leaders and organizations quickly targeted legislative change so as to make the marriage bond a weightier, more durable (and, if only indirectly, religiously-based) commitment. The Covenant Marriage Law was first established in Louisiana in 1997, and similar laws were passed soon after in Arkansas and Arizona. While mainly in Southern states, there is now some kind of covenant marriage legislation afoot in some twenty states, including Minnesota, Iowa, Indiana, and Maryland, which is part of other widespread "divorce reform" legislative activity.

While there has been an increasing amount of public and media-based attention paid to covenant marriage since the Huckabee ceremony, it has so far fallen short of some proponents' early predictions that covenant marriage would "boom" and "could soon sweep the nation." Studies are scant, but the consensus seems to be that numbers are down, and were never really up. Of about 35,000 marriages in Arkansas in 2004, only 164 were of the covenant variety – mostly being conversions of existing marriages. According to Gilgoff (2005), rates are similar in Arizona and Louisiana – with no more than 2 percent of marriages being covenant. Still, it's worth considering what's going on here, now that covenant marriage has at least some salience within the broadening array of marriage debates. (Many proponents attribute the low numbers of covenant marriages to people simply not knowing about the option.)

Covenant marriage, of course, is more than a declaration of traditional marriage; it has very specific, legal dimensions. Advocates for covenant marriage want to offer an alternative to what they see as a blasé, or self-serving, or "test-drive" approach to marriage, since "no fault" divorce was ushered in during the 1970s. In the three states that have actually passed and instituted covenant marriage laws – Louisiana, Arkansas, and Arizona – couples are given a choice between standard marriage and the "CM" option. It's as easy as checking the appropriate box – for the court clerk – but, according to Nock, Wright, and Sanchez (1999), here are the differences for the CM couple:

- the couple will seek premarital counseling – which must include discussions of the seriousness of marriage – and have a signed affidavit (signed by the counselor and the couple) to prove their participation;
- likewise, divorce is only possible if the couple goes to counseling, and after a two year waiting or cooling-off period;
- dissolving a covenant marriage in less than two years requires that one person prove fault on the part of the other. Acceptable faults are felony convictions, abuse, abandonment or adultery. Irreconcilable differences ("we just don't get along") are not acceptable grounds for divorce before two years (2.5 years if you have kids);
- and, couples can "upgrade" to a CM, like Governor Huckabee and his wife.

At the root of CM is the hope of revitalizing a belief in marriage and its sanctity through critiquing the supposed "contract mentality" of recent years. As Gary Chapman argues in *Covenant Marriage: Building Communication and Intimacy* (2003), the legalistic side of marriage is surely important, but the contract mentality has replaced "as long as we both shall live" with "we are committed to each other so long as this relationship is mutually beneficial for us." By contrast, covenant marriage offers deep spirituality and (ideally) a life-long commitment to the other's well being that is "above one's self." As one Louisiana woman put it, "we know that if we have problems, we can't just say I'm leaving" (Loconte 1998).

So, standard marriage is not enough for the advocates of covenant marriage – not in today's world anyway. Making marriage a multiple and tiered system is arguably an intriguing and innovative idea. Having a "menu-driven" approach to wedlock might help couples decide about the meaning of their particular marriage. Of course, if the marriage ante keeps being "upped," it would indeed be ironic if the institutional weight of marriage began to diminish the idea of loving commitment that, for many couples, carries with it a mystical or spiritual understanding. And will adherents of "regular" marriage be seen by some "super-sizers" as opting for a less-than-substantial form of marriage, in other words a "marriage lite" (Zurcher 2004)? For many, the sacredness of marriage cannot be instrumentally imposed, though covenant marriage supporters would surely refrain posing the issue in this way. They might say that they just want to give each marriage every chance possible.

Covenant marriage: political statement or personal choice?

There are many debates around covenant marriage, and some center on the specific problems that exist, or potentially exist, inside of them. Obviously, the fact that it becomes harder to get out of this form of marriage is a major concern in cases of marital violence and abuse. The CM laws state that divorce can be granted in such situations, but many are skeptical that these instances will be "verified" by those charged with that responsibility, which we would presume are mostly pastors and other church-based counselors. (Remember that abuse must be "proved.") Whether women get trapped in CMs remains unclear. Given the recent instigation of covenant marriage, I have not seen any systematic research to argue the situation either way. Predictably, the little research that has been done on CM has unambiguously shown that the large majority of supporters hold highly traditional attitudes about gender and the roles of men and women within marriage (Nock, Wright, and Sanchez 1999), which could itself worry some critics when it comes to issues of abuse.

However, advocates are quick to argue that most marriages fall apart because of "low-level" conflict, where the couple drift apart, often without confronting their problems openly. In this sense, covenant marriage proponents say, "we're not erecting a barricade … we're just putting in some speed bumps" (Loconte 1998). They might also point out that the requirement to seek counseling before marriage – and subsequently, if problems arise – is not something men are often willing to do. As a progressive reform, CM could help men transcend "traditional" codes of masculinity by prompting them to develop effective communication and coping skills.

But then there is the larger issue of its cultural and political significance. On the one hand, proponents are right about the challenges of marriage; however, the supposed moral vacuum or "collapse" that they see behind it – as if statistics reflect ethical stances – has an obvious reactionary subtext. While covenant marriages are hardly widespread, it may not be going too far to say that we are witnessing the latest attempt to redefine marriage along religious and otherwise conservative lines.

According to the website ReligiousTolerance.org, some states are considering abolishing conventional marriage and offering only the covenant version – and obviously this is just when debates about gay marriage are particularly salient. For many, it makes sense that covenant marriage would emerge in the wake of gay marriage initiatives and the passage of the Defense of Marriage Act. Even though we have to make a focused effort to find much in the rhetoric about gay marriage, it is easy to assume that the CM movement is only a knee-jerk political expression. Proponents, though, might say it is simply a way to exemplify God's vision of marriage: "one man, one woman, forever – above their own shifting desires." As far as I have been able to determine, the part about "one man, one woman" is written into the actual leg-islation that is on the books in Louisiana, Arkansas and Arizona. This wording, we must assume, reaches out beyond covenant marriage itself. From this perspective, then, it is no accident that the Huckabee ceremony and all of the subsequent journalistic coverage comes at a time when gay marriage has arguably become the most salient social issue thus far in twenty-first-century America. Gay groups, in fact, were in attendance at the Huckabee event, fundraising and raising awareness about how marriage – any kind of marriage – is not available to same-sex couples.

In this sense, covenant marriage is at least an *implicit* socio-political statement about a "return" to most traditional forms of heterosexual relations. Put another way, *personal understandings and choices about marriage are intersecting with (or becoming articulated within) discourses of social and political reform.* This is tricky because we are not always dealing with, on the one hand, people's solely "personal" concerns about their relationship choices, or on the other hand, an explicit and intentional political backlash. Covenant marriage, in the broadest sense, is a place where a multitude of personal and political strategies are at work – so much so that the two realms are often indistinguishable. Of course, this predicament is nothing new; it is what many theorists and researchers have discussed in terms of the displacement of the private onto the public within the "politics of intimacy," or in debates about "sexual citizenship" and so on. Virtually all intimate choices now intertwine with various "culture wars" about sexuality, morality, and, if only indirectly, marriage itself. Even if covenant marriage only bears a kin-relationship to other more obvious political appropriations of marriage by conservatives, *covenant marriage is implicitly political, whether or not its supporters see themselves in such a light.*

Reflexivity and retrenchment

Whatever the politics of CM supporters, there is something highly *performative* about covenant marriage from a sociological perspective: the willingness to step apart from the crowd, to make one's choice visible and different, to say (and to do so in an almost public way) "this particular alternative is the best way to go." In a strict sociological sense, this development is "anti-traditional," as it makes reflexivity and innovation central to decision-making about marriage. The centrality of therapy in covenant marriage makes it even more so – couples must deliber-ate, disclose their fears, and ostensibly work together. We might say it is "*doing* intimacy" in a world where virtually no one can simply blend into the background and not give voice to their choices (Seidman 2002). Covenant marriage is presumably about creating options, new possi-bilities, and, we would assume, the creation of more satisfying relationships. The equality piece is more ambiguous, but the innovation is there, whether or not one approves of the particular vision. As one advocate put it, "[covenant marriage] has everything to do with giving people more choices" (Nock, Wright, and Sanchez 1999). The difference here, however, is that reflexive processes are paradoxically moving, or hoping to move, in the direction of "tradition," or at least the way that tradition is being defined by the covenant marriage instigators.

This irony of providing more and more choices is not lost on some conservatives. We need only take note of the reactionary discourse about gay marriage to get the gist of the "slippery slope" argument: "so after gay marriage, what's next, marrying your cat?" If CM proponents take this view, we could easily grant covenant marriage the official status of *moral panic.* But it goes further: this slippery-slope viewpoint is one reason why traditionalists themselves are part of the heretofore modest cultural impact of covenant marriage. When given the option of tin-kering or not tinkering with marriage, many invested in orthodoxy and traditionalism will invariably side on the latter approach of sticking with the status quo. If something is so sacred and natural, there is something irreverent and contradictory about breaking it into differing levels and subcategories. It is here that the ironies of tradition/de-tradition come full circle: can reflexivity in intimate life be effectively used to reaffirm heteronormativity, which has historically thrived on the very *absence* of it? Can choice be used to fend off other choices seen as threatening or dangerous? In sum, how can the covenant marriage movement advocate a reflexive program when it comes very close to saying that reflexivity itself is the problem with marriage today?

Whatever one's politics, we are all stuck with ambiguities and uncertainties within our intimate lives. Even those advocating covenant marriages seem to acknowledge this at some level. The question is whether we will move in the direction of developing insidious modes of control and exclusion out of the array of choices emerging, or use the situation as an opportunity for renewal and dialogue. As Jeffrey Weeks (1995) puts it: "In the postmodern world it is unlikely that we will ever rid ourselves of the specter of uncertainty, but its presence might help us to realize that living without certainty is the best spur there is to thinking again about what we value, what we really want." If any program or perspective offers certainty, or even relative security, we had better be careful. In a reflexive world, perhaps there is good reason to trust our distrust.

References

Associated Press (2005) "Thousands Renew Vows in Arkansas," *New York Times*, February 15.

Beck, U. and E. Beck-Gernsheim (1995) *The normal chaos of love*. Cambridge: Polity.

Chapman, G. (2003) *Covenant marriage: building communication and intimacy*. Nashville, TN: Broadman and Holman.

Giddens, A. (1991) *Modernity and self-identity: self and society in the late-modern world*. Stanford, CA: Stanford University Press.

——(1992) *The transformation of intimacy: sexuality, love and eroticism in modern societies*. Stanford, CA: Stanford University Press.

Gilgoff, D. (2005) "Tying a tight knot," *US News and World Report*, February 28.

Loconte, J. (1998) "I'll Stand Bayou: Louisiana couples choose a more muscular marriage contract," *Policy Review* 89 (5).

Nardi, P. (1999) *Gay men's friendships: invincible communities*. Chicago, IL and London: University of Chicago Press.

Nock, S., J. Wright, and L. Sanchez (1999) "America's Divorce Problem," *Society* (May–June) (36): 4.

Plummer, K. (2003) *Intimate citizenship: private decisions and public dialogues*. Seattle, WA and London: University of Washington Press.

Seidman, S. (2002) *Beyond the closet*. London and New York: Routledge.

Swidler, A. (2001) *Talk of love*. Chicago, IL: University of Chicago Press.

Weeks, J. (1995) *Invented moralities: sexual values in the age of uncertainty*. New York: Columbia University Press.

Weeks, J., B. Heaphy, and C. Donovan (2001) *Same-sex intimacies*. London and New York: Routledge.

Zurcher, K. (2004) "'I Do' or 'I Don't' Covenant Marriage After Six Years," *Notre Dame Journal of Law, Ethics & Public Policy* 18 (273).

32

Interracial romance

The logic of acceptance and domination

Kumiko Nemoto

UNIVERSITY OF TEXAS AUSTIN

With globalization and an increasing immigrant population in the United States, the surge in interracial relationships might not be a surprising trend. In fact, the increase in intermarriage and interracial relationships should be a welcome sign in the changing landscape of love, romance, and family, as it fits America's racial-melting-pot image and atmosphere of steadily greater multiculturalism. However, interracial relationships are still far from the norm. While many Americans date someone of another race, fewer marriages cross racial lines. While about 92 percent of all interracial marriages include white partners, only 4 percent of married whites have non-white spouses (Qian 2005:34). In fact, many white Americans remain uncomfortable about interracial intimacy and tend to disapprove of their family members' interracial relationships (Qian 2005:33). Skin color also greatly influences patterns of interracial marriage. The lighter the skin color, the higher the rate of intermarriage with white Americans (Qian 2005:31). Hispanics who label themselves as racially "white," Asian Americans, and American Indians have high rates of marriage with whites compared to those of African Americans. Also, there are distinct gender patterns: 74 percent of the black–white couples involve a black husband and a white wife, and 58 percent of the Asian American–white couples involve an Asian American wife (Qian 2005:36).

The increase in interracial relationships gives the impression that racism and discrimination are lessening in our society. However, the types of interracial couples that are deemed acceptable and desirable continue to be shaped by society's dominant racial and gender beliefs. An increase in dating and marrying across racial lines may not be explained entirely by a decline in racism. Patricia Hill Collins (2004:250) writes, "Crossing the color line to marry interracially challenges deep-seated American norms, yet such relationships may not be inherently progressive." By the same token, Henry Giroux (2006:32) argues that some seemingly oppositional or counter-normative behaviors in fact reveal the logic of domination more than they represent the logic of protest or resistance to the system, much less the logic of liberation. So, what are the dominant images of interracial relationships? What are the ingrained messages in them? In this chapter, I will examine some popular images and interracial relationships and how they express dominant ideologies. Then, drawing on my research on Asian American–white couples, I will explore the racial and gender ideologies that shape these couples and the challenges that are faced by them.

Whiteness and images of interracial couples

Popular culture daily sells hypersexualized racial images and offers aesthetic consumption of racial differences as if such consumption were synonymous with the end of racism and sexism. The cultural images are ambiguous, blurring the line between oppression and nuanced celebration of racial diversity. The images of interracial romance continue to be shaped by traditional themes of white normalcy, whites' exoticization of people of color, male authority, and distinct differences between masculinity and femininity. In many images, white manhood and womanhood continue to represent the norm, with people of color portrayed alongside in an exoticized way.

Even though the popular media claim that "racial mixing" represents an ideal of racial integration, it has also denoted whiteness as a sign of normalcy and ascendancy. In 1993, a multiracial female cyborg appeared on the cover of *Time* magazine as "The New Face of America." Her image metaphorically characterized a future America as increasingly comprising multiracial individuals and couples. At the same time, this young female cyborg represented future multicultural citizenship in a state that would continue to enforce conventional norms of heterosexuality, family values, and white privilege. The "white-enough" appearance of the cyborg, as the face of America, evoked the image of "the future as what will happen when white people intermarry" (Berlant 1997:207), and insinuated that whiteness would remain central to America's race relations. Also, by highlighting race within the private realms of "love," "sex," and "marriage," the cover ensured the continuation of heterosexual unions and family love as solutions for the "problems" of race and immigration (Berlant 1997). Almost 15 years later, media portrayals of interracial couples and multiracial families still reflect what the female cyborg represented at that time: interracial relationships depicted in terms of their approximation to heterosexual unions and the ideal white middle-class family in which traditional male authority figures rule and female caretaker figures serve.

Recent images of interracial couples have apparently gained wide media attention not just because these couples transgress racial lines, but also because they express exotic yet traditional versions of femininity and masculinity. Couples in the media often consist of a white partner with a light-skinned partner of color such as Halle Berry or Jennifer Lopez (Childs 2009). Non-white partners often appear to mirror the white fantasy of hypermasculine or hyperfeminine racial minority images. By portraying interracial couples that represent traditional gender and racial messages, these popular images tell us that interracial couples can be acceptable when they embody attractive racialized femininity and masculinity in which male authority is embraced, whiteness is retained, and American middle-class ideology is sustained.

In addition, images of interracial romance, while aesthetically and romantically appealing in terms of their potentially positive effect on race relations, can erase realities of racial violence and racial hierarchy. They reduce racial differences to a matter of physical appearances and conventional heterosexual romantic norms. Instead of challenging hierarchies and inequalities, these interracial images re-order signs of race and gender according to traditional ideologies, and perpetuate the display of white manhood and white womanhood as dominant – in other words, white men and women as figures served by men and women of color.

Considering the fact that over 90 percent of screenwriters are white (Childs 2009:70), it might not be surprising that images of, and storylines about, interracial relationships in television and film reflect white male desires and fantasies. Interracial relationships are also often portrayed as "race-less" in white-dominated settings (Childs 2009), and race is often represented as a matter of superficial physical differences. Such color-blindness or race-less-ness is a unique aspect of American multiculturalism, and it often entails the exoticization of racial minorities or white-centered assimilation messages (Perry 2002). Neither approach critically engages the issue of power (Nylund 2006). Also, the analysis of interracial couples in contemporary films (Childs 2009) finds repeated instances of the message that white people are not racist; it is racial minorities and their communities, not whites, who oppose and complain about interracial relationships. In many TV programs and films, interracial romances are represented as doomed to fail, thus perpetuating the safe normalization of white couples and same-race unions. The images are also gendered: interracial relationships that appear in the media reinforce white male heroism, with white men depicted as liberal and progressive, certifying their goodness, kindness, and superiority over others (Childs 2009:87).

Popular discourses about Asian American women

Given the dominant hierarchies of race and gender implicit in popular images of interracial relationships, this section looks at how racial and gender ideologies have been historically played out in Asian American–white relationships. Compared to African Americans, a higher number of Asians and Asian Americans marry whites. There are various social factors that could explain the high rate of intermarriage between Asian American women and white men: Asian Americans' overall high education and income, compared to whites and other racial minorities, may be one. But such factors do not explain why Asian American women have a higher intermarriage rate than Asian American men. Also, while Asian Americans are often seen as a "model minority," the question of how Asian American men and women fare as intimate or marital partners of whites has not been much discussed.

Racial stereotypes play a critical role in the dynamics of gender in interracial relationships. Like the stereotype of black men's hypermasculinity, long-existing stereotypes of Asian women as submissive, subservient, passive, and/or hypersexual may serve as critical components in heterosexual attraction. Also, in a culture that automatically equates long dark hair and a thin body with being "feminine" regardless of race, images of the Asian female body are easily marked as representative of a non-threatening femininity. In contrast, Asian men have been often de-sexed and feminized, or hypermasculinized as martial artists or oriental villains. As many researchers have discussed (e.g. Espiritu 2000), these stereotypes of hyperfeminine Asian women and de-sexed Asian men contribute to the maintenance of conventional orders of race and gender centered on the normalcy of whiteness and the dominance of men.

Exotic and hyperfeminine images of Asian American women have long flourished in the United States. Images of Asians and Asian Americans as hyperfeminine have been popular precisely because they complement social and cultural beliefs about American manhood and American family values, in which white men serve as the dominant patriarchal figures and women serve as caretakers of the family. Images of subservient Asian women were repeatedly circulated on military bases in Asian countries during World War II, the Korean War, and the Vietnam War. When a large number of Asian military brides entered the United States in the post–World War II period, interracial marriage was still banned in many states; the images served to reduce racial anxieties stemming from the large influx of Asian women and facilitated these women's assimilation. Hyperfeminine and sexual images of Asian women continue to play a critical role in the transaction of desires and fantasies in cross-border marriages (Constable 2003).

In the 1970s, the model minority stereotype took hold. Asian Americans were viewed as educated and upwardly mobile. Asian and Asian American woman, still imagined as submissive, were increasingly viewed as upwardly mobile and therefore as desirable. These women were good substitutes for white women (who were often viewed as challenging) (Koshy 2005). As a result, Asian American women emerged as exemplars of an alternative femininity which could help men regain the confidence they lost after feminism marked white femininity as more independent and masculine (Koshy 2005).

Subservient images of Asian immigrant women have also complemented America's paternalistic images of nation. That is, these women are welcomed in part because they celebrate America while condemning the patriarchal and non-democratic countries they left. Immigrant women are valued for having the courage to pursue freedom and to escape from their home country's patriarchal constraints (Berlant 1997:195). The women, with few distinctions among them with regard to whether they are "immigrants," "aliens," "minorities," "illegal," or whatever, and who want to "escape" the constraints of their patriarchal families, are seen as suitable markers of model migrant citizens who will be devoted to America (Berlant 1997). Such a gendered immigration discourse has long framed Asian female–white male sexual relationships, especially in the context of military brides who have entered the United States. Thus, the stereotypes associated with Asian women and the immigration discourse have historically served to validate Asian American female–white male couples as "acceptable" gendered unions that can sustain the traditional orders of gender, nation, and family in the United States.

Asian American–white couples

In order to understand the impact of race and gender on the dynamics of interracial relationships, I conducted interviews with 42 Asian Americans and whites who were either in interracial relationships at the time of the interview or had previously been involved in such relationships (Nemoto 2009). I explored couples' race consciousness and social receptions, racialized desires, and gender dynamics. The Asian Americans I interviewed included Chinese, Filipino, Japanese, Korean, and Vietnamese Americans. The individuals ranged in age from their early twenties to their early fifties, and all were heterosexual.

White men interviewed for the study often viewed Asian American women as ideal partners because of their racialized femininity and model minority traits. The stereotypes of Asian American women as hyperfeminine and subservient were frequent responses I received. Likewise, white women referred to Asian American men as having model minority traits or as being domineering. But there are some interesting differences among the couples consisting of an Asian American woman and a white man, relating to whether the woman was a native-born or foreign-born Asian American. Foreign-born Asian American women who lack class mobility, language skills, and a thorough knowledge of US racism and sexism were more likely to adhere to traditional gender arrangements in their dating or marriages, while second-generation Asian American women who date white men often have more education and/or a higher socio-economic status than their white partners. The second- and higher-generation young Asian Americans saw themselves as upwardly mobile and independent, and different from stereotypical Asians. They expressed a preference for white men who possess "egalitarian" traits, which they mentioned were often lacking in Asian American men. Interestingly, many Asian American women, including young second- and higher-generation women who described themselves as being egalitarian and independent, projected highly gendered images onto white men, describing them as being protective breadwinner figures or liberators. Thus, it seems that racial and gender hierarchies have greatly influenced Asian American–white couples. But stereotypes could also be surmounted. For example, Asian American men who possess high class status could repudiate negative stereotypes by exercising power over white women.

In the following section, I discuss some of the findings of my research, with a particular focus on the ways Asian American–white couples were received by family and friends. The Asian American female–white male couples I interviewed reported little social hostility or familial opposition, especially when compared to Asian American male–white female couples; in other words, Asian American women coupled with white men seemed to be much more socially accepted than Asian American men with white women. Some men stated that having an Asian wife was not a problem because of their reputation as good wives. Gary, a 58-year-old businessman who is married to a Korean woman, said, "American men like Asian women. ... I think there's a great acceptance of the Caucasian man marrying an Asian woman. In fact, many of my friends, non-Asian friends, actually say that they envy me because they understand that Asian women are very good wives and very nice ladies." His comment demonstrates the culturally shared notion that Asian women possess the qualities of good wives and also, therefore, reinforce men's sense of masculinity. Gary said, "I think [Asian women] respect the [traditional] values and they tend to be pretty loyal. They exhibit qualities that a lot of American women don't seem to have [such as being] family oriented. [They are] good mothers and good parents."

Some white men noted that the Asian American woman's exotic appearance and small physique is part of their attraction. Peter, a 27-year-old, said that he likes dark-skinned women, and Asian women often caught his eye because of their distinct physical features which he described as "more beautiful than those of whites." Peter associated his second-generation Chinese American girlfriend's thin body with stylish urban femininity, which he thought suited his lifestyle as a musician who performs underground electronic music. Possessing a young Asian woman was a sign of cultural hipness. Peter added, "If you are dating Asian girls, probably it is cooler than if you are dating black girls."

Some men mentioned that, even though they were attracted to Asian women, they were not attracted to other women of color. Patrick, a 28-year-old engineer, had dated a variety of Asian women whom he met in Asian countries when he traveled for work. "I kind of acquired the taste for or the inclination of liking Asian woman," he said. "Black women and Mexican women are different, too. But for some reason, I'm never attracted [to them]." In all likelihood, he has never been attracted to other women of color because his interest lies not in their color but rather in racialized images of traditional womanhood. Of his Filipino engineer wife, Patrick said, "Her nature is [to] try to take care of her husband. I don't think that most American women I've met have been that way ... " Foreign-born Asian American women were often characterized by their white partners as being family-oriented, loyal, and caring. These characteristics apparently played a critical role in some men's attraction to them. The image of Asian women as enhancing men's masculinity bolsters their sense of themselves as authority figures and also contributes to the positive social reception of Asian and Asian American women.

In addition to the stereotype of hyperfemininity, the stereotype of the model minority also adds to the positive image of Asian American women. In my interviews, Asian American women, especially those born in America, associated being Asian with being a disciplined "model minority" and believed this is the reason why they are welcomed by whites. Victoria, a second-generation 26-year-old Chinese American medical student, pointed out that Asian American female–white male couples are extremely common. She said, "All the Asian girls I know have gone out with white guys, basically ... because it's almost popular for white guys to go out with Asian girls." Victoria emphasized that Asian women are desirable for white men. "I know my boyfriend's parents are happy because I'm a lot different from the girls he's gone out with before ... I don't think American girls are quite as respectful as far as how [they] treat another person's family." Victoria's comment illustrates that Asian American women are not merely associated with domestic femininity but also are exemplars of disciplined, respectable womanhood. Peter, a 27-year-old white man, said, "A lot of white women are like spoiled brats. ... A lot of the white women I dated have had codependency issues. They were just overly demanding." Peter says his current Chinese American girlfriend is from an intact family and is professionally ambitious and tenacious, qualities that his white former girlfriends lacked. While these descriptions of model minority traits are well-meant, some of the descriptions, such as "not overly demanding," "not complaining too much," or "not sexually promiscuous," indicate that these men value a conservative, somewhat submissive image of womanhood. They apparently feel that they have more control in their intimate relationships than with white women.

While the white men I interviewed reported few negative responses from their family and friends with regard to their Asian or Asian American girlfriends, many of them did note that things would have been different if they had brought a black woman home. Peter, a 27-year-old multimedia designer, said, "No one ever said anything about Vivian [his Asian girlfriend]. . . But had I come home with a black girlfriend, then some … of my uncles or somebody might have said something about not liking it." Thus, it is not that race does not matter in interracial relationships; it is just that certain racialized femininities, ones that adhere to more traditional gender roles, are more acceptable than others.

Many of the Asian American women I interviewed expressed a preference for white men over men of other ethnic and racial groups, including Asian American men. A 58-year-old first-generation Korean woman believed that American husbands treat women better than Korean husbands do. Similarly, a 38-year-old first-generation Filipina American, who is a mother of two biracial children whom she referred to as "white," talked about her childhood dream to marry a white man. White men, she believed, embody an authentic American middle-class ideal. Considering the fact that whiteness (and its associated Anglo-Saxon middle-class lifestyle) has been circulated globally as a sign of power and an object of desire (Kelsky 2001), foreign-born Asian women's preference for white men over men of other races might not be surprising.

However, most second- or higher-generation Asian American women also explicitly expressed their aversion to Asian and Asian American men, sometimes much more strongly than foreign-born Asian women did. Victoria, a 24-year-old medical school student, was adamant that she would never date anyone other than a white man. She said, "I never dated an Asian guy. … I think that Asian guys are not courteous to women." Grace, a 26-year-old engineer, also never dated Asian men. Grace described them as incapable of dealing with "independent women" like herself. "I am not attracted to Asian guys. … They are not gentlemen. … They are not affectionate. At least the ones I've met. I think my personality clashes with a lot of them. Because I think I'm too independent. I'm too outgoing. A lot of Asian guys like Asian women. . . Either they are dainty or they are pretty or they are. … submissive … " Second- or third-generation Asian American women portrayed white men as being egalitarian, tall, and capable of providing them with what they deserve. Many Asian American women were particularly willing to date or marry white men because they believed these men could provide evidence that they are assimilated, authentic "Americans" who are also independent. Thus, Asian American women's valuing whiteness and white manhood has promoted a mutual attraction between them and white men, bolstering existing racial stereotypes and gender hierarchies.

In the relationships between Asian American men and white women, some of the more successful couples adhered to very traditional gender arrangements. In many of these cases, the Asian American men possessed professional jobs, class status, or career prospects. When minority men exhibit or possess class privileges, and follow the male breadwinner model, they are likely to exercise leverage and power in their relationships with white women, and possibly repudiate the negative racial stereotypes associated with them. However, many negative stereotypes of couples consisting of Asian/Asian American men and white women persist. In contrast with the social acceptance of Asian American female–white male couples, a few white women dating Asian American men reported negative reactions from their families and friends. Emily, a

38-year-old schoolteacher married to a Cambodian American man, used to invite her friends to their home, but eventually stopped. "We had made friends from work, then tried to invite them to dinner. But there's always an air of uncomfortableness that we both detect from these people." Emily has been disowned by her family members since she married her husband; he has rarely met her kin. Karen, a 20-year-old student coupled with a Chinese American man who is studying engineering, remembered her parents mentioning something about their future child. "It wasn't extremely derogatory, but I didn't really like it. They said something like, our children may have a hard time because they will be half-white, half Asian." Karen's friends also expressed concern about her boyfriend. "I said, you know, I am dating somebody and he is Asian. One of my friends made fun of it, and made an Asian joke. The other one said OK. They didn't say oh, that's great. They just said OK. One of them asked me how my parents felt about it." Tracey, a 26-year-old waitress married to a 29-year-old Japanese man, remembered her friends' comments. "They asked me if he had a bad temper or drank too much."

These experiences show that white women coupled with Asian American men encounter less social acceptance than Asian American women with white men. However, this does not mean that Asian American women do not encounter racism. In the same study, most Asian American women described individual encounters with racism, such as name-calling or being dismissed as "foreigners." But the long-popular stereotypes of subservience combined with the logic of patriarchy, in which white men are imagined as protectors and authority figures, validate Asian American female–white male couples and provide them with far more social acceptance than is granted to other types of interracial couples. As I mentioned previously, the public presence of white husbands serves as a buffer or reduces general suspicion toward these women, reducing the likelihood that they will be seen as immigrants, foreigners, or racial minorities (Nemoto 2009:71). Meanwhile, white women with Asian American men are deemed most acceptable when they follow traditional gender arrangements – and even then they might be seen as deviant because they haven't adhered to the logic of white male authority.

In this chapter, I have argued that the dominant racial and gendered ideologies embedded in images and discourses of interracial relationships make certain couples more socially acceptable than others. Even though the rise of interracial dating and marriage gives the impression that racism and sexism are in decline, our images of interracial romance continue to be constructed by traditional ideologies of race and gender. Discourses and the realities of interracial romance do not signify a public welcome for random cross-race relationships. In the case of Asian American–white couples, the high intermarriage rate of Asian American women may largely derive from the dominant stereotype of these women as hyperfeminine and subservient. This stereotype reinforces men's authority, and traditional norms of marriage and the family. These unions therefore do not contradict the dominant ideologies of whiteness, white privilege, or gender inequality. Seen this way, interracial romances may be a more exotic version of the traditional heterosexual union that sustains white privilege, male authority, and America's traditional norms of heterosexual marriage and family values.

References

Berlant, Lauren. 1997. *The Queen of America Goes to Washington City: Essays on Sex and Citizenship.* Durham, NC and London: Duke University Press.

Childs, Erica Chito. 2009. *Fade to Black and White: Interracial Images in Popular Culture.* Lanham, MD: Rowman & Littlefield.

Collins, Patricia Hill. 2004. *Black Sexual Politics: African Americans, Gender, and the New Racism.* New York: Routledge.

Constable, Nicole. 2003. *Romance on a Global Stage: Pen Pals, Virtual Ethnography, and "Mail-Order" Marriage*. Berkeley: University of California Press.

Espiritu, Yen L. 2000. *Asian American Women and Men: Labor, Laws, and Love*. Walnut Creek, CA: Alta-Mira Press.

Giroux, Henry A. 2006. *The Giroux Reader*, ed. Christopher G. Robbins. Boulder, CO: Paradigm.

Kelsky, Karen. 2001. *Women on the Verge: Japanese Women, Western Dreams*. Durham, NC: Duke University Press.

Koshy, Susan. 2005. *Sexual Naturalization: Asian Americans and Miscegenation*. Stanford, CA: Stanford University Press.

Nemoto, Kumiko. 2009. *Racing Romance: Love, Power, and Desire among Asian American/White Couples*. New Brunswick, NJ and London: Rutgers University Press.

Nylund, David. 2006. "Critical Multiculturalism, Whiteness, and Social Work: Towards a More Radical View of Cultural Competence." *Journal of Progressive Human Services* 17(2): 27–42.

Perry, Pamela. 2002. *Shades of White: White Kids and Racial Identities in High School*. Durham, NC and London: Duke University Press.

Qian, Zhenchao. 2005. "Breaking the Last Taboo: Interracial Marriage in America." *Contexts* 4(4): 33–37.

33

Lesbian and gay parents

Situated subjects

Yvette Taylor

UNIVERSITY OF NEW CASTLE, AUSTRALIA

Introduction

What is the current status of lesbian and gay parented families? Have such families moved from conditions of invisibility and hostility towards visibility and respect? The answer varies across socio-cultural contexts. There has been a growth of visibility and rights of lesbian and gay families in the United States and Europe, even as there continues to be a strong assertion of traditional "family values." In my view, same-sex marriage has been over-emphasised in the current citizenship debates, as if such rights would end the discrimination that lesbian and gay parented families experience. But also, too much research and politics around lesbian and gay families assumes a middle-class family, which is now able to feel socially included. This assumption ignores the real class differences between families, both in terms of material resources and in terms of subjective evaluations about what are "good" or "proper" families.

If times are changing in light of socio-legal reform, how do inequalities of class endure in lesbian and gay parental experiences? How, for example, does social class influence the way parents negotiate the schooling of their children as well as children's services provided by the community? Are lesbian and gay parents now the "same" as their heterosexual counterparts, or are their experiences marked by profound differences? What difference does class make in understanding lesbian and gay parents as socially situated subjects, who are sexualised, gendered, and racialised in specific ways?

There is now a wide range of research on lesbian and gay parenting. Perhaps the enduring political necessity to present such families in a positive light has resulted in a sidelining of "harsher" stories, where the classed experiences of parenting have been particularly sidelined and where most studies of lesbian motherhood predominantly sample white, middle-class, educated professional women. So although a now growing research field, much current work on lesbian and gay parenting still overlooks the significance of social class. Even where there has been attention to gendered dynamics and constraints, class, as a crucial component of parental choice and experience, has been neglected. Based on US research, Amy Agigian (2004) is somewhat unique in exploring the intersection between sexuality, race and class in practices of lesbian insemination. Yet, there are other routes to lesbian parenting; and class shapes parenting in myriad ordinary ways such as interactions with social and educational providers and with other parents. I intend to use the concept of social class to refer to the disproportionate alloca-tion of material resources as well as involving values or estimations of worth, for example, judgements about "good" and "bad" parenting. Classed ideas and resources frame ways of doing parenting, effecting too the construction of "respectable," legitimate routes into parenting.

Class and sexuality: intersections

In my book, *Lesbian and Gay Parenting: Securing Social and Educational Capital*, I explore inter-sections between class and sexuality in lesbians' and gay men's experiences of parenting. I examine the initial routes into parenting, the household division of labour, residential pre-ferences, and schooling choice (Taylor 2009). Forty-six lesbian mothers and fourteen gay dads were interviewed across a range of localities in the UK. All of the respondents were white and ranged in age from 18 to 63. Their routes to parenting varied. Most participants (n = 36) had children through previous heterosexual relationships, some of these parents resorted to hetero-sex and now lived open lesbian or gay lives. Respondents who had pursued alternative routes to parenting, such as adoption or assisted insemination, were mostly from middle-class back-grounds. Interviewees were asked to self-identify in class terms, with about half of the inter-viewees identifying as "middle-class" or "lower middle-class" and half identifying as "working-class." While these were broadly congruent with "objective" positioning (including employ-ment, income, and education), several respondents claimed a "working-class" background, often set against their current "middle-class" status. In exploring the ways that class and sexuality frame possibilities, I argue that middle-class lesbian and gay parents seek to protect their children by securing specific educational and social environments which are tied to classed resources.

Examining lesbian and gay routes into parenthood casts light upon the complications involved in achieving and affirming parental status. Lesbian and gay parents often navigate hostile contexts unknown to their straight counterparts. Discrimination and difficulty can be experienced in attempts to access reproductive technologies, creating inequalities which can also be compounded in everyday parental spaces, such as in school settings or in residential locations. Lesbian and gay parents may experience "family," "school," "community" and "home" in quite different ways from their heterosexual counterparts, where there may not be an easy fit into normalised expectations and ways of being. While lesbian and gay parents' "creative" routes into parenting have been evidenced as innovative (e.g. assisted insemination, surrogacy, adoption), this emphasis perhaps sidelines more normative pathways as well as their challenges (Weston 1991; Stacey 1996; Weeks et al. 2001; Agigian 2004). Challenges still persist in accessing alternative routes to parenthood, including compelled interactions with social and clinical providers, such as social workers and medics, who are responsible for considering planned parenthood. Such providers may themselves endorse quite fixed notions of what it means to be a family, making the "creating" of other types of families quite difficult. Moreover, such practitioners are work-ing within legal and social contexts, which often sanction the heterosexual family as the ideal type. Within this already challenging context, some classed advantages and disadvantages can be highlighted, where sexual status may be seen to intersect with class positioning. The emotional, social and material resources which parents are able to draw upon to consolidate and affirm their sense of family is highly depend on class status. For example, the *choice* to become parents was often shaped by class and framed by both implicit and explicit classed "costs." For parents choosing a more "do-it-yourself" approach to pregnancy in accessing sperm donors directly, there were often still costs to negotiate, such as the sperm donor's expenses. Other parents accessed designated but expensive clinics, often also feeling vulnerable about their sexual "outness" and the potential hostility this may invoke from health providers. The choice exercised was often not one of easy access or straightforward privilege. Instead it depended on a knowledge of where good clinics were, at times involving consultation within the broader LGBT community, varying too in the time and finances needed to access these. Both middle-class and working-class lesbian and gay parents face struggles in their routes into parenting, ever threatened by, for example, the (un)known status of donors, legal and clinical costs, custody battles and through the general social disapproval as not being deemed "fit for purpose." While interviewees reported disagreements with (ex-)partners, clinicians, social workers and medics, middle-class status could often partially buffer and protect against these.

Gay and lesbian parented families continue to face discrimination and class-specific challenges. One of the ways that middle-class parents resist stigma is to reframe themselves as more responsible and thoughtful than their heterosexual and working-class counterparts. This claim is based on their experiences as "family planners" who carefully choose when and how they wish to be parents (typically by means of expensive reproductive technologies). Working-class gay (and heterosexual) parents, according to this narrative, often become parents accidentally, or without the same level of thought and agency. Many working-class interviewees had children from previous heterosexual relationships and/or did not have the financial resources to seek out expensive reproductive technologies. Indeed, some working-class parents had not "chosen" to parent, but instead spoke of it as "just happening," continuing a likely (mis)reading of them as "thoughtless" and "irresponsible." In this regard, to the extent that researchers mirror middle-class parents' own accounts, for example, value reflexive choice, their studies will devalue or negate working-class experiences, even calling into question the quality and *legitimacy* of their parenting. In my book, I explore how a middle-class culture of parenting may lead some working-class parents to avoid gay parenting groups and other sites where the narrative of choice and responsibility has a strong framing presence.

To demonstrate the way class and sexuality intersect, a couple of examples are useful here. Having become pregnant through assisted insemination, Gemma, a middle-class lesbian, claims an "active choice" where family doesn't easily "just come packaged," positioning herself against that which "just happens" to "het people":

> You make an active choice … and the vast majority of het people, it just sort of happens to them. You know, very rarely do they actively make the choice. It's interesting talking to women who go for fertility treatment because they have to make the active choice.

Another middle-class lesbian, Jacqui, also contrasts the responsible choice of parenthood with those who come to parenthood unexpectedly and accidentally. In both Jacqui's and Gemma's accounts it is difficult to reconcile notions of "good planning" alongside other interviewees' experiences, where they would not be recognised via the "choice" invoked:

> I think that if you're going to that much trouble to have a child, it must be really wanted. I think that if it's a question of you going down the pub, you're getting pissed and you get laid and you come home pregnant, that child hasn't really been thought about or chosen, or decided on, or anything. I think that when gay people decide they want to have children they put a lot of thought and a lot of effort into it, so it's not just happening to them, they are making choices and I think that's a good thing.

Lesbian and gay parents' "creative" routes into parenting have been observed as innovative and deliberate, foregrounding a reflexive, choosing subject, politically mobilised against expected attacks on their incapacity to parent. All interviewees had to consider and negotiate their relationship to what are considered the "respectable" routes into parenthood. Crucially, respectability often meant an "attack" on the "poor" parenting of others, where "poor" meant the absence of choice and responsibility. The articulation of the middle-class norm of "choice" (family planning) reinforces very conservative notions of who is and is not capable of parenting – revealing the intersection of class and sexuality.

The relevance of class is clearly observed in parental choices and interventions in their children's education. Lesbian and gay parents often spoke of needing to access a good, tolerant and understanding school, which would be able to welcome and recognise their particular family circumstances. Such "tolerant" schools were frequently located in middle-class areas, while schools in working-class areas were often positioned, in a classed contrast, as "intolerant" and failing. Middle-class parents had more resources to negotiate educational routes, just as they could negotiate pathways to parenting, where working-class parents had little choice over educational provisioning. From accessing the "right" school, to having no choice but the "wrong" school, both class and sexuality are relevant in understanding parental expectations and entitlements. Both are intertwined in the construction of educational need, with middle-class parents often stating that being from a different family meant that their child needed special support and an accepting educational environment. The ability of the school to respond to and welcome Carol's lesbian-parented family is a vital part of their inclusion:

> We went together and made sure that they understood who we were and wanted to gauge what their response to us would be as a family and what they would, how they would handle any issues that arose … she [the head teacher] also added that she positively welcomed the idea of us as a family in the school and would be happy to tackle any issues and raise, you know, the issues of lesbian parents with the kids as a part of their development which was great.
>
> *(Carol, 53, middle-class)*

For Carol, the relationship between school and home is a very important and highly constructed one, with expectations and demands placed on the system and the individuals within it. Carol went with her partner into the school and felt welcomed, knowing that their domestic situation was also mirrored in other pupils' families. Interestingly, this particular composition is also seen as a matter of educational "development" more generally where lesbian and gay parented families are seen to embody diversity. Clearly, parents do not arrive at the school gate from "nowhere" – instead they rely on their knowledge and sense of entitlement, which is also connected to their economic status. There are times when such "entitlements" are not straightforwardly guaranteed, given that parents are still often operating in the context of institutional hostility. Yet working-class parents are faced with a double burden of hostility, unable to relocate and spatialise their claims, in accessing a different educational and residential setting (a "good mix" of balanced, tolerant, cosmopolitan space). It is not that such parents are completely "stuck" in place but rather they are unlikely to be recognised in discourses and research which emphasises an expansive sense of choice and of capacities to relocate as essential to "good parenting."

The desire for "good" parental space, such as schooling and neighbourhood, highlights the ways that negotiation of everyday space is often difficult for lesbian and gay parents across the class spectrum. That said, many middle-class parents articulated a desire for a "good mix" in their immediate localities and neighbourhoods. The sense of a "good mix" was articulated in middle-class parents' choices of places where there would be a "mix" of people in terms of race, class and sexuality as well as a "mix" of facilities and services, from good schools to good restaurants and entertainment venues. This "good mix" could suddenly be compromised by the existence of too many of the "wrong" people: working-class and minority ethnic groups were often seen to compromise the balance of a "good mix," threatening this middle-class idealisation of space. The ability to manage and occupy correctly "mixed" space is a classed process, where a "mixed" terrain, as opposed to a homogeneous middle-class setting – or an excessively working-class setting – was considered beneficial, even necessary, in facilitating a sense of belonging and integration.

Middle-class parents are situating their need for space and for "tolerance," desiring to be in a comfortable and accepting space. Yet in doing so, such sentiments and practices reproduce ideas of "intolerant others," situated elsewhere in other kinds of classed places. Thus it seems that both class and sexuality are relevant factors in considering locational journeys and (dis)locations (Weeks et al. 2001; Weston 1991). Carol, for example, tells of her previous, and preferred, "culturally diverse" (intersecting class and race) area, where her child learned and indeed embodied difference. Her child is seen as able to challenge homophobia and articulate "a strong sense of justice," in an "accepting" and "tolerant" environment:

> Hatton Vale … is predominantly Black and Asian and it's a fantastic place to live. It's very culturally diverse and you can get all sorts of exotic foods from your corner shop … and people are pretty well accepting and tolerant of each other. Where we lived was a little tree lined street and was pedestrianised and it was lovely, it was a good place for kids to play. When Abby was out playing in the lane she would hear some homophobic abuse … and Abby always tackled it she has a very strong sense of justice …
>
> *(Carol, 53, middle-class)*

The well-resourced, active, even politicised child is placed at the centre of her environment, commanding attention and visibility, against a "safe," "blended" background.

Paula's strategies of assessment before "coming out" are understandable, as she does not want to risk telling the wrong people. But what is interesting is the ways the "right people" are easily aligned, in her account, with those in a professional status. These dispositions are decoded at the "good" school gate, where Paula encounters other like-minded parents. The "mix" she references encompasses dispositions ("broad mindedness") read off professional status and other "clues":

> Sandbank was quite a kind of mixed area and you could choose whether you were gonna be friendly with people or not … I just try and figure out where their politics are at and how kind of, em, "right on," for want of a better description, people are and it's very hard to say what the clues are. I suppose you just you might start talking about certain … I mean, it is fair to say that people involved in social work you tend to be a little bit more broad minded … so you kind of think, *Guardian* reader type you know so you make, you make it based on those sorts of clues.
>
> *(Paula, 48, middle-class)*

Distinctions occur in imagining tolerant, accepting parents ("right on"), also known through and read off employment positions and credentials. Sarah describes living in a "very middle-class area, it's full of social workers and teachers." At the same time that she is aware of its limitations, she still emphasises the good "mix" of the area, with a range of prices and a range of different types of people. Her physical and subjective situation in space changes in relation to those around her, as she expresses being "obviously" on the lower income bracket, while still seeking a garden, an acceptable level of diversity and, crucially, a good school, as linked to residence. Again, this demonstrates the choice and control which middle-class parents can exercise over their immediate environments:

> Because we wanted a bigger garden and we lived in a part of Birch Field, again, a very diverse area, but lots of cheaper housing, so it had a lot of lesbians living there, often because we are in a lower income bracket. Lots of large racial mix, sort of African, African Caribbean families there, so we were basically looking for a bigger garden and this is the next price range up and still in this side of the city and near a main road, so easy to get into town and what have you. We also had friends up here who knew the area. We knew that the schools were okay – that's about it really.
>
> *(Sarah, 42, middle-class)*

The "knowingness" Sarah speaks of goes beyond friendship ties, also including a sense of the tone, composition and accessibility of the area as a whole (Weeks et al. 2001). Interestingly, all lesbians are situated in the same financial situation if not the very same place. Sarah is also aware that her previous area would be perceived as "professional" and "middle-class," although she experiences her own movement within and between areas as quite "confusing" and "contradictory," in terms of assigning class to such locations. Nonetheless, she still recognises the better choices on offer and the material consequences of such relocation:

> I find it quite confusing or contradictory … I live in an area now where I am surrounded by others who are professionals and would be seen as middle-class and previously we lived in an area where, again, it was big classes of working-class area and I'm now moving back into an area which is very much on the edge of there, of that community … However, I also very much recognise that living on a lower income and often, therefore, you are living in areas on the outskirts of cities and everything that comes with that, that exclusion from society. It will fundamentally affect your opportunities in life and your children's opportunities in life and, therefore, those factors then you may start trying to attach those to a model around class, etc. … this is very much a mixed area, but it gives us choices.
>
> *(Sarah)*

Sarah seemingly more readily identifies with locale than class position, but her account then goes on to detail the intersections between class and parenting (im)possibilities, and the opportunity to "mix" with others, noting varying geographies of choice within this. Importantly, Sarah speaks of having real, material choices – with real material consequences, contrasted with those on the social and geographical "outskirts." With such "good choices" available in the everyday negotiation of space, Sarah is more likely to be also recognised as a "good parent," actively taking parental responsibility and spatialising such claims, even if she also articulates a "confusing" "contradictoriness" in this inhabitation (Byrne 2006; Gillies 2006).

Overall this research seeks to intervene in re-situating the terms of the debate on lesbian and gay parenting, highlights the relevance of the intersectionality of class and sexuality as pertaining to parental (im)mobilities and geographies of choice, where perceptions, experiences and materialities of and in place vary. The "families of choice" literature provides a corrective to "straight and narrow" definitions of families and parenting. Yet it does so often without rigorous attention to the relevance of class, as facilitating and constraining "choice." Broader social and legal changes are also important here, where debates on sexual citizenship move between notions of assimilation/transformation, challenged by attention to the difference that class makes in accessing, claiming and gaining a respectable "ordinary" status. The desire to be the "same" in accessing a range of social spheres — as well as the (im)possibility of being so — may be understood as classed *and* sexualised. In this chapter I've highlighted the limitations and re-circulation of social resources, intersecting with economic capital, where (non-normative) middle-class lesbian and gay parenthood could indeed be troubled but also recuperated in enacting spatial entitlements, choices and movements.

References

Agigian, A. 2004. *Baby Steps: How Lesbian Alternative Insemination is Changing the World*. Middletown, CT: Wesleyan University Press.

Binnie, J. 2004. *The Globalization of Sexuality*. London: Sage.

Byrne, B. 2006. *White Lives: The Interplay of "Race," Class and Gender in Everyday Life*. London and New York: Routledge.

Gillies, V. 2006. "Working Class Mothers and School Life: Exploring the Role of Emotional Capital." *Gender and Education*, 18(3): 281–93.

Stacey, J. 1996. *In the Name of the Family: Rethinking Family Values in the Postmodern Age*. Boston, MA: Beacon Press.

Taylor, Y. 2007. *Working-Class Lesbian Life: Classed Outsiders*. Basingstoke: Palgrave Macmillan.

———. 2009. *Lesbian and Gay Parent: Securing Social and Educational Capital*. Basingstoke: Palgrave Macmillan.

Weeks, J., Heaphy, B. and Donovan, C. 2001. *Same Sex Intimacies: Families of Choice and Other life Experiments*. London and New York: Routledge.

Weston, K. 1991. *Families We Choose: Lesbians, Gays, Kinship*. New York: Columbia University Press.

34

Partners of transgender people

Carey Jean Sojka

STATE UNIVERSITY OF NEW YORK AT ALBANY

People often use the acronym LGBT to signify the identities *lesbian, gay, bisexual,* and *transgender.* Sometimes in addition to LGBT there might also be a Q for *queer,* a second Q for *questioning,* a second T for *transsexual,* an I for *intersex,* a P for *pansexual,* or an A for *ally.* We have expanded this "alphabet soup" of identities beyond only *gay* and *lesbian,* but even as we try to add letters to include more people based on their identities, we often leave some groups out.

The partners of transgender people are one such group. These people and their experiences are often somewhat invisible in gender and sexual minority communities. Perhaps this is because of the diversity of ways that partners of trans people identify. Some may be straight, lesbian, gay, queer, bisexual, pansexual, transgender, non-transgender (also called cisgender), genderqueer, or may have any other number of identities. Because of this, there is no one word or identity that can encompass this group of people.

For some, partnering with a transgender person means nothing different than partnering with other people they may have had relationships with throughout their lives. For instance, a lesbian woman might find herself partnered with a transgender woman and to her, the attraction is about being with a woman whether that person is transgender or non-transgender. For others, the attraction might be predominantly understood as an attraction to transgender people, and they may even identify their desire with terms such as *transamorous* or *transsensual.*

Partners of transgender people are sometimes called simply *partners, significant others* or *SOFFA's* (significant others, friends, family, and allies), or even *tranny chasers,* the latter of which is often considered a derogatory term but may in some situations be claimed by partners in ways similar to the reclamations of *queer, dyke,* or *fag.* Some partners of transgender people were in their relationship before their transgender partner disclosed a transgender identity, and others may partner with a transgender person at some stage during or after a transition. Given the diversity of backgrounds of this group and the myriad ways that partners of trans people identify their desire, their sexualities, and their genders, it may be difficult or impossible to find one term to describe this group as a whole.

The voices and experiences of the partners of transgender people are not always reflected in the research of transgender studies or queer studies. Much of what we know about relationships involving a transgender person comes to us through research that focuses primarily on the transgender person and not on their partner, whether that partner is trans or non-trans. While this research is significant in helping us to understand the meanings that transgender people give to their desire and to their intimate relationships, it is also important to conduct research that involves multiple perspectives, including the perspectives of people who partner with transgender individuals. Focusing on the experiences of partners of transgender people may illuminate aspects of intimacy that might not otherwise be seen in research that only addresses transgender people.

Research which focuses on the experiences of the partners of transgender people is becoming more prevalent, though there are still many unanswered questions about the experiences of these partners. One area that seems to be frequently addressed in current research is the negotiation of the identities of partners of transgender people.

Identities of transgender partners

Sonya Bolus, a non-transgender woman partnered with a lesbian who transitioned to male throughout their relationship, wrote about her own experiences as her partner transitioned. While she experienced some confusion about the transition and how the experience was affecting her own life, she also had positive feelings about her partner's transition. For instance, she wrote that at times "I feel like part of an ancient, unspoken tradition, as one who is particularly 'wired' to partner a transperson" (Bolus 2002:117). Thus, she felt particularly connected to the experience of partnering with a transgender person.

During her partner's transition, Bolus' own identities shifted as well. While not all partners of trans people identify their desire based on the fact that their partner is transgender, Bolus' comment suggests that her transitioning desire might be shaped by her partner's trans status. Bolus continued by noting,

> There are stray moments when I stop in my tracks, suddenly realizing my own transition, how I have also changed. How I am changing even now. On one such day I make a word for myself: *transensual*. And in naming myself, I feel substantial – connected.
>
> *(Bolus 2002:118)*

Bolus is not alone in framing her experiences as a transition; other people who have partnered with a transgender person as they transitioned have noted that their identities and desires may shift or that their understandings of what these mean may become more complex over time. Although the partner may not experience the same transition as their transgender partner, their own experiences may shift their lives and understandings in significant ways that they come to understand as their own transition.

Often, this transition experience of a partner may influence the ways that this person identifies their sexuality. While some studies note that transgender people's sexual desire does not necessarily remain fixed throughout a transition and does not inevitably seem to be heterosexual after transition (Cromwell 1999; Devor 1997; Hines 2007), few studies have focused on the ways that a transition may be related to a partner's potential shifts in identity. While Bolus identified as a lesbian earlier in life, she came to find new terms to better describe herself and her desire such as *transensual*; she also found empowerment through the act of naming herself and her desire. She is not the only one to describe her desire this way, and the identities *transensual* and *transamorous* are becoming better known in trans and queer communities. The desire of people who are transensual or transamorous is neither based on attraction to someone of the supposed "opposite" sex nor attraction to someone of the supposed "same" sex as themselves; in this way, these identities move beyond the heterosexual/homosexual binary toward desire that is defined by attraction to someone who transgresses gender boundaries. Not all partners of transgender people understand their desire in these terms, but it is important to note that some partners choose to define their desire in this way.

Partners may sometimes struggle to understand or to define their sexuality when they are partnered with a transgender person, especially when they feel pressured to define their identities for others. Tiffany, a white non-trans woman who is partnered with an Asian heterosexual trans man, identifies herself as a lesbian. However, when it comes to sharing this information with other people, she finds that her identities can become complicated:

> People are wondering what your sexuality is and, even on quizzes, I get asked on surveys and things like that and I really don't know what to put because I can't put that I'm heterosexual and I can't put that I'm a lesbian. I almost feel like I'm compromising him by saying that I'm a lesbian because he's still female and I don't want to do that.
>
> *(Pfeffer 2008:338)*

Although Tiffany considers herself to be a lesbian, she is aware of many dynamics that influence her identity, including her partner's gender and sexuality. She does not want her identity as a lesbian to discredit her partner's gender identity as a man, but she does not feel that she can identify as heterosexual either. Tiffany feels connected to her lesbian identity and may not want to abandon it; for her, the identity may not discredit her partner's gender, but she worries that others will interpret her identity in such a way. This can make it difficult to explain the complexity of her identities to others outside the relationship.

As Tiffany suggests, relationships with transgender people may often be difficult to define, even by those in the relationship. However, some people seem less concerned about what labels are used to define their relationship. Bernadette, a trans woman, spoke of her relationship with her non-trans partner; when the interviewer asked "Do you think some people see your relationship as a lesbian relationship?" she responded,

> Oh, some people might, but that is their concept of it. I have a relationship with my wife, which is very intimate and loving and has been for the past umpteen years – 40 years – and it isn't any different now than it has ever been and it's very good.
>
> *(Hines 2007:130)*

For Bernadette and her partner, the quality of their relationship was more important than their genders or the classification of their relationship. She did not see the necessity of defining their relationship in one particular way.

The gender presentation of the partner of a transgender person may also relate to the ways that the partner understands their identities and the relationship. Michele, a white, non-transgender self-identified dyke who was partnered with a trans man, said,

> The more I look like a girl and present as a heterosexual girl, the more likely [my partner] is to pass as a boy. And sometimes that makes me uncomfortable because I don't like having my queer identity elided over – especially since I've owned it for so long. ... It makes me angry. It makes me feel invisible. It makes my queer identity feel invisible.
>
> *(Pfeffer 2008:334)*

At this point in time, Michele had identified as a dyke or a lesbian for 14 years, and her queer identity had become important to her. While she believes that her gender presentation affects the ways that her partner's gender may be read in public, she also feels uncomfortable being read as heterosexual. Michele is thus left to negotiate this complicated tension between her own desire to be understood as queer and her seemingly heterosexual relationship.

Partners of transgender people who were a part of queer or LGBT communities before their relationship may feel a sense of loss when their relationship is read as heterosexual. In similar ways, partners in relationships which seemed heterosexual before a transition may also feel a sense of identity loss when their relationship is no longer read as heterosexual. Our identities can become very important, and people may begin to feel that their queer or heterosexual identities are invalidated if others interpret their relationships to be something other than what they had been in the past. For people like Michele, the feelings of queer invisibility can thus be linked to a sense of community and a fear of losing that community.

This tension between preferred and perceived identities may occur in many relationships with a transgender person. However, in relationships where this is the case, not all partners feel the need to resolve this tension. Some may feel comfortable with their identities and the way that the relationship may be read by others even if these seem to conflict.

It is also important to recognize that many relationships in which at least one person is transgender do not look like "heterosexual" relationships; many trans women partner with trans or non-trans women and many trans men partner with trans or non-trans men. Gabriel, a non-trans man who partnered with a trans man said,

> I met a handsome man who I wanted to get to know. Then I was told that he is not just a man but an FTM man. He is still the same attractive and quality person I met.
>
> *(Cromwell 1999:133)*

For Gabriel, the trans identity of his partner did not matter as much as the attraction he felt toward his partner. Their relationship was also not heterosexual. While research on relationships with trans people tends to acknowledge that trans women can partner with women or men, much of the research often overlooks the non-trans or trans men partners of trans men. However, these relationships are perhaps much more common than the research suggests.

Another trans man, Danny, explained what it was like to have sex with men as a man. The interviewer asked him, "What's the difference … between having sex with men now and having sex with men before [transition]?" Danny's response was

> I didn't really. If I did it was oral sex … it was already gay sex … umm … that was a new area. It depends upon your partner's perception. If a man thought I was a woman, we didn't do it.
>
> *(Halberstam 1994:212)*

For Danny, the significant aspect was that when he had sex with a man, that person understood him as a man and understood their encounter as "gay sex." When people confuse gender with sexuality, they may not comprehend why a trans man would be attracted to men; however, if we separate gender identities from sexual identities, it becomes clearer that these may or may not be linked for individuals. Thus, it makes sense that Danny would only have sex with men when his identity as a man was also validated.

It is also important to note that trans people sometimes partner with other transgender people; these relationships, like those that often seem from the outside to be gay or lesbian relationships involving transgender people, are often unexamined in research. Still, the reality is that trans men partner with other trans men, trans women partner with other trans men, and trans men partner with trans women. C. Jacob Hale commented on some of these dynamics:

> What is it when a transfag and a transdyke get together and make magic together with their bodies and hearts? … Whatever else it is, it isn't lesbian or gay or bisexual or heterosexual, because all of those miss the crucial fact that his transsexuality and queerness, her transsexuality and queerness, are a major part of what gets them together in the first place.
>
> *(Cromwell 1999:133)*

Hale notes that in some of these relationships, trans and queer identities may play a large part in the attraction that brings people together. These partnerships, like many involving at least one transgender person, may seem difficult to define. However, the difficulty often arises when others try to fit the relationship into our common categories for sexuality.

Making sense of experiences

As we can see, the experiences and identities of partners of transgender people are quite diverse. Despite this diversity, one important thing to note across these differences is that the experiences of partners are valid in their own right. Partners are not only witnesses to a transgender experience; they also bring their own understandings into their relationships and they potentially encounter changes in their own lives throughout these relationships.

While a non-trans partner of a trans person does not experience what it is like to be transgender, they may have insight into transgender perspectives. Cromwell writes about *transsituated perspectives* that transgender people have because of their experiences of being transgender. He also writes that "nontransgendered people can and do have transsituated perspectives" (Cromwell 1999:129). Thus, a non-trans partner of a trans person may understand a trans experience in distinctive ways even though they may not experience a gender transition in the same way as their transgender partner. Similarly, Halberstam notes that partners are often "a part of the enactment of 'trans-sex' rather than its object or incidental partner" (1994:220), suggesting that partner's experiences are more than periphery; understanding a partner's experiences is essential to understanding the dynamics of their relationships. Therefore, centering the experiences of partners is just as important as centering the experiences of transgender people when addressing this topic.

While further research is needed to conceptualize these experiences and while this work may prove to be complex because of the multitude of identities and experiences of partners of transgender people, it is helpful that even these few voices of this diverse group of people are being included in our research on queer and trans communities. We may be at the beginning stages of bringing these experiences to light in our larger communities, but as we begin to identify the many factors that are important to their identities and relationships, we will ultimately have a clearer picture of what it means to be a partner of a transgender person.

References

Bolus, Sonya. 2002. "Loving Outside Simple Lines." Pp. 113–19 in *GenderQueer: Voices from Beyond the Binary*, ed. Joan Nestle, Clare Howell, and Riki Wilchins. Los Angeles, CA: Alyson Publications.

Cromwell, Jason. 1999. *Transmen and FTMs: Identities, Bodies, Genders, and Sexualities*. Urbana: University of Illinois Press.

Devor, Aaron. 1997. *FTM: Female-to-Male Transsexuals in Society*. Bloomington: Indiana University Press.

Halberstam, Judith. 1994. "F2M: The Making of Female Masculinity." Pp. 210–28 in *Thè Lesbian Post-modern*, ed. Laura Doan. New York: Columbia University Press.

Hines, Sally. 2007. *TransForming Gender: Transgender Practices of Identity, Intimacy and Care*. Bristol: Policy Press.

Pfeffer, Carla. 2008. "Bodies in Relation—Bodies in Transition: Lesbian Partners of Trans Men and Body Image." *Journal of Lesbian Studies* 12(4): 325–45.

Part 6
Sexual identities

Introduction

Sexual identity usually refers to how individuals think of themselves. Do you consider yourself straight? Gay? Lesbian? Bisexual? Transgendered? Transsexual? Queer? Sexual identity is thought to be deeply personal; we find our identities through a process of intense reflection in order to recognize our "true nature." In North American culture, we often think of sexual identity as something innate within the individual that needs to be "discovered." Or we think of sexual identity as a psychological "choice" that individuals must make.

However, most scholars who study sexuality have found that sexual identity is social. They make the case that sexual identity is socially constructed for a few reasons.

First, how do individuals come up with the idea that they should think of themselves as straight, gay, lesbian, or bisexual? Where do they get ideas about what a straight man or a lesbian woman should look like and act like? The very categories that we use – and how we characterize the people within those categories – come from our society. For example, before the mid-1800s, there was no conception of being either a "homosexual" *or* a "heterosexual." Yet people had same-sex sexual or romantic encounters. In the past, individuals who had same-sex acts with one another were often married, had children, and were part of the traditional family structure. Perhaps they thought of their affairs as harmless or as sinful, but these acts did not define who they were as a whole person. People didn't think in terms of having their identities organized around sexual acts. Since the nineteenth century, social changes in Western society have made it possible to think about organizing identity around sexual preferences – changes like how dependent the individual was on the family, how Western culture conceptualized the individual, and the increasingly importance of science for defining people in terms of "normal" and "abnormal" identities.

Second, sociologists think of sexual identity as socially constructed because of cultural differences in how societies think about sexuality. For example, in Denmark, "homosexuality" is fading as a meaningful sexual identity. Instead, Danes increasingly recognize the amazing amount of diversity in people's sexual practices and tastes, and that there are no sex acts that are unique to what we call "homosexuals."

Third, sexual identity is socially constructed in terms of the social role it plays in relations between different groups. How do we know what it means to be a straight man in this culture?

How do straight men come to define how they should act, dress, and look? (Well, in part, by avoiding ways of acting and looking that are associated with being gay.)

A fourth reason for viewing sexual identity as social is that these identities seem very ambiguous and open to varied meanings. Can you be gay only if (as a man) you exclusively have relationships with other men? What if you've had some relationships with women along the way that you've enjoyed? Are you then bisexual? Are you a lesbian if (as a woman) you only fantasize about women? These categories of sexual identity seem extremely slippery.

Approaching sexual identity as social is messy, but interesting. The chapters in this part explore the social construction of sexual identity, using a variety of identities as examples. They raise some interesting questions for all of us to think about.

35
Straight men

James J. Dean

SONOMA STATE UNIVERSITY, CALIFORNIA

From Alfred Kinsey's studies of the sexual behavior of men and women in the 1950s to popular views today, many of us assume that heterosexuality is natural (Kinsey *et al.* 1948; Kinsey *et al.* 1953). In addition, the idea of heterosexuality as a social identity is assumed always to have existed. Recent scholarship, however, has challenged these widespread beliefs.

This chapter examines the social construction of heterosexual identities. I begin by briefly sketching the *historical* development of heterosexual identity over the last 150 years. I then turn to illustrating the social character of heterosexuality by analyzing the relationship between gender and heterosexual identity. In this regard, my focus is on straight men. I want to show how these men use gender to express a heterosexual identity in everyday life. Moreover, I argue that the contemporary development of heterosexual identities, at least in the US, UK and Europe, must be understood in the context of the changing status of gay and lesbian life today. If, as I believe, heterosexual identities are always defined in opposition to homosexual ones, what are the implications of the increased visibility of gays and lesbians for heterosexuals today? How does gay visibility shape straight men's identities?

A history of heterosexual identities

Paralleling research on the history of homosexualities, sexuality scholars have recently begun to study the rise of heterosexuality as an identity. In nineteenth-century America, heterosexual identity did not exist among white middle-class Americans (Katz 1996). Men and women occupied different social roles: men in the world of work and government, and women in the household. Sex norms were centered on marriage. Sex was only permissible as an act of pro-creation in marriage. All non-procreative sex, as well as sex outside of marriage, was disapproved. Marriage was the cornerstone of Victorian life. A proper womanhood, manhood and progeny – not an erotic heterosexual love based on pleasure – were the organizing principles of intimate life among Victorians. Basically, sex was an instinct aimed at reproduction, not the basis of an identity (Katz 1996; Seidman 1991).

Dramatic changes occurred, however, in the early decades of the twentieth century. Women were struggling for civil and political rights, as well as joining the workforce and attending college in large numbers. Also, men were moving from farm and blue-collar occupations to white-collar ones, where the key qualities for white-collar jobs were "feminine" ones, such as the ability to communicate well, to cooperate, and to be agreeable with others. The gender division was changing, men were becoming "feminized" through white-collar occupations, while women were entering the previously exclusive bastions of men: college, the workforce and politics (D'Emilio and Faderman 1988). Many Americans were anxious that gender roles were being blurred and confused. Would this gender confusion lead to the breakdown of marriage and social decline?

Historians argue that heterosexuality played a key role in enforcing a gender order that highlighted the differences between men and women. The notion of the normality and natur-alness of heterosexuality made the idea that men and women are different and complementary seem like a necessity of nature. The norm of heterosexuality, in other words, helped to secure a binary gender order that was weakened by social changes (Chauncey 1994; Katz 1996).

As heterosexuality was seen as a normal part of being a man and a woman, individuals who violated rigid binary gender norms were stigmatized as homosexual. In other words, the norm of heterosexuality shaped a culture of homophobia. Homophobic practices separated hetero-sexuals from homosexuals, denying homosexuals basic rights and respect. In turn, binary gender norms and identities reinforced a norm of heterosexuality, since "normal" men and women exhibited heterosexuality through conventional gender behavior (Chauncey 1994; White 1993).

Today, heterosexual identity is defined as sexual attraction toward the opposite sex (Katz 1996). And procreation, while still used as a justification for the naturalness of heterosexuality, is no longer a necessary part of being heterosexual. New reproductive technologies like artificial insemination make procreative heterosexual relations optional; reproduction no longer requires heterosexual behavior.

Moreover, a heterosexual identity does not have to include a desire to marry or to have a family. It can simply mean opposite-sex attraction. In short, in many societies today heterosexuality, like homosexuality, is increasingly viewed as a distinct identity neither reducible to procreation nor simply the opposite of homosexuality. Heterosexual identities are like other identities, such as being black or white, a man or woman, and display their own patterns or styles.

Gender, homophobia, and heterosexual identity

Let's shift our attention from the history to the sociology of heterosexuality. Recently, I com-pleted research on straight identities (Dean 2005). I was interested in the way straight men and women express a heterosexual identity without necessarily relying on homophobia. In this chapter, I will focus my observations on straight men.

Sexist and homophobic practices are two of the central ways that men project a heterosexual masculinity. That is, for many men, displaying a seamless sense of masculinity in one's self-presentation and behavior conveys a self-identity as straight. This has often meant acting in ways that are openly sexist or belittling of women and femininity. However, such behavior is less tolerated today. So, some men will rely on exhibiting a masculinity that reveals little or no traces of what is culturally associated with femininity. The stereotype of the tough, aggressive, show-no-feelings man expresses this sense of masculinity and heterosexuality.

But also, many men have relied on homophobic behavior to secure a straight identity. Call-ing someone a "fag" or ridiculing individuals believed to be homosexual has been a way to publicly declare a straight identity. My sense is that this is still true in America and many other societies. However, there has been a change in the last decade or so. As gay men and lesbians have become more visible and tolerated, it's become less acceptable to engage in openly homophobic behavior. So, some men rely less on homophobic behavior to convey being straight. My sense is that these men also rely heavily on their masculinity to project a straight identity.

My view is that while some men continue to rely on sexist and homophobic behavior, especially in subtle ways, to convey a straight identity, many men today draw on an exaggerated or hyper-masculine style to convey being straight. I will present three men who rely on a hyper-masculine style to project a straight identity while being more deliberate in managing their relations to women and gays.

William is a 38-year-old white male who grew up in Queens, New York. He joined the army right after high school, serving two years of active duty, and was in the reserves until 1990. He has a shaved head and a solid, jock-like build and attitude. William projects a "hegemonic" style of masculinity through trying to be dominant over other men and women. In particular, through hyper-competitive alpha male practices of trying to beat other men in any possible activity, and in his attempts to win women's sexual attention, he is constantly trying to secure his masculinity and a straight identity.

William projects a sexual identity through sexually objectifying women. That is, he reduces women to their sexuality and their sexuality is understood in terms of his masculine needs. For example, at the very beginning of our interview, he tells me: "Honestly, in regard to relationships with women, bisexual is preferred. I like two girls." He explains to me that what he means by his preference for bisexual women is women who will have sex with both him and another woman at the same time, but who otherwise only have relationships with men. While he says that he has found women in Albany to be less open to this, he says that the most of the women he dated in Las Vegas had no compunction about his preference for group sex. He explains:

> Living in Nevada, most women will do that. It's different than here. People here [Albany, New York], my friend said it once where a woman will go out with a woman exclusively and then go out with a guy exclusively. In Nevada, I would go out on a date with my girlfriend, my girlfriend would want a lap dance. We'd go to a strip bar and we'd have a lap dance just so she could hang out with a girl. Sometimes the dancer would go home with you. Of the women I dated in Las Vegas, probably 75 percent of them were bi, but not bi in the sense that you're thinking where they'll have a relationship with a woman. They have a relationship with men, but they play with girls just because it's the way Vegas is.

William's preference for bisexual women who are willing to have group sex with another woman reinforces his straightness by its association with a hypersexual virility. In his experience in Las Vegas, bisexual women were basically sexual play toys for straight men like himself.

However, William is aware that his straight style can be self-destructive: for example, there is the danger of competitive aggressiveness leading to fights or an inability to emotionally relate to women. For example, while William prides himself on the ability to be competitive with other men, he also realizes the danger in this. He says:

> There is that competitive thing there. You either choose to step up to it or you don't. Who's more of a man. That's it, who's more of a man. I'll go A, I'll go C. You'll go D. What? Motherfucker. I just went Z. That's what it's about. Anywhere you go. It's the ability to go from A to Z in less than thirty seconds flat when everyone else is going B. And that's, either you choose to do it or you don't and if you do it every single day of your life, you'll end up in prison. It's something you gotta ratchet yourself down [from]. But it's the ability to do that when you want to.

However, since William has never been married, and is single and straight, this status creates some tension for him. That is, he knows that others sometimes view being single at the age of thirty-eight as suspect for homosexuality, and this creates some anxiety for him. Thus, in general he maintains clear social and physical boundaries between himself and openly gay individuals, so as to actively project a hypermasculinity that reinforces a clear, straight gender identity. As a result of the boundaries he establishes between himself and gay men, William generally avoids going into gay bars, and he fears having a man flirt with him. He acknowledges this openly:

> I think as a heterosexual guy you have a phobia of being hit on by another guy. That's largely why we don't like to go, like myself, I don't feel comfortable going to Oh Bar [a gay bar in Albany] for a drink. I've been in there before. My friend Alicia dragged me in there one night. I didn't mind. I was there with two chicks, but I felt anxious the whole time. It was a sense of anxiety for me. But you just deal with it. I managed it. I mean I came out in one piece and I was fine. But it's not like, from my perspective, I wouldn't choose to go in there, sit down and have a beer because I wouldn't feel comfortable.

More interesting, however, is that while William maintains a straight identity by relying on a hypermasculine style, he does not express a rabid homophobia. Gay visibility has contradictory effects. While some heterosexuals refuse to associate with gay men and lesbians entirely, others like William integrate them in some way in their lives. For example, although William feels uncomfortable going to a gay bar, he does support gay marriage and have a close gay male friend. William, then, represents the type of straight men who no longer feel the need to construct their heterosexual masculinity through a strong homophobic attitude. That is, gay visibility at times has the effect of uncoupling hegemonic masculinity and virulent homophobia. As gays are viewed as increasingly good and normal, heterosexual men negotiate the establishment of heterosexual masculinity through a variety of identity practices that no longer necessarily depend on strong homophobic attitudes and behavior.

We will see this development even more so in the cases of Jason and Nick, who still rely on gender-conventional behavior to project a heterosexual identity but embrace anti-sexist and anti-homophobic views. Although heterosexual male privilege and status is still central for how men achieve respect in everyday life, heterosexual men also secure their straight masculine status through practices that avoid stigmatizing homosexuals and subordinating women.

Born in 1979, Jason is an attractive young black man. Of average height, he has a lean, muscular build and is wearing loose blue jeans and a windbreaker jacket during our interview. His hair is grown out into a small Afro and he has a dark complexion. Jason is a congenial person who is easy-going but quiet and intensely private. He grew up in Queens and Long Island, New York. He was an only child for most of his life but has a 13-year-old half-brother from his father's second marriage. He was primarily raised by his Jamaican-Indian mother and grew up around his aunt and female cousin. Jason graduated from college two years ago and is working in an administrative job in Albany, New York.

First and foremost, Jason's straight identity is always refracted through the racial lens of his blackness, and this racial lens means that Jason experiences being a (heterosexual) black man as his most salient identity. He says:

> Me being a man and just me being black just automatic throws [sic] out the vision of black man. So that would be my identity, the strongest identity I have. It's not something I try to figure out how to portray to everyone that, "Heh, I'm a black man." It's just something that they see me as. So I just let people see me as what they want to see me as until they find out who I am.

Furthermore, although Jason says that he exhibits some stereotypical feminine behaviors, such as having manicured nails and crossing his legs when sitting, he says that other straight men never notice the clear polish on his nails nor do straight women question his heterosexual identity. However, they do jokingly tell him that he is a "metrosexual." Nevertheless, after a series of questions about whether Jason has ever found himself attractive to men, in which Jason says that he never has, he becomes defensive in answering questions about his masculinity. For example, when I asked him, "How do you think your mother shaped your sense of masculinity?", he replied:

> Well I grew up with her. So I was around her all the time and I didn't turn out feminine. I grew up with my cousin, who's a girl. So I pretty much grew up around women my whole life and I never turned out acting feminine in any way. I guess just the way she acted and the way she portrayed herself. She [his mother] never really, she never really acted like a girl. She never acted sappy or she didn't show that much emotions [sic] to a lot of things.

Similarly, not only does Jason say that he does not act feminine in general, but he does take advantage of his heterosexual male privilege. He says:

> Actually, I'm happy I'm the guy. That does matter to me. We get more advantages. There are so many more things we can do that girls can't do, whether it's hooking up with girls or walking out on the street late at night or just being a guy, not having to be pregnant and going through all those hormones that they do.

Race is always central in the construction of Jason's heterosexual masculinity. He says that his black racial identity positions him within an array of racial stereotypes that convey a secure, straight identity. Whether it's women acquaintances jokingly inferring he has a large penis, male friends insinuating he's good at basketball, or male friends assuming that his associations with women are sexual, his black racial identity carries a sense of exaggerated masculinity and therefore heterosexuality.
Jason says, for instance:

> I mean if you see me around a lot of times you see that I always hang around with girls. They [straight men] never questioned my [straight] sexuality. A lot of people just assume that I have a lot of girls, both guys and girls.

I ask him: "But most straight guys wouldn't hang around with just girls, right? That would be a stereotype for gay men." He replies:

> That could be a stereotype for gay men, but in my case a lot of people seem to just think I have a lot of girls and I'm hooking up with all these girls that I'm hanging out with. Friends think, "Man, you have all these girls. All these girls like you." They never assume that I'm gay because I hang out alone with girls.

While Jason's masculine practices are generally conventional, his black racial identity acts as a kind of inoculation against homosexual suspicion. Indeed, it exaggerates his heterosexual masculinity and sexual prowess, as seen through his friends' assumptions that he has "all these girls." Jason thus reproduces dominant heterosexual masculine identity practices through both letting other men think he has sex with his women friends as well as by his general demeanor of remaining emotionally detached.

However, Jason does not engage in sexist or homophobic behavior. Although he wants to maintain his straight male privilege, he is egalitarian in his views toward women and homosexuals. For example, some of Jason's closest friends are straight and bisexual women and gay men. When I asked Jason why he was not homophobic, he related his experiences of being a racial minority and his desire not to be discriminated against because of who he is. He extends this idea to other minorities in society. He explains:

> Because I'm black and if you look at it from the standpoint of the one time black people were discriminated against by everyone. Why would you discriminate against somebody else? Just put yourself in their shoes because you actually can. Because black people are still discriminated against. So just go to some place else and see how a gay person feels. It's that they can hide it and a lot of times they do hide it and that messes them up inside. So just let them be who they are because you can't hide who you are.

Jason illustrates how gay visibility and rights have successfully framed discrimination against homosexuals as similar to the experiences of discrimination that blacks face. Moreover, he views gays and lesbians as friends and social equals, thus illustrating how heterosexual men do not have to exclude gays and lesbians from their social circles to feel secure in projecting a straight identity.

Nick is one of the few men I interviewed who purposefully blurred the boundaries between homosexuality and heterosexuality. He let others view him as gay at times. By purposefully refusing always to be recognized as straight, Nick challenges the norm of heterosexuality that requires a public presentation as straight.

Nick is a 22-year-old white male who moved to downtown Albany after graduating from a conservative suburban high school in the Capital District. He is an attractive young man who comes across as genuinely nice and amicable. When I asked him what being heterosexual means to him and how important it is to his self-identity, this is what Nick replied:

> It means to me that I'm only emotionally and physically attracted to the opposite sex. But when I think of myself, I don't think of myself as a male heterosexual. Like I'm who I am. What I do with my life, that's who I am, my actions, not my sexual identity.

In high school, Nick assumed that everyone was straight but, after moving to a mixed gay/straight neighborhood in Albany, he changed how he viewed sexual identity.

> Before I was seventeen, I had never met a gay person that I knew of. But when I moved to this area, I started hanging out with people who were gay. I started hanging out with people I didn't know they were gay and I found out later after I became friends with them that they were gay or lesbian. I realized that the lines are so blurred these days that you really can't tell who's gay and straight and just there's no point in trying to assume things. You'll find out anyway.

For example, Nick does not typically say he is straight or mention ex-girlfriends when male patrons at the bar/restaurant he works at flirt with him. He says:

> I get that confusion all the time working in the bar scene. I have guys and girls come on to me. So I know for a fact that I don't project a straight, exact heterosexual or homosexual identity to people who don't know me.

Moreover, because Nick does not view masculinity as tied to heterosexuality, he is not defensive about being viewed as gay at times. It is also the case that in his social world some gay men project a highly conventional masculine sense of self. Gay visibility today means that gays are seen as exhibiting a diversity of styles and gendered presentations of self.

For him, masculinity is about caring for others and protecting them emotionally, economically, and so on. Nick says that he views gay or straight men as capable of being masculine. He explains:

> I think honestly masculinity can be proved by a gay or straight male. I mean it's, I don't know exactly how the gender roles in relationships of gay couples go, like whether or not one person is perceived as the male protector and the other one is the female, like homemaker as classic heterosexual stereotypes. But I perceive masculinity as the male role where somebody looks after them, protects them. It's not somebody who needs to be perceived to be tough, but somebody who provides, who cares, who's affectionate in that role as a man.

For example, Nick's lack of defensiveness about others viewing him as gay is demonstrated through his description of gay men flirting with him, and when he goes to gay bars with friends he is comfortable. I ask him, "So it doesn't bother you when you go to gay bars or hang out with them [gay friends] in gay settings?" Nick replies:

> Homosexuals don't make me feel uncomfortable. It's the same way, the only time I ever feel uncomfortable in a bar is when somebody is a little bit too forward and that happens with straight people and gay people. Although in this area, I do find it a little bit more among the gay community. Like gay men are a little bit more forceful if they find you attractive and they're drunk at a bar. I don't have women grabbing my ass and like touching my chest at a straight bar, but if I go to someplace like Oh Bar or Waterworks [gay bars in Albany] with a couple of friends, it's bound to happen. It doesn't bother me. I almost expect it, but definitely a little bit more forward.

Nick, then, only signals his heterosexual identity when he is interested in a particular woman or when a gay man is explicit in his interest in him. He views sexual identity as only having personal meaning for dating and sex. Like he said, he doesn't think of himself as heterosexual and wants to be judged by his actions. However, unlike most of the heterosexual men I interviewed, Nick both stands up for gay and lesbian rights and does not try to self-consciously project a heterosexual identity, even if he thinks someone might wonder if he is gay. For Nick, being a heterosexual male does not mean being homophobic. Quite the contrary, Nick is an advocate for gays and lesbians and they are a group of people he strongly identifies with as friends and as a community.

In this chapter I've sketched a range of heterosexual masculinities. My research does not deny that many men continue to rely on homophobic and sexist practices in order to convey a straight identity. However, as public or open sexist and homophobic behavior is less tolerated in many social circles, more and more men rely on a kind of hypermasculine presentation to secure a straight identity. This uncoupling or loosening of masculine gender practices from sexism and homophobia represents a significant social change. In the background are broad social changes in gender and sexual patterns.

References

Chauncey, G. 1994. *Gay New York: Gender, Urban Culture and the Making of the Gay Male World, 1890–1940*, New York: Basic Books.

James J. Dean

Dean, J. J. 2005. *Straight Trouble: Gendered and Racial Heterosexualities in the Context of Gay and Lesbian Visibility*, Unpublished PhD dissertation, Albany, NY: SUNY.

D'Emilio, J. and Faderman, L. 1988. *Intimate Matters: A History of Sexuality in America*, New York: Harper & Row.

Katz, J. N. 1996. *The Invention of Heterosexuality*, New York: Plume Books.

Kinsey, A., Pomeroy, W. and Martin, C. 1948. *Sexual Behavior in the Human Male*, Philadelphia, PA: Saunders.

Kinsey, A., Pomeroy, W., Martin, C. and Gebhard, P. 1953. *Sexual Behavior in the Human Female*, Philadelphia, PA: Saunders.

Seidman, S. 1991. *Romantic Longings*, New York: Routledge.

White, K. 1993. *The First Sexual Revolution: The Emergence of Male Heterosexuality in Modern America*, New York: NYU Press.

36

Sexual narratives of "straight" women

Nicole LaMarre

STATE UNIVERSITY OF NEW YORK AT ALBANY

When it comes to sexual identity, nothing is as "straight" as it seems. Today, when someone asks about a person's sexuality, more often than not they are referring to whether or not the person is straight, bisexual, or gay. However, sexuality is comprised of many facets, including desires, fantasies, and sexual acts. Sexual orientation, or self-identification of sexuality based on the gender/sex of preferred partners, is only one aspect of sexuality. Recent research suggests that, although people may identify as one orientation or another, their sexual practices, desires, and fantasies have a fluidity that challenges the notion of fixed sexual identities. This essay will address this sexual fluidity by looking at the sexual narratives of several women. My interviews suggest that a critical rethinking of how heterosexuals negotiate sexual identities is vital to understanding the social organization of sexuality in contemporary American society.

The trouble with sexual identity

Many social groups and institutions are organized around sexual orientation. For example, "Focus on the Family" is established on a shared belief in the normalcy of heterosexuality and conventional, two-parent households. Other family rights organizations, such as the now defunct "Love Makes a Family of Connecticut," are centered on lobbying for same-sex marriage rights for LGBTQ families. Despite the fact that these two groups have vastly different goals, they share a common foundation; they each construct individuals and families around fixed sexual identity categories. One group advocates for the advancement of heterosexual families and the exclusion of everyone else and the other promotes equal rights for LGBTQ families. While grouping people together by sexual orientation may be politically useful, as it unites people through their common goals, it is a strategy that raises some troubling concerns.

For instance, gay and lesbian organizations have had an often tenuous relationship with bisexuals, whose goals sometimes differ from that of homosexuals. Lesbian and gay organizations have sought to gain rights by presenting homosexuality as a natural condition, unchangeable by the person or anyone else. On the other hand, bisexual organizations have fought to make room for multiple desires and to blur the boundaries between heterosexuality and homosexuality. Furthermore, groupings based on sexual identity are problematic because its members may not agree on key issues. For example, not all heterosexuals argue for the exclusion of homosexuals, and some homosexuals view same sex relationships as a conscious choice, others as a biological trait, and still others as a combination of both (Whisman 1996).

In a heteronormative society, where heterosexuality is institutionalized and naturalized to the point where it is seen as the basis of family and society, sexual identities become highly politicized because they are a gateway to social privileges (Warner 1994). By asserting that heterosexuality is a natural condition, and by promoting this notion in the media and other institutions, heterosexuality is left unexamined. How often do we assume people we meet are heterosexual? At the beginning of teaching large lecture classes on sexuality or gender, I begin by asking the class when they think heterosexuality emerged as an identity. Inevitably, there are always some who say "since the dawn of time." However, heterosexuality as a sexual identity only emerged in the twentieth century (Katz 1996). Before this time, sexual acts between individuals of the opposite gender were understood simply as a behavior. Today, however, sexual behaviors are almost always associated with having a sexual identity. For instance, many of us would see anal sex as probably something that gay men do, while vaginal sex is something heterosexual women do. Yet these sex acts can be experienced by anyone, heterosexual, homosexual, or otherwise.

If heterosexuality is socially constructed and its definition historically specific, what are the understandings of heterosexuality today? Do individuals who we think of as heterosexual also have desires or fantasies or behaviors that contradict this identity? Are there significant differences among "heterosexuals" such that the identity term (heterosexual) is not very helpful in describing the sexuality of that population? Do all heterosexuals have the same understandings of sexual identity and similar sexual experiences? Is sexual orientation significantly more complicated than social discourses allow?

Heterosexuality and heteroflexibility

Researchers have explored women's sexual narratives to uncover the wide range of sexual experiences of heterosexual and homosexual women (Carr 2006; Rust 1993). They have shown that women are likely to engage in an extensive array of sexual behaviors throughout their lifetimes, some of which transcend categorization as heterosexual or homosexual. Take the Madonna and Britney Spears kiss on MTV's VMA show, or Katy Perry's recent hit "I Kissed a Girl." Are any of these women strictly heterosexual? Some feminists and sociologists would argue they are exemplary of heteroflexibility, where the political context of sexual decisions is glossed over by explanations of idiosyncrasy and personal choice (Diamond 2005). The media has come under fire for failing to recognize heterosexuality as a hegemonic social institution that exerts considerable pressure on individuals. More specifically, the media will often portray women who are sexually and emotionally involved with one another. However, in the end at least one (if not both) of these women will be shown to "choose" a man (e.g. the 2001 movie *Kissing Jessica Stein*). Heterosexuality is presented as only an individual choice concealing its status as a social institution. Still, the media is recognizing the fluidity of sexuality and the limitations of binary understandings of sexual identity.

How do heterosexual women account for their heterosexuality? Furthermore, how are "straight" women using the categories of sexual orientation to interpret their sexual experiences and desires? Does the category of heterosexuality serve to accurately describe individual sexualities when sexual behaviors and fantasies are explored? In order to investigate these questions, I conducted a qualitative study in 2007 that examined how young adult, self-identified heterosexual women accounted for their heterosexuality. The interviews centered on exploring the relationships between women's sexual behaviors, desires, fantasies, and personal definitions of heterosexuality.

Exploring heterosexuality: fluidity between sexual identification, acts, and desires

My study focuses on the sexual narratives of young adult (18–25 years old), self-identified "straight" women. The analysis shifts between the sexual desires of participants and the accounts they provide of their sexual identity in order to explore the contradictions in their sexual narratives. These women's narratives are vital to shedding light on how contemporary sexualities are limited by social constraints at the same time that individuals are experiencing increased fluidity in their sexual identities.

It is my observation that while many women continue to rely on binary sexual categories (hetero/homo) to understand their sexual orientation, there are some women who refuse to identify as gay, straight, or otherwise. Moreover, they do this regardless of whether or not they would be socially defined as heterosexual, homosexual, or bisexual. This finding is especially significant because it suggests that some women's overall sexualities are transcending the expectations of normative heterosexuality (and normative homosexuality). Furthermore, regardless of how the women self-identified, their narratives underscore a level of sexual fluidity that challenges rigid identity categories. For many of these women, the label of "heterosexual" did not reflect the depth of their sexual experiences and desires.

I will present three narratives. These indicate that heterosexuality (and for that matter homosexuality) is not sufficient for categorizing sexuality, as sexuality is far too complicated to reduce to gender/sex preferences. The first two narratives reflect the contradictory character of heterosexual narratives. That is to say, these women assert a strong straight identity but their sexual narratives suggest otherwise. The third narrative illustrates the possibilities that exist when sexual orientation is abandoned as a social category altogether.

When I first spoke with Alice she was in a long term relationship with her boyfriend of four years. I met up with Alice, a 22-year-old teacher, in her apartment to talk about her personal approach to sexuality. After self-identifying as a heterosexual, I asked Alice what, in her opinion, would make someone a homosexual. She responded, "I don't think you can be gay unless you have sex with someone of the same sex." She used actions, rather than desires or fantasies, as the basis for establishing a heterosexual/homosexual identity. Alice noted that even though a person may fantasize about a person of the same sex, it does not make them a homosexual unless they act on that desire.

Later in the interview, Alice specified that her favorite and most satisfying sexual act was oral sex. She said that she does not orgasm or enjoy sex with her boyfriend without oral sex, and would not continue to date him (despite their long history) or anyone else if they would not engage in cunnilingus. She went so far to say that she does not enjoy penetration (penile) with her boyfriend and cannot orgasm through penetration alone. When I asked her why oral sex was her favorite act, she said, "It's just really important to me, I don't know if it's the power or the control, but I really don't like penetration and don't get anything out of it. I really need [oral sex] to orgasm."

In terms of her sexual fantasies, Alice spoke about how she had a recurring fantasy of a woman "going down" on her. She further disclosed that the fantasy of oral sex with a woman was a source of eroticism for her; "I usually just picture a female going down on me [while having sex with her boyfriend], not a specific person just someone of the same sex going down on me." She also described watching lesbian pornography to turn her on. Despite the fact that she had often thought about being with a woman sexually, Alice had never had an intimate encounter with a woman. Although Alice initially identified as a heterosexual, after we had discussed her fantasies and desires she modified her statement, saying, "OK, how about this? I'm a heterosexual with bisexual tendencies. Until I have sex with a female I will still consider myself a heterosexual."

The contradiction between her "heterosexual" identity and her non–heterosexual fantasies were stated in a very frank way. Alice's sexuality was not limited to heterosexual desires or normative heterosexual acts (as she expressed distaste and even an aversion to penile penetration), regardless of her self-identification as a heterosexual. When I asked Alice if she thought she could have a pleasurable experience with a woman if she met one that she really liked, she replied, "Sure, I think it could be hot." Even though she found women desirable and erotic in a way she did not express about men, she relied on binary, restrictive definitions of her sexuality based on the gender/sex of her partners. While it is arguable whether or not Alice is truly "straight," the importance of her narrative lies in exemplifying the complexity of sexuality in a person who holds to a rigid sexual identity.

Diane also identified as a heterosexual. She was 22 years old and a graduate student in cultural studies. What I found most interesting in talking with Diane is that, unlike Alice, Diane detailed having intimate encounters (short of "going all the way") with several women. Although she identified as a heterosexual, her understanding of sexuality was less constricted by normative heterosexual expectations. She explained that sexuality

> depends on who the person is, what their sexual history is. For me personally, I see myself as a straight woman, but I think that really for anyone if the right person came along it wouldn't matter what sex or gender or anything they were. And I feel the same way about myself. I do find women attractive, you know I've never particularly met one who you know, tickled my fancy … I'd say sexual identity is just one part of my personality …

Diane was very open in discussing her sexual history with me, and downplayed gender/sex preference as a defining part of sexuality. Although she identified herself as heterosexual, she talked at length about one woman who she had "made out" with on several occasions, and with whom she almost had a sexual relationship. While she never had sex with the woman, she "totally would have." Now she asserts that not having sex ultimately saved their friendship.

Diane went on to discuss sex acts that satisfied her, as well as the fantasies that she had and how they played out in her sexual relations. She enjoyed penetration (penile, finger, and sex toy), and oral sex the most because it "sort of feels like you're more in control sometimes, like they're doing you a service. It's somewhat of a power issue." She said that, without being able to engage in those acts, there would have to be sufficient passion in other aspects of a relationship to compensate. Power and control were important to her sexual satisfaction, particularly when engaging in oral sex and in BDSM (bondage, domination, sadism and masochism) activities, including tying up and whipping her partners.

I asked Diane about her sexual fantasies. She talked about "voyeurism" and "exhibitionism" in the form of public sex. She used an example of a sexual encounter on a vacation:

> I recently went on a [trip] and the last night I was there I ended up meeting this guy and we went for a walk and ended up having sex in the branches of some low growing trees. Essentially it ended up being a walled off section, so we were kind of in the tree so yeah, we'd hear someone walking close by and we'd freeze, but you know someone looking from where we were you could see the lights of a club on one side and signs for restaurants on the other and yeah that was just cool.

Part of the construction of normative heterosexuality is that sexual acts are not only between two consenting adults, but also that it occurs in private. Diane breached these norms by repeatedly engaging in public sexual acts, acts that were an integral part of her fantasies and sexual desires. Not only did Diane breach the heterosexual contract by partaking in public sex, but also by specifying that exhibitionism and BDSM were more fundamental to her sexual satisfaction than the gender/sex of her partner.

I went on to ask Diane if she could rate the importance of gender/sex preference in relation to other aspects of her sexuality. She explained that, "It depends on the individual. I could see a man who is very attractive and we hook up one night and it's fantastic but personality wise and intellectually he's a jerk. While he's pretty to look at and great in the sack, you don't want him to open his mouth or see him on a regular basis." Rather than saying gender/sex or sexual acts were more important, she said that it was more of a combination of the two in a particular individual that mattered. For Dianne, her attraction to a person could not be reduced to the person's gender/sex alone. Diane expressed being attracted to both men and women. The types of sexual acts the person engaged in were at times more important than what her sexual partner had "underneath their clothes." Yet Diane did not dismiss the importance of the combination of masculinity and femininity in her intimate companions. She described being sometimes turned on by the masculinity and assertiveness of her sexual partners, but other times enjoying a "softer" feminine companion. Contrary to normative heterosexual expectations, opposite sex attraction was not the sole determinant of Diane's heterosexuality.

Before we ended the interview, I asked Diane if she could say what made someone a heterosexual or a homosexual. She said that it depended on who someone is attracted to overall; "It's based on who looks good to you." Thus, if someone was predominantly attracted to people of the opposite sex, he or she would be a heterosexual. Bisexuals would be individuals who have equal attraction for men and women. Her definition of sexual orientation did not capture the fluidity that Diane herself experienced in gendered desires. Despite expressing her occasionally strong attraction for women, Diane continued to define herself as a heterosexual. In doing so, Diane reduced the variances in her sexual history, and adopted a label that failed to capture the multiplicity of her desires. By adopting a public heterosexual identity, Diane rendered her non-normative heterosexual desires and sexual experiences invisible. Overall, Diane was open to experiencing non-normative sexual acts (like BDSM, exhibitionism, and intimate encounters with women), but fell short of rejecting binary, exclusionary sexual categories.

Contrary to the first two interviews, the third interview is an example of a woman who society would regularly identify as heterosexual but purposefully rejects such a label. Hannah was a 21-year-old college student who majored in business. When I asked Hannah how she self-identified sexually, she said,

> I'm pretty open I guess. And we [my brother and I] were actually talking about this … I would be like oh she's really pretty and my brother would be like oh no no no, you're not gay at all [implying that I was]. So I don't, well like I think about it but I never actually dated a woman um, but like, well, I don't know if there's a name for it. Because I'm attracted to both men and women and usually to men that are more masculine but sensitive, and females that are more masculine. So I don't know.

She stated that "it's usually easier to say that I'm straight" because she has only had sexual experiences with men. When I asked her what she would say if someone asked if she was heterosexual or homosexual, she responded, "I'll tell pretty much what I just told you; that I'm attracted to both [men and women] but I've only hooked up with guys. I'm actually not that shy about it."

Unlike Alice or Diane, rather than purposefully portraying a "straight" identity, Hannah often found herself annoyed when people assumed her heterosexuality;

> Sometimes I get annoyed with people's assumptions about me and I'll be like what's wrong with that because I have a lot of friends who have gone through a lot of crap and so when people talk about sexuality I try to correct their assumptions. I think that's important … I try to correct [people's assumptions] as soon as I'm comfortable …

In terms of her favorite sexual acts, Hannah identified choking, submission, and the use of sex toys as important to her sexual satisfaction. Although she noted that, "I really like toys and I think they are fun. There are so many things you can do," she also expressed frustration when her "lovers" were not open-minded about incorporating sex toys into sexual encounters. Hannah went so far as to specify that she would not have a sexual relationship with anyone should they refuse to participate in the above activities. Hannah explained that she enjoys being submissive in her sexual relations. As she often found herself in an aggressive role in her public life, playing a submissive role in her erotic life was exciting to her.

Although Hannah only had a few intimate encounters with women, none of which went "all the way," she often thought of being with another woman while masturbating. Hannah's personal fantasies and erotic desires for other women were an integral part of her sexuality. She went on to explain that she felt the sexual acts she participated in were more important than the gender/sex of her sexual partners. "It wouldn't matter to me if it [having sex] was with a guy or a girl actually." If she were to be rigidly categorized as a heterosexual, Hannah felt that she would have had to "give up expressing my desires for other women." Hannah was not comfortable identifying as a heterosexual because she felt it would limit her freedom of choice. Hence, her discomfort with restrictive labels led Hannah to reject binary categories. Similarly, Hannah expressed discomfort at being labeled bisexual, as many bisexual women she knew eventually ended up with men and denied their desires for women.

I asked her at the end of the interview if she felt it was possible to draw borders around sexual identities. She replied, "I think it is too complicated. I mean I'm not attracted to every man, just like I'm not attracted to every woman. So, I don't think I put much stake in it [sexual orientation] because I don't think it's possible [to categorize people]. I mean you may be surprised you haven't met everyone in the world." Hannah actively sought to correct people's assumptions because she felt sexuality was too complicated to be captured by any one orientation. The transgression of sexual categorization was an attempt to maintain her freedom to experience her desires however she wanted.

In the end, all three of the narratives portray women who experience a wide variety of sexual desires, fantasies, and acts. Although all three women's stories strayed from normative expectations of heterosexuality, only Hannah actively distanced herself from being labeled a heterosexual. As this research suggests, women's experiences and understandings of heterosexuality vary greatly from person to person. For some, heterosexuality is a matter of a dominant sexual attraction to the opposite sex. Yet for others, heterosexuality is contingent upon the gender/sex of the people you actually have sex with; sexual desires need not be limited to the opposite sex. Some heterosexual women fantasized about other women but said they had no desire to act on their fantasies. Interestingly, a number of heterosexual women interviewed were very open to having sex with women but lacked the opportunity. No two accounts of heterosexuality were the same. When we look past the political meaning and organization of heterosexuality we see that no two heterosexuals are alike. In fact, few people are "100 percent straight." Moreover, a handful of women in the study, like Hannah, actively rejected being categorized. What does this renunciation and transcendence of sexual orientation mean?

Conclusion

A thorough exploration of women's sexual narratives demonstrates that many heterosexuals have desires and experiences that contradict their sexual identity. Although socially perceived as a static identity, the label "heterosexual" describes very little about an individual's overall sexuality. Heterosexual women do not necessarily experience an absence of same sex desires or sexual encounters. Furthermore, heterosexual women may have very different interpretations of what heterosexuality means. This underscores the complexity of sexuality and the narrowness of contemporary discourses regarding heterosexuality. On the one hand, these interviews show the ongoing reliance of many American women on sexual binaries in contemporary society. On the other, the interviews illustrate that some women are able to experience desires and fantasies that are not limited by normative expectations of heterosexuality. Based on sexual orientation alone, "straight" women have little in common sexually aside from their self-identification as heterosexuals.

These interviews dispel the notion of heterosexuality as a fixed identity. Thinking back to the organizations mentioned earlier, heterosexuality is less a natural condition today than it is a means of politically organizing groups of people. Through its organization around normative heterosexuality, "Focus on the Family" maintains the illusion of the fixity and constancy of heterosexual identities. The illusion has the effect of naturalizing opposite sex attraction and making it a basic organizing principle of Western societies. This accounts for the continuing reliance on sexual orientation because it continues to have meaning in social institutions. But heterosexuality tells us little about individual sexualities. Today, heterosexuality maintains its privilege on an institutional level.

Certainly there are some women who may kiss other women solely for the benefit of teasing or stimulating men. Scholars often dismiss these women's experiences as examples of hetero-flexibility, or argue they exemplify the heterosexualizing of female same sex desires. To some extent this may be true. However, women like Hannah are actively working to challenge the rigidity of sexual identity categories. Hannah's narrative illuminates the possibility of creating a society without fixed or rigid sexual borders, and perhaps without the exclusive norm of heterosexuality. Furthermore, it is possible that these women's accounts are the first step towards creating a society that values personal choice and experience over sexual conformity cloaked by an appearance of sexual freedom.

While identity politics have been important in gaining sexual rights in our society, the underlying problem may not be the privileged status of heterosexuals. The true problem lies in societies' reliance on oppositional, dualistic categories that pit groups of people against one another. Rejecting static sexual identities may be the key to "undoing" oppression based on sexual orientation.

References

Carr, C. L. 2006. "Bisexuality as a Category in Social Research: Lessons from Women's Gendered Narratives." *Journal of Bisexuality* 6(4): 27–47.

Diamond, L. M. 2005. "'I'm Straight, but I Kissed a Girl': The Trouble with American Media Representations of Female–Female Sexuality." *Feminism Psychology* (15): 104.

Katz, J. N. 1996. *The Invention of Heterosexuality*. New York: Plume Books.

Rust, P. 1993. "'Coming out' in the Age of Social Constructionism: Sexual Identity Formation among Lesbian and Bisexual Women." *Gender and Society* 7(1): 50–77.

Warner, M. 1994. "Introduction." In *Fear of a Queer Planet: Queer Politics and Social Theory*, ed. Michael Warner. Minneapolis: University of Minnesota Press.

Whisman, V. 1996. *Queer by Choice: Lesbians, Gay Men, and the Politics of Identity*. New York: Routledge.

37

Lesbians

Interview with Tamsin Wilton (1952–2006)

UNIVERSITY OF WEST ENGLAND

Tamsin spent the early years of her working life as a schoolteacher, a bookshop manager, an arts administrator, a vision mixer in an artists' TV studio, and a freelance illustrator/cartoonist. Oh, and as an "enthusiastic" heterosexual. It wasn't until her late thirties that she fell in love with a woman and decided that a lesbian life suited her much better. At around the same time, prompted by the ignorant and inhumane response in Britain to the HIV/AIDS epidemic, she signed up for an MSc in gender and social policy and joined Bristol Polytechnic (later to become the University of the West of England) as a researcher on an AIDS education project. She was never sure which was more traumatic – becoming a lesbian or becoming a social scientist! Almost two decades and more than ten books later, she became the UK's first Professor of Human Sexuality, an honorary member of the Gay and Lesbian Association of Doctors and Dentists, and became internationally known for her work on the political and personal aspects of lesbian identity and sexuality, the social and cultural issues surrounding AIDS, and the complex relationship between sexual behaviours, identities, and wellbeing. She died from an aneurysm in 2006.

When did the idea of a lesbian as a sexual identity emerge?

The idea of "lesbianism" emerged as part of what I call "the sexological project." The "homosexual" was a nineteenth-century invention. The new science of sexology had come up with the idea that homosexual people were members of a third sex. Early pioneers of the science of sex invented the notion of homosexuality and lesbianism as *conditions* or as *referring to distinct human types* in order to rescue us from the earlier idea that same-sex activities were immoral and should be criminal. So, I think we can date the idea of a lesbian "identity" from around that time.

What was it like to be a lesbian in the 1950s and early 1960s in Great Britain?

Lesbian life in the UK in the 1950s and early 1960s was very much a risky, underground affair. There were very few places where women could meet, and little sense of a lesbian subculture outside major cities. I was lucky enough many years ago to have as neighbours an elderly lesbian couple. They had met during the Second World War, when Iris left her abusive husband to live with Eliza, and they set up home together in a traditional working-class district of

Bristol. As I think was probably often the case, everybody *knew* but nothing was ever mentioned. Eliza dressed like a man, acted like a man, worked like a man and could be taken for a man, whilst Iris dressed and acted like any other housewife in the street. The first time Eliza admitted the true nature of their relationship to anyone, and the first time she said the word "gay" aloud, was when Iris died. Like Eliza and Iris, most women lived lives of anxious secrecy, and many in that older generation continue to do so.

How did the women's movement in the 1970s change the meaning and social life of being a lesbian?

The impact of the second wave of the women's movement on lesbians in Britain was immense. Politicizing lesbian identity, apart from anything else, took away the shame of sexual "perversion" and replaced it with a far more powerful and empowered position – that of being in the vanguard of the army of women which was going to overthrow the patriarchy!

For the first time, women-only social events were held in every town and city, and this meant that there were far more places where it was safe for lesbians to socialize. More women started to experiment with lesbian relationships and, although it would be almost impossible to quantify, it seems likely that the number of women who identified as lesbian increased dramatically.

There was, of course, a downside to all this. The invention, by a British group of activists called the Leeds Revolutionary Feminists (LRF), of the notion of the *political lesbian* was experienced as an insult and an attack on lesbian sexuality by women whose lesbian identities and relationships pre-dated feminism. The definition of the political lesbian was: "a woman-identified woman who does not fuck men." The "new" lesbians, whose first allegiance was to the feminist struggle, began to censure many elements of lesbian culture and sexuality. Everything from butch/femme to s/m was labelled "male-identified," and lesbians who took part in such activities were pushed out of feminist spaces. I went on the annual Lesbian Strength March in London that year, and was astonished to see "politically right-on" lesbian feminists handing out leaflets demanding that women in s/m gear or wearing leather be excluded from the march, and from the party at the Lesbian and Gay Centre where the march was due to end up.

Things reached stalemate with the advent of HIV/AIDS. Some lesbians went so far as to publish statements to the effect that AIDS was nothing to do with lesbians, whilst others – myself included – got on with the business of trying to get information about just what the risks were, and producing educational material for dykes about safer ways of having sex and injecting street drugs. The need to produce explicit safer sex materials, and the fact that gay men were making good use of "pornographic" imagery to promote safer sex and save lives, suddenly meant that the debates around porn got a whole lot more complex, and the fiery battles between different kinds of feminists about lesbian sexuality simply fizzled out.

Can you describe some of the chief ways that being a lesbian today is different from being a lesbian in the 1970s and 1980s?

I think that the meaning of sexual identity has changed. One way to gauge this change is to look at popular culture. Although there is still a lot of homophobia around, there is also a broad strand of popular youth culture which regards homophobia as silly and uncool. Club culture is sexually playful, and images of girls snogging each other are everywhere – though there is another side to this, in that there are far fewer images of blokes snogging each other, and a certain sense that the girls snog each other to turn the blokes on. So I don't think you can regard this as a completely positive phenomenon! Also, there are troubling ethnic and class

261

issues. The "urban" music scene (polite euphemism for black music) incorporates elements of serious homophobia, particularly in the lyrics of "ragga" singers from Jamaica, so I imagine it may be less easy for lesbians from minority ethnic communities.

Also, consider British television, which is very different from American television – far more liberal on the whole. We have less of a problem from mouthy right-wing christian fundamentalists, so lesbian and gay characters and storylines are run-of-the-mill television fare. The barriers here were broken by a soap opera, *Brookside*, which broadcast the first prime-time lesbian kiss in 1989, and then by a television adaptation of Jeanette Winterson's novel, *Oranges are Not the Only Fruit*. Now it is obligatory for every soap opera to have at least one gay male character and one or two lesbians.

I think this increased tele-visibility of lesbian and gay sexualities, together with widespread disgust at the virulent homophobia which was unleashed in response to the first cases of HIV/AIDS in Britain, has led to a far more tolerant attitude and a recognition of sexual diversity. The young lesbians I meet are so relaxed and at ease in their sexual identity that it makes me rather envious! I don't think they have much idea about what it feels like to have to conceal the truth about your sexuality in order to survive. When interviewing lesbians, I have found, too, that younger lesbians are far less hung up about sexual contact with men. They don't feel that having had sex with men in the past (or even in the present) disqualifies them as "real" lesbians.

Do young lesbians relate to their bodies and sexuality differently than those from an older generation?

My observations are that lesbians are far more inclined to follow current fashion – which at the moment is all about exposing as much metal in your belly-button as possible and letting your bottom-cleavage hang out of your jeans. There has been a real blurring of the gay–straight boundaries in relation to fashion. I saw my first eyebrow-full of steel rings at Gay Pride in 1989 and felt quite faint; now, of course, piercings are routine on everyone (except me!). I have a suspicion that Madonna, in particular her coffee-table book *Sex* and the Blonde Ambition tour, has had more to do with the "gaying" of mainstream popular culture than has been recognized, but I want to spend more time working on this idea before I hold forth on my "Madonna theory."

Do you think there are any major differences between the politics of lesbianism in the UK and in the US?

There are, in global terms, more similarities than differences between lesbian politics in the US and Britain. Having said that, there are some significant differences. Probably the most important is that we don't have a written constitution here in the UK (being a monarchy, we are "subjects" of her majesty rather than "citizens" of a state), so there are no constitutional rights to underpin the legal process when trying to establish lesbian and gay rights. The European Union has been our salvation, since they have come up with human rights legislation which prohibits discrimination on the grounds of sexual orientation.

Another difference is that right-wing christian fundamentalism is not such an issue here. This is not to say that religion is not a problem; far from it. Ironically, it is the American congregation of the Church of England which ordains gay bishops, not the British one, and the Archbishop of Canterbury seems to be powerless to prevent the Church breaking apart over this issue (but then, many in the church think women bishops are against the will of God, so we are dealing with a nineteenth-century mind-set really!). There are also current problems with the New Labour Government under Prime Minister Tony Blair, whose Cabinet contains a lot of church-goers. This means that they draw back from supporting lesbian and gay rights when those rights come into conflict with religious belief. Laws prohibiting discrimination on sexual orientation grounds in the workplace, for example, have an opt-out clause for faith-based organizations and individuals of strong religious conviction.

Many of the services which are privately run in the US are state-administered and publicly funded in Britain. The state school system, for example, is extremely important as an LGB political issue, since almost every child passes through it. Issues such as homophobic bullying and education about sexuality are therefore very live for groups such as Stonewall, which lobby for LGB rights. It is, for a variety of reasons, highly unlikely that Britain will ever have a specialist school or college for LGB youth, such as those found in the States.

I want to ask you about your research on representations of lesbians in movies. In the US there has been a new gay visibility in movies, but lesbians are still much less visible. What is the situation in the UK?

The issue of lesbian visibility in film is probably about the same here as it is in the US, since almost all films shown in British cinemas are from Hollywood! However, there are plenty of "art house" cinemas which show films from independent studios in Europe, the Middle East (particularly Iran), Japan, China, India and Australia. Some fabulous lesbian and gay cinema has come out of Australia (e.g. *Desperate Remedies* and *Priscilla, Queen of the Desert*) and these are widely shown in British art house cinemas. There is also an annual Lesbian and Gay Film Festival, hosted by the British Film Institute in London, which tours to major cities such as Edinburgh and Bristol, and this includes lots of small-budget lesbian-made films and videos.

However, I suspect that the most important difference lies, once more, in our television networks. Because both the BBC and Channel Four (an independent channel which is a terrestrial commercial broadcaster) have a public service remit, and Channel Four in particular has a duty to serve minority communities. Channel Four broadcast the first-ever weekly magazine programme aimed at a lesbian and gay audience in 1989. It was called "Out on Thursday," and ran for five years. The BBC has adapted Sarah Waters's novels *Tipping the Velvet* and *Fingersmith*, and Channel Four shows the US show *Will and Grace*, and it ran *Ellen* over here too. None of this means that lesbians are now well-represented on British television. Gay men are far more visible, partly because there is an honourable British tradition of camp stand-up comedy (and most of the camp stand-up comics have been gay, though until recent times their sexuality was a strange kind of open secret). People like Julian Clary and Paul O'Grady (aka Lily Savage) are very popular, and although lesbian comics such as Leah Delaria have been given shows, they have not tended to last very long.

Lobbying by groups such as Stonewall and the Campaign for Press and Broadcasting Freedom has been very successful in banishing offensive coverage of lesbians from the television screens, so most of what we see is actually quite carefully done. Real-life lesbians are often to be seen on "reality" shows of various kinds (two friends of mine are currently being filmed for a show about how to pay off your mortgage in two years!) and Alex Parks, an "out" lesbian from Cornwall, won Fame Academy last year. All in all, things are a lot better than they used to be. However, there is still a lot of trivialization and sensationalism, and the rubric "this programme contains lesbian sex scenes" is still used as a way to increase the straight male audience.

Do you think that there are any important differences between British and Hollywood movies with regard to the way lesbians are portrayed?

It's difficult to compare Hollywood movies with British movies, simply in terms of size and resource base, but I tend to see the two industries as following pretty similar paths when it comes to showing lesbians on screen. In this respect, as with most matters to do with sex and sexualities, British popular culture mirrors that of the US rather than that of European countries such as France or Germany, where attitudes tend to be more accepting. On the other hand, what we might call "educated" British culture tends to draw more upon that of mainland Europe, but, in relation to the cinematic arts, this is a relatively small audience which is content to visit art-house cinemas. Many of the most innovative and positive cinematic representations of lesbians have come from the non-English-speaking European countries, and the audience for dubbed or subtitled films is largely drawn from the educated minority.

Mainstream British culture, of course, is also touched by the puritanical religious values which drove the Pilgrim Fathers across the Atlantic, and this is one of the factors shaping a peculiarly British attitude to all things sexual and to deviant sexualities in particular. This is reflected in cinema. If you think of earlier films, such as *The Killing of Sister George* or *The Children's Hour* it is clear that, while storylines are sympathetic to the plight of the socially excluded lesbian, to *be* a lesbian is presented as a very unfortunate state indeed. This is something of a contrast to *Madchen in Uniform* ("Girls in uniform"), a German film which presents a subtle and sophisticated critical analysis of the inhumanity of gender roles as part of a rather tender lesbian love story. Certainly it is not coincidental that many of the earliest sexologists, who argued for the human rights of lesbian and gay people, were German.

Anyone wishing to gain insight into the British attitude to sex should spend some time watching the *Carry On* series of comedy films. These, with their broad, cartoonish representation of gender and of sexuality, are a strangely accurate reflection of the contradictions inherent in our approach to the erotic. The same characters – among them Hattie Jacques's fat, frustrated spinster, Barbara Windsor's big-breasted dumb blonde, Kenneth Williams's arch homosexual and Sid James's ever-leering, "up for it," working-class rogue – are present in just about every *Carry On* film. Although figures of fun, there is no spite or malice in these films. In an early exposition of "don't ask, don't tell," everyone *knows* that Kenneth Williams (in person and in character) was gay, but, whilst his campness is gently mocked, it is also celebrated. Similarly, whilst it is made clear that the characters played by Hattie Jacques – generally domineering figures of petty female authority such as hospital matrons – are women made furious by sexual frustration, there is a degree of sympathy in the mockery directed at their plight. Significantly, whilst the films are stuffed with gay jokes, there is never so much as a glimpse of lesbian possibility.

This, too, is an accurate reflection of the British attitude to lesbians, which has always been that the best way to prevent lesbianism is to act as if lesbians didn't exist. Whilst Queen Victoria's famous refusal to believe that such acts were possible is the stuff of legend, it is a matter of historical record that, during a 1920s Parliamentary debate on legislation intended to include lesbianism in the Sexual Offences Bill, one peer protested:

> It would be made public to thousands of people that there was this offence; that there was such a horror ... Is there any necessity for it? How many people does one suppose are really so vile, so unbalanced, so neurotic, so decadent as to do this? ... you are going to bring it to the notice of women who have never heard of it, never thought of it, never dreamed of it.

Clearly, the *Carry On* films are carrying on an established British tradition. By representing a highly sexualized cinematic universe in which there are no lesbians, the films represent and reproduce a cultural strategy for erasing lesbian possibility. It is for this reason that lesbian feminists in Britain (and the US) identified "lesbian invisibility" as one of the key tools of male supremacist cultural production.

I'd like to touch on your research on the British healthcare system. What are the chief problems lesbians face in accessing medical services?

Lesbians in the UK do have problems accessing healthcare. Again, the situation is unlike that in the US, since the two healthcare systems could hardly be more different. Our National Health Service (NHS) is funded from the public purse, and aims to provide healthcare free at the point of need from cradle to grave. Although the economics of this are now under considerable challenge as a result of demographic changes in the UK population (where aging baby-boomers are threatening to outnumber the working-age population) and of an increasingly globalized free-market economy, it is still the case that this is what the NHS does, indeed, manage to provide.

Thus, whereas lesbians in the US may have problems affording healthcare in the first place (lacking access to the economic privileges of masculinity), that is not the case in the UK. Rather, problems faced by lesbians in relation to the healthcare system are entirely due to heteronormativity and to what might be called institutional homophobia.

Despite the claims of various researchers – some of which have been, frankly, ridiculous – there is nothing to distinguish the lesbian body from the non-lesbian body. Moreover, almost everything which the women's health movement has learned about the health issues confronting "women" may be traced back to heterosexual activity and identity. This has two implications: the first is that the "women's health movement" has, in fact, been the *heterosexual* women's health movement; and the second is that lesbianism is likely to be beneficial to women's health. Here we see that heteronormativity – the unreflexive assumption that heterosexuality is some kind of default state and not to be problematized – carries negative implications for everyone. Whilst lesbian women may be put at risk because little attention has been paid to our health needs, non-lesbian women may be deprived of the health information they need because the potential risks of heterosex are not recognized or acknowledged.

In Britain, as everywhere, the most direct problem confronting lesbians who seek health care is institutional homophobia. The personal prejudices of health and social care workers may have devastating consequences, and here it is the lingering "respectability" of homophobia in British society which has to be challenged. Many doctors, for example, are christian, and exploit their religious beliefs to justify refusing to treat lesbians or gay men. A very recent research project carried out around London found that some primary care practices were simply refusing to allow openly gay men to join their lists, on the ground that they were "a religious practice." In the context of widespread hostility towards lesbians and gay men, many health and social care professionals are simply not given the information they need in order to provide good-quality care to this group, and do not have their prejudices challenged in the course of their professional training.

This may result in some practitioners maintaining attitudes and beliefs which are quite grotesquely homophobic. At a study day for midwives at the John Radcliffe Hospital in Oxford a few years ago, I was approached by one midwife who had listened in great agitation to my lecture on midwifery services for lesbian mothers. This midwife demanded to know what was done with "the boy babies" of lesbian mothers. Since all lesbians fervently loathed all men, she explained, surely they would simply dispose of their infant sons by murdering them. She supposed that social services were aware of this, and that any lesbian who gave birth to a son would immediately have that baby taken into care by the local social service team. Her worry was that some lesbians might give birth secretly, in their own homes, and she was asking me, in all seriousness, how those infants might be protected from their murderous, man-hating mothers! My appalled insistence that this was no more than a product of her imagination seemed to fall on deaf ears, and I have worried ever since that this woman is continuing her work as a community midwife with her extreme homophobic fantasies intact.

This, and other evidence gathered by researchers, suggests that all health and social care practitioners need to be given information about how to meet the needs of their lesbian service users and patients in basic training, and that it needs to be made clear that homophobia is unprofessional and that homophobic behaviour towards patients is a disciplinary offence.

The long, hard graft of making the NHS aware of this has borne fruit. The British Medical Association (BMA), the Royal College of Nursing, and the Royal College of Midwifery have all published guidelines on the treatment of lesbian and gay patients, and the Gay and Lesbian Association of Doctors and Dentists (GLADD) is now consulted by the Department of Health (DoH) and the BMA for advice. The DoH has established an External Reference Group on Sexual Orientation, and the colleges and university departments where doctors, nurses, and other practitioners are trained are increasingly concerned to offer their students the knowledge and skills they will need to offer good-quality care to their lesbian and gay patients.

Have lesbians organized to reform medical institutions and have they tried to develop alternative healthcare options?

The positive change within the healthcare system in Britain could not have taken place without the activism of lesbian healthcare professionals and service users. Almost all of the research evidence used to demand action has come from lesbian researchers. This has been essential since, until very recently, such research would simply not have been funded. It is, unsurprisingly, lesbians within the healthcare professions who have pushed for the issue to be addressed within their professional groups. Lesbian midwives and lesbian (and gay) nurses put pressure on their Royal Colleges to develop guidelines, and lesbians working in higher education have produced the resources to enable improved training to take place.

It has been very much a case of seeing what needs to be done, recognizing that nobody else is going to do it, and doing it yourself. It was, for example, precisely that kind of process which led to the publication of my own books, *Sexualities in Health and Social Care* (a textbook for health and social care students) and *Good For You: A Handbook of Lesbian Health and Wellbeing*, which remains the only British health guide for lesbians.

Lesbian genito-urinary medicine (GUM) clinics have been established in Oxford, Glasgow, and in two London hospitals, and these not only offered unprejudiced and accepting care to lesbians, but also provided extremely valuable research evidence to demonstrate that lesbians *do* get cervical cancer and sexually transmissible infections and that we *do* need screening, particularly cervical smears (pap smears) and other tests which non-lesbian women tend to get in the course of their routine encounters with the reproductive health services. Lesbians travelled long distances to attend these lesbian-specific services, but many are now less well attended and some have closed altogether. It is difficult to know whether this indicates that mainstream services have improved so much that lesbians no longer require special clinics, or whether services simply collapse when key staff move on.

Any concluding thoughts on the differences between lesbian life in the US and UK?

I would have to say that we are both like and unlike the US. This is not surprising, since there has always been a lively two-way relationship between Britain and the European mainland, and our histories are linked still more intimately than is the case for the US. Our welfare state is greatly beneficial to lesbians, and we are geopolitically close to countries like Sweden, Denmark, and Holland, whose attitudes to sexuality are tolerant, cultured, and sophisticated. It is inevitable that lesbians who have experienced at first hand the intoxicating sense of social acceptance which prevails in these countries will be empowered to demand something similar in their homeland.

It is also significant that Britain, for all its imperial history, is much, much smaller than the US, and far more crowded. Whereas the pink dollar represents the potential for real political power in the US, that is never going to be the case on this side of the Atlantic. Our demands for acceptance, therefore, have to be based on philosophical and political arguments about justice, fair play, and equality, rather than on economic power. This is another reason why we have looked to Europe, rather than the US, for support.

A final, important point is that attitudes seemed to change for the better quite dramatically with the demise of Prime Minister Margaret Thatcher's Conservative administration. Why this is, I am not yet sure. Certainly it has something to do with HIV/AIDS, and a lot to do with Section 28 (intended to stop local authorities promoting homosexuality by banning the public funding of books, plays, leaflets, films or any other material showing gay relationships as normal), and the determination of public-service broadcasters to defy a right-wing government which wanted to silence every mention of lesbian and gay existence. As I have indicated, I think Madonna played a significant role too, though this remains to be properly discussed. It is the nature of social and cultural change that it is understood only with hindsight, and then the explanation for it is as likely to be guesswork and story-telling as any other kind of historical narrative. Whatever conclusions are drawn, things are looking up for lesbians in the UK.

38

The disappearance of the homosexual

Interview with Henning Bech

UNIVERSITY OF COPENHAGEN, DENMARK

Henning Bech is Professor of Sociology at the University of Copenhagen, Denmark. Among his English language publications are *When Men Meet: Homosexuality and Modernity* (1997: Cambridge: Polity Press; and Chicago: University of Chicago Press) and "Report From A Rotten State: 'Marriage' and 'Homosexuality' in 'Denmark'", in K. Plummer (ed.), *Modern Homosexualities: Fragments of Lesbian and Gay Experiences* (1992: London and New York: Routledge).

Do lesbians and gays in Denmark view homosexuality as an ethnic identity as many do in America?

Until quite recently, Denmark was ethnically very homogeneous, so there is no tradition of establishing identities and groups in terms of ethnicity. Apart from that, you will find pretty much the same range of identity constructions in Denmark as in the rest of Western Europe, Australia, and North America. What is specifically interesting about Denmark is the trend towards the *disappearance* of all kinds of homosexual, gay, lesbian, and queer identities. Many people with strong same-sex sexual interests are beginning to think and speak of themselves in terms of *taste*. Thus, they do not see themselves as possessing a gay, lesbian, or queer identity. Instead, they speak of having a taste or a sexual preference, like someone may have a preference for classical music, football, or vegetarian food.

Is this development specific to Denmark?

In many parts of the Northwestern world (including, as usual, Australia and New Zealand), you will find trends towards the disappearance of identities associated with same-sex sexuality. Such identities tend to appear when the lives of homosexuals are really different from those of heterosexuals, especially if homosexuals are oppressed and struggle to claim a normal or natural identity. Homosexual identities would tend to disappear if there was no longer much need for legitimation, or if their lives no longer differed very much from other people's. But the way in which disappearance takes place is different in different contexts.

In the US, there is a trend towards "normalization." For many Americans with same-sex interests, their lives are not structured by the need to conceal, and are not dominated by shame, guilt, and fear. Instead, they have integrated their homosexuality into their conventional social worlds in ways that differentiate according to the level of openness they consider appropriate and desire. In some European countries, there are trends toward a somewhat different kind of "normalization." Here, same-sex "sexual" desires and practices are increasingly being considered socially and publicly legitimate, provided they are constructed in accordance with conventional norms of conduct. Sweden would be the exemplary case. In other European contexts, such as in Denmark, the "disappearance" of the homosexual involves a different pattern. Here, lifestyles, character traits, and outlooks among most Danes are increasingly looking like those that have been characteristic of the homosexual.

Could you explain this Danish "disappearance of the homosexual" in greater detail?

Since the 1960s, there has been a comprehensive equalizing of the life conditions of "heterosexuals" and "homosexuals". Both groups, *and* this is true for both women and men, have developed similar lifestyles. Thus heterosexuals, too, understand that marriage and the nuclear family are not necessarily the only choice; they, too, get divorced and establish different types of intimate arrangements and families. They, too, experience promiscuity and serial monogamy, and establish networks of friends as a supplement or an alternative to family networks. They, too, enjoy the pleasures of anal or oral sexuality – or enjoy watching them on public TV. They, too, experience gender as more of a choice or site of play rather than as natural and fixed. In short: any feature that you might consider to be specifically homosexual is becoming increasingly common among all Danes.

Thus, the homosexual disappears, but in a specific way. Not primarily by becoming like heterosexuals or "integrated" and "normalized." Rather the opposite. What was specifically homosexual, or might be imagined to be so, disappears in the sense that all Danes, regardless of sexual preference, are adopting similar lifestyles and intimate arrangements. In this sense we may speak of a "*homo*-genizing" of ways of life. Consequently, in many regards it is perhaps more adequate to speak of the disappearance of the heterosexual as a specifically socio-cultural creature, rather than of the homosexual. What remains of the divide is merely a matter of sexual or erotic taste, and this is something entirely different from the idea of the homosexual as a separate human type or identity. Thus, we are witnessing the *end* of the homosexual.

Why is this development so prominent in Denmark?

One important factor is that women entered the labour market in vast numbers during the 1960s and continue to stay there now. Women's participation in the labour force almost equals that of men – and notably, throughout their lives. Moreover, the vast majority of women who work hold full-time jobs. Thus, they are accustomed to earning their own money and having a life outside the home.

Further, the Danish welfare state plays an influential role. If people are guaranteed an acceptable level of financial and social security, they will not fear living outside the "traditional" family and experimenting with their lifestyle. In Denmark, the economic foundation for living outside traditional family and gender structures is established through the development of a relatively prosperous economy with high rates of employment, high salaries, as well as a high level of state-guaranteed support for those out of work: unemployment benefits, old age benefits, and other kinds of support. Importantly, these benefits are given to the individual, and not to the family (or to the male "head" of the family). Moreover, there is a highly developed, publicly organized system of institutions for child-care. It is by now almost a commonplace among feminist researchers that the welfare state is "women-friendly." It improves the conditions for women's autonomy. Also, the Danish political culture is open to women's participation. Obviously, there is no developed welfare state in the US.

A further factor is the strong cultural ideology of "*frisind*." The term literally means "free mind" or "free spirit." It does not simply denote permissiveness, but enlightened tolerance in matters of personal conduct, combined with a social commitment to establishing the material, social, and educational conditions for individuals to think and live as they prefer. Obviously, ideals do not always correspond to realities; however, it is an ideology that is widely supported by all major groups in Denmark. This national ideology encourages individuals and groups to think and live as they wish. It does not specify norms for how people should live.

Is there no suppression in Denmark?

Certainly there is suppression. Denmark is far from being an ideal society in relation to sexuality and gender. There are still homophobia and heterosexism. However, there is comparatively little of it. In the mass media, there is hardly any negative mention of homosexuals. A population survey in 1999 showed that only 7 percent of those surveyed indicated a strong aversion to homosexuals. This figure may already be outdated. Since then, a Minister of State has been invited to the Royal New Year Ball with his male partner; the Prime Minister of the "Conservative" government has publicly announced that he is personally in favour of church weddings for homosexual couples; and a Parliamentary spokeswoman for what many consider to be the most reactionary, almost "fascist," party lives openly in a registered partnership.

Some might think that "registered partnership," or homosexual marriage, means that gays are imitating straights. What's your view?

I know this is how many Americans, and also some Europeans, think. They argue that lesbians and gay men may be tolerated, but only if they live in accordance with heteronormative standards. Gays that live differently are exposed to raging homophobia. However, registered partnership was introduced in Denmark in 1989 against the backdrop of changes in the social meaning of marriage and the family. For most Danes today, entering a marriage is no longer associated with convictions of lifelong duration, monogamy and the strict separation of tasks and authority along gender lines.

But aren't there gay institutions like in the US?

People from abroad sometimes ask me, "Well, are there no gay bars left then?" Of course there are. Gays and lesbians (to use these terms as shorthand) still go to gay and lesbian bars, discos, parks, porn cinemas, bathhouses, restaurants, cafés and the like. However, the meaning of these places is changing as the homosexual disappears and is superseded by a culture of sexual taste. People come together for the sake of cultivating a taste, pursuing an erotic preference, or to enjoy the proximity and warmth of being together. Indeed gay and lesbian life is still going on in its variety. Accordingly, we may conclude that the introduction of registered partnership has not led all gays and lesbians simply to imitate some middle-class straight model.

Some Americans have argued that allowing gays and lesbians to marry will cause the decline of or weaken the family because they will introduce promiscuous lifestyles and gender distress. What's your view?

I realize that my own work on the introduction of registered partnerships in Denmark has in fact been invoked by the US right wing to support this argument – for instance by Stanley Kurtz of the influential conservative think tank "The Hoover Institution" at Stanford

University. So let me be very clear on this: *There is nothing in my work that would support this kind of argument*. Homosexuals did not seduce heterosexuals to take over homosexual lifestyles. And homosexual marriage is not the cause of changes within the family – rather, such changes are part of the backdrop permitting the introduction of registered partnership. Besides, I do not agree with the association by US conservatives of homosexuality with the moral weakening of the family. Such a thing occurs when people stay together in marriages that do not work, transforming the home into hell for each other and the children; and where people are forced to live according to roles and rules that restrict them unnecessarily. Perhaps US conservatives should rather concentrate on the role of racism, poverty, and the lack of social security to understand real challenges to the wellbeing of US citizens.

Are there any major challenges facing lesbians and gay men in Denmark?

The influential National Organization for Gays and Lesbians (founded in 1948) has concentrated on combating legal discrimination. There are still a few discriminatory laws. For instance, doctors are not allowed to assist a woman at insemination, if she is not married to a man or lives in a "marriage-like" relation with a man. Yet this is not simply the result of homophobia or heterosexism. The support for this legislation has to do with fantasies about the importance of fathers; and in their contemporary Danish version, these fantasies are related to women's wishes of living a life outside the home *and* their reluctance to give up power over it.

To fight legal discrimination is important work. However, there is reason to expect that what remains of discriminatory laws will disappear within a few years. Other agendas are coming to the fore.

Journalists often contact me and ask one of three questions. First: should we not introduce legislation on "hate crimes" like they have in the USA? I reply that this would not be wise. There are rather few assaults on homosexuals in Denmark, and of those many – perhaps most – of them are committed by immigrants with a Moslem cultural background. Moreover, violent assaults are punishable anyway. In the Danish context, introducing "hate crimes" may well help create an unnecessary atmosphere of fear that is hardly beneficial to those with same-sex sexual interests. And in a social climate where the Danes are rapidly developing ever less negative attitudes, what would be the political gain of depicting them as generally being liable to hate crimes?

Journalists will also ask: shouldn't we demand the state to investigate if homosexuals are overrepresented among suicides as a result of homophobia? However, there is no reason to expect any overrepresentation – unless, as in Norway, all this lamentation about suicides conjures up so much anxiety for those "coming out" that they might as well commit suicide immediately.

Journalists and others will also ask: what about homophobia in the world of sport? But maybe what we are finding here is often something else: perhaps some version of what I have called "absent homosexuality" – where same-sex sexual wishes are conjured up and at the same time denied. Moreover, must all erotic and sexual interests among men, or among women, publicly declare themselves to be homosexual? Is some men's reluctance to physical homosexuality perhaps a way of protecting intense, possibly also intensely erotic, male desires that are guarded in order to avoid a simplifying labelling as "homosexual"? And how often are we, in the telemediated world of sports and elsewhere, witnessing what I call the "post-homosexual sexualization" of men for men and of women for women – now that no shadow can fall over these relations from the vanishing homosexual? Perhaps it is worth investigating such relations in the world of sport empirically *and* without in advance locking oneself up within the optics of homophobia?

So gay, lesbian and queer politics are irrelevant in Denmark?

From the viewpoint of my analyses, it would seem adequate and fruitful to develop a kind of politics (or non-politics) of disappearing homosexuality, disappearing homophobia, disappearing heteronormativity. This would imply maxims such as the following ones.

1 *Say nothing.* Example: You are invited to participate in a television programme intended to debate the topic of homosexuality. As your opponent they have managed to excavate some fundamentalist priest from the depths of Jutland. So: *say nothing*, i.e. do not participate in the television programme. In a situation of an advanced trend towards the disappearance of the homosexual, old ideologies of homosexuality (including hostile ideologies) only survive by being revived through contradiction.

2 *Praise the heterosexuals* for being so nice, enlightened and welcoming. In a situation of an advanced trend towards the disappearance of the homosexual there is no reason to use the whip. Progress is advanced by encouragement.

3 *Don't say the usual.* Do not repeat the old narratives from the history of homosexual identity constructions. The arguments that gays and lesbians are inherently respectable *or* revolutionary lose credibility as the majority of the population is living in ways that are just as "alternative", or at least would not reject the idea that they might come up with the idea of doing so. Above all, the argument that homosexuals are different by nature is problematic. First, no one knows whether homosexual preference comes from nature, childhood, heaven, or joy. Second, the argument on nature is a double-edged sword. It is adduced with the hope that the reference to nature would establish the right to practice same-sex pleasure and love. However, trying to identify a homosexual "nature" does not at all prevent science and society from wanting to change that nature and eradicate the homosexual – by way of brain surgery, castration, hormonal treatment, psychoanalysis, and so on.

4 *Say something different.* Invent new stories; search through the history of scholarship and science in order to wheedle elements of other truths out of it; create new horizons for concrete investigations. Apart from stories, in themselves relieving, of vanishing disparities and with a happy end, one might envisage histories/herstories of coquetterie, flirtation, and seduction; narratives of wonderful infatuations with hairy legs; and tales of erotic tastes, of jointly cultivating the esthetics connected with them and delighting in the very proximity and warmth of thus being together. In this respect it is certainly possible to gain inspiration also from those dimensions of American queer scholarship that point beyond the horizon of specific US circumstances.

Finally, I must emphasize that my considerations on politics were sketched *from the perspective of the disappearance* of the homosexual. In the everyday world we are still some distance away from this *happy end* – and that goes for Denmark too. Moreover, moralism has a way of always being poised, ready to jump in and condemn sexual pleasures as being "abnormal." In this situation it is no doubt necessary to use a variety of political arguments and tools – those we know from the history of homosexual identity construction as well as the kind of "non-politics" I outlined above.

39

Gay men and lesbians in the Netherlands

Gert Hekma and Jan Willem Duyvendak

UNIVERSITY OF AMSTERDAM, NETHERLANDS

Since the 1970s the Netherlands can be regarded as one of the most liberal countries with regard to sexual politics. It transformed from a country that was strongly religious and conservative in sexual morals to one that is highly secular and liberal in affairs of sexual morality. Around 1970, the Dutch changed from positions that rejected divorce, pornography, prostitution, homosexuality, contraception, teenage sexuality to more liberal views on all these topics. The change of climate was followed by a change in laws. Divorce was made easier, pornography and prostitution were decriminalized and contraception was made generally available. The criminal law, containing different ages of consent for homosexual and heterosexual sex (21 versus 16 years), was changed; both were set at 16. Contraceptives were made available to all postpubescent women in the 1970s and became part of medical care provisions.

Amsterdam has known a vibrant gay culture since the 1950s and its Red Light District has become a major tourist attraction. In 1973, gays and lesbians were allowed to serve in the army. Marriage was opened for same-sex couples in 2001, the Netherlands being the first country to do so. Prostitution became legal in 2000. However, street prostitution is strictly controlled in the towns where it is permitted, and many city councils have forbidden it. The existing bordellos are regulated for reasons of safety, health, policing and taxing. Cities cannot outlaw them, as prostitution is regarded as normal labor.

Why exactly these changes took place in the Netherlands during the sixties and seventies is not entirely clear, but they have had such a tremendous impact. The liberal sexual culture of the Dutch is partly a result of a political culture that is based on the idea of the separation of state and church. Sexual affairs are viewed as the private business of Dutch citizens and should not be regulated by the state. The Dutch inherited this secular model of political culture from the French.

The sexual revolution of the 1960s had a powerful impact on the Netherlands. In part, this relates to a broad change that occurred in the Netherlands, the so called depillarization of society. Until the 1960s, the Netherlands had a type of social organization in which all citizens were members of a distinct community or "pillar" – Roman Catholic, Protestant or Humanist. These "pillars" were encompassing for the individual. For example, each had its own schools, church, media, political representatives, and culture. This community-based social order collapsed in the sixties as a result of increased social and spatial mobility, individualism, creeping secularism, and the rise of a national media. The two social groups (pillars) that had been most in favor of a strict sexual morality, the Catholics and the orthodox Reformed Calvinists, were influenced by psychiatrists and social workers to reconsider their sexual beliefs and values. In the course of the sixties, these religious orthodox groups relaxed their ideas of sexual morality. This change of opinion among the more orthodox groups made it easier for the majority of the population to support a liberal sexual morality.

Of course, the sixties also witnessed the rise of the youth, student and feminist movements that supported sexual choice and variation. The relative strength of the sexual reform movements, and the lack of resistance by religious and political authorities, resulted in a rather easy transition to a liberal sexual culture. Parallel to this development, Dutch society became highly secular (nowadays 50% of the population are non-believers) while the religious pillars and parties lost their predominant position. A fundamental value change occurred, resulting in the fact that since the 1980s the Dutch are among the most "post-materialist," liberal people of the world. There is a new, moral majority of a clear progressive signature.

The rise of a gay and lesbian movement

In 1969, psychiatrist Wijnand Sengers declared that homosexuality was not a pathological problem, but that homosexuals nevertheless could have psychological problems just like heterosexuals. His research concluded that he could not find one convincing case of a homosexual whose sexual orientation had been changed to heterosexual. It would be better to help homosexuals to adapt to their preferences and social situation, which included referring them to gay organizations. He was not the first to declare that homosexuality was not a disease, but this time his profession accepted this position. He set out to help homosexuals.

At the same time, priests and clergymen set out to tell the public that the homosexual should be accepted. There was still a discussion whether homosexuals should live a chaste life, but the general feeling among clergy was that they should be accepted. In 1971, the parliament decided to get rid of the only existing criminal law targeting homosexuals. Until the sixties homosexuality was generally considered to be a sin, crime, and disease and now, within 10 years, it was none of these things. This was a radical change.

These changes led to discussions in the gay and lesbian movement about their social and political goals. Generally, the movement favored the aim of social integration and acceptance. However, the Federation of Student Working Groups on Homosexuality and later the lesbian groups, Purple September and Lesbian Nation, and the male group Red Faggots, criticized integration as the chief goal of the movement. These more radical groups advocated that society be changed allowing for greater visibility and acceptance of sexual and gender variation. The issue of whether gays and lesbians should seek assimilation or social change remains a point of debate to this day. The heterosexual population may have embraced gays and lesbians in their roles as sons and daughters, and as comedians on television but, radicals argue, isn't Holland still overwhelmingly heterosexual?

Actually, a homosexual movement in Holland began as early as 1946, but it really took off in the sixties. Initially, the major organization was the Culture and Recreation Center, which, in 1964, became the Dutch Society for Homophiles COC and in 1971 Dutch Society for Integration of Homosexuality COC. It became a serious cultural and political force that attracted general attention. In 1967, the Schorer Foundation was established to provide psychological care for homosexuals. Before the AIDS crisis in the 1980s, the movement had already succeeded in becoming a part of society and the government. Gay and lesbian groups were established in political parties, trade unions, universities, the army and the police, medical care, and the churches. And, with the AIDS crisis, and its rippling effects throughout society, the government, medical authorities and representatives of the gay movement met and set up a committee that would prepare medical care, prevention activities and counseling. Gays and lesbians were becoming part of the government. Soon, the first openly gay politicians were elected and the agenda of gay rights was now on the agenda of the state.

Since the early eighties, the annual gay parade has moved from Amsterdam to other towns, following the logic that such a demonstration of gay and lesbian visibility was more important for people in the provinces. When it was held in 1982 in Amersfoort, centrally located on the Dutch Bible Belt, local youth attacked gays and lesbians and unprecedented violence broke out. It created uproar in Dutch media and politics and led to the enactment of gay and lesbian anti-discrimination policies on a local and national level. Soon there passed an Equal Rights Law (1993) that extended equal legal, social security, housing, pension, legacy, and asylum rights to gays and lesbians.

In many respects, AIDS proved a turning point. Cooperation between the gay and lesbian movement and local and national authorities took place. This cooperation followed the Dutch model of bringing representatives of "minority" groups or communities into the government with the aim of eliminating discrimination or establishing tolerance and equality. In this case, gays and lesbians were appointed to take responsibility for political decisions regarding AIDS and gay/lesbian rights. The system worked generally well, but raised dissenting voices. Nonetheless, openly gay men and lesbians were represented in various political bodies. Eleven of the 150 Dutch MP's (member of parliament) in 2000 were openly gay or lesbian. The question remains though what this type of political representation means for establishing real equality and acceptance.

Since the early 1980s a strong subculture – more for gays than for lesbians – developed: gay and lesbian sport clubs got for instance a strong stimulus from the Gay Games that were held in Amsterdam in 1998. In general, it was non-political groups that flourished, such as organizations for hikers, traditional dancers, lovers of old timers, book clubbers, and so on.

Same-sex marriage

When the issue of homosexuality and marriage first hit the Dutch media in 1968, it was estimated that about 90,000 homosexuals were in straight marriages. Although doctors had often advised homosexuals to marry to get rid of their homosexual desires, this strategy was seen as wrong from the late 1960s on. Marriage would not change sexual orientation and married homosexuals made their partners, children and themselves unhappy.

Through AIDS and the urgent medical problems it created, gay men had learned the importance of legal recognition for issues such as housing, social security, hospital visits, pensions, and inheritance. Although some social institutions and businesses offered something like domestic partnership benefits, these benefits did not include national rights and benefits. After several years of steady social and political pressure, "registered partnerships" were established for both same-sex and other-sex couples in 1997. Giving full marital rights was a step too far for the liberal-socialist government at that time. But three years later its successor administration decided to open up marriage for same-sex couples and give them the same rights as other-sex couples. The first marriages of gays and lesbians were celebrated in Amsterdam on April 1, 2001. The large majority of the population now supports gay marriage, and even the Christian-democratic party, which initially opposed the law, now accepts it and has even an openly gay married man as MP.

The question of identity and politics today

When it comes to identity, most gays and lesbians in the Netherlands prefer to keep it low key. They will often say, "my homosexuality is just one part of my personality." However, the attention in the media to critical pronouncements by imams on homosexuality, and a growing awareness of antigay violence, especially among recent immigrant communities, makes it clear that homosexual emancipation is an ongoing project: legal change has not guaranteed social change. Some gays and lesbians will now be open and visible, while others decide to stay in the closet out of fear of consequences, for example, teachers.

The absence of strong sexual identities parallels the lack of spatially concentrated gay and lesbian communities. The bigger towns in the Netherlands have their "gay districts," mainly places where bars are located. These locations, however, are always used for other public functions as well. The Amsterdam leather district, for example, is in the Red Light District where English hooligans, tourists and the people who come for the world of prostitution sometimes mix uneasily with the leather men. Although many gay men live in the inner cities, they have not created "ghettos." This is difficult because housing associations and urban authorities distribute most housing in cities. Most Dutch gays and lesbians also have little inclination to live in exclusively gay or lesbian neighborhoods. The same holds true for social life. Partly as a result of Dutch tolerance, gay men and lesbians often choose to live in places that are gay-friendly. Also in the Netherlands gays and lesbians tend to migrate from places where they face intolerance and discrimination to places that are more gay-friendly. This lessens the necessity for them to create their own organizations. The main field of special socializing, apart from the world of bars, has become sport. Even in this sphere, most sports organizations will proudly declare that they welcome straight people.

Also, gays and lesbians are under pressure from straight people and the media not to create separate organizations because "we are so tolerant that you don't need them." This is the common line when gays and lesbians organize their own institutions and events, for example with the Gay Games in 1998. Since the decline of the time when the Dutch were organized into distinct communities (pillars), liberal and progressive Dutch have been critical of attempts to create separate communities by Muslims, ethnic minorities or homosexuals.

With the opening up of marriage for same-sex couples there are no provisions in civil or criminal law that discriminate against homosexuals. The legal fight for gay rights is effectively at an end. As a result, most Dutch citizens believe that homosexual emancipation is finished. They argue that there is no longer any need for a movement. But these legal changes have proved no guarantee for social acceptance of gays and lesbians. Several reports made clear that teachers have become less willing to come out of the closet and that gay men have to face verbal and physical abuse in certain urban neighborhoods, especially those with a high percentage of ethnic minorities. The self-congratulatory complacency that has become a landmark in Dutch discussions on homosexual emancipation appears to be unrealistic. Homosexuality is still a problem. Authorities such as school boards or policemen continue to refuse to defend gay and lesbian rights. Since the Gay Games, many straight and some gay people say that gays and lesbians should not be so open so as not to offend others. And, some people say, that given the availability of bars and discos and marital options for gays and lesbians, they don't need to flaunt their sexual expressions in public

A chief source of conflict around homosexuality concerns the Muslim community. Keep in mind that about 10% of the Dutch population are recent immigrants. The major groups are Surinamese, Turks and Moroccans. Almost all of these immigrants are Muslim. Within the Muslim religious community homosexuality is condemned. The first ethnic party with a political program, the Arab-European League, has identified three main targets: prostitution, homosexuality and alcohol. Not only has the Muslim community challenged the Dutch culture of tolerance but it has made being gay very hard for Muslim individuals. Recently, they have established their own bars in Amsterdam. Gay Muslims also established a successful foundation

"Yoesuf," which provides information on Islam and homosexuality, organizes workshops and offers social support.

Sexual attitudes now

The Dutch are highly ambivalent about the gains of the sexual revolution. They are citizens of the country that most profited from it, but often people complain that "we have gone too far" or "perhaps we should return to the morality of the fifties when Holland was a safe and pleasant country." Gay cruising areas have become controversial and as the public demands their closure, some city governments comply. Women who are "promiscuous" are still labeled "sluts." Erotic postcards, that staple of the Amsterdam tourist industry, had to be removed from visible places on the streets after complaints of some tourists. At the same time, women prostitutes who are visible in Red Light Districts are spared criticism. The reputation of Amsterdam as a gay or sex capital is somewhat in decline. Tourist Information Boards are reluctant to provide the relevant information although half of the visitors to Amsterdam come for the Red Light District or gay venues. Notwithstanding all changes that have occurred in the field of moral politics, the Dutch continue to feel unease and ambivalence when it comes to the day-to-day concerns of sexuality.

Bibliography

Jan Willem Duyvendak, "The Depoliticization of the Dutch Identity, or Why Dutch Gays Aren't Queer", in: Steven Seidman (ed.), *Queer Theory/Sociology*, Cambridge, MA and Oxford, 1996, pp. 421–438.

——"Identity Politics in France and the Netherlands: The Case of Gay and Lesbian Liberation", in: Mark Blasius (ed.), *Sexual Identities – Queer Politics*, Princeton, NJ and Oxford, 2001, pp. 56–72.

Gert Hekma, "Imams and Homosexuality. A Post-gay Debate in the Netherlands", in: *Sexualities* 5:2 (2002), pp. 269–280.

——"How Libertine is the Netherlands? Exploring Contemporary Dutch Sexual Cultures", in: Elizabeth Bernstein and Laurie Schaffner (eds), *Regulating Sex: The Politics of Intimacy and Identity*, New York, 2005, pp. 209–224.

Judith Schuyf and André Krouwel, "The Dutch Lesbian and Gay Movement. The Politics of Accommodation", in: Barry D. Adam, Jan Willem Duyvendak and André Krouwel (eds), *The Global Emergence of Gay and Lesbian Politics*, Philadelphia, PA, 1999, pp. 158–183.

Steven Seidman, *Difference Troubles. Queering social theory and sexual politics*, Cambridge, 1997, Ch. 12. A.X. van Naerssen (ed.), *Gay Life in Dutch Society*, New York, 1987.

40

The bisexual menace revisited

Or, shaking up social categories is hard to do

Kristin G. Esterberg

SALEM STATE COLLEGE, MASSACHUSETTS

What is bisexuality? Is it an identity that a person holds, something one *is*? Is it a behavior, something one *does*? Is it stable? Or does it shift and float and change? Is bisexuality distinct from heterosexuality and homosexuality? Is it a little bit of both, or neither? Does bisexuality have the potential to end sexual categories altogether, or does it constitute a new, third category?

In the early part of the twenty-first century in America, bisexuality seems to be both everywhere and nowhere. Popular magazines like *Newsweek* and *Essence* proclaim that bisexuality is "coming out" and "out of the closet," and movies like *Kissing Jessica Stein* increasingly experiment with bisexual flirtation. At least in some quarters and on some college campuses, bisexuality seems highly visible, chic. Yet at the same time many bisexuals themselves argue that they are almost completely invisible – socially erased. While to some commentators and social critics the "bisexual menace" might seem to be knocking at society's door, bisexual invisibility may be far more common.

Talk about bisexuality abounds. Bisexuality is seen by some as the "natural" state of sexuality – what everyone would "naturally" be before society has its way with you. Yet others argue that bisexuality doesn't exist. Bisexuals are "really" straight or gay or something else – or would be, if society hadn't had its way with them. In popular discourse, bisexuals are often seen as a menace. Called "vectors of disease," bisexuals are blamed for bringing AIDS and sexually transmitted diseases to "innocent" wives and children, and as polluting the "purity" of the lesbian community. Bisexual desire is seen as raging out of control, as bisexuals are portrayed as sexual swingers having multiple, simultaneous erotic relationships with "anything that moves" (as the title of one bisexual journal ironically put it). Bisexual sex is inevitably seen as group sex – a tangle of sweaty, unidentified body parts engaged in multiply perverse acts. And bisexuals are seen as hopelessly confused: fence-sitters, unable to make up their minds about what they "really" are.

At the same time, in at least a few quarters, bisexuals are lauded as post-modern, chic, and truly queer. In an historical moment in which traditional concepts of identity are increasingly being challenged, bisexuality seems to fit the bill. Unlike more vanilla monosexuals – lesbians, gay men, straights – bisexuals alone have the ability to "mess with" dualistic thinking about sexual identity. Because bisexuality does not fit neatly into the dominant categories – neither homosexual nor heterosexual, but both/and – bisexuality is sometimes seen as the sexual category to smash all sexual categories.

A series of oppositions

In popular discourse, bisexuality has primarily been defined as a series of oppositions. In one formulation, bisexuals and transgenders are seen on one side, the "queer" side, versus gay men and lesbians on the others. In this version, lesbians and gay men are seen as more conventional – monogamous, more like straights. The move toward same-sex marriage and civil unions for same-sex partners in Massachusetts and other states serves to highlight this divide. Same-sex desire as practiced by married same-sex partners is socially conventional; bisexual desire is seen as perverse. Sometimes this perversity is lauded, as when queer activists seek to deconstruct social labels, seeing them as oppressive and a source of social control. At other times this queerness is criticized as perverted and wrong – not only by right-wing activists but also by gay men and lesbians themselves.

Another scenario, promoted at least at times by the mainstream lesbian and gay movement and by many bisexuals themselves, sees lesbians, gay men, and bisexuals as having many interests in common. In this formulation, bisexuals are presumed to share a common base of oppression with lesbians and gay men. Bisexuals are lumped together with lesbians and gay men (lesbigays), who must unite against heterosexist oppression. Because all three desire – at least potentially, in the case of bisexuals – those of the same sex, and because this desire is socially stigmatized and legislated, the common interests of lesbians, gays, and bisexuals in ending oppression are emphasized over potential sources of difference.

In yet another scenario, lesbians are counterposed with all of those who "love men." From the vantage point of lesbian feminism, bisexuals are seen as trading on heterosexual privilege and selling out the lesbian movement. In a patriarchal and sex-obsessed world, lesbians alone (and primarily feminist lesbians) are seen as standing firm against patriarchy.

Finally, in an opposition that is far more often put forward by bisexual people themselves than by others, monosexuals – lesbians, gays, and straights – are counterposed to bisexuals. Here, monosexuals are seen as rigid, overly focused on gender as a basis for relationship, while bisexuals are seen as truly flexible and able to overcome differences based on gender.

Why are these oppositions important? First, they reflect deeply held assumptions about the dualistic nature of Western thought. In modern Western thought, the individual, who is presumed to have something called a self, reigns supreme. Prior to the mid-to-late nineteenth century, individuals simply did not *have* something called a sexual identity. Some time around the latter part of the nineteenth century, the terms homosexual and heterosexual entered into common parlance in Europe and the United States, and by the end of the twentieth century became the predominant way in which sexual desire was organized. By the late twentieth century, a Western man who experienced desire for men could hardly resist being labeled homosexual.

In addition, we tend to see things in terms of binaries: male/female, hetero/homo, black/white, dominant/subordinate. Because of the binary structure of Western thought, we tend not to recognize intermediate categories like bisexuality or transgenderism. When we do, we tend to interpret them in terms of the dominant category (Ault 1996). Thus, bisexuality is often treated in conjunction with homosexuality or lesbianism and rarely considered in its own regard.

These oppositions also reflect people's fears about bisexuality. For lesbians, gays, and straights, whose understandings of themselves are rooted in a clear separation of homosexual and heterosexual, male and female, bisexuality can raise powerful fears. For straights, bisexuality raises the dangerous specter of the pleasures of same-sex desire. For lesbians and gays, bisexuality raises the possibility of having to rethink one's own sexuality, acceptance of which is often hard-won. Especially for those who are immersed in a lesbian or gay community and politics, the loss of identity can be devastating.

These oppositions, too, tell us about shifting political alignments. Debates about the nature of bisexuality reflect political questions as much as empirical ones. They force lesbians and gays to revisit the question of political strategy. Contemporary lesbian and gay organizing reflects what some have called an "ethnic" model of identity. According to this model, lesbians and gays are an identifiable, relatively "fixed" percentage of the population and, like other "minority" groups, in need of civil rights protection (Duggan and Hunter 1995). The recent task of the lesbian and gay movement has been to develop a community and politics along ethnic community lines, with relatively firm boundaries between members and nonmembers, and to press for civil rights – especially in the areas of marriage and employment discrimination. Bisexuality poses a challenge to this model. If sexual identities are neither rigid nor fixed, then what are the implications for a unified lesbian and gay community?

Race, culture, bisexuality

The debates about bisexuality also highlight that sexual categories are essentially social constructions and, especially in the case of bisexuality, fuzzily constructed ones at that. The emphasis on identity in modern Western culture raises particular questions in thinking about race, culture, and bisexuality. Different societies in different time periods clearly organize sexuality differently. When we look cross-culturally, we find ample evidence of what we might call bisexual behavior. Yet we find relatively few examples of bisexual identity. So, for example, anthropologist Gilbert Herdt has extensively documented same-sex behaviors among the Sambia of Papua New Guinea (1997). In this society, all adolescent males experience a period of ritual same-sex expression with an older male. As adults, the males sexually initiate adolescent boys into adulthood, and most adult males also enter into sexual relationships with women. Are all Sambian men bisexual? Not according to the concepts of their culture. What does it mean to use such a term outside of its cultural context?

Similarly, many sociologists and anthropologists have documented what some have called a Latin model of homosexuality (or sometimes Latin bisexuality). In many Latin American societies, men may engage in sexual behavior with both men and women. As long as the men play an active ("insertive") role, they are not considered homosexual or bisexual. They are, simply, "normal" men. Yet the men who play a "passive" role are seen as homosexual – even if they also engage in sexual behavior with women. In this model, males who engage in sexual activity with other men are not considered homosexual, as long as they otherwise play culturally approved masculine roles. On strictly behavioral grounds, one might call those who play an "active" role bisexual, for they are often married or have relationships with women. But again, no word for bisexuality exists in this socially structured form of sexuality.

In the contemporary United States, African-American and Latino men who engage in sexual relationships with other men may be more likely than European American men to also maintain relationships with women. They may be less likely to think of themselves as gay or bisexual or to participate in a gay men's community. There are a number of reasons why this may be so. Racism within white gay men's communities is surely one reason. At the same time, in a racist society men of color may need and desire to retain connections to their families of origin and to their racial/ethnic communities. These kinds of connections are crucial for the survival of people of color.

The HIV/AIDS epidemic highlighted the gap between identity and behavior for many men of color, as men who had never identified themselves as gay or bisexual were stricken by the disease. Men who were "in the life" may or may not have disclosed their romantic and sexual relationships with men to others. Yet most rejected the label "gay" or "bisexual" as having far more to do with whites. Does this make the men bisexual, even if they do not think of themselves that way?

Class, too, is surely important. Poor and marginalized men and women are far more likely to be imprisoned or to engage in prostitution than the affluent and whites. The prison experience brings with it opportunities for same-sex sexual behavior for both women and men (something some social scientists have called "situational" bisexuality or "secondary" bisexuality). Yet prisoners and male prostitutes may very well not think of themselves as bisexual. Again, what does it mean to call someone bisexual who does not think of him or herself in that way? On the other hand, what does it mean to think of bisexuality as mainly a "white" phenomenon?

Bisexual identities

Debates around race, culture, and sexuality inevitably lead us to question what it means to be bisexual. If we define bisexuality as simply behavior – sexual desire or activity with both men and women – then we miss something important. Is a lesbian who occasionally sleeps with men "really" bisexual even if she continues to think of herself as lesbian? Is a married man who occasionally fucks men really bisexual, even if he thinks of himself as straight? What about a gay man and a lesbian who have sex with each other on occasion? Is theirs queer sex? Bisexual sex? Straight sex? What about virtual sex? If a woman exchanges sexual email with someone she thinks is female but is "really" male and writing from a female persona, is that straight sex? For whom? What is sex, anyway? What particular combination of body parts and desires have to come together in order for something to be called sex?

It's far more fruitful to think about the question of identities and to acknowledge fully the slippages between identities, desires, and behaviors. How do people come to think of themselves as bisexual? What does bisexuality mean to the people who think of themselves in that way? How might these change over time? Instead of seeing bisexuality as indelibly rooted in behavior, it is important to think about how individuals come to understand themselves as bisexual – and to consider how individuals reshape those understandings over time and context. Just because one is bisexual today, one might not be tomorrow.

When we shift to a focus of identity, we can begin to challenge the notion that sexual identities are fixed, essential, or unchanging. In my earlier research (Esterberg 1997), for example, I examined the identity accounts, or stories, that bisexual women in a Northeast community in the United States used to understand their experiences. Rather than seeing identities as fixed or essential parts of the person, I argued that identity accounts arise within the particular communities and social settings in which women (or, for that matter, men) find themselves. As women make sense of their desires, attractions, and relationships, they come to see themselves in culturally available terms. As a bisexual movement developed through the 1980s and the 1990s, women who experienced desire for both men and women could increasingly think of themselves as bisexual. This was a social category that simply didn't exist in other cultural times and places.

In the particular community I studied, I identified four dominant accounts of bisexual experience. Some of the women I interviewed thought of themselves as "not quite heterosexual." Their bisexuality consisted of an openness to experiences with women, even though they had primarily had erotic and romantic relationships with men. Others saw themselves as openly, sometimes proudly bisexual. These women tended to be active in creating a politicized bisexual presence within the lesbian/gay community. A third account was expressed by women who came to see bisexuality from the vantage point of lesbian feminism. These women had previously thought of themselves as lesbian; in coming to understand their desire for men, they came to think of themselves as bisexual. A final group of women rejected the impulse to label their identity at all, preferring to see their sexuality as fluid, in the moment. Labels – even seemingly expansive ones like bisexuality – felt restrictive.

Bisexuality, monogamy, and choice

If bisexuality is socially constructed, what does this say about the question of choice? Although heterosexuals, lesbians, and gay men also have the capacity to exercise choice in acting on their sexual desires, the question of choice retains greater significance for bisexuals. Even if individuals do not necessarily choose *desire*, a position many formerly lesbian bisexuals claim, they can certainly choose to act on it or not. They can choose whether to embrace the identity or not. This is not all that much different from others. Married couples, after all, typically don't have sex with all those whom they might like to (at least not if they wish to remain married). But the questions of choice and monogamy are inflected differently for bisexuals.

Social conservatives seize upon the question of choice and argue that a same-sex choice is a sinful one (or, in more secular terms, an antisocial one). Issues of choice are tricky among the left as well, and especially among feminist lesbians. As a political ideology, lesbian feminism valorized women's political, social, and economic relationships with other women. Lesbian feminism held out the possibility to heterosexual women that they, too, could become lesbian and move out from under men's patriarchal domination. In this way, bisexuality became perceived as a threat to lesbian visibility and solidarity, and bisexual women were seen as traitors. In the face of the mainstream lesbian/gay movement, too, which has built a political strategy on the claim that sexuality is biologically based, immutable, and fixed, bisexuals raise the possibility that sexual orientation is not so fixed after all, a position that many in the lesbian and gay movement see as undercutting their political position.

By its very nature, bisexuality also raises the issue of monogamy. Although, of course, there need be no necessary relationship between the potential for relationships with both sexes and actually having them, this distinction is not often made. Some critics go so far as to argue that bisexual monogamy is, by definition, impossible. In my earlier study, one interviewee argued that one's a lesbian if one's involved with a woman, straight if involved with a man. One could only be bisexual, in this schema, if one were involved with both a man and a woman at the same time.

Kenji Yoshino (2000) argues that gays and straights alike have an interest in defining themselves in opposition to bisexuals through the institution of monogamy. First, monogamy is a societal norm. And although straights, with their access to legal marriage, have perhaps greater investment in that norm than gays and lesbians do, monogamy has in recent years become a social norm among many American lesbians and gay men – especially as gay marriage and civil partnerships become legal in a few states. Some gays, Yoshino argues, distinctly wish to "retire" societal stereotypes of gay promiscuity.

Bi politics, bi movements

Where does this leave us, in thinking about bisexuality, visibility, and bisexual action? The 1980s and 1990s saw a flowering of bisexual organizing in the United States, as bisexuals sought to counter their invisibility. This period saw the creation of a number of autonomous organizations, groups, networks, and newsletters. Several path-breaking anthologies were published, and bisexuals – many of them movement-affiliated – appeared on numerous daytime TV talk shows (Gamson 1998).

One strategy bisexual activists used extensively entailed alignment with the lesbian/gay movement, and an attempt to force lesbians and gays to include bisexuals in their organizing. This strategy has been successful, at least to a limited extent, as many mainstream lesbian/gay activists added the word "bisexual" to their organizations and activities, and others moved to names such as "Spectrum" or "Rainbow Coalition" that at least on the face of it included bisexuals. Still, the inclusion of bisexuals under a lesbigay umbrella is by no means certain.

Others sought to organize under a queer umbrella. The rise of queer politics in the 1990s may have been a more welcome home for those bisexuals who valued the transgressive nature of their sexuality. If queer activists sought to challenge traditional dichotomies of gay/straight, male/female, then bisexual activists fit right in. Queer organizing also represented a more youthful "in your face" style of activism, anathema to some within the more staid lesbian and gay movement. Yet the queer umbrella, while it may have sheltered a diverse group of practices, individuals, and organizations, also functioned as a "cloaking device," serving to render bisexuality invisible (Ault 1996).

Especially within these conservative times, bisexual organizing holds enormous challenges. Despite repeated public "discoveries" of bisexuality, the issue of bisexual invisibility is paramount. In becoming visible, however, bisexuals run the risk of creating a fixed identity. Identities, as queer and post-modern theorists have argued, are inherently limiting and subject individuals to social regulation. Yet they are also at least potentially liberating, by enabling like individuals to mobilize around shared concerns. The attempt to organize around bisexual identity thus poses the danger of fixing boundaries and limiting possibilities at the same time as it creates possibilities for women and men to articulate their desires and create a public space for them.

Learning from some of lesbian feminism's mistakes, bisexual organizers have sought to remain open about inclusion and the nature of bisexual identity. As a group that has been most subject to erasure, bisexual organizers are sensitive to the needs for individuals to define themselves. But can bisexual organizing ultimately avoid an ethnic model of social movement organizing? That remains to be seen. And over the last few years, as the nation moves further to the right, there seems to have been relatively little bisexual organizing.

Bye-bye binary? The missing potential of bisexualities

What are the chances that sexual identities as we know them today will actually disappear? Will bisexuality usher in an era of unlabeled sexuality? Are we at the brink of just such a queer moment, in which the hetero/homo divide collapses into an unlabeled ambisexuality, in which gender plays no more role in sexual choices than eye color or the way someone walks or cuts their hair? The existence of those who prefer not to take an identity, who prefer to remain unlabeled, might hint at such a possibility.

More than ever, however, I remain skeptical. We are deeply mired in a period of prolonged conservatism, in which play around gender boundaries seems increasingly anachronistic. Queer organizing seems distinctly a thing of the past, and there seems little social movement organizing that celebrates anything queer or transgressive. The phrase "queer nation" itself sounds hopelessly last century, and I see little on the horizon to take its place. The most prominent lesbian/gay social movement organizing seems focused on the issue of marriage and civil unions – an issue that seems, at least on its face, designed to solidify the differences between bisexuals and others.

If there's any hope for change in our thinking about bisexuality, it may come from the greater visibility of transgendered individuals and activists. Because their bodily existence shakes up the categories of male and female, masculine and feminine, transgendered men and women may shake up sexual identities as well. Yet even here I remain skeptical. The tenacity with which heterosexuals hold onto heterosexual privilege and the deeply institutionalized nature of heterosexual life, on the one hand, combined with the deep investments that lesbians and gay men have made in their sexual identities and movements, on the other, lead me to believe that the collapse of binary thinking is not imminently on the horizon. Perhaps the best we can hope for is the realization that sexuality is far more complex than previously recognized. That, by itself, would be no small thing.

References

Ault, Amber. 1996. "Ambiguous Identity in an Unambiguous Sex/Gender Structure: The Case of Bisexual Women", *Sociological Quarterly* 20(3): 107–22.

Duggan, Lisa and Nan D. Hunter (eds). 1995. *Sex Wars: Essays in Sexual Dissent and American Politics.* New York: Routledge.

Esterberg, Kristin. 1997. *Lesbian and Bisexual Identities: Constructing Communities, Constructing Selves.* Philadelphia, PA: Temple University Press.

Gamson, Joshua. 1998. *Freaks Talk Back.* Chicago, IL: University of Chicago Press.

Herdt, Gilbert. 1997. *Same Sex, Different Cultures.* Boulder, CO: Westview Press.

Yoshino, Kenji. 2000. "The Epistemic Contract of Bisexual Erasure", *Stanford Law Review* 52(2): 353–461.

41

Bisexualities in America

Interview with Paula C. Rodríguez Rust

SPECTRUM DIVERSITY LLC, SPECTRUMDIVERSITY.ORG

Paula C. Rodríguez Rust is a sociologist specializing in bisexuality and sexual identity. She has conducted two major research studies, including the International Bisexual Identities, Communities, Ideologies, and Politics study, and published two books, *Bisexuality and the Challenge to Lesbian Politics* (1995) and *Bisexuality in the United States* (2000). She lives with her partner of 21 years, Lorna, and their four children in central New Jersey.

How have American popular images of bisexuality changed in the last couple of decades?

There have been many changes in popular images of bisexuality during the past few decades. In a nutshell, during the 1970s bisexuality was "chic." On the heels of the (hetero)sexual revolution and the gay pride movements of the 1960s, the social atmosphere in the United States favored sexual experimentation. Sexual openness and experimentation, including with members of one's own sex, was seen as healthy and liberating; old sexual mores were considered stifling and repressive. Popular news magazines ran stories with titles like "Bisexual Chic: Anyone Goes" (*Newsweek*, May 13, 1974) and "Bisexuality: The Newest Sex-Style" (*Cosmopolitan*, June 1974). Bisexuality was fashionable. College students, "hip" people, Janis Joplin, and David Bowie were doing it. Heterosexuals, lesbians, and gay men were doing it.

The advent of HIV/AIDS changed this image. Once gay men became labeled a source of HIV, bisexuals – who were suddenly transformed in the public mind from curious, carefree (male and female) college students to married men with children who lurked around public restrooms – became seen as the conduit through which HIV would pass from the gay community to heterosexuals. The implication was that gay men and bisexual men had done something to deserve HIV, but that heterosexuals were innocent victims. As long as HIV had been largely confined to gay and bisexual men (and a few other socially marginal groups such as Haitians), there was little public concern about the disease, and little funding was allocated toward finding treatments and cures. But when heterosexuals began contracting the disease, gay and bisexual men were blamed for spreading the disease instead of being recognized as the first victims, and funding was suddenly available for HIV research. Popular news magazines warned wives that their husbands might be bisexuals who would bring HIV home to them and their children. *Redbook* warned readers about the "secret life of bisexual husbands" (1993) and *Cosmopolitan* published "The Risky Business of Bisexual Love" (1989).

Meanwhile, however, the bisexual political movement was gaining in numbers. Having begun decades earlier, during the 1980s the bisexual movement became more visible and outspoken. As the GLB community responded to AIDS with increased visibility and political action, the bisexual movement also gained fervor in response to AIDS-related accusations and characterizations. Several new bisexual organizations, including the Boston Bisexual Women's Network, formed during the 1980s. These organizations challenged negative characterizations of bisexuals in both mainstream and gay/lesbian publications, and by the 1990s popular magazines had a new take on bisexuality. *Time* rediscovered bisexuality in "Bisexuality: What Is It?" (1992) and *Newsweek* published "Bisexuality emerges as a new sexual identity" (1995). In the 1990s, bisexuality was portrayed as a lifestyle that challenged traditional conceptualizations of sexuality. No longer a fad for heterosexuals, lesbians, and gay men who wanted to experiment, bisexuality "became" a sexual orientation, and bisexuals became a social and political group in the public eye. This trend has continued into the new millennium, although the issue of same-sex marriage has eclipsed bisexuality in the public eye. The news media's memory of bisexuals as a visible readership segment might be fading; the *New York Times* might have chosen a different headline if the story "Straight, Gay, or – Lying? Bisexuality Revisited" (July 5, 2005) had been printed in the 1990s. In the year 2005, however, this headline sparked an organized and comprehensive response from bisexual activists that reflected the sophistication of the contemporary bisexual political movement.

Do you think there is any connection between the increased visibility and tolerance of gays and lesbians and the broader acceptance of bisexuality?

It is tempting to argue, simply because gays, lesbians, and bisexuals are all "sexual minorities," that public acceptance of one form of non-heterosexuality would tend to lead to acceptance of other forms of non-heterosexuality. I'm not convinced of this, however. The growing acceptance of gay men and lesbians has changed our cultural conception of sexuality from one involving heterosexual men and women only, to one involving heterosexual men/women and gays/lesbians. It's simply a new social conception of sexuality; there's nothing inherent in it that would make it any more amenable to further change than any earlier conceptualization of sexuality. After all, "heterosexuality" is itself a relatively new concept; but ask most people on the street, and they will tell you that the nuclear heterosexual family, within which heterosexual men and women are defined as such by their sexual attractions to each other, is the original "tradition." This is not true. For example, marriage in nineteenth-century English culture was based on social and economic compatibility, not sexual desire. Two people who married each other because of sexual passion were considered fools, because such passion fades and could not be the basis of a lasting marriage. Individuals found their sense of self in their relationships to their families as mothers, fathers, wives, and husbands. The idea of defining oneself in terms of one's sexual desires toward other people would have seemed grossly self-centered and inappropriate. Men and women married each other and had sex with each other, but the concept of "heterosexuality" as a *sexual orientation* dates back only to the late 1800s (Katz 1995). Furthermore, the "nuclear" family is a preferred family form only in particular cultures and historical periods; for example, many cultures emphasize extended or multigenerational families, not nuclear families, and many cultures consider the entire community or village – not just two parents – responsible for the welfare and upbringing of children. Yet today in the United States we call the nuclear heterosexual family the "traditional" family form; historically speaking, change is forgotten in the public mind soon after it happens.

Although greater acceptance of lesbians and gay men might not necessarily lead to greater acceptance of bisexuality, we can all – gays, lesbians, bisexuals, the transgendered, and the intersexed – help each other gain acceptance and equal rights by standing together and supporting one another. Sometimes we don't support one another, and sometimes the in-fighting within a minority is more damaging than the larger struggle with a dominant society. In other words, if lesbians and gay men don't support the rights of bisexuals, and if lesbians, gay men and bisexuals don't seek to understand and support transsexuals and intersexed people and vice versa, we all weaken each other in our efforts to build a world in which all forms of gender and sexuality are respected.

This is true for all minorities, not only sexual and gender minorities. As minority members, we can struggle against our own oppression while accepting social prejudices against other groups, or we can use our own experiences of oppression to understand others as well and become part of a larger struggle against injustice. For example, white lesbians and gay men do not necessarily understand racism any better than white heterosexuals, so lesbians, gay men, and bisexuals do not necessarily understand and support each other any more than heterosexuals understand what it's like to be a sexual minority in this society. But we *could* use our own experiences to understand the experiences of others, and the more we make an effort to understand each other, the more united we will all be – across differences in sexuality, as well as gender, race, ethnicity, ability, age, social class, culture, religion, height, weight, etc.

I believe that it is the responsibility of members of socially privileged groups – for example, heterosexuals, whites, the able-bodied – to understand the privileges they have as members of these groups, and to participate in the struggle to create a society in which everyone is equally respected for who they are. If you are white, how often do you walk into a store and wonder if store security is watching you because of your race? Probably never; not having to worry about what other people think of you because of your skin color is part of your race privilege. *Make yourself aware of the effect of your whiteness on your life* by asking yourself once in a while how you would be experiencing your life if you were African-American or Latino/a. If you are able-bodied, how often do you plan to go somewhere – a store, a theater, a friend's house – and wonder if you'll be able to get up the steps into the door? Assuming you will be able to get in is your privilege. If you are heterosexual, do you think about marriage and assume that you will be able to marry the person you love? Same-sex couples can marry in Massachusetts, but not in any other state in the USA, and nor in the eyes of the federal government, which means even married same-sex couples in Massachusetts do not receive the same rights as married heterosexual couples. If you are lesbian or gay, how often do people tell you your sexuality simply doesn't exist? Bisexuals are often told they don't exist, and that they should make up their minds whether they are lesbian/gay or heterosexual. It might be uncomfortable for heterosexuals to stand up for LGBTI rights, and it might be uncomfortable for whites to stand up for the rights of people of color – after all, we don't want to offend someone by using the wrong words because of our own ignorance and, anyhow, it doesn't seem to affect us in a negative way on a daily basis so it's easy to put off until we have some spare time – but if the privileged don't speak out, who is left to do all the talking and fighting? The same people who have already been doing the suffering, the fighting, and the talking.

Are there differences among men and women with regard to bisexuality?

Research has found average or typical differences between bisexual men and bisexual women. However, any statement that takes the form "bisexual men are like this, whereas bisexual women are like that" would be an overgeneralization. There are more differences among bisexual men, and among bisexual women, than there are between the genders. The largest differences among bisexuals correspond to the cultural contexts within which bisexuality is found, rather than gender. Many people stereotype bisexuals as people who "need" both male and female partners, or who are very promiscuous and can't be monogamous. This is not true. Bisexuals, like lesbians, gay men, and heterosexuals, can be celibate and they can be monogamous. Think about it; a heterosexual woman who chooses to remain celibate is still heterosexual, right? What makes her heterosexual is her sexual attraction to men, or maybe her expectation that some day she will fall in love with someone and that person will be a man. She doesn't need to have sex with a man to be a heterosexual. Bisexuality is the same. Most people who identify themselves as bisexual do so because they are sexually attracted to both men and women, or because they could see themselves in a romantic relationship with either a man or a woman. Bisexuals don't "need" sex with both men and women; they are simply more open to the possibilities than heterosexuals, lesbians, and gay men who find only one gender sexually interesting.

There are many forms of bisexuality. Some bisexuals find one monogamous lifetime partner – what makes them different from lesbians, gay men, and heterosexuals is that this partner could have been either a man or a woman. There is also serial monogamy, in which an individual has one partner at a time. This is a pattern for many people, including lesbians, gay men, heterosexuals, and bisexuals – the difference is that for bisexuals, over the years their partners might include both men and women. Some people experiment with both men and women when they are young, and then decide as adults that they are really only interested in one gender or the other, so they identify as lesbian, gay, or heterosexual in adulthood although their sexual history is bisexual. Other people grow up believing they are heterosexual and might even marry someone of the other sex, and then later in life discover an interest in people of their own sex, so they divorce and find a same-sex partner. They might identify first as heterosexual and later as lesbian/gay, but their *behavioral history* is bisexual. Some bisexuals live in open committed relationships, meaning that they have one primary long-term or lifetime partner, but agree with that partner that both of them are free to have secondary relationships with other people as well. Polyfidelity is a committed relationship among more than two adults; for example, it could be two men and two women living in sexual fidelity with each other. Just as among heterosexuals, lesbians, and gay men, there are bisexuals who have many sexual partners over time, people who have one-night-stands or anonymous sex with many different people, and people who are celibate. Unfortunately, because of social misunderstanding and disapproval of bisexuality, lesbianism, and gayness, some bisexuals are secretive about their same-sex interests. This leads to other patterns of bisexuality: for example, individuals who are heterosexually married but who also have sex with people of their own gender without their spouse's knowledge.

The most interesting differences between bisexual men and women concern not individual-based statistics, but the cultural and social differences in how bisexuality is experienced by men and women. Weinberg, Williams and Pryor (1994) found that both bisexual men and women reported that it is easier to have sex with men, but easier to fall in love with women. This is not surprising; although we have come a long way in terms of gender equality, boys are still expected to strongly desire sexual contact, whereas girls are taught to value emotional relationships and romance. Consequently, both bisexual men and women tend to have more male than female sex partners (e.g. Rosario *et al.* 1996; Weinberg, Williams, and Pryor 1994). This means bisexual men have more homo-sex, whereas bisexual women have more hetero-sex. The basic difference, however, lies not in bisexual men and women themselves – it does not result from higher Kinsey attraction scores among bisexual men than among bisexual women, for example – but in the world of potential partners in which both bisexual men and women live. Bisexual men and women live in the same world, that is, a world in which male sex partners are more available than female sex partners, but the consequences are different – more heterosexual contact for women, but more homosexual contact for men.

Another interesting difference existed in the bisexual political movement during the 1980s. In many political movements, as in many other domains of social life, men tend to be more visible and in more leadership roles than women. However, because more gay/bisexual men than lesbian/bisexual women contracted HIV infection during the 1980s – a period of growth for the bisexual political movement – many of the most visible bisexual leaders during this time were women. Many of the men who might have been involved in the bisexual movement were sick, deceased, caring for sick loved friends and partners, or occupied with fighting for HIV funding. Many of the women, on the other hand, had had political experience because they were involved in other social movements of the 1960s and 1970s, such as the counter-culture and feminist movements, so they came to the bisexual movement well-prepared to make a difference.

Is there any evidence that more young men and women today are experimenting with bisexuality or identifying as bisexual? How would you explain this?

I believe that young people today are more likely to identify as bisexual than in previous generations, and that they are doing so at younger ages. Previous generations grew up in time periods when being lesbian or gay, not to mention bisexual, was either not talked about or more severely condemned. You were assumed to be heterosexual, and that was it. Today, although bisexuality does not receive much public attention, lesbian and gay issues are talked about in the national media. Television shows contain gay characters, and newscasters report on the progress of same-sex marriage rights. The experiences of Ellen DeGeneres are a chronicle of the way in which lesbians and gay men have been portrayed in the public media over the past couple decades. During the 1970s, 1980s, and 1990s, young people in urban areas began to have access to social services for sexual minority youth, but people in suburban and rural areas and youth in certain parts of the country still had nowhere to go to receive positive information about being gay or lesbian, let alone bisexual. Many young people who were gay, lesbian, or bisexual did not find any positive information or like-minded peers until college – and many did not find it even then.

During the past fifteen or so years, however, the explosion in the internet and in youth access to the internet has led to a whole new world. Individuals who belong to many different minorities – racial minorities, sexual minorities, political minorities – can find each other today in a way never possible before. People who live in small towns can now find others who are like them through the internet. Young people who are wondering about their sexuality can find other young people who are wondering or who have come out on the internet. Information and support is available to anyone with an online hookup and a little privacy. Today, it is hard to imagine the person who has not at least heard of lesbianism, gayness, and bisexuality.

It is still difficult for most young people to come out. However, with all the information and support available today, it is undoubtedly easier for young people who do feel attracted to members of their own sex to recognize these feelings and develop a positive lesbian, gay, or bisexual identity. Young people are also very creative when it comes to sexual identity. It's more OK than ever before to simply be "Questioning" or to make up your own identity. So, I think bisexual identity is becoming more common, and young people are coming out at younger ages, but also that young people are feeling freer to simply explore their sexualities without worrying so much about putting labels on it.

How possible is it today, in America, to practice bisexuality and not identify as bisexual?

Quite possible. Most individuals who describe themselves as attracted to both men and women, or who have had sexual contact with both men and women, do not identify as bisexual (e.g. Laumann *et al.* 1994). First of all, many people still subscribe to the belief that "you are either lesbian/gay or heterosexual," or they define bisexuality in terms of having *equal* feelings or experiences with men and women, so they identify as lesbian/gay or heterosexual based on the preponderance or importance of their experiences with same-sex as against other-sex partners. They are not in denial or lying about their sexuality; they are simply defining sexual orientation in terms of *preference* for one gender or the other and describing themselves honestly within that paradigm. Other individuals discredit either their same-sex or their other-sex experiences by saying they were "experimental," or "just a phase," and therefore not relevant to their "true" sexual identity. Whether these experiences were *really* "experimental" or not is a question of perspective, not a question of fact, and so, therefore, is the question of whether such people are *really* lesbian/gay/heterosexual, or really bisexual. "Sexual orientation" is a culturally constructed concept with different meanings to different people, in different ethnic contexts, and in different historical time periods.

Personally, I feel that any way an individual wishes to define their sexuality should be respected by others. For example, if a woman has had both male and female partners but chooses to define herself as a lesbian because she does not believe in bisexuality and her feelings for women are stronger, then that's fine with me. As a scientist, however, I take a different point of view. I do not feel that it is appropriate for scientists to conduct research using methods that do not recognize the existence of bisexuality. Imagine a natural rainbow: this rainbow is continuous; it is not divided into separate colors. Different cultures divide the rainbow into different numbers of colors; as few as three or as many as one hundred. Modern Western culture divides the rainbow into six or seven basic colors, each of which is in fact a "category" which covers a range of light wavelengths. Three of these categories are red, orange, and yellow. Ask me if the color "orange" exists. Well, it's a matter of perspective. Certainly, the wavelength of light that we call orange exists, but we could have divided the rainbow differently. We could have made a single division between red and yellow, and called everything on one side "red" and everything on the other side "yellow." Then, what we now call orange would, depending on whether it's more reddish or more yellowish, be called either red or yellow. Then, orange would not exist. But how useful would that be? As culturally constructed as it is, the name "orange" is useful, and it would seem odd to eliminate it by defining the concept out of existence. The same argument applies to bisexuality. There are people who clearly identify as bisexual, feel attracted to both sexes, and have sex with both men and women; why on earth would we not want a concept we can use to describe these people, and why on earth would anyone want to tell them they are not bisexual? Culturally, the reasons many people feel compelled to protect the "gay/straight" mindset in which bisexuality does not exist are understandable – they are the self-protective reasons that many people prefer to pretend that things they fear or don't understand don't exist – but it's not a very realistic, respectful, or open-minded way to live in the world.

Finally, is there any evidence regarding patterns of bisexuality among different ethnic or racial groups? If not, what is your impression as a scholar of bisexuality?

I will answer this question primarily in terms of culture, rather than race or ethnicity. Sexual patterns and meanings correlate with culture, not with biological characteristics such as skin tone or eye shape. Obviously, traditional cultures arose among particular racial groups, and the concept of "ethnicity" combines elements of both race and culture, but given mass world migration and acculturation it makes more sense to talk about cultural differences in sexual patterns than about racial or ethnic differences. The very idea of having a sexual identity, and of basing this sexual identity on one's personal sexual feelings or behaviors, is particular to contemporary "Western" or "Anglo" culture. So, the concept of a "bisexual identity," not to mention a "bisexual lifestyle," is culturally specific. Bisexual behavior, on the other hand, is found among people in many cultures. This behavior, therefore, carries very different meanings and takes very different patterns in different cultures. There has been more research on these differences among men than among women.

Considerable ethnographic research has been conducted on Latino constructions of sexuality, often in comparison to Anglo constructions of sexuality (e.g. Carballo-Diéguez and Dolezal 1994; Matteson 1997; Almaguer 1993). For the purpose of illustration here, I will describe the differences between Latino and Anglo sexual constructions in very broad strokes. In contemporary Anglo culture, sexual identity is based on one's own sexual desires or attractions and experiences with either males or females. The heterosexuality of a Latino, on the other hand, is more strongly based on his family relationships – his status as husband and father and his commitment to those roles. The fact that he might also have had sex with men, possibly before his marriage when heterosexual opportunities were restricted by the emphasis on chastity among Latina women, does not detract from his heterosexuality as long as he takes the insertive role during sex and displays appropriate *machismo*. "Gay men" are defined not in terms of the fact that they have sex with men, but in terms of the *pasivo* or receptive role they take during that sex and in terms of their gender presentation. In Latino culture, therefore, what an Anglo would call "bisexual behavior" is a cultural phenomenon that takes place among *heterosexual* men. In contrast, in Anglo culture, a married man who has sex with men on the side would probably be considered a "closeted gay man," not a heterosexual. There is some evidence of racial and ethnic differences in rates of bisexual behavior and identification resulting from cultural differences in the construction of sexuality. This evidence, and the underlying cultural differences, are reviewed in depth in Chapter 22 of *Bisexuality in the United States* (Rodríguez Rust 2000).

In some ethnic and racial minority communities in the United States, homosexuality and bisexuality are characterized as influences of white culture and a sign of the rejection of one's own ethnic culture in favor of acculturation – or selling out – to a more powerful white culture (e.g., Tremble, Schneider, and Appathurai 1989; Chan 1989; Icard 1986). An individual who is coming out as bisexual, lesbian, or gay amid these attitudes risks being told that they are rejecting their ethnic, racial, or cultural identity by adopting a bisexual or gay identity. They might even be told that they are rejecting their family and their racial or ethnic community. The irony is that in many of these traditional cultures, homosexuality was not condemned as much as it was in earlier northern European cultures. For example, the Chinese term "passion of the cut sleeve" refers to the tender story of Han emperor Ai-di, who cut off his sleeve rather than wake his male lover who was sleeping on it (Hinsch 1990). In China following the Cultural Revolution, homosexuality was portrayed as a capitalist perversion brought in from the West, and today Chinese-American youth in the USA might be told they are rejecting their Chinese heritage by identifying as lesbian, gay, or bisexual. In contrast, European-American youth with light-colored skins do not have to struggle with conflict between their ethnic and their sexual identities and lifestyles. For white lesbians, gay men, and bisexuals, not having to "choose" between or struggle to "integrate" their sexual and their racial/ethnic identities is another aspect of racial privilege.

Concluding thoughts?

In recent history, each generation confronts new social problems, and each generation builds on the solutions of previous generations. Although there will always be struggles between people who wish to retain traditional values and those who value change, it seems that over time we have been moving toward greater acceptance of diversity. Different types of people are no longer isolated from each other. We have more opportunities to get to know each other, to understand each other, and to celebrate – not just tolerate – these differences. There is no contradiction between pride in one's own way of life, form of love, or cultural heritage, and understanding and appreciation of other ways of life, loves, or heritages. We are enriched by our differences, and we are all responsible for ending discrimination and social prejudice so that we can create a world in which we can all participate fully and enrich each other by our difference.

References

Almaguer, Tomás. 1993. "Chicano men: A cartography of homosexual identity and behavior", in Henry Abelove, Michéle Aina Barale, and David M. Halperin (eds), *The Lesbian and Gay Studies Reader*, New York: Routledge.

Carballo-Diéguez, Alex and Curtis Dolezal. 1994. "Contrasting types of Puerto Rican men who have sex with men (MSM)", *Journal of Psychology and Human Sexuality* 6,4: 41–67.

Chan, Connie. 1989. "Issues of identity development among Asian-American lesbians and gay men", *Journal of Counseling and Development* 68,1: 16–21.

Hinsch, Bret. 1990. *Passions of the Cut Sleeve: The Male Homosexual Tradition in China*, Berkeley: University of California Press.

Icard, Larry. 1986. "Black gay men and conflicting social identities: Sexual orientation versus racial identity", *Journal of Social Work and Human Sexuality* 4, 1/2: 83–92.

Katz, Jonathan Ned. 1995. *The Invention of Heterosexuality*, New York: Dutton.

Laumann, Edward O., John H. Gagnon, Robert T. Michael, and Stuart Michaels. 1994. *The Social Organization of Sexuality: Sexual Practices in the United States*, Chicago: University of Chicago Press.

Matteson, David R. 1997. "Bisexual and homosexual behavior and HIV risk among Chinese-, Filipino-, and Korean-American men", *Journal of Sex Research* 34, 1: 93–104.

Rodríguez Rust, Paula C. 2000. *Bisexuality in the United States: A Social Science Reader*, New York: Columbia University Press.

Rosario, Margaret, Heino F. L. Meyer-Bahlburg, Joyce Hunter, Theresa M. Exner, Marya Gwadz, and Arden M. Keller. 1996. "The psychosexual development of urban lesbian, gay, and bisexual youths", *Journal of Sex Research* 33, 2: 113–26.

Rust, Paula C. 1995. *Bisexuality and the Challenge to Lesbian Politics: Sex, Loyalty, and Revoluton*, New York: New York University Press.

Tremble, Bob, Margaret Schneider, and Carol Appathurai. 1989. "Growing up gay or lesbian in a multi-cultural context", *Journal of Homosexuality* 17, 1–4: 253–67.

Weinberg, Martin S., Colin J. Williams, and Douglass W. Pryor. 1994. *Dual Attraction: Understanding Bisexuality*, New York: Oxford University Press.

42

Multiple identities

Race, class, and gender in lesbian and gay affirming Protestant congregations

Krista McQueeney

UNIVERSITY OF NORTH CAROLINA CHAPEL HILL

The sociological study of identity spans complex terrain. Social psychologists have been studying identity – the meanings through which we define ourselves, and others define us, as particular kinds of people – since the 1930s. Most sociologists make three assumptions about identity. First, identities are not inborn, they are *socially constructed* – we learn them in childhood (largely from parental figures), and continue to (re)learn them throughout our lives. This means that identity is not merely idiosyncratic: it is shaped by the cultural and social conditions of our lives. Second, identities are *fluid*: they can change over time and across situations. Who I say I am, or who you perceive me to be, may not be who I will say I am (or who you perceive me to be) five minutes, five months, or five years from now. Third, we *perform* identities in social interaction. By seeing people as actors who perform identities differently over time and across contexts, sociologists recognize that individuals have agency in the creation of self. One may act differently, for instance, with parents than with friends. These assumptions stem from a perspective in sociology called symbolic interaction, which holds that humans actively interpret the social world. We interpret the world in our own terms, but the world is not of our own making. As such, our identities – for example our sexuality, race, class, and gender – are both shaped by and reshape the world around us.

These insights have had far-reaching effects for understanding identity as a social – not a biological – construct. But we still have far to go in understanding how people experience *multiple identities* – for example, race, class, gender, and sexuality – in daily life and how these multiple identities intersect and shape each other. Many sociologists analyze one identity (for example, sexuality) at a time, as if it were separate from other aspects of the self. Others see identity (for example, race) as a variable that helps predict a given outcome (for example, income). Seeing identities in this way treats all members of a social group as the same, thus masking important differences among group members. As feminists of color have pointed out, identities are not additive: we cannot understand social experience by simply counting the oppressions (for example, racism plus sexism plus heterosexism) people face. After all, identity is about the quality, not the quantity, of one's experiences. Instead, identities emerge from the experiences and consciousness tied to one's position within intersecting and mutually reinforcing social systems (for example, racism, sexism, heterosexism). This view of identities, and the systems of oppression that shape them, as multiple and interconnected is known as intersectional feminist theory.

Intersectional feminist theory, introduced in the 1980s by feminists of color, has important implications for the study of sexual identity. As Patricia Hill Collins (2000: 11) explains, intersectional theories "view race, class, gender, sexuality, ethnicity, and age, among others, as mutually constructing systems of power. [Yet] because these systems permeate all social relations, untangling their effects in any given situations or for any given population remains difficult." Despite this difficulty, intersectional theory calls sociologists to attend to the multiplicative effects of heterosexism and homophobia for gays and lesbians of color, many of whom are already harmed by racism, classism, and sexism. How does their social location within multiple, interlocking systems of inequality define their experience and consciousness differently from, say, white lesbian women and gay men, or black heterosexual women and men? Studying sexual identity through an intersectional lens calls us to look beyond the everyday categories people use to define sexuality – lesbian, gay, bisexual, transgender, heterosexual – to recognize how these identity categories intersect with other bases of identity (for example, race, class, gender, religion). When we consider sexual identity, we must strive to understand not only how an individual experiences and performs an identity as a *sexual* being, but also as a member of racial/ethnic, class, gender, and other social groups. Intersectional theory shifts the focus from one aspect of a person's identity to the multiple systems that shape our consciousness, experience, and behavior.

In this chapter, I will draw on data from three years of participant observation and interviews in two lesbian and gay affirming Protestant churches in the Southeast US – one predominantly black and the other predominantly white – to illustrate how an intersectional perspective complicates and deepens our understanding of sexual identity. As Wilkins (2004) argues, sociologists can conduct more thorough analyses by examining social inequality through distinct, but interconnected, lenses. For example, an analyst might consider the consequences of race and sexual identity performances together, and then consider other identity combinations, such as race and gender, or gender and sexuality. It is important to make clear the identity lens one foregrounds. In the rest of this chapter, I will draw on examples from the study of black and white lesbian and gay Christians to illustrate these points. Though the churches I studied had both white and black gay male congregants, my comments will be limited to black and white lesbian women. Before discussing the intersections of these women's identities, though, I will provide a brief background on prevailing views of homosexuality in Christianity.

Homosexuality and the Christian church

For each of the major branches of US Christianity (Evangelical, Catholic, and mainline), the dominant view of homosexual sex is that it represents an "abomination before God" (Melton 1991). These branches affirm the dignity and worth of all people – including lesbian women and gay men – as reflections of God's image. Even so, mainstream Christian beliefs and practices regard male–female marriage as the only acceptable context for sexual activity. Thus, in most Christian traditions, lesbian women and gay men are welcomed in the Christian community only so long as they abstain from "sinful" same-sex activity.

In contrast, the churches I studied embraced what Hunter (1991) calls a "progressive" worldview: they believed the Christian faith must evolve as the culture advances. For example, members pointed out that most Christians no longer adhere to the Old Testament "law codes" that prohibit having sex during menstruation, eating shellfish, or wearing mixed-blend clothing.

If we as a culture have come to view these behaviors as acceptable, and, conversely, such biblically sanctioned arrangements as slavery and women-as-property as unacceptable, why do we still consider homosexual sex sinful? The word "homosexual," they noted, was not even invented until the turn of the twentieth century (and there was no concept of loving same-sex relationships in biblical times). Still, the images of homosexual promiscuity and deviance that circulate in the broader church and culture informed how lesbian and gay Christians redefined their sexual identities and practices as compatible with Christian belief. To dispel the "immoral" images they confronted, lesbian and gay members engaged in a group process of sexual identity reconstruction. They drew on the resources at their disposal to present themselves as good people – people of faith – despite their homosexuality. Importantly, all gay men and lesbian women did not have the same resources at their disposal to accomplish this. The resources they deployed to fashion themselves as normal and moral people were inextricably linked to the systems of racism, classism, sexism, and heterosexism that shaped their lives.

Race-ing sexuality

For the lesbian women in these churches – both black and white – performing a sexual identity that fit with Christian morality was a race project. All of the black lesbian women and gay men I interviewed regarded race as their primary identity. Many echoed Joy, a 42-year-old black lesbian, who said:

> The first lessons I learned from my parents were, number one, I was black, and I should never be ashamed of being black. Number two, people are gonna mistreat me because I'm black … I had to be strong … and not trust white people cause they'll betray you in a minute … So being black was how I saw myself … sexuality came later, it wasn't as important.

As adults, many black lesbian women struggled to find a place where they belonged. In coming out, they found their support system in the black community (and church) threatened. Nor did they feel they fit in predominantly white gay and lesbian communities and institutions. As 32-year-old black lesbian Erika said: "The black community, even the church, is not accepting. The pastor of the church I grew up in kicked me out when I was nineteen … [because] he thought I was gay. But the gay community, you know, the clubs and everything, it's pretty much all white … So I just feel a lot of times like, where do I fit?" Like Erika, many black lesbian women felt caught in a marginal space between the (white) lesbian and (black) heterosexual worlds. This had important implications, as we will see, for the performance of (black) lesbian Christian identity.

In contrast, white lesbian women did not grow up with a sense of racial difference. In a culture that privileges whiteness, their race was "unmarked" (Phelan 1993); it was invisible to them (and many others). As Emily, a 36-year-old white lesbian, said in an interview, "I always considered myself a good person. I was nice, everybody liked me, I mean, I accepted Jesus Christ as my personal savior when I was thirteen … but [after coming out] I struggled for years with, am I good, or am I not?" Given their racial privilege, most white lesbian women viewed sexuality as their most salient identity, since many saw it as their first experience of marginality and difference. As their awareness of same-sex desire grew, they (and/or others) often questioned whether they belonged in their home churches. For white lesbians like Emily, their view of themselves as good people was threatened. Still, their racial membership remained intact. Coming out as lesbian or gay did not jeopardize white lesbian and gay churchgoers' place in a valued "white community" to the degree that it did for black lesbian women and gay men.

The social locations these lesbian and gay Christians inhabited shaped their performance of lesbian and gay Christian identity. For example, some of the black lesbians in the predominantly black church I studied *minimized* their sexuality – they privileged "Christian" as the most valued identity. For example, Pastor Paula, the 37-year-old black lesbian minister of the mostly black church I studied, preached:

> In my house, we worship the Lord. So if there's anyone who still thinks their sexuality gets in the way of having a relationship with Jesus, you need to talk to me. Because despite all the garbage people tell us, y'all, we're Christians first and foremost … When are we just gonna realize that our sexuality is no big deal? God loves us for who God made us to be, and our sexuality has nothing to do with that.

By minimizing sexuality as less important than the Christian identity, black lesbian women and gay men upheld a view of themselves – and presented themselves to others – as normal, faithful black people who just happened to be lesbian or gay (as God created them). In contrast, I never heard *white* lesbian women minimize their sexuality. Given cultural representations of black female and male sexuality as exotic, promiscuous, and sexually predatory (e.g., hooks 1992; Collins 2000), many in black churches (Douglas 1999) and black communities (Dyson 1996) have discouraged open discussion of non-marital sex. As a result, for black gay and lesbian Christians to highlight sexuality may have meant further rejection from white society *and* the black (heterosexual Christian) community. By minimizing sexuality, they affirmed that they were moral black people committed to uplifting the race. In contrast, white lesbian women, especially those who were middle class, inhabited spaces of privilege that offered them more resources – both ideological and material – to integrate their sexuality with a view of themselves as normal, faithful Christians. The cultural meanings attached to whiteness and middle classness offered them resources to perform "good Christian" selves that were unavailable to black (especially working-class) lesbian women due to racism, classism, and heterosexism.

Seeing lesbian and gay Christians' identity performances through a race lens adds depth to our understanding of how intersecting systems of power shape identity. Many studies of lesbian and gay Christians have focused on white, middle-class gay men, who constitute the majority of worshipers in gay and lesbian affirming churches nationwide. However, without considering how lesbians and people of color perform Christian identity, these studies inadvertently privilege white, middle-class gay male experience. Much of this research treats sexual identity as separate from other bases of identity: analysts tend to ignore, for example, how race, class, and gender shape white gay men's Christian identity construction. Indeed, white gay men's Christian performances *are* shaped by race, class, and gender inequalities. Yet, without including the experiences of lesbians and people of color, our ability to recognize "unmarked" identities (for example, whiteness and maleness) is inhibited. In turn, our grasp of how people manage sexual and religious identities remains incomplete.

Race-ing gender

Seeing gender/sexuality through a race lens, for example by taking black and white lesbians' Christian identity performances together, can help us flesh out the possibilities and limitations of intersectionality in daily life. As feminists of color have noted, treating "woman" as a universal category privileges white, middle-class, heterosexual experience (for example, Anzaldúa and Moraga 2002). By seeing identity and experience through an intersectional lens, we can better understand how women's (in this case, lesbians') experiences and identities are shaped by their differential locations within racism and classism.

In the churches I studied, white lesbians often drew on their "unmarked" (Phelan 1993) identities as white and middle class to challenge the notion of a "good mother" as exclusive to heterosexual women. For example, when I asked how she thought other church members viewed her, Peggy, a 42-year-old white lesbian, said:

> We have a great family, I mean our family is kind of different than everybody else's, but we have the same struggles, and the same trials, and the same joys that any other family with a 4-year-old has. And I think that's how we're seen in the church, as just another family with a young child.

Like Peggy, many white lesbian women in monogamous couples performed (gendered) identities as mothers to dispel the image of lesbians as enemies of the traditional family. They drew on the privileged (but unmarked) resources attached to their social location as white, middle-class women to present themselves as normal and moral people whose families were the same as heterosexuals'. After all, they encountered "the same struggles, and the same trials, and the same joys [of] any family." The implication was: *I may be different sexually, but my experience as a mother makes me the same as a straight (and white) woman.*

Even in the black church, white lesbian couples were privileged as mothers. Black lesbians, many of whom were working-class and had children from previous heterosexual relationships, never used motherhood to perform good Christian identities. Neither in interviews nor in the group ritual of "prayers and praises," in which congregants came forward to pray for their needs and give thanks for their blessings, did I ever hear a black lesbian woman invoke her identity as a mother as a basis for being a good Christian (even on Mother's Day). In fact, the only time I heard a black (single, working-class) lesbian invoke her identity as a mother was in a personal testimony. Vera said:

> In my early twenties, I found myself a single mother. I never held down a job before, y'all. You know, they say love makes a family, and that's really nice, but money keeps a family together. And with my boys, I never felt I could raise 'em right … they needed a man in their lives. Now I love my kids, anyone who knows me will tell you I love my kids more than life itself, but I just could not shake the feeling that I was a bad mother. So there I was, a single mother, working at Wal-Mart, doing what I could. And, you know, I did things I'll always regret. I gave my kids up to family members 'cause I thought they could raise 'em better than I could … when my brother-in-law took me to court, the things he said about me being a bad mother, the people I had influencing my kids – and you know what I mean, y'all – it's been a struggle. But God worked it out, thank you Jesus!

In the end, Vera felt a sense of victory in getting her children back. But she did not claim a "good mother" identity. Her class status (and her race, marital, and sexual identities) constrained her from crafting an identity as a "good mother" and threatened her sense of self as a good Christian. She gave up her children (something a good Christian would never do) because she felt she was unable to provide the sort of Christian family – that is, a male–female marriage – that would raise them right.

The white lesbian women in these churches were committed to inclusiveness. Even so, their performance of motherhood reinstated white, middle-class families as the cultural norm. By performing "good mother" identities, white lesbian couples drew on the race and class resources at their disposal. It was they – not working-class black mothers – who had the race privilege to fit normative (Eurocentric, middle-class, heterosexual) notions of motherhood and family. Because they also had class resources to afford *in vitro* fertilization or international adoption, and the couple status to more closely perform the traditional family, their identity performances were convincing. In this way, white lesbians successfully claimed a place in the predominantly heterosexual church they attended and enjoyed a sense of dignity and self-worth as good Christian women. Still, by drawing on a culturally dominant notion of white, middle-class motherhood to normalize their lesbian identities, they inadvertently reinforced a cultural view of poor, "unwed" black mothers as inferior (Collins 2000). Deploying the "good mother" identity was, you could say, a way of signifying whiteness and middle-class status – but without doing so explicitly. That is precisely how unmarked identity categories work, and why those who possess them have a subtle, nearly invisible form of power.

Conclusion

Analyzing sexuality together with other identities (for example, race, class, gender, religion) is difficult. But discerning *the consequences* of multiple identity performances for inequality is even harder. One way to examine the consequences of multiple identities, as they play out in daily life, is to consider identities separately or in tandem. By doing so, we can see the consequences of multiple identity performances for one or two systems of oppression at a time. I will use this approach here for lack of a better alternative.

Seen through a race lens, black lesbian women's minimizing strategy transgressed racial boundaries. To question heterosexuality disrupted a conventional notion of "authentic black-ness" upon which the idea of a "black community" currently rests. Given white racism, many blacks regard unity and sameness as vital to black solidarity. Thus, to highlight sexual differ-ence – and question sameness – is an act of transgression. It is also risky, since white, middle-class culture has stereotyped black people as hypersexual. By minimizing their sexuality, black lesbian women tried to fit into the black heterosexual world. Yet, they did not deny their sexuality entirely. They affirmed: "This is who God made me to be." Thus, they challenged black churches and communities to be more inclusive and accepting.

Seen through a sexuality lens, however, minimizing sexuality left heterosexism intact because it downplayed the importance of sex and sexuality. For some it meant staying in the closet. Without challenging the beliefs and practices in the church and broader culture that condemn homosexuality and privilege heterosexuality, black lesbian women could claim a sense of dig-nity and self-worth as normal black people and good Christians. Still, their quest for change in the Christian church was constrained by heterosexism, as it intersects with racism. Maintaining an identity as a "real" black Christian meant, for many, downplaying sexual difference and, for some, passing as straight.

Seen through a gender lens, white lesbians' "good mother" identity performances reinforced conventional femininity. One of the primary conventional gender expectations for women is to nurture others (Bartky 1995). By presenting themselves as good mothers, white lesbian women assumed and reinforced conventional gender norms that disadvantage women (for example, women are expected to perform the lion's share of undervalued, often unpaid, caring work). As we have seen, this performance also reinforced racism, since it (re)created white, middle-class lesbian women as the worthiest mothers. That black lesbian women (also owing to their social location as working-class and single) did not draw on motherhood as a resource to perform Christian identity echoes the call from intersectional feminists to attend to differences among women. As we have seen, race and class have important implications for lesbian women's everyday experiences and performances of identity. These differences must not be ignored. Though white lesbian women challenged the heterosexist notion of lesbian women as unfit mothers, their performance of identity did not liberate lesbian women as a group. Indeed, only those closest to white, middle-class heterosexuality had cultural currency to normalize themselves as mothers.

To understand sexual–religious identity negotiation, one must also consider other identities that shape people's lives. As this analysis shows, considering race, class, gender, and sexuality together reveals the necessity of studying "intersectionality" empirically. These findings indicate that challenging one boundary (for example, sexuality) may reinforce others (for example, gender and race norms). Examining how people experience multiple identities will be a crucial tool to understand how this paradox plays out in everyday life and how it might be solved.

References

Anzaldúa, Gloria and Cherrie Moraga. 2002. *This Bridge Called My Back: Writings By Radical Women of Color.* Berkeley, CA: Third Woman Press.

Bartky, Sandra. 1995. "Feeding Egos and Tending Wounds: Deference and Disaffection in Women's Emotional Labor". In Mary Rogers (ed.), *Power, Dignity and Social Structure: Readings in Multicultural Social Theory.* New York: McGraw-Hill.

Collins, Patricia Hill. 2000. *Black Feminist Thought: Knowledge, Consciousness, and the Politics of Empowerment.* 2nd edition. New York: Routledge.

Douglas, Kelly Brown. 1999. *Sexuality and the Black Church: A Womanist Perspective.* Maryknoll, NY: Orbis Books.

Dyson, Michael Eric. 1996. *Race Rules: Navigating the Color Line.* Reading, MA: Addison-Wesley.

hooks, bell. 1992. *Black Looks: Race and Representation.* Boston, MA: South End Press.

Hunter, James Davidson. 1991. *Culture Wars: The Struggle to Define America.* New York: Basic Books.

Melton, J. Gordon. 1991. *The Church Speaks on: Homosexuality.* Detroit, MI: Gale Research.

Phelan, Peggy. 1993. *Unmarked: The Politics of Performance.* New York: Routledge.

Wilkins, Amy. 2004. *Sex and Sensibility: Gender, Race, and Class in Three Youth Cultures.* Doctoral Dissertation, University of Massachusetts, Amherst.

Part 7
Sexual institutions and sexual commerce

Introduction

Many of us think of sex as a personal feeling or desire. As individuals, we experience sex as a passion of varying and fluctuating intensity. We may worry about too little or too much passion. We may also worry about whether we have the right or normal sexual desires and levels of intensity. Some of us may worry about whether sexual desire may lead us to inappropriate, even criminal, behavior.

Our individual desires are, however, socially regulated. Laws, and ideas of appropriate and inappropriate or normal and abnormal behavior which we acquire from our social environments, provide guidelines or rules that control our sexual feelings and conduct.

Moreover, society establishes social settings or arrangements that are understood by citizens as sexual environments. These social settings are socially approved spaces to be sexual. We can call these sexual settings and arrangements "sexual institutions." Examples of sexual institutions are dating rituals, proms, weddings, sex shops, adult theaters, escort services, brothels, cruising areas, and singles bars. These institutions stimulate or encourage sexual feelings and regulate them. When we enter a sexual institution there is a heightened focus on sexual feelings, fantasies, and possibilities, but also an awareness that there are rules governing our behavior.

Sexual institutions are then legitimate social spaces to be sexual. For example, gay bathhouses are places for sex between men. It may be that some men also go to bathhouses to meet friends, but the culture and social organization of the bathhouse makes it clear that this is a setting whose purpose is sex. Typically, after paying an entrance fee, men deposit their clothes in a private room or locker. They stroll through the dark halls and rooms of the bathhouse either naked or with just a towel. Everyone in the bathhouse understands that they will be looked at, and will look at others, with an eye to sexual possibilities. Spaces are established in the bathhouse for the purpose of sex, such as private rooms or darkened public rooms. While the bathhouse is a highly sexualized social setting, there are rules regulating sexual behavior. For example, sex must be consensual, individuals can end sex and exit from a sexual encounter at any time they wish, and there are no extended obligations or commitments that accompany a sexual encounter.

As strange as it may seem, the gay bathhouse has many things in common with a very different sexual institution, marriage. Marriage is a sexual institution. Sex is expected and indeed sexual satisfaction is a standard to judge whether a marriage is working or successful. The institution of marriage also controls and regulates sexuality. For example, in many countries marriage is accompanied by a norm of monogamy or the expectation of sexual exclusiveness between spouses. Adultery may be a crime or viewed as a moral violation of the spirit of marriage.

Sexual institutions are settings for legitimate sex. These institutions sexualize the self, encourage or incite sexual feelings, create the expectation of sexual expression, and at the same time organize and regulate sex. In this part, you will be introduced to a wide range of sexual institutions – from weddings and marriage to gay circuit parties and internet dating sites. Whatever else you may learn from these readings, we hope that you come away with the understanding that, as much as sex is a personal and often an intimate matter, it is also about social institutions that organize and control our sexualities.

43

One is not born a bride

How weddings regulate heterosexuality

Chrys Ingraham

STATE UNIVERSITY OF NEW YORK AT PURCHASE

All aspects of our social world – natural or otherwise – are given meaning. Culture installs meaning in our lives from the very first moment we enter the social world. Our sexual orientation or sexual identity – or even the notion that there is such a thing – is defined by the symbolic order of that world through the use of verbal as well as non-verbal language and images. Heterosexuality as a *social* category is much more than the fact of one's sexual or affectional attractions. What we think of when we talk about heterosexuality or refer to ourselves as heterosexual is a product of a society's meaning-making processes. In reality, heterosexuality operates as a highly organized social institution that varies across nations, social groups, culture, history, region, religion, ethnicity, nationality, race, lifespan, social class, and ability. In America and elsewhere, the wedding ritual represents a major site for the installation and maintenance of the institution of heterosexuality.

The title of this chapter pays homage to French feminist Monique Wittig whose classic and provocative essay "One is Not Born a Woman" examines what she calls the political regime of heterosexuality and its requisite categories of man and woman. She argues that the category of woman and all of the meaning attached to that category would not exist were it not necessary for the political regime of (patriarchal) heterosexuality. For the purpose of this chapter, the same holds true of the taken-for-granted category of bride. While it may seem obvious to most that one is not born a bride, in reality many women see themselves as following a naturalized path toward heterosexual womanhood.

But how did this contrived and constructed social practice become naturalized? The task of examining this taken-for-granted social arrangement requires a conceptual framework capable of revealing how heterosexuality has become institutionalized, naturalized, and normalized. Any attempt to examine the institution of heterosexuality requires a theory capable of understanding how this institution with all its social practices such as dating, proms, and Valentine's Day, is often viewed by many of us as natural.

The heterosexual imaginary

French psychoanalyst Jacques Lacan's concept of the "imaginary" is especially useful for this purpose. According to Lacan, the imaginary is the unmediated contact an infant has to its own image and its connection with its mother. Instead of facing a complicated, conflictual, and contradictory world, the infant experiences the illusion of tranquility, plenitude, and fullness. In other words, infants experience a sense of oneness with their primary caretaker. Louis Althusser, the French philosopher, borrowed Lacan's notion of the imaginary for his neo-marxist theory of ideology, defining ideology as "the imaginary relationship of individuals to their real conditions of existence." The "imaginary" here does not mean "false" or "pretend" but, rather, an imagined or illusory relationship between an individual and their social world. Applied to a social theory of heterosexuality the *heterosexual imaginary* is that way of thinking that relies on romantic and sacred notions of heterosexuality in order to create and maintain the illusion of well-being and oneness. This romantic view prevents us from seeing how institutionalized heterosexuality actually works to organize gender while preserving racial, class, and sexual hierarchies. The effect of this illusory depiction of reality is that heterosexuality is taken for granted and unquestioned, while gender is understood as something people are socialized into or learn. The heterosexual imaginary naturalizes male to female social relations, rituals, and organized practices and conceals the operation of heterosexuality in structuring gender across race, class, and sexuality. This way of seeing closes off any critical analysis of heterosexuality as an organizing institution and for the ends it serves (Ingraham 1994, 1999). By leaving heterosexuality unexamined as an institution we do not explore how it is learned, how it may control us and contribute to social inequalities. Through the use of the heterosexual imaginary, we hold up the institution of heterosexuality as fixed in time as though it has always operated the same as it does today. This imaginary presents a view of heterosexuality as "just the way it is" while creating obligatory social practices that reinforce the illusion that, as long as one complies with this naturalized structure, all will be right in the world. This illusion is commonly known as romance. Romancing heterosexuality is creating an illusory heterosexuality for which wedding culture plays a central role.

The lived reality of institutionalized heterosexuality is, however, not typically tranquil or safe. The consequences the heterosexual imaginary produces include, for example, marital rape, domestic violence, pay inequities, racism, gay-bashing, femicide, and sexual harassment. Institutionalized heterosexuality and its organizing ideology – the heterosexual imaginary – establishes those behaviors we ascribe to men and women – gender – while keeping in place or producing a history of contradictory and unequal social relations. The production of a division of labor that results in unpaid domestic work, inequalities of pay and opportunity, or the privileging of married couples in the dissemination of insurance benefits, are examples of this.

Above all, the heterosexual imaginary naturalizes the regulation of sexuality through the institution of marriage, ritual practices such as weddings, and state domestic relations laws. These laws, among others, set the terms for taxation, healthcare, and housing benefits on the basis of marital status. Rarely challenged – except by nineteenth-century marriage reformers and early second-wave feminists – laws and public- and private-sector policies use marriage as the primary requirement for social and economic benefits and access rather than distributing resources on some other basis such as citizenship or ability to breathe, for example. Heterosexuality is much more than a biological given or whether or not someone is attracted to someone of another sex. Rules on everything from who pays for the date or wedding rehearsal dinner to who leads while dancing, drives the car, cooks dinner or initiates sex, all serve to regulate heterosexual practice. What circulates as a given in Western societies is, in fact, a highly structured arrangement. As is the case with most institutions, people who participate in these practices must be socialized to do so. In other words, women were not born with a wedding gown gene or a neo-natal craving for a diamond engagement ring! They were taught to want these things. Women didn't enter the world with a desire to practice something called dating or a desire to play with a "My Size Bride Barbie," they were rewarded for desiring these things. Likewise, men did not exit the womb knowing they would one day buy a date a bunch of flowers or spend two months' income to buy an engagement ring. These are all products that have been sold to consumers interested in taking part in a culturally established ritual that works to organize and institutionalize heterosexuality and reward those who participate.

Heteronormativity

A related concept useful for the study of the heterosexual imaginary and of institutionalized heterosexuality is heteronormativity. This is the view that institutionalized heterosexuality constitutes the standard for legitimate and expected social and sexual relations. Heteronormativity represents one of the main premises underlying the heterosexual imaginary, again ensuring that the organization of heterosexuality in everything from gender to weddings to marital status is held up both as a model and as "normal." Consider, for instance, the ways many surveys or intake questionnaires ask respondents to check off their marital status as either married, divorced, separated, widowed, single, or, in some cases, never married. Not only are these categories presented as significant indices of social identity, they are offered as the only options, implying that the organization of identity in relation to marriage is universal and not in need of explanation. Or try to imagine entering a committed relationship without benefit of legalized marriage. We find it difficult to think that we can share commitment with someone without a state-sponsored license. People will frequently comment that someone is afraid to "make a commitment" if they choose not to get married even when they have been in a relationship with someone for years! Our ability to imagine possibilities or to understand what counts as commitment is itself impaired by heteronormative assumptions. We even find ourselves challenged to consider how to marry without an elaborate white wedding. Gays and lesbians have maintained long-term committed relationships yet find themselves desiring state sanctioning of their union in order to feel legitimate. Heteronormativity works in all of these instances to naturalize the institution of heterosexuality while rendering real people's relationships and commitments irrelevant and illegitimate.

For those who view questions concerning marital status as benign, one need only consider the social and economic consequences for those who do not participate in these arrangements or the cross-cultural variations that are at odds with some of the Anglocentric or Eurocentric assumptions regarding marriage. All people are required to situate themselves in relation to marriage or heterosexuality, including those who *regardless of sexual (or asexual) affiliation* do not consider themselves "single," heterosexual, or who do not participate in normative heterosexuality and its structures.

One is not born a bride, and yet to imagine oneself outside of this category is to live a life outside of the boundaries of normality and social convention. To live outside this contrived and constructed social practice is to live on the margins of society, excluded from the social, legal, and economic rewards and benefits participation brings. To resist membership in the heteronormative social order – as bride or as groom – is to live with the penalties and challenges to all those who resist. It means living a life where you have to defend your sexual loyalties on a daily basis – are you straight or are you gay?

Weddings

To demonstrate the degree to which the heteronormative wedding ritual regulates sexuality we must begin with an investigation into the ways various practices, arrangements, relations, and rituals standardize and conceal the operation of institutionalized heterosexuality. It means to ask how practices such as weddings become naturalized and prevent us from seeing what is at stake, what is kept in place, and what consequences are produced. To employ this approach is to seek out those instances when the illusion of tranquility is created and at what cost. Weddings, like many other rituals of heterosexual celebration such as anniversaries, showers, and Valentine's Day, become synonymous with heterosexuality and provide illusions of reality that conceal the operation of heterosexuality both historically and materially. When used in professional settings, for example, weddings work as a form of ideological control to signal membership in relations of ruling as well as to signify that the couple is normal, moral, productive, family-centered, upstanding citizens and, most importantly, appropriately gendered and sexual.

To study weddings means to interrupt the ways the heterosexual imaginary naturalizes heterosexuality and prevents us from seeing how its organization depends on the production of the belief or ideology that heterosexuality is normative and the same for everyone – that the fairy-tale romance is universal. It is this assumption that allows for the development and growth in America of a $35 billion-per-year wedding industry. This multibillion dollar industry includes the sale of a diverse range of products, many of which are produced outside of the USA – wedding gowns, diamonds, honeymoon travel and apparel, and household equipment. Ironically, the production of these goods frequently occurs under dismal labor conditions where manufacturers rely on a non-traditional female workforce, indirectly altering cultural norms in relation to heterosexuality and family. In Mexico, Guatemala, and China, for example, the effect has been to shift the job opportunities away from men with the consequence of significant levels of domestic violence and femicide. Sexual regulation in these locations is directly related to the gendered division of labor working to produce goods that support the American heterosexual imaginary. Veiled in the guise of romance and the sacred, these social relations conceal from view the troublesome conditions underlying the production of the white wedding.

When you think of weddings as "only natural," think again! This process of naturalization begins with children. By targeting girls and young women, toy manufacturers have seized on the wedding market and the opportunity to develop future consumers by producing a whole variety of wedding toys, featuring the "classic" white wedding, and sold during Saturday morning children's television shows. Toy companies, generally part of large multinational conglomerates that also own related commodities such as travel or cosmetics, work to secure future markets for all their products through the selling of wedding toys. Mattel, the world's largest toymaker and a major multinational corporation, has offices and facilities in thirty-six countries and sells products in 150 nations. Their major toy brand, accounting for 40 percent of their sales, is the Barbie doll – all 120 different versions of her. Mattel's primary manufacturing facilities are located in China, Indonesia, Italy, Malaysia, and Mexico, employing mostly women of color and at substandard wages. Annually, Mattel makes about 100 million Barbie dolls and earns revenues of $1.9 billion for the California-based company. The average young Chinese female worker whose job it is to assemble Barbie dolls lives in a dormitory, sometimes works with dangerous chemicals, works long hours and earns $1.81 a day.

The staging of weddings in television shows, weekly reporting on weddings in the press, magazine reports on celebrity weddings, advertising, and popular adult and children's movies with wedding themes or weddings inserted, all work together to teach us how to think about weddings, marriage, heterosexuality, race, gender, and labor. Through the application of the heterosexual imaginary, the media cloak most representations of weddings in signifiers of romance, purity, morality, promise, affluence or accumulation, and whiteness. Many newlyweds today experience their weddings as the stars of a fairy-tale movie in which they are scripted, videotaped, and photographed by paparazzi wedding-goers, not as an event that regulates their sexual lives and identities along with those of the laborers who make their wedding possible.

The contemporary white wedding under multinational capitalism is, in effect, a mass-marketed, homogeneous, assembly-line production with little resemblance to the utopian vision many participants hold. The engine driving the wedding market has mostly to do with the romancing of heterosexuality in the interests of capitalism. The social relations at stake – love, community, commitment, and family – come to be viewed as secondary to the production of the wedding spectacle.

The heterosexual imaginary circulating throughout the wedding industry masks the ways it secures racial, class, and sexual hierarchies. Women are taught from early childhood to plan for the "happiest day of their lives." (Everything after that day pales by comparison!) Men are taught, by the absence of these socializing mechanisms, that their work is "other" than that. If they are interested in the wedding it is for reasons other than what women have learned. The possibilities children learn to imagine are only as broad as their culture allows. They are socialized to understand the importance of appropriate coupling, what counts as beauty, as appropriate sexuality, what counts as women's work and men's work, and how to become "good" consumers by participating in those heterosexual practices and rituals that stimulate their interests and emotions and reap the most rewards.

One is not born a bride. One learns to comply with the social and cultural messages that flow to and through the wedding ritual. It is the rite of passage for appropriate heterosexual identity and membership. It is everything but natural.

References

Ingraham, Chrys. 1994. "The heterosexual imaginary", *Sociological Theory* 12 (2): 203–19.
——1999. *White Weddings: Romancing Heterosexuality in Popular Culture*. New York: Routledge.

44

Change and continuity in American marriage

Erica Hunter

STATE UNIVERSITY OF NEW YORK AT ALBANY

From the time we are children, the general expectation is that we will grow up to find some-one with whom we want to spend our lives in marriage. Many of my friends who have gotten married cannot provide an explanation of *why* they decided to get married apart from that it just seemed like the next step in their relationship. But why would someone think about questions such as "why do you want to marry?" in our society? After all, marriage provides couples with many personal benefits, such as public recognition of their love and the fulfillment of childhood dreams.

However, marriage plays other roles in our personal lives and society, such as legally binding two lives together and creating heterosexual relationships as normal. When we think about what it means socially to become married, it forces us to examine marriage as a social institution. Marriage is not simply an agreement between two people. Marriage is a legal and social contract, and an institution that includes romance and weddings that reinforce gender roles and heterosexuality.

The institution of marriage

As an institution, marriage has several purposes in our personal and social lives. First, marriage is seen as a legitimate marker of one's transition into adulthood and brings with it the responsi-bilities and privileges that come with being an adult, such as living independently from one's parents, engaging in a sexual relationship, and starting a family of one's own. In addition, marriage helps legitimize a couple's relationship in the eyes of their friends and family. Couples are generally expected to marry after dating for a while as a way of moving forward with their relationship, and to display their commitment to one another. Couples who decide to cohabit, or live together without getting married, will often transition into marriage or separate within five years; only a small percentage of couples who cohabit continue to live together without becoming married after five years. Since so many couples choose either to marry or to end their relationships, one can imagine that cohabitation allows couples to see if they are compatible for marriage. Couples who choose to cohabit without plans to marry often feel pressure from friends and family to marry in order to commit themselves symbolically to each other.

Examining marriage as an institution allows us to understand the impact it has on our lives as members of a society. When a couple marries, they are granted thousands of benefits from both local and national governments and employers. Social security, tax benefits, legal protections (including the right not to testify against your spouse and the ability to make medical decisions on behalf of one another), immigration rights, and healthcare benefits are automatically granted to partners in a marital relationship; those who do not or cannot marry often lack these legal protections or must find other ways to secure some of these privileges for their relationship. The passing in the USA of the Defense of Marriage Act (1996) limits non-married couples' abilities to secure benefits provided by the national government by recognizing only other-sexed relationships as able to legally marry and receive the benefits it provides to legally married couples.

Marriage also works to legitimate heterosexual relationships. First, the relationship between marriage and sexuality is created and maintained through gender expectations and roles. For example, children – who often are not thought of as being sexual – are raised in a heterosexual framework that includes the expectation that they will eventually fall in love with someone of the other sex, marry, and raise a family of their own. Even definitions of what it means to be male and female are constructed in ways to produce them as complementary, thus creating an illusion that men and women need each other to form a complete union. Second, the frequency and acceptance of heterosexual marriage work to reinforce it as a normal, natural practice. In addition to the general expectation that one will marry, heterosexual marriage is celebrated, even made sacred, in our society. We congratulate newlyweds and hope for the best for them. This social expectation to marry is real: over 90 percent of the population will marry at least once in their lives. Whatever our personal reasons are for getting married, it is an institution that reinforces the idea that heterosexuality is the natural and normal way to be.

Marriage as a changing institution

Increases in cohabitation, high divorce rates, and legal pressures from same-sex couples for legal recognition of their unions have led some observers to claim that the state of marriage today is in jeopardy. However, an examination of the history of marriage will reveal that marriage is an institution in constant transition, both in what it looks like and the meanings it has for those who engage in it. This section will briefly examine the historical changes in marriage in the United States in the nineteenth and twentieth centuries. Although the USA has a rich history of family diversity, this history will focus mostly on white, middle-class couples. Other issues, such as interracial and same-sex relationships, will be mentioned as examples of major shifts in how our understandings of marriage and love relationships have changed.

Marriage historically served an important role in organizing the lives of individuals. Through most of the eighteenth and early nineteenth centuries, there was a strong reliance on farm- and family-based production. Men and women married for familiar reasons, such as to combine family wealth and to maintain reliable, stable relationships with neighbors. This also caused marriages to be divided on racial and socioeconomic lines. The focus of marriage was social; individuals generally did not marry for feelings of love because such relationships were seen as being unstable and unlikely to succeed. What was considered an attractive mate varied based on gender. Men often looked for wives who could assist with the family farm and/or whose family could provide the best dowry or bride's wealth to his family. Women looked for men who would be stable, reliable providers. In addition, the family was one of the only institutions through which people experienced their world. Work, education, religion, and family creation were mostly done within the family and marriage. Marriage also affected individuals on the personal level, by providing norms and regulations regarding their roles within marriage and family. These expectations were based on a gendered and age-based system, so that men/women and children/adults had different, complementary roles within the family to perform. The way marriage was institutionalized assured the survival of individuals and their families; a poor choice in marriage partners could literally mean success or failure in life. The need for differentiated roles within the family, and the large role of procreation in marriage, also construct marriage as an inherently heterosexual institution.

Marriage began to change in the second half of the nineteenth century. The rise in individualism started to pull people away from their birth families in favor of marrying and creating families with partners they chose. In addition, the development of industry and wage labor provided options to men who did not want to farm. Income gained from wages allowed people to purchase many of the necessities that they had once relied on their families for, such as food, housing, and clothing. As outside institutions such as the workplace started to reshape the way that individuals lived, so too did they reshape the way that people viewed marriage and family life. No longer did couples have to marry based strictly on what was best for their families or to make sure they would live a secure life – wage labor provided them with an opportunity to take care of themselves if the need arose. These events led to an increase in individuals moving away from their families and choosing to marry for reasons of love. No longer were individuals forced to marry for survival but, for the first time, couples were able to marry because they wanted to share their lives.

This change in how marriage was understood also reshaped the relationships between married couples. No longer were both partners working at home to provide subsistence for their families. With men moving outside the home into the workforce, women were left at home to take care of household and childcare. This transition developed the "ideology of separate spheres," or the idea that men's and women's work should occur in different spheres: men's lives would focus on work and the public sphere, while women would attend to the domestic needs of the family and home.

This shift brought about several changes in the ways intimate life was understood. Couples viewed their intimate relationships as being rooted in companionship, and their relationship was supposed to promote personal happiness. The size of the family decreased and couples spent more time caring for children. Because marriage was slowly becoming based on personal happiness, individuals now wanted a right to divorce.

However, this increase in individualism and freedom in marriage was constrained by race. Throughout the nineteenth and twentieth centuries, federal laws limited marriage to couples of the same race. However, laws against interracial marriage did not mean that racially mixed couples would not form relationships or have children. It was not until the landmark case *Loving vs. Virginia* in 1967 that laws against interracial marriage in the United States were declared unconstitutional. Interestingly, the historical arguments against interracial marriage mirror contemporary arguments against same-sex marriage, such as if we allow interracial/same-sex marriage then people will want to marry their cousin/sibling/dog. Marriage is not a static institution but changes as the larger society changes.

Today, marriage has lost some of its influence as competing institutions, such as the workplace, the peer group, and education, replace many of the functions historically served by the family. In addition, these institutions are shaping how people live their lives. For example, increased enrollment in higher education and longer hours in the workplace remove individuals from their families for longer periods. In addition, these institutions often provide companionship and social support. Marriage is no longer the only marker of becoming an adult. Today, graduation from college, buying one's first home, or starting gainful employment, also indicate the passage to adulthood. Current trends such as delayed marriage, declining fertility, the cohabitation option, the greater visibility of same-sex couples, have had the effect of making marriage more a matter of individual choice than social obligation.

While the meaning of marriage has been historically fluid, marriage has always retained its institutional influence in the regulation of sexuality. Even today, the influence of marriage in the promotion of heterosexuality is strong, from the passing of the Defense of Marriage Act in 1996 to the general expectation starting at a very young age that we will all become either handsome grooms or blushing brides. Even though people today spend a smaller percentage of their lives married than ever before, the expectation remains that they desire and seek marriage as the best arrangement for their personal, sexual, and social lives. Laws and social pressures that subtly label heterosexuality as normal and ideal, while stigmatizing all nonheterosexual and nonmarital practices, support marriage.

Marriage, gender, and sexuality

While not all societies have historically practiced exclusively heterosexual marriage based on complementary gender roles, this relationship type has been dominant in the United States. From early in their lives, children learn how to perform masculinity or femininity as is consistent with their sex. As children learn gender roles from their families, including the proper way to dress and the appropriate way to interact with others, they also are subtly taught how to be heterosexual. If a little boy likes to have tea parties with his female friends, his parents may try to correct his behavior and get him interested in more masculine activities, such as playing sports, in an effort to teach him masculine behaviors. Those who perform their gender poorly are often suspected of being homosexual because of the strong association assumed between gender roles and one's sexuality. For example, being masculine in the United States is directly related to being attracted to women and desiring them sexually.

Heterosexuality is often viewed as the ideal basis of marriage because of the different gender roles men and women are expected to play in marriage. For example, when we think of the "traditional" family of years past, we think of a breadwinning father who supports a homemaking wife. Even today, with many mothers in the labor force, the different roles or tasks each spouse is expected to perform are often based on gender. Women still do a majority of household and childcare work, and men, although not generally the sole financial provider, are still expected to be the primary breadwinners and have less responsibility for childcare. This understanding of marriage and families as needing people of different genders in order to function well constructs heterosexual relationships as normal.

The idea of complementary gender roles within marriage is based on the idea that this institution is organized for the procreation and raising of children. The general expectation for young boys and girls is to form a couple, which causes children and adults to view heterosexuality as a biological given. Children are expected to exhibit gender-appropriate (hetero) sexual and romantic desires. Girls and young women are often told to wait for their Prince Charming before engaging in sexual activity. They are expected to show interest in boys by having crushes on them and planning their weddings, which are also considered the most important event of their lives. Boys, in turn, are expected to prove their masculinity by having sexual relationships with many girls before settling down with a "good girl" – that is, a girl who is a virgin or at any rate not too experienced. Images of heterosexuality as the natural and right way to be are part and parcel of the institution of marriage.

The images and ideas about marriage in America are so tightly linked to notions of complementary gender roles that it is difficult for many of us to imagine same-sex couples as families. While there remains much diversity in families today, we still find that same-sex couples are assumed to take on complementary gender roles within their intimate relationships. Terms such as "top" and "bottom," used to describe active/passive or male/female sex roles within same-sex sexual relations, help to bring heterosexual imagery to these relationships. Since same-sex couples by definition consist of two men or two women, they are understood as needing to conform to a heterosexual model, despite research that shows that both same-sex and other-sexed couples experience a great deal of diversity in how they experience gender within their intimate relationships.

Marriage: a declining or a changing institution?

Family sociologists often note that delayed marriage, less time spent in marriage, and decreased fertility suggest that marriage is no longer a basic need for survival. Today, people can choose to marry or not. However, the wider freedom to choose marriage does not mean that it is in decline. It seems clear that marriage has retained one of its most basic functions: the regulation and reproduction of heterosexuality. While one can make an argument that there has been a weakening of marriage, I would reply that as long as marriage exists it will promote heterosexuality as the most natural arrangement. Moreover, whatever the institutional reality, marriage remains an idealized state of how we should live. While cohabitation and childbirth outside of marriage are becoming increasingly common, many who participate in these practices still want to marry someday. They do not see their cohabitation and procreation as permanent alternatives to marriage. Individuals who cohabit often marry or separate, poor couples often delay marriage until they have the assets to "make it work" yet still have children, and children, regardless of their family structure, are generally assumed to want to grow up and get married. Marriage is still the ultimate goal for most people.

There has also been some debate among sociologists as to how marriage is changing. Some sociologists argue that marriage is becoming deinstitutionalized, or that the institutional roles of marriage, such as creating household units, having and raising children, and providing a basis for learning gender roles, are increasingly being replaced with a model of marriage as an institution designed to fulfill personal development. While some fear that this shift will result in the decline of marriage, I would argue that there is a positive aspect in these changes. These changes could lead to a social policy that acknowledges and supports diverse types of intimate arrangements and families. Currently, some of the benefits associated with marriage are designed to help couples care for themselves and their children, but a majority of these benefits could – and, I think, should – be shared with others in non-married families. In a nation that claims to be pro-family, it seems ironic that law and policy tend to support only families based on marriage. If we extended benefits to individuals in different types of families, we would do a much better job at strengthening families. Policies like this would not undermine marriage but would promote couple relationships and strong families.

45

The political economy of sexual labor

Interview with Elizabeth Bernstein

BARNARD COLLEGE

Tell us a little about yourself

My research occurs at the intersection of the sociology of sexuality and feminist approaches to law and policy. My two books, *Temporarily Yours* (University of Chicago Press, 2007) and *Regulating Sex* (Routledge, 2005), explore the interplay between transformations in political economy, modes of state regulation, and sexual practices and identities in the post-industrial West. My current research examines the coordination of political-economic and religious interests in the development of recent US policies pertaining to the "traffic in women." Throughout all of this work, my agenda has been to illuminate the moral and political convictions that motivate particular sets of social actors and to situate policies pertaining to gender and sexuality within a broader field of social, political, and economic relations.

By training, I am a qualitative sociologist who draws from a combination of participant observation, in-depth interviews, and discursive analysis to ground my theoretical claims. Because my work seeks to connect "micro" with "macro" levels of social transformation, my ethnographic approach is both multi-sited and multi-perspectival. I situate my scholarship within sociological lineages that seek to understand local behaviors and identities in terms of their enabling political-economic and historical conditions. In my writing, I place my own ethnographic research in explicit dialogue with a broad array of empirical and theoretical work on contemporary political economy and cultural transformations, engaging with scholarship from anthropology, history, political theory and law in addition to sociology and inter-disciplinary gender and sexuality studies. In contrast to social researchers who aspire to apprehend their data in the absence of any contaminating theoretical apparatus, my own research agenda has developed with an aim to address specific and evolving sets of paradoxes and questions.

Currently, I am a member of the women's studies and sociology departments at Barnard College, Columbia University, where I teach courses on the sociology of gender and sexuality; trafficking, migration, and sexual labor; and contemporary social theory.

For Temporarily Yours, *a research project on contemporary forms of prostitution, you employed a number of methods for researching different aspects of sex work. Could you discuss the different approaches you took and explain why you chose them?*

My primary methodological approach for *Temporarily Yours* was ethnographic – meaning I spent a long time talking to, following around, and "hanging out" with diverse participants in the sex industry. However, the focus of my research evolved a lot over the course of the nearly 10 years that I was working on this book. It actually began as a study of the San Francisco Task Force on Prostitution, which had been formed to look into the possibility of reforming prostitution policy in the city. Initially, I had been intrigued by the abundant media coverage of the Task Force, which suggested that the feminists, prostitutes' rights activists, and neighborhood representatives that formed its core were considering legalizing prostitution (a solution which each of the above groups had historically opposed) and even contemplating such controversial public policy solutions as city-run brothels or municipal licensing. I wondered if and under what guise prostitutes' concerns were being represented in these considerations, who was doing the representing, and which (if any) feminist position would predominate when it came down to the nitty-gritty of policy reform. Most importantly, I was concerned about what the likely impact would be – for sex-workers and other city residents – if the proposed reforms should come to pass.

Most of the prostitutes' rights leaders who held seats on the Task Force told me that they were either currently working as prostitutes or had worked as prostitutes in the past. Yet I was soon to discover that only a few had any experience with street prostitution – the main focus of the Task Force's attention. As I got to know them and the organizations they represented, I came to have a better understanding of the complexity and diversity of local prostitution markets, and the different social realities they entailed. At this point, I decided to expand my project to include participant observation with sex-workers working in diverse ways and at diverse levels, so that I might test empirically my growing suspicion that the dynamics and meanings of prostitution varied systematically across social space. I became particularly interested in the contrast between the self-employed sex workers that I had met in activist groups like COYOTE, and the lived realities of commercial sex work for those who walked the streets.

Like a series of ever-widening concentric circles, my project expanded outward for several years, as I reached for broader and broader contexts to make sense of what I saw. In 1998, I learned that Sweden and the Netherlands were in the process of the revising their prostitution policies, and that both countries had assembled task forces similar to the one that I had served on in San Francisco. These two cases were of particular interest to me because Sweden and the Netherlands had both been hailed as "gender utopias" by various groups of feminist activists and the press, yet the two countries were changing their laws in opposite directions: Sweden was implementing a criminalization model, while the Netherlands was legalizing the sex trade. I realized that by looking together at the cases of San Francisco, Amsterdam, and Stockholm, I would be able to compare the lived dynamics of contemporary prostitution under three different legal regimes, in cities that shared a number of common features, including size, economic infrastructure, and reputations for being socially progressive.

Of these different ways of researching the social contexts of sex work that you undertook for Temporarily Yours, *which was the most difficult and why?*

As many ethnographers have noted, the most difficult aspect of social research is "studying up," rather than studying down or horizontally. People with social power – e.g. state agents, middle-class social activists, the police – are the least likely group to be willing to share their opinions or the intimate details of their lives. Even though there were certain things that made my research with policy makers easier to conduct than my research with sex workers (such as the fact that this research generally took place in comfortable indoor settings and during normal business hours), figuring out the state's interests in regulating the sex trade was the hardest nut for me to crack.

My fieldwork with street-based sex workers was actually much easier, and was facilitated by some crucial collaborations. The San Francisco-based prostitutes' rights activist, Carol Leigh, had been doing condom distribution amongst street prostitutes for over a year by the time I met her. She was enthusiastic and welcoming when I asked if I might join her, and we spent the next six months as research and outreach partners. With her 15-year tenure as a prominent local activist, Carol was instrumental in introducing me to a vast network of sex workers who were important informants for this project.

This is not to suggest that my research on the streets did not present me with serious challenges. In his book, *Distinction*, the sociologist Pierre Bourdieu cautions that when researchers attempt to understand social others through a provisional and deliberate engagement with their worlds, the result is likely to be perceptions of these worlds which still derive from the researcher's own habitus.[1] On the streets, there were clearly degrees of social distance that made my provisional entry into this world possible in the first place (such as being white and middle class) and which also allowed me to return home to my own comparatively safe and comfortable surroundings at the end of the night. These social disparities were politically as well as methodologically troubling to me, and led to my growing activist engagement in sex workers' rights issues. They also led to my decision to orient my street-based research around problems that were relevant to the sex workers themselves. When I announced my intention to investigate the police treatment of streetwalkers (which was something that the women on the streets complained about routinely) and indicated that I was prepared to go undercover as a "decoy" and to be taken to jail along with everyone else, the sex workers were very enthusiastic.

What large-scale social changes in the economy have impacted sex work?

There is an abundant literature on the transformations that have taken place within the global economy over the last 30 years. Numerous sociologists have traced the nature and significance of post-industrialism and the emergence and impact of the service economy and the new information technologies, as well as ensuing socio-demographic changes.[2] While sociologists of the family and of culture have extended this project, few commentators have linked post-industrial cultural formations to the changing nature of sexuality.

One of the key arguments of *Temporarily Yours* is that the proliferation of forms of service work, the new global information economy, and "postmodern" families peopled by isolable individuals have produced another profound transformation in the erotic sphere. Both the traditional "procreative" and the modern "companionate" models of sexuality are increasingly being supplemented by a sexual ethic that derives its primary meaning from the depth of physical sensation and from emotionally bounded erotic exchange – what in the book I call *bounded authenticity*. Whereas in the domestic sphere, relational sexuality derived its meaning from its ideological opposition to the marketplace, bounded authenticity bears no antagonism to the sphere of public commerce. It is available for sale and purchase as readily as any other form of commercially packaged leisure activity.

Another important way that contemporary economic transformations and sex work are linked is through the gentrification of post-industrial cities and the decline of streetwalking as a commercial sexual form. From the fall of 1994, when I first began my study, to the early part of 1997, street prostitutes in San Francisco were steadily "pushed" by police sweeps deeper and deeper into the Tenderloin. By 1997, local politicians and police had made a more definitive decision regarding street prostitution in San Francisco: they decided to eliminate it. As in other US and Western European cities, rigorous, combative policing became a frontline strategy for purging sex workers and other marginalized populations (such as the homeless and the mentally ill) from newly desirable downtown real estate. With increased police crackdowns on street-walking, a new array of spatially dispersed sexual services emerged to take its place. In this way, transformations in the forms and functions of urban space were accompanied by changes in the social geography of commercial sex.

Similarly, how has information technology been changing sex work?

Sex workers were among the first and most consistent beneficiaries of the technological inno-vations that defined the "new economy." The internet has reshaped predominant patterns of sexual commerce in ways that some sex workers have been able to benefit from. At the same time that street-based sex workers have been more severely policed, for many indoor sex workers it has become easier to work without third-party management, to conduct one's business with minimal interference from the criminal justice system, and to reap greater profits by honing one's sales pitch to a more elite and more specialized audience.

By advertising through specialty websites, sex workers can pitch their ads towards clients with an interest in their specific physical characteristics (e.g. fat women, older women, Asian women), or in the precise sexual services for which they can offer expertise (e.g. tantra, sado-masochism, erotic massage). Many such sites are even linked to client websites which feature restaurant-style "reviews" of their services. The erotic review sites that clients frequent are also subdivided by market niche. For example, there are some websites that are geared specifically towards budget shoppers, while other websites contain links to escorts' "blogs," in which the day-to-day musings of the sex worker are intended to serve as a window into her personality. There are also a number of websites such as *Craig's List* where sex workers can advertise if they are interested in working sporadically or informally, and where ads for sex workers appear unobtrusively between the headings for computer help, event planning, and real estate.

How different is sex work from other types of service work that require emotional labor on the part of women?

The sociologist Arlie Hochschild originally devised the term "emotional labor" within the context of her research on airline stewardesses, for whom smiling and the production of cheerfulness are often part of the job. She argued that "this kind of labor calls for a coordination of mind and feeling," and draws on a source of self "that we honor as deep and integral to our individuality" (Hochschild 1983:7). Since Hochschild first devised the term, various scholars have found it to be a useful analytic tool for understanding the kinds of caring work that women are called upon to perform in many different labor sectors, including such arenas as childcare and domestic work, nail salons, bar hostessing, and sex work.

The insecurity and transience of contemporary social life have led some people to divest emotional meaning from their private-sphere relationships, reinvesting it instead in market relations, both as workers and as consumers. Through reliance on such things as psychotherapy, child care, domestic labor, and take-out cuisine, they seek to provide their lives with the necessary "services" – and emotional meaning – that individuals of an earlier era could expect to secure in noncommodified, private-sphere relationships. What Hochschild has termed "women's uneasy love affair with capital-ism" is made all the more acute when we consider that many of the flourishing sectors of the late-capitalist service economy, including sex work, are commercialized refinements of services that women have historically provided for free (Hochschild 1997: 221).

You interviewed some male sex workers in your study. Were their experiences different than the women's?

In the post-industrial cities where I conducted my research, male sex workers comprised approximately a third of the overall market. For methodological rather than substantive reasons, my ethnographic research on the streets did not include a sustained focus on male sex workers. The men tended to concentrate on different strolls and did not typically mix with the women that I worked with. Among indoor sex workers, however, gender divisions were less enforced, and my research was able to encompass the experiences of both women and men. Many of the indoor female and male sex workers that I met attended the same activist meetings, advertised in the same venues, and at times even shared clients.

That said, there are also some important differences between the experiences of male and female sex workers that should be highlighted. Socially and politically, male sex workers are less visible than female sex workers, and they are not arrested anywhere near as frequently. Some researchers have also stressed male sex workers' greater propensity to talk about their own experiences of pleasure – as opposed to simply work – in their performance of sexual labor. What I found in my research was that indoor male sex workers often took great pride in offering an experience of bounded authenticity to their clients. When female sex workers offered this, they would call it the "girlfriend experience" in their ads. Many of the male sex workers that I spoke with boasted that the best purveyors of the "girlfriend experience" were actually men. As one sex worker that I interviewed insisted, "You'll hear people talk about 'cold, mechanical, detached.' But to me … it's like a sacred, wonderful, beautiful thing to do for other people and to get money for doing that."

Building off the idea of purchasing a "girlfriend experience," there are a number of commentators who say that we are undergoing a "pornification of society" where the boundaries between "normal life" and those of the world portrayed by sex workers are blurring. Does this idea have any resonance for you? If so, what do you think is behind this trend?

It's true that a significant transformation of public culture has occurred, one which is in need of more serious theorizing than the moralizing commentary of the Religious Right (and certain feminists) have offered. Two of the most tangible markers of the new public culture of sexual commerce have included the mainstreaming and ubiquity of pornography and the normalization of commercial sexual products for female consumers (e.g. lingerie, sex toys, and instructional videos). It should also be noted that, despite recent challenges posed by a rising tide of sexual conservatism, the sex workers' rights movement has continued to flourish.

But it is also important to recognize that the normalization of sexual commerce and the policing of the most "deviant" corners of the industry have occurred simultaneously. Notably, all of the developments that I list above occurred during the very same period when public streetwalking was being eliminated from major urban centers and a new global panic around Third World and child prostitutes was gathering steam. In New York City, at the very same moment that streetwalkers and porn stores were being banished by Rudolph Giuliani's infamous zoning ordinances, new members-only erotic events were being mainstreamed for a white, middle-class clientele, who crowded into upscale sex parties by the hundreds. At the same time that Times Square's Harmony Burlesque Theater was shut down, Victoria's Secret was replacing the district's "live nude girls" with mannequins posed as strippers and donning frankly pornographic lingerie. Meanwhile, the ethos of the strip club continued its spread into privatized spaces, as "cardio-striptease" and pole-dancing classes became staple features of the home video market and city gyms.

The simultaneous trends of greater normalization and greater policing are best explained by situating them in terms of broader post-industrial transitions, including the gentrification of urban space, transformations in intimate relations, and changing social norms around gender and sexuality – especially for the affluent middle classes.

There have been a number of scholars who have questioned whether sex work should be legalized and/or regulated. How did your research on sex workers influence your views on this question?

In recent decades, states and municipalities throughout North America, Australia, and Western Europe have sought to contain a burgeoning and diversifying sex trade through a variety of innovative measures – from stepped up enforcement against the perpetrators of "quality of life" crimes to the legalization of brothel keeping to increased client arrests. At the same time, "pro-sex" as well as "anti-prostitution" feminists have argued for an array of competing legal remedies, advocating on behalf of diverse forms of legalization or criminalization.

Few commentators, however, have situated their analyses within the context of post-industrial transformations of sexuality and culture. My comparative research in San Francisco, Amsterdam, and Stockholm (cities which employ three very different legal regimes) demonstrates that the failure to situate sexual commerce within a broader political-economic framework can lead advocates to argue for opposing tactics which, once implemented, might have surprisingly similar effects on the ground. Whether sex work is decriminalized, legalized, or criminalized, the interests of real estate developers, municipal and national politicians, and business owners may overshadow the concerns of feminists and sex workers.

What is arguably most remarkable about the disparate array of legal strategies that Europeans and North Americans have implemented in recent years is how singular they have been in effect: the overarching trend has been toward the elimination of prostitution from city streets, coupled with the state-facilitated (or de facto tolerated) flourishing of the indoor and online sectors of the sex trade. In San Francisco, Amsterdam, and Stockholm, three quite disparate versions of policy reform in the late 1990s resulted in a common series of alterations to the social geography of sexual commerce: the removal of economically disenfranchised and racially marginalized streetwalkers from gentrifying city centers; the de facto tolerance of a small tier of predominantly white and relatively privileged indoor sex workers; and the increased policing of illegal migrant workers, pushing them further underground. While the divergent components of national and local cultures, histories, and regulatory strategies are by no means irrelevant to the configuration of sexual commerce in these cities, the shared realities ushered in by larger patterns of political economy have been more definitive in shaping its predominant forms. In all three cases, the common focus of state interventions has been upon eliminating the visible manifestations of poverty and deviance (both racial and national) from urban spaces, rather than the exchange of sex for money per se.

What are you researching now?

My current research analyzes the social construction of "sex trafficking" in discourse and policy, both within the United States and transnationally. Over the course of the last decade, a good deal of political attention – but scant empirical research – has been dedicated to decrying "the traffic in women" as a dangerous manifestation of global gendered inequalities. Within the United States, the advocacy of evangelical Christian and secular feminist actors has served to grant the issue of human trafficking unprecedented prominence in both the Bush and the Obama administrations. In my new research, I take as a departure point my earlier research with migrant and domestic sex workers and the diverse social actors that attempt to regulate their movements. As an ethnographer, I have been attending state- and activist-sponsored policy meetings as well as evangelical Christian "pray-ins" in order to investigate the strategies and ambitions of the unlikely coalition of conservative Christians and feminist activists who have pressed this issue. The commitments and activities of these two groups are important to look at because they have produced policy transformations on a scale unparalleled since the White Slavery scare of the Progressive era.

Any final thoughts?

In most debates about the moral and social significance of sex work, commentators' own assumptions regarding the proper relationship between the spheres of sex, intimacy, and commerce are left unstated. Ethical and political evaluations of prostitution often apply an unstated norm by presuming it to consist of a timeless set of practices and meanings. I suggest instead that normative discussions of sexual labor begin with an understanding of the socially and historically specific meanings that affix to commercial sexual transactions and to intimacy and sexuality more generally. Practices of sexual commerce ought to be situated squarely within contemporary economic and cultural currents, rather than regarded as exceptions to be judged apart.

Notes

1 Pierre Bourdieu, *Distinction: A Social Critique of the Judgment of Taste* (Cambridge, MA: Harvard University Press, 1984: 372–73). In Bourdieu's work, the term "habitus" refers to socially specific capacities to think, feel, and act in particular ways. As such, the term connects individual and social levels of experience. For a brief discussion of the term and its usage in Bourdieu's work, see Loïc Wacquant, "Habitus," *International Encyclopedia of Economic Sociology* (2004).
2 See, for example, Daniel Bell, *The Cultural Contradictions of Capitalism* (1978), David Harvey, *The Condition of Postmodernity* (1990), Gøsta Esping-Andersen, *The Three Worlds of Welfare Capitalism* (1990), Robin Leidner, *Fast Food, Fast Talk* (1993), Sherrie Turkle, *Life on the Screen* (1995), and Manuel Castells, *The Information Age* (1997).

References

Hochschild, Arlie. 1983. *The Managed Heart*. Berkeley: University of California Press. Page 7.
——. 1997. *The Time Bind*. New York: Metropolitan Books. Page 221.

46

Sex sells, but what else does it do?

The American porn industry

Chris Pappas

UNIVERSITY OF MINNESOTA, MINNEAPOLIS

When I tell friends, family and students that I study pornography, the smiles and giggles are instantaneous. It is difficult to find the correct language to describe research on such a topic that cannot be converted into a joke about the stigmatized and deviant aspects of pornography consumption – for the comedians, it's as simple as placing methodological terms like "research," "investigate," "examine," etc. in quotation marks to shift their meanings from statements of scholarly interest and intent to confessions of "prurient interests." While I understand why people laugh, and often play up it to keep students' attention, I do feel that unfortunately it reproduces stereotypes about what is, in reality, one of the most crucial sites in debates over gender, sexuality, and culture. Pornography represents a vital and active mode through which pass various strands of thought, research, and practice about gender, sex, sexuality, culture, inequality, social movements, law, crime and deviance, politics, identities, media, morals, work, organizations, and economics. The depth, breadth, and diversity of topics and issues available through the study of pornography have often been cast as vicious polemics, wherein perspectives are often reduced to simplistic binaries. Much of what academics know about pornography comes from the "pornography debates" within feminism in the 1970s and 1980s, where pornography was cast as a causative factor in the subjugation and abuse of women. The shadow of these debates still looms large over the study of pornography, and in doing so complicates and even denies a productive research site wherein questions of the social construction of sexuality can be asked and answered.

In this brief chapter I contrast the conceptualization of pornography as a social problem (in both "traditional" obscenity-oriented and anti-pornography feminist perspectives) with contemporary perspectives that attempt to understand porn as a profitable and influential cultural industry. Special attention is paid to the production and consumption/reception of pornography, as well as to previous social scientific research of this controversial and continuously contested issue. I should note that my discussion here focuses exclusively on pornography in the American context; when seen in global perspective, many key dynamics change.

What is pornography?

I shall not today attempt further to define the kinds of material I understand to be embraced within that shorthand description; and perhaps I could never succeed in intelligibly doing so. *But I know it when I see it* ...

(*Supreme Court Justice Potter Stewart, Jacobellis v. Ohio, 1964, emphasis added*)

When most people try to define pornography, they usually focus their definitions on some sort of sexually explicit material intended to cause sexual arousal. However, within this relatively straightforward understanding lies a highly politicized and contentious struggle for meaning. More often than not, pornography is framed as a social problem, and is almost always connected to some notion of obscenity or otherwise unwanted behavior. Conservatives on the right claim that pornography contributes to moral decay and corruption; radical feminists on the left argue that pornography is a tool used to uphold the patriarchy, sexism, and the continued devaluation of women. In all of this, there seems to be little agreement on what actually constitutes pornography. Like Potter Stewart's infamous definition above, the boundaries of obscene and proper, sacred and profane, erotic and vulgar, always seem to be in flux; no-one can agree on the criteria which make something pornographic.

Another way to understand the issue can be gleaned from a stereotypical childhood experience. When first confronted with art appreciation in grade school, teachers and parents alike face an enormous amount of difficulty in explaining to their students/children the difference between naked and nude; that is, the difference between an objectionable and inappropriate presentation of unclothed human bodies and the proper and artistic, and thus highly valued, presentation of those same bodies. At a technical level, there is often very little that distinguishes one from the other. What the children are actually learning and – the parents and educators hope – internalizing, are the social and cultural norms surrounding morals and behaviors, but also coded understandings of power and social status: how to integrate one's own body, literally and figuratively, into the social body.

Of course, the difficulty in making distinctions between proper nudity and offensive pornography did not stop various people from trying to legislate such a distinction. In 1973 the US Supreme Court set the precedent for defining unprotected obscenity (Miller v. California). It utilized the "Miller Test," composed of three conditions: the "average person," applying "contemporary community standards," must find that the work "appeals to the prurient interest"; that the material in question depicts, "in a patently offensive way," sexual conduct; and, to be obscene, it must be found that "the work, taken as a whole, lacks serious literary, artistic, political, or scientific value" (the SLAPS test).

The problem here, of course, is that the components of the test are still vague and difficult to define in an analytical fashion. There can be endless debate about what constitutes the average person and how to determine what they would find offensive. It is not as if there has been a large, national survey asking people to rank various sexual practices. "Contemporary community standards" is a difficult concept because, as sociologists, we know that community standards are always changing – often faster than we think (or would like) – and that communities are usually composed of a vast amount of diverse ideas. And the "SLAPS" test leaves the door wide open for thorny debates about what constitutes literature, art, politics, or even value.

There was fierce debate over many sexually explicit films, like "sexploitation" films from the 1950s and 1960s such as Russ Meyer's *Faster Pussycat! Kill! Kill!*, and various sex-focused horror films, as well as sexually explicit art house films, mostly foreign, like those of Italian directors Fellini and Bertolucci, or Swedish director Vilgot Sjöman's *I Am Curious (Yellow)*. It should be noted, though, that while this list includes some of the greats of avant-garde cinema and newly ordained classics of retro-camp pop art, there were far more forgettable movies whose sole purpose was to make a buck showing nudity and sex, like fallacious foreign "documentaries," here in quotes because, while they marketed themselves as social scientific or otherwise academic movies about other cultures, they existed for no other reason than to show nudity and/or sex. Films could show all the racy subject matter they wanted, but throw in disingenuous warnings at the end so they could be claimed to have political or educational value. Such pretensions were nothing more than ways to defend against the SLAPS test. Think back to the grade-school students learning about art: it is hard enough to teach them the distinction between naked and nude, but now they must be taught to differentiate, say, art from pop culture, or literature from comic books, and so on. Such distinctions are constantly questioned in America these days, making it very hard to create such boundaries, much less enforce them.

Feminists define pornography

A similar attempt to define pornography came from second-wave (1960s and 1970s) feminists. During the early years of the women's movement, feminists had organized around a variety of economic, health, and social justice causes (wages and occupational choices, birth control, abortion, sexual violence, prostitution, etc.), but also around a variety of cultural issues. Arguing that aspects of American culture devalued women, feminists sought to challenge egregious examples of sexism in movies, books, music, and so on. Moreover, many feminists, a lot of them having previously worked on anti-sexual violence campaigns, claimed that such cultural symbols taught and reinforced notions of male supremacy and gender/sexual inequality, and that taken together they created a "rape culture," or a context wherein the sexual abuse of women was normalized and justified.

An obvious place to make such a case was the relatively new and rapidly expanding pornography industry. While pornography has existed in most societies throughout history, the 1970s saw the rise of the adult/XXX movie, as well as the peak of circulation for most pornographic magazines, and the spread of adult movie theaters, bookstores, and other sex-oriented businesses. Some feminists tried to make a distinction between "erotica" and pornography, the former being – to use the language of the period – a non-violent, egalitarian, loving form of sexually explicit material, as opposed to pornography's hateful, violent, exploitative version. Other feminists, most notably Andrea Dworkin and Catherine MacKinnon, attempted to pass anti-pornography ordinances in many cities that established pornography as a civil rights issue and gave women who participated in the making of pornography or who were abused due to pornography a way to challenge their abusers in court. The problem, again, was that the criteria used to define pornography could not be standardized. The same criteria used to ban pornographic films would also make many soap, shampoo, gym/fitness, and vacation commercials pornography. While many cities tried to pass such ordinances (Minneapolis, Indianapolis, Cambridge, MA, for example), they were always vetoed by mayors or struck down on First Amendment grounds.

To understand where the anti-pornography feminists were coming from, you may want to compare debates about pornography to contemporary debates about violence in TV and video games, or concerns over "gangsta rap" in the 1990s. The arguments follow a similar logic: that such cultural products cause unwanted behavior and contribute to social ills. In fact, in the 1980s, a lot of the then-groundbreaking research on media effects was used to bolster anti-pornography arguments. Data came mainly from psychologists, who tried to show that, in laboratory situations, men felt more animosity towards women after viewing pornography, especially pornography that was considered violent (Donnerstein 1984). However, by the mid-1980s, the media effects body of research had been unable to demonstrate any reliable effects that pornography had on attitudes and behavior towards women (Donnerstein, Penrod and Linz 1987). Indeed, the two most established and cited researchers began to criticize anti-pornography feminists for the ways in which they were interpreting and otherwise using their data. The "Meese Commission," initiated by Ronald Reagan in 1986 to examine the dangers of pornography, wherein many radical feminists testified alongside conservatives, had been severely criticized for being politically motivated and ignorant of the available data.

Who makes pornography, and who buys it?

Anne McClintock (1992) states: "Far from being simply a free-speech or private-fantasy issue, porn is a giant, high-profile, multi-billion dollar international business that draws on the most sophisticated electronic systems, vast personnel divisions, teams of technicians, secretaries and market analyzers, fleets of transport vehicles and global distribution networks" (McClintock 1992: 128). All of the controversy surrounding pornography, most of which attempts to condemn it, belies the fact that pornography remains one of the most popular, influential, and certainly profitable forms of pop culture. Estimates of the pornography industry's annual profits range from one to tens of billions of dollars, and most of those estimates don't even include internet pornography.

We can assume that access to pornography is a contributing factor here. While the only way to see pornographic films in the 1970s was to go to adult movie theaters and the like, the rise of the VCR, cable TV, and now the internet has given individuals easy access to sexually explicit material. In fact, it is often argued that pornography is the primary reason the VCR boom occurred, and that pornographic rentals make up the bulk of the video rental business. Indeed, the argument goes that pornography rentals are the only way independent "mom and pop" video stores can stay in business and compete with giant companies like Blockbuster; there is even a XXX version of Netflix, the popular DVD rental-by-mail service.

It is not just increased access that makes pornography so popular. While at one time those in the pornography industry – the actors and directors and so forth – were outcasts in the eyes of Hollywood and the American public, they are now fetishized, caricaturized and curious but still popular stars. In the 1980s, no one would admit to knowing a pornographic actor; today, people like Ron Jeremy and Jenna Jameson have large cult followings, best-selling books, are the subjects of documentaries, and have appeared in major Hollywood and TV projects. Even obscure figures like directors and producers such as Adam Glasser, aka "Seymour Butts," have starred in their own reality TV series.

This is all sociologically significant, as it indicates the importance sexual culture has to American culture overall. That is, the emergence of pornography as a massive industry, rather than an underground or criminal enterprise, shows the ways in which morals, beliefs, and in some cases sexual practices were changing. The phenomenon of the porn industry acts as a space wherein people negotiate, reinforce, or change their attitudes about what is right and wrong, normal and deviant, sexy and gross, etc., from what turns them on to how they identify.

Let's take an example. In the 1950s, Alfred Kinsey's research, published in 1947 and 1953, brought sexuality to the forefront of debate in America, unintentionally causing a shift in attitudes and behavior that would become better known as the "Sexual Revolution." Kinsey's work, while methodologically flawed, caused an immense public debate about the sexual morals and practices of America; citizens were shocked to read about the high rates of extra- and pre-marital sex, homosexuality, and a variety of other stigmatized sexual practices and identities. In the same year as Kinsey's volume on the sexuality of women (1953), Hugh Hefner launched *Playboy*; the first issue, containing nude images of Marilyn Monroe, sold out in record time. Taking his cues from Kinsey, Hefner wanted to bring what he considered "real" sexuality to the American male, and wanted to see more openness about sex and sexuality than the conservative morals of the day allowed. While his actions drew extreme controversy, the magazine went on to have a monthly circulation in the millions. Following Hefner's initial success, and in a relatively short time, the pornography industry, once an underground network of petty thieves and social outcasts, established itself as a major commercial and cultural force, highly organized and increasingly accepted as legitimate. As for Hefner, he succeeded in creating a new and influential form of masculinity that incorporated new attitudes about sexuality and consumer behavior; the now-clichéd joke about "reading it for the articles" seems to be truer than most think. *Playboy* was not simply about the pictures; through its editorial content, journalism, articles, and advertisements, the magazine acted as a primer for men whose social roles had been shaken up by the vast changes brought about in the post-World War Two era. The sex industry, *Playboy* in this case, gave men the ability to claim identities in which sex and sexuality were normal and everyday, not just the domain of the stereotypical patron of peep shows – "raincoaters" in the pornographic vernacular.

Consumers of pornography

If we want to argue that pornography had become the domain of "normal" citizens and their "everyday" lives, as opposed to the domain of perverts and deviants, then we should know who consumed pornography. A cursory look at the General Social Survey (GSS), a large, national, representative survey of opinions and attitudes, shows that while attitudes about pornography have remained somewhat similar over the last twenty or so years, the number of people who have seen a pornographic film has steadily increased, this amidst the culturally accepted (but possibly changing) notion that no one talks about or admits to using pornography. (Although, with the pornography industry releasing somewhere in the neighborhood of 15,000 films per year – again, not including internet content – it almost seems impossible not to see a XXX movie these days.) It is for these very reasons – stigma and so on – that the GSS is still not the best way to get data about pornography's audience. Indeed, there is no adequate data source that can account for pornography's audience beyond the market data that tells us that it sells very well.

However, we do know that pornography's audience is not exclusively male – women have become the fastest-growing audience for pornography. They remain the most coveted demographic that pornography producers want to attract, so much so that major changes in the content of pornography have occurred. That is, the sex industry began to shy away from its status as an exclusively straight male domain, and began to market its products towards couples – note the shift in language from sex toy to "marital aid." (However, the debate over whether this shift from men-only to couples porn has been substantial beyond industry PR rhetoric is suspect, due to the limits of the available data.) Gay and lesbian pornography is also very popular and profitable, and increasingly accepted in the mainstream of the industry. In fact, there is a pornographic product for almost any social category and any sexual fetish, identity or passing interest that one could conjure, from racial and ethnic groups to various types of role playing and so forth.

The production of pornography

However, just because the industry creates products for these groups does not mean that the representations are always genuine, egalitarian, or fair. The pornography industry has traditionally been very racist, so much so that people who performed with African-American actors were blacklisted and cast out of the industry. Representations of racial and ethnic sexualities remain extremely stereotypical and often offensive, as do many representations of sexual minorities and certain fetishes. This is not to say that all representations are unfair, or that things have not changed. Various African-American, Latino, and Asian actors have recently become highly-paid superstars, and minority-owned and controlled production companies have sprung up.

The other surprising finding about the making of pornography is that it remains one of the few professions wherein women make a lot more money than men. In fact, women performers wield a great deal of power: they choose who they perform with, what they will do, when they will work, and in some cases they name their salary. Men, on the other hand, are for the most part subject to the women's decisions, and make on average about one-half to two-thirds less than most women (Faludi 1999: ch. 10 gives a fascinating overview of the gender dynamics of the porn industry). This phenomenon is recent, and in stark contrast to the porn industry's beginnings. In the 1970s, only those who produced and distributed films made money. The performers and directors, mostly either struggling actors or sexual libertines, made next to nothing. A particularly significant horror story from this era comes from Linda Lovelace (real last name Marchiano), porn's first superstar from its first critical/financial success (*Deep Throat*, in 1972) who testified many times and published books claiming that she had been forced, sometimes at gunpoint, to perform by her abusive husband, one of the film's producers. Throughout the 1980s actors in the industry were treated unfairly through low wages, unfair contracts, and little protection against various health risks (causing heroic efforts by women in the industry to establish support services for medical and mental health). Nowadays, due to the increasing popularity and profitability of the industry, the collective effort of various advocates and activists inside and out of the industry, and the entrepreneurial dealings of various major stars, working conditions remain for the most part fair.

Some people find women's participation in pornography, both as part of the audience and as part of the production, to be empowering, and argue that it demonstrates the importance of women controlling their own sexuality. Others argue that the higher wages exist only because women still have to exploit themselves to make money. Cornell (2000) collects the most important pieces from all sides of the debates. Duggan and Hunter (1995) offer arguments in favor of women participating in pornography. Dworkin and MacKinnon (1988) offer reasons against. But through the debates we again see the sociological significance of pornography. Like the schoolchildren learning the norms of social behavior at the city art gallery, controversies around pornography give us insight into how this form of popular culture reinforces, liberates, or otherwise affects our understandings of power and the social order.

Conclusion

I began by discussing the history of contemporary pornography through the lens of various legal attempts to define and regulate it, and placed this in the context of the feminist debates about pornography. While both of these perspectives are crucial for understanding pornography – indeed, the free speech and violence debates have been nearly synonymous with the study of pornography since the time of the Cold War – new perspectives on pornography need not reproduce these historical debates; there is little to say that has not been said. This is not to say that such concerns are not important – censorship remains an unfortunate political reality in America, and sexual violence a disturbing and appalling social reality. However, as we continue to acquire quality data about pornography, we can more accurately analyze its overall significance and influence; with better tools and better information, we may be able to shed new light on such phenomena. Part of this new approach involves taking pornography seriously as a massive, highly organized popular industry, and treats with equal respect those who watch, buy, produce, and protest against pornography as important players in a field that, in relatively quick time, has become one of the primary arenas wherein social power (and social inequality), social pleasure (and social pain), and social identities (and social anonymities) are negotiated, arranged, and enforced, a site where we can witness the construction and maintenance of the sexual lives of American citizens and American culture.

References

Cornell, Druscilla. 2000. *Feminism and Pornography*. Oxford: Oxford University Press.

Donnerstein, Edward. 1984. "Pornography: Its Effects on Violence Against Women", in Neil Malamuth and Edward Donnerstein (eds), *Pornography and Sexual Aggression*. Orlando, FL: Academic Press.

Donnerstein, Edward, Steven Penrod and Daniel Linz. 1987. *The Question of Pornography: Research Finding and Policy Implications*. New York: The Free Press.

Duggan, Lisa and Nan D. Hunter (eds). 1995. *Sex Wars: Essays in Sexual Dissent and American Politics*. New York: Routledge.

——1997. *Sex Wars: Sexual Dissent and Political Culture*. New York: Routledge.

Dworkin, Andrea and Catherine A. MacKinnon. 1988. *Pornography and Civil Rights: A New Day for Women's Equality*. Minneapolis, MN: Organizing Against Pornography.

Faludi, Susan. 1999. *Stiffed: The Betrayal of the American Man*. New York: William Morrow.

McClintock, Anne. 1992. "Gonad the Barbarian and the Venus Flytrap: Portraying the Male and Female Orgasm", in Lynne Segal and Mary McIntosh (eds), *Sex Exposed: Sexuality and the Pornography Debate*. New Brunswick, NJ: Rutgers University Press.

47

Sex workers

Interview with Wendy Chapkis

UNIVERSITY OF SOUTHERN MAINE, PORTLAND

Wendy Chapkis is an Associate Professor of Women's Studies and Sociology at the University of Southern Maine. She is editor of two anthologies published by the Transnational Institute in Amsterdam, *Loaded Questions: women in the military* (1979) and *Of Common Cloth: women in the global textile industry* (co-edited with Cynthia Enloe; 1983), and author of two books, *Beauty Secrets: women and the politics of appearance* (South End Press; 1985) and *Live Sex Acts: women performing erotic labor* (Routledge; 1997). Her current research is on medical marijuana use and the "War on Drugs" (*Dying to Get High*; co-authored with Richard Webb, New York University Press, forthcoming).

How is it that you came to study sex workers?

I don't really see myself as "studying sex workers." That sounds too much like Dian Fossey studying the great apes. I think of myself as studying the practices and meanings of prostitution for women.

Like most women of my generation, I grew up with my mother's understanding that sex was about both pleasure and danger. What defined sex was male pleasure and what haunted sex was the risk to women of rape, pregnancy, and loss of reputation.

I came of age twenty years later than my mother, in the late 1960s and early 1970s. The difference was profound. In a time of free love and women's liberation, the innocence of virginity was far less compelling than carnal knowledge. And in the age of the pill and legal abortion, some of the dangers associated with sex seemed to recede. But while free love might have been packaged as a revolutionary practice, getting paid for it was not. Despite my misgivings about the practice, I was pretty sure that it was an incomplete understanding of exploitation to define it as someone getting paid for what I was willing to do for free. While men clearly benefited from the institution of prostitution, I wondered who benefited from making criminals of women charging for sex.

How did your sociological and feminist colleagues respond to your research interests?

I started formally studying sex work while in graduate school in the 1980s and early 1990s, at the University of California at Santa Cruz. At least one of my mentors in sociology feared that I was turning away from serious issues (such as global economic inequality) to focus on sex – though of course the two are deeply interconnected. Perhaps he was just concerned that I would make myself unmarketable after first publishing a book about women and beauty standards and then following it up with a dissertation about commercial sex. In general, though, sociology has been pretty receptive to my work. I have experienced somewhat more hostility within feminist circles, including some versions of women's studies.

Why did you choose to study sex work in Amsterdam, the Netherlands?

I have a complex and long-standing connection with the Netherlands. During my undergraduate studies, I enrolled at the University of Amsterdam for a year. Then, after graduation, I returned to the Netherlands for most of a decade (from the mid-1970s to the mid-1980s) to work at the Institute for Policy Studies' international center – the Transnational Institute in Amsterdam. I was both impressed with and infuriated by Dutch culture. On the one hand, it offered a hopeful contrast to the United States of the Reagan years: the Netherlands was a successful social democracy with a deep commitment to both collective responsibility (in the form of a generous welfare state resulting in low rates of poverty) and individual rights (demonstrated through the de facto decriminalization of marijuana use and prostitution). It had a vibrant women's movement. But it also had the lowest rates of female employment in Western Europe. Dutch national identity emphasized "tolerance" but, at the same time, my experience living in the Netherlands as a woman with a moustache was one of unremitting and very public harassment.

When I returned to the United States in 1985 to attend graduate school, I had no sense that the Netherlands would figure prominently in my future research. But as I became reacquainted with sexual politics in the US, I began to draw comparisons between the two settings. America in the 1980s was enmeshed in the so-called "sex wars," with feminists deeply divided over commercial sex. I had just come from a decade in a country with both an active women's movement and a very visible and legal prostitution sector.

As I began developing a research focus for my dissertation, I decided to confront head-on my own ambivalence about prostitution, to begin to examine why commercial sex had become such a central issue in contemporary feminist politics, and to explore whether prohibition of prostitution (which made criminals out of participants) in fact improved the lives of prostitutes in the US. The Netherlands, with its decriminalized prostitution sector, seemed like a perfect counter-example for purposes of comparison.

Can you talk about some of the problems you encountered researching sex workers? For example, was it difficult to gain their trust and did you have to get approval by any government agencies?

Fortunately, neither in the US nor in the Netherlands are government agencies in a position to decide whether sex workers are allowed to speak with researchers. The only state officials I worried about were law enforcement officers in the United States – and then only because I was concerned that the women I interviewed were admitting to engaging in criminal conduct. For that reason, I asked all of my interview subjects whether they wanted to be known by name or to remain anonymous. For safety reasons – that is, to reduce the possibility of police harassment – many of the women I interviewed in the US did ask to be anonymous. Some Dutch sex workers, though far fewer, also requested anonymity; sex work might be legal in the Netherlands but it is still stigmatized.

Trust is, of course, critical in such circumstances. I wouldn't have had any access if the women I wished to interview didn't have some measure of confidence in me as an ally. I worked hard to establish my credentials as a feminist advocate of prostitutes' rights before I began soliciting interviews. In the town in which I lived in California, for example, I organized a political alliance between sex workers and (other) feminist activists to protest against police raids on the local massage parlors. Regardless of our views on prostitution (and they were very mixed within the alliance), we all agreed that closing women's places of employment did nothing to empower them and, in fact, meant that many of them had to resort to working in more isolated and dangerous settings – out of their own homes or on the streets.

Similarly, when I returned to the Netherlands in 1993 to do comparative research, I volunteered with the Dutch prostitutes' rights organization, the Red Thread, as a way to be of service before asking for their time and their experiences.

I can't imagine skipping that step and simply approaching women working the streets, out of their homes, behind the windows, or in the clubs, and asking for an interview, without first having made clear what was at stake for me and offering to be of use. Once I had begun doing interviews, sex workers referred others to me.

I was fully aware that, by establishing access through work with activist organizations, my sample was skewed toward women who were politically involved and who tended to see their involvement in prostitution as work. I attempted to deal with this bias both by being explicit about it in my writing and by making a conscious effort to find women who did not share that sense of commercial sex as potentially empowered work. For example, I contacted the Dutch anti-trafficking organization, the STV, and asked them to provide me with interview data with women who had been victims of forced prostitution. Those interviews were the only ones I did not conduct myself but rather gathered through the organization's own staff; trust and familiarity were clearly critically important for women in situations of forced prostitution.

But it is also important to say that I believe sex workers share their stories with researchers not only because they trust us but also because they see us as useful to them. A common misconception is that sex workers are passive objects used by clients and by scholars for our own pleasures and purposes. In fact, of course, sex workers are also active subjects with their own set of interests. I was well aware that sex workers were using me to help get their stories out, to build sympathy and greater respect for those in prostitution, and – in the United States – to help make the case that their lives were made more difficult and more dangerous by the criminalization of their trade.

What ideas did you have about sex workers before you began your research, and did this change in the course of your research?

My ideas about sex workers have always been complicated and often contradictory. Before I began talking with women in the trade, I imagined some of them to be women with very restricted options motivated by desperation (for money or drugs) and forced by circumstance to surrender control over their bodies to dangerous strangers. I also often imagined some of them to be proudly renegade women who were sexual outlaws, women who made conscious and instrumental use of men's ability and desire to pay for sex, who embraced the stigma of the whore and rejected the social controls meant to discipline women's erotic lives. What I found once I entered the field was that both of these representations are true and that neither is adequate. Women's lives are rarely models of complete victimization or absolute empowerment. Prostitutes are no exception.

How did sex workers understand selling sex? Were they really able to approach their work as "just work"?

This kind of question is impossible to answer. There is no one understanding among sex workers of what it is to sell sex or even what it would mean to say that something was "just work." I believe the question arises in part because of a widespread sense that sex is uniquely difficult to commodify and that the process of doing so necessarily causes unique distress to the worker involved. But it is my sense that it is not the exchange of sex for money that is the cause of most of the difficulty within prostitution; instead it is the poor conditions under which that exchange takes place.

In addition, like many forms of service work, prostitution involves some measure of emotional labor. The challenges of performing emotional labor in other fields have been well described (see Arlie Hochschild's *The Managed Heart*,[1] for example). Some workers are more effective at establishing and maintaining emotional boundaries in those professions than are others. And, because prostitution – like all service work – is interactive, much depends on the behavior of the client. If a client is respectful and demands no more than what has been negotiated, the ability to create and maintain boundaries is enhanced. The intensity of the work also affects how well a worker can maintain a sense of the job as manageable. Working too many hours, seeing too many clients, earning too little money, or being treated with disrespect, all can contribute to worker distress.

But here I must emphasize that it is crucial to recognize that these challenges are not unique to prostitution. Most work shares some of these challenges, especially stigmatized or low-status work, work in the service sector or underground economy, and work that is physically and emotionally demanding. To imagine otherwise undermines our ability to understand prostitution as work and to imagine how to improve the conditions under which it is practiced.

Do you have a sense of how being a sex worker affected their sexual and social relationships outside of work?

I do think that "relationship strain" is an occupational hazard facing many sex workers. A sex worker has to create a clear distinction for herself and her partner between work and intimacy. Even if this is possible for the worker herself, her partner may struggle with it. In addition, the "whore" stigma clearly affects how sex workers are perceived outside of work by those who know what kind of work they do. A sex worker has to deal with both titillation and condemnation.

Could you describe a typical day at work for one of the sex workers you studied?

I find myself resisting this question. It feels both voyeuristic and impossible to fully answer. No single sex worker is representative, no particular form of sex work is "typical." Those differences among sex workers are more characteristic than the details of any one sex worker's day. Among the women I interviewed for *Live Sex Acts*,[2] a typical day was waiting for the phone to ring, talking to some guy, and hoping he shows up (Samantha working out of her home); watching the mirrors that reflect the action on the street to decide if you want to encourage a potential client or instead to turn your back, to apply more lipstick, and to wait until he passes by (Ans working behind the windows in Amsterdam); working the afternoon shift in a place with no windows, chatting up a few clients and realizing you'll have to get them drunk to at least make some money off the bar (Jo doing time in a "really chic" sex club); working the streets all night giving quick blow jobs and discovering you can make more money if you pack a dildo and pretend to be a boy instead of the underage girl you actually are who is trying to get enough money together to leave a sexually abusive home (Sandy discussing being a teenage streetworker); trying to give head in a photogenic fashion under hot lights and really enjoying the challenge of trying to make it all look effortless (Nina on the porn set); scheduling five, or maybe at most ten, clients in a whole week for a lengthy sensuous massage session where the men know that they are entering your temple and must behave respectfully (Vision). There is no typical form of sex work, no typical sex worker.

Are there differences between sex workers in the Netherlands and in the United States?

This question too is difficult to answer. The problem with the question is that there are enormous differences between sex workers within each of those countries; which American sex worker and which Dutch sex worker should we take as the model in order to compare them with each other?

It is more useful to discuss the important differences in national context, in the social and political conditions under which sex work is practiced. The Netherlands has a reasonably intact social welfare system that provides at least basic support for all legal residents of the country, including housing assistance and healthcare. Drug addiction is understood to be a medical not a moral or criminal problem, and assistance to addicts is available. Dutch women working in prostitution are therefore less likely than their American counterparts to be doing so simply to survive. On the other hand, in many large Dutch cities – such as Amsterdam – many sex workers are not legal residents but rather undocumented immigrants who do not have access to the Dutch social welfare safety net. In addition, many migrant sex workers must earn enough money in the trade not only to support themselves but to send much needed income to family members in their home country.

The most important difference between the practice of prostitution in the Netherlands and in the US is the legal status of the trade: sex work is legal and regulated in the Netherlands while it is prohibited and criminalized in the US (except for several counties in Nevada). In the context of legal prostitution, the police become a potential resource for sex workers rather than an additional risk. When prostitution is legal, sex workers can discuss fully and openly with clients what services are provided (and what are not) and at what price. In the US, sex workers must negotiate in haste in an attempt to avoid police entrapment and arrest.

Once again, however, the advantages of legal prostitution exist only for legal residents of the Netherlands. The many undocumented migrants working in the Dutch sex trade have none of those protections. For them, much like their American counterparts, the police are feared, and deportation, if not arrest, is a constant risk.

Feminists have been divided in their view of women's sex work. Some see it as another form of gender exploitation, while others see it as an issue of women's worker rights. Where do you stand on this debate?

The short answer is that it is both another form of gender exploitation and an issue of worker's rights. It is surely not a coincidence that the vast majority of clients are male while the majority of sex workers are female. Prostitution is yet another social arena in which women perform undervalued service work, work that serves men.

But one of the crucial points here is that prostitution is far from unique in this respect. Women are over-represented throughout the service sector and under-represented in higher-paying occupations. I find it very unhelpful to separate out sex work as if it were uniquely exploitive of women.

In this area of women's work, it is crucial that women be allowed to organize, publicly to demand their rights as workers, to insist on the dignity and respect owed any worker, owed any woman. That is made much, much, more difficult when sex work is criminalized and relegated to the underground economy.

And yes, sex work is also about sex. Women and sex are closely linked in our culture – women's sexual status is still defining for many women: virgins, wives, and mothers have a protected status denied to sluts, dykes, and whores. Sex, in other words, is used to separate the good and virtuous from the bad and disposable.

This is a distinction that feminists have been fighting for decades. I believe that it is imperative for the current generation of women's rights activists to recognize that, as long as a woman is prohibited from deciding the terms under which she will engage in sexual activity – whether for pleasure or profit or reproduction – no woman is free. In other words, the struggle of sex workers for legal rights and cultural respect is a shared struggle. We all lose when a whore is a woman who deserves whatever she gets and when a sexually active woman is an object of ridicule unless she is engaged in satisfying her conjugal and reproductive duty.

What do you see as the prospects for a sex worker rights movement in the US?

The movement is well underway. Sex workers in this country have been engaged in collective political action since at least 1973 when COYOTE (the San Francisco-based sex worker self-advocacy organization) was formed. COYOTE and other sex worker rights' organizations around the country continue to demand the decriminalization of sex work, improved working conditions, and respect for the men and women performing erotic labor.

In the past decade, at least one group of sex workers in the US successfully unionized and gained collective representation – the exotic dancers at the San Francisco club, the Lusty Lady.[3] The workers not only won union representation in 1996, but in 2003 they bought the business and created a sex worker cooperative. But many forms of sex work are much more difficult to unionize both because most sex work is criminalized in the US and because, even in the legal sectors such as exotic dancing and pornography, workers are most often considered "independent contractors" rather than employees. For this reason, much of contemporary sex worker organizing has been grassroots, informal and educational.

Over the past twenty years, sex workers have begun to add their own voices to those of researchers in writing accounts of the sex trade.[4] In addition, sex workers are writing and publishing magazines directed at those in the trade, including such periodicals as *Danzine*, *Spread*, and *Hook*.

Clearly, sex workers are continuing to come out and, in the process, are making clear that there is no clear and easy distinction between "them" and "us." And it seems to me that Third-Wave feminists seem to be heeding the call to link feminist campaigns for control over our own bodies to the struggles of sex workers for self-determination.

Of course, all of this is happening in the midst of a well-organized anti-sex moral panic in this country, as evidenced by abstinence-only sex "education" in the public schools, the continuing refusal of the FDA to approve over-the-counter sales of the morning-after pill; attacks on abortion rights; new laws prohibiting equal marital rights for same-sex couples; the Bush Administration's policy of denying funding to international family planning, AIDS, and anti-sex-trafficking organizations which support a woman's right to an abortion or which refuse to condemn the practice of prostitution. Clearly sex worker organizing – like all organizing around sexual rights – is facing powerful resistance.

But sex workers, like others engaged in intentionally non-reproductive sex, will not accept state-mandated second-class citizenship. Despite recent right-wing successes in seizing control of the state apparatus, this is not a stable moment for reactionary politics. The right's embrace of violence, repression, and religious intolerance depends too much on fear. Fear is not an emotion that can be mobilized indefinitely. The wheel is turning; a politics that offers more than fear and that acknowledges complexity not moral certainty will return. And I see sex workers among those who are on the front line of a politics of social justice, compassion, and pleasure.

Notes

1 Hochschild, Arlie (2003) *The Managed Heart: Commercialization of Human Feeling*, University of California Press.
2 Chapkis, Wendy (1997) *Live Sex Acts: Women Performing Erotic Labor*, Routledge.
3 Query, Julia and Vicky Funari (2000) *Live Nude Girls Unite*. Documentary film distributed by First Run Features.
4 For example, see contributions by sex workers to the following anthologies: Delacoste, Frederique and Priscilla Alexander (eds) (1998) *Sex Work*, Cleis Press; Nagle, Jill (ed.) (1997) *Whores and Other Feminists*, Routledge; Whisnant, Rebecca and Christine Stark (eds) (2005) *Not for Sale*, Spinifex Press. See also autobiographical monographs by sex workers, such as: Burana, Lily (2003) *Strip City*, Miramax Books; Eaves, Elizabeth (2004) *Bare*, Seal Press; Egan, Danielle (2005) *Dancing for Dollars, Paying for Love*, Palgrave Macmillan; Sprinkle, Annie (1998) *Post-Porn Modernist*, Cleis Press; Tea, Michelle (2004) *Rent Girl*, Last Gasp Press.

48

Conflicts at the tubs

Bathhouses and gay culture and politics in the United States

Jason Hendrickson

STATE UNIVERSITY OF NEW YORK AT ALBANY

Gay bathhouses, affectionately referred to as "the tubs," are commercial establishments where men gather for sexual encounters. They can be found in many large and medium-size US cities, and operate as private membership clubs. Bathhouse patrons pay a nominal membership fee and then can choose to rent either a locker, to store their clothing, or a private room, typically equipped with a small bed, a nightstand and a hook for hanging clothing. The amenities inside bathhouses often include saunas, steam rooms, stages for live performances, video screens upon which pornography is projected, and small gyms. Today, some bathhouses have even added high-speed internet connections to the services they offer. In the US, bathhouses have served as meeting places for men interested in sex with other men since at least the turn of the twentieth century. They have played an important part in the development of modern gay identities, politics and culture.

Inside the bathhouse

Bathhouses are organized around the pursuit of sex. Consider, for example, the physical layout of most bathhouses. The interior of the typical bathhouse is a labyrinth of hallways lined with private rooms that encourages a constant flow of men, usually clad only in the towels wrapped around their waists. The often continuous parade of men cruising the hallways provides a steady stream of potential partners. Some men choose to stay in the rooms that line the hallways. These men usually sit or lie on the beds inside the private rooms, with their doors left open so that the passing men can view them and they can check out the passing men. Every bend in the hallway or open door offers the promise of more potential sexual partners.

Verbal communication in bathhouse hallways is kept to a minimum. Too much chatter in the areas of the bathhouse set aside for sexual encounters could shatter the erotic ambiance. Men visiting bathhouses have developed a unique system of codes and cues that allow people to negotiate sex with minimal verbal communication. Sexual encounters are initiated and negotiated largely through a number of non-verbal cues. For example, sustaining eye contact is a sign of sexual interest. When a man sees someone in whom he's interested, he will fix his gaze on the man. If the man returns and holds the gaze, it's an indication that he shares the attraction. Breaking eye contact indicates that a man is not interested in a sexual encounter with a particular person.

Not everyone in the bathhouse is cruising the hallways. As we have seen, some men choose to sit or lie on beds inside the private rooms with the doors left open. Here, too, a system of signs has been developed to help them negotiate sexual encounters. The position in which a man is lying inside his room usually indicates what type of sexual experience he's seeking. Likewise, whatever sex toys or other sexual paraphernalia (for example, dildos, bondage equipment) a man has on display in his room is an indication of his sexual tastes.

While bathhouses are organized around the pursuit of sex, many men develop non-sexual relationships there as well. Indeed, for some men, bathhouses serve as a social hub and a source of new friends. Patrons who frequent a bathhouse on a regular basis sometimes form and maintain friendships with other regular patrons. Bathhouses provide many spaces not usually geared toward sex – for instance, lounges, snack bars and sunning decks. These areas provide bathhouse patrons with other social spaces, when they are not engaged in sexual pursuits. Here, men can communicate more freely without disturbing the sexual atmosphere of the areas primarily dedicated to sexual pursuits. Many men spend a good portion of their time in the bathhouse catching up with the friends they've made there in the spaces set apart from the primary cruising areas. Indeed, for some men, bathhouses serve many of the same social functions as bars. Bathhouses are places where men can both meet new people and catch up with friends. In this way, bathhouses serve a variety of needs – sexual and social – for many gay men.

Bathhouses and gay identity

Bathhouses played a central role in the development of a distinct homosexual, and later a gay, identity in the US. In the early twentieth century, most people did not consider themselves heterosexual or homosexual, straight or gay. During that period, being a "real man" or a "real woman" was what was important. Sexual attraction and desire were thought to be an expression of gender. As historian George Chauncey (1994) has documented, in New York City in the early part of the century, the sexual world was divided along gender lines into "fairies" and "normals." Fairies were effeminate men who desired sex with "normal," non-effeminate men. Having sex with fairies did not imply a distinct homosexual or gay identity for "normal" men. Bathhouses contributed to the emergence of distinctions based on the gender of one's partner – the emergence of heterosexual and homosexual identities – over distinctions based on a person's gender performance.

Bathhouses offered gay men a relatively safe place where they could meet and forge ties with other gay men. Outside of bathhouses, gay men often risked harassment, blackmail, and violence. Inside bathhouses, gay men were shielded from police who might harass or arrest them, hustlers who sought to exploit them, and violence that could result from approaching the wrong man. It was within the protected space of bathhouses that gay men came to value sex with other gay men and where they were able to form social connections with one another (Chauncey 1994).

The mid-century saw an increase in the persecution of gays and lesbians. In the post-World War Two period, gays were fired from their jobs, exposed in local newspapers, and represented in the media as menacing threats to children, the family, and the nation. The public places where gays and lesbians gathered came under attack. Bars that catered to gays could have their liquor licenses revoked. Parks and other cruising grounds came under intense surveillance. Gay men arrested in bars, parks, or other places for offenses such as solicitation or lewd behavior – the charges that police often used against gay men – could lose their jobs, families, and their standing within their communities. Through all of this, bathhouses continued to provide a relatively safe and secure place for gay men to meet other gay men for sex and socializing (Berube 1996).

The gay movement that emerged in the late 1960s and early 1970s fundamentally transformed the meaning of homosexuality. In the early post-war years, homosexuality was most often viewed as a sickness, a sin, or a crime. Gay men and lesbians, influenced by the social movements of the 1960s, turned their sexual identities into a source of pride. This movement demanded public visibility for gays. "Coming out" – publicly declaring one's sexual identity – became the ultimate political act. In this context, gays began to form distinct gay areas in many cities. The number of gay bathhouses proliferated during the 1970s as gays developed areas that catered to their interests. For many gay men, bars and bathhouses became the center of social life. Many gays of this generation saw bathhouses as a place where new forms of intimacy and sexuality could be explored. As we'll see, this view was not shared by all.

While gay bathhouses have occupied a prominent place within the development of gay culture and communities, they have also generated much conflict and debate. Some gays have viewed bathhouses as a site of sexual freedom and creativity, while others have viewed them as reproducing standard and repressive forms of sexuality. Bathhouses have served as sites for debate over sexual repression and liberation, gender, the proper and effective response to the AIDS epidemic and, indeed, the meaning and place of sex and sexuality. The place of bathhouses in gay culture and politics has been rife with conflict, as will be made clear below.

Bathhouses and sexual liberation

The gay movement that emerged in the late 1960s and early 1970s did not merely wish to legitimize gays alongside heterosexuals; it sought fundamentally to change the meaning and place of sexuality and intimacy in society. Many gay activists of this period were critical of what they viewed as a repressive sexual regime. Gay activists wished to develop a sexually liberated society by challenging repressive sexual norms.

A sexually liberated society was thought of as one in which sexuality would be diffused throughout society. Gay activists at this time believed that sex could serve as the basis for a number of different types of relationships. They shunned monogamy, which they viewed as an alienating exercise of ownership that reduced partners to property. Sex, according to these activists, should not be viewed through the lens of property relationships. Rather, it should be seen as an activity that promotes intimacy and connectedness. These activists viewed sex as a pathway to intimacy rather than as an expression of intimacy. They asked: If sex is a pathway to intimacy, why not use it to create more intimate bonds with more people? The bonds of intimacy achieved through sex could serve as the foundation for an entire community. In this context, some viewed bathhouses as a place where relationships based on intimacy and sexuality could generate a sense of belonging and community.

Gay liberationists at this time were also intent on exploring pleasures and the body. Liberationists were often critical of a sexual regime that narrowed and limited sensual and sexual expression to the genitals and to orgasms. Bathhouses and other public cruising grounds such as backroom bars, sex clubs, and the like were often touted as laboratories for creating new forms of unrepressed sexuality (Moore 2004). Many gay men, for example, explored sadomasochism (SM) in the bathhouses, sex clubs, and backroom bars that catered to SM interests. SM advocates often claim that pleasure is not focused solely on genitals, nor is it always, or even usually, achieved through orgasm. In SM, the entire body, not just the genitals, can be an erogenous zone. As well, relations of power between SM partners and the esthetics of SM can be eroticized.

For some gay men of this time, then, bathhouses were places where repressive sexual norms could be challenged and where new types of relationship and forms of pleasure could emerge. At the very least, bathhouses represented for some people a place where they could explore and celebrate their sexuality without apology, and in the company of others who felt the same (Bell 1979).

Gender

Not all gay activists believed that bathhouses could serve as a site of sexual liberation. Bathhouses cater primarily, if not exclusively, to men, and some activists argued that bathhouses and other sexual cruising grounds promoted a narrow, masculine approach to sexuality (Blevins 1977). According to these critics, bathhouses encouraged a pleasure-oriented approach to sex. This approach was thought to separate sex from emotional connection and meaningful relationship outside of sex. The activity in bathhouses was organized around quick, anonymous, and impersonal encounters that were unlikely to lead to the vision of sex and intimacy championed by gay liberationists.

Bathhouses promote objectification and alienation, according to critics. The types of encounters that take place in bathhouses reduce the participants to mere bodies and body parts to be used for easy sexual gratification without any significant emotional, intimate, or social connection. These critics also point to the terms that gay men use to refer to their sexual partners as evidence of sexual objectification. Sexual partners are often described as "numbers" or "tricks," terms that don't acknowledge a partner's subjectivity. Men evaluate each other exclusively in terms of their physical attractiveness. Those who do not meet expected standards of sexual attractiveness, or those who are considered too old, are marginalized and often ignored. Also, critics argued that this approach to sexuality alienates people from themselves (Blevins 1977). In bathhouses, men in pursuit of sexual gratification use their own bodies as tools. They are not encouraged to explore their thoughts and feelings about sex, intimacy, relationships, or community. If men in bathhouses are treating themselves and their partners as mere instruments, they are unlikely to create new types of relationships and new forms of community based on intimacy and pleasure.

Not all gay activists viewed sexual objectification as necessarily bad. Objectification was bad, some activists argued, only when it becomes static and non-reciprocal – for instance, when men always objectify women and women always remain sexual objects, never subjects (Wittman 1992). Those who defended bathhouses against charges that they encouraged sexual objectification argued that people should be able to enjoy being both sexual objects and subjects.

AIDS

While bathhouses generated a fair amount of conflict during the 1970s, the emergence of AIDS in the early 1980s intensified and increased the urgency of debates about bathhouses. Even before the HIV virus had been identified or the routes of its transmission were known, it appeared that AIDS was sexually transmitted and people were being encouraged to limit the number of their sexual partners and change their sexual practices. By the mid-1980s the role of bathhouses in the transmission of HIV became the topic of much heated debate. Were bathhouses the site of sexual freedom, or the site of disease and contagion? Were placing restrictions upon or closing bathhouses warranted for public health reasons, or were such measures a homophobic response by government officials? Were gay bathhouses a site for the transmission of a new disease, or were they places for effectively disseminating information about how to protect oneself from the disease? These were among the primary questions that emerged in the 1980s in response to the AIDS epidemic.

In an attempt to slow the spread of HIV, proposals to close bathhouses were made in both San Francisco and New York City. Public health authorities, politicians, and some AIDS activists pointed to evidence that suggested that the more sexual partners a person had, the more that person was at risk of contracting HIV. Bathhouses, these people argued, provided an environment that encouraged multiple, often anonymous, sexual contacts and thus increased the odds of HIV transmission. By closing the bathhouses, public health authorities and AIDS activists hoped to decrease the transmission of HIV. The proposals to shut down bathhouses provoked acrimonious debate.

Perhaps the most common argument against closing bathhouses was that such measures would violate civil liberties, namely the right to privacy and the right to association. Some saw the impending closures as the first in a series of civil liberties violations directed specifically toward gay men. Proposals to close bathhouses to slow the spread of AIDS were a veneer that masked the real goals of such measures: to erase the visibility and sexual freedoms won by the gay movement. The fear these opponents expressed was that, if legislation and city ordinances shut down gay bathhouses and legal authorities enforced these restrictions, soon gay bars would also be closed; if the state banned sex at gay bathhouses, soon all gay sex would also become criminalized.

Other opponents to bathhouse closures viewed the proposals as an assault on the unique gay male sexual culture of which the bathhouses were considered a part. These opponents recognized gay bathhouses as important social institutions that had evolved to meet the needs of many gay men. They also maintained that the people who called for bathhouse closures conflated gay sex with unsafe sex. They pointed out that gays have historically been viewed as sick or pathological. When a new and deadly sexually transmitted disease appeared that primarily affected gay men, the public was quick to return to viewing gay sex as inherently dangerous. Gays who advocated the closure of bathhouses had internalized society's view of gay sex as "dirty." Opponents to forced bathhouse closures rightly pointed out that gay sex is not inherently risky, in terms of HIV, nor does it matter where sex takes place. What matters is that a person takes measures to protect himself and his partners. HIV can be transmitted as easily in a bedroom as in an orgy room at the tubs.

Finally, some AIDS activists opposed proposals to shut down the bathhouses on the grounds that measures to close bathhouses to help combat the spread of HIV were misguided, if not inimical, to the effort to combat HIV. Rather than seeing bathhouses as sites that contribute to the spread of HIV, these activists argued that bathhouses were ideal places to combat the spread of AIDS. Bathhouses were especially effective sites to disseminate information about reducing the risk of contracting HIV. Bathhouses often passed out brochures, condoms, and lube, and displayed posters to educate gay men about safer sex. Closing the bathhouses, these activists argued, would only disperse gay men seeking sex to parks, streets, or even just to their bedrooms, where they could not so easily be reached with prevention messages. Additionally, these activists saw bathhouses as a place where gay men could create sexual norms that promoted safer sex. These activists reasoned that, since the men who frequented bathhouses were concerned about their health and valued bathhouses and the unique sexual culture of gay men, they would make changes in the sexual culture that would help protect them and ensure the survival of their sexual institutions. These activists also recognized the importance of bathhouses as an institution that has evolved to serve the needs of gay men. Bathhouses offered a relatively safe environment for gay men in which they could express their sexuality at a time when they were often persecuted and harassed. Now, bathhouses could help gay men adjust to the new health crisis. Indigenously created safer sex messages were likely to be more effective than messages created by public health authorities.

Bathhouses and the meaning of sex

At the center of most of the debates on bathhouses is the broader meaning and place of sex in people's lives. Should sex be about expressing intimacy and love within the context of an established, ongoing relationship? Or should it be about pleasure? Is sex fundamentally a private experience? Or does sex permeate society, even providing a foundation for community? Is pleasure-oriented sex really degrading to participants? Or can different forms of intimacy be achieved in relatively anonymous sexual encounters?

Evidence for the constellation of many of these underlying questions can be seen in the debates described above. Consider the position of gay activists who viewed bathhouses as sites for sexual liberation. These activists challenged many prevailing norms about sexuality: most fundamentally, they challenged the very idea that sex is a private experience that should be confined to bedrooms and monogamous partners. Sexuality should permeate all aspects of society, according to these activists. Sex should be used as a vehicle for generating a multitude of social relationship. Indeed, sex could serve as a foundation for achieving community.

Critics of bathhouses who protested on the grounds that they promote a narrow and masculine approach to sexuality also presented questions about the fundamental meaning and place of sex in people's lives. Sex, according to these critics, should involve intimacy and mutuality. They viewed sex that was primarily pleasure-oriented as degrading to participants and held that sex that is "merely" for pleasure promotes sexual objectification and alienation. Socially legitimate sexuality entails treating one's partners with respect and dignity, as people with a full complement of emotions, interests and desires that should be acknowledged. Defenders of bathhouses who replied to charges that bathhouses promoted a narrow masculine approach to sex argued that sex oriented to pleasure is not necessarily degrading to participants. They argued that people have the ability and desire to be both sexual subjects and sexual objects.

The debates about bathhouses that emerged in the context of AIDS centered primarily on the issue of sexual freedom. For example, should society have the right to control the sexuality of its members if it's done in the name of preserving public health? Those who argued against bathhouse closures on the grounds that the closures would violate people's civil liberties argued that people should have a fundamental right to be sexual in any way they choose. Even if people's sexual behavior could potentially pose risks to them, society was viewed as not having the right to limit or interfere with people's sexual choices. Those who argued that bathhouses are an important part of the sexual culture that gay men have created made a similar claim. The sexual culture and institutions gay men created in the face of social repression are highly valued by many gay men, and this culture and its institutions should not be taken away. Finally, the AIDS activists who argued that bathhouses could be used to create community norms about safer sex also made claims about sexual freedom. They argued that gay men should be able to create sexual norms out of the cultural and institutional resources that they already have available to them. Indigenously created norms are likely to be more effective than those imposed from the outside by public health authorities.

References

Bell, Arthur. 1979. "The Bath Life Gets Respectability", in Karla Jay and Allen Young (eds), *Lavender Culture*, New York: Jove/HBJ.

Berube, Allan. 1996. "The History of Gay Bathhouses", in Ephen Glenn Colter *et al.* (eds), *Policing Public Sex: Queer Politics and the Future of AIDS Activism*. Boston, MA: South End Press.

Blevins, Steven. 1977. "Sexism in the Bars, Baths, and Bushes", *Gay Community News* 4(44): 5.

Jason Hendrickson

Chauncey, George. 1994. *Gay New York: Gender, Urban Culture, and the Making of the Gay Male World, 1890–1940*, New York: Basic Books.
Moore, Patrick. 2004. *Beyond Shame: Reclaiming the Abandoned History of Radical Gay Sexuality*. Boston, MA: Beacon.
Wittman, Carl. 1992. "A Gay Manifesto", in Karla Jay and Allen Young (eds), *Out of the Closets: Voices of Gay Liberation*. New York: New York University.

49

Queering the family

Mary C. Burke and Kristine A. Olsen

UNIVERSITY OF CONNECTICUT

The word "family" conjures up different thoughts for different people. For some of us it means love and support, the people we can always depend on. For others it means strained relationships and obligations. Some of us may think specifically about the people in the household we grew up in or the one we live in now, while others may think of an extended group of relatives and even ancestors. Still others may not think of kin related by blood or marriage, but instead focus their thoughts on their closest friends and loved ones. And regardless of the particular images we have of family, many of us probably think of the family as involving a private part of our lives. However, in reality it is anything but.

Historically, the family has been a key site of both biological reproduction and the reproduction of gender norms and roles. In terms of biological reproduction, this means that the family, specifically the culturally and legally sanctioned heteronormative family, has been a key site for the bearing and rearing of children. In terms of the reproduction of gender roles and norms, it means that the family has traditionally been one of the first places where gender is acquired. This includes the reproduction of the gendered division of labor, which assigns specific tasks and responsibilities based on gender that are then passed on to subsequent generations through the process of socialization. For instance, in the "traditional" heteronormative nuclear family model, which includes a married man and woman and their dependent children, the father is responsible for economically supporting the family (the "breadwinner") while the mother is responsible for taking care of the home (the "homemaker"). Given the centrality of the family in both these forms of reproduction, other major social institutions, chief among them the state, are deeply involved in the life of families, including promoting a specific notion of the ideal family.

Glance even briefly at the most recent census data and it is hard to miss the diversity of family forms. Or better yet, start talking to the people you go to school with, work with, or count among your friends, and even more nuanced variations on the family will emerge. Some people are raised by one person – a mother or father, an aunt or uncle, a grandparent, or an older sibling – while others are raised by two or more adults – a mom and dad, two moms, two dads, foster parents, step parents, grandparents, or all the folks on a commune. However, despite these varied configurations, there is a clear distinction between reality and ideology or what our society projects as the ideal family.

The reality is that families differ. They differ across time, across cultures, and within a particular society. However, in terms of ideology, some families are better than others and certain families are not even recognized. Ideology is a body of ideas that is used by members of an institution or group to justify a given social order. The heteronormative nuclear family model is currently the dominant family ideology. In an era where the traditional nuclear family form accounts for less than 7 percent of all households in the US, it is easy to brush this description off as outdated. Yet this form of the family continues to be idealized in US society.

Despite this continued idealization, "alternative" familial arrangements are doing much to challenge taken-for-granted assumptions about the meaning of family. In this chapter, we discuss two recent LGBT (lesbian, gay, bisexual, transgender) challenges to the norm of the heterosexual nuclear family. First, we consider several ways in which LGBT families and same-sex marriage are changing the ways that gender has been reproduced in families. Second, we highlight how alternative insemination (AI) and second-parent adoption, particularly as they are utilized by LGBT individuals and partners, challenge views of the family as a key site of biological reproduction. In the course of these discussions, we will highlight three institutions that powerfully shape the family as we know it in the United States: marriage, medicine, and law.

Family and gender

From the "gayby boom" to the solemnization of gay and lesbian couples in cities as far away as New Paltz, NY, and San Francisco and to the legalization of same-sex marriage in Massachusetts, LGBT families have received an increased amount of attention over the past decade and a half in the US. Same-sex marriage in particular was considered a key issue in the outcome of the 2004 election. Eleven states featured ballot initiatives on the topic. The Republican ticket made headlines when George W. Bush and Dick Cheney split on the issue of a proposed constitutional amendment banning same-sex marriage. And the Democratic ticket caught flak on the matter – John Kerry for hailing from the infamous state of Massachusetts, and John Edwards for "outing" Cheney's daughter during the vice-presidential debate. These issues have attracted such a large amount of attention and fueled so much debate because LGBT families present challenges to certain ideas of gender which are central to the ideal of the heterosexual nuclear family. In particular, arguments about gender complementarity, male and female role models, and "proper" gender roles are at the heart of opposition to same-sex marriage.

Gender is a particularly salient social category in American culture. It is often noted that gender is the first identity prescribed to us when we are born. New parents are well aware of this fact given the frequency with which they are asked, "Is it a boy or a girl?" However, while gender infiltrates all aspects of our life, family has historically been a key site of the reproduction of gender roles and norms. Take for instance the history of marriage in Anglo-American family law. According to Weitzman and Dixon (1999: 316–17), legal marriage, traditionally grounded in the Christian conception of marriage as a holy union between a man and a woman, historically included five important features:

1 it limited marriage to a single man and woman;
2 it dictated that legal marriage be monogamous;
3 it dictated that the intended purpose be the bearing and rearing of children;
4 it established a hierarchical relationship among family members (husband as head of household with wife and children as subordinates); and most importantly
5 it required a division of family roles and responsibilities based on sex.

Surveying these five features reveals that four of the five features of Anglo–American marital law, considered the foundation of the family, pertain explicitly to gender.

However, the family is not a fixed entity. The institution of family is constantly changing. Historically, we have seen a myriad of changes to the gender norms on which the institution of family has been formed. Some particularly significant challenges have been the increasing number of women in the workforce and the concomitant rise in dual-earner households, the advent of no-fault divorce laws, and the rise in single-parent families. Each of these changes challenged the gender hierarchy and division of labor that form the basis on which the institutions of marriage and family were formed.

A new challenge has emerged in the form of same-sex partners and LGBT families. In the US, we assume that part of being male and thus masculine is to be attracted to women. In this sense, homosexuality has often been treated as a form of gender deviance. For instance, when gays and lesbians protested against the inclusion of homosexuality in the American Psychological Association's (APA) manual on psychological disorders, they were rejecting both the pathologization of homosexuality and the identification of homosexuality with a gender disorder (Coombs 2001: 398). Furthermore, in many cultures, engaging in same-sex sexual activity is not, in and of itself, enough to earn a person the label of gay or homosexual (Cantu 2000). Instead, it is the individuals who transgress gender norms that are labeled as homosexual. Only the man who took the "women's position" would face the stigma of being a homosexual. Furthermore, even though homosexuality is typically no longer treated as a gender disorder in the US, stereotypes about effeminate gay men and masculine lesbians persist in American culture.

Yet the challenges posed by same-sex partners and LGBT families go well beyond this point. Take, for instance, mother–mother–child relationships. As we have already suggested, the heterosexual nuclear family not only acts as a model of what "real" families should look like but also renders different family forms inferior. Sullivan (2001) argues that lesbian co-parent families are not even recognized as families. This is especially true for non-birthmothers in these families. However, while the ideology of the heteronormative nuclear family operates to render these mothers invisible, their existence presents a constant challenge to our normative conceptions of gender and family. Because, unlike their birthmother partners, these women's identities as mothers are not based on biological maternity, they must constantly declare their status as mothers (Sullivan 2001). In this sense, each time they claim the status of mother to a doctor, a teacher, or a stranger, they force others to confront unstated assumptions about the gender composition of two-parent families.

Same-sex partners and parents also pose a threat to the gender division of labor that has been central to the American family. While some families are more egalitarian than others, the majority of heterosexual families involve some division of labor based on gender. Sometimes, this division is quite strict, with the female operating as a full-time housewife and the male working outside the home. Even in heterosexual dual-earner households, women continue to be responsible for more of the household tasks, creating what some have deemed a second shift for women (Hochschild 1997). This parental division of labor plays a significant role in gender socialization in families. Same-sex couples and LGBT families necessarily challenge this division. In a relationship between two men, one or both of them will be performing domestic tasks that in most heterosexual families are associated with women. Gender norms lose their social force and relevance in same-sex families. While people may (seriously or jokingly) wonder "who's the daddy?" or "who's the wife?," such distinctions do not apply. In this sense, same-sex partners also provide their children with a very different understanding of what family is, one that challenges assumptions about gender roles and norms.

Like lesbian and gay couples, transgender and transsexual individuals and couples also challenge hegemonic conceptions of what it means to be a family as well as normative ideas about gender. Transgender individuals and their families raise questions about the very concepts of male and female. For instance, think about what might happen if a court decides that sex reassignment surgery does not make an individual born biologically male a "true female." The transsexual who understands herself as female, living and representing herself as such, would not be able to marry a man, but could arguably marry another woman. While this couple would be legally viewed as heterosexual, this label hardly seems applicable.

While LGBT families must continue to confront the hegemony of the heteronormative nuclear family, an ideology that renders their families inferior if not invisible, their struggles continue to bring change. Second-parent adoption, partnership benefits, and same-sex marriage are all increasingly salient topics both in the US and abroad. As LGBT families become more visible and reshape cultural ideas and public policy, they will not only challenge assumptions about what families look like but also the ways that the family has historically reproduced gender. Indeed, they even have the potential to challenge our very conceptions of gender.

Family and procreation

Marriage and family are not static institutions. In the US today, the heteronormative nuclear family persists as a cultural ideal, but this is a relatively recent model of social organization, dating from mid-eighteenth-century Europe (Coontz 2005). For much of modern history, family has been a central economic and political institution. In earlier times, marriage was a social and legal contract that created political alliances and cooperative ties between communities, and served as the basis of property distribution, securing inheritance within families. Despite the modern cultural ideal of marriage as a bond of love and commitment, until very recently this institution was used primarily to create a family unit that provided a pool of labor resources and ensured paternity so that property could be transferred from one generation to the next. Indeed, the predominance of arranged marriages throughout history speaks to the interdependence of marriage and procreation. Although we may like to think that marriage is all about love, many of society's institutions have a vested interest in marriage, and regulate it accordingly.

Marriage is often shaped by factors relating to race, class, and gender. Marriages are often arranged along class lines, either explicitly, as in the case of arranged marriages, or implicitly, as people meet through common social networks. In the US, the prohibition of slave marriages in the antebellum south reinforced the slave owner's jurisdiction over his property. Anti-miscegenation laws, aimed at preventing "mixed-race" children, existed in parts of the US as recently as 1967. Currently, the majority of industrialized nations allow only opposite-sex couples to marry legally and to access the multitude of rights and benefits marriage offers. In many US states, second-parent adoption is illegal, or at the very least heavily regulated. What this form of exclusion and regulation reveals is the privileging of the procreative, implicitly heterosexual couple. Yet this legal and cultural precedent does not go unchallenged. In this section we consider recent LGBT challenges to two institutions, medicine and law, that have a fundamental impact on the way that we think about family, gender, and procreation. The new reproductive technologies (NRTs) and family law simultaneously provide opportunities, as well as constrain the ways that families are created. Here we focus on how same-gender couples' experiences with reproductive medicine and family law reveal the ways that hegemonic discourse legitimizes some families while delegitimizing others. However, these interactions also reveal how LGBT families challenge existing cultural assumptions, including the relationship between marriage and procreation, and between sexuality and procreation.

Alternative insemination (AI) procedures such as donor insemination (DI) and *in vitro* fertilization (IVF) have had a significant impact on the ways that families are formed, and how they are being legally recognized. On the one hand, these procedures and related technologies allow for the separation of sex from procreation, and the strengthening of reproductive freedoms. Donor insemination, an assisted fertilization technique where sperm from a known or anonymous donor is used to achieve conception, has allowed countless childless couples and single women to bear children. For lesbians who want to become parents, DI offers a relatively simple, low-tech procedure for achieving this end. At the same time, state-wide laws and employer policies are increasingly providing some level of legal protection to lesbian and gay families. These technologies have made it possible to create what Kath Weston (1991) has termed "families of choice."

Although assisted-conception techniques have been around for over a century, in recent decades the medicalization of reproduction and professionalization of AI have resulted in a flood of specialty clinics, services, and practitioners to aid single women and childless couples in conception. Some of these facilities, particularly on the US east and west coasts, now openly cater to lesbian clients. For those who can afford the service, the sperm bank and physician-assisted insemination have largely replaced more informal methods, such as those arranged through friends and acquaintances using an appointed semen "courier." At infertility clinics, semen specimens are carefully screened for abnormalities, and potential donors often undergo extensive physical and psychological evaluations before being meticulously catalogued by race/ethnicity, religious affiliation, height and weight, and even personality type.

Yet despite these new medical opportunities afforded to women and different types of couples, the field of medicine is permeated with a biomedical discourse that constructs AI as an "infertility treatment" for heterosexual couples. In order to qualify for insurance coverage of physician-assisted, AI-related expenses, a "childless couple" (the requisite unit of treatment) must be diagnosed with "infertility," defined by the American Society of Reproductive Medicine (ASRM) as "*a disease* that exists when a couple has tried to conceive for 12 months during which time they have had intercourse [sic] without the use of contraception" [emphasis added] (in Agigian 2004: 48). Operating within the confines of biomedical discourse, practitioners act as gatekeepers, controlling access to AI procedures by screening candidates for their worthiness. Located outside of the heteronormative nuclear family model, lesbian couples who wish to use physician-assisted insemination must present their inability to conceive a child sexually as an illness that requires treatment.

However, in using fertility treatments and creating families, lesbian parents also challenge dominant notions of family. AI allows women to create families without legal fathers, thus disentangling procreation from heterosexuality. Same-gender, two-parent households with children provide an alternative family pattern to that of the heteronormative nuclear family. The invisibility of LGBT families that results from the apparent "naturalness" of the heteronormative nuclear family structure is being challenged on multiple levels. Increasingly, gay- and lesbian-headed families are depicted in contemporary media. In some school systems, teaching materials such as *That's a Family!* aim to provide elementary-aged children with an understanding of, and respect for the diversity of family forms that exist. Although controversial, children's books such as *Heather Has Two Mommies* and *Daddy's Roommate* depict gay and lesbian families in a positive light. Same-sex families have also gained varying levels of legal recognition in some states through the implementation of domestic partnership, civil union, and same-sex marriage.

However, once AI-assisted families have been formed, family law does not easily, if at all, recognize lesbian families. As evidenced by numerous child custody court cases, lesbian and gay parents comprise a class of individuals that do not fit the ideological definition of family, which includes a married man and woman and their dependent children. Measured against this ideal, lesbian and gay families are often deemed illegitimate. Legal discourse intercedes in the lives of families by using the heteronormative nuclear family model as the standard against which all families are measured.

As Katherine Arnup and Susan Boyd (1995) argue, lesbian custody cases reveal how parental "fitness" is often used to deny custody or visitation to the non-birth, or "de facto" parent. A family that does not include a married mother and a father is automatically defined as unstable. Such a family may be subject to invasive actions by the state, such as additional hearings, mandatory counseling, and, in some cases, the granting of parental rights to a donor who may have had no hand in raising a child conceived with his sperm. In *Ward v. Ward* (1996), Florida's Supreme Court awarded custody of an 11-year-old girl to her father, who had previously served a prison sentence for murdering his former wife, rather than allow her to remain in the custody of her lesbian mother.

In many custody hearings, the priority of "finding a father" reflects the predominance of the married, two-parent family ideal. In fact, the institution of marriage is associated in legal thinking with family stability, while those who are unmarried are viewed as unstable, and therefore unfit parents. For lesbian mothers in particular, parental "fitness" is determined based on the good mother/bad mother dichotomy. The "good mother" is, of course, heterosexual. Through the lens of heterosexism, "lesbian mother" becomes a contradiction of terms. Thus it is not uncommon for lesbian mothers to "act straight" at custody hearings in an attempt to retain custody of their children (Arnup and Boyd 1995: 82–3). Although family law idealizes the heterosexual two-parent family, custody hearings may actually highlight the assumptions and contradictions involved.

Conclusion

Family is a seemingly universal institution. Although its form and function varies considerably from one society to the next, this form of social organization, at the most basic level, distinguishes members of the in-group from those of the out-group. But family is also a site where both laws and norms regulate behavior. Marriage is one way that families are legally recognized. As we have discussed, family is a place where gender roles are learned. The gender division of labor organizes tasks and responsibilities along gender lines, as the breadwinner/homemaker model demonstrates. LGBT families challenge assumptions about sex and gender by questioning the seemingly natural relationship between them.

LGBT experiences with reproductive medicine and family law reveal the power of a society that assumes a norm of a heterosexual family to limit alternatives. At the same time, as we've seen, families are changing and becoming more diverse. In particular, lesbian and gay families are challenging our ideas of family. Lesbian alternative insemination results in the creation of families that don't fit the heteronormative nuclear family model. While access to AI procedures continues to be controlled by the medical community and regulated by health insurance providers, the very existence of these services supports the separation of procreation from sex. As women negotiate reproductive medicine, they find ways to create families within the confines of biomedical discourse. LGBT interactions with family law reveal a similar pattern of strategy and negotiation. Increasingly, judges make rulings that respect the position of "social parents," and the autonomy of the LGBT families. Medicine and family law are not necessarily oppressive and exploitative of LGBT families. Rather, they provide a context of both opportunities and constraints within which individuals make unique choices about the extent to which they will engage the system on its terms. Often they and their families are co-opted, undermined, or delegitimized by these institutions; but sometimes the contradictions they raise break new legal and political ground.

References

Agigian, Amy. 2004. *Baby Steps: How Lesbian Alternative Insemination is Changing the World*. Middletown, CT: Wesleyan University Press.

Arnup, Katherine and Susan Boyd. 1995. "Familial Disputes? Sperm Donors, Lesbian Mothers and Legal Parenthood." In Didi Herman and Carl Stychin (eds), *Legal Inversions: Lesbians, Gay Men, and the Politics of Law*. Philadelphia, PA: Temple University Press.

Cantu, Lionel. 2000. "Entre Hombres/Between Men: Latino Masculinities and Homosexualities." In Peter M. Nardi (ed.), *Gay Masculinities*. Thousand Oaks, CA: Sage Publications.

Coombs, Mary. 2001. "Transgenderism and Sexual Orientation: More Than a Marriage of Convenience." In Mary Bernstein and Renate Reimann (eds), *Queer Families, Queer Politics: Challenging Culture and the State*. New York: Columbia University Press.

Coontz, Stephanie. 2005. *Marriage, A History: From Obedience to Intimacy or How Love Conquered Marriage*. New York: Penguin Books.

Hochschild, Arlie. 1997. *The Second Shift: Working Parents and the Revolution at Home*. New York: Avon Books.

Sullivan, Maureen. 2001. "Alma Matter: Family 'Outings' and the Making of the Modern Other Mother (MOM)." In Mary Bernstein and Renate Reimann (eds), *Queer Families, Queer Politics*. New York: Columbia University Press.

Weitzman, Lenore J. and Ruth B. Dixon. 1999. "The Transformation of Legal Marriage Through No-Fault Divorce." In Arlene S. Skolnick and Jerome H. Skolnick (eds), *Family in Transition*. New York: Longman.

Weston, Kath. 1991. *Families We Choose: Lesbians, Gays, and Kinship*. New York: Columbia University Press.

50

Pleasure for sale

Feminist sex stores

Alison Better

BRANDEIS UNIVERSITY, MASSACHUSETTS

Sex stores can be found in many communities across America. These stores are not standardized or regulated, but have several features in common. Sex stores may sell pornographic media, sex toys and novelties, sexual accessories and devices, and sexually charged humor items. The Supreme Court, through a series of first amendment cases, legalized sex stores in the 1960s. These early sex stores (since the 1960s) catered almost entirely to male clientele and often had pornographic video viewing rooms on the premises. They were designed without windows so customers would not be seen. Such stores often had a reputation for being taboo, dirty, and a menace to the community. As time progressed, sex stores have diversified, both in terms of their atmosphere and their audience. Now, several different sorts of sex stores operate across the country, each catering to different pleasure needs and potentials.

Nonetheless, it is important to note that today several states still criminalize the sale of sex toys. The most restrictive law is in Alabama, where it is not legal to sell sex toys. It is lawful for Alabama residents to own and use toys, provided they were purchased elsewhere. Though several appeals to the 1998 law prohibiting the sale of "any device designed or marketed as useful primarily for the stimulation of human genital organs" have been filed, the Alabama Supreme Court has upheld the state ban in a September 2009 ruling (Chandler and Velasco 2009). However, a loophole exists in the law that toys can also be purchased if they are for "a bona fide medical, scientific, educational, legislative, judicial, or law enforcement purpose" (Brantley 2009). In January 2009, Coweta County, Georgia passed an obscenity ordinance that "prohibits sale or distribution of obscenity," and prohibits anyone from "knowingly" selling, or possessing with the intent to sell, "any device designed or marketed as useful primarily for the stimulation of human genital organs" (Campbell 2009). The state of Mississippi also made the sale of sex toys illegal while allowing citizens to own toys. A Texas ban on promoting or selling sex toys was overturned in 2008. The Texas ruling also overturned any bans on the sale of sex toys in Louisiana and Mississippi as it was heard by the Fifth Circuit Court of Appeals covering those three states. Given this legal context, the following discussion of sex stores does not apply to every US state.

Traditional sex stores

Upon opening an opaque and imposing door and walking into one traditional sex store, I am immediately confronted by a display of sex toys advertised as novelties. Toys intended to provide sexual pleasures are presented on shelves and a selection of lingerie and stockings lined the wall. Many of these packages are covered in graphic images of people using the products, often topless women in suggestive poses giving the camera direct eye contact, luring the viewer through the packaging. On the wall opposite the lingerie stands a large desk raised off the ground with two men working behind it who watch the movements of the customers. The back half of the store is lined with several aisles of shelves filled with pornographic videos with titles like *Big Boobs Power* or *Barely Legal Innocence 9* that run the length of the floor.

Traditional sex stores can be found in a variety of forms in almost every state in America. They market pornographic films and sexual goods. These stores often have a variety of sex toys and other sexual products. In addition to locally owned adult bookstores and sex shops, there are several large chains of traditional sex stores in America, including Amazing, Romantix, The Lion's Den, and Castle Megastore. Traditional sex shops sell a variety of goods, ranging from gag gifts and novelties like penis-shaped pasta and drinking straws and bachelorette party favors to vibrators to pornographic videos. Such stores are often located on well-traveled main roads or in shopping districts surrounded by other retail shops. They are well-marked and well-lit.

Some traditional stores are more "hardcore." Hardcore sex shops sell the same merchandise as the traditional shops, while fostering a more sexually charged atmosphere. Hardcore shops are a subset of traditional stores where sex acts or sex work may take place on the premises. This usually takes the form of peep booths or video booths and enclosed areas where customers can pleasure themselves while watching a pornographic act (either on video or live) located in a section of the store. Unlike average traditional sex stores, hardcore sex stores are often located in either urban vice districts or in unmarked, windowless buildings outside of city limits.

While traditional sex stores are well-marked and well-lit on the outside, they are often environments shrouded in secrecy and anonymity on the inside. Through my fieldwork in sex stores, I've noticed that patrons do not look at one another and store clerks serve mostly as theft deterrents. Products are arranged on shelves or hooks in rigid plastic packaging, often decorated with pornographic images of a person using the product. These stores can sometimes seem dirty or seedy to patrons; many women I have spoken to as part of a larger study of sex stores have mentioned uncomfortable or frightening experiences including harassment and sexual overtures while shopping at traditional sex stores. This environment is exciting and titillating to some, while it is overwhelming and off-putting to others.

Feminist sex stores: a new type of sex shop

I entered into a brightly lit room through a frosted glass door. A table to my left offered information about events of interest, including an amateur porn night, women's and trans health care, and the local GLBT community newspaper. To my left was a selection of condoms and lubricants, with testers available for each product. Along the back wall were displays of vibrators, many labeled phthalate-free. There was a large selection of silicone vibrators which are easy to clean as well as dual action or "rabbit" vibrators that simultaneously provide clitoral and vaginal stimulation. A sample of each toy was out of its packaging and on a shelf. The electric toys were plugged into an outlet for testing. Further along this wall were anal toys and men's toys, including vacuum pumps and cock rings. Other sections of the store contained dildos and harnesses as well as trinkets and gifts. A nearby table displayed glass dildos and hand-carved wood dildos that look like sculptures. A small room off the main space contained books (both educational and erotic), fetish gear, including whips and gags, and a small selection of pornographic videos for purchase. The clerks were positioned behind a counter that spanned a wall of the store and some walked around asking if they could be of any help as I shopped.

Feminist sex stores began to emerge in response to women's discomfort with traditional sex stores. Since specialized sex retail environments often serve as the only option for the purchase of pleasure goods, traditional sex stores were once the only place to buy sex toys. The first feminist sex shop in America, Eve's Garden, was opened in New York City in 1974. It was quickly followed by Good Vibrations in 1977, a sex shop in San Francisco. Until the early 1990s, these two stores were the only sex stores focusing on feminist ideals and women's sexual pleasure. Since 1991, 23 feminist sex shops emerged in the United States and the current total of feminist sex stores is 26. These stores are in cities both large and small, and occasionally in suburbs just over city limits. Some are small franchises with multiple locations.

Five features are present in all feminist sex shops: (1) Feminist sex shops are committed to understanding the process of their inception and the importance of connections to the past and also to other feminist sex stores; (2) They maintain the importance of safe spaces for women (many stores today are rephrasing this to include people of all genders and sexual orientations); (3) They exist to fill needs in their communities; (4) They promote the importance of healthy and pleasurable sexual lives; (5) To this end, they provide information and education about sexuality.

Feminist sex store creation and cooperation

Feminist sex shops understand that the process of their creation and their history are important. By telling the stories of their creation, current owners share the knowledge with anyone else seeking to bring a safe space for different sexual identities into their community. Current business owners help out aspiring ones as they begin to build new stores around the country. Though store owners do not often interact with one another in person since they live in different cities, it is clear that they identify as part of the same community and are working both together and separately to ensure access to information and products to help all people reach their sexual and pleasure potentials. Many of these stores provide information about their owners, founding, and company history on their websites and in other public information about the store. Though the stores are all independently owned and operated, feminist sex store owners see themselves as part of a larger movement to create a safe space for education and enhancing sexual potentials.

This alignment of political ideals with providing a sex-positive retail environment was also found by Meika Loe, who conducted a case study of a feminist sex store, which she calls Toy Box. Her focus was on the structure of the business and how they balanced political ideals and profits (Loe 1999:706). Through her observations at the store and office, and through interviews with staff and owners, Loe was able to look at changes over time in this feminist business. The store wanted female customers to "come away from visiting the store convinced that sexual pleasure was one's birthright and one's path toward liberation and empowerment" (Loe 1999:713). In addition to selling products, they were selling a pro-sex ideology. In the early 1990s control of the store moved from its owner to its staff, who began making decisions for the business and later became worker-owners in 1992 (Loe 1999:717, 723). The store continues to be successful as it changes over time. Toy Box has transformed its business structure and ownership, yet remained entrenched in feminist values (and changed with them over time).

Safe shopping spaces

For several of the women who opened the feminist sex shops, uncomfortable experiences at traditional sex shops led them to their consciousness-raising "click" moment about the validity of women's sexuality. These feminist pioneers felt that women should have a place to go to explore and learn about their sexuality and to buy well-made sexual aids and other products. Their own open-mindedness about sexuality had brought them into traditional adult stores, but even with their comfort about sexuality, they were intimidated and saw nothing in the stores that catered to their needs. These experiences led each of these women to the same decision: to open a sex store that would cater to women's needs and be a safe place to shop for and explore their desires.

It should be noted that one of the only sociological studies on sex store shopping did not find female consumers to be particularly uncomfortable in that sexualized space. Dana Berkowitz (2006) writes about gender performance in pornographic establishments. This study is based on her fieldwork at the XTC Center (a pseudonym), a traditional sex store open 24 hours a day, seven days a week in the Southeast United States. Berkowitz found an equal number of men and women shopping at the store and looked at their patterns of shopping behavior. She examined four types of shopping configurations, woman alone, man alone, a group of women, and mixed gender. She found that men shopping alone displayed two different types of masculinity, swagger and confidence amongst the "video voyeurs" and weakness and nervousness among the "petrified patrons" (Berkowitz 2006:593–94). Women shopping alone here shopped with confidence, marching over to the section where vibrators were displayed, thoughtfully choosing their purchases, and asking the clerk questions (Berkowitz 2006:596). She found women embraced sexual agency in this setting. Women in groups tended to act more reserved than women shopping alone, a finding not echoed in my own observations. Berkowitz found the deviant nature of the setting shifted the usual gender norms while patrons were shopping.

In regard to providing safe spaces, in my own research on sex shops, I have found that many women are uncomfortable with the traditional male-focused sex retail establishments and are seeking a safer and more welcoming alternative as they seek to enhance their sexual pleasures.

The shopping experience in adult bookstores is uncomfortable for many women who report feeling watched and find many of the items for sale unappealing. Products in traditional sex shops are oriented to heterosexual men, with naked women appearing on many of the products' packaging. Also, the neighborhoods that housed adult bookstores are sometimes dangerous as these stores were often located in urban vice districts.

The feminist sex shops that women opened differed from traditional adult bookstores in a variety of ways. The storefronts were approachable and located in safer neighborhoods. Stores were painted in soothing light colors and played soft music. Samples of each product were on display on shelves or tables, and customers were invited to see how the products felt. Many sex toys were repackaged to remove pornographic images. Staff members were knowledgeable and approachable and willing to help customers make successful purchases. Many stores wrote up instruction sheets and care information for women to bring home with their purchases so they could safely use and store their new toys.

Filling community needs

Feminist sex shops seek to serve a larger purpose in their surrounding community. Several feminist sex shops have become contemporary outposts for feminist activism and community development. Some of these stores have hosted sexuality discussion groups on topics such as the differences between erotica and pornography, defining sex, and polyamory to raise community consciousness about sexuality. Other stores have held book clubs and knitting groups in their retail spaces. Stores across the country have sponsored educational centers that enhance the community impact of the retail store. Several feminist sex stores have spun off outside educational centers, including the Center for Sex and Culture in San Francisco and the Center for

Sexual Pleasure and Health in Rhode Island. These spaces focus on sexuality education and activism.

Sexual health and pleasure

Sexual health is important to all feminist sex shops. One Midwest feminist sex store was created by a sex educator/counselor and a physician. The store sees itself more as a sexuality resource center and provides detailed sex information on both its website and the retail store. Visitors to the store's website or retail locations have the opportunity to ask questions of a medical doctor and co-founder of the store. Information and advice can be found on the website answering questions about all aspects of sexuality, ranging from advice about reproduction, anatomy, and menopause to libido and orgasm. This store sees itself as a place that combines sexual health and pleasure. Several other feminist stores are staffed by sexuality educators and sexual health practitioners.

Another way that concern with sexual health is evident in feminist sex stores is the way they have handled the sales of jelly plastics. In recent years it has become known that certain types of materials used in the making of sex toys can be bad for people's health. Jelly plastics, often used for vibrators and other sex toys, contain toxic phthalates. In addition to leaching toxic gases into the air, this material can cause reproductive harm and is able to be absorbed through skin (Furniss 2006). These materials are also carcinogenic. Furthermore, jelly plastic is harmful as it is porous and not able to be sterilized. This means that bacteria, mold, and fungus can live in a jelly plastic sex toy with no way for the toy to be sanitized.

Feminist sex stores often do not carry any product made with jelly plastic. Although some stores continue to sell them (since customers enjoy their low price), they explain the risks and problems to the consumer and advise them to use a condom with any jelly plastic toy. Stores that are committed to the health and safety of their clients often test products before sale for the presence of phthalates or seek manufacturers who use materials that are phthalate-free. The owner of a Minneapolis sex store founded a consumer advocacy group called Coalition Against Toxic Toys (CATT) to educate the sex toy industry on the harms of some of the products on the market. CATT aims to stop the production of harmful and toxic sex toys. These stores understand sexual health to be a right and refuse to let unsafe, harmful, or toxic products in their stores.

Sexual education

Each feminist sex shop provides workshops and classes on location. Though different courses are taught in each city, these ventures share a common thread. Each class is aimed at continuing to liberate sexuality by both educating participants and working to raise their sexual consciousness. Classes focus on pleasure and confidence in one's sexuality, learning about sex acts, kink, and burlesque, including classes titled "Talk Dirty to Me: The Art of Erotic Talk," "Cheap Sex Workshop," and "Knotty Thoughts: the Eroticism of Rope." Workshops are also offered on flirting, strip-tease, communicating about sex, masturbation, and a variety of sex practices.

Conclusion

Sex-positive feminism seeks to empower women to have agency over their sexuality and sexual pleasure. To this end, the women who founded feminist sex stores embody this new feminism, both in their retail establishments and in their communities. Raising sexual consciousness through feminism, coupled with anger over the lack of resources available for women's sexual gratification in traditional sex stores, led a small group of women to change the landscape of understanding about sexuality and pleasure through the creation of a new site for sexual commerce, feminist sex shops. These shops continue to impact both their customers and their community, opening up dialogue about healthy sexuality and pleasure and making products available to help pursue these ideals.

As feminist sex stores continue to grow, new generations of people of all genders and sexualities find ways to meet their sexual needs and explore the depths of their sexual pleasures through these retail and community spaces. These stores have an impact on their community that surpasses our usual perceptions of retail stores. While most business owners seek entrepreneurship, feminist sex shops go beyond mere commerce and have positioned themselves also as sites of sexual consciousness raising, education, and empowerment. Through openness and education, feminist sex stores help contribute to new understandings of pleasure and sexuality in America.

References

Berkowitz, Dana. 2006. "Consuming Eroticism: Gender Performances and Presentations in Pornographic Establishments." *Journal of Contemporary Ethnography* 35: 583–606.

Brantley, Mike. 2009. "Alabama Sex Toy Ban: Court Rejects Challenge." *The Press Register*. http://blog. al.com/live/2009/09/alabama_court_rejects_challeng.html. Accessed March 17, 2010.

Campbell, Sarah Fay. 2009. "Coweta Passes Tighter Obscenity Ordinance." *The Times-Herald*. www. times-herald.com/Local/Coweta-passes-tighter-obscenity-ordinance-646015. Accessed March 21, 2010.

Chandler, Kim and Eric Velasco. 2009. "Alabama Supreme Court Upholds Sex Toy Ban." *The Birmingham News*. www.al.com/news/birminghamnews/metro.ssf?/base/news/1252743369276790.xml&coll= 2. Accessed March 17, 2010.

Furniss, Candace. 2006. "Sex Toys and the Revolution." *Confluence* 12(2). www.stlconfluence.org/article

Loe, Meika. 1999. "Feminism for Sale: Case Study of a Pro-Sex Feminist Business." *Gender and Society* 13 (6): 705–32.

Part 8
Sexual cultures

Introduction

We often think of sex as a solitary affair, or as something two people do together. But sex can also be linked to group life. In many societies, sex has become a reason for forming communities and cultural identities. The gay and lesbian community is one example. So are Sadomasochists and young people who share a common hip-hop culture. In these cases, individuals share a common social location, and share a set of practices that relate to sex.

The chapters in this part discuss sexual cultures in three ways. First, sexual cultures can emerge when a group of people, by virtue of their sexual practices and tastes, are stigmatized or even criminalized by the wider society. Sadomasochism is a good example of this. Sadomasochists are individuals who derive sexual pleasure from inflicting or receiving pain or humiliation. Even though this is a consensual activity, many Western societies have made S/M criminal. The medical and psychiatric community still treats it as a psychological disease. Given their marginalization, people who practice S/M have come to see each other as possessing a unique, common identity. They have built a community based on this identity, and they try to educate the broader society about their sexuality.

Second, sexual cultures can emerge even when individuals are not particularly marginalized or stigmatized. Individuals might form a common sexual culture simply by virtue of the fact that they have sexual tastes that vary from the mainstream. Feederism is a perfect example. Feederism refers to individuals who find food and body fat sexy. Feederism is not illegal, or even stigmatized, but it does vary from the mainstream. While such individuals might have always existed, it has only been recently that they have formed a community based on their sexual desires and practices. Gay circuit parties are another example of a sexual culture that has formed within the broader gay community. Circuit parties are attended by gay men who have stylized a certain version of masculinity in their look, dress, and attitude. Circuit boys have well-toned, muscular bodies, and they eschew the notion that gay men are necessarily effeminate. Circuit culture is sort of like a community within a community, having emerged in order to cultivate a very specific style or aesthetic.

Third, the idea of a sexual culture can refer to individuals who share specific sexual styles that develop around an art form or specific form of popular culture. Take music, for example. Music has, at least since the 1950s and the advent of Rock 'n' Roll, been an artistic medium in which sexual meanings circulate. Today, hip-hop is a musical/dance medium where sex is often a dominant theme. Sometimes music cultures simply reflect the sexual values of the mainstream. In rock culture, rock stars (always men) are valorized for their ability to have sex with "groupies" (always women). Similarly, much of hip-hop reflects a misogynist and heterosexist style that degrades women and homosexuals. Sometimes, though, music cultures challenge dominant sexual norms. Alternative rock groups openly espouse tolerance toward gays and lesbians. And there is an increasing number of female hip-hop stars who openly challenge and poke fun at the way male hip-hoppers objectify women.

You might wonder how so many interesting sexual cultures – the gay community, feeders, sadomasochists, circuit boys and so on – have come to exist. Certainly there is a wider variety of sexual cultures than there were just 50 years ago. The internet is one reason. Through cyber culture, individuals can meet a wider variety of individuals, and they can do so anonymously. Cyber culture makes it possible for individuals who once may have had a difficult time meeting to find each other – as is the case with disabled people, but also feederists, gay people, sado-masochists, men on the "downlo," and even heterosexuals. Cyber culture, because it is anonymous, also gives people the opportunity to experiment with their sexual identities and styles in ways they might not have otherwise.

Sex, then, may become a key feature of group life. This is especially true in the contemporary era when we are witnessing the proliferation of a wide variety of sexual identities and cultures. Hopefully, this part will convey a sense of this sexual inventiveness.

51

Sexual liberation and the creative class in Israel

Dana Kaplan

THE HEBREW UNIVERSITY AND THE OPEN UNIVERSITY, ISRAEL

The story of the history of sexuality is often told as a shift from a traditional, repressed sexuality to a contemporary liberated and hedonistic sexuality. But this conventional view ignores the importance of class in shaping sexual cultures. By and large, during the nineteenth century in many Western societies, there were two opposing ideologies of sexuality. There was a middle-class, "respectful" sexuality, and, from the perspective of the middle class, there was a lower-class, deviant, permissive sexuality. In the course of the twentieth century, however, this division has been reversed. Today, working-class sexuality is often considered conservative and restrained while a culture of sexual fulfillment and intense sexual pleasures have been idealized by the middle class. For this class, sexuality has gradually become an important way for selves to express their individuality.

In this chapter I explore the way social class shapes sexuality. Specifically, I examine the significant role pleasure and notions of liberation play in middle-class sexuality. The common view is that the sexual revolution of the 1960s had the effect of blurring class boundaries, and sexual liberation became universal. I have my doubts. In any event, I will explore everyday understandings of sexuality among the new, creative middle class in Israel. I will argue that notions of liberated sex invoke a sense of individuality and entitlement among this class. By describing sex as a "fun" leisure activity and by endorsing sexual experimentation, members of this class express their individual personalities in the context of a post-industrialized Israel.

Israel is usually described as a society which is undergoing a shift from collectivism to individualism. From a society unified around a hegemonic Zionist pioneering ethos, Israel is increasingly becoming a pluralistic and globalized society. This change is evident in the economic, cultural and ideological spheres. In the economic sphere, a state-centralized economy has, from the mid-1980s, undergone a profound process of privatization. This economic liberalization has encouraged a service economy and a flourishing hi-tech industry. In the cultural sphere, consumerism has become a new way of life for many Israelis. Middle-class Israelis have turned out to be enthusiastic consumers of the new leisure and lifestyle goods provided by a new culture industry. For example, the media environment is saturated with new privately owned TV channels, airing global and commercial content. Similarly, many Israelis have begun shopping in American-style malls, enjoy an elaborate dining scene (from global fast food chains to exquisite restaurants), and carefully design and decorate their homes.

The post-industrialization of Israel is also apparent in a shifting value system, from collectivist to individualist values and from traditionalist to modernist values. This shift is expressed also in a relaxation of sexual norms. By and large, there has been a normative shift from sexual Puritanism to more liberal views regarding sex and homosexuality in particular. Yet, despite a growing sexual individualization, Israel remains a family-oriented society with a positive attitude towards procreation, as is evidenced by high marriage and birth rates compared with similar, post-industrial societies. This mixture of family values and relative sexual tolerance makes Israel a remarkable case study for examining the relationship between sex and class. Further, this tension between the more traditional inclination towards family life and the tendency to experiment with sex reinforces the ways in which my interviewees interpret their sexuality as a true exploration of an individualized self.

My point of departure draws from the sociologist Pierre Bourdieu's analysis of the new French middle class. He claims that this class has shifted from a "duty to [a] fun [sexual] ethic." In Bourdieu's analysis, sexual freedom and sexual satisfaction are seen as essential for flagging membership in this class. Intense sexual pleasure is a marker of class status. Yet there has been relatively little research into the class aspects of the quest for intense sexual pleasure. In general, social research on sexuality emphasizes the role of gender rather than class. Furthermore, the sexual culture of the privileged, which is based on a discourse of liberation and self-realization, is not usually seen as class-distinctive. Consequently, the specific ways in which sex is enmeshed in the class experiences of the middle class remains under-explored. This chapter reports on my preliminary research into the role of sexuality in the new middle classes in Israel.

Based on in-depth interviews with middle-class heterosexual men and women in Israel, I will explore two ways in which this class expresses itself through its approach to sexuality. First, sex is approximated to art and to a bohemian way of life. Sex is given an artistic, avant-garde and transgressive meaning. Second, sex is said to indicate a "well connected" person and someone who endorses a "fun" lifestyle. Both the view of "sex as art" and "sex as a lifestyle" accentuate a middle-class culture that puts a premium on individualism and self-expression.

Sex as art

In 1954, a sociologist reviewing Kinsey's book on female sexuality predicted that "in an America which is coming to honor leisure and play … not only is our interest in sex capable of infinite elaboration through all the arts, but intercourse itself is likely to gain recognition as art." Half a century later, Shusterman (2006) argues that art and sex have been unjustly assigned to separate spheres. He argues that sex is an everyday kind of aesthetic experience. My interviewees also approached sex and art as interconnected.

An insight into sex as art is given by a middle-aged academic man, a BDSM (bondage, domination, sado-masochism) master. His sexual journey has taken him to the canon of Western S& M erotic literature. He has also read psychoanalytic scholarship as well as surfed "the cage," an Israeli BDSM website, and watched artistic erotic movies for inspiration and knowledge. This has helped him to contextualize his new found sexual taste within a sophisticated, artsy, libertine heritage. But BDSM is also related to another form of artistic outlet – writing. Examining the largest Israeli BDSM virtual community reveals that members express cultural know-how by writing erotic literary pieces. Writing beautifully, that is, being witty, kinky and racy, is the most common activity in this site. In the BDSM world, writing is also a bodily practice, as when the "master" writes on his "slave's" skin. Our BDSM interviewee is apparently in the habit of writing aphorisms as well as verbal abuse all over the body of his long-time "slave." The aesthetization of BDSM is related both to its aristocratic social history but also to its distinctive theatricality.

This theatricality, that was always there [in my sex life], and it is meant to create some kind of a drama in sex. Many times this drama surpasses sex and it is not directly sexual. It can even be a simple thing, like abstaining from getting naked. As far as I'm concerned, sex should not necessarily start or even continue with nudity.

Theatricality is a way to make sex a powerful aesthetic and erotic experience.

BDSM practitioners are not the only sex artists I discovered. Apparently, one can consider oneself a creator of a superior kind of life even by practicing a more normative – if quite kinky – sexuality. A sense of transgressiveness can be achieved by the simplest means, for example, by not having sex in a bed or preferring "a more disorganized atmosphere," as a male interviewee says. Many of the interviewees perceive some sexual acts as less acceptable and hence more risky and interesting. For example, both women and men report engaging in anal sex, which until recently has been culturally associated with the stigma of homosexuality. Thus, when a senior manager in the NGO (non-governmental organization) sector says she "recently became interested in the ass," this speaks not only to the expanded tolerance of homosexuality but to an ethic that aims to push the sexual envelope. For the new middle classes in Israel, gay culture has come to epitomize coolness. The construction of anal eroticism as a positively "dangerous" and "risky" adventure and its incorporation into heterosexual lives can therefore be interpreted as part of the middle-class politics of "cool."

Artistic creativity is shown in the aesthetization of sex and the elevation of the sexual act to the level of art. One interviewee considered the sexual encounter itself as an out-of-the-ordinary experience. For him, the enactment of a "good fuck" is like the creation of a master-piece for an artist. Sex assumes a kind of transcendent, almost "sacred" value. "Now [when we come] is a good time to die. Like, if I'd died, I would die happy." The aesthetization of sex is also related to a heightened awareness of one's own and one's partner's body. Men and women of the creative class are familiar with their personal turn-ons and turn-offs, and can easily ver-balize them. Moreover, they are aware of the fine-tuning of their bodies when they feel sexual, and are reflexive in identifying the specifics of their desire. A woman says: "Sometimes [when] I'm exhausted, there is something in the weight of [my] body that arouses me sexually." Another interviewee spoke of "sexual competence" as "acknowledging the ability to extract from the body fun and pleasure and to really connect to it. [...] [it's] the way you conduct yourself, [your] thoughts, speech, etc."

In these examples, we can see that feeling sexual is a capacity originating from a heigh-tened awareness of one's body and potential bodily pleasures (to feel aroused when exhausted, or to be aware of one's erotic potential). For the creative class, genuine sexual pleasure entails going against conventional sexual norms or scripts. Sexual excitement is often triggered by being acutely aware of one's specific erotic desires and a willingness to transgress social norms. Like an artistic creation, sexual excitement and pleasure emanate from within the self.

The experience of liberated sex is understood as an expression of authenticity, as it is pre-mised upon an ability to connect body, mind, and self expression when being sexual. Being a sexual person is constructed as an experience of mind/body release and uninhibited flow. For example, a woman says,

There is the satisfaction [per se], but there is also everything that surrounds it. It's a kind of a satisfaction-package. ... This satisfaction is definitely related to having a good orgasm, but it is also so much more. It's not only about coming. I also gain satisfaction from the situa-tion, from the totality of what's happening.

For this woman it is more exciting and fulfilling to be in a sexual mood and to plan a sexual scene than it is to just "come." Sexual satisfaction is thus related to building up to the thrill (such as having a get-away weekend) and not just the act of having sex or the orgasmic moment. In this respect, it is significant that the individual is responsible for generating sexual excitement. One of the clearest expressions of this tendency is being able to be clear about one's sexual needs and to communicate them. Sexual sophistication is thus not about possessing a special skill or technique; nor is it synonymous with being sexy and desired by others. It is a particular disposition towards the body and its pleasures. For the interviewees, sex is not an instinctual drive or act. Rather, it is a learned capacity, which can be cultivated and developed. For example, many interviewees reported that they have gradually learned how to touch and be touched in more pleasurable ways.

The "cultivated" sexual disposition – rather than the "natural" sexual instinct – is similar to what Bernstein (2009) describes in her study of educated, middle-class female sex workers. This new kind of prostitute, she contends, professionalizes her sexual labor by perfecting her sexual skills, such as giving a better massage or becoming a certified sex therapist. But sexually pleasing customers is not the only thing that matters. In fact, in order to successfully market the sexual commodity they offer, these women also strive to perfect an authentic sexual experience. As professional middle-class women, they want to get aroused and experience sexual pleasure with customers. In this regard, and similar to many other service-oriented occupations, they bring their class-based cultural capital to work. But even in a much less "service" oriented atmosphere, cultivating and perfecting one's own pleasure capacities is a serious task.

If "sex work for the middle classes" simulates real-life intimacy, then "non-commercialized" middle-class sex may take the shape of a game. Most of the interviewees emphasize the pleasure of fantasizing, flirting, being "players." They may be sincere – but they are still only players. For example, a female photographer says that her favorite part of intimacy is the falling in love phase, and the sweet agonies that go along with it. Then, she is "horny for days and days" and so she comes "in a second."

Interestingly, there is a gender difference in cultivating the capacity for sexual pleasure. Whereas men stress that, over time, they have learned to please their partners; women talk of becoming more attuned to their sexual needs. In the interviews, men express their masculinity by saying that they are now better lovers than before, more attuned to the "female body," and can make women come better or faster. For example, an academic described how his wife has helped him to be a better, more considerate partner in their marriage. When asked if she was as dominant in their sex life, he replied that "No, [not] in sex. It was something *I* have started exploring and investigating, [it was important for me] to see what makes *her* feel good … , that the point in having sex would be to make her come, that she would feel good with it." Women, on the other hand, tended to construct the ability to take pleasure in sex as a "long forgotten" and reawakened capacity, usually (but not always) as a consequence of a love affair outside marriage. But both men and women underscore their ability to create a pleasurable sexual act, indeed to construct sex as a total pleasure-experience. This is understood as a sign of a sophisticated, avant-garde self.

Sex as lifestyle

As we have seen, being sexually skillful and playful is understood as an expression of a unique and creative self. But an interest in sex is also the backdrop against which they, as typical members of the creative class, can demonstrate their market skills and ability to relate to people. For example, a male interviewee who is a senior insurance agent admits to sometimes closing large-scale deals in a *ménage à trois* with a customer and his wife. Others say their friends know all about their active, fulfilling sexual life, and that they openly discuss "their good sex life" with friends, as well as with business acquaintances. By talking of sex they also increase their reputation and status.

But sex doesn't have to mix with business to be valuable. Interviewees portray sex as part of an endless endeavor of self-improvement. The association of sex and self-care is not surprising, given that fitness and health are essential in the lifestyle of the middle classes. In particular, men emphasize the importance of a culture of self-improvement through bodily and sexual fitness and health. They stress the importance of smelling good, going to the gym, having tattoos, eating well, and, of course, having good sex. In their discourse, sex is not constructed, however, in terms of sexual health or sexual functioning, but rather as taking good care of oneself. Similarly, sex is not discussed as a luxury but rather as a matter of living a high "quality" and sophisticated life. Thus, a highly successful lawyer identified himself as a dedicated and expert host. He enjoys inviting friends over for a tasteful, freshly self-cooked dinner made from the best, freshest and most exquisite ingredients. "I live intensively. If I entertain friends, then I entertain with a million things. I'm constantly stressed out, in my life, in my demand for quality," he says. However, he states, "when I entertain as I like to, I do it for myself. I enjoy the experience of creating it." For him, the attraction lies in being able to create a fine dining experience.

The analogy between food and sex connoisseurship is a recurrent theme in many of the interviews, especially for the men. These "new men" like to cook for their families, go out to ethnic as well as expensive restaurants, invite friends over and experiment with sex, whether anal sex, group sex or attending sex clubs. In this vein, a revealing fantasy of a male interviewee is one in which he cooks dinner for two secretaries and, eventually, "something [sexual] happens." Similarly, when asked to explain what "sexual enjoyment" means for him, another male interviewee compared sex to a range of other lifestyle options that bring pleasure, such as eating out, buying clothes and owning a car.

> What is it that you gain from dining in a nice restaurant? Go have McDonald's! What is it there to gain? In the morning I purge it anyway! What did I gain? More calories? [But] do you enjoy!? Why would you buy a beautiful piece of clothing? Why would you have a nice dinner? Why buy a nice car – and [yet] you don't see the rewards of the most important thing – physical pleasure.

These examples show that sex is placed in the sphere of the everyday and is not formulated as something "sacred" and apart from the "profane." Whereas the importance of sex lies in that it brings pleasure, this is not a crudely bodily pleasure. Instead, sex is conceived of as an opportunity for self-exploration and expression. Similar to the consumption of food or fashion, sex is implicitly divided into more and less sophisticated kinds of pleasures.

In contemporary Israeli life, a refined taste no longer relies only upon the consumption of highbrow cultural products. Rather, it is more often a creative process, whereby consumers interact with cultural forms. Instead of simply purchasing commodities, consumers are increasingly active in creating their own, exciting consumption experience. Thus, going to the gym, drinking coffee in the local Italian-looking café or spending a few hours in the flea market looking for vintage clothes is no less important than the actual body, cup of coffee or piece of clothing one purchases. This, I believe, is why the sex/food analogy is so prevalent in the interviewees' discourse. Food and dining have become a total consumer experience in contemporary times. In many ways, sexual activity can also indicate a playful, creative self.

An interest in sex is sometimes presented as part of a "total" lifestyle of self-refinement and sophistication. The ordinary and easy way in which my interviewees discuss their sexual lives entails considerable cultural wit and social sophistication. The willingness, even enthusiasm with which they share intimate details from their lives is related to what Hey (2005) describes as a distinctive, new middle-class disposition of "excitation." Hey argues that a flexible occupational market blurs "the market/self-interest/social/sexual interest nexus." In the creative occupations, workers are expected to express a very strong yet controlled "shameless pushy" personality (Hey 2005:863). It appears, then, that being a sexually oriented person is a way of relating to people and presenting such a strong personality.

Conclusion

I have argued that sexual liberation is part of the culture of the creative class in contemporary Israel. In this sense, class shapes sexuality. The categories of "sex as art" and "sex as a lifestyle" are related to two significant capacities of the creative class. One is the ability to evaluate sexuality in aesthetic terms; the second is the capacity for self-promotion. These two capacities are extremely significant and beneficial to those who hold them within a capitalist order. In contemporary societies, and this is true of Israel, there has been a shift from corporate, organized capitalism to a global, networked capitalism in which culture itself is a huge business. From a society of producers, we have turned into a society of consumers. The market offers a variety of lifestyles and identities to choose from or construct. However, even in the face of such transformations, class has not disappeared from the social landscape. To a large extent, the freedom to choose and nurture individual lifestyles is a class-based privilege (Bottero 2004).

In consumer-oriented capitalism, unlike industrial capitalism, artistic hierarchies, gender roles, and the separation of labor from leisure and the private from the public sphere are constantly shifting, if not eroding. In this new reality, class differences are ever more subtle. For example, sociologists of culture convincingly show that popular and everyday cultures are more significant than highbrow and canonical cultures in differentiating between classes. Thus, in the past, a privileged social position was related to the conspicuous consumption of high art. But in contemporary capitalism, class-based tastes are largely expressed through skills such as the appreciation and interpretation of art, rather than owning expensive art. More importantly for the current discussion, the aesthetic sphere expands from the artistic to broader social terrains and new cultural forms. In this regard, my interviewees constructed sex as a form of art. For them, sex is one such social sphere of everyday aesthetization.

The creative class also signals its privileged social position by emphasizing self-promotional skills. I explored this notion through the category of "sex as a lifestyle." Here, sex is more than a sign of an artistic sophistication. It also enables social interactions, or strengthens social ties and demonstrates one's communicative skills. In contemporary Israel, where employment flexibility requires flexible workers, the demand from the creative class to present an "authentic self" (unique and special) is institutionalized in the sphere of work. Yet the search for authenticity expands to society at large. For example, according to Bauman (2007), acquiring social value and recognition increasingly depends on the ability to cultivate "subjectivity." By this he means that social standing is strongly related to being communicative and unique, and to projecting a distinctive self-identity to others.

The men and women I interviewed talked about sex using terminology taken directly from the culture of contemporary capitalism. Corporations and people alike are supposed to not only "look sexy" on the outside but also to "be sexy" on the inside. People are expected to project and convince others of their "creative and romantic subjectivity" (Adkins 2008:187). Certain subjective states, like "ease," "flow" or "audacity" may prove personally and economically advantageous. In other words, creativity, sophistication, flexibility, and self-promotion are not only indicators of a "good" sexual citizen but a potentially "good" economic prospect.

It was not long ago that sex was considered a private, personal matter, at least normatively. Sex has now entered the public sphere, and it is commodified in a variety of ways. For instance, sex is commonly used by the media to promote and sell commodities. Sex is also a commodity in itself, part of a global economy of cyber-pornography, sex tourism, trafficking or sex work. Yet, sex does not only promote consumption. More significantly, having sex can feel like shopping. When there are more sexual options to choose from, sex becomes a site for cultivating a sense of individual identity and a social lifestyle. We may have more sexual partners during our lifetime than in the past. We may also experience a "consumerist" type of sex life in which we continuously expect new and exciting pleasures. In this marketplace logic, "we are urged to resist prior (conventional/oppressive/just plain boring) forms of intimacy in much the same way that we are urged to throw out or update last year's wardrobe" (Blum 2002:853). Yet if sex is similar to modern consumer culture and indeed part of this culture, then, like consumer culture itself, sex is also organized along class lines.

Finally, against the backdrop of a "sex industry," the creative class can associate themselves with an elevated kind of sexual experience. By conceiving sex as both aesthetic and a type of social interaction, rather than a merely "biological" act, they can approach sex as a form of self-expression and authenticity. These men and women move easily in the world of aesthetic objects and intense experiences, as they refine their capacity for sexual pleasure. This capacity is class-based.

References

Adkins, Lisa. 2008. "From Retroactivation to Futurity: The End of the Sexual Contract?" *NORA: Nordic Journal of Women's Studies*, 16(3): 182–201.

Bauman, Zygmunt. 2007. *Consuming Life*. Cambridge: Polity.

Bernstein, Elizabeth. 2009. "Sex Work for the Middle Classes." *Sexualities*, 10(4): 473–88.

Blum, Virginia L. 2002. "Introduction: The Liberation of Intimacy: Consumer-Object Relations and (Hetero)Patriarchy." *Antipode*, 34(5): 845–63.

Bottero, Wendy. 2004. "Class Identity and the Identity of Class." *Sociology*, 38(5): 985–1003.

Bourdieu, Pierre. 1984. *Distinction: A Social Critique of the Judgment of Taste*. Cambridge, MA: Harvard University Press.

Gershuny, Jonathan. 2005. "Busyness as the Badge of Honor for the New Superordinate Working Class." *Social Research*, 72(2): 287–314.

Hey, Valerie. 2005. "The Contrasting Social Logics of Sociality and Survival: Cultures of Classed Be/ Longing in Late Modernity." *Sociology*, 39(5): 855–72.

Shusterman, Richard. 2006. "Aesthetic Experience: From Analysis to Eros." *Journal of Aesthetics and Art Criticism*, 64(2): 217–29.

52

Internet sex: the seductive "freedom to"[1]

Dennis D. Waskul

MINNESOTA STATE UNIVERSITY, MANKATO

The lascivious lure is blunt: hundreds of thousands of "XXX pics," "steaming hot live hardcore sex shows," "the sexiest erotic stories – both text and audio," "hardcore chat 24/7," "adult games" and "the hottest new XXX videos." Although many sites claim "something for everyone," the primary allure is apparently for those who prefer "vixens," "sluts," "nymphos," "whores" and "insatiable girls that bear it all for you" – often of a "cum guzzling" variety who "take it up the ass" from "huge" "throbbing" "cocks" that "stuff" and "pound" "pussy" until they "burst," "explode," and "erupt" a "giant load in her pretty face." "No holes barred." "What are you waiting for?" "Cum inside now." "Free Preview." "FREE." "Instant Access." "Join Now." "No Credit Card Required." Indeed.

According to the motto of Cybererotica – one of the most significant industry leaders in e-commercial pornography – the internet is a place "where fantasy meets reality." However, this particular intersection of fantasy and reality – decidedly androcentric, often misogynistic, aggressive, sometimes violent, and frequently packaged in a carnivalized form of grotesque degradation (see Langman 2004) – is chiefly the product of the hucksters of commercial internet pornography. If the motto of Cybererotica is correct, then this fantasy meets *commercial* internet reality: relatively low start-up costs, the most cost-efficient technology of reproduction to date, a product consumers "access" without distribution expenses, and an instant global market of actual and potential credit card consumers who pay to (click and) play. For these reasons, commercial internet pornography is driven by the market and market competition as much as by consumer demands. Indeed, commercial internet pornography may reveal much more about e-commerce and the internet marketplace than about sexuality (see Perdue 2002).

The situation is quite different when one need not "pay to play" – a form of erotic computer-mediated experience most often called "cybersex." Among those familiar with this sort of activity, cybersex strictly refers to erotic forms of real-time computer-mediated *communication*. Rather than a passive consumption of relatively static pornography, cybersex entails active, interactive, and creative communication with others through typed text, live digital video, sometimes spoken voice (by use of computer microphones), or some combination thereof. Cybersex is typically (but not necessarily) an anonymous experience: participants generally know one another only through a self-chosen screen name (often a name like "BustyBabe," "HungHunk," "SWF4U," or "BiGuy"); while intimate sexual desires are expressed, participants rarely share personal identifying information. Although people may pay a fee – for client software, to a service provider, or an internet "virtual sex worker" (typically a webcam performer) – participants in an authentic cybersex encounter have no ulterior economic motive. In an authentic cybersex encounter, erotic internet communications are strictly for fun and free; motives approximate those of other free-will sexual encounters: desire, expression, intimacy, play, experimentation, arousal, and/or orgasm.

Cybersex is primarily experienced in one of two forms. Cybersex can be a purely textual activity: two or more people connected by a computer network send each other sexually explicit messages that discursively perform an erotic encounter. Chiefly found in internet chat and instant messaging environments, "hot chat" is a written sexual conversation – much like phone sex, only typed instead of spoken – a form of coauthored interactive erotica. Cybersex can also be experienced by use of digital cameras. Using relatively inexpensive "webcams," cybersex participants may not only type to one another but also watch (as they are watched) in live streaming video. Unlike hot chat, webcam cybersex is less about "coauthored interactive erotica" and more about exhibitionism, voyeurism, "I'll show you mine if you show me yours," seeing and being seen nude, masturbating, involving other clandestine sexual pleasures, and even engaging in sex acts with one or more persons "in the flesh" that are shared with one or more persons "in the virtual" (akin, perhaps, to a virtual *ménage à trois*, virtual soft-swinging, or a virtual orgy). The differences between text cybersex and webcam cybersex are not trivial. In the next sections I will briefly detail the distinct nature and expressed motives and virtues of both text and webcam cybersex.

Text cybersex

Text cybersex is a form of discursive role-playing intended to inspire sexual imagination and fantasy. By describing actions and responding to chat partners, participants pretend they are involved in an actual sexual encounter. For this reason, the quality of "hot chat" typically depends on extensive sexual and communicative literacy. In other words, "good" text cybersex depends on the ability to use *words* to evoke vivid, rich, visceral mental images and sequences of events – which is precisely what the participants in my studies of cybersex repeatedly suggested:

> An active imagination and expansive vocabulary help. Using predictable expressions is a little ho-hum. Just saying "I want to suck your dick" is unlikely to arouse many people.
> There are only so many ooohs and mmm hummms you can type.

Text cybersex is purely about "typing dirty", it involves neither touching nor seeing bodies (other than one's own). For this reason, participants are generally free to assume a wide variety of imaginative roles and otherwise playfully toy with alternative vicarious experience. As several text cybersex participants told me:

> Cybersex allows the freedom of sexual expression. Cybersex allows a person to be whoever or whatever they want to be!!
> It's erotic, it turns me on – the mystery of it. Not knowing who is really on the other end is really erotic – you can be anything. I may stretch truth, and live out fantasies … it allows you to be with whoever you want – no inhibitions.
> You can do anything you want and you can picture anybody you wish.
> Sometimes I pretend I'm a woman. I've also invented experiences (like 3 somes). … Cybersex enables me to play out fantasies … it allows you to take your dreams one step closer to reality.

According to many text cybersex participants, these experiences provide a means to learn new sexual techniques, discover or explore new turn-ons, and vicariously experience arousal in ways they would not (or could not) in everyday life. Consequently, text cybersex participants often described the experience as meaningful, highly valued, and full of perceived therapeutic overtures:

> With cybersex I learned stuff I didn't know, like maybe how to do some things better. Everyone should try it!
>
> Since I've started chatting with people online, I've been walking around in this perpetual state of arousal! It's wonderful! I mean, perpetual, never ending, I'm always thinking about sex, coming up with new ideas, listening to other people's fantasies and expressions and learning things I never knew existed!
>
> Whether a guy or a girl sends me a private message and wants to talk, it's usually very exciting. I am 32 years old and think I am only now reaching my sexual prime, and I don't know that I'd have discovered certain things about myself without it. I never thought I could be so free with my emotions and fantasies, and it's even spilled over into my real life, I mean now I feel free about talking about my sexuality (bi-sexuality) with other people openly, now that I've discussed it with myself first (which basically is what I'm doing here, talking to a nameless, faceless person, i.e., ME!).
>
> I guess the reason I do it is because it is a safe medium by which to explore sexually. To experiment with those aspects of sex that you have not yet explored. To enhance your sex life through the use of new ideas that are learned with a new sexual partner, without risk. It is also a way to be excited sexually without the performance anxiety that is present in face-to-face encounters. It is a way to express yourself sexually in a way you may not feel comfortable doing in a relationship.

Clearly, these cybersex participants view "hot chat" as a context to explore the surfaces and depths of sexual desire, imagination, and fantasy. Because it is purely typed text, these cybersex participants describe the experience as providing unprecedented "freedom of sexual expression," "to be whomever or whatever they want"; a safe medium to explore and experiment with sex. While there are obvious limits to these alleged "freedoms" (see Waskul, Douglass, and Edgley 2000), one cannot deny that in a medium of words (and words alone) people are generally "free" to present themselves as whomever (or whatever) they want – generally "free" to indulge desires and fantasy in a context that is generally "free" of stigma (and other social sanctions) – even if those expressions tend to adhere to relatively conventional sexual and gender scripts. Indeed, it is precisely these freedoms that Cleo Odzer (1997: 43) cites in a frank description of her internet sex life:

> With the freedom to be and do anything, I had sex with three men once. Posing as a man, I had sex with a woman. Posing as a gay man, I had sex with a man. I had sex with a man who was posing as a woman. I learned all about S&M, as the sadist and the masochist. I had all sorts of sex in every new way I could think of.

Webcam cybersex

In contrast, "webcam" cybersex is all about looking at bodies, having one's own body gazed upon, for the explicit purposes of sexual arousal. Consequently, because live streaming video reveals fleshy facts, people are not free "to be whomever or whatever they want." Certain physical characteristics are apparent, for the most part, and all the more so when clothing is removed: gender, race, physique, attractiveness, weight, even a rough approximation of age. Consequently, webcam cybersex may similarly excite sexual imagination and fantasy, but the experience has everything to do with bodies – namely, seeing and being seen as sex objects. As several webcam cybersex participants told me:

> When someone is turned on by watching me, it make me feel that I'm sexier than I truly believe I am … it's nice to get compliments on … the body … I just think it's sexy that people can masturbate and think of me, little ole me.
>
> Having a few dozen guys tell you how hot you are, etc., really gives you a great outlook on how you see yourself sexually. Positive reinforcement!
>
> [Webcam cybersex] feels wonderful! Of course, it makes me feel like he desires my body. … As you can see, I'm a pretty good size woman. I'm not uncomfortable about it on here. I feel as desirable as the ladies who are much smaller than me. As a matter of fact, I feel very sexy and seductive on here.
>
> I enjoy most the emotional uplift I get from people telling me I am beautiful. I need to feel that I'm still attractive … It's just good to have people tell you you are still attractive.

This is easy to understand – it feels good to be told one is attractive, sexy, and desirable. For these cybersex participants the excitement others receive from seeing them nude is repaid by the comforting knowledge that one's body *is* appealing. As these quotes also illustrate, this is particularly the case for people who feel disenchanted with their body as an object of sexual arousal. Often this disenchantment has everything to do with perceptions of their physical appearances, especially regarding age and weight. As one man explained: "Being 48, it makes me feel attractive when someone compliments me on the body." Another explained, "It feels good when others compliment me. I feel like, even though I'm overweight, I am accepted by them."

Even so, it is misleading to conclude that webcam cybersex is all about aged and overweight people congratulating one another on their continued sexiness. A great number of webcam cybersex participants are highly attractive 20- and 30-year-olds. Yet, they too often share a similar disenchantment, but for different reasons. In fact, these webcam cybersex participants most often relate their disenchantment to marriage and long-term partnerships. For some, the problem is related to the routinization of their normal sexual activities and the desire for a different experience. As one woman told me, "My main reason for being here is to be sociable, hoping to meet that Mr. Right even though I'm married and have a very active sex life at home. The ROUTINE part sucks!" A man told me something very similar: "I've been in a long-term relationship for almost 5 years, and this way I can remain faithful to that while still getting off with hot guys from around the world." However, for most participants I interviewed, the desire for different sexual partners and novel erotic experiences is less important than what webcam cybersex does to re-enchant a sense of their body as an object of sexual arousal.

Murray Davis (1983: 119) once wrote: "[M]arriage seems almost intentionally designed to make sex boring." We may add that long-term sexual relationships also tend to make our bodies boring. In time, being seen nude by one's lover becomes so commonplace that our sexual generators simply run out of gas or otherwise lose their erotic power. Thus, it makes sense. When our own nudity no longer generates appreciative erotic power, a person may come to feel undesirable, unattractive, inadequate, and thoroughly unsexy. For this reason, some participants discover webcam cybersex useful in refueling a connection to their sexual body and rejuvenating their perceptions of the power of that body to generate eroticism:

I've been with my wife for so long now that our bodies aren't as exciting as they once were. Our sex life is ok, but without that special quality I sometimes feel like a piece of furniture around the house. When someone is excited about seeing me in all my nudity I suddenly feel sexually awake again.

Hubby is older than I am. He knows nothing of this. I'm not a complainer but he does not have the passion or desire, or at least he doesn't know how to show me. ... it's hard for him to tap into the part of my brain that triggers stimulation. I'm a very erotic person. The feeling of being naughty is a turn-on too. See, I'm bad, but I love it.

These expressed motives and virtues – of both text cybersex and webcam cybersex – are not particularly surprising. It's hardly shocking to discover that people who engage in cybersex tend to appreciate the experience. However, magnifying the obvious is often worthwhile: people who engage in cybersex tend to find the experience sexually arousing, but they also frequently report other pleasures that have everything to do with exploring, expressing, and cultivating a sexual imagination as well as acquiring new looking-glasses by which they assess themselves as an object and subject of sexual pleasure. Furthermore, exploring these "obvious" dynamics sharply contrasts with much published literature on cybersex, a majority of which seems quite intent on magnifying problems, dangers, and moral issues. Indeed, moral panic regarding cybersex, some of which I will address in the next section, is all too common.

Cybersex and moral panic

There seems no shortage of either "problemizers" or "problematizing" regarding the internet. For example, psychologist Kimberly Young is most known for her questionable assertion that "Internet Addiction Disorder" has reached epidemic proportions in the United States (in 1998 she estimated there were five million "addicts") and that the internet is a "millennial addiction" (1998: 28). Similarly, the subtitle to a book edited by Al Cooper *et al.* (2000) apparently plagiarizes filmmaker George Lucas: Cooper seeks to expose *The Dark Side of the Force*. However, unlike the movie *Star Wars*, in Cooper's apparent version of the movie fiction "the force" refers to the internet and "the dark side" of sex and pornography. Cooper (Cooper *et al.* 2000; Cooper 2002) and a growing cadre of associates have sought to provide an empirical foundation for "cybersex compulsivity," its health risks, and the appropriate "treatment." Unlike the run-of-the-mill "internet addict" that so deeply concerned Kimberly Young, these scholars suggest that cybersex – not the internet – is the "drug of choice" (Delmonico *et al.* 2002: 147, 149). Indeed, a quick review of the published literature on cybersex reveals an obvious bias: a large proportion examines sex on the internet as a form of "sexual addiction," "compulsive" behavior, and otherwise a manifestation of a "hypersexuality" disorder.

The prevalence of these problematizing literatures is curious considering that most researchers report that 1 percent (or less) meet *their own* definitions of internet "sex addicts" or "cybersex compulsives" – far less than the expansive literature on the subject might suggest. In fact, the number is so small that even the most well-known scholars of "cybersex compulsivity" (see Cooper *et al.* 2000: 19) are forced to admit that "[t]hough the focus of this article is sexually compulsive behavior on the internet, it bears reiterating that one of our major findings was that for the vast majority of respondents, surfing the internet for sexual pursuits did not lead to significant difficulties in their lives." However, apparently unwilling to accept the findings of their own study, Cooper *et al.* (2000: 20, 24) followed up this statement by claiming that there really *are* more compulsive cybersex addicts who dangerously flirt with the internet because "a significant portion (possibly between 27 and 42%) are likely to be in denial about the true severity of their issues," and that, "[i]n any case, the use of chat rooms for sexual pursuits should be a red flag and something to which clinicians should pay particular attention." Cooper *et al.* (2000: 25) conclude by likening "cybersex compulsivity" to a rampant drug addiction, suggesting that 200,000 Americans are likely to be "addicted" to sex on the internet, which they suggest is "a hidden public health hazard."

I do not deny that some people become compulsive about sex on the internet, but to characterize an empirical one percent as *really* more indicative of a speculative 27–42 percent is at the very least questionable, clearly hasty, perhaps poor science, possibly arrogant, and maybe self-serving. In fact, given the evidence offered, suggesting that sex on the internet might represent a "hidden public health hazard" may even qualify as irresponsible. When scholars are apparently unwilling to accept the findings of their own studies, choosing, instead, to gloss empirical data in lieu of hunches about what they "think" might be more accurate, we should *all* raise an eyebrow of suspicion.

When they are not concerned about the alleged hazards of internet sex to a person's own "health," many scholars are concerned about the perils to a person's relationships with others. This is particularly the case in literature examining what has come to be called "virtual infidelity." While, once again, I do not deny that internet sex can represent problems with "new infidelity" (Glass 2003), nonetheless upon closer examination the problem becomes more complex than is often presumed. For example, in *Cybersex Exposed*, Jennifer Schneider and Robert Weiss (2001) dedicate an entire chapter to "The Cybersex Widow(er)." Schneider and Weiss provide rich ethnographic data on 100 people (97 women and three men) who "felt" they lost their partners to cybersex. Significantly, several people cited by Schneider and Weiss freely acknowledge previous real-life infidelities; as one person said: "My husband has actually cheated on me with a real partner, and it *feels no different!*" (2001: 105; emphasis in original). Although Schneider and Weiss skirt the point, it seems reasonable to presume that a history of violated trust is a significant variable to consider in the tribulations endured by these so-called "cybersex widows." Even more interesting are many accounts from respondents who appear mostly distraught by *masturbation*. Consider, for example, just a few words cited by Schneider and Weiss (2001: 89–90; 93):

> I knew my husband was masturbating all the time, but I thought it was my fault, that I just wasn't attractive enough for him. When I found pornography files on his computer going back five years, everything made sense. ... I thought I was not good enough because I did not look like the girls in the computer pictures. I thought if I dressed and looked better, it would keep him interested. Eventually, I gave up competing with his masturbating and chose not to have sex with him. His behavior has left me feeling alone, isolated, rejected, and less than a desired woman. Masturbation hangs a sign on the door that says, "You are not needed. I can take care of myself, thank you very much."

Obviously, for these respondents in Schneider and Weiss's study, masturbation within marriage is a "problem." Yet, oddly, Schneider and Weiss gloss the masturbation issue and attribute the trouble to "cybersex." Once again, I do not deny that internet sex can pose difficulties for committed relationships, but clearly there is more to the story than first appears. Pinning these fidelity problems on "cybersex" may be convenient and attention-grabbing – but is it accurate?

I suggest that these problematizing studies are more about morality than social science. Even more, these moral positions are often based on highly questionable assumptions. On one hand, they regularly hinge on questionable determinist views of the effects of media. On the other hand, they are often based on equally questionable essentialist views of sex, sexuality, children, women, men, and the nature of committed relationships (especially marriage). While this is not the place for a full critique of these studies (some of which *do* have merit), I merely suggest a more critical stance on the all-too-easy claims regarding the hazards, dangers, perils, and risks of internet sex. Indeed, as Steven Stern and Alysia Handel (2001: 283, 289) have neatly pointed out, contemporary concerns about sex on the internet are nothing new: "they are part of a recurring pattern in which people worry about the use of new technology for sexual purposes" and "focusing too heavily on these details might distract us from a complete understanding of sexuality on the internet."

Discussion

Like cars and telephones, computer networking technologies bestow a seductive freedom – the "freedom to" (Stoll 1995: 234). In the case of internet sex, the "freedom to" can assume many and multiple forms: the freedom to experiment with the surfaces and depths of one's desires and fantasies; the freedom to present one's self and body alternatively; the freedom to indulge sexual interest with relatively minimal fear of consequence (either physical or social); the freedom to see and be seen as both a sex object and a sex subject to whatever degree one feels comfortable; the freedom momentarily to shed social roles (faithful partner, monogamous spouse, dedicated parent, or whatever); the freedom to play, explore, and discover in ways that one might not (or cannot) in everyday life. One way to characterize these various "freedoms to" is a simple recognition: the internet bestows the freedom to "be" without "being" in a "space" without "place" (see Waskul 2005). On the internet, everybody is any body, and any body is nobody in particular. Likewise, on the internet, everywhere is any where, everyplace is any place, and anywhere is nowhere in particular. Consequently, the internet provides a context, medium, and environment in which people have the "freedom to" slip through the cracks of otherwise mundane everyday life.

It is not surprising that circumstances like these evoke moral condemnation, from many sources (religious, political, legal, social-scientific, and so on). To whatever extent we believe that the whole of a person – sexual or otherwise – is rightly found in an individual's over-socialized roles of society (occupational, family, romantic, etc.), then any "crack" that allows people freely to shed those roles will be deemed a threat to moral and social order. At the very least, as scholars of the social world, it is worth recalling that such a view is the antithesis of many influential theoretical perspectives and conceptual frameworks which detail the nature of human social life (see Waskul 2005). Regardless, internet sex is potentially "sex off the leash" – a form of sexual expression that exists outside of most formal social controls – and that is precisely why it tends to offend some people while also posing a tantalizing draw for others. As Cleo Odzer (1997: 113) rightly points out, "To society, the worst use of sex, of course, is as a means to an end that's not socially sanctioned." The motives and virtues of internet sex certainly represent one such "means to an end that's not socially sanctioned." Perhaps those who adhere closest to Augustinian or Freudian views of sexuality – viewing sex as a potentially dangerous source of both destruction and evil – would agree that unsanctioned sexuality is a timeless peril that requires faithful and vigilant guards. Perhaps others might see sexuality as infinitely more than a person's behaviors, something that includes thoughts, dreams, desires, and fantasies that are not so easily contained by social control – too much of which might result in monstrous expressions. Perhaps others will merely find it all ironic, amusing, and playful. Others still might simply remain fascinated by it all. Indeed, in the final analysis, internet sex is much like many other subjects and experiences – it might well be assessed by how it uniquely moves you.

Note

1 I would like to thank Phillip Vannini and Matthew Bernius for their gracious reviews of early versions of this chapter.

References

Cooper, Al. (ed.) 2002. *Sex and the internet: A Guidebook for Clinicians*. New York: Brunner–Routledge.

Cooper, Al, David Delmonico, and Ron Burg. 2000. "Cybersex Users, Abusers, and Compulsives: New Findings and Implications." In A. Cooper (ed.), *Cybersex: The Dark Side of the Force*. Philadelphia, PA: Brunner–Routledge.

Davis, Murray. 1983. *Smut: Erotic Reality/Obscene Ideology*. Chicago, IL: University of Chicago Press.

Delmonico, David, Elizabeth Griffin, and Patrick Carnes. 2002. "Treating Online Compulsive Sexual Behavior: When Cybersex is the Drug of Choice." In A. Cooper (ed.), *Sex and the Internet: A Guidebook for Clinicians*. New York: Brunner–Routledge.

Glass, Shirley. 2003. *Not Just Friends*. New York: The Free Press.

Langman, L. 2004. "Grotesque Degradation: Globalization, Carnivalization, and Cyberporn." In D. Waskul (ed.), *Net.SeXXX: Readings on Sex, Pornography, and the Internet*. New York: Peter Lang.

Odzer, Cleo. 1997. *Virtual Spaces: Sex and the Cyber Citizen*. New York: Berkley Books.

Perdue, Lewis. 2002. *EroticaBiz: How Sex Shaped the Internet*. New York: Writers Club Press.

Schneider, Jennifer and Robert Weiss. 2001. *Cybersex Exposed: Simple Fantasy or Obsession?* Center City, MN: Hazelden.

Stern, Steven and Alysia Handel. 2001. "Sexuality and Mass Media: The Historical Context of Psychology's Reaction to Sexuality on the Internet." *Journal of Sex Research* 38 (4): 283–91.

Stoll, Cliff. 1995. *Silicon Snake Oil: Second Thoughts on the Information Highway*. New York: Doubleday.

Waskul, Dennis. 2002. "The Naked Self: Being a Body in Televideo Cybersex." *Symbolic Interaction* 25 (2): 199–227.

——2003. *Self-Games and Body-Play: Personhood in Online Chat and Cybersex*. New York: Peter Lang.

——(ed.) 2004. *Net.SeXXX: Readings on Sex, Pornography, and the internet*. New York: Peter Lang.

——2005. "Ekstasis and the Internet: Liminality and Computer-Mediated Communication." *New Media & Society* 7 (1): 45–61.

Waskul, Dennis, Mark Douglass, and Charles Edgley. 2000. "Cybersex: Outercourse and the Enselfment of the Body." *Symbolic Interaction* 23 (4): 375–97.

Young, Kimberly. 1998. *Caught on the Net: How to Recognize the Signs of Internet Addiction – and a Winning Strategy for Recovery*. New York: John Wiley and Sons.

53

The time of the sadomasochist

Hunting with(in) the "tribus"

Darren Langdridge

THE OPEN UNIVERSITY, UNITED KINGDOM

Sadism and masochism were unknown medical terms until the late nineteenth century, when the psychiatrist Richard von Krafft-Ebing introduced these labels to refer to the very particular, and indeed sometimes quite peculiar, behaviors of some of his patients. Later still, Freud (1905) brought the terms together to produce the label of sadomasochism, which remains in widespread use today to describe sexual activity involving bondage and/or the infliction or receipt of pain or humiliation: a sadist preferring to bind the other, inflict pain and/or humiliation, whilst a masochist preferring to be bound, receive pain and/or humiliation. These acts of description had a much more profound impact than simply drawing public attention to behaviors that have been known for many hundreds of years, however. For with recognition by the medical profession, the people engaged in these practices were at once demonized and subject to the control of the state through the twin arms of the medical and legal professions. Of course, some of the behaviors described by Krafft-Ebing and Freud were non-consensual acts of violence, perpetrated on unwilling victims. But others were not, instead being fully consensual acts sought out for the pleasure they afforded. This crucial distinction remains at the heart of the dispute over the legitimacy of sadomasochism as a sexual practice/identity that may be pursued by consenting adults.

In this chapter I outline the ways in which sadomasochists have forged new sexual sub-cultures in the US and UK; that is, distinct communities of people engaged in similar practices. With this in mind, I highlight the way in which safe, sane, and consensual practice forms the basis for membership of most sadomasochistic sub-cultures. First, however, it will be necessary to provide some context to the discussion of S/M as a sub-culture through consideration of the way in which S/M has been the subject of medical and legal attention.

The medical gaze and the resistant sadomasochistic subject

Since 1886 the medical profession has continued to describe, theorize about and "treat" people who engage in sadomasochistic sex. Most often this has involved the medical profession working with people engaging in non-consensual acts of sexual violence. However, work with this population has then often been applied to all people who engage in S/M. This is rather unfortunate since this particular process serves to conflate consensual and non-consensual practices (and people), with research priority invariably given over to that which is non-consensual. Only rarely has the medical profession sought to explore the meaning of such practices amongst people happily and consensually engaging in them for the pleasure they afford, fully cognisant of what they are doing. Sadism and masochism are still classified as psychiatric disorders within the Diagnostic and Statistical Manual of the American Psychiatric Association (DSM IV – 1994) and the International Classification of Diseases of the World Health Organization (ICD 10 – 1992), the two most widely used psychiatric diagnostic manuals. Like homosexuality some thirty years ago, consensual sadism and masochism are considered alongside rape and child sexual abuse as individual psychopathologies. The inclusion of these diagnostic categories and the continuing difficulties encountered with the medical profession are in large part due to the influence of early psychoanalytic understandings of sadomasochism, which considered it a developmental disorder along with homosexuality and indeed pretty much anything other than heterosexual sexual intercourse. There are, however, ongoing campaigns in both the US and the UK to have these diagnostic categories removed from future editions of DSM and ICD.

As mentioned above, the medical categorization of sadomasochism operates to do much more than simply describe a group of sexual behaviors. The power of medicine to pathologize has long been recognized, and this is particularly apparent with sadomasochism, where the voice of the participant has been drowned out by the voice of the medical professional. But whilst participants' voices have historically been silenced, this appears to be changing, as sadomasochism becomes a sexual story (cf. Plummer 1995), gaining wider recognition and acceptance. More recently, there has been a growth in sociological and psychological research that has sought to give voice to practitioners themselves with the aim of understanding the meaning of these practices/identities. Unlike much medical research, this work does not attempt to impose a pre-determined, culturally and morally conditioned, theoretical framework on people, but rather seeks to give priority to the voices of practitioners themselves so that their own meanings are prioritized.

Operation Spanner and the legal battle for the sadomasochistic body

Opposition to S/M has not only been medical but also legal, and "Operation Spanner" serves as a key example of the way in which the state has sought to mark off what is and what is not acceptable, with regard to consensual sexual practice, in the UK at least. In December 1990, sixteen gay men were convicted for engaging in consensual sadomasochistic sex – in an operation codenamed "Spanner" by the police investigating the case. The men were either fined, or imprisoned for up to four and a half years, depending on the perceived severity of the acts in which they were involved. Even though none of the men required medical treatment, the injuries were deemed serious enough to warrant prosecution. They appealed to the House of Lords (Regina v Brown and others, 1994) and the European Court of Human Rights (Laskey v United Kingdom, 1997, 24 EHHR 39), both of which turned down their appeals. In the UK High Court the defence of consent was denied since, according to Mr. James Rant QC, the presiding judge, it was the role of the law to draw the line "between what is acceptable in a civilised society and what is not." Furthermore, it was decided that sadomasochism, unlike decorative piercing, tattooing, or contact sports (such as boxing), should not be exempt from the law of assault. Whilst these men have now been released from prison, the campaign to clear their names and prevent the imprisonment of others engaged in consensual sadomasochistic sex continues (see online at http://www.spannertrust.org (accessed March 17 2006)).

The Spanner case raises a number of important issues and, in particular, the importance of the intersection of gender, sexual identity, and sexual practice. All the defendants were gay men, and there is evidence to suggest that this may have been an important factor in their prosecution. In another similar case, where a husband branded his initials on his wife's buttocks (Regina v Wilson, 1996), the court accepted the defence of consent in spite of the act being serious enough to fall under the legal category of assault occasioning actual bodily harm, as it did in the Spanner case. In this case, the courts stated that consensual activity between a husband and wife in the matrimonial home was not a proper subject for criminal prosecution. One wonders what the view of the court would have been if the wife had branded the husband, or if two lesbians had branded each other with their initials. The implications of even more complex intersections, with for instance race and ethnicity, nationality or disability alongside gender, sexual identity and sexual practice, are also worth considering. For there is not one set of sadomasochistic behaviors but many different sadomasochistic behaviors; not one sadomasochistic practitioner but many different sadomasochistic practitioners; not one sadomasochistic community but many different sadomasochistic communities. S/M citizens may be white, male, middle-class and able-bodied, or black, female, lesbian and disabled, and every variation in between. Privilege may be accrued with one aspect of a person's identity or practice whilst simultaneously denied by another. With so much diversity, state authorities will find it increasingly difficult to regulate such practices/identities but, as the Spanner case demonstrates, they may well try, even if it involves the gross oversimplification of such diversity in the pursuit of prosecution, for the spurious desire to draw the line between what is and what is not acceptable in a civilized society.

Sadomasochistic sub-cultures

A number of factors have led to the growth of new sadomasochistic sexual sub-cultures, including, of course, the simple desire to meet others with similar sexual interests/identities. However, a number of other factors have coincided in recent years to bring about the rise of these new communities in the West, including: the growth of urbanization and industrialization enabling autonomous personal lives to develop; oppressive state interference in people's personal lives and the resistance that this engenders; changes in communication and the mass media; the emergence of individual stories of personal suffering, pain, and then triumph; the (very recent) rise of positive psychotherapeutic and medical professionals encouraging the story; and the development of an interactive social world ready to hear the story (cf. Plummer 1995). These factors have been similarly identified as key elements in the emergence of the lesbian and gay movement and the attempts of lesbians and gays to gain equality and social justice. Indeed, the rise of S/M has in many, though not all, ways followed a similar path to the rise of the lesbian and gay movement in the 1970s and 1980s. Furthermore, Giddens (1991) argues that in these late-modern times we are witnessing a transformation of intimacy. One consequence of this is the emergence of "plastic sexuality" – sexuality with a focus on pleasure rather than on either reproduction or romantic love. The recent prominence of S/M may be viewed as part of a culture of sexual pleasure.

Sadomasochism, as a new sexual story, certainly appears to be in the ascendancy. S/M has appeared in: film ("9 and ½ Weeks," "Blue Velvet," "Crash," "Quills," "Tie me up, Tie me down," "Sasayaki (Moonlight Whispers)," "Wild At Heart"); television (advertisements, including Calvin Klein and Häagen Dazs, and programs such as "Buffy The Vampire Slayer," "Twin Peaks," and numerous "late-night" documentaries); music (from "The Velvet Underground" and "REM," to "Twisted Sister," and from "Robbie Williams" and "Kylie Minogue," to "Eminem" and "Marilyn Manson"); literature ("Coming to power," "Consensual Sadomasochism," "Leatherfolk," "Public Sex: The Culture of Radical Sex," "Screw the Roses, Send me the Thorns," "SM101," "The Topping Book: Or, Getting Good at Being Bad") and so on. The list is almost endless, and continually growing. Much of this represents a watered-down version of S/M, but still it seems that the public appetite is there, as is a media willing to feed this hunger.

But sadomasochistic communities are complex things. As noted previously, there is not one S/M community or sub-culture but a myriad of communities serving a myriad of purposes. Unity and division can be seen within and between such communities, and radical differences in identity work and practice witnessed. Some communities consist of members relating to each other much like family members, caring for each other and ensuring that all involved feel a sense of belonging. Other communities will be much more transient, driven primarily by desire and fuelled by a commercialism similar to that within many contemporary lesbian, gay, and bisexual communities. Indeed, there has been tremendous growth in the commercial S/M scene, with clubs emerging in major cities catering for pretty much every desire. Cutting across these different communities will be structural variations. In particular, communities are more often than not structured by sex and sexual orientation. Distinct scenes exist for gay men and lesbians, as well as straight men and women. Bi and trans people may find a home in one or both of these communities, or instead create an alternative queer space in which such binary divisions matter much less. Other structural factors, such as class or race, may also play a part. Research shows that, on the commercial gay S/M scene at least, there remains a dominant white, middle-class male population, although it is worth noting that this appears to be changing with increasing numbers of working-class, black and Asian men inhabiting previously white, middle-class spaces. Finally, people engaged in S/M may embrace or resist S/M as an identity at different times and in different places. For some, S/M is their primary identity, with man or woman, gay or straight, working-class or middle-class, all secondary or sometimes not important at all. For others, S/M describes all or part of their sexual practice rather than their identity, and membership of S/M communities may or may not be important as a consequence. This complexity makes it difficult to speak of S/M as a distinct sub-culture, and instead I argue S/M communities are better understood as "neo-tribes" (Maffesoli 1996).

The concept of the "neo-tribe" has been growing in popularity in cultural studies as a heuristic for understanding the ways in which nebulous communities might serve the needs of their members in a time still dominated by a culture of individualism. Sadomasochistic sub-cultures provide very clear examples of neo-tribes. Unlike sub-cultures, S/M communities are fluid and dynamic, coming together through a sense of sexual belonging rather than through structural or political factors. S/M practitioners will enter a community for the sense of belonging it engenders, and then leave it in search of another. Many will also be members of multiple communities, living out multiple (sometimes competing) identities. Maffesoli (1996) seeks to re-work the notion of a tribe, moving away from traditional anthropological under-standings, through a consideration of the way the individual has increasingly served to function as *the* key feature of social life, in the West at least, for the last half century. There have of course been communities in recent years in which the individual gave way to the group, but these communities have tended to be fixed, structured by race or class. Very recently, however, we have witnessed the rise of new forms of communities in which people come together for "mutual aid, conviviality, commensurality [and] professional support" (Maffesoli 1996: 69). That is, these communities function to enable people to bind together, fulfilling the deeply felt need to experience a sense of belonging in countries where individualism dominates. Weinzierl and Muggleton (2003: 12) describe the "*tribus*" (collection of neo-tribes) thus:

The "tribe" is also "without the rigidity of the forms of organization with which we are familiar; it refers more to a certain ambience, a state of mind, and it is preferably to be expressed through lifestyles that favour appearance and 'form'" (Maffesoli 1996: 98). Tribes do not therefore exhibit stable practices of inclusion and exclusion – they are integrative and distinctive at the same time. These new network socialities seem to encourage plural, fluid, and part-time rather than fixed, discrete, and encompassing group identities – individuals are able to flow between multiple signs of identity conceptions.

S/M communities provide very good examples of neo-tribes in the making. Here there is little that is static, with much that is played out in terms of appearance and form: two key characteristics of neo-tribes (Maffesoli 1996). Motifs appear and disappear, are changed and manipulated, as new desires emerge and take center-stage. Surface appearance and form is emphasized through bondage, leather, rubber or metal, along with the skin, of course, as the final material to be enjoyed by practitioners. Tattooing, branding, and other forms of body modification also play an integral part in many S/M communities. Membership of most S/M communities is also not fixed, with practitioners moving within and between communities as they seek out acceptance and support along with the gratification of desire. What is crucial, however, is the attitude of the practitioner, and in particular their desire (or not) to subscribe to the norms of the neo-tribe they seek to join.

In the following section I draw on recently published work on S/M (Beckman 2001; Langdridge and Butt 2004, 2005; Taylor and Ussher 2001), along with publicly accessible material written by S/M practitioners on the internet, to highlight the ways in which S/M practitioners produce and refine rule systems for the neo-tribes they have created. In particular, I focus on the active maintenance of a robust notion of consent in S/M communities, and the ways in which community members regulate this through advice, support, and active intervention. At all times the focus will be on giving voice to practitioners themselves, in stark contrast to much previous work on this topic where the theoretical perspective of the researcher has led to the silencing of the researched.

Negotiating safe, sane, and consensual S/M

"Safe, sane, and consensual" is a phrase very familiar to S/M practitioners, for it has emerged as *the* central rule for most, though not all, S/M practice. Indeed, for many within S/M communities any sex which is not safe, sane, and consensual is abusive and to be avoided at all costs. Safe play involves safety at a number of levels. First, there is the physical safety of the people involved in the "scene" (the term for any situation where people are engaging in S/M sex). This often involves careful negotiation before a scene, ongoing discussion throughout a scene, the use of "safewords" (an agreed code word/s which means the scene must stop or slow down), the provision of equipment to aid safe play (like condoms, gloves, strong scissors) and so on. Safe play is also likely to involve careful negotiation around mental safety to avoid those involved in a scene panicking or feeling used or abused. This may include considerable "aftercare," where people spend time soothing any injuries and ensuring that there is no unwanted emotional aftermath. Sane play is in many ways connected with safe play, especially where emotional safety is concerned. This particular feature of S/M has arisen, at least in part, as a response to pathologizing medical understandings of S/M which suggest that the people involved are in some way psychologically damaged and therefore unable to consent in an informed way. Practitioners take care before and during scenes to check out the mental health of partners as best they can. In public spaces, like S/M clubs, many of those present will act as arbiters of what is sane play and will often intervene if it is thought the scene is going too far. This is more difficult to regulate in private settings, but responsible S/M practitioners will take care of each other and seek to ensure their play is sane – real and grounded – at all times.

Finally, most S/M practitioners will only play if it is fully consensual. This means playing only with adults and actively negotiating consent at all stages of a scene. Maintaining a robust notion of consent is particularly important within most S/M communities for both the safety of practitioners as well as the perception from much mainstream sexual culture that S/M involves abuse. However, consent is a complicated issue and, as will be shown below, considerable thought and discussion is given to the meaning of consent within the context of sadomasochistic sex.

Langdridge and Butt (2004) investigated websites produced by S/M practitioners with the aim of exploring the stories being told therein. They found two main discursive themes in their analysis: one concerned with rejecting pathological understandings and therefore ensuring the play was sane; and another was concerned with the explicit negotiation of consent. Safety was also a key issue identified for practitioners, in line with safe, sane, and consensual practice. The theme concerned with rejecting pathological explanations was particularly focused on countering the beliefs that S/M is the product of childhood trauma and that people engaged in S/M cannot form satisfactory loving relationships; both ideas psychoanalytic in origin. Unlike early discourses of homosexuality, there were few attempts to identify a cause (or causes) for one's sadomasochistic behavior, but rather a simple rejection of pathological psycho-medical discourses. This discourse served to offer up a notion of pluralistic sexuality, where S/M was not seen in opposition to, but rather as an extension of, "vanilla" sex. This, along with the increasingly public nature of sexual identities, may play an important part in practitioners feeling little need to search for causes for their behaviors.

The second major theme identified by Langdridge and Butt (2004), which was concerned with the explicit negotiation of consent, involved the active explication of oral and written contracts serving to establish the psychological boundaries for safe, sane, and consensual sex. Sadomasochistic sex, unlike most other forms of sexual activity, often employs explicit contracts between practitioners. These contracts offer up a particularly powerful challenge to institutionalized power inequalities through parody, as contracts are constructed to undermine masculine hetero-normative understandings of sex and sexuality by, for instance, mimicking the traditional marriage ceremony. Parody has been a particularly powerful tool for queer activists and it appears that S/M-ers also employ this strategy in an attempt, deliberately or not, to undermine the structural inequalities that form the foundation of institutionalized oppression. The way in which safe, sane, and consensual practice is practically employed can be vividly seen in the following "submissive Bill of Rights" (reproduced only in part here), which is being continually modified, updated, and reproduced across the web and then used within D/s relationships (Dominant/submissive relationships):

> You have the right to be treated with respect. Not only do you have this right, you have the right to demand it. Being submissive does not make you a doormat or less of a person than anyone else. The word "submissive" describes your nature and in no way diminishes you as a human being. You have the right to respect yourself as well.
>
> You have the right to be proud of what you are. Being a submissive is nothing that should ever bring you shame or feelings of reproach. Your submissive nature is a gift and should always be a source of pride and happiness.
>
> You have the right to feel safe. Being a submissive should not make you feel afraid, insecure or threatened. Submission is not about living on the edge or flirting with fear. In any situation you should feel safe or there can never be true surrender. ...
>
> You have the right to say NO. Being submissive does not take away your right to have dislikes or negative feelings about things. If something is happening or about to happen

that you feel strongly opposed to, it's your duty to speak up. Remember, failing to com-municate the word NO is the same as saying YES. ...

You have the right to be healthy. Health involves your physical, mental and emotional wellbeing. Any relationship, D/s or otherwise, that causes you to suffer physically, mentally or emotionally, beyond your limits, is abuse. ... Being a submissive does not give anyone the right to harm or injure you in any way. The D/s community will stand behind you if you should encounter such a situation but you are the one who has to make them aware before they can help.

There are many similar documents employed within S/M communities. Contracts are drawn up for D/s relationships where the parties explicitly contract all aspects of their relationship. This will include all aspects of safe, sane, and consensual practice, with statements about playing safely and respecting limits, commitment to each other, and agreement around specific sexual practices. As Langdridge and Butt (2004) point out, these contracts may also serve to parody other contractual relationships, most often the marriage contract but also employment contracts and business service contracts. This playful aspect of S/M, along with the loving commitment that practitioners will often have for each other, is often lost on those looking from the outside, who see only violence and pain. Beckman (2001) and Taylor and Ussher (2001), in their qua-litative studies with S/M practitioners, similarly stress the centrality of consent. One participant in Taylor and Ussher's (2001: 298) study described the process of negotiation thus:

We"ll write to one another at some length and then we'll probably sketch out some kind of sequence of events ... everything is pretty well planned out not in chapter and verse but so we'll have a rough idea of what's likely to happen and where the respective limits are.

(E)

This kind of explicit negotiation around a scene and consent are common in longer-term S/M relationships, although, of course, not the same for all S/M encounters. Indeed, in many S/M scenes, especially in commercial S/M venues, the partners may never have met before and may engage in very little conversation. However, even in these situations consent continues to be negotiated, though often non-verbally. For instance, a submissive may move into a sling, voluntarily indicating their consent to be fucked or fisted, and often then voice or signal to the dominant to get condoms or gloves. Ongoing interaction between the practitioners will also involve the active negotiation of consent, as a dominant moves to fist and a submissive moves their hips away to indicate their refusal. So, even here, in the most casual of sexual encounters, we can see boundaried play that is at once safe, sane and consensual – the central requirement for membership of most, if not all, S/M neo-tribes.

Conclusions

This chapter has sought to highlight the growth of S/M neo-tribes and the way in which these communities have developed new rule systems to both protect members and challenge negative stereotypes. In spite of the considerable efforts by those engaged in consensual S/M, however, there is ongoing resistance to these particular sexual sub-cultures from the state, principally through the twin arms of the legal and medical professions. In spite of this, or perhaps in part because of this, there has been the proliferation of S/M communities in which members can come together for mutual pleasure and the support that belonging can engender. These emer-ging neo-tribes highlight the ambiguity, fluidity, and complexity of belonging, and the way in which communities give themselves boundaries through the active creation and maintenance of rules and regulations. To this end, S/M neo-tribes provide a place for people outside the mainstream sexual culture to fulfil their desires in a way that is safe, sane, and consensual – surely the *sine qua non* for good sex, regardless of the form it takes?

References

Beckman, A. 2001. "Deconstructing Myths: The Social Construction of 'Sadomasochism' Versus "subjugated Knowledges' of Practitioners of Consensual 'SM'". *Journal of Criminal Justice and Popular Culture*, 8 (2): 66–95.

Freud, S. 1905. *Three Essays on the Theory of Sexuality*. Standard Edition, Vol. 7 (ed. and trans. J. Strachey). London: Hogarth Press.

Giddens, Anthony 1991. *The Transformation of Intimacy*. Cambridge: Polity.

Langdridge, D. and T. Butt 2004. "A Hermeneutic Phenomenological Investigation of the Construction of Sadomasochistic Identities". *Sexualities* 7 (1): 31–53.

——2005. "The Erotic Construction of Power Exchange", *Journal of Constructivist Psychology* 18 (1): 65–73.

Maffesoli, M. 1996. *The Time of the Tribes: The Decline of Individualism in Mass Society*. London: Sage.

Plummer, K. 1995. *Telling Sexual Stories: Power, Change and Social Worlds*. London: Routledge.

Taylor, G. W. and J. Ussher 2001. "Making Sense of S&M: A Discourse Analytic Account", *Sexualities*, 4 (3): 293–314.

Weinzierl, R. and D. Muggleton 2003. "What is 'Post-Subcultural Studies' Anyway?" In D. Muggleton and R. Weinzierl (eds), *The Post-Subcultures Reader*. Oxford: Berg.

54

Secret sex and the down low brotherhood

Justin Luc Hoy

UNIVERSITY OF ILLINOIS, CHICAGO

In 2004, author and activist J. L. King appeared on the Oprah Winfrey TV show to discuss a phenomenon that was beginning to appear more and more in the mainstream media: the *down low* or *DL*. King introduced the down low to Oprah and millions of her viewers across the country as a startling new subculture of black men who had sex with other black men, but still identified as exclusively heterosexual. King based much of his information concerning this phenomenon on his own experiences as one of these men. He also relied on a report issued by the Centers for Disease Control (CDC) released in 2001 that estimated a 30 percent HIV infection rate among black men. The majority of men who comprised this 30 percent reported that they had engaged in sexual intercourse with other men. However, many of these men still self-identified as "straight." Suddenly, newspapers like the *Los Angeles Times* and the *New York Times* started running full-page spreads on this new and alarming sexual subculture of black men. Women who had been infected with HIV by their "down low" spouses began to surface in cover stories and exposés, and men like J. L. King began talking to the media about their lives on the down low.

This slurry of media attention evoked strong reactions in both the black community and among whites. Black women were scared that their husbands were on the down low and sleeping around with men behind their backs. Whites attributed this seemingly deviant behavior to the assumed old-fashioned or homophobic nature of the black community. Indeed, nearly everyone had something to say about the down low. But, through the media frenzy, very few efforts have been made to understand the sociological dynamics of the down low. Why do black men stay on the down low? What are the sociological implications that revolve around the down low? Is the down low a *black only* phenomenon? Having raised such questions, it is essential to examine the most popular ideas concerning the down low, and to look at the issue critically through a sociological lens.

Creating a space: havens in a heartless world

In his book about the down low, J. L. King (2004) presents his readers with a dilemma that he claims every down low man faces. Most of these men have a professed desire to be straight, and they enjoy all of the rights and privileges associated with heterosexuality. King, like many of his down low brothers, was married, had children, and professed interest in women even while having sex with men. In the end, though, how *could* these men be straight and still be having sex with men?

King refutes the idea that he and his down low brothers are gay, and initially rejected the idea that they are bisexual. Rather, he states that, while the act of having sex with men is homosexual, the core of him is heterosexual. In fact, King (2004) and other DL men are critical of the gay community and attempt to distance themselves from gay men. They draw on stereotypes of gay men as "drag queens or sissies," while claiming to be *real men* (Denizet-Lewis 2003: 4). King and other DL men assert their privilege as men to be the traditional heads of households, hold women responsible for preventing their sexual decisions as down low men, and claim their sense of masculinity is different and, in fact, superior to gay masculinity. Are King and his down low brothers trying to create a unique social space for themselves by not identifying as gay, but not quite fitting into a traditional heterosexual masculinity?

If one thinks about where a black, down low man stands socially, he may already feel at a social disadvantage due to racism and domination by a white majority. From black peril, or the white-constructed fear of black men as rapists, killers, women-stealers, etc., to the pronounced economic disadvantage they have in the workplace compared to white men (see Reskin and Padavic 2002), black men possess what R. W. Connell (1995) calls *spoiled masculinities*. A black, down low man, were he open about his sexual practices, would be considered homosexual by most. As homosexuality also represents a spoiled masculinity, down low men could suffer an additional sense of devaluation and inferiority. Moreover, down low men risk disapproval from their own family and community if their practices are discovered. In response to these risks, King and his down low brothers protect their threatened, already spoiled masculinities by overemphasizing their "straight," "real man" qualities, and by downplaying their sexual desire for other men.

King and down low men still face a problem within the black community. While King may reject accusations that he and his down low brothers are homosexual, the black community may shun down low men if they are exposed. Black communities often have their own culture of homophobia in which homosexuality is seen as a white phenomenon that afflicts *weak* brothers or sisters. Being gay can be seen as an abandonment of the struggle for black civil rights and cultural integrity (Collins 2004). Blacks wish to avoid an association with homosexuality in order to avoid further social marginalization. Clearly, this type of homophobia poses problems for men on the down low because it potentially exposes them to disrespect and losing their status as "normal," straight black men. As a result, many black men who live on the down low may feel that they are without a community, having rejected the gay community and having been rejected by the black community. The down low, then, exists as a new community or subculture, forged by men who could not fit anywhere else.

Theorizing the down low

Why do down low men need to live on the down low? I briefly consider the sociology of gender and sexuality.

We are a culture organized about norms that associate maleness with masculinity and femaleness with femininity. Men and women are expected to exhibit the appropriate gender traits and roles that society has assigned them. Many people assume these gender norms and roles to be natural. In the most general sense, men are expected to be strong, decisive, and aggressive. Indeed, the *good* man is assumed to be the boss, whether at work or at home. He is in charge. Women, on the other hand, are expected to be nurturing, supportive, and submissive. The woman is at the man's disposal. While gender norms and roles have and continue to change, there still exists male domination and female subjugation in most of our social activities, even sex.

Gayle Rubin (1993) argues that sexual behaviors can be placed on a moral continuum. Some types of sexual behaviors are labeled as good, and some are labeled as bad. What is labeled as good and what bad depends greatly on which individuals and groups have power. In American society, *wholesome* sex is often limited to consensual sex between same-race couples, preferably married and definitely heterosexual. Individuals whose sexual practices deviate from this ideal are disapproved of to varying degrees, from mild disapproval to criminalization.

Men who live on the down low may experience many benefits for identifying as heterosexual, but may also experience the burden of stigma and great risk for their sexual encounters with men. Such great risks attached to being exposed as a man who has sex with men could very well lead down low men not to disclose their behavior to their female partners. Telling a female partner may feel like one is losing masculine privilege, and many down low men feel that women must take responsibility for protecting themselves even though they might not be aware of their partner's down low experiences. In this regard, King says that he wrote his book for the women of down low men, so *the women* can protect themselves from men on the down low. This denial of responsibility by down low men is indicative of the reality of men's sense of social superiority and privilege.

Is the down low a black phenomenon?

The down low is not just a black problem, nor is it exclusive to any racial, ethnic, or sexual group. Indeed, men of various groups have been engaging in down low behavior for many years. Consider the fact that the great American composer, Cole Porter, was a married man who had sexual encounters with men on numerous occasions. Cole Porter was white. Recently the former governor of New Jersey, Jim McGreevey, a white man, resigned after confessing he had a male lover. He made his resignation announcement with his wife beside him.

The difference, however, between these white men who lived on the down low and the black men who are widely implicated in these practices is one of position and power. While all of the men involved in the down low risk stigmatization and devaluation if exposed, black men face a much more difficult time reconciling their practices with where they stand in society. While white men can continue to have closeted sex with other men, or be embraced by a white-centric gay community by virtue of their white privilege, black men are not in a position to do either without societal ridicule. On one hand, the racism and internal homophobia encased within the gay community discourages black men from adhering to a gay identity. On the other hand, the black community fears including these men at the risk of further marginalization. Even when black men who have sex with other men forge a new space to practice their desires on the down low, both white and black citizens, along with the media, pathologize them as sexually deviant and dangerous.

While the health risks of the down low are apparent, we should note that the down low is much deeper than simply a group of lecherous black men looking for secret sex. Rather, the down low is a reaction to a society that systematically oppresses people based on their respective races, genders, and sexualities. Certainly, when we see the marginalized (the black and gay communities) oppressing the marginalized (down low men), such a system vividly comes to life. As long as such oppression occurs, we will see sexual communities like that of the down low manifest themselves as political and inclusive spaces for those who have no other communities to turn to. Even then, however, such communities will stand before more socially dominant groups and risk criticism and hatred. The ultimate question, then, is how fractious must identity movements become before the marginalized begin to recognize commonalities in difference and strive to end oppression rather than criticize and subjugate one another for no apparent benefit?

References

Collins, Patricia Hill. 2004. *Black Sexual Politics*. New York: Routledge.

Connell, R. W. 1995. *Masculinities*. Berkeley: University of California Press.

Denizet-Lewis, Benoit. 2003. "Double Lives on the Down Low." *New York Times*, August 3.

King, J. L. 2004. *On the Down Low: A Journey into the Lives of "Straight" Men who Sleep with Men*. New York: Broadway Books.

Reskin, Barbara and Irene Padavic. 2002. *Women and Men at Work*. London: Sage.

Rubin, Gayle S. 1993. "Thinking Sex: Notes for a Radical Theory of the Politics of Sexuality." In Henry Abelove *et al.* (eds), *The Lesbian and Gay Studies Reader*. New York: Routledge.

55

Wait ... hip hop sexualities

Thomas F. DeFrantz

MASSACHUSETTS INSTITUTE OF TECHNOLOGY

Summer 2005, driving home from the gym in Bull City (Durham, NC, if you don't know), FM radio cranked. A new beat catches my body. Hot and lean. I ride its tones downward, catching the finger snaps in between the throaty, falling and rising bassline that asks a question then answers itself in one continuous swoop. Funky, hot, and full of potential, the spare beat is only a basstone and a fingerpop, but it is defiant and inevitable as it commands me to move my shoulders, my neck, my pelvis. A whispering male voice draws me toward the radio speaker; for a moment, I focus only on the sound and its desire for me to pay attention to its musical imperative. "Wait till I show you this ... You will never get enough."

Like any hip hop academic – corny as that may sound – I rush home, fire up the laptop, and Google the hook. In seconds I get it: Ying Yang Twins, the lead single from their just-released CD *United States of Atlanta*, and the version I heard in my car was a "clean" version of a "dirty" song. I download the real deal. In anticipation, I position the laptop speakers and let loose the preferred, original, explicit version. This is more like it. The beat bounces just as hard in its insistent groove, but now the rhyme sizzles with exhortations to flirt, to give head, to fuck, switch positions often, and finally the provocative hook – "Wait till you see my dick ... Gonna beat that pussy up." I laugh, incredulously, at the inelegant rhyme, and immediately forward the tune to everyone I can think of. Within days, it seems to be the only song I hear, at parties, on the radio, at the gym, in the club.

Ironically for the hit single "Wait (The Whisper Song)," hip hop is broadly conceived as never being about waiting for anything, always about sex, and seldom about whispering. So how did "Wait" achieve such an effect in the popular imagination? What made it the radio and club hit of the summer? The anecdote of my first hearing of the tune demonstrates several important tenets of hip hop. This music is portable, easily separated from its original local context. It thrives in public and private transcripts, with "secret" versions of songs easily available to fans in the know. "Wait" demonstrates a laughable misogyny, at once humorously boastful and patently rude. It is not precious – it flashes into and out of pop consciousness aggressively, making its statement and generating buzz before moving, just as quickly, out of circulation, making way for the next cycle of hits and misses. Most importantly, the music demands dance, and predicts playful interaction in some social space – the club, the gym, and possibly (although, not probably) the bedroom.

Hip hop offers an array of obvious and urgent questions surrounding sex and sexuality. Is hip hop truly obsessed with depictions of sex and sexuality? What kinds of depictions are most prevalent? What depictions are resisted by hip hop hedz, and why? How do sex and sexuality feed hip hop into world markets? How has a global marketplace for hip hop accelerated a demand for sexually explicit musical materials? How has hip hop come to stand for a youth sensibility that conjures perverse behaviors – as often social as sexualized – practiced as oppositional rituals to an increasingly corporate-controlled mainstream? Are hip hop sexualities different from other kinds of sexualities?

Hip hop histories

Constructing answers to these questions transports us to the complex areas of popular culture and marketplace culture. Hip hop, a constellation of esthetic practices imbued with undeniable focus on style, emerged as the first post-civil-rights manifestation of black expressive culture in the United States. Its four constituent elements consist of B–Boying/B–Girling, which includes breakdancing and the physical attitude of hip hop; writing, which includes graffiti and visual representations of hip hop; dj'ing; which includes turntabilism and the aural component of hip hop; and emceeing, which includes rapping and spoken-word poetry, the narrative aspect of hip hop. Each of these elements is bound by what some call the fifth element of hip hop – knowledge, or consciousness, which allows hip hop to inspire productive change among its participants, whether they be artists or fans. While each of these elements also has some relationship to representations of sex and sexuality, emceeing, or rapping, holds the most profound implications for a consideration of sex and sexuality defined by contemporary popular culture.

The history of hip hop can be easily aligned with African-American creative practices that stretch from the blues and jazz traditions of the early twentieth century. In general, these practices interwove boasting and toasting – that is, competitive bragging about one's abilities, and celebrating the achievements of another – with the musical accompaniment of the day. African-American culture has long prized a comfortable connection between spirituality, physicality, and sexuality in its performance traditions. These performances allow for: ecstatic release of energy; the call-and-response of performer and witness in service of communication; and a commitment to the well-being of the gathered community for the performance. Importantly, they are also built upon the willingness of witnesses to be amazed and surprised by the performer. Taken together, these esthetic aspects of performance led directly to the place of sexually-charged lyrics in hip hop music. Some hip hop, like some of the blues before it, connects audiences through boastful stories of sexual encounters staged as bragging rituals about near-impossible events.

Race is an issue here. The blues, like hip hop, attracted many denouncers as it gained popularity, and particularly as it moved from African-American contexts, where sex might be discussed as part of a constellation of human activity, to white-dominated public venues that denied conversations about sex and sexuality. In line with the fear of miscegenation that haunted white domination of black bodies in the United States, the suggestion of sex by African-Americans created anxiety for whites resistant to social mixing. So, while an extensive library of raunchy blues lyrics has been documented from the first decades of the twentieth century, few, if any, of these songs received airplay on commercial radio. For example, the suggestive lyrics to "Long John Blues," a popular song recorded by Dinah Washington in 1948, attracted attention from moralists: "I went to Long John's office and told him the pain was killin' … / He told me not to worry, that my cavity just needed fillin' … / He took out his trusted drill / And he told me to open wide / He said he wouldn't hurt me / But he'd fill my hole inside / Long John, Long John, you've got that golden touch / You thrill me when you drill me, and I need you very much." Songs in this tradition functioned by innuendo and intrigue, with a heavy dose of tongue-in-cheek humor that surrounded their performance and reception. Too easily, African-American expressive cultures like blues dancing and singing were characterized as patently immoral and lascivious, without redeeming artistic consequence. In this way, sexualized African-American popular culture fed into an ancient American consciousness that considered black bodies as sub-human and animalistic in comparison to demure, civilized white bodies.

Hip hop follows the blues, but differs dramatically because of its relationship to technologies of mass production. As hip hop emerged, youthful emcees quickly created a strand of boastful narratives that attracted audience attention with outlandish tales of sexual stamina and virility. But changing public standards allowed these raps with suggestive lyrics to receive commercial airplay, and an ascendant music video industry capitalized on sexualized imagery as a major selling point for hip hop. As the market solidified and expanded, its producers veered more aggressively toward sex, and exploited the racist, but popular, presumptions that affiliated young bodies of color with rampant, excessive sexuality. As hip hop achieved commercial exposure unprecedented for previous black expressive cultures, so did its most sexualized lyrics, and typically without regard to the political consequences that these representations engendered in mainstream contexts.

Back in the day

The earliest mainstream hip hop rhymes offered innocent and almost naive depictions of courtship and sexual curiosity. Playful emcees taunted each other and the object of their affection in raps like "Roxanne, Roxanne," a 1984 recording by the group UTFO, which told a story of guys trying to talk to a girl on the street. As the rap progressed, each emcee was rejected by Roxanne, which allowed the next prospect a chance to horn in on her with his best lines. Almost immediately an answer rap – "Roxanne's Revenge," released by Roxanne Shanté in 1984 – confirmed the elasticity of rap for sexual politicking. Set to a beat borrowed from the first record, the 14-year-old female rapper dismissed the UTFO emcees and boasted about her own qualities and abilities as an emcee.

Other answer-back recordings followed immediately, and the market for sexualized bravado in rhyme hardened. Emcee Positive K achieved a big success with "I Got A Man" in 1992, a party track that suggested an inviolable war between the sexes, performed, in a little-noted irony, by the emcee as both the male and the female voices. While underground hip hop had long embraced explicit depictions of sexuality, as in Akinyele's notorious 1993 release "Vagina Diner," it held few aspirations toward commercial radio. But, by 1995, the success of LL Cool J and LeShaun's "Doin It" confirmed the crossover possibilities of sexually-charged rap, with simulated foreplay and sex acts integral to the narrative drive of the track. Set to a sample borrowed from Grace Jones, the song, while still playful, exuded an undeniably explicit sensibility in its references to particular sexual acts, a sensibility amplified by the accompanying music video directed by Hype Williams.

LL Cool J (born James Todd Smith) established himself as a rap sex symbol. Having taken his moniker as a sexualized boast – Ladies Love Cool James – his performances solidified the persona of a romantic thug, a hypermasculine African-American man who operates as a stylish, considerate lover. LLJ began this arc of his career with raps like "'Round the Way Girl" (1990), a sort of "everyman" narrative celebrating a diversity of women of color seldom described by mainstream media. As LLJ boasted about the kinds of girls he hoped to date, he also confirmed, in rhyme, fashion trends and style prerogatives of the day. In videos, LLJ often capitalized on his sex appeal by appearing shirtless and smiling seductively at the camera.

LLJ's mainstream success predicted the rising popularity of sex in media representations of hip hop, as well as the preferred terms of female participation therein. In LLJ's videos, women typically functioned as silent, dancing props who could bolster the ego of the emcee. The abundance of voiceless female bodies in these videos led quickly to the late-1990s phenomenon of "video hoes," scantily clad women of color, who performed lewd gestures toward an unblinking camera. While dancing girls have long been a trope of American entertainment, the hypersexualized imagery of hip hop music videos approached a pinnacle of degradation unimaginable before the advent of music video. Probably the most extravagant use of women as background material came in Nelly's notorious "Tip Drill" video (2004), directed by Benny Boom. Set at a house party in a lavish mansion, dozens of women in bikinis and high heels demonstrate booty-popping moves and simulate sex acts with each other and the emcees. The women here are moistened, available, silent, and unfailingly willing. This depiction of available flesh echoed longstanding American conceptions of black bodies as sexually provocative and predisposed to physical labor. In this realm of music videos, hip hop created little space for nuanced dialogue across gender about sex or sexuality.

Let's talk about sex

While mainstream conversations about sex in popular culture are few, many scholars have noted that hip hop offers a public platform for some women to talk, frankly, about sex. Some rappers, including Queen Latifah and the groups T.L.C. and Salt n Pepa, established their mainstream reputations in the 1990s as straight-talking women who brought a no-nonsense attitude to the public discourse surrounding sex. But these rumblings of public conversation almost always occurred in heterosexist terms that valorized masculine domination. For example, some female emcees adopted the mainstream's misogynistic attitudes toward sex in an attempt to express an empowerment of female sexuality. Emcees including Missy Elliot and Foxy Brown promoted a pop-sensibility of sex-positive women in control of their sexual destinies, in recordings that offered directives for men to fulfill the rapper's sexual needs, as in the 1996 Lil' Kim track "I Don't Want Dick Tonight," which concluded its hook, "Eat my pussy right!" Some of these efforts led to action beyond hip hop as a realm of entertainment: Jimmie Hatz, a condom company founded in 2003, aggressively promoted its products as a hip hop consumer item. In the main, however, female rappers and singers working in hip hop embraced highly sexualized personae that confirmed heterosexist fantasies of women entertainers as commensurate with professional sex workers.

Hip hop has produced its own resistant recordings that critique mainstream preoccupations with misogyny, most famously in DJ Vadim and Sarah Jones's spoken-word anthem "Your Revolution" (1999). Conceived as an antidote to the hypersexualized depictions of women in hip hop, the song answered back an expansive string of hit songs with a wry rejection of their terms of engagement. In a relaxed but direct cadence, Jones dismissed LL Cool J and others as she explained: "Your revolution will not find me in the backseat of a jeep / With LL, hard as hell, you know doin it and doin it and doin it well / Nah come on now / Your revolution will not be you smacking it up, flipping it, or rubbing it down / ... Your revolution will not happen between these thighs." The song achieved a modest underground following without commercial airplay; in an ironic twist, the Federal Communication Commission sanctioned a

Portland, Oregon, radio station for airing the song in 2000, claiming that it defied decency regulations. Three years later the ruling was overturned and fines were dismissed, but by then the song had received national attention as a harbinger of how hip hop could critique itself and its own representations of sexuality, even if it functioned within a larger mainstream context committed to maintaining a heterosexist orthodoxy.

Queer hip hop practices

March 2000, cruising Tempe, Arizona, with a pal in a drab rental car. Headed to an underground queer African-American club we found out about – somehow. Talking about Lauryn Hill's visionary hip hop, realized on a spiritual plane with its R&B roots intact; and D'Angelo's hot-as-hell nude video for "Untitled (How Does It Feel?)," we land in the parking lot – folks are dressed as they want to be for a Saturday night: some cats in shiny suits, others in baggies; glam women in tight dresses arm in arm with big mamas sporting work boots. Once in the door, the vibe is positive and happy. A small club, with a dance floor at one end, and some already jumpin', jumpin' to Destiny's Child. The deejay shouts out to a sister at the back, grooving high as the new tune bleeds into the air – a sinister pizzicato string sample sets a mood of insistent menace. The beat drops. A tinny, electronic assemblage, built from a synthesizer and a drum machine, with a hyperactive break that comes around every chorus. A cheer erupts from the crowd. The dance floor fills, and we get out our versions of the wop and the shake, even as Juvenile rhymes, "Girl you workin with some ass yeah, you bad yeah / Make a nigga spend his cash yeah, his last yeah / Hoes frown when you pass yeah, they mad yeah / … Got a nigga schemin' large yeah, on the hard yeah / A smooth little broad yeah from out the projects / A nigga do a trick yeah, on the dick yeah … Girl, you looks good, won't you back that ass up / You'se a fine motherfucker, won't you back that ass up." The music calls for a dance that rises up through the shoulders and the neck for the break, but settles down, hard, for some deep booty-banging at each and every release.

The anecdote of my dance in an Arizona club demonstrates that queer hip hoppers may respond to the social imperatives of the music in much the same way that straight fans do; the music may contain calls for particular dances in rhyme as well as in the musical structure and content. In the dance space, the misogyny or homophobia of a rhyme can be easily disregarded as celebrants communicate with their bodies. Some hip hop rhymes may be read as queer in their particularity: rhymes like Sir Mix-A-Lot's "Baby Got Back" (1992), or Juvenile's "Back That Ass Up" (1999) explore a fetish of anatomy that attempt to normalize particular unstated African-American erotic desires. The "queerness" of a fetish of the rump here – as with the penis of the Ying Yang Twins' "Wait … " – suggests how hip hop can create space for alternative conversations about sex, conversations that would not happen in other musical contexts. Hip hop's focus on sex can attract queer interest, even when its overt message is heterosexual.

Like previous African-American popular music forms, hip hop has bolstered the continued practice of dances based in the expert manipulation of isolated regions of the body, especially the pelvis. These dances, now many generations removed from historical contexts of fertility rituals that likely inspired them, can be extremely difficult to achieve and perform well. In this, music videos often depict masterful dancers engaged in social dances that could be considered salacious by some. After all, expertise in hip hop dance is valued by hip hoppers in any venue, and an explicit focus on the possibilities of the body attracts people of any gender or sexual persuasion to these dance practices. From B-Boying and B-Girling, through C-Walking and poplocking, to rumpshaking and bootypopping, hip hop's beats reveal and confound the body in rhythmic motion.

But the body and its dances needn't be conceived only in terms of how they predict sex or sexuality. Access to hip hop culture, including its dances, reaches beyond any limits prescribed by mainstream conceptions of what sex looks like, sounds like, or seems to be. As emcees take up more outlandish stances and create more ribald imagery in rhyme about sex, be it normative, queer, or entirely unexpected, it may continue to be true that dance contains the glue that ties hip hop sexualities together.

56

Gay men dancing

Circuit parties

Russell Westhaver

ST. MARY'S UNIVERSITY, NOVA SCOTIA, CANADA

Introduction

When it comes to thinking about sexuality and sexual identity we often direct our attention to our biology, genes, hormones, or to what took place while we were in our mother's womb. And at one level it seems relatively obvious that sexual identity is informed by our biology. We all live in a body comprised of cells, neurotransmitters, blood, hormones, organs, muscles, and other tissues. In light of our biomass, it almost seems absurd to suggest that who and what we are isn't linked to our biology. As sociologists, however, we want to be cautious about a purely or primarily biological understanding of sexuality. Unlike other biological dimensions of being human, like breathing or digestion, our sexuality is an intimate (and sometimes violent) social experience – which is to say that our sexuality is always produced and experienced in relation to others. Even in our most solitary masturbatory fantasies and dreams we are always involving others, even if they are not actually present.

The social dimension of sexuality becomes particularly apparent when we recognize that our experiences and conversations about sexuality are never *just* about sexuality. When we talk about our sexuality or experience something as sexual, it is always linked to what it means to be a man or a woman, to where we live, to how much money we make, to the type of work we do, and to the time period in which we live. Consider this: the kind of sexual person you are is very different from the kind of sexual person your parents were when they were your age. And your own experiences and conversations about sexuality are very different than what might be experienced by your contemporaries in equatorial Africa. In short, how we understand and experience our sexuality changes over time and across cultures; it means different things to different people at different times.

The social dimension of sexuality also becomes apparent when we recognize that the sexual lives people *want* to lead are often not the sexual lives people *can* lead. Sexuality is never just about biomass; it is also about who has the *power* to be "sexual" in particular ways. Same-sex marriage is an example. If sexuality were only a matter of biology, if it had no *social* component – and had no meaning in relation to others – then gays and lesbians would be able to get married. Another example involves concerns about the number of people we have sex with or where we have sex. If sexuality were only a biological matter, then having multiple partners would not appear scandalous and no one would care about who you choose to invite into your bed, back alley, sex club, dungeon, or hot tub – or what you did with them once they got there. But clearly the marriage of gays and lesbians and the sorts of sexual practices in which people engage are practices that most of us care about in some way for some reason.

For all of us, then, our sexuality is experienced in relation to a breathtakingly complex set of meanings which we understand and live through various social relations of power. With its focus on biophysical processes and structures, biology is not well equipped to deal with the power-laden meanings and interpretations of sexuality. If we are biological creatures, then we are also equally social, meaning-making creatures that must contend and live with differential access to power, prestige, and privilege. Thus, what is necessary for any balanced understanding of sexuality is an account that brings meaning and power to the forefront of our analysis. Part of the general purpose of this chapter is to show how something that feels like a biological certainty is also a social affair. Significantly, however, seeing our personal experiences in terms of meaning and power is often difficult – particularly when it comes to sexuality, which often feels like a deep biological certainty. To illustrate how sexuality is a social and political affair, we need a concrete example. To this end, I want to invite you to dance.

Circuit parties

Between 1998 and 2002 I conducted ethnographic research on circuit parties (Westhaver 2005). Circuit parties are rave-like events – very large, all-night dance parties which attract thousands of attendees. Well-known DJs offer continuously mixed music, the events run between six and upwards of twelve hours, and attendees spend the vast bulk of their time dancing. Unlike raves, however, circuit party attendees are primarily – almost exclusively – gay men. Indeed, this is one of the defining features of a circuit party; they are events that are intimately about being a gay man. By examining how attendees understand their participation in circuit parities, we can begin to get a sense of how our sexuality is not merely a matter of biology, but also an experience that must necessarily be understood in terms of meaning and power.

This begins to become apparent when we reflect on what a circuit party means for attendees: many attendees understand circuit parties as dance events for gay men that centre on friendship, community, and bonding. The importance of these meanings becomes particularly vivid as attendees rely on kinship metaphors to capture their experiences. As one attendee said, "I think there is definitely some kind or some sense of family." Framing the circuit in terms that are associated with one of the most intimate relationships we can have suggests that the circuit is important because it can invoke feelings of safety and belonging:

> As gay men we're brought up all our lives thinking that there is something wrong with us. It's always something that we have to fight for or strive for within ourselves, within our families, in society. So when you grow up you always hide it – and then you come to a big event with 20,000 people and you don't have to hide it anymore.
>
> *(John)*

In this light, it becomes clear that circuit parties are similar to Gay Pride parades, allowing attendees to confirm who they are:

> It's memorable because at a circuit party you see so many gay people all being happy about being gay, expressing themselves. When you see people who are having no issues with it, no problem at all and are just having fun, well you just get right into it, you just feel so good about yourself.
>
> *(John)*

391

From this, we can argue that the circuit party is a means by which a sense of community is made possible and where being gay is celebration. John put it most clearly when he said: "I think circuit events are an outlet to forget about what society has conditioned us to think, and forget about what we learned since we were kids." This means that the circuit experience is linked in important and complex ways to the lack of power gay men have in the context of a world that does not generally value or even tolerate same-sex desire (Bardella 2002; Bollen 1996; Lewis and Ross 1995a). In short, being a gay man dancing at a circuit event is a political affair – it makes sense in relation to the power others are able to exercise over the lives of some gay men.

We can see this complex interplay between meaning and power more clearly if we begin to reflect on how some attendees think about gender. When I interviewed Frank, he observed that there is rarely, if ever, any male violence at a circuit event. He compared this to non-gay night clubs and dance parties, noting that one can always anticipate some sort of male violence at these events. Frank believed that gay men are a "different gender." Frank's comments are interesting and useful for two reasons. On the one hand, they help to illustrate that sexuality is never simply about sexuality. In the context of the circuit, gay men's sexuality is also deeply connected to the meaning of being a man. On the other hand, as will become apparent in the following pages, the kind of masculinity that emerges through the circuit is not really too "different" from conventional notions of gender, suggesting that attendees' sexuality is deeply connected to the politics of being a man.

"The look – it's kind of a beefy tough macho thing"

This interplay between sexuality and gender becomes particularly apparent in the pronounced emphasis on bodily appearance that is part of the circuit experience. Circuit ephemera – promotional material, websites, magazine ads, program guides – is often the first point of access attendees have to a circuit event. The glossy figures gracing circuit advertisements are invariably muscular, gym-toned bodies, with broad shoulders, well-defined arms, v-shaped backs, and washboard abdominals. At parties, images of men chiselled into varying forms of perfection are frequently projected onto screens around the dance floor, and buff, semi-clad go-go dancers gyrate on pedestals above the crowd. So, while the circuit is a celebration among gay men, it is also a celebration of a particular kind of gay man – one that is buff, well built, and muscular.

It is not difficult to argue that this aesthetic is studied and deliberately crafted. Marc noted:

> I think there is a new clone that has a certain kind of tattoo and a certain kind of haircut and a certain kind of beefiness that you see a lot at circuit type events – it looks pretty cookie cutter. So that's the look – it's kind of a beefy tough macho thing.
>
> (Marc)

This tattooed, butch, and macho configuration of masculinity is further emphasized by the (very) loose themes holding parties together. Many parties are organized around military, leather, or jock themes, where symbols of a normative Western masculinity help fill in the details of "the look":

> Guys were milling about in half-formed queues with all the right get up: combat boots, cargo pants, some uniforms, buzz-cuts, and captain's hats. At the leather event it was the same: lots of harnesses, chains, chaps, heavy black biker-looking boots, leather caps, more than a couple decked out in what looked like leather armour – gauntlets of leather that looked like some sort of medieval scale-mail covering the arm up to the shoulder – very gladiator like.

There is, then, a concerted effort on the part of attendees to exercise and realize a particular experience of masculinity through both dress and gesture. Frank summed this up when he told me:

> I think it's a celebration of masculinity for sure. So you want to epitomize everything masculine about you. That's where the facial hair comes in; chest hair is coming back, the big muscles: everything that can epitomize male sexuality and being a man is epitomized on these dance floors.
>
> *(Frank)*

While this exercise is carried out with more or less intensity, more or less success, and more or less commitment on the part of individual attendees, it would be difficult to argue that the realization of masculinity, through an approximation of "beefy tough macho" symbols, is not intimately connected to the circuit experience.

This is no more apparent than in the way dancing is subtly gendered. Certainly each attendee brings a unique style to his dance, but a notable degree of similarity exists across individual dancers in terms of the rigidity and stiffness of the movements. Peculiar to this physical configuration is its emphasis on masculinity. There is little bending at the waist, only small degrees of torsion in the upper body, legs remain relatively straight, with arms slightly bent and held close to the body – mimicking at times, ever so slightly, a boxer's pose. Curling hands into a fist and punching the rhythm of the music out above one's head, clasping one fist in the other hand above the head in a way that begins to emphasize abdominals and intercostals, and hooking thumbs into pockets or belts, all suggest that what characterizes the circuit is not merely dancing but a dancing interpreted and enacted through notions of masculinity.

It can certainly be argued that music with more vocals invariably leads attendees to raise their hands above their head and scream appreciatively, suggesting that attendees are just as likely to dance in a manner that is considerably less masculine than the above argument allows for. It is telling, however, that any hand gestures above the shoulders are jokingly identified as being "above the fag line" or "big girl moves." Equally telling is the way in which the music which invokes this type of dancing is regularly referred to "fluffy," "girl music," "pretty," and "light," while music which does not fall into this category is framed as "hard," "edgier," "dark," and "dirty." At one level, jokes about "big girl moves" are, of course, just that: jokes. At another level, however, jokes, as gentle as they might be, are also policing mechanisms which function, in subtle ways, to gender the dance as masculine. Jokes identify the speaker with and – in no easy and direct way – constrain speaker and listener to a "beefy tough macho" configuration of masculinity.

What these reflections on the circuit experience and "the look" begin to suggest is that, for attendees, being a gay man dancing is never just about being gay; it is also deeply implicated in a notion of masculinity. We are never purely sexual creatures; our sexual identities are always lived out in relation to other aspects of ourselves, like where we live, how old we are, or, in this case, our gender. An important aspect of the interplay between sexuality and gender for a gay man dancing in the context of this circuit is that "the look" – and all that it entails – privileges a relatively normative notion of masculinity. And as sociologists we know that, when some things are privileged over others, we must also begin thinking about relations of power. For example, to make a critique – even jokingly – that someone dances with "big girl moves" is a kind of insult that gains its force and effect from a broader set of social relations of power that privilege masculinity over femininity. In terms of the circuit experience, we can think about power in two ways. On the one hand are relations of power that privilege masculinity over femininity and whose effects play out primarily within the circuit party experience. On the other hand are relations of power that privilege straight over gay and generally contextualize that experience. Both sets of power relations produce and maintain attendees' sexual self-understandings.

Policing the "feminine element"

Ben's comments about *"the look"* are helpful for thinking about how attendees' sexuality is shaped by relations of power which privilege men:

> I think the circuit is about a very loose sense of community. We like the music, the dancing and the visualisation; everyone is body focused. Or at least a large segment of those of us who go to these parties are body focused. And I think that's why we go – the fun, the music, but also the look. At times it reaffirms our sense of community, who we are – our likes or our dislikes in some respects – and that's a positive thing.
>
> *(Ben)*

Ben's comments are interesting because he tells us that "the look" helps reaffirm gay men's "sense of community." Importantly, however, as this esthetic "reaffirms our sense of community, who we are," it also functions as a means of marking "our likes or our dislikes." Andy's candidness about this is very helpful for illustrating how this shapes attendees' experience:

> Circuit events for me – especially in Miami and Los Angeles – are very body conscious things. When you don't have the body, you are out of the group.
>
> *(Andy)*

As an esthetic category, *"the look"* positions some attendees in relation to others, such that those able to approximate *"the look"* occupy a more legitimate social position within the circuit's hierarchy of value. Gay men who have *"the look"* occupy a relatively superior social position in relation to those who do not. It would not be difficult to imagine how this dynamic might lead some gay men to have a less than positive – or at least conflicted – understanding of themselves.

This exclusion also emerged as Andy told me that what appealed to him about circuit parties was the presence of a North American masculine sensibility that was, in his experience, absent among gay men in his native Holland. For Andy, gay men in Europe had less to prove by being more masculine, due to a higher degree of legislative equality. He said that such that gay men in Europe:

> … can be more open about being gay. So a lot of guys don't develop their masculinity and they don't have to act differently during daytime. The point is that they also behave very gay – all queeny and they are all busy with their hands in the air. And I don't feel associated with that. Most of them behave very queeny – their interests are different. Everything straight boys do, most gay guys don't like. So they don't like to play snooker, they don't like to work out.
>
> *(Andy)*

For Andy, the circuit is about a particular kind of masculinity – where "gay men can be masculine" – which he uses to distinguish himself from those who "behave very queeny." Whether or not there is a distinct kind of North American masculine sensibility is open for debate. The important point is that in Andy's estimation the circuit is about a particular kind of masculinity, one that might, at some level, be read as a "straight" masculinity – or at least one that is not "queeny."

Andy's comments suggest that the masculine sense of self realized through the circuit is not simply about approximating *"the look,"* but is also realized through a policing of what, in effect, undermines that masculinity: femininity. We can see this exclusionary exercise take place in relation to what one attendee called the "feminine element" in other gay men:

> He's tall – taller than me – and really lean. He's having fun dancing and he is all over the place. Arms in the air, doing some sort of Whitney Houston or Celine Dion thing mixed up with a Ru Paul sashay. He reaches out to touch the stage/podium thing in front of him and then does this stripper pose, arching his back, looks over his shoulder, spins around and throws his hands in the air. A guy beside me has been watching him – turns to me and says, "Can you believe that girl? I hate that."

While what this speaker said was not heard by the man dancing, it does reveal how an adoration of a particular kind of masculinity – one that does not express anything that might be construed as "queeny" – is part of the circuit experience. Clearly, there is little room for "the feminine element" in the circuit. This hierarchy is significant: it creates and maintains kinds of interaction where some men are valued as objects of desire and others are not, creating possibilities for action for some and denying this power to others.

Significantly, as much as the above participant is policing gay men dancing (particularly those within ear-shot), Andy's comments also suggest to us that attendees also police the presence of "the feminine element" in themselves. For example, I asked Alex to tell me about his worst circuit experience:

> I was dancing with this guy who I was having this really really incredible connection with. And then he started to put his hands down my pants and I had no dick at that moment because I was like so high. I think I had like a micro-phallus. And I was so embarrassed and I didn't want him touching me. And he went away and I went into this paranoid thing, thinking, "He went away because I had small dick." And I kind of got all weirded out.
>
> *(Alex)*

It is interesting that Alex's worst circuit experience is about the discomfort he felt as his dance partner began to put his hands in his pants. Note that Alex's difficulty was not with the prospect of another man putting his hand in his pants – but rather with what that man might find once he did so: "I had no dick at that moment because I was like so high. I think I had like a micro-phallus. And I was so embarrassed and I didn't want him touching me." In the context of an event that is so clearly about masculinity, the absence of that signifier most closely associated with masculinity – an erect, or at the very least functioning, penis – created a significant amount of anxiety for Alex. Indeed, we can understand Alex's anxiety in term of the degree to which he felt he was able to measure up to all that "*the look*" entails. When it comes to a list of "everything that can epitomize male sexuality and being a man," the flaccid, unresponsive penis is not likely to be found. It is, in fact, the antithesis of the masculinity associated with a "beefy tough macho thing." Alex, in effect, excludes from himself the fullness of what it means to have a body that does not always respond in the way we want. By refusing to embrace this vulnerability, Alex renders – and accepts – himself as a kind of masculine failure, effectively disempowering himself.

"Can be more open about being gay"

We have, then, a process where social relations of power privileging masculinity over femininity shape attendees' understandings of themselves as sexual creatures. Attendees' experiences of themselves as gay men are constrained by others – "when you don't have the body, you are out of the group" – which informs a kind of self-policing, where a gay identity is anxiously constrained within a particular hyper-masculine configuration. Importantly, however, while aspects of the circuit exclude certain members from full participation in the circuit experience and while aspects of the circuit also encourage the exclusion of parts of the self from the self, the hyper-masculine images associated with a "beefy tough macho thing" must also be understood in terms of social relations of power that contextualize the circuit experience in particular and the lives of gay men in general.

Andy's comments about the degree of legal equality gay men experience in Europe compared to North America – that European gay men "can be more open about being gay" – are useful for thinking about how the social relations of power contextualizing the circuit experience also come to inform and shape that experience. His comments remind us that gays (and lesbians) live in a broader context of homophobia, where they are, in greater or lesser degrees, reviled because of the fact that they desire members of their own sex/gender. Indeed, as Andy suggests, we might understand the pursuit and veneration of "*the look*" as a (less than perfect) strategy for finding a place in this less than tolerant world. Part of the hatred extended toward gay men is an effect of how they are perceived as failed men. "Real" men do not desire men; for a man to desire another man is to risk being treated as a kind of masculine failure.

It is true, of course, that in the urbanized West there has been a gradual and uneven melting of conventional gendered messages – witness the rise of the "metrosexual"concept – but our understandings of gender are still very normative in their structure:

> If the sex–gender system of "metropolitan gay identity" has abandoned conventional notions of gender hierarchy such as those of the Latin American model, where manhood is associated with the dominant role, residues of a hostile ideology which conceptualizes femininity and passivity as inferior still haunt it.
>
> *(Bardella 2002: 87)*

With the aid of a gym membership, a willingness "to work out," and the right attitude, it is possible to desire men and yet avoid the spectre of "the feminine element." A big, buff, and well-built, masculine-looking man can fend off the suggestion that he is not "really" a man more successfully than one who is not equipped with the conventional signifiers or symbols of what "real" men are about. For some, this solution is, at best, a partial one; at worst, it is a poor one. By embodying the ideas associated with normative masculinity gay men are "in fact eroticizing the very values of straight society that have tyrannized" the lives of gay men (Kleinberg 1987: 123). Whether or not this solution on the part of circuit attendees – and gay men more generally – is successful, it does begin to highlight how social relations of power contextualizing the circuit experience – and gay men's lives more generally – are part and parcel of the experiences of sexuality within the circuit experience.

Conclusion: enervating the biophysical architecture

In short, what a gay man dancing at a circuit event can illustrate for us is this: sexual identity is a poetic and political affair. We can parse this out in two ways. First, sexuality is never simply about sexual desire. Who we desire is clearly linked to other aspects of our lives. In the context of the circuit, sexual identity (desiring men) is also linked to what masculinity means (a desire to be a man) – a link that becomes apparent when we pay attention to "*the look*." Second, this interplay between sexuality and gender is held together – motivated – by social relations of power. In terms of the circuit party experience, sexual identity is experienced through relations of power that privilege masculinity over femininity, made most apparent in the way "*the look*" is used as a marker of inclusion and exclusion: "When you don't have the body, you are out of the group." Equally important, however, is the way relations of power which contextualize the circuit – relations of power which generally privilege straight over gay – also shape attendees' sexual self-understandings. In light of a broader context of homophobia, the circuit is a place where a gay man can try to resist, through an approximation and veneration of "*the look*," cultural codes that render men who desire men as failed men. In effect, the circuit is a place where a gay man can, with more or less success, dance his way to becoming a gay man.

This interplay between meaning and power helps teach us that it is not merely biology that holds our sexual identity together; rather, we hold our sexual identity together because we have (or do not have, as the case may be) the power to make some meanings stick together in particular ways. Indeed, as Alex's anxiety illustrates, our sexual and gendered identity is hardly a straightforward expression of our body's architecture. By all accounts, the simple presence of his penis – what we take to be a biological marker of being a man – should leave no doubt in Alex's mind about his status as a gay man. But given what it means to be a gay man dancing at a circuit event, this biological marker actually threatened his self-understanding. We can, I think, summarize these observations by concluding that, when it comes to our existence as sexual creatures, understanding the biophysical architecture of the body is not enough; we also need to understand how this architecture is enervated by meaning and power.

References

Bardella, Claudio. 2002. "Pilgrimages of the Plagued: AIDS, Body and Society." *Body & Society* 8: 79–105.

Bollen, Jonathan. 1996. "Sexing the Dance at Sleaze Ball 1994." *The Drama Review* 40: 166–91.

Kleinberg, Seymour. 1987. "The New Masculinity of Gay Men, and Beyond." in M. Kaufman (ed.), *Beyond Patriarchy: Essays by Men on Pleasure, Power, and Change*. Toronto and New York: Oxford University Press.

Lewis, Lynette A. and Michael W. Ross. 1995a. "The Gay Dance Party Culture in Sydney: A Qualitative Analysis." *Journal of Homosexuality* 29: 41–70.

——1995b. *A Select Body: The Gay Dance Party Subculture and the HIV/AIDS Pandemic*. London: Cassell.

Westhaver, Russell. 2005. "'Coming out of Your Skin': Circuit Parties, Pleasure, and the Subject." *Sexualities* 8: 367–94.

Part 9
Sexual regulation and inequality

Introduction

When we hear the word "regulation," what probably comes to mind are laws, policies, and rules that government bureaucracies enforce. For example, the US Department of Transportation has explicit regulations governing airline safety. These policies mean that we can only take some items aboard a plane (knives are not allowed), that there are certain things we are not supposed to say on a plane (like making threats), and certain behavior that is not permitted (like smoking in the plane's bathroom). If this is what comes to mind when we think of regulation, then what does *sexual regulation* mean? After all, we don't have security guards watching to make sure we say and do certain things before having a sexual encounter. We don't fill out forms and go through inspections to determine whether or not we can have sex, or have checklists that instruct us about federally-approved sexual practices.

Sexual regulation is obviously different from airline safety regulation. However, it's not as different as one might initially assume. There *are* in fact federally-approved sexual practices. Likewise, sexual regulation does involve ideas about: safety; what kinds of behaviors are allowed or forbidden; what should and should not be said; and inspection. For example, federal laws and policies concerning everything from healthcare to taxes show that there *is* a federally-approved sexuality – a straight, married couple where the husband works and the wife stays home to care for children. Or the military policy of "don't ask, don't tell" also demonstrates that homosexuality is federally disapproved of. Moreover, there are also laws that define what is considered sexually "obscene" and therefore what can and cannot be said.

But there is also more to sexual regulation than just government laws, rules, and policies. Other institutions regulate sexuality as well. For example, medical doctors espouse definite ideas of what constitutes "safe" sexual practices. Most religions, including Christianity, have explicit rules about what sexual behavior is permitted and forbidden. And therapists and other mental health professionals regularly perform "inspections" in the form of mental health examinations which delve into an individual's sexual past to determine whether the individual is sexually normal or "pathological" in some way.

Reviewing this list, we can see that sexual regulation differs from airline regulation in three important ways. First, determining how sexuality is regulated involves deeper interpretation and analysis than following a government checklist of forbidden and permitted actions. Second, the "regulators" of sex and sexuality are far more varied than a centralized government bureaucracy; they include other institutions like religion, schools, or health providers, as well as the cultural beliefs into which we are socialized. Third, sexual regulation does not *only* involve formal laws, policies, and rules, but also norms, beliefs, and social practices.

Sexual regulation is about social control – encompassing all the means society has of getting people to conform through every social institution. It encompasses formal laws, rules, and guidelines; for example, laws that govern who can have sex with whom, or who is considered a legitimate citizen with full human rights based on sexual identity. It encompasses the moral guidelines concerning sexual behavior that are espoused by religions like Christianity. And sexual regulation includes ideas of appropriate and inappropriate (or normal and abnormal) behavior that shape and control our sexual beliefs, feelings, and actions. It encompasses the taken-for-granted assumptions we have been socialized to hold about men and masculinity and women and femininity. All of these things tend to socially control in some way – that is, they encourage us to conform. Through following government policies, or the gendered scripts we are taught, the religious beliefs we were raised in, the school environments where we're encouraged to mock others sexually for not fitting in, we are indelibly shaped by sexual regulation.

57

Sexuality, state, and nation

Jyoti Puri

SIMMONS COLLEGE, BOSTON, MASSACHUSETTS

- Decriminalize homosexuality
- Pakistan does not have any gays
- Brazilian women are hot!
- http://www.missworld.tv/
- Sex with a girl below 16 years is rape
- Our values are strong, ours is a chaste nation
- Don't ask, don't tell, don't pursue
- She's easy, she's American

Familiar phrases bring us face-to-face with sexuality's inseparability from the state and the nation. We live with such sentiments and policies every day without thinking twice about them. Precisely because the impact of nation and state on sexuality is so routine, it all seems unremarkable. Perhaps the spark of sexual desire set off deep within one's core reinforces the belief that sexuality is personal, private. Nothing could be further from reality; social institutions matter tremendously to issues of sexuality. When pushed to consider which institutions matter, we easily concede the usual suspects – family, media, peer groups, school, and religion. But the above phrases starkly remind us that nations and states are equally important to sexuality, if not more. Think about it: it is easier to ignore parental injunctions about your sexual behavior than what the state sees as sexually legal. This chapter presents a case for how nations and states bear on matters of sexuality and why this is too crucial to ignore.

It is helpful to have definitions of key terms such as nationalism, nation, and state, and that's where I start each of the sections, before going on to draw the connections with sexuality. The chapter is organized into two main parts, one on nationalism and nation and the other on the state. Even though there is overlap between the two concepts and what I have to say about each of them in terms of sexuality, this is an effective way to remind ourselves that the two concepts are not the same. For examples, I focus mostly on India and the USA. The idea is to blend useful examples that may be less familiar to the primary readers of this book with what seems familiar, but the purpose is the same: to question the links between sexuality, nation, and state.

Nationalism and nation

Let's start by defining the tricky thing that is nationalism, and the sibling concept, nation. You may wish to try this as we go, but, when I think of nationalism, coming up with an associated list of things is far easier than a crisp definition: flags, wars, passports, patriotism, and so on. One reason making it harder to abstract a definition is the near impossibility of imagining a world without nations; they seem so ... what's the word? ... normal that stating exactly what nationalism is, or what a nation is, is tough. All the more important to pin down the definition. Consider this: nationalism is the belief and practice aimed at creating unified but unique communities (nations) within a sovereign space (states). Said in a different way, nationalism is the belief that a people = nation = state.

Nationalism comes before nation; the *idea* and belief in the (north) American nation came before the Declaration of Independence and the creation of the nation of America, and the United States of America became the sovereign state. More than one nation co-exists in the USA, although unequally – America, Nation of Islam, Cherokee Nation, Queer Nation (now almost defunct), among others. Nationalism is inherently neither good nor bad; rather, it is an abstract idea that unifies us but also separates us from others. We are linked as individuals to a broad collective and, along with others, we become part of a nation that seems uniquely ours. The flip side of each nation as a unique unified entity is to specify how it is different from another. It ought to be difficult to come up with 192 national stereotypes (that's how many nations are recognized by the United Nations), but nevertheless we seem to be able to – the British are stoic, Koreans are hard-working, Americans are loud, Chinese are cheap, Jamaicans are lazy.

Nationalism is a powerful principle, a powerful promise. Power is the ability to make things happen, and nationalism's ability to whip up sentiment and movements, to unify people or divide them, and create policy is awesome. Nationalism has inspired movements of independence (for example, Bangladesh), resistance to oppression (Palestine), a sense of community in times of social crisis (terrorist bombings in Madrid and London), but also genocide (Bosnia), invasion (US in Iraq), war (India–Pakistan), and militarism (South Korea). I don't know of anything more precious to a person than her/his life. And what more sobering measure of nationalism's power is there than the fact that sacrificing one's life or taking the life of another in the name of the nation is considered the highest good?

Nationalism is not merely powerful in the sense of the "power of nationalism"; nationalism is itself a form of power. As a form of power, nationalism is a mechanism of social regulation. Why do I say that? Because we cannot imagine our lives without this social structure; because we are told that it is the highest form of community, over family or religion, to which we owe allegiance; because we are raised within the parameters of national cultural values, and draw from within our sense of self/identity; because we experience kinship with other people whom we have never met, and hatred for people from another nation whom also we have never met, as a result of nationalism; because it works by permeating our desires, not through force, but by making us complicit in policies and ideologies in the name of the nation.

The promise of nationalism is that we are all essentially the same and equal as citizens – a flawed promise, if there ever was one! No nation has been able to ensure genuine equality to its entire people while recognizing differences of race, ethnicity, gender, sexuality, social class, language, religion. It is not a matter of getting it right, of fixing the flaws of nationalism. In fact, the inequalities are not simply incidental but are built into the national social and legal infrastructures; law, military, government, schools, skilled professions in the US, for example, are remarkably skewed in terms of class, gender, and race. And these limitations of nationalism are directly relevant to sexuality.

Nationalism on sex and the nation's sex

Nationalism's greatest impact on matters of sexuality is by defining what is normal and abnormal, what is respectable and what is deviant. The fundamental link between respectable sexuality and nationalism is that ideals or customs of dominant groups are endorsed as national ideals, and are socially and legally enforced. The flip side of this respectable sexuality is what becomes designated as abnormal or deviant. Curiously, heterosexuality frequently corresponds to what is respectable and normal, and deviance to homosexuality.

In India, the norms for adult sexuality are quite unambiguous – it belongs within marriage and is meant to procreate no more than two children. But what lies beneath the marital bed? If this were true, HIV/AIDS would not be affecting young (primarily 15–44 years of age) sexually-active persons mostly through heterosexual contact (85.7 percent of transmissions). Whether true or not, for normal sexuality to have influence, abnormal sexuality must also be whipped up. Perhaps no greater misconception exists than the fact that Indian Muslims, the main minority group, are increasing rapidly. This increase is wrongly attributed to rampant male Muslim sexuality and the desire to increase proportions relative to Indian Hindus. The irony is that Hindus vastly outnumber any other religious group in the population, at more than 84 percent, and the threat posed by Indian Muslims and their male sexuality is fabricated but widely believed. Already declining birth rates among Muslims are expected to stabilize at 14 percent of the nation's population. So much for rampant male sexuality (notice the absence of any regard for Muslim women's sexual desires, or their wish for contraceptives).

Women are especially spotlighted when it comes to specifying respectable sexuality. Rape is undoubtedly seen as a form of sexual deviance, but under particular circumstances it can reveal national ideologies about sexual respectability. In May 2005, a young student in New Delhi was kidnapped and sexually assaulted in a moving car by four men. The incident struck a raw nerve in the city that is now called the rape capital of India. English-language newspapers reporting on the assault showed restraint, and in one case even reported on the brave determination of the young woman to put aside her grief and trauma and help the police in nabbing the suspects. But individual persons were less impressed or felt less constrained about expressing their opinions. What dominated their reactions was that this young woman was from northeastern India and that she was walking with a friend at two in the morning. Offensive stereotypes of women from the northeast, labeling them as sexually promiscuous and as unrespectable, were more pronounced in these reactions than the expectation that each person, and all women, have a right not to be touched without their consent. The implications were that this young woman is un-Indian and un-respectable, which doesn't condone the rape but purports to explain how she became the victim of sexual assault. Such can be the tragic and offensive logic when sexuality is part of the domain of nationalism.

If something is to be underlined here, then it is this: the issue is one of who belongs in the national community and who doesn't, and sexuality – normal, respectable – is the litmus test of belonging. The paradoxical catch is that some, by virtue of their religious affiliation, their ethnicity, their gender, their social class, are never going to be seen as sexually respectable and, therefore, as part of the national community. Norms of Indian sexuality, or for that matter North American sexual respectability, are specific to class-, gender-, race-, and sexual-orientation. It is curious to me that college-going women in the US worry about how many sexual partners they can have and under what circumstances (one-night stands, for example) before they need to consider their reputations. Interestingly enough, these are worries shared by some friends in India who are older than the college girls by several years.

Nowhere are the issues of belonging to the national community more precarious than for those who identify as lesbian, gay, bisexual, transgender, or queer. How national communities include or exclude their sexual minorities varies; the recently-won right of lesbians and gays to marry, in Spain (2005) and Canada (2005), is about equal citizenship and recognition in the eyes of the nation. More frequently, though, people are excluded either explicitly or through omission on the basis of sexual orientation or because they are transgendered. When was the last time a presidential address in the US made mention of gays and lesbians as an essential and equal part of the national community? This is omission. Current US President Bush has only mentioned them in the context of direct exclusion, by saying that marriage can only exist between a man and a woman.

The disturbing paradox is that, even as lesbians, gays, bisexuals, and transgendered people may be omitted, made invisible in the national community, they are also subject to unusual scrutiny. Another crime committed in New Delhi in 2004 starkly illustrates this point. This time, an upper-class gay man, Pushkin Chandra, and his friend were brutally murdered by two working-class men – as it turned out, over an argument about documenting their sexual activities. The English-language media brought to bear tremendous pressure on the police to solve the crime, but in an outrightly scurrilous manner. Inflammatory articles about "gay lifestyles," their deviant, upper-class, Westernized and, therefore, un-Indian sexual behaviors, littered the newspapers. The police, in their turn, went on a witch hunt within the gay networks of New Delhi, surveilling gay men, browbeating, threatening, and tracking them. The police officer who supervised the solving of the crime confirmed this in a conversation. Sexuality rights activists rightly questioned the role of the media in whipping up a voyeuristic revulsion against gay men in general and placing them at the edges of the national community. As Pramada Menon poignantly said, "One person's death has brought an entire community into focus. Newspapers are suddenly full of stories about homosexual life – and not in a celebratory way. ... A stray incident has been used to stereotype them all and an already marginalized community is being pushed further into the margins."

What I have been doing in this section is noting the obvious ways in which nationalism and sexuality are connected, even though their specific connections will vary by case. I have been also making connections where they may not be so obvious. The idea is that if we start to recognize how nationalism and sexuality are connected, we are more likely to question and undo them. By way of that, here is a summary of the key points made in this section. First, nationalism shapes sexuality by defining what is normal, indeed, respectable. Second, the dominant groups determine the norm of respectable sexuality, which establishes who belongs to the national community. Third, gender, sexual orientation, race, religion, class are among the key social dimensions to determine belonging to national community. Fourth, the nation itself can take on sexual meanings. For example, citizens may associate national identity with exclusively heterosexual citizens. What I am getting at in this point is that, implicitly and sometimes explicitly, nations are seen as heterosexual. This is exactly what happens when the nation is thought of as a community of heterosexuals or when the nation becomes personified as a young desirable woman or as the heroic soldier fighting for family, community, and nation.

State

It is time to underscore a point that is couched in the above discussion, and to segue to the state. We don't think anything of using the concepts of nation and state interchangeably, but any attentive political science student will remind us they are different. The linking together of nation and state, or the equation that a people = nation = state, is itself a modern artifact of nationalism. That's why the terms seem confusing, redundant. The state is a sovereign demarcated territory, and more. It is a set of cultural institutions that generate ideologies (for example:

the state is all-powerful), establish administrative policies and procedures (for example: monitoring populations), and enforce them through direct and indirect violence (for example: police and the law). A mouthful of a definition for something that seems awfully boring, no? For all the passion and love the nation inspires, one is hard pressed to find an ode to the state.

So, let's see if we can get to the importance of the state in another way. A student wakes up one morning and goes about her routine. As she gets dressed and heads out of the door, she will not recall that the building she inhabits, her apartment, the kitchen appliances and bathroom fittings, the car that she drives, the university that she attends, are all made possible by fulfilling a long list of state and federal laws. She will not note the police on the streets (for the most part), the post office that she drives by, and the traffic lights at the intersection. She is less likely to forget about the taxes that are withheld from her weekly paycheck or the year's financial aid package. All of this has to do with the presence of the state in our lives, and this is just the start of the list. The TV that she watches, and the communication and broadcast laws, are easier to forget, but it's harder for her to ignore that the content is monitored. The point is that so fundamental a structure is the state in our lives that we see it selectively, and it would have to stop functioning for us to fully appreciate its relevance. This, its semi-invisibility, along with the more obvious institutions such as police, military, law, and government, is what gives the state tremendous power.

State on sex

Sexuality is no exception to the impact of the state in our lives. If one is eligible to have sex, with whom, of what kind, under what circumstances, where, whether sex aids or contraceptives are used, are all matters subject to regulation by the state. And we think sexuality is a personal matter! My point is not that the state is an evil big brother; Hollywood movies have already contributed enough to that myth. That we imagine the state as the evil monster is only a means of working through our anxieties about its impact in our lives. I would rather have us recognize the power of state ideologies, the institutionalization of power in state institutions, and the impact of an intricate administrative machinery. This does not happen in tandem or function smoothly, but can be messy, inconsistent, even contradictory (what happens when a lesbian couple gets married in Massachusetts but the marriage is not recognized in another US state, or under some federal laws?).

Nothing better illustrates the power of the state on issues of sexuality than the mobilization against Section 377 of the Indian Penal Code. The law can be summarized as the "sodomy law," which prohibits "sex against the order of nature." That is really to say, it prohibits anal and oral sex. This poses a problem for heterosexual couples who incorporate a range of sexual techniques. This most certainly poses a problem for gay men and lesbian women, because "sex against the order of nature" is thought to inherently include consenting sex between two adult women or two adult men. Not just anal or oral, but any sex between them could be interpreted as unnatural. Introduced by the British in 1860, this law is not just out of date but it is inconsistent with a cultural past that did not impugn persons with alternative sexualities. Notably, the law is not widely used to prosecute individuals but it contributes to a contemporary culture of violence and intolerance of transgenders, lesbians, gays, and bisexuals in India. It is most typically used by the police, thugs, and opportunists to harass, threaten, blackmail, and extort money and sex. Section 377 of the Indian Penal Code indicates how sexuality is regulated by the state; how it institutionalizes intolerance for some sexualities; how the belonging of lesbians, gays, transgenders and bisexuals in the Indian national community might be unjustly precarious but the state has the power to enforce the injustice through the police, the courts,

HIV/AIDS policies, etc. Is it any wonder that there is gathering momentum across India to change Section 377 and to decriminalize homosexuality? Here's hoping.

Earlier, I noted that same-sex sexualities are more systematically targeted; this would include state institutions. Notwithstanding a few nations, gay, lesbian, and bisexual women and men are the objects of regulation by the state through denial. What do I mean by that? In the US, the fact that same-sex couples cannot marry outside the state of Massachusetts, or openly serve in the military, is deeply problematic not just because it limits personal choices. These prohibitions withhold the benefits of citizenship that the state extends to married couples or citizen-soldiers. The other side of this denial is the promotion of heterosexuality by the state. And is it easier to concede the point that gay, lesbian, bisexual, and transgendered people are often denied the privileges enjoyed by heterosexual women and men? Is it harder to concede that hetero-sexuality is openly or subtly promoted by the state? If so, the reason is that we don't *see* the privileges of heterosexuality. The power of the norm is what makes it disappear from sight: precisely because it is normal, we stop noticing it. Think about the innumerable laws and pro-cedures – inheritance, marriage, birth and adoption, health proxy, death, tax exemptions, par-enting, work-related insurance and benefits, home ownership and loans that implicitly say – for heterosexuals only! This is the unequal impact of the state on sexuality.

Sexualizing the state

So far, in this section, the discussion has focused on the state's impact on sexuality. What if we were to turn the lens around? What if we were to look at the state through the lens of sexu-ality; to sexualize the state, as it were? I think it is an exercise worth doing. For one thing, it would tell us more about how the state promotes and privileges heterosexuality. I am sure you've noticed or heard of the rising tide of Christian right-wing backlash against sexual and gender minorities in the US which began in the 1990s and continues to date. The backlash is unabated but not unchallenged. One such challenge to the right comes from scholar Lisa Duggan (1994), who calls for "disestablishment strategies." This is how Duggan explains dis-establishment strategies: to show how the state constantly privileges heterosexuality; and to take the position that the state ought to *stop* its promotion. To make this point, she draws a parallel to why the state ought to remain secular. Think about it: if one of the founding principles of the US state is that it is secular, and not partial to any one religion, then why not have the same approach to sexuality? Why privilege a certain form of sexuality constantly and systematically? The state should divest itself of such heterosexist biases, Duggan rightly declares.

For a second, I think it's important to sexualize the state because it takes us beyond a one-way analysis of the impact of the state on sexuality. We typically see the impact of the state on same-sex sexualities, commercial sex workers, and on other marginalized groups. But, why not analyze the state? Sexualizing the state makes us do the hard work of analyzing how it is thor-oughly infused with issues of sexuality. By this, I don't mean just the laws, policies, and ideol-ogies regulating sexuality, heterosexuality, and same-sex sexualities. I mean all of the same that don't appear to be directly about sexuality but whose pre-occupations with issues of sexuality are never far behind (for example, US citizenship laws that are not obviously related to sexuality but, in fact, privilege heterosexuals). This approach moves us away from treating the state as a singular cohesive unit that unrelentingly privileges heterosexuality and marginalizes all else.

This is not meant to be confusing. In this section, I have argued that the state is implicated in privileging and promoting certain sexualities. I have also argued that the state is not cohesive, monolithic, or a singular unit; indeed, it is a messy, inconsistent and contradictory set of insti-tutions. The additional point that I am making here is that it is politically important to see the state as inconsistent, and to identify when and where the state does not privilege heterosexuality (for example: the decriminalization of homosexuality in the US through Lawrence vs Texas, June 2003; the August 2005 ruling by the California Supreme Court that both lesbian parents are to be seen as a child's mothers even after their relationship is over). To take the position that there are no inconsistencies in the state would be to see it as all-powerful (which it is not), would ignore social change (which has occurred), and would identify strategies for further change (in all spheres of life). Put another way, sexualizing the state is necessary for seeing how state power operates, and for challenging it.

Conclusion

It is hard to predict how familiar you are with the concepts of nationalism, nation, and state. It is equally hard to predict to what degree these concepts interest you. I hope this chapter has been successful in its aim to help you see the intertwining of sexuality with nationalism, nation, and state. I also hope that understanding connections of sexuality to these concepts has tweaked or enhanced your interest in issues of nation and state. What I would like to underscore is that nation and state have an impact upon sexuality in ways that affect our personal and collective lives. In the same vein, it is important to recognize the ways in which matters of sexuality are diffused into the nation and the state. It's a matter of recognizing the complex intertwining of sexuality with nation and state, precisely so that we can question how sexuality is regulated by these social structures. If there is one thing I would like you to take away from this chapter, then it is this: we need to challenge how nation and state create inequalities between normal and abnormal sexuality on the backs of women, transgenders, and men, who are socially marginalized because of their sexual orientation, race, gender, social class, or religion.

References

Duggan, Lisa. 1994. "Queering the State", *Social Text* 39: 1–14.
Hobsbawm, Eric J. 1990. *Nations and Nationalism since 1780: Programme, Myth, and Reality*, Cambridge: Cambridge University Press.

58

Iran's sexual revolution

Pardis Mahdavi

POMONA COLLEGE, CLAREMONT, CALIFORNIA

On November 4, 2009, thousands of young Iranians poured onto the streets of Tehran to protest the fraudulent election of Mahmoud Ahmadinejad in June of the same year. As much as for what it commemorated, this day was important for what it demonstrated – namely that a social movement had become political. November 4, 2009, was the 30th anniversary of the hostage-taking in the US Embassy in Iran, often referred to as the Iranian Hostage Crisis. The 1979 taking of American hostages in Tehran sent a strong signal to all of Euro-America. Through their actions, members of the Iranian Revolution were saying that "This is a new Iran," and that they would not be under the thumb of the United States or Western powers or the Shah, Iran's monarch. Revolutionaries claimed the Shah was leading Iran down a path of decadence, "westoxication" (or *gharbzadegi* as it was called), that meant the country was straying from core ideals and values. During the Iranian Revolution, the Shah was overthrown and Iran underwent a regime change.

In November 2009, the scene on the streets of Tehran resembled the mass demonstrations that had led to the Iranian Revolution 30 years previously. Young people, disenchanted and frustrated with a regime that does not embody their hopes and dreams for Iran, took to the streets, coalescing behind a leader and movement referred to as the *Sabze*, or Green Movement. The process (set in motion after the fraudulent election of President Ahmadinejad on June 12) is part of a social movement that has been building amongst various groups of Iranians within the country, most prominently spurred by Iran's sexual revolution, multiple women's movements (religious and secular), and civil and political reform movements.

A sexual revolution which has been taking place in Iran since the late 1990s, has coalesced with other movements (women's rights, minority rights, etc.) and has developed into the political movement known as the Green (*Sabze*) Movement. This movement was, until recently, without a leader and a definite agenda. Groups found their leader in the presidential candidate Mir Hossein Moussavi, who was (according to opposition leaders) denied his rightful place as the president of Iran by a corrupt regime. The Green Movement is about more than Moussavi. This movement is about Iranians communicating through their actions to the global public that they are not happy, that they want a change in their political system, and that they want to reclaim their full rights as citizens.

In this paper I chronicle the trajectory of what began as a sexual revolution and social movement among certain groups of middle- and upper-class young Iranians in Tehran, and then move from sexual politics to the civil rights movement we are witnessing in Iran today. I focus on the transformation of a sexual movement into a political movement in post-revolutionary Iran. I will first situate the current Iranian social movement in relation to other sexual and civil rights movements across the globe.

Sexual revolutions and social movements in Euro-America

This is not the first time the world has seen an association between sex, civil rights and social revolution. Sex, drugs, and rock-n-roll were key components to the countercultural sexual revolution in the United States and Europe in the 1960s and 1970s. The sexual revolution that took place in the United States in the 1960s (and similar versions of social movements taking place in parts of Europe around the same time), set the stage for larger social movements that culminated in changes in attitudes towards social justice, equality, and the self.

In the United States, the 1960s were marked by shifting views on sexuality, gender relations and social recreation. The US sexual revolution was about more than changing views of sexuality and intimacies; it was about a search for authenticity, claiming autonomy and resisting authority (Allyn 2001; Escoffier 2003). During this time, youth experimented with sexual relations outside of traditional familial arrangements and heteronormativity. A series of inter-connected movements emerged that included the struggle for civil rights, women's rights, minority rights, the rights of the disabled, and lesbian and gay liberation. These movements were often connected to broader justice issues such as anti-poverty, low-income housing, unionization and so on.

The prevailing attitude underlying this sexual revolution and its accompanying social movements (often captured under the umbrella phrase "counterculture"), was a profound distrust of authority, and a resistance to "the establishment," or the government. This distrust was fueled by a series of events including President Eisenhower's 1960 deception over the U-2 incident, the botched Bay of Pigs invasion in 1961, skepticism towards the investigation into the assassination of President Kennedy in 1963, the resistance to the Vietnam War, and a number of clashes between activists/protesters and the police. Activists in the counterculture movement began pointing at the shortcomings of the US government and questioning law enforcement (this was a time when words like "pigs" and "fuzz" entered the vernacular to refer to policemen).

Though opposition movements were not a new occurrence in the history of the United States, the counterculture movement had a series of defining characteristics which set it apart from its predecessors. First, and perhaps most importantly, was that this movement seemed to be driven by young people. Many of today's "baby boomers" were leaders of these social movements, and students were at the heart of the counterculture on university campuses. The baby boomers were seeking to break free from the repression of the 1950s, and sought to transform notions of social justice, tolerance and equality. Furthermore, resistance to authority through civil disobedience was a centerpiece of activism. Finally, its culture of experimentation extended from the body and gender roles to dress and drugs. The societal shifts set in motion in the 1960s are still being felt to this day.

In Eastern Europe, countercultural movements spread rapidly as a series of collective reactions to the harsh authoritarian regimes of the Soviet bloc. The Hungarian Revolution of 1956 was perhaps the first instance of a civil rights social movement in Eastern Europe; it was met with a harsh crackdown by the Soviet government. This was followed in 1968 by Czechoslovakia's "Prague Spring" which laid the groundwork for the Velvet Revolution that took place in Czechoslovakia in the late 1980s.

In Western Europe, countercultural movements spread rapidly to major European centers such as Amsterdam, Berlin, London and Paris. The German student movements of the 1960s and the French general strikes of 1968 were manifestations of the counterculture. In Britain, the emergence of the "New Left" was a movement of leftist activists that first centered on labor unions and then expanded into a broader movement seeking social justice, tolerance and equality for different populations. The UK, like the United States, was also home to counter-cultural influences, giving birth to pop groups like the Beatles and the Pink Floyd and to many types of countercultural style movements such as the Mods, the Rockers, the Teddy Boys and the Punks (Hebdige 1981).

These social movements were about challenging established views on politics, gender, the body, and the self; they were also broad movements for social justice and cultural change. They relied on activism on the streets, but also on cultural productions such as music, and the "body politics." Civil disobedience and opposition to "the establishment" were manifested through dress, music, and lifestyle experimentation as well as public protests. These various aspects of the counter-culture combined in the United States and parts of Europe to push for major socio-political change.

Iran's sexual revolution

During the summer of 2000 I went to Tehran to write about the daily lives of young people. When I arrived, the phrase constantly on the minds and lips of the youth with whom I spoke was "sexual revolution," a phrase that would keep me coming back to Iran for the next seven years. The phrase "sexual revolution" or *enqelab-i-jensi* (in Persian) was one that ordinary Ira-nians used. Young people and their parents would talk about a change in the discourse around sexuality and especially heterosexuality and heterosocial relations. These changes were referred to as *their* sexual revolution. By "sexual revolution" they often meant a change in the ways communities of young people think, act, and talk about sex. This sexual revolution was just one part of a larger movement that my interviewees referred to as a sociocultural revolution, or *enqelab-i-farhangi*. This social movement encompassed behaviors such as pushing the envelope on Islamic dress, sexual behaviors, heterosocializing, the creation of an underground rock-n-roll scene, driving around in cars playing loud illegal music, partying, drinking, dancing and so on. Basically, the sociocultural revolution involved young people doing what they aren't supposed to do under current clerics' interpretations of Islamic law.

The Islamic Republic of Iran (IRI) is governed by Islamic law (or the *Shari'a*). The many meanings of *Shari'a* are complex and vary depending on who is interpreting the laws and how. In this chapter, I refer to Islamic law as it has been interpreted by members of the clerical regime in power in Iran since the Revolution, though I acknowledge that this is just one set of inter-pretations of Islamic law. This version of Shari'a law contains strict rules on comportment, lei-sure, sociality and sexuality. Shari'a mandates, among other things, that women and men should interact minimally before marriage. For example, this means that an unmarried young man and woman seen in the company of one another without a chaperone could technically be arrested and punished since young men and women are not to spend time alone with one another. Opposite-sex young people should limit their interactions to conversations at school, in groups, or in the presence of family members. Furthermore, this version of Shari'a mandates that women should be covered in "proper" Islamic dress (ideally a cloak from head to toe, hiding any bodily shape). Islamic law, as interpreted by the Iranian "morality police," also mandates a somber comportment and devotion to higher powers as the main source of pleasure and recreation. In 2006, President Ahmadinejad rolled out a new "Morality Plan" that sought to re-enforce his vision of Islamically approved behavior and comportment. It is important to note that what may seem to those of us in the West to be superficial or casual behaviors (such as wearing make-up, attending underground parties or gatherings, and driving around in cars playing music deemed illegal by members of the regime) is understood as potentially risky political behavior in Iran.

Under this interpretation, everything in Iran becomes political and politicized. It has politicized Islamic dress, certain types of music, and even certain websites. Examples include internet bans on sites such as Facebook Orkut, or Friendster, and the banning of many popular Iranian bloggers, underground rock musicians, and film makers. Those who violate its rules are harassed, punished, or sometimes forced to leave the country. Many young people in Iran have become inspired to engage in political activism through their involvement in these social movements.

This movement began (as have other sexual revolutions in other parts of the world at various points in history) among the middle and upper middle class in Tehran – the most urban center – and then moved to other socioeconomic groups in other parts of the country. What began as a small movement seeking to shift attitudes about morality, comportment and sexuality in Tehran quickly broadened to a larger focus on the body, sociality, and comportment in opposition to what many young people view as a repressive regime. Young people, in an attempt to subvert the fabric of morality woven by the Islamic regime in power in post-revolutionary Iran, are using their bodies and social behaviors including sexual activity, recreational drug use, and the creation of an "underground" music scene (sex, drugs and rock-n-roll) to challenge the regime (Mahdavi 2009).

A movement led by youth

The sexual revolution is led by educated, restless youth and is changing sexual and social discourses, redefining pleasure and recreation, and leading some young people to become involved in the larger movement pushing for general social change. Today, 70 percent of Iran's population is under the age of 30. Literally *children of the revolution*, many of these young people were born during or right after the 1978–79 Iranian Revolution which led to the Islamic Republic of Iran. Urban young adults who comprise almost two-thirds of Iran's population are highly mobile, highly educated (84 percent of young Tehranis are currently enrolled at university or are university graduates, with 65 percent of these graduates being women) and underemployed (there is a 35 percent unemployment rate amongst this age group). Many are also highly dissatisfied with the current regime, and use their social behaviors to resist what they view as a repressive government.

Having fun and carving out spaces for recreation have been politicized by Islamists in power (Bayat 2007) who seek to regulate social activities and cleanse the public sphere of "morally questionable" behavior. Behaviors deemed "morally questionable" differ based on interpretation, but can range from small things like wearing excessive make-up or bright colors, to public displays of affection, to drug use and sex work.

"Me wearing lipstick," noted Mahnaz, a 20-year old beautician, "is more than just looking good, it's about pissing off them, the morality police, and about me getting satisfaction." Another young man talked about the meaning of resistance to him: "Look, this regime, the one in power, they are all about taking away fun," explained Ali Reza, a 22-year-old student from Tehran University. "They are so focused on what we do, they made fun political, so we use our fun, we use our day-to-day looks, fashions, and fun times to tell them we don't care what they think. This is us resisting," he added. Another young woman commented on the regime's focus on make-up and expressed her confusion. She lamented:

> What I'm trying to understand is, why can't I do *namaz* (prayer) wearing nail polish or make-up? Why do I have to wipe those things off for doing *namaz*? Why can't I present

myself to God the way I want to? The way I present myself to my friends? I have so many questions, the regime is full of contradictions, and then they wonder why we don't want to follow.

Her boyfriend Saasha, a 21-year-old religious studies major, took her sentiments one step further.

> They sit for hours and tell us, when you want to enter into the bathroom, enter with the right foot. If you sit on the floor, cross this foot over this one. Ay, *Khoda* (God)! We are really out of it, this regime is really out of it. This is what they want to teach us. They want to focus on going to the bathroom, and when and where to have sex. There are more important things like dealing with our huge unemployment or traffic problems, but they have chosen these things to focus on, so this is how we fight back, by focusing our attentions on social, sexual and cultural relations (*ravabet*)."

Many of the young people I spoke with said that they had decided to often engage in "extreme" behaviors to challenge the Islamic regime. Notes Ashghar, a young jewelry salesman residing in the northern part of Tehran:

> The regime complains about the youth and our cultural revolution. But it's their own fault that the young people have become like this. They breed this version of Islam. They tell us *this* is our culture, Islam. It has been beaten into us, and we don't like it, so us young people, we reject everything that has to do with religion or their version of culture. Why do we want to move to be more Western? They hate the West; by default we love it!

Young people emphasized that they were exploring their sexuality, engaging in a sexual revolution that they see as a movement for social change, and they are trying to renegotiate intimacy, citizenship, and a sense of self in ways that challenge the current regime.

Inspired by the women's movements and reform movements (movements pushing for a reform of principles of Islamic law) the sexual revolution started to take hold as a social movement and led some young people to begin to move from sexuality activism to a larger push for social justice and equality. Azar, a 23-year-old student at Azad University in Tehran, explains:

> For me, well it started out about looking good, having fun, and dating. But then I saw the politics behind what we were doing. I saw that it meant something, that it was threatening. I began to see things differently. I began to view my actions as my rights, and that's how I got involved in pushing for social change.

Azar's comments echo at least a dozen other interviewees who told of a similar trajectory. In the aftermath of the fraudulent election of Ahmadinejad in June 2009, these movements began to coalesce in the Sabze Movement.

Civil disobedience in the Sabze Movement

"The personal is political" was the phrase that echoed across the United States during nation-wide civil rights protests. Just as civil disobedience was the primary strategy in the counter-culture of the United States and Europe four decades ago, so too is this the strategy employed by members of the Green Movement in Iran today. Though met by violent responses from the regime's Revolutionary Guard and police, the activists of the Green Movement continue to pursue peaceful means of resistance. They have employed creative strategies such as the currency campaign. This involved marking various money bills with slogans criticizing the hypocrisy of the regime and calling for social justice. For example, Rial and Toman (Iranian currency) bills were marked with slogans from the opposition movement (such as a one-dollar/toman bill bearing the slogan "Where Is My Vote?") have increased exponentially, with each slogan a call to others to engrave their large bills with slogans demanding freedom of speech and a return of individual autonomy. The government attempted to take these bills out of circulation but found that there were so many of them that it would lead to a financial collapse if it were to do so.

This movement is perhaps one of the largest and most profound examples of civil disobedience the region has seen in decades. The protests led by the Green Movement involve activists walking, sometimes silently, other times chanting "God is great," a slogan used during the Iranian Revolution to oust the Shah. This slogan has been reclaimed by the opposition to signal that God is now on the side of the opposition and that the actions of the regime violate the ideals of Islam. The Green Movement also distributes images and videos that show members of the Revolutionary Guard and police using violence against peaceful protesters. During the bloodiest clashes between the opposition and Revolutionary Guards that took place on December 27, 2009, video clips showed police harassing, shooting, and even using their cars to run over the protesters. By contrast, the protesters were shown trying to stop the violence. One prominent clip showed a scene where protesters outnumber policemen. Instead of violently clashing with the police, the protesters had formed a human wall, backing the police into a corner so that they could not use violence on other activists. Another clip featured a woman who threw herself on top of a policeman in order to prevent him from hitting her and her co-protesters. She was not trying to hurt the man, but rather using her body as a shield to stop him from hurting others.

Gender in the Sabze Movement

Similar to the counterculture of the US and Europe, activism around issues of sexuality and gender have played a major role in shaping the contours of the Green Movement. Many of the protests are led by women and involve men and women protesting side by side, thereby challenging norms requiring gender segregation. Furthermore, many of the public leaders and icons of the Sabze Movement have been women. For example Zahra Rahnavard, wife of the opposition leader and presidential hopeful Hossein Moussavi, was an important part of his campaign; she was often seen standing by her husband, holding his hand at times, and has been a key political figure during and after the campaign. There is also the martyred figure of Neda Agha-Soltan, the young woman gunned down during the early weeks of the protests in June. Her face and story have become a call to action for the Green Movement.

More importantly, there has been the use of the *hijab* (head covering for women) by men, a public demonstration of gender-bending that serves as a call for equality by the activists. This campaign began during and after the arrest of one of the opposition activists, a student leader by the name of Majid Tavakoli, who was arrested after a speech that was highly critical of the regime in early December of 2009. Following his arrest, the authorities published photographs of Tavakoli wearing the hijab as he tried to flee the police. The police published these photographs to shame him as one of the public figures of the Green Movement by portraying him as unmanly and cowardly. This strategy backfired on the regime, however, when the pictures became a symbol of a grassroots movement with hundreds of men posting online photographs of themselves in *hijab*, with captions reading "We are all Majid." In the protests that have followed, many men have been seen wearing head coverings in a public statement against the regime.

The hypocrisy of the regime has also been highlighted by evidence of the rape and torture of political prisoners. In particular, the use of rape has been pointed to as evidence that the regime has lost touch with Islamic values. The fraudulence of the mass trials, combined with the heavy use of violence by members of the Revolutionary Guard, have contributed to a large-scale delegitimization of the regime and what it purportedly stands for.

Looking ahead

What started as a sexual revolution and a series of small-scale social movements has become a large-scale civil disobedience movement. What seemed to some outside observers as young people falling prey to the pitfalls of "sex, drugs, and rock-n-roll" has evolved into a social and political movement that is now challenging the Iranian Islamic regime. As was the case with countercultural movements in the United States and Europe, social movements can often combine to become forces of broad societal change. Today, the sexual revolution, combined with the women's movement and minority rights movements, has led to a far reaching civil rights movement, the likes of which the country has never before seen, and which will certainly change the future of Iran.

References

Allyn, David. 2001. *Make Love, Not War: The Sexual Revolution: An Unfettered History*. Boston, MA: Little, Brown.
Bayat, Asif. 2007. "Islamism and the Politics of Fun." *Public Culture*, 19(3): 433–60.
Escoffier, Jeffrey (ed.) 2003. *Sexual Revolution*. Philadelphia, PA: Running Press.
Hebdige, Dick. 1981. *Subculture: The Meaning of Style*. 2nd ed. New York: Routledge.
Mahdavi, P. 2009. "Who Will Catch Me if I Fall?" in A. Gheissari (ed.), *Contemporary Iran: Economy, Society, Politics*. Oxford: Oxford University Press.

59

Christianity and the regulation of sexuality in the United States

Joshua Grove

STATE UNIVERSITY OF NEW YORK AT ALBANY

Despite predictions that religion would fade as societies modernized, this has not happened. Religion, especially Christianity, continues to play a major role in Americans' lives – their personal and public lives. This chapter discusses the roles that various Christian denominations play in defining and regulating sexuality. I will discuss how Christianity has been a key social force in shaping sexual attitudes and influencing social policy and laws. In this sense, Christian churches are caught up in the politics of sexuality in America. I will illustrate this by discussing the relationship between the church and homosexuality. Finally, prospects for change are considered.

What is conventional Christianity?

By conventional Christianity, I include the Christian denominations with the largest member affiliation rates in the country. This includes the following families of churches in order of national size: Roman Catholic; Baptist (Southern and National Conventions); Pentecostal (Churches/Assemblies of God); United Methodist; Lutheran (Evangelical Lutheran Church in America and Missouri Synod); Presbyterian Church USA; US Episcopal Church; and the United Church of Christ. Although this is not an exhaustive list, most Christian denominations are similar in their responses to questions of sexuality and conduct. Furthermore, I will contrast the policies of these conventional churches with other religious groups, such as Unitarian Universalism and Reform Judaism.

Regulating sexuality

It should come as no surprise that Christianity has had a significant influence on how we define and *feel* about sex. Perhaps more importantly, Christianity also condemns and at times punishes sexual behavior deemed deviant or inappropriate. In conjunction with other social institutions such as the economy and government, religion creates sexual hierarchies. At the top of this hierarchy is heterosexuality. Not all heterosexual types, however, maintain this position of power.

Religious doctrines and moral teachings are key factors in enforcing the *normative status of heterosexuality*. This means that only heterosexuality is considered in line with Christian values. Only heterosexuality is natural and moral. But it is not just heterosexuality that is viewed as sacred. Good Christians must conform to a particular set of behavioral norms, such as marriage, monogamy, and creating and raising a family. Within much of conventional Christianity, individuals who deviate from these sexual norms become outsiders or less than fully respected Christians. This has made the inclusion of gays and lesbians a very difficult undertaking, as it clashes with the heterosexual ideal.

Within Roman Catholicism, heterosexual marriage is celebrated as a *sacrament*. A sacrament is a religious rite or ritual celebrating a sacramental occasion, such as a wedding, baptism, or communion. In short, sacraments represent the belief in God's grace and in Jesus Christ. Sacraments are the foundation of Christian theology and practice. Conventional Christian denominations teach that sex is to be restricted to marriage, and argue that this is only open to heterosexual couples. And although marriage may not be an official sacrament in every Christian denomination, it continues to be one of the most celebrated institutions in all of Christendom.

Members of the Christian Right and Moral Majority have been arguing for decades against the gay and lesbian movement, declaring that homosexuality is destroying the nation and the family. In fact, popular evangelical Rev. Louis P. Sheldon has just released a book entitled *The Agenda: The Homosexual Plan to Change America*. "The homosexual agenda is an attack on everything our Founding Fathers hoped to give us. But I am convinced that we can witness a tremendous victory, and with God's help, we shall overcome." Overcome what? The author and his supporters believe that homosexuality is a choice and the gay and lesbian community is trying to convert heterosexuals into homosexuals. These groups of Christians fear that homosexuality will lead to the ultimate decline of family values, which really means the decline of a specific and narrow idea of family – heterosexual, married with children, wife as mother and father as breadwinner. It is clear that same-sex marriage is not likely to be supported by conservative Christianity at any time soon.

Aside from not being able to marry, gay and lesbian couples of conventional Christian denominations are forbidden from having their unions blessed. In addition, gay and lesbian persons are not able to become clergy. The single exception to this rule is the United Church of Christ, which ordained its first openly gay member, the Rev. William Johnson, in 1972. In the summer of 2005, the Evangelical Lutheran Church in America Church-Wide General Assembly voted to uphold their policy excluding gays and lesbians, but only by a narrow margin. The policy also states that "any church policy that seems to approve of such behavior is a betrayal of the authority of Scripture and an ignoring of the natural order." The natural order here, of course, is normative heterosexuality, where sexuality is *assumed* to be inherently a function of biology, meant for monogamous marriage and childrearing.

These exclusionary policies have implications for heterosexual clergy as well, specifically those who are sympathetic to the gay and lesbian movement. In 1999, the Rev. Greg Dell, a United Methodist minister in Chicago, was convicted of breaking church law when he blessed the union of a same-sex couple. He was punished by being suspended from the ministry until he promised his Bishop in a letter that he would not "officiate at another such union, as long as the rule against them remained." In late 2003, members of the US Episcopal Church experienced the first election of an openly gay bishop, Rev. Gene Robinson. Voting members faced a great deal of social pressure to line up for or against him. Indeed, many heterosexual pastors who supported the election of Robinson met with mixed reactions when they returned to their home dioceses. By promoting the image of a sexually inclusive church, proponents of gay and lesbian religious participation risk some of the same consequences as gays and lesbians themselves.

To be sure, the way clergy behave is crucial to the growth of congregations. However, the sexual views of the clergy also influence the beliefs and behavior of the members in their faith communities. In other words, if the pastor doesn't support same-sex marriage, why should we?

Disagreements about questions of sexual morality often turn faithful adherents toward other religious alternatives, or, turn them away from organized religious practice altogether. Never before in American history has spirituality and religion been more diverse, with a growing number of people describing themselves as spiritual and *not* religious. Since religion is often in competition with other social institutions to attract members, they must be mindful of shifts in public attitudes.

Prospects for change

Why have many congregations and churches begun to welcome the gay and lesbian community into their folds? Changes in public opinion and laws greatly affect the ways in which conventional churches respond to questions of sexuality. It seems clear that, in the last decade or so, the attitudes of Americans towards gays and lesbians have changed considerably. Jeni Loftus (2001) analyzed personal opinion data from 1973 through 1998 to track America's growing acceptance of gay and lesbian persons. She found that Americans are much more tolerant and inclusive than even fifteen years ago. In 1973, just over 70 percent of those surveyed believed homosexuality was "always wrong." By 1998, this number dropped to 56 percent. Along these same lines, in 1987 only 13 percent reported homosexuality was "not wrong at all." In 1998, this number increased to over 30 percent. It will be interesting to see how these numbers change over time as the visibility of gays and lesbians continues to increase.

Since the late 1960s, the rise in the visibility of the gay and lesbian community has been unprecedented. More gays and lesbians are out of the closet and openly celebrating their relationships, fighting for the right to marry. There are gay and lesbian small-business owners, corporate managers, lawyers, doctors, teachers, and yes, elementary school teachers. Gays and lesbians are even in Congress, their voices represented by gay and lesbian public servants such as Congressmen Barney Frank, Jim Kolbe, and Tammy Baldwin. As I see it, this increased social visibility of the national gay and lesbian movement has been fundamental to its success.

Changes in public attitudes toward the gay and lesbian community often translate into positive court decisions and government legislation. This, of course, does not happen without the considerable political influence and labor of gay and lesbian lobbying groups. Consider the recent decision of the Massachusetts State Supreme Court that led the state to recognize same-sex marriage as of April 2005. This is the first state in the union to allow same-sex marriage, following the same legal precedents as Canada (2005), Belgium (2003), the Netherlands (2001), Spain (2005), and the UK (2005). In Vermont and Connecticut, a gay or lesbian couple is able to acquire a license for a civil union. Similarly, California, the District of Columbia, Maine, and New Jersey offer same-sex domestic partner benefits. In cities around the USA, such as Seattle and New York, these benefits are available to city employees.

While this progress is important, gays and lesbians still face serious opposition. The most powerful of these groups is the conservative branch of Christianity. Make no mistake, religious ideals and principles often find their way into politics and government. In 1996, President Clinton signed into law the Defense of Marriage Act (DOMA), defining marriage as a legal relationship between a *man* and a *woman*. This also gave states the right to decide for themselves how to deal with same-sex marriage. Imagine if each state were to regulate heterosexual marriage and not recognize the union between your mother and father, your best friend and his/her spouse, or perhaps your own marriage.

Should states be permitted to make those decisions on your behalf? Many politicians not only believe this, they have also proposed the Federal Marriage Amendment (FMA), which would amend the United States Constitution. In effect, the FMA would define marriage, *on the national*

417

level, as the union between a man and a woman. This would overturn any state decision supporting same-sex marriage. This, of course, stems partly from the religious convictions of politicians, as well as the Republican base, which is highly influenced by the Christian Right. Thus, although it is crucial to celebrate the victories of the gay and lesbian movement toward full inclusion, such as same-sex marriage in Massachusetts, it is also necessary to be aware of the losses and possible obstacles to these political goals. This demonstrates how, even in secular components of society, religion still maintains significant influence.

Change within the American church

A sign of dramatic change in the status of gays in America is that there are many religious faiths, including some conventional Christian denominations, which fully include gays and lesbians in their ministries, as both clergy and laity. Gay and lesbian clergy currently serve in churches, hospitals, university campuses, and counseling centers across the country in *most* religious traditions, regardless of policies and doctrines. Some of these pastors still live in the closet because their passion for the ministry overrides their need to be free from its sexual regulation. Other pastors work with congregations that are accepting of lesbians and gay men, even when threatened by the administrative hierarchies of their denominations.

To be sure, change is happening everywhere within conventional Christian denominations. The United Church of Christ (UCC) ordains gay and lesbian persons and has done so for over thirty years. In 1985, the UCC General Synod adopted the resolution known as "Open and Affirming," which publicly declared that those of all sexual orientations are welcome to the life and ministry of the church. This was meant to encourage local congregations to adopt an open and affirming statement, letting the gay and lesbian community know that they are welcome. In addition, the United Church of Christ has a specific branch of ministry known as Lesbian, Gay, Bisexual and Transgender Ministries. This has been quite successful.

However, not all attempts made by the United Church of Christ to promote inclusion have been accepted with open arms. For example, when the UCC launched a multi-million-dollar campaign in 2005 to promote inclusivity, television networks NBC and CBS refused to air their commercials, arguing that they were too controversial. Specifically, the commercial begins with two bouncers protecting the entrance to a church and deciding which people are "good enough" to attend services. Then, on the television screen, you read: "Jesus didn't turn people away. Neither do we." A voiceover then announces the United Church of Christ's commitment to Jesus's extravagant welcome: "No matter who you are, or where you are on life's journey, you are welcome here." The ad can be viewed online at http://www.stillspeaking.com/resources/indexvis.html (accessed 21 March 2006). Fortunately, networks including ABC Family, Discovery, History, Travel, and TV Land have aired the commercial.

This progression of the United Church of Christ is important because, since 1998, it has been in "full communion" with the Evangelical Lutheran Church in America, Presbyterian Church USA, the Reformed Church, and the Disciples of Christ. This involves an agreement in the ways in which Gospel messages are preached, as well as sharing communion and growing together in word, ministry, and Christian teachings. In fact, in the Lutheran, Presbyterian, and Reform Church, margins of victory for those opposed to gay and lesbian inclusion have become smaller and smaller over the past decade. The Evangelical Lutheran Church in America, Presbyterian Church USA, United Methodist, and US Episcopal Church each have national programs ministering specifically to the gay and lesbian community.

One example is Lutherans Concerned/North America, which is a private organization supporting the inclusion of gay and lesbian persons into the Lutheran Church, and into Christianity in general. In 1984, they initiated a program entitled "Reconciling in Christ," which is similar in nature to the United Church of Christ's "Open and Affirming" statements. If a Lutheran congregation decides officially to open their doors to the gay and lesbian community, they do so through an official statement known as "Reconciling in Christ." The same is true for Presbyterians, where the accepting congregations are known as "More Light Churches." For Episcopalians these churches are known as "Oasis Churches," and in United Methodism they are called "Reconciling Congregations."

It is also possible that these changes in attitudes and church-wide discussions on sexuality stem from religious faiths outside of conventional Christianity. Founded in 1968 by the Rev. Troy Perry, the Metropolitan Community Church became the world's first church established primarily for ministry to the gay and lesbian community. With almost 300 congregations spread across twenty-two countries, the Metropolitan Community Church has a long history of celebrating positive images of gay and lesbian Christians and fighting for social equality.

Unitarian Universalism has consistently supported the full inclusion of gays and lesbians, not only in church policy, but also in secular, governmental politics. In 1987, the Unitarian Universalist Association (UUA) General Assembly voted overwhelmingly to initiate the "Welcoming Congregation" program to educate its members about the inclusion of gay, lesbian, bisexual, and transgender persons. In fact, Unitarianism has acknowledged the role of the church in the oppression of sexual minorities and vowed to challenge this form of injustice. In 1973, the UUA created the Office of Bisexual, Gay, Lesbian, and Transgender Concerns. The main purpose of this office is to promote education across Unitarian churches and foster ecumenical cooperation among different religious faiths. Today, Unitarian Universalism is growing in membership and is a supportive, encouraging environment for *any* person who is interested in a spiritual community and social advocacy.

The support of gay and lesbian persons can also be seen in Reform Judaism. In 1996, the Central Conference of American Rabbis, serving almost 2 million Reform Jews, condemned government attempts to ban gay marriage. Moreover, in 2000 they officially gave rabbis the right to preside over civil ceremonies blessing same-sex unions. To be certain, Reform Judaism does not view this issue as being about gay rights or women's rights. Rather, this is about *human* rights, and they urge people to view it in the same way.

Conclusions

I hope that this chapter raises questions in your mind about how religion regulates sexuality in the United States. How would you feel if you were told the love you had for your partner was cursed by God? Would you believe it to be true, dedicate yourself to celibacy and not question the authority of that which condemns you? In part, this has been the reaction of many gay and lesbian Christians throughout the world, and throughout history. Unfortunately, it has been the core teaching of sexuality in most conventional Christian denominations, which have only recently opened the doors of discussion about sexual morality outside of heterosexual marriage. It may take some time before significant progress has been achieved. Patience, as they say, is indeed a virtue.

Many men and women have spent a great deal of their lives believing that they would be damned to hell and social marginalization if they expressed a gay or lesbian sexual identity. We can only hope that, as time passes and more people are educated, homophobia will fade into the past. I urge you to challenge any individual, group, or institution that condemns a person simply for being gay or lesbian. Indeed, you may find that you have to challenge your own perceptions of morality and sexuality. Some take for granted the privileged status of heterosexuality; empathy and compassion are achieved only when you step outside of yourself.

References

Publications

Black, Dan, Gates, Gary, Sanders, Seth, and Taylor, Lowell. 2000. "Demographics of the gay and lesbian population in the United States: Evidence from available systematic data sources." *Demography* 37(2): 139–55.

Loftus, Jeni. 2001. "America's liberalization in attitudes toward homosexuality, 1973 to 1998." *American Sociological Review* 66(5): 762–82.

Oswald, R. F. 2002. "Resilience within the family networks of lesbians and gay men: Intentionality and redefinition." *Journal of Marriage and Family* 64(2): 374–83.

Patterson, Charlotte. 2000. "Family relationships of lesbians and gay men." *Journal of Marriage and Family* 62(4): 1052–69.

Seidman, Steven. 2002. *Beyond the closet: The transformation of gay and lesbian life*. New York: Routledge.

Stacey, Judith and Biblarz, Timothy J. 2001. "(How) does the sexual orientation of parents matter?" *American Sociological Review* 66(2): 159–84.

Weston, Kath. 1991. *Families we choose: Lesbians, gays, kinship*. New York: Columbia University Press.

Websites for further information

www.catholic.org [Roman Catholic Church]
www.elca.org [Evangelical Lutheran Church in America]
www.hrc.org [Human Rights Campaign]
www.mcc.org [Metropolitan Community Church]
www.pcusa.org [Presbyterian Church USA]
www.rj.org [Reform Judaism]
www.stillspeaking.com [United Church of Christ Advertisement for GLBT Inclusion]
www.thomas.loc.gov [U.S. Library of Congress]
www.ucc.org [United Church of Christ]
www.umc.org [United Methodist Church]
www.uua.org [Unitarian Universalism Association]
www.vatican.va [Vatican: The Holy See]
www.whitehouse.gov [U.S. White House]
http://en.wikipedia.org/wiki/Category:LGBT_civil_rights [Encyclopedia of GLBT civil rights]

60

The marriage contract

Mary Bernstein

UNIVERSITY OF CONNECTICUT

Many girls and young women dream of a beautiful white wedding, where they can be queen for the day. For young men, the idea of marriage often marks the transition into adulthood, a time when they become responsible adults rather than immature playboys. For men, marriage also confirms their heterosexuality, as a middle-aged single man can easily be suspected of being gay. Marriage is seen as a mark of maturity and earns social status for the married couple. However, if we look beyond the lavish weddings, we can see that marriage is more than just a white dress, bridesmaids' gowns and lots of gifts. Marriage is a legal contract. Historically, marriage laws have served to regulate sexual behavior and enforce gender roles and notions of racial and national purity. Socially, families that do not meet the romantic notion of the husband, wife, and children, are considered deviant. Politically, marriage is promoted as the solution to reducing crime, eradicating poverty, and expanding health insurance. Advocates of same-sex marriage point out that marriage provides benefits to the couple that can be obtained in no other way.

In this chapter I examine the history of marriage as a legal contract, and its relationship to procreation and gender roles. Then I look at the ways in which marriage is promoted by current public policy as a way to solve a variety of social problems. Finally, I briefly consider the debate over same-sex marriage to understand why so many lesbian and gay couples want the right to marry.

Marriage for procreation

The intended purpose of marriage has historically been for procreation, and so the law regulates the sexual lives of married couples and unmarried individuals with that goal in mind. At its most basic level, until 2004, when the state of Massachusetts began to issue marriage licenses to same-sex couples originating from that state, marriages in the USA could only take place between one man and one woman. In fact the law even dictated what sexual acts couples were allowed to perform. The so-called "sodomy" statutes forbade what was once called "the abominable and detestable crime against nature." In practice, this included any oral–genital contact or anal contact between partners, whether married or not (Bernstein 2004). The last of these laws was overturned in 2003 in the US Supreme Court case *Lawrence v. Texas*. Fornication by unmarried adults was also once prohibited in most states in the country. Infertility, or a failure to consummate a marriage, could be used as grounds for divorce. Thus the only lawful sex, historically, was vaginal intercourse by married couples for the purpose of procreation. Those couples unable to procreate could divorce. Marriage laws also prohibit bigamy and polygamy, as well as extra-marital relations, all of which would get in the way of producing legitimate children. Even when these sex laws were not enforced, their existence served as the state's symbolic effort to promote sex for procreation within marriage and to decry any other expressions of sexuality that did not fit into the form of a monogamous married relationship where sex was solely for the purposes of procreation. Thus the law enforces what can be termed "heteronormativity" – that is, sexually monogamous marital relationships geared toward procreation (Bernstein and Reimann 2001).

Historically, procreation as a goal of marriage was an economic necessity. By having children, families could increase their household workforce, which was particularly important, for example, in farming families where the children worked in the fields beside their parents. Peasants would often delay marriage until a pregnancy occurred, in order to verify the woman's fertility. Upper-class men who needed legitimate heirs would divorce their wives for failing to produce children. Of course, at the time, no one considered that it might be the man, rather than the woman, who was infertile. Marriage for love, rather than strictly for procreation, is a relatively new phenomenon, one that has emerged slowly over the past 200 years (Coontz 2005).

Since one of the primary goals of marriage was to produce children (Weitzman and Dixon 1999), government feared that allowing interracial couples to marry would produce children who were "mixed-race," thus "diluting" the white race (*Loving v. Virginia*). Laws against interracial marriage, known as antimiscegenation laws, served to maintain "racial purity." In the 1960s, Mildred and Richard Loving, an interracial couple, decided to challenge the antimiscegenation laws. Married in the District of Columbia, the Lovings' marriage was lawfully recognized until they moved to Virginia, where their marriage was considered illegal. The Lovings turned to the Court to pursue their right to marry. The case, *Loving v. Virginia*, eventually made its way to the US Supreme Court. In 1967, the Court ruled in favor of the Lovings and overturned all the remaining laws against miscegenation. In its verdict, the US Supreme Court stated: "The fact that Virginia prohibits only interracial marriages involving white persons demonstrates that the racial classifications must stand on their own justification, as measures designed to maintain White Supremacy" (1018–1019). Marriage laws also served to maintain national purity in a curious intersection of gender inequality and xenophobia. For example, until the mid-twentieth century, if a woman who was a US citizen married a man who was not a citizen, then she would lose her US citizenship. In cases where an American man married a foreign woman, however, the man would not lose his citizenship, attesting to women's precarious status as citizens. Today, same-sex couples are not allowed to marry.

Marriage and gender roles

Historically, the marital contract was built on and served to enforce a sexual division of labor. When a man and woman married, any property that she owned became his upon marriage and she was no longer allowed to enter into her own contracts. The wife took the husband's name and, of course, she was not allowed to vote. After all, the man was considered the leader of the family and it was assumed that his political interests reflected the interests of his family, including his wife and children. It was not until the late 1800s, with the passage of the Married Women's Property Act, that married women were allowed to own their own property. It was not until 1920 that women in the US won the right to vote. Despite these changes, the law continued to enforce gendered roles within marriage. For example, as late as the 1960s, husbands, not wives, were allowed to sue for a loss of personal services such as housekeeping and sexual relations. Rape within marriage was not considered a crime by most states until the 1980s because it was considered the wife's duty to have sex with and produce legitimate children and heirs for her husband (Coontz 2005).

Over the past 120 years or so, many of these gendered and racialized aspects of the marital contract have entered the dustbin of history, so that the US marital contract now treats husbands and wives mostly the same. What this means is that the law treats marriage as a partnership and (although this varies by state) upon the dissolution of the marriage, divides property equally. Under conditions of continued gendered inequality, however, this means that in practice divorced women fare much worse financially than divorced men, because their earnings are on average substantially lower than men's earnings.

Although marriage has become increasingly based on love over the past 200 years, rather than being about "acquiring in-laws, jockeying for political and economic advantage" (Coontz 2005), it is still a legal contract. So, in the USA, what laws are covered by the marital contract? More than one thousand federal laws, and hundreds of laws in each state, are covered by the marital contract. These laws rest on assumptions about the emotional bonds between spouses, take for granted that marriage is the best environment for raising children, and presume certain economic relations between partners (Chambers 2001), protecting both the children and the parents.

Because the law assumes close emotional ties between spouses, in the event that one spouse becomes physically incapacitated, the law gives the other spouse the right to make any medical and financial decisions for the partner who is ill (including whether or not to donate the partner's body parts upon their death). If a third party injures a married person, the partner can sue for a loss of "consortium" or companionship. Should a married person die intestate (without a will), the law makes the partner the rightful beneficiary of the inheritance. Upon divorce, the law also regulates child custody, visitation, and child support (Chambers 2001).

The law also makes certain assumptions about the financial relationship between married partners, treating the couple as a single economic unit which helps to promote a gendered division of labor. If only one spouse works, then that spouse pays less tax than she/he would if she/he filed as a single person. However, if the partner also works outside the home, then the couple pays *more* tax than they would pay if they both filed as single people. As a result, some couples choose not to marry because they would rather not pay this extra tax, what some have termed a "marriage penalty." In families where the husband earns substantially more than the wife, the couple may decide that it is economically unwise for the wife to work outside of the home, because her earnings would not offset the extra tax the couple would have to pay (Chambers 2001). Technically, this problem would also arise if the wife earned substantially more than the husband, but in the vast majority of cases the wife's earnings are significantly lower than her husband's. If the couple has children, then it is even more likely that the wife's earnings would not pay for childcare, thus making it economically wiser for the wife to stay home and take care of the children. Thus, under the realities of economic inequality based on sex, tax laws promote a gendered division of labor in the home. Although the law no longer enforces a gendered division of labor in the home, married women continue to spend significantly more time on housework and childcare than their husbands, even when both are employed full time.

Marriage as the solution to social problems

The term "family" carries great emotional and cultural force. Although lawyers, sociologists, and psychologists all mean different things by the term "family," the privatized-nuclear family holds a sacred place in the American psyche and is embedded in most major social and legal institutions. As an ideal type, *The Family* consists of a legally married (biologically male) husband and a (biologically female) wife, approximately two children, and the obligatory dog or cat. Although a wife may work, her primary responsibility remains taking care of the home, husband, and children; while the husband's main task is breadwinning, though he may, on occasion, deign to "help out" around the house. Although clearly not representative of the majority of American families (Bernstein and Reimann 2001), this view of *The Family* is hegemonic, and has been called an "ideological code" (Smith 1999: 159) or a "privileged construct" (Weston 1991: 6). Heteronormative assumptions about appropriate gender roles underpin the hegemonic view of family and are appropriated by policymakers as a way to detract attention from the structural causes of social problems.

Historically, "the traditional family" – or the "modern family" as Stacey (1996) terms it – is a recent and, in light of demographic trends, a rather short-lived phenomenon (Coontz 1992, 2005). Industrialization and urbanization prompted massive changes in family life throughout the nineteenth and twentieth centuries worldwide. The material need for extended families diminished, children lost in economic but gained in emotional value, nuclear families became smaller, and, as the lifespan lengthened and economic dependencies decreased, marriages for life were no longer the reality for an increasing number of couples. As a result, families come in all shapes, sizes, and colors, ranging from "traditional" families to couples without children, single-parent families, step families, and families of choice whose members are not always related by marriage, blood, or law (Stacey 1996; Weston 1991).

Despite the heterogeneity of contemporary family forms, families that deviate from the ideal type of the "modern family" are judged inadequate. For example, immigrant and poor families, and families of color, have drawn criticism from conservatives and liberals alike for their diverse, nonconforming family organizations. Their difference from the ideal of the white, bourgeois, native-born family was and continues to be interpreted as the primary source of each group's social problems, and of society's ills in general (Coontz 1992; Rubin 1994).

Daniel Patrick Moynihan's report (1965), for example, sparked a decades-long debate about the relationship between African-American family structures – extended kinship networks and lower rates of marriage – and the plight of blacks in America. Many commentators attribute poverty within the black community to African-American family structures. In response, other researchers see the low incidence of two-parent married African-American couples as a result of racism and poor economic opportunities (Wilson 1987). In either view, African-American families are compared to white, middle-class families, and seen as deviant. The main difference between conservative and liberal critics lies in whether they blame such families for their "deviation" or attribute these "deviations" to structural factors.

The state not only continues to promote the heterosexual nuclear family as the norm but is pouring billions of dollars into promoting marriage as a way to overcome a variety of social ills. In short, marriage is not only ideologically important, it has become an important goal of public policy and is used as a way to detract attention from structural issues such as those related to poverty or a lack of health insurance.

A failure to marry, rather than the lack of job opportunities, affordable and safe childcare, and educational opportunities, is often said to be the cause of poverty. Promoting marriage, rather than promoting economic self-sufficiency, has become an important part of US welfare policy. In 1996, then-President Clinton signed a bill to abolish Aid to Families with Dependent Children (AFDC), a public assistance program that provided a minimum income for the poor. Laden with assumptions that poor women were sexually promiscuous or irresponsible, as well as a failure to recognize the gendered nature of the labor market, the Personal Responsibility and

Work Opportunity Reconciliation Act of 1996, like much of US welfare policy, attempted to encourage marriage as a way to move poor women and their children off the welfare rolls. More recently the Bush administration proposed spending $1.5 billion dollars in programs designed to promote marriage rather than to reduce poverty in other ways. These programs include counseling and courses in conflict resolution. Thus, for many of the poor, marriage is defined and promoted as a primary way to achieve economic independence from the state, rather than looking at the structural causes of poverty. The *New York Times*, for example, stated: "the fiscal lift that occurs when middle-class couples marry and combine resources does not come about in neighborhoods where jobs have long since disappeared and men in particular tend to be unskilled and poorly educated" (*New York Times* 2004). Sociologist Barbara Risman points out the problem with marriage promotion programs. She says: "When people don't get married, including the poorest of people whom these projects are aimed at, it's not because they don't believe in the institution of marriage. They don't have the financial resources to make it work" (quoted in Barrett 2004).

Similarly, marriage is often posed as the solution to a lack of available healthcare. Unlike many Western countries, the United States does not provide universal healthcare for its citizens. In fact, in the United States, millions of working Americans and their children do not have health insurance. Rather than promote universal health insurance, the Bush administration is working to promote marriage as a way to provide health insurance to poor women and children. The idea is that, by marrying, poor women will be able to gain health insurance through their husbands. This policy fails to take into account the fact that millions of working men do not have health insurance to pass on to their wives and children. Poor people in general do not have healthcare, and marriage is no guarantee that they will get health insurance. Criticizing individuals for not being married distracts attention from discussing the lack of affordable health insurance.

Same-sex marriage and the future of marriage

Historically, marriage was inextricably tied to procreation and the enforcement of gender roles, as well as to maintaining notions of race and national purity. While antimiscegenation laws are no longer in place, and the law no longer dictates that procreation be strictly linked to marriage, public policy condemns those who do not conform. While the law no longer enforces a strict gender hierarchy within marriage, common practice and continued economic inequality between men and women often have the same effect of promoting a gendered division of labor that leaves women in a disadvantaged position. Homemakers are dependent on husbands, and women who work outside the home must work a "second shift" of housework and childcare in addition to their paid work responsibilities (Hochschild 2003).

Given this history of marriage as an institution that privileges certain kinds of relationships at the expense of others, marriage's ties to procreation and maintaining gender roles, lesbians and gay men have debated the wisdom of pursuing same-sex marriage as a goal (Bernstein and Reimann 2001). However, even those lesbians and gay men who feel that they themselves would not get married believe that lesbians and gay men should not be denied access to the right to marry. Same-sex marriage advocates point out that marriage provides social recognition for valued relationships. A wedding provides friends and family an opportunity to congratulate the couple and provide support for their relationship. From a legal standpoint, while any couple (same- or different-sex) can draw up wills, this is an expensive process, and it is impossible to privately contract access to the thousands of federal and hundreds of state laws that are involved in the marriage contract. Furthermore, the legal rights that come with marriage are comprehensive, and are especially important in protecting children. For example, the ability to marry would assure that both parents in a same-sex couple have the right to make medical decisions when a child is sick or hurt and would protect the rights of both parents and children in the event that parents separate or one parent dies. While some states allow the partner of a same-sex couple to adopt the legal child of her/his partner, this is an expensive and time-consuming process. The right to marry would eliminate the need for such second-parent adoptions in most cases. Others argue that the separation of procreation from heterosexual marriage as witnessed by the current "gayby" boom, and the fact that by definition there is no division of labor based on gender roles for same-sex couples, will transform the institution of marriage. Time will tell how much lesbians and gay men will transform the ever-changing institution of marriage in the United States, as same-sex couples in Massachusetts have won the right to marry and activists pursue that right in other states.

References

Barrett, Barbara. 2004. "Does Marriage Need Government's Help?" *Newsobserver.com*. Available online at http://www.ncsu.edu/news/dailyclips/0104/012004.htm (accessed 21 March 2006).

Bernstein, Mary. 2004. "'Abominable and Detestable': Understanding Homophobia and the Criminalization of Sodomy." In Colin Sumner (ed.), *Companion to Criminology*. Oxford: Blackwell.

Bernstein, Mary and Renate Reimann (eds). 2001. *Queer Families, Queer Politics: Challenging Culture and the State*. New York: Columbia University Press.

Chambers, David L. 2001. "'What If?' The Legal Consequences of Marriage and the Legal Needs of Lesbian and Gay Male Couples." In Mary Bernstein and Renate Reimann (eds), *Queer Families, Queer Politics: Challenging Culture and the State*. New York: Columbia University Press.

Coontz, Stephanie. 1992. *The Way We Never Were: American Families and the Nostalgia Trip*. New York: Basic Books.

——2005. *Marriage, a History: From Obedience to Intimacy, or How Love Conquered Marriage*. New York: Viking.

Hochschild, Arlie. 2003. *The Second Shift*. London: Penguin.

Moynihan, Daniel Patrick. 1965. *The Negro Family: The Case for National Action*. Washington, DC: Office of Policy Planning and Research, U.S. Department of Labor.

New York Times 2004. "Heartless Marriage Plans." *New York Times* 17 January.

Rubin, Lillian. 1994. *Families on the Fault Line: America's Working Class Speaks about the Family, the Economy, Race, and Ethnicity*. New York: HarperCollins.

Smith, Dorothy E. 1999. *Writing the Social: Critique, Theory, and Investigations*. Toronto: University of Toronto Press.

Stacey, Judith. 1996. *In the Name of the Family: Rethinking Family Values in the Postmodern Age*. Boston, MA: Beacon Press.

Weitzman, Lenore J. and Ruth B. Dixon. 1999. "The Transformation of Legal Marriage Through No-Fault Divorce." In Arlene S. Skolnick and Jerome H. Skolnick (eds), *Family in Transition*. New York: Longman.

Weston, Kath. 1991. *Families We Choose: Lesbians, Gays, Kinship*. New York: Columbia University Press.

Wilson, William Julius. 1987. *The Truly Disadvantaged: The Inner City, the Underclass and Public Policy*. Chicago, IL: University of Chicago Press.

61

Healing (disorderly) desire

Medical-therapeutic regulation of sexuality[1]

P. J. McGann

UNIVERSITY OF MICHIGAN

Sex matters – to individuals, to be sure, but also to social groups. Consequently all societies define and enforce norms of how to "do it," with whom, when, where, how often, and why. Yet how such sexual norms are enforced, indeed which acts are even considered to *be* sex ("it"), varies tremendously. In some cases sexual regulation is informal, as when girls or women admonish one another to control their sexual appetites lest one gain a "reputation." In others, regulation is more formal, as when a female prostitute is arrested and sentenced for her sexual misconduct. Of course, the legal system is not the only institution that formally regulates acceptable and unacceptable sexual practices. Religion also helps construct and enforce ideals of normal sex, defining some acts as sinful, others as righteous. In both cases, the moral language of sin and crime renders the social control aspects of legal and religious sexual regulation apparent.

But what of therapeutic approaches, as when a girl viewed as having "too much" sex is referred to juvenile court for "correction" of her incorrigibility? Is not intervention then for the girl's own good? Might it, for example, derail her developing delinquency, perhaps even prevent her subsequent involvement in prostitution? And what of the prostitute herself? What if rather than sending her to jail we instead direct her to therapy – based on the belief that a woman who sells her sexuality to others must, *obviously*, be sick? Do these therapeutic approaches also count as sexual regulation?

Here it is helpful to speak of social control, a broad concept that refers to any acts or practices that encourage conformity to and/or discourage deviations from norms (Conrad and Schneider 1992). From this perspective a medical-therapeutic response to violations of sexual rules *is* a form of sexual social control. However, in contrast to the transparently moral language of law and religion – good/bad, righteous/sinful, right/wrong – therapeutic regulation of sex relies on more opaque dichotomies of health and illness, normality and abnormality. Although such terms may camouflage the moral evaluation being made, the result is the same; whether the means are legal, religious, or therapeutic, a negative social judgment is made and a sexual hierarchy is produced (Rubin 1993). A dichotomy of good versus bad sexual practices, good versus bad "sexual citizens" (Seidman 2002), is thus created and enforced:

> Individuals whose behavior stands high in this hierarchy are rewarded with certified mental health, respectability, legality, social and physical mobility, institutional support, and

427

material benefits. As sexual behaviors or occupations fall lower on the scale, the individuals who practice them are subjected to a presumption of mental illness, disreputability, criminality, restricted social and physical mobility, loss of institutional support, and economic sanctions.

(Rubin 1993: 12)

Medical-therapeutic approaches – medicine, psychiatry, psychology, social work, and juvenile justice – are part of a web of practices that help define and enforce a society's sexual hierarchy and sexual norms. The "helping" ethos of therapeutic approaches, however, disguises their regulatory dynamics and effects. An illness diagnosis provides a seemingly positive rationale for restricting or changing sexual behaviors found to be disturbing; intervention is, after all, *for our own good*. Even so, what is considered a sexual disorder may have disciplinary consequences. Whether or not a sexual activity is "really" a dysfunction or even causes distress for those diagnosed, individual sexual choices deemed non-typical are curtailed, and sexual culture is restricted in the name of health.

Some consider such matters the proper province of politics rather than medicine. Cloaked in the garb of sexual health, therapeutic intervention seemingly depoliticizes judgments of sexual normality and abnormality. This sleight of hand renders medical-therapeutic regulation of sex an insidious form of social control, a way to induce conformity to sexual norms while seeming not to do so. What's more, an individual need not be under the direct care of a helping professional to suffer the repressive consequences of therapeutic sexual regulation. Medical images of normal sexuality filter out of therapeutic settings into other institutions and everyday life. There they inform commonsense notions of sexual abnormality, illness, and perversion. Expert medical knowledge also helps legitimate the criminalization of non-standard sexual practices (Rubin 1993). These understandings simultaneously construct what we think of as sexually normal, healthy, and proper. In this way, sexual disorders reflect – and help reproduce – a society's sexual norms. Intended or not, medical-therapeutic approaches to sex enforce sexual ideals.

This chapter explores some of the politics of "healing" disorderly desire. Using three contemporary sexual difficulties – erectile dysfunction, gender identity disorder, and sexual addiction/compulsion – I show how medical-therapeutic approaches shape and direct sexual expression. Some forms of regulation are directly repressive; they limit or deny sexual options construed as unnatural, abnormal, or unhealthy. Other forms of medical-therapeutic regulation are more subtle; their "normalizing" dynamics work by producing cultural ideals of natural and healthy sexuality. The ostensibly objective medical model of sex is especially important in this regard. It provides both the taken-for-granted understanding of what "sex" is (and is for) and the reference point from which sexual abnormality and sexual disorders are defined. As we shall see, this intertwining of the individual and cultural levels, and of repressive and normalizing forms of power, is a central dynamic in medical-therapeutic sexual regulation. Moreover, given that some individuals who "have" sexual disorders suffer neither distress nor impairment, it seems that diagnostic categories are not purely scientific entities, but social constructs that reflect social and political dynamics and concerns.

Medicalized sex and medical social control

When something is "medicalized" it is conceptually placed in a medical framework. The "problem" is then understood using medical language, typically as a disorder, dysfunction, disease, or syndrome, and is approached or solved via medical means (Conrad and Schneider 1992). A "sex offender," for example, might be sentenced to rehabilitative therapy rather than prison, or a man concerned about his homosexual desire might consult a psychiatrist rather than a priest. Although such medical-therapeutic regulation may be less punitive than criminal or religious sexual intervention, medicalizing sex produces positive and negative results.

On the plus side, defining sexual difficulties as medical problems may make it easier for people to talk more openly about sex and thus seek information and advice. Accordingly a medical approach to sex may enhance individual sexual pleasure. Yet medicalization also raises the possibility of "medical social control" (Conrad and Schneider 1992) – in this case, the use of medical means to increase conformity to sexual norms and/or to decrease sexual deviance. Prescription drugs, talk therapy, behavioral modification, negative or aversive conditioning, and/or confinement in a juvenile or mental health facility, can be enlisted to ensure adherence to sexual norms. Even without such direct medical intervention, viewing sex with a "medical gaze" often leads to a limited, biologically reductionist understanding. Stripped from its social context, sexual *difference* may become sexual *pathology*.

Medical social control sometimes has a slippery, elusive character. When individuals consult therapeutic professionals regarding sexual matters, they typically anticipate alleviation of sexual distress rather than restriction of sexual freedom. For their part psychiatrists, doctors, therapists, and social workers may neither intend nor understand their therapeutic practice as tools of sexual repression. Despite this mismatch of intent and effect, therapeutic intervention has regulatory consequences. The "promiscuous" girl can be held against her will in a mental or juvenile justice institution. The man who desires multiple sex partners might be forced to remain monogamous and to refrain from masturbation lest his sexual "addiction" overtake him.

Sexology and its legacies

Although some of our categories of sexual disease are new, medicine and sex have long been entangled in North America and Europe. Sexology, the science of sex, originated in mid-nineteenth-century Europe when physicians such as Magnus Hirschfeld, Richard von Krafft-Ebing, and Havelock Ellis turned their attention to sexual behavior. At the time Europe was caught up in a cultural mood of scientific rationality, evolutionism, and fantasies of white racial superiority. These currents inspired detailed scientific description of sexual diversity, and the delineation of sexual practices into normal and abnormal types. The latter were dubbed "perversions" and seen as sickness rather than sin. With the emergence of sexology, formal regulation of sexuality shifted from predominantly religious to secular modes of social control. Regulation of deviant sexuality thus became the province of medical authority (Foucault 1990).

Commonsense understandings of categories of disease view them as morally neutral descriptions of states of un-health. Yet even cursory consideration of the malleability of sexological categories shows that sexual disorders reflect more than just the accumulated sexual knowledge of the time. Forms of sexual behavior once considered abnormal and diseased are now "known" to be a normal part of sexual health. Some sexual illnesses reflect the normative standards of more powerful groups at the expense of those with differing sexual tastes and less power. And some sexual disorders seem more like reflections of prevailing cultural currents rather than actual sexual dysfunctions.

Masturbation, for example, was once the disease of "Onanism" (Conrad and Schneider 1992). A dangerous illness on its own, "self-abuse" was also a sort of gateway disease – a disorder that could so weaken the afflicted that he might fall prey to other perverse "infections" such as homosexuality or sadism. Now, though, masturbation is considered a "natural" (even if private) part of healthy sexuality; in fact, masturbation is prescribed as a therapeutic treatment for some sexual disorders, such as "premature ejaculation" (ejaculation that occurs before coitus) or "anorgasmia" (inability to orgasm). Healthy and normal sexual practices may also become disordered or unsavory over time. Visits to female prostitutes, for example, were once part of the prescribed treatment for male (but not female) "lovesickness." Massage of female external genitalia by a doctor or midwife was once the preferred treatment for "hysteria" (Maines 1999). However, in most locales today the former is illegal and the latter might be considered sexual misconduct or abuse. The female "psychopathic hypersexual" illustrates how disease categories reflect cultural concerns. Female sexual psychopaths "suffered" from an excessive amount of sexual desire at a time when it was "known" that girls and women were naturally modest and chaste, or at least sexually passive. Interestingly, the hypersexual female diagnosis emerged at the end of the Victorian era – a time of changing gender relations and rising anxiety over the increasing independence and agency of women. The psychopathic hypersexual diagnosis reflects these concerns and codifies the violation of normative gender standards as disease. Finally, the declassification of homosexuality as a mental disorder in response to social and political developments outside psychiatry is the example *par excellence* that disease categories rest on more than scientific facts (Conrad and Schneider 1992). One wonders: if historical categories of sexual disease are so obviously shaped by non-scientific factors, might the same be true of contemporary constructions of normal and abnormal, healthy and diseased sex?

The medical model of sex

Although many concepts from classic sexology are no longer accepted, there are continuities between nineteenth- and twenty-first-century medical approaches to sex. The thrust to describe and delineate the diversity of sexual practices and types persists. So, too, does the "medical model" of sex. This view posits sex as an innate, natural essence or drive contained in and released from the body. Bodies, in turn, are understood as machine-like composites of parts. When the parts are in proper working order, bodies are able to achieve their functional purposes. Sexual organs become engorged as blood and other bodily fluids accumulate in anticipation of sexual activity. These changes, as well as sexual drives, patterns of sexual behavior, and even sexual types (bi, homo, hetero), are understood as universal properties of individuals independent of society. Cultural variation in sexual practice is seen as relatively superficial; changes in surface social details do not alter the deeper biological reality of sex (Tieffer 1995). Because reproduction is considered the natural function of sex, the medical model depicts heterosexuality as natural and neutral, not in need of explanation or scrutiny – unless, that is, something goes awry with the hydraulic sexual machine. Thus, nineteenth-century sexology and modern sexual science have mostly observed, described, and catalogued deviations from or problems with sex oriented toward reproduction.

The contemporary Human Sexual Response Cycle (HSRC) is the iconic embodiment of this approach. First conceived by Masters and Johnson in the 1960s, the HSRC describes a presumably universal pattern of physiological changes that occur during "sex": excitement, plateau, orgasm, and resolution. In the "excitement" stage, for example, penises become engorged with blood and vaginas lubricate in preparation for "sex." Most medical-therapeutic professionals concerned with sexual disorders now rely on a three-stage derivative model of desire, arousal, and orgasm. Despite its supposed scientific neutrality – the HSRC model was based on seemingly disinterested laboratory observation of heterosexual genital intercourse – the HSRC has been critiqued as heteronormative and androcentric, and for reifying a limited understanding of "sex" as the cultural sexual ideal (Tieffer 1995).

Although the array of potentially normal human sexual activity is vast, HSRC constructs only a narrow range of acts relating to coitus (penile–vaginal intercourse) as constituting "sex." Other forms of sexual activity are relegated to "foreplay" – preparatory, albeit pleasurable, preparations for the "real thing." Forms of sexual activity that do not culminate in coitus are viewed as perverse substitutions for, or distractions from, the real thing (Tieffer 1995). Oral sex followed by heterosexual coitus may be normal foreplay, for example, whereas oral sex in the absence of coitus is considered abnormal or dysfunctional. The HSRC thus constructs both what *should* and *should not* be done during normal sex. In so doing the HSRC helps constitute "sex" itself.

What, for example, comes to mind when one person says to another, "We had sex"? Despite the nearly endless possibilities (given the number of bodies and body parts that may or may not be involved, variations in sequence, pace, position, sexual aids or toys, and the like) the meaning of "We had sex" is typically unproblematic in everyday life. In fact, a common response might be a titillated "Really! How many times?" The answer to this question is also typically unproblematic, given that we know both what "sex" is and what "counts" as a time. Now, though, let's make it explicit that the two people who "had sex" are of the same sex. Did the meaning of "having sex" change in your mind? What counts as a "time" now? Will your answer change if our partners are male, female, or transgendered? What if we add a third or fourth participant? Is the sex that was had still the *normal* kind? Or does it now appear abnormal, maybe even *sick*, despite being consensual and mutually pleasurable?

The HSRC is also critiqued as androcentric (male-centered), given that the orgasm in question is the man's. Clinically, male ejaculation/orgasm marks the transition to the "resolution" stage. As such, male orgasm is the basis of counting how many "times" sex occurs, or even if sex is "had" at all. Moreover, although the HSRC codifies "foreplay" as an official part of sex, there is no category of "afterplay" – such as sexual activity focused on female orgasm after the man ejaculates. Even adding this concept, though, leaves coitus intact as the defining sexual moment. The (heterosexual) male's orgasmic experience thus defines "sex," whereas female orgasm is not considered. Indeed, female orgasmic pleasure is not a necessary part of real sex. Female orgasm does not count, at least not from the perspective of the supposedly universal and natural HSRC – unless, that is, the counting concerns "abnormal" female sex response. Since at least 70 percent of women do not achieve orgasm from penile–vaginal penetration alone, the HSRC focus on coitus and male ejaculation as the goal and purpose of "sex" renders most women sexually unhealthy, defective, disordered, or dysfunctional (Tieffer 1995). Despite these shortcomings, sexual activities that diverge from the HSRC are defined as abnormal, pathological, deviant, unnatural, dysfunctional, and disordered.

Sexual disorder in DSM

"DSM" is short for *Diagnostic and Statistical Manual of Mental Disorder*. Published by the American Psychiatric Association, DSM is a professionally approved listing of diagnostic categories and criteria. It is the central text for those working in the mental and sexual health fields in the USA, and the key to second-party reimbursement for medical-therapeutic services. DSM has undergone four revisions since its initial publication in 1952. A roman numeral in the title denotes placement in the revision sequence: DSM-II in 1968, DSM-III in 1980, DSM-III-R in 1987, DSM-IV in 1994, and DSM-IV-TR in 2000. Categories of disease are refined and re-conceptualized over the course of these editions. Sometimes this results in a disorder being relocated within DSM's typological system, as when homosexuality shifted from psychopathic personality disturbance (DSM-I) to type of sexual deviance (DSM-II); sometimes it leads to the complete removal of a disorder, as when homosexuality was left out of DSM-III.

The most recent DSM lists three major classifications of Sexual Disorder: Paraphilias, Sexual Dysfunctions, and Gender Identity Disorders. "Paraphilias" include exhibitionism, fetishism, frotteurism, pedophilia, sexual masochism, sexual sadism, transvestic fetishism, and voyeurism. (Many of these types were the original "perversions" described by nineteenth-century sexology.) "Sexual Dysfunctions" concern impairments or disturbances related to coitus. Three subtypes directly mirror the derivative HSRC model: disorders of desire, disorders of arousal, and disorders of orgasm. The fourth subtype, pain during coitus, also reflects the centrality of coitus in constructing the sexual dysfunctions. The last major classification of sexual disorder in DSM is "Gender Identity Disorders." With subtypes for adults and children, these disorders represent deviations from "normal" gender embodiment.

DSM facilitates communication among an array of sexual helping professionals with diverse training, specialization, and institutional placements and practices. Using DSM categories, individuals as varied as a social worker with one year of postgraduate academic training, a psychiatrist with over ten years of medical and clinical training, or a college intern working in a residential juvenile treatment program, can communicate with one another. This is helpful, to be sure. But the shared language of DSM may also make the sexual disorders seem less politically contested and more objectively real than they really are. This may, in turn, make it more difficult for practitioners to recognize the biases built into DSM diagnostic categories. Far from being neutral classifications, the major DSM categories of sexual disorder encode normative assumptions of sexuality. Paraphilias delineate that which we should *not* do sexually; sexual dysfunctions reflect incapacities in what we *should* do; and gender identity disorders concern how we should appear and who we should *be* while doing it.

One way to avoid uncritically replicating these biases is to rename the major types of sexual disorder based on their ideological effects rather than naming the types based on their relationship to coitus. "Sexual dysfunctions," for example, seems a neutral and comprehensive term; in reality it is a specific reference to *hetero*sexual dysfunctions of penile–vaginal intercourse. Consider instead "disorders of prowess" – disorders based on one's compromised ability to engage in coitus. We could similarly disrupt the heteronormativity of HSRC and speak of "disorders of appetite" – disorders of too much or too little desire to engage in coitus, and/or having desires that do not include or that extend beyond coitus. Finally, "gender violations" seems an apt tag for forms of gender expression and embodiment that violate the traditional gender styles underpinning normative heterosexuality. Having linguistically interrupted diagnostic business as usual, I now turn to some specific disorders and consider how each reflects and reproduces dominant North American sexual norms and the sexual hierarchy built on them.

Sexual disorders and the maintenance of ideal sexuality

Some people do experience distress in relation to sexual matters. Treatment of sexual disorders may alleviate such distress and thereby enhance sexual pleasure. This does not mean, however, that medical-therapeutic intervention does not also produce negative consequences or operate in repressive fashion. Moreover, since some of the DSM's sexual disorders are not necessarily *dysfunctions* but violations of dominant sexual norms, therapeutic intervention may enforce conformity to the dominant sexual ideal. Sexual codes, though, are political, ethical, moral, and existential matters – not medical ones. While bringing one's sexual practices into line with prevailing sexual norms may alleviate individual distress, it also obscures the social, cultural, and ideological sources of sexual difficulties.

The Western sexual ideal has become less oriented to procreation and more pleasure-based over time. This new "relational" sexual code (Levine and Troiden 1988) understands sexual activity as creating, expressing, and enhancing a couple's intimacy, and mutual sexual pleasure is accordingly thought of as a normal part of healthy sex. This does not mean, of course, that anything goes. Ideally sexual pleasure occurs within an on-going committed monogamous relationship between two conventionally gendered people of "opposite" sexes (Rubin 1993). In some locales homosexuality may be approaching this sexual ideal – provided, that is, the same-sex couple and their relationship is otherwise normal: the partners are committed to one another, their sex is an expression of love and caring, and they are, like heterosexuals, either masculine men or feminine women (Seidman 2002). Ideal sex occurs in private, is genitally centered (as per the HSRC construction of coitus as "sex"), and is caring rather than aggressive or violent (Rubin 1993). Individuals who engage in such normal sex are good sexual citizens, while those who engage in non-normative sex are thought of as bad. The latter are perceived as immoral, abnormal, unhealthy, diseased, perverted and socially dangerous (Seidman 2002).

Erectile Dysfunction: a prowess disorder

At first glance it may be hard to grasp how improving a man's erection may be a form of sexual regulation and repression. Certainly treatment of Erectile Dysfunction (ED) holds the promise of increased sexual pleasure! It also, however, channels pleasure toward particular sexual acts and body parts in a manner that reflects and reinforces the limited HSRC construction of coitus as the be-all and end-all of "sex." The focus on erections also helps reproduce traditional masculinity and associated stereotypes of "natural" male and female sexuality.

Previously known as the psychological and interpersonal disorder of "impotence," ED is now understood as a physiological impairment of arousal. ED has recently risen to prominence alongside the increased visibility of drug-based treatments; indeed, the discovery of a pharmacological treatment is intertwined with the discovery that impotence is "really" a hydraulic and mechanical disorder. In this, the "Viagra age" (Loe 2004) is emblematic of the biological reductionism that often results when sex is medicalized. The individualized focus removes sexual problems from their interpersonal, social, and cultural contexts. ED thus seems a purely medical rather than a political matter.

The proliferation of penile fixes – Viagra, Cialis, Levitra, and the like – has made it possible for many men to achieve the full, long-lasting erections they desire. The penile fix has also raised expectations and created new norms of male sexual performance. In the Viagra Age it is easy enough to rebuild him, make him bigger, harder, and get him that way faster regardless of his age, fatigue, or emotional state. With the little blue pill and some physical stimulation a real man can get the job done, whether or not his heart is in it. That the perfect penis is now but a swallow away reinforces the cultural understanding of male sexuality as machine-like, uncomplicated, straightforward, and readily available. This reinforces the commonsense view that men are "about" sex whereas women are "about" relationships, while constructing female sexuality as complicated and mysterious (Loe 2004). These contrasting images of male and female sexuality reflect the notion that men and women are "opposite" sexes. This gendered assumption in turn bolsters the seeming neutrality of heterosexuality as complementary opposites that "naturally" attract the other. In this way ED reflects and reinforces heteronormative cultural ideals of sexuality *and* gender.

The ED treatment focus on producing erections "sufficient" for penetration also disciplines the sexuality of individual men. For starters, it directs attention to preparing the man for "sex" – understood, of course, as coitus. While this constructs sex in an image of male orgasm, it also constrains the realm of pleasurable and culturally valuable sexual activity. The phallic focus comes at the expense of the man's other body parts and their pleasures, and construes other sexual activities, including other types of intercourse (anal or oral), as less than the real thing. The phallic focus even deflects attention from the wider possibilities of pleasure linked to other penile states (the soft penis, for example, or movements between soft and hard). Preoccupation with the size and "quality" of erections also reinforces a sexual "work ethic" that emphasizes active male performance rather than sexual enjoyment and/or receptivity. The man's sexuality is thus restricted and restrained, his potential pleasures lessened. Pharmaceutical ads disseminate these messages widely in their depictions of ED treatments as being for caring, committed heterosexual couples rather than, say, homosexual couples, single men, men who masturbate or use pornography, or men who engage in multiple-partner sex (Loe 2004).

Gender Identity Disorder: a gender violation

The gendered nature of ED and its treatment suggests the close coupling of traditional gender and normative sexuality. As Seidman (2002) points out, good sexual citizens are gender-normal citizens: their gender identities and expressions fit traditional gender images and understandings. Thus, normal sex occurs between individuals whose gender styles and gender identities are seen as appropriate for their sex category – men are masculine and see themselves as male; women are feminine and see themselves as female. The gender identity disorders reflect and reinforce these essentialist understandings of the "natural" relationship between sex category, gender identity, and gender embodiment, by pathologizing alternative configurations of sex and gender (McGann 1999). Non-normative ways of doing gender – a feminine man, for example – and atypical gender identities – such as a female-bodied person who identifies as male – are examples of clinical "gender dysphoria." Whether or not their ego functioning is impaired, they experience distress related to their condition, or other psychopathology exists, gender dysphoric individuals, including children, may be diagnosed with and treated for Gender Identity Disorder (GID). Although a GID diagnosis can have the positive result of facilitating access to medical technologies of bodily transformation, it does so by constructing gender difference as disease. GID thus also provides a rationale for medical social control of gender difference – an especially troubling possibility for gender-different children.

When GID first appeared in 1980, it included two types of diagnostic criteria. One concerned impairments in cognitive functioning centered on sexual anatomy, such as a boy thinking his penis ugly or wishing he did not have a penis, or a girl insisting that she could one day grow a penis. The other diagnostic criteria were thought to indicate the child's desire to "be" the other sex. In actuality, however, these criteria focused on cultural violations of gendered appearance or activity norms – boys who look and "act like" girls, for example. Although a child need not demonstrate distress regarding the condition – in fact, DSM notes that most children deny distress – a child had to demonstrate *both* the cognitive functioning and cultural criteria to be diagnosed. That is, a child could not be diagnosed with GID on the basis of cultural gender role violations alone. This two-tiered diagnostic requirement has weakened over subsequent DSM editions. Since 1994 (DSM-IV) it has been possible to diagnose a child as gender disordered based *only* on cultural criteria – that is, based only on the child's violations of social standards of traditional masculinity and femininity in the absence of demonstrated impairment of cognitive function. Thus, a girl with short hair, whose friends are boys, and who refuses to wear dresses, may now "have" GID. In effect, the diagnostic net has widened; a tomboy considered normal under DSM-III-R became abnormal in DSM-IV.

Interestingly, this expansion of GID has occurred alongside the removal of homosexuality from DSM-III and the increasing "normalization" of homosexuality in everyday life (Seidman 2002). None the less, organizations such as Focus on the Family publicize and support therapeutic treatment of gender-different children in order to stave off their future homosexuality. Because children can be and are diagnosed and treated solely for gendered appearance and role violations, GID enforces our cultural gender dichotomy and our understanding of hetero-sexuality as the natural attraction of gendered opposites (McGann 1999).

One need not be gender-dysphoric oneself to suffer GID's disciplinary effects. As noted earlier, medical judgments of health and illness influence everyday life understandings. In this case the construction of atypical gender as illness discourages gender openness and fluidity for all. GID also regulates sexual expression directly by limiting normal sex to that which occurs between traditionally gendered people; cross-dressing sex play by individuals who are otherwise gender-normal, for example, is "known" to be abnormal or perverse. The sexuality of gender-atypical but non-dysphoric people is also distorted by GID. The wholly normative heterosexual desire of a "tomboyish" woman may be invisible to her potential partner, for example. Alter-natively, her erotic draw to males may be dismissed as unbelievable or insincere since she is, *obviously*, a lesbian, based on her appearance (McGann 1999).

Sexual Addiction/Compulsion: a disorder of appetite

At times the terms "sexual addiction" and "sexual compulsion" are used interchangeably; at times they refer to different disorders. Neither is currently listed as an official mental disorder in the DSM. None the less, patients are treated for sexual addiction/compulsion, books and arti-cles are published on the disorder, practitioners are trained in its treatment modalities, ther-apeutic institutions specialize in it, and TV documentaries such as Discovery Health's *Sex Mania!* present it as a valid diagnostic category. Sexual addiction/compulsion is thought to be similar to other chemical or behavioral dependencies, such as those on alcohol or food. In practice, the diagnosis can refer to nearly any sexual behavior deemed "excessive" in the therapist's or clinician's professional judgment. In this, sexual addiction is a near-perfect obverse of the prevailing sexual ideal, the dark shadow of the good sexual citizen. As with GID, many individuals diagnosed with sex addiction deny that their disorder causes them distress or harm, and helping professionals often have to work long and hard to convince their "patients" that they are in fact "sick." For this reason sexual addiction aptly illustrates how disease categories crystallize political differences regarding sexual norms. It also shows how disease categories reflect the social currents and concerns of their origin.

Sexual addiction was "unthinkable" in the relatively sexually permissive, sex positive 1970s (Levine and Troiden 1988). At the time sex was seen in a more recreational, pleasure-based light and therapeutic concern consequently focused on "Inhibited Sexual Disorder" (Irvine 2005). But in the 1980s and the early days of the AIDS epidemic, fears of sexual chaos came to the fore and therapeutic attention turned instead to excessive – thus dangerous – sexual desire. As the dominant sexual ideal shifted from a recreational to a relational code, forms of sexual expression that had been normalized in the 1970s were pathologized as addictive and compulsive (Levine and Troiden 1988).

Gay men were at first thought to be especially prone to sex addiction. Indeed, the gay press worried that the diagnosis was a medical form of homophobia, a way to pathologize behavior construed as deviant by the hetero majority, but that was normative within some gay commu-nities (Levine and Troiden 1988). While gay male acceptance of anonymous and/or public sex may have initially swelled the sex addict rank, heterosexuals also "suffer" from the disorder. Straight women who deviate from relationally-oriented monogamous sex may be considered addicts, for example. A broad range of sexual activity outside of coital monogamy is considered indicative of addiction/compulsion, including multiple partners (at the same time or as succes-sive couplings), "frequent" masturbation, the use of pornography, "recreational" sex (sex solely for pleasure), anonymous or public sex. Sex addiction also manifests within the otherwise sexually normal hetero couple, as when one partner desires coitus more frequently, and/or wants to engage in activities in addition to or instead of coitus. In these cases a therapist may tip the balance in favor of the more traditional partner by elevating one personal preference as "normal" while deeming the other compulsive or addictive. Here, use of the term "lust" rather than "desire" in the sex addiction literature reveals a moral evaluation masquerading as neutral medical description. Other morally charged "retro-purity" terms are also common in the sexual addiction literature, such as promiscuity, nymphomania, and womanizing (Irvine 2005).

Although the activities presumed indicative of sexual addiction or compulsion may be atypical, they are not inherently pathological. It seems, then, that medical ideology has retained the theme of morality but has done so in seemingly apolitical terms. The sex addict diagnosis codifies prevailing erotic values as health (Levine and Troiden 1988). This move privileges a certain style of sexual expression while marginalizing others. Indeed, the sex addict diagnostic guidelines read like a description of a dangerous sexual citizen. The construction of sexual activities not oriented toward coitus, polyamorous relationships, and non-relational, pleasure-based sex as illness ends political debate on these matters before it begins.

Sexual disorders or disorderly sex?

Medicalized sex is not necessarily the enemy of pleasure. As Rachel Maines (1999: 3) documents regarding the preferred treatment of hysteria: "Massage to orgasm of female patients was a staple of medical practice among some (but certainly not all) Western physicians from the time of Hippocrates until the 1920s." This example is titillating, of course. It is also instructive: it points to the necessity of separating the therapeutic professional's *intent* from the potentially repressive *effects* of therapeutic intervention, and to the importance of viewing both in the context of cultural understandings of sex and eroticism. The clinical phenomenon of "hysterical paroxysm" certainly looks now to be orgasm. But in a cultural moment that understood vaginal penetration as necessary for "sex" to occur it was seen instead as the climax of illness. Just as the physician treating the hysterical patient did not necessarily intend to incite his patient's pleasure, contemporary helping professionals may not intend to restrict the sexual freedom of their patient-clients.

Medical-therapeutic sexual regulation works at the cultural level via a normalizing dynamic that constructs a limited range of sexual activity as healthy, natural, normal sex. Medical-therapeutic regulation also works repressively directly on individuals, limiting their sexual choices and/or serving as justification for coercive "therapeutic" responses to non-normative sexual variation. Both dynamics and more are apparent in the sexual disorders just discussed. Erectile dysfunction illustrates the strait-jacket that is the medical model of sex. It also shows the chameleon-like nature of medical social control; therapeutic response to a sexual problem can simultaneously enhance and reduce pleasure. GID demonstrates how medical constructions of "normality" at the cultural level intertwine with the individual level; the enforcement of normal gender on individuals reinforces the cultural concepts of gender that the naturalness of heterosexuality is built on. Together, ED and GID show that one need not be diagnosed to have one's sexuality regulated by medical-therapeutic approaches. Finally, much like the female hypersexual diagnosis, sexual addiction/compulsion demonstrates the political danger that arises when illness categories embody prevailing erotic ideals. At such times sexual disorder can be wielded as a "baton" to force erotically unconventional individuals to adhere to sexual norms (Levine and Troiden 1988). Perhaps then, rather than speaking of sexual *disorders* – a term that suggests objective disease and dysfunction – we could more accurately speak of *disorderly* sex: sex that is socially disruptive, sex that disturbs the dominant cultural sexual ideal.

As individuals attempt to negotiate or realize increased sexual freedom, by seeking, for example, to engage in consensual but non-normative sexual acts, to form atypical sexual partnerships, or to increase their sexual activity outside of prevailing cultural standards of frequency or duration, we would do well to keep in mind something we might call "Oliver's predicament." Oliver Twist's simple request – "Please, sir, may I have some *more*?" – is an illustrative instance of appetite exceeding the capacity (or *willingness?*) of those in charge to satisfy desire. Like Oliver, individuals often stand vulnerable and alone, looking upward meekly into the face of more powerful persons or social forces such as widespread public support for a cultural sexual ideal (for example, monogamy) and/or for medical diagnosis as abnormal (for example, sex addict) of those who violate such ideals. In comparison to credentialed medical-therapeutic "experts," individual "perverts" lack credibility to speak on their own behalf – to argue, for example, that while their choices may be different that does not make them "sick." And even if allowed to so speak, experts who know better may deem the simple request for "more" to be evidence of the pervert's pathology. Moreover, culturally-defined sexual ideals regarding valid forms of sexual activity and relationship are institutionally supported (defining marriage as the union of two rather than three persons, for example); such institutionalization confers legitimacy, value, and power such that questioning or challenging the norm seems to threaten disorder.

Medical diagnoses may be preferable when other definitional options include depravity (you sinner! you freak!) or personal moral failing (how *could* you?). But medical neutrality is false neutrality given the negative social judgment that is illness (Irvine 2005; Conrad and Schneider 1992). The helping ethos and humanitarian ideal of medicine may obfuscate but does not negate the reality that therapeutic intervention in sexual matters has disciplinary effects. Disease categories are forms of power that enshrine and enforce prevailing sexual standards in the name of sexual health. Disorders of desire are thus as much about the *social* body as they are about the corporeal one. Medical-therapeutic discourse, though, disguises the ways in which the personal has always been political when it comes to sex.

Note

1 This work was supported in part by NIMH Grant T32MH19996, and benefited from many stimulating discussions with Kim Greenwell.

References

Conrad, Peter, and Joseph Schneider. 1992. *Deviance and Medicalization: From Badness to Sickness*. Philadelphia, PA: Temple University Press.

Foucault, Michel. 1990 (1978). *The History of Sexuality*. New York: Vintage.

Irvine, Janice. 2005. *Disorders of Desire* (2nd edn). Philadelphia, PA: Temple University Press.

Levine, Martin P. and Richard R. Troiden. 1988. "The myth of sexual compulsivity." *Journal of Sex Research* 25, 3: 347–63.

Loe, Meika. 2004. *The Rise of Viagra: How the Little Blue Pill Changed Sex in America*. New York: NYU Press.

Maines, Rachel P. 1999. *The Technology of Orgasm: "Hysteria," the Vibrator, and Women's Sexual Satisfaction*. Baltimore, MD: Johns Hopkins University Press.

McGann, P. J. 1999. "Skirting the gender normal divide: a tomboy life story." In Mary Romero and Abigail J. Stewart (eds), *Women's Untold Stories: Breaking Silence, Talking Back, Voicing Complexity*. New York: Routledge.

Rubin, Gayle S. 1993. "Thinking sex." In Henry Abelove, Michele Aina Barale, and David M. Halperin (eds), *The Lesbian and Gay Studies Reader*. New York: Routledge.

Seidman, Steven. 2002. *Beyond the Closet: The Transformation of Gay and Lesbian Life*. New York: Routledge.

Tiefer, Leonore. 1995. *Sex is Not a Natural Act and Other Essays*. Oxford: Westview Press.

62

Schools and the social control of sexuality

Melinda S. Miceli

UNIVERSITY OF HARTFORD, CONNECTICUT

The question of whether or not schools should teach students about sexuality has been one of heated debate since the early twentieth century. The simple fact remains that schools do teach students countless lessons about sexuality, in a variety of ways, every single day. As social institutions through which every citizen passes, schools have an enormous amount of power to influence the beliefs and values of young people. In this chapter, I analyze some of the ways that public schools shape America's sexual culture by looking at their informal and formal curriculum, culture, and their sex education policies. My chief claim is that schools have tried to promote what is considered a "normal" and "respectable" sexuality, that is, heterosexuality, conventional gender sexual norms, and an ideal of marriage and family. Lately, some students have begun to challenge some of these sexual norms.

School culture and the social control of sexuality

Critical theorists seek to understand all the ways in which power is exercised and resisted in educational institutions. Pierre Bourdieu argued strongly from this perspective that schools have considerable social power because they appear to be neutral transmitters of the best and most valuable knowledge. Hence, dominant groups within schools can purposefully transmit inequalities and the process will be viewed as objective and fair. Schools have promoted what Bourdieu and others (e.g. Sears 1992; Giroux and McLaren 1989) have called a hegemonic curriculum, which simultaneously legitimizes the dominant culture and marginalizes or rejects other cultures and knowledge forms. The concept of hegemonic curriculum, and the closely related concept hidden curriculum, have been well documented in research into educational institutions and practices since the 1960s.

Early studies examined the ways in which upper- and middle-class, white and male culture, history, morals, behaviors, norms and values are taught and enforced in schools through the power of a hegemonic process where they are also naturalized, neutralized, and made invisible. Over the past decade and a half several studies of school culture have included an examination of a hidden sexuality curriculum in schools (Sears 1992; Epstein 1994; Miceli 1998; Best 2000; Irvine 2002; Kehily 2002). These studies have documented that normative heterosexuality is rather explicitly enforced by the culture of most schools. In overt ways it is enforced by the immense visibility of heterosexuality within the school environment – in the halls, in the cafeteria, at after school activities and functions, etc. The ways in which students, as well as teachers and administrators, incorporate heterosexual activities, behaviors, and language into the social aspects of the school establish and enforce a culture and ideology in which heterosexuality is exclusively the norm of acceptable behavior, discussion, and even feeling.

In some ways, it seems that the explicitness of heterosexuality is so immediately obvious to anyone who has spent even a few hours in any school that it is foolish to remark about this as a sociological analysis. However, as with many things, the salience of this observation is largely dependent on an individual's perspective. Heterosexual behavior and language are integrated and normalized within school culture to such a degree that they have become the natural, and often considered the "neutral," school environment or culture. Things like male–female displays of attraction and affection, discussion of opposite-sex relationships in the halls and classroom, school dances, proms, anti-gay jokes and insults, and the harassment of gay and lesbian students are not viewed as "explicitly heterosexual." These activities are generally perceived merely as a natural school environment and youth culture. However, there is a myriad of ways in which the norm of heterosexuality and the prescriptive behaviors for males and females it enforces, are constructed and maintained through the organized and spontaneous interactions among students and between students and faculty.

This normative heterosexuality not only represses and stigmatizes same-sex interactions, but also dictates a carefully gender-scripted form of heterosexuality, what Best (2005) calls the "hetero-romantic" norm that prescribes specific behavioral norms for males and females. Fulfilling these "hetero-romantic" norms is important to proving one's masculinity or femininity and to winning acceptance into peer culture. Best (2005) sheds light on how these things are constructed by the pinnacle US high school event, the senior prom.

> An event like the prom, as it comes into being through the relations and talk of its participants, embeds normative meanings about heterosexuality and gender in school and the culture beyond. Young women (and young men) come to understand their experiences and identities in terms of these cultural meanings and in this way, sustain the culture of high school as a heterosexual one in which heterosexuality and gender inequality are normative features. Significantly, it becomes virtually impossible for young men and young women to narrate this school event and thus, their schooling and identities, without mention of gender and heterosexual codes … Understanding how events like the prom legitimate specific ideological practices through its celebration of heterosexual romance is important to understanding how identities and cultural meanings are constructed through day-to-day life in contemporary American institutions.
>
> *(Best 2005: 210–11)*

Best's ethnographic study of high school proms illustrates how completely scripted this event is by gender inequalities and romanticized ideals of heterosexuality. The significance of this event, which is one night in a person's life, is amplified through its embeddedness in the culture of the high school experience. The prom is established as one of the most defining moments of high school and the teenage years, given as much or more significance as academic achievements and graduation. The importance of this event is further constructed through the mass media – teen magazines, television shows, popular music, and a long list of films whose plots revolve around the prom. In these ways having an ideal romantic prom night is a gendered accomplishment marking an important achievement in femininity (for young women the look, the dress, and getting her date to treat her well are the most significant things) and masculinity (for young men securing an attractive date and ending the evening with sex are the markers of success) and represents acceptance into the valued world of adult heterosexual relationships.

This "hetero-romantic" discourse of the prom plays a powerful role in educating adolescents about the acceptable and expected behavior governing heterosexual relationships. This is not the only lesson about the heterosexual requirement for manhood and womanhood that students receive in school; it is more like the final exam, testing years of accumulated knowledge. Social research has documented that, throughout their school years, throughout their primary and secondary school years, students are continually socialized into traditional binary gender roles. There are countless messages sent to students by faculty, administrators, and through the curriculum about preparing themselves for their future adult role in a committed – preferably by marriage – monogamous heterosexual relationship. Central to these lessons, in both the formal and the hidden curricula, are instructions about how to be properly masculine or feminine as a means of achieving the desired relationships and displaying one's heterosexuality to others. Key to proper masculinity, of course, is refusal of anything weak, sensitive, soft, nurturing – in other words, all things feminine. Key to proper femininity, conversely, is rejection of assertiveness and strength, but most importantly the acceptance of the compulsion to strive for a standard of feminine beauty set by what heterosexual men desire in women. For both male and female students, failure to do this through the correct gender performance carries the punishment not only of rejection from the opposite sex, but also through accusations of being a fag, a dyke, gay or queer. All of the lessons about correct gender behavior and the norms of heterosexuality are intimately and constantly tied to the stigmatization of homosexuality.

Being lesbian, gay, or bisexual in high school

Examining the lives of gay high school students (as well as of those students who are perceived to be gay) reveals much about the ways in which educational institutions seek to enforce cultural gender and sexual norms, and to control and shape the knowledge and meanings about sexuality available to students. I spent three years observing a community center-run support group for lesbian, gay, and bisexual teenagers, and conducting in-depth interviews with thirty of these teenagers about their school experiences (Miceli 1998, 2005). The subject of the "heterosexual culture" of schools came up frequently in these discussions. In the words of two of the students I spoke with:

> "Everything throughout the entire educational system is heterosexual – boys girls, boys girls, boys girls – heterosexuals are everywhere and we have to accept them. We don't have a choice, they're the mainstream. Then there is us. We have to accept them, but they do not have to accept us."

> "At school you have to watch a completely straight place. You have to watch girls and boys holding hands; girls and boys flirting with each other. And when you are gay you realize that everyone does it so subconsciously. Everyone's flirting with each other. Even just mannerisms, not exactly flirting, it's just their straight world. Everything. And you have to watch it, and then you realize that you are not a part of it. You are just sitting in the back of the class trying to get the hell out of there."

The underlying theme of most of these conversations was that the school environment provides "straight" students with the freedom to express themselves with a wide range of acceptable behaviors, while gay students' freedom of expression is extremely limited at best, and severely persecuted at worst.

Often a support group discussion that began with one member's expression of frustration over some behavior they felt they had to hide at school would escalate into a flooded discussion, spoken in tones of frustration and pain, often masked by sarcasm, of how the norm of heterosexuality engulfed them every day at school. The students described school culture as one in which there is almost continuous discussion and concern about heterosexual relationships and dating, talk about heterosexual sex, constant open heterosexual flirtation, and regular preparation for some social event such as a football game, a school dance, or the prom. Generally, in conversation about these things, there was an interesting mixture of mocking humor and laughter at what support group members thought to be the "silliness" or immaturity of straight students' "obsession" with these activities; resentment of heterosexual students' freedom to flaunt such conversations and behaviors; and anger over the ways in which this heterosexual culture denies, makes invisible, or makes abnormal the existence and expression of lesbian, gay, and bisexual students' feelings and relationships. Many lesbian, gay, and bisexual students experience normative heterosexuality as a central part of the beliefs, values, and skills that schools are trying to teach. This culture of heteronormativity binds heterosexual students to one another and to the school, while it excludes and punishes gay students for their failure to conform.

Gay students experience schools as places that are not only explicitly heterosexual but also explicitly intolerant of homosexuality and gender non-conformity. Experiences of harassment by lesbian, gay, bisexual, and transgender (LGBT) students were common in my own qualitative research and have been well documented on a national level in the USA by several large-scale surveys of high school students. One example of such a study is GLSEN's (gay, lesbian, straight education network) "The National School Climate Survey: The School Related Experiences of Our Nation's Lesbian, Gay, Bisexual and Transgender Youth." This survey has been conducted bi-annually since 1999 to monitor how gay students experience schools. The results of the 2003 survey of 887 LGBT students from across the USA largely highlight the persistence of wide-sweeping problems for LGBT students. Findings in the report include the following: 84 percent of LGBT students reported they have been verbally harassed; 82.9 percent stated that teachers or administrators rarely, if ever, intervened when they witnessed homophobic comments; 55 percent of transgender students reported being physically harassed because of their gender identity; 41 percent of lesbian, gay, and bisexual students said that they had been physically harassed because of their sexual orientation; and 64.3 percent of LGBT students reported that, because of their sexual orientation, they felt unsafe at school (GLSEN 2003). GLSEN grades every state based on how well they protect and meet the needs of LGBT students. In 2003, forty-two states received a failing grade.

The prevalence of this harassment provides empirical evidence for the assertion that normative heterosexuality is structured and enforced by schools. In many ways schools teach students to understand sexuality as a binary of heterosexuality and homosexuality in which heterosexuality is the natural, normal, desirable form of affection and self-expression, and homosexuality is deviant, immoral, and punishable. Most students learn through their years at school that the stigmatization of homosexuality is as normal and acceptable as heterosexuality.

The existence of gay and lesbian people is rarely if ever discussed directly anywhere in the curriculum of most schools. Without accurate information about gay and lesbian people, students, both gay and straight, are more likely to accept and internalize negative stereotypes of gay people and misinformation about homosexuality. The absence of information about homosexuality and the sexual identity of gay and lesbian historical, literary, political, artistic, etc. figures is generally regarded by school officials as taking a "neutral" stance on sexuality. However, it is in reality an example of how schools act as agents of social control over sexuality by being the gatekeepers of the knowledge about sexuality deemed appropriate or relevant to teach to students.

This assertion is further supported by an examination of the controversy that has arisen in the past twenty years as gay, lesbian, bisexual, and transgender students and their allies have tried to make changes to the culture and curricula of schools. Beginning in isolated locations in the northeast in the late 1980s, and expanding through the 1990s, LGBT students and their heterosexual friends began to seek safe and supportive places for themselves in schools. What came to be called gay–straight alliance clubs or GSAs were established by students with the goals of meeting with peers who were interested in discussing issues revolving around being LGBT, thought to be LGBT, or being supportive of sexual diversity in high school; to educate the school community about the negative effects of homophobia; and to work at making changes to the culture and policies of schools to make them safer and more tolerant places for all students. Since the first GSA was formed in 1989, more than 2,000 have been established across the USA, with the largest concentrations in California and in the northeast. In this time many lawsuits have been filed and won to establish the rights of LGBT students to be protected from harassment and homophobic attacks in schools and to form officially recognized school GSA clubs.

Such efforts have been met with fear, resistance, and sometimes outrage. The reaction to efforts to make schools more inclusive of gay students and less tolerant of homophobic attitudes and anti-gay harassment exposes the entrenched normative heterosexuality of schools and demonstrates just how entrenched many people are in protecting this institutionalized means of controlling sexuality. The conflict over this issue closely mirrors the debates over sex education. At the heart of the struggle over both issues is a disagreement over what about sexuality should be silenced and what should be spoken. However, as Foucault instructed, what is silenced speaks volumes.

Sex education and the social control of sexuality

Michel Foucault argued persuasively that Western societies simultaneously repress and obsess over sexuality. Sexual speech is both amplified and silenced. The patterns of what about sex is spoken about and what is silenced is not random, but rather both are part of the weave of power relations and social control. According to Foucault it is a mistake to conclude that, as Western cultures increased the amount of sexual speech and the number of arenas where sex is discussed, the less sexuality is repressed and controlled. Conversely, it is incorrect to conclude that, in spaces where sexual speech is forbidden or regulated, it is successfully repressed or absent. Foucault argued that a concerted effort to control the sexuality of youth began in the eighteenth century, with schools being a logical target of rules and regulations. However, he argued:

> It would be less than exact to say that the pedagogical institution has imposed a ponderous silence on the sex of children and adolescents. On the contrary, since the eighteenth century it has multiplied the forms of discourse on the subject; it has established various points of implantation for sex; it has coded contents and qualified speakers. Speaking about children's sex, inducing educators, physicians, administrators, and parents to speak of it, or speaking to them about it, causing children themselves to talk about it, and enclosing them in a web of discourses which sometimes address them, sometimes speak about them, or impose canonical bits of knowledge about them, or use them as a basis for constructing a science that is beyond their grasp – all this together enables us to link an intensification of the interventions of power to a multiplication of discourse. The sex of children and adolescents has become, since the eighteenth century, an important area of contention around which innumerable institutional devices and institutional strategies have been deployed.
>
> *(Foucault 1990: 29–30)*

Sex education classes introduce direct and purposeful sexual discourse into the regulated space of the school where it was previously confined to the hidden curriculum. Janice Irvine (2002) argues that "[s]ince the sixties, as openness about sexuality in popular culture has intensified, U.S. communities have fought over whether to allow discussions about sexual topics in the classroom. At stake is what is in the best interest of young people. The history of sex education in America is part of long-standing efforts to regulate sexual morality through the control of sexual speech" (2002: 4). In her book, *Talk About Sex: The Battle sover Sex Education in the United States*, Irvine provides a detailed historical account and a sophisticated sociological analysis of these battles and how they fit into larger power struggles to control cultural norms, beliefs, and values.

The idea of formal sexual education classes in schools was first proposed in the early twentieth century by a collection of moral reformers, which included suffragists, clergy, temperance workers, and physicians dedicated to eliminating venereal disease. From the beginning there was disagreement about the specific content and aim of sex education classes, and yet agreement that accurate information about sexuality needed to be taught for the good of public health. This group also felt that the restrictive measures of the Comstock laws that sought state restriction of virtually all public discussion of sexuality, including sex education and contraception information, had to be combated (Irvine 2002). Contemporary conflicts between advocates of abstinence-only and proponents of comprehensive sex education are situated in this long-standing tension between those who feel that the public is best served by limiting children's access to information about sexuality and those groups who feel that public health problems are caused by a lack of such information.

Comprehensive sexuality education stresses abstinence for youth, and it also provides information on contraception and abortion. The Sex Information and Education Council of the United States (SIECUS) was founded in 1964, and has become the leading advocate of comprehensive sexuality education programs being integrated into schools at all levels. SIECUS and its supporters argue that students should receive age appropriate information on subjects like human reproduction, anatomy, physiology, sexually transmitted diseases, masturbation, and homosexuality, and engage in discussion of sexual values. "Advocates of comprehensive sex education endorse what they consider to be the therapeutic potential of open and informative sexual discussion in the classroom. They believe that silence has fostered ignorance, shame and social problems like teen pregnancy and sexually transmitted diseases. They view sexuality as positive and healthy and they generally support gender equality and acceptance of sexual diversity" (Irvine 2002).

Opponents criticize SIECUS's model of sexual education as irresponsible and misinformed. These groups argue that providing students with information about sexual practices, such as the use of contraceptives, has contributed to rising levels of adolescent sexual activity, sexually transmitted diseases, and teenage pregnancy. Since the 1960s conservative Catholics and Christian fundamentalists have founded a variety of political organizations in order to fight for regulation of sex education. These groups are part of the religious right, and opposition to sex education has bolstered their social movement to restore traditional sexual and gender values and norms to American culture (Irvine 2002). One of many strategies for achieving this goal is restricting the sexual discourse young people are exposed to. Carefully controlling or eliminating sexual discussion from school, they argue, is essential to efforts to protect children and adolescents from the "dangers" of sexuality and to reinstating sexual morality to the culture (Irvine 2002).

Michelle Fine (1988) and others have argued that the struggles over sex education are not only about broadly whether "talk about sex" in schools is appropriate or not, but also, through what is said and what is unsaid, to specifically define appropriate sexuality for males and females. Fine's (1988) investigation into the content of the prevalent sex education programs in the United States concluded that "within today's standard sex education curricula and many public school classrooms, we find: (1) the authorized suppression of a discourse of female sexual desire; (2) the promotion of a discourse of female sexual victimization; and (3) the explicit privileging of married heterosexuality over other practices of sexuality" (1988: 30). The sex education programs that Fine refers to emerged in the early 1980s as a result of the Adolescent Family Life Act (AFLA), the first federal law specifically passed to fund sex education. The AFLA, which is still in use and has become increasingly funded and expanded since, was written by conservative Republican senators with the goal of ending premarital teen sex and therefore teen pregnancy and teen abortion (Levine 2002). Because it is girls who get pregnant and have abortions, they became the target of the abstinence education programs. These programs, Fine (1988) and others have argued, teach girls to fear their own sexuality, to view sex as dangerous and harmful, and to guard themselves from becoming the victims of their own or males' uncontrolled sexuality. In this discourse of abstinence education, young women are held responsible not only for controlling their own sexuality but also for preventing their own victimization.

This approach to sex education in the United States contrasts sharply with that taken by many other countries. In countries like Sweden, France, Germany, and The Netherlands the approach is to educate students about sexuality in all of its aspects so that they can develop healthy and responsible sexual attitudes and behavior. Judith Levine argues that studies of sex education in other countries prove that their more comprehensive approach has been successful.

> In many European countries, where teens have as much sex as in America, sex ed starts in the earliest grades. It is informed by a no-nonsense, even enthusiastic, attitude toward the sexual; it is explicit and doesn't teach abstinence. Rates of unwanted teen pregnancy, abortion, and AIDS in every Western European country are a fraction of our own; the average age of first intercourse is about the same as in the United States.
>
> *(Levine 2002: 98)*

Interestingly, surveys on public opinion about sex education constantly find that the majority of Americans support a more comprehensive model. "In fact, the degree of consensus reported in national surveys about sex education is striking. A 1998 national survey found that 87 percent of Americans favor sex education and of those 89 percent believe that, along with abstinence, young people should also have information about contraception and STD prevention" (Irvine 2002). Despite public opinion, the issue of expanding current sex education curricula more often than not sparks intense local controversies and makes national headlines. In addition, despite the opinion polls, the federal government has continued to increase its funding of abstinence-only programs and the religious right has continued to have a loud voice in the discourse of sexuality.

> In 1997, the U.S. Congress committed a quarter billion dollars over five years to finance more education in … abstinence. As part of the omnibus "welfare reform bill," the government's Maternal and Child Health Bureau extended grants to the states for programs whose exclusive purpose is teaching the social, psychological, and health gains to be realized by abstaining from sexual activity. In a country where only one in ten school-children receives more than forty hours of sex ed in any year, the regulations prohibit funded organizations from instructing kids about contraception or condoms except in terms of their failures. In a country where 90 percent of adults have sex before marriage and as

many as 10 percent are gay or lesbian, the law underwrites one message and one message only: that "a mutually faithful monogamous relationship in the context of marriage is the expected standard of human sexual activity." Nonmarital sex, educators are required to tell children, "is likely to have harmful psychological effects."

(Levine 2002: 91)

These debates over sex education curricula are a prime example of the efforts to regulate sexual discourse, knowledge, and behavior, and of the fact that schools are central arenas in this power struggle. The amount of energy, resources, and passion spent by all sides on efforts to control what schools teach about sexuality indicates the impact schools have on the broader social control of sexuality.

References

Best, Amy L. 2000. *Prom Night: Youth Schools and Popular Culture*. New York: Routledge.

——2005. "The Production of Heterosexuality at the High School Prom", in Chrys Ingraham (ed.), *Thinking Straight: The Power, the Promise, and the Paradox of Heterosexuality*. New York: Routledge.

Epstein, Debbie (ed.). 1994. *Challenging Lesbian and Gay Inequalities in Education*. Buckingham: Open University Press.

Fine, Michelle. 1988. "Sexuality, Schooling, and Adolescent Females: The Missing Discourse of Desire." *Harvard Educational Review* 58: 29–53.

Foucault, Michel. 1990. *The History of Sexuality: An Introduction, Volume 1*. New York: Vintage Books.

Giroux, Henry A. and Peter McClaren. 1989. *Critical Pedagogy: The State and Culture Struggle*. Albany, NY: SUNY Press.

GLSEN. 2003. *The 2003 National School Climate Survey*. New York: GLSEN.

Irvine, Janice M. 2002. *Talk About Sex: The Battles over Sex Education in the United States*. Berkeley: University of California Press.

Kehily, Mary Jane. 2002. *Sexuality, Gender and Schooling: Shifting Agendas in Social Learning*. New York: Routledge.

Levine, Judith. 2002. *Harmful to Minors*. Minneapolis: University of Minnesota Press.

Miceli, Melinda S. 1998. *Recognizing all the Differences: Gay Youth and Education in America Today*. Doctoral Dissertation. Ann Arbor, MI: University of Michigan.

——2005. *Standing Out, Standing Together: The Social and Political Impact of Gay–Straight Alliances*. New York: Routledge.

Sears, James T. 1992. *Sexuality and the Curriculum: The Politics and Practices of Sex Education*. New York: Teachers College Press.

63

Law and the regulation of the obscene

Phoebe Christina Godfrey

UNIVERSITY OF CONNECTICUT

Have you ever asked yourself what is meant by the word "obscene"? If you were asked to list specific words, acts, or books, or to describe images that you thought qualified as obscene, what would you include and would your list and descriptions match those of your friends, your parents, your grandparents, or even people from another culture and/or country? Or would you, like Supreme Court Justice Stewart in *Jacobellis v. Ohio* (378 U.S. 184, 197 [1964]), refuse to define it but then declare "But I know it when I see it"? Even the effort to look the word up in Webster's US Dictionary is no help, since one is merely provided with vague and fluid synonyms such as "lewd," "filthy," "lascivious," "indecent," and "disgusting." As a result, one is left feeling rather confused and unsure of what constitutes an obscenity, let alone an obscenity law or how such laws could be made or applied.

This chapter will therefore argue that obscenity and that which is considered obscene is not inherent in the written word, printed image, or act, but is socially defined. Linked to this idea that obscenity is socially defined will be the assertion that any laws created to control it are of necessity vague and thus difficult to apply. Furthermore, obscenity laws (like most laws) are, in their origin and their application, linked to power relations within a particular society. Finally, in order to demonstrate these claims, a brief historical overview of the origin of American obscenity laws and their application will be given.

Obscenity laws as a system of social control

To be human is to engage in the creation of meaning through laws, including social norms that on a collective level constitute the basis and the structure of any given society. Laws are the official rules by which any given society is organized and which usually have a formal punishment attached if violation occurs. Social norms are like laws but have a less stringent punishment and define behaviors deemed by any given society to be seen as normal and thus acceptable. For example, in one society for women to go topless could be seen as normal – hence a social norm – while in another – say our own in the USA – such an act might be seen at the least as a violation of a social norm and/or even illegal, depending on state law. A social norm can therefore also be a law, depending on how serious a society views the particular behavior and consequently its infraction. Either way, laws and social norms are socially constructed and determined in general by the overall consensus of the larger group or society. Furthermore, both act as a constant means of controlling individual behavior for the supposed benefit of the whole.

Thus, societies, and their members, define themselves by their social norms or laws and in particular by those most fundamental laws that are termed taboos (such as the near universal incest taboo), as well as those that form the basis of religious duality. Religious duality is the human tendency to categorize acts, people, and things into simplistic notions of good and evil, right and wrong, sacred and profane, moral and immoral, acceptable (there is significantly no antonym to "obscene" listed in the dictionary) and obscene. In fact, as the sociologist Emile Durkheim stated, "The fundamental categories of thought, and thus of science, are of religious origin" (Durkheim 1992: 89). In other words, all societies have ideas about what is right/good and wrong/evil but there is almost no universal consensus, and thus such categories can be understood as being socially constructed. For example, concurring with Durkheim in terms of the social construction of right and wrong is a quote from Hamlet, one of Shakespeare's most forlorn and philosophical characters, who claimed that there is no such thing as good and evil, only thinking makes it so. Likewise there is no such thing as an obscenity, only thinking makes it so. More concretely, only making a social norm or a law stating that some word, act, book, or image is obscene makes it so, and makes it then possible to control people's behavior.

Key to an understanding of the role of laws, including obscenity laws, in all societies, is to recognize that their essential function is to control people's behavior while creating social cohesion, as in the duality of "us" – those who follow the laws and are considered good – and "them" – those who don't and are considered not good. To merely create or state a law or social norm is meaningless without the means to implement it through the use of force. This most often necessitates an unequal power relationship between the creator or overseer of the laws and those who must follow them – as with, say, "God" and humans, government and citizens, rulers and the ruled, rich and poor, men and women, parents and children. Likewise, the role of religious institutions and/or governments is to ensure that the behavior of believers and/or citizens is controlled, and to do so there must be the means whereby punishments, both subtle and severe, are administered. Furthermore, the very existence of religious institutions and/or governments depends on their ability to implement, using the threat of force to varying degrees, their chosen laws. Implementation most often also depends on the ability of religious institutions and/or governments to justify and legitimize those same laws and their set punishments in the event of non-compliance. The concepts of legitimation and justification are the ways in which authority groups explain why they condemn some acts, behaviors, beliefs, and even people, and not others. Declaring, for example, anal sex as obscene must be followed by a reason why. It is possible to claim that anal sex is obscene just because it is, but usually claims to the authority of religious morality based on what "God thinks" help solidify a particular perspective or law, increasing the possibility for control. Thus, a religious institution and/or government's measure of power is generally predicated on the degree to which they can control people's behavior through, as put forth by Michel Foucault, a "multiplicity of force relations" (Foucault 1992: 475). These "force relations" can appear normal and thus benign as a result of socialization, education, and indoctrination to those who follow the norms, or they can appear more overtly coercive and oppressive to those who resist. The coercive and oppressive qualities would involve mental and physical violence, the degree of which varies depending on the particular society and, within that society, on the particular situation and individual involved.

Role of ideology

Linked directly to the control of people's behavior on the part of a ruling institution, like a government, is the production of ideology that includes the defining of "Truth." Ideology can be generally defined as a collection of ideas put forth by a particular society as representative of what that society believes as meaningful or true. In relation to obscenity, this would mean defining and classifying what "obscene" is, despite the obvious fact that its very definition is and remains highly subjective, hence Justice Stewart's remark about "knowing it." To better understand the power dynamics within a particular society, it is helpful to think in terms of a social class structure – the different levels of power based on economic position. In relation to ideology it can be said that, in general, it is the ruling class – those that control the resources of a given society – that also control to varying degrees the production of knowledge, including what is understood by all as being true. Karl Marx, the German political economist, succinctly expressed this concept when he stated that "[t]he ideas of the ruling class are in every epoch the ruling ideas, i.e. the class which is the ruling material force of society, is at the same time its ruling intellectual force" (Marx 1974: 212).

In other words, those with the power to control the resources of a given society also and of necessity control to varying degrees the ways in which that society understands itself, as well as the world around it, including ideas of morality and laws. Thus, the ruling class is the class that generally has the means to create, distribute, enforce, and legitimize its ideas, making them in simple terms the "only" acceptable ideas and thus the laws. Furthermore, the ruling class is able to decide what counts as true, and even as "the Truth." In addition, in most societies power and control are articulated by means of not only social class but also gender relations, as in male domination through patriarchy, as well as race/ethnic relations, for example, as in white supremacy. The overlapping of such systems of control based on interlocking systems of oppression (and privilege) along the lines of social class, race, gender, and sexuality form what Patricia Hill Collins has termed a "matrix of domination" (Collins 1992: 553). These social categories, like the category of obscenity, are socially constructed in that they vary across time and place and are linked to expressions of social power. A person's position in society is greatly dependent on the ways in which his/her gender, race, social class, and sexuality are defined both in relation to his/her body and in relation to his/her society/social group. It is in the area of sex that the distinct meanings of gender and racial categories are most regulated, not only by social norms but also by laws, such as in who can have sex with whom (in terms of gender, as in homosexuality; race, as in interracial relations; and social class, as in a princess and a poor boy … etc.). Under what conditions (age of consent laws, and marriage within which it is religiously sanctioned … etc.)? In what locations (both in terms of physical place, as in the bedroom and not the church; and where in the human body, as in the vagina and not the mouth or anus)? What it means (sacred, sinful … etc.)? What can be written/depicted about it? And what or who is and is not considered obscene and why?

Thus, like all laws and social norms, obscenity and obscenity laws are clearly socially con-structed and are linked to larger ideological and institutional expressions of social control and power. Since they are socially constructed and do not exist in any absolute form outside of a particular social context, they have changed over time and will continue to change according to the specific beliefs, tastes, needs and discriminations of any given society, and specifically that society's ruling class. Definitions of obscenity and its codification into laws have been used and continue to be used to control people's behavior, creative work, and sexual expression, through the threat of punishment that can vary from social shaming to criminal arrest.

A brief history of US obscenity laws

As the United States became increasingly more complex and urbanized with the advancement of industrial capitalism, the need for social control and cohesion increased. The development of such social institutions as public schools, police/criminal justice systems, and medical institutions were all highly instrumental in ensuring greater levels of social control over larger groups of people who were living closer and closer together. In the US, government fears at this time of the unruly Northern urban masses, many of whom were newly-arrived immigrants, were as common as were the already existing fears of slave rebellions in the South.

In 1835 President Andrew Jackson recommended that Congress prohibit mail that could potentially incite slave rebellion in the South. Then, in 1842, Congress enacted its first anti-obscenity law authorizing the customs office to seize "'obscene and immoral' imported prints or pictures (but not printed matter)" upholding the belief that such "filth" was a foreign thing (Tone 2001: 4). What is interesting to note in the enactment of these two laws is that, although controlling slaves was primarily economically motivated while controlling supposed obscenity was primarily socially motivated, both ultimately enhanced government regulation of stigmatized groups – slaves and consumers of pornography. By the 1860s it seemed that in fact the United States was capable of producing and distributing through the mail its own version of "obscene pictures and books," and so Senator Jacob Collamer of Vermont demanded that the federal government do something to control what he termed "a very great evil" (Tone 2001: 5). The result was Collamer's bill of 1865 that made it a misdemeanor punishable by a fine to mail any "obscene book, pamphlet, picture, print or other publication … [of] vulgar and indecent character" (Tone 2001: 5).

Yet who was to decide which particular book, pamphlet, etc., was obscene and which was not? Amusingly the issue was left up to the discretion of the postmaster to discern if an item was "obscene" or not, thereby giving that individual (and presumably his nominees) the right to randomly read people's mail and potentially (if they were lucky enough) people's obscene mail.

Tying into these original obscenity laws regarding the mail, in 1868 the *Hicklin* doctrine set forth to test material for obscenity based on the question as to whether or not it had a "tendency" to "deprave and corrupt those whose minds are open to such immoral influences" (de Grazia 1992: xi), with children and young girls being the obvious imagined "victims." In the US, this law was used to suppress works of great literature, sending to prison, for example, the publisher of the novels of the famous French author Emile Zola. Following this legal standard was the passage in 1873 of the first of the federal anti-vice laws known as the Comstock law. Named after Anthony Comstock who, as the secretary of the New York Society for the Suppression of Vice, presented Congress with his personal collection of "abominations," including "racy playing cards, contraceptive rubber goods, and such salacious dime novels as *The Lustful Turk*" (McGarry 2000: 9). At first fairly innocuous, the Comstock law ballooned into a century of laws focused on the censorship of published material (including such literary masterpieces as James Joyce's *Ulysses*), the policing of sexuality, the governing of traffic in sexual literature and pornography sent via the mail, including information on birth control and abortion. The censorship of these diverging materials was all done in the name of obscenity and its alleged potential to do "moral harm."

Uses and abuses of obscenity laws

It is important to note how the definitions of obscenity and its corresponding laws change. Sexual literature and pornography, for example, have always existed in human societies and certainly existed in the US prior to the Comstock law. This is not to say that such items would not have been frowned upon by religious institutions and individuals as violations of religious morality and of social norms, but they were not thought to need federal regulation and criminalization through laws. Why at this particular historical juncture did questions of obscenity reach an increased level of interest, fear and even moral panic to merit government regulation (McGarry 2000: 9)? Possible answers range from: an increase in secularism whereby religion became increasingly irrelevant and therefore less able to exercise social control, particularly in the area of sex (religious/sexual issues); the rise in urban working-class populations from immigration and rural migration (social class issues); the beginning of women's call for suffrage and questions about a "woman's place" (gender issues); abolition and the racialization of America's cities, again as a result of immigration (racial and ethnic issues); as well as a combination of all and not to mention other possible factors.

The point is that, having once set down the laws, they could now be used not only to control supposed "vice" that may have in fact been offensive – like, say, child pornography – but also to control anyone or any group or any ideas (as in Jackson's desire to control literature that could incite a slave rebellion, or the later suppression of women's suffrage and reproductive rights) deemed undesirable by the state. In other words, because obscenity, and correspondingly obscenity laws, have always lacked a clear and measurable definition, application of the laws has been completely subject to the whims and interests of the state in the most opportunistic ways. Thus, to varying degrees, literature promoting contraception, references or displays of homosexuality, prostitution, or even just sex in general have been labeled as obscene and therefore policed by "good" citizens and state authority alike. Likening the promotion of contraception with pornography by labeling both as obscene is highly problematic and allows one to see how difficult, and at times even absurd, the policing of the dissemination of ideas, information, literature, art can be, regardless of content.

In the late nineteenth and early twentieth centuries social changes resulting from abolition and the women's suffrage movement actually increased the application of the Comstock law, as suffragettes like Ida Craddock became increasingly involved in the promotion of sex education and contraception. In Craddock's case, as a result of publishing sex education manuals that were deemed obscene she was imprisoned in five jails and two mental institutions (in 1902, rather than serve another prison sentence, she committed suicide). Such legal suppression of women's rights and their access to health information and contraception continued even after women got the vote in 1920. Margaret Sanger, another pioneer of women's reproductive rights, was also subject to numerous arrests. She fought tirelessly for the legalization of contraception against the Comstock law, and in 1933 finally succeeded to get the courts to agree that diaphragms were for medical purposes and should not be subject to obscenity laws. This, however, did not stop both the application of the Comstock law in other areas of American society, nor did it mean that birth control would be widely accepted socially until about the 1960s (Tone 2001).

Literature and the application of obscenity laws

As for the application of the Comstock law to literature, take for example the case of James Joyce's masterpiece *Ulysses*. In 1918 this magnificent novel was published in installments in the Chicago-based literary journal *The Little Review*, started by the feminist Margaret Anderson. However, on October 4 1920, Anderson and her partner Jane Heap were arrested and charged with publishing obscenity by John Summner, who had after Comstock's death taken his place in 1915 as secretary of the New York Society for the Suppression of Vice (de Grazia 1992: 7). Anderson and Heap lost their case and were fined a hundred dollars, and were forced to cease publishing *Ulysses*. Now the irony here is that *Ulysses* is by no means a sexually explicit novel, and certainly not by today's standards. In fact, the scene thought to be "obscene" involved a man looking at a young woman's legs as she was sitting on the grass and leaning back. However, according to the application of the law at the time, it was considered obscene and thus banned. As a result it was not published in the US until 1933, when Supreme Court Judge John M. Woolsey ruled that in fact it was *not* obscene, in that it did not "arouse lust" (perhaps disappointingly) in him nor in any of the other judges. Thus Judge Woolsey set a new measure for obscenity that would question whether or not the work "arouse[d] lust in the 'average person'" (de Grazia 1992: xii).

Yet, despite the attempt to set a standard, such a measure fails to recognize how cultural, historical, ethnic, and even gender-specific the arousal of lust happens to be, and that there really is no "average person." What in fact was being taken as the "average person" was that which represented the dominant group, which in our society happened to be (and still is) upper-class white males (and in particular judges). It was they, as the earlier quote from Marx affirms, who would be setting and enforcing the supposed moral standard for all.

It was not until 1957 that the Supreme Court addressed "the question of whether literature dealing with sex should be protected by the First Amendment." According to the Court, "literature was protected, but … 'obscenity' was not" (de Grazia 1992: xii). Yet how "obscenity" and "literature" were being defined and understood still remained highly subjective. In 1964, in the Supreme Court case involving Henry Miller's *Tropic of Cancer,* Justice William J. Brennan Jr. included the more liberal notion that, in order for something to be obscene, and hence deemed illegal, it had to be "*'utterly without'* literary, artistic, scientific, or other social value" (de Grazia 1992: xii; emphasis mine) – a definition that now allowed for pornography and other sexually explicit materials to be entitled to First Amendment protection (de Grazia 1992: xii).

The most recent definition given for obscenity resulted from the case *Miller v. California* (413 U.S. 15, 24 [1974]) that began in 1973 and involved four illustrated books and a film, all on aspects of sex. This case caused the Supreme Court Judge Chief Justice Burger to revise and subsequently strengthen the definition of obscenity by adding three basic guidelines: (a) whether "the average person applying contemporary community standards" would find that the work, taken as a whole, appeals to prurient interest; (b) whether the work depicts or describes, in a patently offensive way, sexual conduct specifically defined by applicable state law; and (c) whether the work, taken as a whole, *lacks serious* literary, artistic, political, or scientific value (*Miller v. California*, 413 U.S. 15, 24 [1974]; emphasis mine). Furthermore, there was a change from *national* standards to *local, community* ones, which allowed for more traditionally religious states such as those in the South to set their own more conservative standards.

Immediately one should once again notice the vagueness, especially, with the addition of the word "*serious*" and the fact that the standard would be set by "the community." Communities would no doubt have their own interpretations, agendas, and moral frameworks that could differ greatly either in degree or in kind from the person/persons under the scrutiny of obscenity laws. Thus the state, as well as "average" citizens, could demonize and even control the behavior and sexual tastes/interests of seemingly non-conforming, and/or non-religious, and/or just unique individuals.

Obscenity laws in the US today

Now you may think that, even though many obscenity laws in all their variations remain on the books, their application is a thing of our less sexually liberal past. Today we have adult bookstores, Britney Spears almost naked on TV, websites promoting and selling every kind of sexual "desire"/"perversion," all capitalizing on the multi-million-dollar sex industry and all of it seemingly legal, give or take some extremes – for example child pornography and snuff movies (where someone, usually a woman, is actually killed). However, although most would agree that banning child pornography and snuff movies is a good thing, and that children should be protected from explicit references and/or displays of sex, there obviously remain many gray areas where no consensus exists. Regardless, obscenity legal cases still take place and many still seem to make little sense when compared to all that is considered legal.

One such case took place in Texas in 2000 when Jesus Castillo, a seller of adult comic books, was charged with two counts of obscenity and sentenced to 180 days in prison, given a $4,000 fine and one year of probation. The Texas State Appeals Court upheld the conviction. However, his prison term was suspended. He did have to pay $4,000 and serve one year of unsupervised probation. The Supreme Court denied Castillo's petition for "writ of certiorari" (a decision by the Supreme Court to hear an appeal from a lower court) in 2003, and so the Texas court's ruling put forth by the prosecutor "that Comic books are for kids" (Weiland 2003) held, and possibly the application of the law that the comic books lacked "*serious* artistic value."

Once again, how these terms were being defined and who decided the supposed obscenity of the comic books is not apparent. Furthermore, it should be asked why this one seller of *adult* comic books (not children's comic books, as the court seemed to ignore) was convicted in this particular case and not the other untold numbers who sell porn DVDs and magazines in adult stores throughout Texas and the country? What purpose is thus being served here, and why are police being used to arrest comic booksellers and not "genuine" criminals? Although the court argued that children could buy these comic books (the store was across from an elementary school) and therefore they could possibly be "morally harmed," it can be argued that much of the violence children watch on television leads them to be "morally harmed." Furthermore, the sale of guns to anyone over 18 does not prevent children from getting hold of them, though this fact does not keep guns off the store shelves, nor does it result in the arrest of the sellers. And when it comes to causing moral and physical harm, certainly guns outrank any supposedly obscene comic book or magazine. Thus there is a multitude of contradictions embedded in our existing obscenity laws, and, not surprisingly, no clear answers, which means that the use and apparent abuse of obscenity laws remain completely at the discretion of the local, state, and even federal authorities.

Conclusion

Having begun by asking you to define obscenity, it is hoped that having finished the chapter you are in fact no closer to your definition than you were at the start. There is no set definition of "obscenity," and thus any laws that do attempt to limit and ultimately to control it are doomed to both failure and abuse. This is not to say that there shouldn't be some laws that attempt to protect children from moral harm. However, when it comes to the supposed protection of adults, this becomes much more problematic, especially if that protection is in opposition to the First Amendment. Furthermore, in recognizing how the rule of law itself creates the very categories and meanings of the behaviors it claims to be controlling, it becomes evident that obscenity laws are like self-fulfilling prophecies. By criminalizing what people do for pleasure, and which most often doesn't harm others, criminals are guaranteed. Obscenity laws, despite the state's best efforts, obviously do not stop people from producing, selling, buying, enjoying sexually explicit materials (including, in some Southern states, sex toys). Rather, obscenity laws randomly and often seemingly irrationally criminalize some people some times for some acts (Koppelman 2005: 1635).

The criminal justice system is not separate from the social structure, which includes the socially constructed vagaries of oppression and privilege embedded in the interlocking categories of social class, race, gender, and sexuality. In other words, the vagueness of the obscenity laws has enabled them, and still does, to be differentially applied according to different levels of social, economic, and political power. Hence such laws have in many cases been more about stigmatizing certain individuals or groups while perpetuating racism (slavery), sexism (issues of contraception), homophobia (homosexuality), than prohibiting anything that could be considered obscene. And this, perhaps more than anything else, should come under the seemingly indefinable definition of "obscene."

References

Collins, P. H. 1992. "Black feminist thought and the matrix of domination", in C. Lemert (ed.), *Social Theory: The multicultural and classic readings*, Boulder, CO: Westview Press.

de Grazia, E. 1992. *Girls lean back everywhere: The law of obscenity and the assault of genius*, New York: Random House.

Durkheim, E. 1992. "The cultural logic of collective representation", in C. Lemert (ed.), *Social Theory: The multicultural and classic readings*, Boulder, CO: Westview Press.

Foucault, M. 1992. "Power as knowledge", in C. Lemert (ed.), *Social Theory: The multicultural and classic readings*, Boulder, CO: Westview Press.

Koppelman, A. 2005. "Does obscenity cause moral harm?", *Columbia Law Review* 105: 1635–1679.

McGarry, M. 2000. "Spectral sexualities: Nineteenth-century spiritualism, moral panics, and the making of U.S. obscenity law", *Journal of Women's History*, 12(2): 8–29.

Marx, K. 1974. "The German ideology", in E. Fromm, *Marx's concept of man*, New York: Frederick Ungar.

Tone, A. 2001. *Devices and desires: A history of contraception in America*, New York: Hill & Wang.

Weiland, J. 2003. "CBLDNews: Supreme court refuses Castillo case", available online at http://www.comicbookresources.com/news/newsitem.cgi?id=2666 (accessed 21 March 2006).

Part 10
Sexual politics

Introduction

We live in a world where, at least in most countries, heterosexuality is the norm. In many nations, heterosexuality is not simply a sexual preference of the majority of people – it is an institutional force that organizes social life.

In a world where a narrow version of heterosexuality is institutionalized as the norm, individuals – nonheterosexual and heterosexual – sometimes become the target of social efforts to stigmatize and even criminalize their behavior or identity. A wide variety of social institutions – the law, the criminal justice system, education, the mass media, and so on – might be enlisted to control and punish specific sexualities. When this happens, individuals might organize to contest these forms of social discrimination or oppression. Sexual politics is about social conflict about which sexual desires, acts, identities, and relationships should be socially supported and which should be socially punished and repressed.

By far the best examples of sexual politics come from the lesbian and gay community. Since the 1950s, lesbian and gay people have been organized against the social institutions that have criminalized them and made them into second-class citizens in America and elsewhere. Gays and lesbians have fought discrimination in the workplace and housing. They have fought to have their sexuality de-criminalized. They have organized against homophobic depictions in the mass media. Especially during the 1980s and 1990s, gay people fought against homophobic laws and social policies that stigmatized and endangered gay people with AIDS. By far the most heated political challenges gays and lesbians have faced recently is on the front of marriage. Gays and lesbians have challenged marriage laws that exclude their relationships. They have also fought to challenge the limited definition of what constitutes a family. All of these battles – against the criminal justice system, marriage and family, the media, and public opinion – are examples of sexual politics.

Of course gays and lesbians are not the only people to have organized around sexual political issues. Although AIDS politics grew largely out of the gay community, many other people (especially people of color, and people in the developing world) are now organized to resist the discrimination people with AIDS face from pharmaceutical companies and world governments. Many people have protested against the way certain sexual images and ideas are censored by the government and mass media. Ida Craddock was a woman who was arrested for publishing sex education manuals in the early twentieth century. She and others protested against laws which the government used to define obscenity. Prostitutes and sex workers in recent years have organized to demand the legalization of prostitution, as well as social benefits like healthcare. These are all examples of sexual politics, too.

What about mainstream, ordinary, average heterosexuals – do they have sexual politics? The answer is yes, especially in America. In response to what they view as a permissive sexual culture, conservative heterosexuals have organized politically against divorce and homosexuality. As America and other places become more accepting of a wider variety of sexual expressions and lifestyles, defenders of a narrow, "traditional" version of heterosexuality have become increasingly outraged and vocal. The covenant marriage movement is one example. In a covenant marriage, heterosexuals promise not only to marry each other, but to abide by much more rigid rules should they decide to divorce. Heterosexuals have also organized to exclude gays from the right to marry. They have attempted to change sex education curricula, arguing that an "abstinence only" education promotes moral, healthy sexual behavior amongst youngsters. Most of these struggles have been articulated as a defense of "the traditional family" and "family values."

In this part of the book, we present a wide variety of examples of sexual politics – liberal, conservative, gay, straight, and otherwise. You'll learn about the various marriage battles, sex education, AIDS politics, the politics of sex workers and gender/sexual conflicts in America. You'll be treated to a really interesting discussion of the differences between gay and lesbian politics in the Netherlands and the US. There is also a fascinating interview about the politics of sex education with a leading scholar in the field. In all of these essays, you will see that sexual politics is simultaneously personal, cultural, and institutional.

64

Gay marriage.
Why now? Why at all?

Reese Kelly

STATE UNIVERSITY OF NEW YORK AT ALBANY

Currently, the most polarizing issue in the United States regarding the gay and lesbian community is gay marriage. The dominant agenda in the lesbian and gay (L/G) movement is the fight for legal recognition of same-sex couples. The theme of gay marriage is presently on the rise, with coverage of political demonstrations, weddings and commitment ceremonies, and civil rights court proceedings. The most noteworthy illustration of the gay marriage issue in popular culture is its importance in the 2005 US presidential election. Alongside the September 11 terrorist attacks and the war in Iraq, gay marriage, often disguised as "family values," stood as a key point of contention among most of the candidates. But why now? Gays and lesbians have been challenging society and the courts for the right to marry since the early 1970s. What is so unique about the current social climate that marriage is the leading gay issue?

Tolerated but not equal

Let's start with the emergence of the L/G movement in the late 1960s and early 1970s. During this time people were fired from their jobs as teachers, hospital workers, and state employees because of their actual or suspected homosexuality. The representation of gays and lesbians in the media was negative, if at all. Bars and clubs were raided nightly, limiting the available social space for people to be open about their homosexuality. Consequently, the gay and lesbian movement spawned in the 1970s focused on visibility, self-affirming identities, and ending discrimination based on sexuality, mirroring other civil rights movements of the time.

Lesbians and gays who did fight for the right to marry were but a small minority within the gay and lesbian movement. The movement was driven by a young generation of gay and lesbian activists who believed that marriage was a patriarchal heterosexual institution that upheld the oppression of gays and lesbians. To them, gay marriage was the antithesis to their agenda of freedom from society's dominant institutions. Both national and local gay and lesbian organizations ignored the issue of marriage, saw it as a hopeless cause, or more commonly, had higher priorities. Accordingly, the 1970s was a decade of fighting for a self-affirming positive gay or lesbian identity and fighting off social stigmas not for adult concerns, such as gay marriage.

Beginning in the 1980s and 1990s, marriage became part of the larger fight for gay and lesbian equality due to three major social factors: the impact of AIDS, the growing visibility and integration of gays and lesbians in society, and a growing middle-aged L/G population. All of these factors contributed to a change in the L/G movement from tolerance to a politics of equality. AIDS had considerable influence on the direction of the gay and lesbian agenda during the 1980s and early 1990s. First recognized in 1981, HIV, the virus that causes AIDS, surfaced as the "gay plague," leading to hundreds of thousands of deaths among gay men by the early 1990s. The fear, ignorance, and complacency on the part of the medical community as well as of the general public forced the issue to the front of the gay and lesbian political agenda. The AIDS crisis became a platform for pinpointing specific legal and social acts of discrimination towards gays and lesbians. The origin of many AIDS-related issues was that gays and lesbians had no legal partner status. More specifically, health coverage, visitation rights, inheritance and residency rights were a necessity for those infected as well as their partners.

Also during this time, the residual effects of the gay rights movement could be seen in the media's representation of gays and lesbians. In the late 1980s and increasingly through the 1990s, mainstream television and film began to have gay characters and present issues unique to gay culture. The most notable movie, *Philadelphia*, confronts issues of workplace discrimination and AIDS. A few years later, Ellen DeGeneres became the first openly gay character (and actor) in a leading role on US prime-time television, and Pedro Zamora became the first openly gay and HIV-positive reality television star on MTV's Real World, San Fransisco. Gay people, more than ever before, were becoming part of the cultural landscape. Unfortunately, depictions of gays and lesbians were heavily based on stereotypes, while television shows that offered nuanced portrayals were often canceled. The overall gay presence in the media reflected a growing tolerance, if not quite acceptance, of gays, a widespread decriminalization of homosexual behavior, and more so, the increasing number of Americans who were "coming out" about their gay, lesbian, and bisexual lifestyles. The heightened visibility of gays and lesbians reminded all Americans of the existence of gay culture and its demand for equal rights.

In the late 1980s and early 1990s we also see an increasingly middle-aged and coupled gay population. Of those who came out of the closet during the 1960s and 1970s, many sought long-term relationships, contrary to the stereotype of the promiscuous gay man. Many lesbians were also coupling off and starting families with children from previous marriages, through adoption, and through *in vitro* fertilization. These gay families expressed the need for rights to which only married heterosexuals had access, such as second-parent adoption, healthcare benefits, and hospital visitation rights. In regard to the law, only the biological parent had rights to the child. In the case of a separation or death, the non-biological parent had no legal recourse to gain custody, even partial, of shared children. An even more common occurrence in child custody discrimination was that gays and lesbians who had children from previous heterosexual marriages often lost custody in divorce settlements. Even if it was in the best interest of the child, emotionally or economically, to remain with the gay parent, courts often ruled in favor of the heterosexual parent for fear of raising the child in an "unsuitable household." The need for parental rights became part of the agenda of gay rights organizations.

By the mid-1990s, then, gays and lesbians faced a complicated and often contradictory combination of social acceptance and discrimination. The L/G movement had shifted from a politics of tolerance to a politics of equality, including employment rights and struggles in academia over knowledge. They were becoming progressively more visible in culture, and national gay and lesbian organizations were on the rise and gaining economic and political strength. Former President Bill Clinton even claimed that gay people were a part of his "vision" of America. Nevertheless, there were still no laws protecting them from workplace, housing, and family discrimination in most states. Moreover, in contradiction to Clinton's campaign promise to include gays in America's "vision," he enacted two federal laws endorsing the national discrimination against gays and lesbians. The first law, in 1993, was the "Don't ask, don't tell" military policy banning gays from being open about their sexuality or engaging in homosexual acts while in military service. Furthermore, Clinton signed the Defense of Marriage Act in September 1996, which allows each state to recognize or deny any marriage-like same-sex relationship which has been recognized in another state. It also defines marriage as a legal union between one man and one woman only. Accordingly, gays and lesbians, although accepted by the dominant culture, were accepted on the condition of being second-class citizens, restricted from access to two of America's principal social institutions, the military and marriage.

9/11, and the politics of fear

Through the late 1990s and into the new millennium, the United States, as a whole, experienced considerable contradictions, with a rise in social acceptance and certain legal protections for gays, but also a rise in political conservatism. With the exportation of jobs to other countries and the response to the 9/11 attacks, there is a budding culture of anger and hostility towards anyone who is seen as an outsider. The "other" or "outsider" is seen as a threat to the lives of the everyday American. Although this fear is mostly directed at Americans with Middle-Eastern, Mexican, or Asian heritage, it has also spread to include anyone who is considered to be "unpatriotic." In regards to sexuality, those who are perceived as "unpatriotic" are predominantly single mothers and gays. To be "patriotic" by the current dominant standards one must be heterosexual, married, and family-centered. Religious activist and dominant spokesperson for the Christian Right Jerry Falwell went so far as to claim that gays and lesbians were part of the reason for the 9/11 attacks. Led by President George W. Bush, conservative politicians aim to promote "family values" which enact discriminatory legislation against gays and lesbians. The most notable of these campaigns is a constitutional amendment to protect marriage, proposed by President Bush in February of 2004. This amendment would define marriage as being between only a man and a woman, leaving states to define other legal arrangements for same-sex couples. Although it is highly unlikely that this amendment will actually be ratified, the impact of such an amendment would sanction homophobia and discrimination as a national policy.

Although 9/11 helped shape a conservative political climate, gays and lesbians have not retreated into the closet. Instead, gays are moving into the mainstream and the battle for sexual justice grows ever more public. Gay characters can be found in almost every prime-time television show, and in major movie box office hits such as *As Good As It Gets*. Many popular TV programs focus solely on gay culture, such as *Queer Eye for the Straight Guy* and the two Showtime hits *Queer as Folk* and *The L Word*. Gay culture is being disseminated from US urban meccas such as San Francisco and New York City's Chelsea Village to suburban areas across the country, such as Oak Park, Illinois, and Somerville, Massachusetts. Furthermore, gay culture is no longer confined to those who identify as gay, as one can see with the invention of the "metrosexual," a clean-cut, well-dressed, urban-dwelling heterosexual man. Moreover, a more radical faction of the gay and lesbian movement, the queer movement, is gaining popularity among the younger generation, predominantly college students. The queer movement calls into question what we define as man/woman and heterosexual/homosexual. It aims to break down the dichotomous categories of sex, gender, and sexuality by turning assumptions about what is normal and natural on their heads. Thus, as gays become a larger part of the dominant culture, the queer agenda continues to be a driving force for broader social and legal change.

Moreover, despite some serious setbacks to the movement, gays and lesbians have achieved a significant number of civil rights advancements in the past decade. In the private sector, many companies have made domestic partner benefits available and adopted anti-discrimination poli-cies. By 2004, almost half of the United States' Fortune 500 companies offered same-sex partner health insurance and other benefits (Chauncey 2004: 117). On the state level, almost half of the states allow second-parent adoption in some jurisdictions, if not the entire state (Human Rights Campaign 2004). There are also approximately a dozen states which allow protection from workplace discrimination for state employees based on sexual orientation (Human Rights Campaign 2004). The most significant legal advancement, however, was the 2003 Supreme Court decision in the *Lawrence v. Texas* case that sodomy laws are unconstitutional. In other words, the US Supreme Court ruled that private sexual conduct is protected under the con-stitution, ending legal discrimination against homosexual sex acts. The growing visibility and integration of gay culture, and the struggle against an increasingly conservative national politics, have set the stage for marriage to be the fighting ground for gay and lesbian civil rights at this time.

Changing gender roles and changes in marriage

To understand some of the passion behind the gay marriage debate, we must look at some key social forces that have changed the institution of marriage. In particular, I want to comment on changing gender aspects of marriage.

Consider that the role of motherhood has been somewhat uncoupled from marriage. Many women are today raising children on their own as a result of divorce, teenage pregnancy, or simply choosing not to marry. Workforce participation has allowed many women to opt out of marriage, for they can rely on their own salary instead of seeking out a second income through marriage. Moreover, the stigma attached to being single has lessened over the years due to the overwhelming number of single adult women, with or without children. Although this social trend has prompted conservative rhetoric regarding the need for marriage and the family, these alternative family structures have poked holes in the notion that a nuclear family is the only legitimate option.

More generally, the changing roles of men and women have dramatically altered the social organization of marriage. Only a few decades ago, men and women had distinct roles in mar-riage. Women were relegated to the home, subservient to their male partners, and were expected to be the primary caregiver in the family. In contrast, men were expected to be dominant heads of households and primary breadwinners, with little obligation for childcare. Nowadays, women are less constrained to the private world of their homes and participate, at least minimally, in the public corporate world. As a result, women generally have more financial independence, giving them leverage in delineating familial duties. Also, the notion of masculinity seems to be loosening up a bit. There is less of a stigma attached to "stay-at-home" husbands or to those men with less earning potential than their wives. Additionally, gay couples and non-nuclear family arrangements provide examples of alternative roles for all family members that are not necessarily gender-specific. The home, and more specifically marriage, is becoming a place of intimacy and commitment between equals, and gender roles are less constraining or defining.

Alternatives to marriage

There are a few alternatives to marriage for gays and lesbians who cannot legally marry and for those who merely choose not to. Currently, Massachusetts is the only state that has legalized gay marriage; however, Governor Romney has pushed clerks to ask for proof of in-state residency for gay couples. Therefore, gay residents of the other forty-nine states have to be resourceful in finding options to legitimize their relationship status and accrue partner benefits.

The first step towards accruing marriage benefits for gay couples was the advent of "domestic partner" (DP) status, which allows non-married couples to gain marriage-like benefits from private agencies. For instance, health benefits, bereavement and sick leave, and pension benefits offered by employers are increasingly available to "domestic partners" of the employed. Some employers ask for proof of codependence to qualify for DP benefits, while others require registry with the city or town of residence. DP benefits are available mostly to gay couples who cannot legally marry, but in many instances are offered to heterosexual cohabiting couples as well. A substantial number of corporations and professions offer DP benefits, the first being the software company Lotus in 1992. DPs vary in the extent of included benefits, from very few to matching those given through marriage. Moreover, DP benefits are insufficient because they do not involve any federal recognition of an intimate relationship, and therefore DP benefits cannot be carried across states or claim any federal-level benefits such as tax breaks.

The legal status available to gays and lesbians which comes closest to marriage is a civil union, obtainable in Vermont, and most recently in Connecticut. In short, civil unions provide most, if not all, benefits and rights of marriage on the state level. Healthcare benefits, second-parent adoption, hospital visitation, and state tax benefits can be acquired through civil union status. However, these rights, as well as the status of the civil union, are only recognized within Vermont. For example, civil unions can only be terminated in the state they were given. Also, as with DP, the federal benefits conferred to married couples – over 1,000 in total – are not applicable to civil unions. Unlike DP benefits, civil unions are only open to those couples who cannot legally marry. Not only are the benefits of civil unions unequal to those of marriage, the mere fact that they exist as a separate status just for gay people symbolizes a powerful inequality in our legal system. Simply put, civil unions are not equal to marriage in practice and principle.

Should lesbians and gays be allowed to marry?

There are three general arguments in the gay marriage debate: the anti-marriage side, the pro-marriage side, and a queer critique of the place of marriage in our society. It is important to keep in mind that people of any sexual orientation or political identification can and do align with each of the sides. Many heterosexuals support gay marriage, just as some gays are passionately against it.

The anti-gay marriage side emphasizes the notion that marriage and heterosexuality are the cornerstones of the Judeo-Christian tradition. Critics of gay marriage appeal to the bible, which claims that the relationship between Adam and Eve is the foundation of civilization. The bible also explicitly states that a man should not lie with a man as he lies with a woman. As a society that rests on Christian foundations, marriage in America must be restricted to heterosexuality in order to preserve its moral and social coherence. Those who are against gay marriage also believe that heterosexual marriage provides the right moral environment for a healthy family. Marriage encourages family values such as monogamy, respect for authority, and the importance of the differences between men and women. Homosexuals are stereotyped as being unable to have stable relationships and dangerous to healthy gender development in children. For many critics, homosexuality is the very antithesis of a healthy family and society.

The pro-gay marriage side argues that, whether or not gays and lesbians want to marry, they should have the right to decide. The argument from the anti-gay marriage side that marriage is a religious matter is misleading. In fact, marriage is a civic or legal relationship between the two individuals and the government. Marital status confers more than 1,400 government-recognized rights and benefits. Individuals may choose to have a religious marriage, but the institution of marriage is a secular legal affair. Moreover, it is important to note that those who argue for gay marriage continue to define marriage as, ideally, a long-term, loving commitment that should be valued and respected. Other than having a same-sex partner, they believe that many gays are already in such long-term relationships or wish to commit to relationships based on shared love and commitment. Also, pro-gay marriage advocates argue that, since the right to marry is viewed as part of being a first-class citizen, denying this right to gays consigns them to a second-class status.

There is a third party to the gay marriage debate, the so called "queer" position. The term "queer" is less a sexual identity than a viewpoint that questions the privileging of certain specific social norms, identities, and institutions as normal and beyond question. Queers are critical of marriage because it is the one intimate arrangement that the state sanctions as natural and preferable. What's wrong with this? Queers argue that, by conferring recognition and rights on marriage, the state renders all other non-marital relationships as inferior. A state-recognized institution of marriage creates a division between marriage, which is respectable, good, even ideal, and other intimate and family arrangements which are less than ideal, if not viewed as deviant and abnormal. Queers also make the compelling point that it's not only gays and lesbians who are disadvantaged by associating marriage with many exclusive benefits, but the poor and many non-white people are disadvantaged because less of them marry. In sum, queers do not advocate the inclusion of gays and lesbians into the institution of marriage, but the extension of full marital benefits to all who need them.

The controversy of gay marriage is complicated, and, as I hope to have shown, it affects people of all sexual orientations. Fortunately, whether or not gays are eventually able to marry, the dispute does not stop us from deciding who we choose to love, in what ways, and for however long.

References

Chauncey, George. 2004. *Why Marriage?: The history shaping today's debate over gay equality.* New York: Basic Books.

Human Rights Campaign. 2004. "HRC Marriage Center." Available online at http://www.hrc.org (accessed March 23 2006).

Warner, Michael. 1999. *The Trouble with Normal: Sex, politics and the ethics of queer life.* Cambridge, MA: Harvard University Press.

65

The US Supreme Court and the politics of gay and lesbian rights

Gregory Maddox

SOUTHERN ILLINOIS UNIVERSITY CARBONDALE

Because American law is based on the premise that all persons are entitled to equal justice under the law, unpopular positions are more likely to be heard in the courts than in the legislative and executive branches of government. This makes the judiciary, particularly the Supreme Court, increasingly important instruments of social change in the United States, as many groups seek to have their voices heard there. *Social movements* can best be thought of as groups of people seeking some kind of change in the social order, and usually for every social movement there is a *countermovement* whose goal is to resist the change that social movements advocate. These groups can be large or small, centered on a specific issue or around broad ideals, and can be highly organized with a rigid hierarchy or loosely organized with no clear structure. Social movements and their countermovement opponents must seek validation from the state, and can do so in different ways. They may appeal to a large enough number of people for legislatures or executives to act on their behalf. If social movements represent minority viewpoints, however, this popular support may be difficult to arrange. Thus, the courts may be the only refuge for these groups.

No court has as much authority in the United States as the Supreme Court. Its nine justices have the final word on interpreting the law, including the ultimate authority to interpret the US Constitution. The cases heard before the Supreme Court affect public policy, nationally, as opposed to the local jurisdiction of the lower courts, so social movements as well as their countermovement opponents prefer to have cases heard there because of the larger impact of a potentially favorable decision.

Decisions by the justices are often divided, and consequently so are the opinions of the Court. The opinion representing the views of the justices on the winning side, even if decided unanimously, is referred to as the *majority opinion*, and the *dissenting opinion* represents the views of the justices in the minority. In addition, justices may write separate *concurring opinions*, in which they agree with the majority or the minority but differ on specific matters found in the majority or dissenting opinions. Although only the majority opinion holds the binding legal outcome for the case, its legal *precedent*, all the opinions written in a case are important. Within them are points that might be addressed in future cases, rationale behind the decisions, or implications for society resulting from the case. Thus, the Supreme Court often acts as an arbitrator where cultural boundaries between accepted and unaccepted aspects of society are negotiated as questions of law by its nine justices.

Numerous instances of social movements successfully relying on the Court for social change are found throughout American history, most notably during the term of Chief Justice Earl Warren. The Warren Court heard a number of cases sponsored by the NAACP, one of the most successful social movement organizations in history, including the 1954 landmark *Brown v. Board of Education of Topeka* which struck down the notion of "separate but equal" in public schooling for black Americans. The Warren Court also decided a number of cases protecting the rights of criminal defendants, including *Gideon v. Wainwright* (1963), which requires legal representation for criminal defendants regardless of ability to pay, and *Miranda v. Arizona* (1966), responsible for the now famous "Miranda Warnings." Other social issues have been affected by Court cases, and by cases in other Courts. The case of *Griswold v. Connecticut* (1962) established a constitutional right to privacy. The Court, under Chief Justice Warren Burger, decided the cases of *Furman v. Georgia* (1972), which placed a moratorium on capital punishment, and *Roe v. Wade* (1973), which legalized abortion based upon the right to privacy found in *Griswold*. All of these cases became tremendously important to social movement organizations and counter-movement organizations because of the new interpretations of civil rights for various groups of people they represented. Because of its role in arbitrating negotiations of cultural boundaries, we can look at the Supreme Court as a vital catalyst for social change.

Gay and lesbian civil rights organizations form another such social movement that has, on several occasions, looked to the Court for relief from a deviant cultural status or for acknowledgment as being within accepted cultural "boundaries." Most important to this process is the dynamic "relationship" between movement and countermovement organizations, and how this relationship influences collective identity. *Collective identity* is "the shared definition of a group that derives from members' common interests, experiences, and solidarity" (Taylor and Whittier 1992: 105). There is a great deal of research showing how a group's collective identity influences its *framing activity*, or the methods used to convey its ideas and beliefs to others. (See Hunt, Benford, and Snow 1994 for further insight on framing activity and collective identity.) Through their use of these framing activities, their messages, which convey aspects of their collective identities, are presented to the Court.

In this chapter, I investigate how the Court is used to mediate negotiations over cultural boundaries. In addition, I show how collective identity affects, and is affected by, the Court's decisions. As examples of these processes, I examine the content of the *amicus curiae* ("friend of the court") briefs filed in three landmark lesbian and gay civil rights cases. Such briefs serve the Court by representing the interests of groups and individuals not party to the legal action yet affected by potential decisions. Past research has suggested that *amicus curiae* briefs are becoming increasingly important to the Court, and has further suggested that social movement and countermovement organizations have increasingly used these briefs to address the Court.

The cases

I chose three particular cases, *Bowers v. Hardwick* (1986), *Romer v. Evans* (1996), and *Lawrence v. Texas* (2003), because they were among the most important cases heard in the area of gay, lesbian, and bisexual boundary formation, based upon several aspects. First was the gravity of the issue to be decided in each case. The *Bowers* case sought to determine whether intimate consensual homosexual acts were outside cultural boundaries to the point of being considered criminal activity. The *Romer* case sought to determine whether gays, lesbians, and bisexuals warranted protection from discrimination as a class of people. The *Lawrence* case revisited the issues in the *Bowers* case after some fifteen years of change in cultural attitudes towards homosexuality. These areas of case law affected interaction within society as a whole, and ramifications from the decisions handed down held potential consequences for millions of Americans; therefore, these cases attracted the most attention, not only that of gay and lesbian organizations and their opponents, but also of the media and the public at large. Because of such attention, groups and individuals together spent millions of dollars on *amicus* briefs on both sides of the issues with the hope of influencing the Court.

Second, these cases were heard over a span of time when public sentiment towards homosexuality was rapidly changing. Furthermore, this time difference allowed for change in the makeup of the Court. Only three of the nine justices who heard the *Bowers* case in 1986 remained on the Court to hear *Romer* in 1996 and *Lawrence* in 2003.

Third, although the background or points of case law covered in each of these cases may differ, the process of filing and the potential utility of the *amicus* briefs to the Court remained constant. How the organizations made use of their briefs in light of their collective identities and these circumstances thus becomes important in determining if and how they make a difference to the Court's decisions, and consequently to boundary formation.

In the following sections, I will discuss each of the cases and their briefs within their cultural context to show how notions of collective identity can be observed. Through this, we can see the framing activities that groups used to link their beliefs to those of the justices in attempts to influence the Court towards favorable decisions.

Bowers v. Hardwick (1986)

The post-World War Two era was significant in the development of a positive collective identity for lesbians and gays in the US (Engel 2001). Beginning with the homophile organizations of the 1950s and early 1960s, through the liberationist organizations of the late 1960s and 1970s, lesbian and gay organizations were gaining success in changing popular notions of homosexuality. Around the country, local governments began to include lesbians and gays in ordinances protecting groups from discrimination. The federal government ended official discrimination against gays and lesbians in federal employment. The American Psychiatric Association removed homosexuality from its recognized list of mental illnesses. Gay and lesbian leaders were even invited to meet with officials in the White House. This era seemed to represent to lesbians and gays a period of slow but steady improvement, but throughout the 1960s and 1970s, as gay organizations pushed for rights, countermovement organizations grew against them. Public battles, such as Anita Bryant's antigay "crusades" in the late 1970s, drew national attention to this cultural conflict and galvanized fundamentalist religious organizations. Groups like the Moral Majority grew, in part, because of a growing social awareness of a "homosexual agenda," which could be used as a means for mobilizing conservative Christians across the country. This cultural conflict would soon grow into an all-out war.

In the early 1980s, a strange new "gay cancer" began to spread within the gay community, and as it became the epidemic known as AIDS, the cultural battle lines between social acceptance and deviance changed. Schroedel (1999) noted that studies of the time period suggested that gay men were "among the least liked groups in America" (1999: 90). This unpopularity naturally extended into the political arena as well. With conservative president Ronald Reagan in the White House and little support in Congress, homosexual rights organizations were having little success in furthering a legislative agenda, and realized they needed to find a voice elsewhere. The case of *Bowers v. Hardwick* became the opportunity for millions of lesbians and gays to be recognized, if not as equals, then at least not as criminals. In this case, police arrested Michael Hardwick for violating Georgia's sodomy statutes after inadvertently discovering him having sex with another man in his own bedroom. Although criminal charges against him were not pursued, Hardwick brought suit against the state of Georgia for relief against the enforcement of this statute and the case eventually made its way to the US Supreme Court.

This case was of tremendous importance to lesbian and gay civil rights groups; if it was not won, who knew how long it would be before another chance to end criminalization would come? It was equally important to countermovement groups dedicated to preventing the advancement of homosexual rights. So, as the case came before the Supreme Court, groups on both sides appealed to the Court through *amicus curiae* briefs in the hopes of a favorable decision. Thirteen briefs were filed, representing forty different individuals, organizations, or states. Of these thirteen briefs, four were filed in support of Georgia's right to criminalize sodomy and nine briefs were filed in support of gay and lesbian rights. It is interesting to note that many of the groups filing briefs in support of lesbian and gay rights were not gay and lesbian organizations. Examples include the National Association of Women, the Association of the Bar of the City of New York, and the American Jewish Congress; the American Psychological Association and the American Public Health Association jointly filed a brief, and a brief was filed representing a number of liberal or moderate Protestant Christian organizations.

Throughout the briefs filed by groups favorable to gay and lesbian civil rights, the right to privacy was framed as the dominant theme, and not the "acceptability" of gays and lesbians. All of the nine briefs filed on this side of the issue were centered on the belief that all Americans should expect a constitutional right to privacy, and little mention of the growing acceptability of lesbians and gays was made. In fact, two of the briefs actually mentioned that their organizations were not necessarily in favor of granting acceptance for gays and lesbians, but felt strongly enough about privacy issues to warrant their participation in the case.

Countermovement organizations were not so reluctant to address their beliefs regarding the acceptability of gays and lesbians; each of the four briefs used beliefs of immorality as the basis for persuading the Court not to decriminalize sodomy. These briefs noted Biblical injunctions and the long Judeo-Christian history of criminal statutes punishing homosexual behavior. In addition, briefs argued that the idea of privacy as extended by the Court in earlier cases should not be extended to homosexual behaviors because such behaviors have always been specified as criminal throughout British and American legal history.

The opinion of the Court in *Bowers*, written by Justice White, did not specifically refer to any brief, but the main issues that Justice White used in his opinion were the same issues framed in countermovement briefs, suggesting that these countermovement groups were successful in their framing activities. The main point of the decision handed down was simply that no right to privacy existed that would allow for the protection of homosexual sodomy, even in the home. Instead, the decision stated, striking down the criminal statutes would, in effect, *create* a fundamental right to practice homosexual sodomy. Chief Justice Burger, in his concurring opinion, made plain the similarity between his beliefs, as stated in his concurring opinion, to the interpretive frames commonly extended in the four briefs filed against lesbian and gay rights: traditional moral values and historical legal criminalization of sodomy, especially homosexual sodomy. By taking the prerogative to write a separate concurring opinion that allowed him to include his strong beliefs, Burger reinforced the immorality of homosexuality as a matter of law.

Justice Blackmun wrote the dissenting opinion in this case. It should be no surprise that, as author of the *Roe v. Wade* decision based on privacy issues, he focused much of his dissent in this area. He noted, as did most of the briefs in support of the respondent, that this case involved an act that was of an intimate nature, more so because it occurred in the bedroom of the respondent's home. Blackmun often criticized the majority opinion, and referred to the references of history and tradition in countermovement briefs (as well as Chief Justice Berger's concurring opinion) as "blind imitations of the past." In this manner, Blackmun was perhaps suggesting that the importance of changing social opinions of lesbian and gay acceptability should have been considered.

The effects of the *Bowers* decision were immediately felt throughout the lesbian and gay community, affecting its notions of collective identity. As the lack of any official response to the AIDS crisis was leaving many lesbians and gays with the feeling of abandonment by their government (Gould 2001), this decision was seen as reinforcement of this feeling. New organizations were forming to mobilize support around victims of AIDS. Many new groups, such as the Human Rights Campaign and the National Gay and Lesbian Task Force, worked within the same mainstream political system that older liberationist groups once resisted. In addition, radical groups such as Queer Nation and ACT-UP developed by capitalizing on the anger of many gays and lesbians, bringing record numbers out of the closets and into the streets. In so doing, notions of lesbian and gay collective identity were changed, and these changes lasted throughout the 1980s. The presidential election of 1992 again made lesbian and gay rights an issue, and with the election of President Clinton, who claimed to support advances in lesbian and gay civil rights, progress seemed to have been made, though it often seemed a slow, uphill fight.

As groups mobilized around gay and lesbian rights and around those suffering from AIDS, their countermovement opposition continued to grow and strengthen as well. In fact, the advancement of the Christian Right within politics and society helped set the stage for the second case where boundaries were negotiated.

Romer v. Evans *(1996)*

In part because of increased efforts of lesbian and gay groups in response to AIDS and apparent advances in gay and lesbian civil rights, a majority in the state of Colorado voted in the November general election of 1992 to adopt an amendment to the state's constitution which forbade the state, its agencies, and its political subdivisions (that is, local governments) from enacting, adopting, or enforcing any statute or policy that would provide special protections against discrimination for homosexuals and bisexuals. Several individuals, joined by many governmental bodies in Colorado, instituted a lawsuit in state courts against "Amendment 2," as it was called. The suit claimed that Amendment 2 violated several provisions of the US Constitution. The trial court in Denver issued an injunction against the enforcement of the amendment. This forced Governor Romer (ironically, against his personal wishes) to appeal to the Colorado Supreme Court to overturn the lower court's decision, which it did not do. Consequently, as governor, he was forced to petition the US Supreme Court.

Organizations on both sides of the issue filed *amicus* briefs, and did so in larger numbers than had participated in the *Bowers* case; here, twenty-six *amicus* briefs were filed, representing 110 individuals, organizations, or governmental entities. Nine of the twenty-six briefs were filed in support of Amendment 2, and seventeen were filed in opposition to it. Groups as diverse as the NAACP, the National Education Association, the American Bar Association, and the American Federation of State, County, and Municipal Employees joined the American Psychological Association and others who filed briefs in *Bowers* to support lesbians, gays, and bisexuals before the Court in *Romer*. Likewise, many new groups joined the filers opposed to lesbian, gay, and bisexual rights in this case. What makes this case such an interesting contrast to its predecessor, though, was that the position taken by lesbian and gay groups and their allies and the position taken by countermovement groups were effectively switched. Whereas in *Bowers*, countermovement groups had argued that gays and lesbians were too deviant to be considered within the bounds of cultural acceptance, they instead argued in *Romer* that gays and lesbians were not a class of people that lay beyond cultural boundaries so as to require "special protections." On the other side of the issue, groups who argued in *Bowers* that lesbians and gays were socially accepted and should be considered within the boundaries of the mainstream were forced to argue in *Romer* that lesbians, gays, and bisexuals, as a class of people, were victims of cruel and often violent discrimination that warranted protection under antidiscrimination statutes.

Several briefs filed by countermovement groups noted the successes lesbian and gay organizations enjoyed through their recent mobilization efforts. Some countermovement groups even suggested that, because lesbian and gay groups were so wealthy and powerful, they themselves required protections for their religious liberties, such as in the raising of their children and in the free expression of their religious speech. Perhaps because of cultural gains towards acceptance by lesbians and gays, virtually no mention of immorality existed within countermovement briefs. So, in just ten years since *Bowers*, countermovement organizations changed their framing tactics, often taking a seemingly defensive position to cultural changes resulting from gay and lesbian advances in civil rights.

Justice Kennedy wrote the opinion of the Court in *Romer*, which struck down Amendment 2 as unconstitutional. The decision shared many of the same arguments used in the *amicus* briefs filed against the Amendment, again suggesting the success of framing activities. The basis of his opinion was in three parts, the first of which suggested Amendment 2 put lesbians, gays, and bisexuals into a solitary class and withdrew from them equal protection from harm. The second part of Justice Kennedy's opinion noted that, by the wording of the amendment to preclude their involvement in the political process, lesbians, gays, and bisexuals were subject to a special disability that others did not face, such as the need for further constitutional amendments for remedy of grievances. The third reason for striking down Amendment 2 was that no legitimate state interest was served by it other than making homosexuals unequal to everyone else, which he stated Colorado could not do.

In writing the dissenting opinion of the Court, Justice Scalia began by suggesting that the amendment was little more than an attempt to preserve the traditional moral values. He further noted that it was well within a state's right to single out homosexuality, and noted the precedent from *Bowers* as rationale. In addition, he suggested that what the majority deemed "animosity" towards homosexuality was based on their own elitist attitudes that did not represent the true will of the people.

This case seemed to indicate that, as a matter of law, lesbians, gays, and bisexuals were a minority group needing protection from discrimination – in effect, placing them outside the boundaries of cultural acceptance. Regardless, lesbian and gay civil rights organizations framed the case as a victory. Instead of framing themselves as a minority needing protection, groups now claimed that the Court protected them from attack by the Christian Right and conservatives. This perceived progress, as well as progress with a recently elected president claimed as an ally, propelled the lesbian and gay civil rights movement forward. Social movement organizations, in part through technological advances like the internet that allowed for mobilization with less risk of publicity for closeted lesbians, gays, and bisexuals, continued to grow in both numbers of members and amount of resources. The growth of the movement made the third case even more important, and more visible, than its predecessors.

Lawrence v. Texas *(2003)*

In terms of viewing lesbians and gays as equal Americans under the law, the *Romer* decision's application of equal protection helped to detract from perceptions of second-class citizenship for gays and lesbians. There remained in certain jurisdictions, however, the criminal sanctions against sodomy upheld in *Bowers*, which could be used against them. Lesbian and gay civil rights organizations were looking for a case that could be used to overturn that decision and take away the threat of these criminal sanctions and the stigma that accompanies arrest and prosecution. In Texas, they found such a case, and with virtually identical circumstances as *Bowers*. Gay and lesbian organizations, as well as their countermovement opponents, suddenly found themselves in another boundary negotiation process before the Court with the case of *Lawrence v. Texas*.

In this case, there was a total of twenty-eight *amicus* briefs filed, only a slight increase over the amount filed in the *Romer* case, though the amount of briefs filed was more balanced between the two sides in this case. Fifteen of the twenty-eight briefs were filed in support of Petitioner Lawrence, asking the Court to end the criminalization of sodomy, and thirteen were filed supporting the state of Texas, asking the Court not to overturn the statute. More interesting, however, was the tremendous increase in the numbers of interested parties sponsoring these briefs. Instead of the 110 organizations, individuals, and government entities filing in *Romer*, there were now 236 in *Lawrence*.

As was the case in *Romer*, countermovement opposition rarely contained specific examples of framing around the issue of morality. Briefs mentioned morality only generally, and in relation to specific issues, such as in their belief in states' rights to promote moral values, rather than as a universal condemnation of homosexuality, as was prevalent in *Bowers*. On the other side, however, briefs filed by some gay and lesbian groups and their allies in *Lawrence* actively embraced a moral position: discrimination against lesbians and gays is morally wrong. Their argument was that discrimination against homosexuals was "irrational animus," seeming to continue the frame that arose in the *Romer* case.

Justice Kennedy again wrote the opinion of the Court, based on the application of sodomy laws against gays and lesbians as a violation of their liberties under the Due Process Clause under the 14th Amendment. In so doing, the Court overturned its precedent in *Bowers*. In his opinion, Kennedy criticized *Bowers*'s reliance upon proscriptions against homosexual sodomy as having "ancient roots." He cited information contained in *amicus* briefs to show that such proscriptions were, in fact, relatively recent. He later cited briefs in reference to the issue of whether prosecuted cases of homosexual sodomy involved acts occurring in the privacy of the home. Next, he cited *amicus* briefs that provided historical data pertaining to equal enforcement of sodomy laws to heterosexuals as well as homosexuals. Finally, to show that reliance on *Bowers* has eroded within the US and abroad, Justice Kennedy cited briefs that noted that many other nations have taken actions to protect the rights of homosexuals.

Justice Scalia wrote the dissenting opinion in the *Lawrence* (2003) case. In it, he took issue with many of the points raised by Justice Kennedy in the majority opinion. First, he referred to the historical assumptions regarding homosexuality that he claimed justified the *Bowers* decision. He next raised the point that states have an interest in promoting public morality, a point common in briefs filed by countermovement groups. More interesting, however, was his suggestion that the Court had merely taken a side in the "culture war," influenced by the "so-called homosexual agenda" (*Lawrence v. Texas*, 18). Scalia warned that, although the majority decision in *Lawrence* does not address the issue of same-sex marriage, it certainly opens the door to such boundary negotiation processes in the future, and groups on both sides of the civil rights issue began gearing up for the next confrontation. Although statutes remained on the books that allowed for detrimental treatment of gays and lesbians in employment, military affairs, and family issues, it was perhaps because of repeated mention of the issue in *Lawrence* that same-sex marriage became the next apparent battleground.

Framing the *Lawrence* decision as another victory over conservatives and particularly the Christian Right, lesbian and gay groups continued mobilizing with renewed vigor, relying on perceptions of progress to increase membership and resources. Likewise, their countermovement opponents used the *Lawrence* decision as a means for increased mobilization in their fight against infringement on their religious freedom. Just when this boundary negotiation takes place has yet to be decided, but one thing is sure. This process will likely involve increased numbers of organizations, governmental bodies, and individuals as *amicus curiae*, and their briefs will continue to attempt to influence the decision of the Court as representations of their interpretive frameworks and their collective identities.

Summary

For some time, social movement organizations and their countermovement opponents have increasingly realized the importance of using the Supreme Court as a mechanism for social change across the United States. This is a logical choice, for, with the right case, groups can implement national social change by influencing the decisions of only nine justices, rather than 535 legislators and the president. As more and more social movement and countermovement organizations use the Court to negotiate cultural boundaries of acceptance and deviance in this manner, it becomes increasingly important to understand this process.

There are numerous examples in past research that illustrate how social movement organizations frame their message in the hopes of linking their ideological framework to that of other individuals or groups. Previous research has indicated that these framing processes are very informative in determining an organization's collective identity. In this chapter, we investigated one example of how social movement and countermovement organizations' collective identities influence, and are influenced by, the process of negotiating cultural boundaries before the Supreme Court. We have looked at particular examples of framing activity, *amicus curiae* briefs filed before the US Supreme Court. In these briefs, lesbian and gay civil rights organizations, working with and in opposition to other organizations as interested "friends of the Court," sought to influence the decision of the justices towards a favorable outcome. In so doing, they present a snapshot of their collective identity. Furthermore, we can see through this negotiation process how the outcomes of these decisions have determined the cultural boundaries between acceptability and deviance for lesbians and gays in the United States, further affecting their collective identities.

Because of the timing of the *Bowers* decision, during the height of the AIDS crisis, the decision against lesbians and gays had a strenuous yet uniting effect on their collective identity. Lesbian and gay organizations were able to grow because of the anger and bitterness toward the government woven into the community's collective identity. They capitalized because mobilization efforts struck this common chord among lesbians and gays, and because groups raised the awareness of AIDS and the issue of equality for all Americans among the public. Out of a period marked by a deep dislike of lesbians and particularly of gays, these organizations grew strong enough to change the collective identity of their countermovement opposition, as we saw in *Romer*. No longer was the issue of immorality central to these organizations' collective identity; instead, we saw countermovement groups framing their message around the defensive posture of "protecting their religious liberties." The favorable decision in *Romer* further energized lesbian and gay organizations. So successful were these groups in mobilizing members and resources that, in less than a decade, lesbian and gay rights, for the first time, became a serious issue during a presidential election. By the time of *Lawrence*, some ten years later, countermovement organizations had strengthened around the ideology of protecting religious liberty. These groups had adopted as part of their collective identity the need to thwart what they saw as the "homosexual agenda." The briefs filed in *Lawrence* were filled with such references, making this negotiation of cultural boundaries, if not a holy war, then definitely a cultural war.

As social movement organizations on both sides of the issue prepare for the next major battle in this war, likely to revolve around same-sex marriage, it appears that all eyes will focus on the Court in anticipation of further decisions in the boundary negotiation process. In addition to mobilizing membership and resources, these groups keep an eye on the make-up of the Court. Because of the advancing years of some justices, the replacement and confirmation process of justices in the Senate will become increasingly important, not merely to the boundary negotiation process, but, as we have seen, to the collective identity of millions of lesbian and gay Americans.

Furthermore, as the battle between gay and lesbian organizations and their countermovement opponents plays out, it will be interesting to see other negotiation processes as they develop before the Court. As important as the Court was in determining collective identity for lesbian and gays in the twentieth century and into the twenty-first, it is likely the Court will begin hearing more important cases involving the transgendered. In so doing, not only will it be settling boundary negotiations and shaping the collective identities of these groups, it may well be determining our cultural definitions of gender, the very basis of what it means to be male and female.

Cases cited

Bowers v. Hardwick 478 U.S. 186 (1986).
Lawrence et al. v. Texas 539 U.S. 558 (2003).
Romer v. Evans 517 U.S. 620 (1996).

References

Engel, Stephen M. 2001. *The Unfinished Revolution.* New York: Cambridge University Press.
Gould, Deborah. 2001. "Rock the Boat, Don't Rock the Boat, Baby: Ambivalence and the Emergence of Militant AIDS Activism." In Jeff Goodwin, James M. Jasper, and Francesca Polletta (eds), *Passionate Politics: Emotions and Social Movements.* Chicago, IL: University of Chicago Press.
Hunt, Scott A., Robert D. Benford, and David A. Snow. 1994. "Identity Fields: Framing Process and the Social Construction of Movement Identities." In Enrique Larana, Hank Johnston, and Joseph R. Gusfield (eds), *New Social Movements: From Ideology to Identity.* Philadelphia, PA: Temple University Press.
Schroedel, Jean R. 1999. "Elite Attitudes towards Homosexuals." In Ellen D. B. Riggle and Barry L. Tadlock (eds), *Gays and Lesbians in the Democratic Process.* New York: Columbia University Press.
Taylor, Verta and Nancy Whittier. 1992. "Collective Identity in Social Movement Communities: Lesbian Feminist Mobilization." In Aldon Morris and Carol McClurg (eds), *Frontiers in Social Movement Theory.* New Haven, CT: Yale University Press.

66

The politics of AIDS

Sexual pleasure and danger

Jennifer Gunsaullus

INDEPENDENT SCHOLAR, SAN DIEGO, DRJENNSDEN.COM

AIDS began creeping into our national psyche almost twenty-five years ago, and by the end of 2003 it was estimated that 1,039,000 to 1,185,000 individuals in the United States were living with HIV/AIDS (CDC 2005). The government of the United States was slow to respond to the growing epidemic in the early 1980s, largely due to the association of the disease with the socially stigmatized population of gay men. In fact, the disease was initially named GRID, Gay Related Immune Disorder. None the less, through monumental efforts, gay rights activists were able to raise awareness and funds to target prevention efforts, care for the infected, and change the public perception of the disease (Cohen 1999). Recently, though, there has been greater recognition that the demographic profile of HIV/AIDS has changed. The "face of AIDS" is no longer primarily middle-class, white gay men, but lower-income African-Americans and Latinos. And while women in the United States only account for 22 percent of AIDS cases, heterosexual African-American women represent the majority of these cases (CDC 2005). This chapter explores the role of AIDS politics in the growing epidemic and the rise of AIDS activism, including attempts to change the ideology of sexual behavior and the role that community-based organizations have played in addressing the disease in their communities. Although AIDS is an entirely preventable disease, the complexity of the interaction between social, psychological, and biological factors has led to its status as a global crisis.

AIDS politics, AIDS activism

It is commonly stated in HIV prevention efforts that "AIDS does not discriminate." On the face of it this is accurate, because the disease itself does not "care" who it infects. However, the political nature of AIDS means that it infects and affects parts of the population differently. Referring to the "politics" of AIDS means considering how social factors such as power and inequality come into play with the spread of the disease and the reaction it provokes. Mainstream initial responses (or lack of responses) to the disease revealed who was considered expendable in society, namely gay men, injection drug users, and prostitutes (Cohen 1999). From its inception in the early 1980s, AIDS activism has had a distinctive character when compared to other social movements and the responses to other diseases. One of the fundamental reasons for this is the clearly social character of HIV/AIDS that disproportionately affects specific subcultures and communities, groups that are already marginalized or considered to have deviant identities. Steven Epstein (1996) explains: "If AIDS were not deadly, if it were not associated with taboo topics such as sex and drug use, and if the groups affected were not already stigmatized on other counts, such linkages between identity and illness might be of little consequence" (1996: 11). And just as AIDS has its distinct politics, so do the groups largely affected by the disease, hence "gay politics" or "black politics." While there is great variety within these classifications, the groups' dominant beliefs and leaders determine the direction of activism in response to this social crisis. Although activism is often understood as direct and confrontational protests in support of a cause, this chapter also includes many less overt forms of activism. Activism in the AIDS movement has emerged in many shapes, from small, everyday activities such as delivering food to AIDS patients, to the creation and display of the AIDS quilt, to large-scale protests with international media coverage.

AIDS activism for white gay men

In the United States the AIDS crisis was initially identified with white gay men, and this population was the first actively to protest against the public portrayal of the disease and to demand funding and attention. Through the political and social organizing of the gay rights movement prior to AIDS, many white, middle-class men already possessed the community and institutional contacts and organizational skills to address this new problem affecting their community and putting their identity in jeopardy (Epstein 1996). Early AIDS activists, primarily those in gay and lesbian communities, organized quickly in response to the threat of the disease due to the death of loved ones, the stigma of the disease, and the lack of governmental response. PWAs (Persons With AIDS) and activists in the movement perceived the disease itself and the government's inaction to stem the infection as political threats to their rights as citizens. The majority of early activists were infected themselves, or closely affected by the disease through caring for sick loved ones and the death of family members and friends (Tester 2004).

While activism assumed many forms, the most outspoken activists in the early AIDS movement were members of the organization ACT UP. It is difficult to speak of AIDS activism without conjuring up images of the controversial grassroots organization ACT UP, whose political activism garnered much media attention. ACT UP initially formed in 1987 in New York City in the primarily white gay and lesbian community to generate an organized front to attack the government's indifference to AIDS policy and politics. Using compelling slogans such as "Silence = Death," they identified as a "diverse, nonpartisan group, united in anger and commitment to direct action to end the AIDS crisis." Their first public demonstration in March 1987 on Wall Street in New York was well covered by the media. It served as a model for their precisely coordinated demonstrations that conveyed a political message in a practical way (Rimmerman 1998).

This organization's nonviolent civil disobedience tactics were modeled after those of the African-American community in the civil rights movement. Such campaigns use unconventional means to attract public and media attention through boycotts, demonstrations, and marches. In their dedication to radical democracy, ACT UP did not develop any formal structure or spokespeople/leaders. ACT UP's largest impact has been with the AIDS drug industry and demanding changes to hasten the process in the way the US Food and Drug Administration (FDA) approves AIDS drugs. Other areas of activism have included pressing for health insurance coverage for experimental drug therapies, implementing a needle-exchange program at the federal level, federally-funded condom distribution, and pressure on pharmaceutical companies to reduce the prices for AIDs-treatment drugs. In light of the shifting demographics of the disease, ACT UP has attempted actively to recruit women and African-Americans and Latinos to their ranks (Rimmerman 1998). While some activists of color within ACT UP were frustrated by the narrow focus on drug approval processes or the racist actions of other members (Cohen 1999), ACT UP's constituency has evolved with the changing demographics of the disease to include significantly greater numbers of low-income individuals and people of color, as well as expanding into the global politics of AIDS (Kim 2001).

AIDS activism in African-American communities

White gay men were not the only ones affected by the disease, but they were the most vocal and organized. Early in the spread of the disease, statistics revealed that African-Americans were disproportionately infected with HIV/AIDS, although this was receiving little media or research consideration. While African-American communities were experiencing rising infection rates, political activism was not a response to it. Even within the major institutions and organizations of African-American communities, such as the Church and civil rights organizations, there was little acknowledgment of the impact of the disease (Cohen 1999). In contrast to white gay men and lesbians, the African-American communities' identity and affirmation of self was not being challenged through the political reaction to AIDS. Many other reasons also account for the delayed response to the disease, including: belief that is was a "white" disease; lack of public discussion about sexual behavior; homophobia and the subsequent denial of the possibility of AIDS in their communities; other more far-reaching community concerns (for example, police brutality, civil rights, poverty); and conspiracy theories that AIDS was created by the United States government (Cohen 1999). Also, unlike the early activists in the AIDS movement who as white men had greater cultural capital (for example, education, money), Cohen (1999) argues that, due to racial marginalization, "the majority of African-Americans still lack the political, economic, and social resources necessary to participate actively in the decision-making that significantly influences and structures their lives" (1999: 9).

However, parts of the African-American community did respond immediately in the AIDS movement, specifically gay men. Black gay men faced challenges that were both similar and different to those of the mainstream AIDS activists and those most affected early by the disease. Informal responses to the crisis involved caring for loved ones dying from AIDS, which largely relied on the social networks of family and friends already in place. On the more formal level, black gay men responded by challenging the lack of attention towards the problem from dominant organizations as well as from leaders within the African-American community. Their formal leadership in the early response to AIDS primarily took shape in conference planning, the provision of AIDS services to those who would otherwise not receive assistance, and community education to raise acknowledgement of and attention to AIDS. Before the support of national organizations such as the NAACP or the Urban League, or the formation of an African-American AIDS infrastructure, gay and lesbian activists in communities of color initiated two of the earliest national conferences on AIDS for people of color. None the less, "black politics" precluded the integration of "gay politics," as race was a more strategic political identity (Cohen 1999). Currently, however, many AIDS organizations exist both nationally and as community-based organizations to tackle all aspects of HIV/AIDS in African-American communities.

The politics of gender also slowly surfaced in the understanding of AIDS politics, as women were more likely to be infected and to require unique prevention education tactics and support as PWAs. The growing impact on African-American women has not received substantial political attention as an important social issue from the government. For example, in the vice-presidential debate in the fall of 2004, when queried about the impact of HIV/AIDS on African-American women, neither election candidate was aware of the problem.

For African-American women, appearance in AIDS politics initially took the form of "innocent victims" – heterosexual women who unwittingly contracted AIDS from their "bisexual" boyfriends or husbands (Cohen 1999). Media and popular constructions of morality and guilt aside, gender and race, as well as social class and other demographic characteristics, intersect and impact upon women's risk for HIV in ways not easily understood or addressed by mainstream AIDS activists and organizations. Multiple social factors put females in the United States at heightened risk for contracting HIV and other STIs (Sexually Transmitted Infections). Cindy Patton (1998), a leading theorist on women and AIDS, argues: "The fact is, class, ethnicity, and gender structuration conspire to place some women at extraordinary risk of having unprotected sex … " (1998: xii). The factors that place particular women at increased risk also contribute to keeping these women from acting on their own behalf to enact a political response (Patton 1998). Non-white, low-income women have had little opportunity in the past two decades to mobilize in the AIDS movement, as compared to gay men, because of gender, race, and socioeconomic limitations, as well as a lack of recognition of the problem within their communities (Cohen 1999). Because of the lack of activism and acceptance of the problem, the women who are most at risk for contracting HIV and STIs often do not perceive themselves as such.

Sex-positive ideology

An ideology is a framework through which individuals interpret what is "normal" or "right" and "wrong," and through the use of these norms and values it confers legitimacy in society. It is a concept that "refers to the systems of belief that frame and guide our general understanding of, and interaction in, the world" (Cohen 1999: 41). The public response to AIDS is highly linked to ideological beliefs about sex, sexuality, and morality (Epstein 1996). Sexual behavior has long been regulated through religious teachings and political groups. The advent of AIDS strengthened the resolve of many religious and political leaders to regulate and control the behavior of those practicing outside the normative standards for sexual behavior (that is, only within the realm of adult heterosexual, monogamous marriage). Sex and education related to sexual topics in the United States has often been equated with danger, disease, and immoral deeds (Irvine 2002), and these negative judgments are often used to perceive and define the behaviors of gay men, sexually active women, or racial ethnic minorities.

In response to this, one approach to HIV/AIDS prevention and education is the attempt to reclaim positive sexuality for these groups and offer a sex-positive ideology. AIDS researcher Steven Epstein asserts that "AIDS activists have sought to challenge the ideological linkages between sex and death and put forward 'sex-positive' programs of AIDS prevention that assert the right to sexual pleasure and sexual freedom" (1996: 21). Programs that espouse sexually explicit language or pictures, or ones that overtly approach sexual activity as positive and plea-surable, stand in stark contrast to government policies to promote abstinence, and sex only for married heterosexual couples (Palmer 2004). However, stigmatized sexual behavior can carry shame and guilt for those involved, thereby compromising self-esteem and impelling sexual behavior into hiding. This can consequently mean that risks associated with sexual behavior are not consciously considered or are not perceived as significant threats. The importance of a sex-positive approach was immediately recognized by gay activists who "claimed free and public sexual expression as integral to their sexual and social identity" (Palmer 2004: 272) and argued that "safe sex" was as erotically pleasurable as unprotected acts.

Some prevention programs targeting heterosexual women of color have also adopted a sex-positive perspective that attempts to validate the sexual behaviors of women and women's control over their sexual health. However, there has not been the same type of pro-sex public advertisements associated with female sexual behavior as for gay men. For women, these messages are more likely to appear in private contexts, such as all-female workshops that "eroticize" safer sex. These types of programs are more likely to be created in organizations that target African-American women than those targeting other women of color. Such programs offer safer sex options that also validate and cater to women's sexual desires and pleasure through presenting sex toys for masturbation or as a safer alternative to intercourse, a variety of condoms and lubricant options, and innovative ideas for sensual erotic activities. For example, in one community organization with a women's prevention program targeting African-American women deemed at-risk for HIV, the prevention educator encouraged masturbation and self-exploration for women. She discussed using all five senses to delve into what turns women on, as alternatives to penile–vaginal penetration. The highlight and climax of the program was the presentation of a large assortment of sex toys and games, including cards, handcuffs, lingerie, dildos, vibrators, a plastic light-up penis gun, butt plugs, videos, and books. The overall goal was to create a culture of sexual empowerment for women that combines safety issues and choice with pleasure.[1]

Role of community-based organizations

One path for activism to emerge, and for the variety in AIDS politics to be addressed, is through the formation of community-based organizations (CBOs). Much less controversial overall than ACT UP, and rarely appearing in the mainstream media, these organizations focus on filling the prevention education and AIDS service needs of their immediate communities in culturally sensitive ways. A profusion of HIV- and AIDS-related organizations were created to address the AIDS crisis, particularly in urban areas. Unlike organizations fighting any other disease, the number of national and local-based organizations created to address HIV and AIDS is monumental (for example, in New York City between 1981 and 1998, 166 organizations were formed to address HIV/AIDS). Chambre (1999) argues that the growth of so many organizations is likely to be due to the changing nature of the HIV/AIDS virus as well as to racial, ethnic, and community politics. Since new information was constantly surfacing about how to treat and prevent the disease and who was being affected, various communities believed they were best situated to address the evolving problem. As well, leading health organizations, such as the World Health Organization and the Centers for Disease Control and Prevention, emphasize the need for communities to define and implement prevention education programming representative of their particular community's needs. By the mid-to-late 1980s, the United States government and public health departments realized that community involvement would be necessary in enacting prevention programming and effective social service delivery for infected individuals (Chambre 1999).

The label "community-based organization" (CBO; or non-governmental organization, NGO, in other countries) refers to a nonprofit, self-directed organization whose "goal is to meet the community's self-defined needs. The CBO is located within the community, its leadership comes from the community, and it is staffed by members of the community being observed" (Van Vugt 1994: 13). Community-based organizations have a history of providing valuable public health services and, due to the AIDS crisis, have recently grown tremendously. Since these organizations are led by members of the community they serve, they are in a unique position to reach the needs of at-risk populations due to their proximity, cultural sensitivity, and intimate knowledge of the values and health beliefs of their cultures. Ideally, the environment of mutual respect (that is, nonjudgmental and supportive) and cultural sensitivity cultivated in CBOs encourages participants to protect themselves from disease (Van Vugt 1994). The HIV prevention efforts by CBOs in the United States are believed to have had a significant impact on decreasing the spread of HIV infections. Some founders of early racial ethnic organizations believed that gay organizations were acquiring a disproportionate percentage of the funding through their role in defining AIDS politics and policy. The assumed critical role of culture in prevention led to racially specified CBOs. And for some of these CBOs, one of the impetuses for formation or to broaden services to include HIV/AIDS was the available public funds and contracts for minority areas (Chambre 1999).

In the AIDS crisis, CBOs have served their communities in numerous ways. In the early 1980s many formed as ASOs (AIDS Service Organizations) to provide support and care for AIDS patients and their families. As more formed and the technologies, demographics, and funding around the disease changed, many CBOs became multi-service organizations. Although not an exhaustive list, the multi-service CBOs of today may provide: HIV prevention education workshops; peer education and intervention; HIV support groups; HIV treatment education; street outreach; needle exchange programs; HIV testing sites; harm reduction initiatives; media campaigns; discrimination assistance; community organizing; policy analysis; links to medical care and appropriate housing; translation services; casework and counseling; and adolescent outreach. The work of community-based organizations has been crucial in increasing the recognition of AIDS and providing needed services in non-white communities (Cohen 1999).

In spite of all the organizations addressing HIV/AIDS, Chambre (1999) points to a scarcity in services targeting women and families. However, in the latter stages of the AIDS crisis, community-based organizations have created more programs specifically targeting women of color, with the goal of reducing the transmission of HIV and other STIs to the at-risk women within their communities. Educators within these CBOs seek out women in their communities to receive their prevention education and services, as many women most at-risk or infected are least likely to seek out such services. CBOs are based on the principle that educators and service providers will have a greater impact in their communities if they not only look like their clients, but have lived similar lives, are trusted, and speak the same cultural "language" (Van Vugt 1994).

Global AIDS politics

Although this chapter has outlined the growth of AIDS activism, alternative sexual ideology, and CBOs in response to the politics of AIDS within the United States, AIDS is clearly a much greater concern at the global level. Of all AIDS cases worldwide, 85 percent of individuals are located in the poorer countries of the world (Boone and Batsell 2001). Sub-Saharan Africa has been particularly hard-hit, with a lack of leadership, cultural sexual norms, and poverty all contributing to the spread of AIDS. Non-governmental organizations, located within areas struggling with the disease, are a primary source for education and services, and ideally promote reform at the political and policy level, and partner with the state to enact effective programming. However, since many NGOs in parts of Africa have parent organizations from Western countries, and because many political leaders have avoided tackling the AIDS issue, the relationship between government and NGO has been mediated with distrust, and has been less than complementary (Boone and Batsell 2001). None the less, as in the United States, those hardest hit by the disease are playing a large role in making decisions and providing aid. Activism is a compelling and valuable method to enact social change and compassion for this devastating disease both domestically and globally.

Note

1 This data is based on information gathered through my doctoral dissertation fieldwork.

References

Boone, Catherine, and Jake Batsell. 2001. "Politics and AIDS in Africa: Research Agendas in Political Science and International Relations." *Africa Today* 48(2): 3–33.

CDC (Centers for Disease Control and Prevention). 2005. "Basic Statistics." Available online at http://www.cdc.gov/hiv/topics/surveillance/basic.htm (accessed March 24 2006).

Chambre, Susan. 1999. "Redundancy, Third-Party Government, and Consumer Choice: HIV/AIDS Organizations in New York City." *Policy Studies Journal* 27 (4): 840–54.

Cohen, Cathy. 1999. *The Boundaries or Blackness: AIDS and the Breakdown of Black Politics*. Chicago, IL: University of Chicago Press.

Epstein, Steven. 1996. *Impure Science: AIDS, Activism, and the Politics of Knowledge*. Berkeley: University of California Press.

Irvine, Janice M. 2002. *Talk About Sex: The Battles Over Sex Education in the United States*. Berkeley: University of California Press.

Kim, Richard. 2001. "ACT UP Goes Global." *The Nation* 273: 17–18.

Palmer, Janet B. 2004. 'Let's Talk About Sex, Baby': Community-Based HIV Prevention Work and the Problem of Sex." *Archives of Sexual Behavior* 33 (3): 271–5.

Patton, Cindy. 1998. "Preface." In Nancy L. Roth and Katie Hogan (eds), *Gendered Epidemic: Representations of Women in the Age of AIDS*. New York: Routledge.

Rimmerman, Craig A. 1998. "ACT UP." In Raymond A. Smith (ed.), *The Encyclopedia of AIDS: A Social, Political, Cultural, and Scientific Record of the HIV Epidemic*. Carried by permission of Fitzroy Dearborn Publishers. Available online at http://www.thebody.com/encyclo/actup.html (accessed March 24 2006).

Tester, Griff M. 2004. "Resources, Identity, and the Role of Threat: The Case of AIDS Mobilization, 1981-1986." *Research in Political Sociology* 13: 47–75.

Van Vugt, Johannes P. 1994. "The Effectiveness of Community Based Organizations in the Medical Social Sciences: A Case Study of a Gay Community's Response to the AIDS Crisis." In Johannes Van Vugt (ed.), *AIDS Prevention and Services: Community Based Research*. Westport, CN: Bergin & Garvey.

67

The pro-family movement

Tina Fetner

MCMASTER UNIVERSITY, HAMILTON, ONTARIO, CANADA

We often think about our sexuality as very private and personal. However true this might be, sexuality is also social in a number of ways. One of the clearest examples of the social aspect of sexuality is the recent "culture war" in the United States, which is largely a struggle over what the social rules governing sexuality should be. Should comprehensive sex education be provided to students through public education? Should same-sex couples be allowed to marry under the law? Should pregnant women have the right to decide whether they get an abortion? What about girls who are under 18 years old? These issues about sexuality certainly have a profound impact on people's personal lives. The policy battles over these issues, however, are taking place in the public sphere, fought by activists and politicians.

Much of this activism is in response to the many changes in the social norms governing sexuality in the United States over the last thirty years or so. The fight for women's equality, the "sexual revolution," and the growth of lesbian and gay communities are a few of these important changes, but they are not the only ones. For example, cultural changes marked by an expansion of the consumer sphere means that advertising for consumer products reaches every nook and cranny of our daily lives. The use of sexually suggestive images in advertising has provoked many to declare that we live in a "sex saturated" environment.

In response to these and other changes, a social movement has emerged to lobby for the return of stricter norms governing sexuality. This social movement has been known by a number of names, such as the Moral Majority, the Religious Right, the New Christian Right, and the Pro-Family Movement. Though the pro-family movement gained public notoriety in the 1990s, it actually began in the 1970s and has been active ever since. This social movement has been particularly successful at integrating its issues into the agenda of the Republican party, and so it has become a very powerful social movement in the United States today. This chapter will trace the history of this social movement and discuss the implications for a number of social policies governing sexuality.

What is the pro-family movement?

The pro-family movement is a group of social movement organizations that share both a wide-ranging conservative political agenda and a (primarily evangelical) Christian identity. For the pro-family movement, these two are closely tied together, in that their religious perspective informs their political goals, such as legalizing prayer in school and criminalizing abortion. Though the movement claims to be concerned with building strong families, their policy goals reach far beyond the institution of the family. For example, pro-family activists advocate ending medical research that uses stem cells, stopping legalized gambling, and eliminating some topics from being discussed in schools.

While the pro-family movement is a self-identified Christian movement, it is important to remember that not all Christians, nor all evangelical Christians, are pro-family activists. Many evangelical Christians have diverse opinions on each of the issues supported by the pro-family movement, and even people who join the movement might feel strongly about one of the movement's issues, but disagree with the movement's stance on other issues. In any social movement, there is much more diversity among members than we might see at first glance. Pro-family leaders add to the confusion by frequently making statements that imply that all Christians agree with their political goals. By making claims about "the Christian perspective" on one policy or another, pro-family activists try to make it sound like millions of Christian Americans agree with them, even though this is often not the case.

History of the pro-family movement

How did the pro-family movement come to be? Why is it so much stronger in the United States than in other, similar countries? The answer lies in the unique history of evangelical Christianity in the United States, out of which this movement was born. Ironically, the roots of what makes this social movement so powerful lie in evangelical Christians' historical belief that politics had no place in the life of good Christians. I will explain.

Through much of the middle of the twentieth century, Christian evangelicals were dedicated to withdrawal, not only from politics, but also from what they perceived to be immoral secular influences. From the 1930s through the 1960s, evangelical Christians were dedicated to building alternative social networks, religious and educational institutions as a shield from the cultural influences of the outside world. Many Christian evangelicals thought that popular music was a particularly evil influence on children, as was the sexual content of magazines, films, and television.

Public schools presented material which contradicted biblical literalism, evangelical Christians' faith that the bible is the true word of God rather than a metaphorical representation of God's message. Because of this particularly evangelical Christian understanding of the bible, parts of the curriculum were contentious, even before the days of sex education. For example, the teaching of evolution in science classes contradicts a literal reading of the bible, which says that God built the world in six days. In response, evangelical Christians retreated from the secular world, built private, independent schools, libraries, and other institutions that supported their own values and ideology.

They developed networks among churches, as well as bible institutes, summer camps and other religious retreats, television and radio networks, videos and a host of other Christian children's books, bible study pamphlets, and so on. These Christian institutions and media turned out to be very popular, and soon evangelical Christian organizations had amassed incredible financial resources and membership numbers, and had created wide informational networks and an ideological consistency among their members that would turn out to serve political ends very well. Of course, none of this was intentional during the era of retreat from secular politics, but all of that changed in the 1970s, when one group of evangelical Christians decided to stop retreating and start changing the secular world through political activism. These evangelical Christian church networks, schools, radio stations, television shows, and publishing houses, and the distinctly Christian values and identity they created, became the backbone of the pro-family movement.

The development of the pro-family movement

Two important grassroots movements preceded the pro-family movement and influenced it greatly. The first was the fight against the Equal Rights Amendment of the early 1970s, led by Phyllis Schlafly, which was responsible for defeating the legislation that would have added this language to the US constitution: "Equality of rights under the law shall not be denied or abridged by the United States or by any state on account of sex." Schlafly's multi-state crusade was among the first examples of grassroots activism for conservative social causes, and her organization, the Eagle Forum, is still one of the leading pro-family groups in the United States. The second important movement is Anita Bryant's fight against gay rights in the late 1970s. American sweetheart and former beauty queen Anita Bryant led a series of grassroots efforts across the country to repeal local legislation protecting gay men and lesbians from discrimination. In her 1977 auto-biography, *The Anita Bryant Story*, Bryant says, "homosexuals cannot reproduce – so they must recruit. And to freshen their ranks, they must recruit the youth of America."

Both of these movements were successful in their legislative goals, and they set an example to some conservative Christian leaders that politics and evangelism can go together. Jerry Falwell was reluctant at first to enter politics, because he worried that his followers would reject his active participation in the secular world. But Bryant's work demonstrated that conservative Christian evangelicals supported secular activism, and he founded the Moral Majority in 1979, with a plan to integrate an evangelical Christian agenda into mainstream party politics. Falwell's success in building a national movement led to the emergence of other organizations that built coalitions with Republican party insiders to create what the media called the New Christian Right. This brand of Christian activism was quite successful in integrating conservative social policy concerns into the platform of the Republican party at both national and state levels over the course of the 1980s. The Moral Majority's voter registration drives signed up both unsa-tisfied Christian Democrats and nonvoters to the Republican party.

In the 1990s, the relationship between conservative Christian activists and the Republican party became even stronger, despite the objections of more moderate Republicans. Some pundits in the 1990s predicted that the Republican party's turn toward a socially conservative agenda would create a crisis in the party, which has a long history of opposition to the gov-ernment intrusion into personal matters. This, however, did not come to be, as the pro-family movement's influence on the Republican party continued to grow throughout the 1990s and into the current century, culminating in the election of President George W. Bush, a born-again Christian who supports the platform of the pro-family movement.

What began in the 1970s as a group of conservative Christian political outsiders writing let-ters and carrying picket signs has turned into a powerful political force with great influence in the legislative and executive branches of the federal government, as well as many state and local governments across the nation. The various organizations in the movement took up multiple issues and packaged them into one "pro-family" agenda. Critics complain that this pleasant-sounding tag hides an agenda to undermine the separation of church and state in the United States. In fact, many pro-family leaders have been quoted stating explicitly their desire to create a system of "Christian governance" for America. Today, they continue to exert great influence on many laws and policies governing sexuality.

Pro-family activism and sexuality

Many items on the pro-family agenda have to do with restricting sexuality and reversing some of the changes in sexual norms that have occurred over the past several decades. Pro-family activists fight for policies that limit the sexual freedoms of individuals and censor sexual information, especially from young people. Below, I outline a number of the pro-family movement's priorities regarding sexuality.

Sexuality in television, music and film

Pro-family activists are concerned with the amount of sexually suggestive material in the media these days. They take a variety of paths to try to limit the sexuality published through television, music, and film. First, they advocate boycotts of particular shows and songs that they find offensive. They publish guides for parents to limit sexually suggestive materials their kids view and listen to. They also pressure businesses to refuse to sell music or DVDs that are offensive, and they encourage their supporters to patronize the stores that adopt such policies.

In addition to the sexually suggestive material available for general consumption through television, radio, and the film industry, the pro-family movement is also concerned with sexually explicit material, or pornography. Some pro-family activism has shut down local adult film stores, created local zoning laws that limit where these stores can be opened. These days, however, sexually explicit material is no longer relegated to the back rooms of video stores and the dark, seedy parts of town; it is easily accessed in people's homes over the internet. The pro-family movement is working to censor internet pornography through federal legislation. These anti-pornography measures have broad public support that goes well beyond the pro-family movement itself.

Sex education in public schools

One of the biggest battles the pro-family movement continues to fight is for limits on information on sexuality in public schools. In the beginning of this fight, the pro-family movement made direct arguments for censorship of this information. As time went on, pro-family activists became more politically savvy, arguing *for* what they call "abstinence-only" sex education, rather than *against* sex education in general. However, abstinence-only sex education is more about keeping scientifically accurate information from students than providing them with sex education. For example, abstinence-only educators can only talk about pre-marital sex in terms of the problems it causes. Critics of abstinence-only curricula contend that some programs even go so far as to include inaccurate information, such as the myth that condoms have holes in them bigger than the HIV virus, in order to scare young people away from having sex.

Abstinence-only sex education is one of the pro-family movement's biggest policy victories. In 1996, special funding for abstinence-only education was established by the federal government, meaning that resource-starved public schools have an incentive to provide this sort of sex education curriculum, rather than more comprehensive and accurate education. In 2001, this funding was extended, and continues to increase each year. There are no federal funds dedicated to comprehensive sex education at this time.

Civil rights for lesbians and gay men

The fight against civil rights for lesbians and gay men has been a longstanding plank in the pro-family movement's platform. Currently, this fight is taking the form of opposition to laws that recognize marriage between two people of the same sex. However, this is not the only anti-gay position of the pro-family movement. The movement also opposes extending anti-discrimination legislation to include lesbians and gay men, not to mention bisexuals and transgender people.

That is, pro-family activists want the law to allow landlords to be able to refuse housing to people who are gay or lesbian, and to allow businesses to fire people just for being gay, and allow restaurants, hotels, and other service providers to have the legal right to refuse to serve lesbians and gay men.

The pro-family movement also has attempted to block kids from forming Gay–Straight Alliance groups in their high schools. These groups are extracurricular social clubs that provide a safe space for kids to talk about sexuality, and often have a diverse mix of straight, gay, lesbian, bisexual, or "questioning" youth (those who are unsure of their sexual identities), as well as kids who don't follow traditional gender norms. Though a federal law dictates that public high schools cannot discriminate against extracurricular groups based on the content of their discussions, the pro-family movement has supported those high schools that have tried to shut these groups down.

Abortion

Abortion is a very contentious issue in America, with people holding very strong feelings for or against making this procedure available to pregnant women. The pro-family movement is squarely positioned on the "pro-life" side of this debate, and works diligently to restrict women's access to abortion. This battle occurs in a number of venues, including the "front lines" of medical clinics that provide abortions or abortion counseling. Picketers protests outside these clinics, and often try to convince women who enter the clinics to change their minds about getting an abortion.

Another front in this battle is legislative, and although the US Supreme Court has determined that women have a constitutional right to choose to terminate their pregnancies, the pro-life and pro-family movements have urged legislators to curtail that right whenever possible. They have successfully limited the number of women who have access to abortion by implementing parental consent and parental notification laws that require pregnant women under the age of 18 to obtain signatures from their parents before they can obtain an abortion.

The impact of the pro-family movement

The success of the pro-family movement on some issues, and their ongoing battles on other issues, have an impact upon different groups in different ways. Below, I look at the pro-family agenda through a few different lenses.

Youth

From the pro-family perspective, keeping information about sex away from young people is tantamount to protecting children from harm. But there is little acknowledgement by pro-family activists that youth, those years between sexual maturity and legal adulthood, is an age category that is distinct from childhood. Thus, the pro-family agenda does not distinguish small children in grade school from high school seniors.

Many pro-family policies are targeted at youth. Some, like abstinence-only sex education, make it more difficult for young people to get accurate information about condoms and other birth control, rape crisis assistance, and options such as emergency contraception, or the "morning after pill," which prevents pregnancy when taken soon after sexual intercourse. The pro-family movement has successfully lobbied five states to adopt policies that prevent teachers from discussing homosexuality in the classroom, and dozens of others to require parental permission before youth can participate in such a discussion.

Other policies have direct impact upon young people's bodies and physical well-being. Parental consent requirements for abortion procedures put young women's choices in the hands of their parents. And the pro-family movement's opposition to anti-bullying laws mean that schools will be less safe for lesbian, gay, bisexual, and transgender kids.

Women

Restricting access to abortion is one pro-family policy that directly impacts on women's lives. The pro-family agenda includes reversing the 1973 Supreme Court decision, *Roe v. Wade*, which determined that abortion is a constitutional right. Pro-family activists are hopeful that new judicial appointments to the Supreme Court will set the stage for a legal challenge to this historic ruling.

Other pro-family policies have a disproportionate impact on women, such as restrictions on the distribution of emergency contraception and legal protections for pharmacists who refuse to fill prescriptions for birth control pills. Other policies that restrict women's sexuality include bans on the vibrators and other sex toys that many women use to achieve orgasm. The pro-family movement would also like to change marriage laws to make it more difficult to get a divorce, which will be the most harmful to women who are victims of domestic violence.

Women outside of the United States are also affected by pro-family policies. The pro-family movement's successful implementation of the "Mexico City Policy" (commonly known as the "global gag rule") in US foreign policy means that federal funds will not go to any foreign aid organization that provides abortions, refers women to abortion providers, or even discusses abortion as an option with pregnant women. Other pro-family-supported foreign aid policies, such as de-emphasizing condom use in HIV-prevention efforts in Africa, will cost both women and men their lives.

Lesbian, gay, bisexual, and transgender people

Lesbian, gay, bisexual, and transgender people are major targets of the pro-family movement, which claims that lesbian and gay people are a threat to the family. Pro-family activists actively oppose same-sex marriage, and they have succeeded in writing new laws to prevent lesbian and gay couples from marrying in thirty-eight states, even though same-sex marriage is only available in Massachusetts and same-sex civil unions are only recognized in Vermont.

Marriage is not the only anti-gay item on the pro-family agenda. As I have mentioned, the pro-family movement also opposes anti-discrimination protections for lesbian, gay, and transgender people. They also want to exclude sexual identity from states' hate crimes laws, and they work to prevent lesbian, gay, bisexual, and transgender people from adopting children or becoming foster parents.

Sexual politics as social movement politics

Each social policy, whether it is at the level of the federal government or the local school board, has a direct impact on the way that individuals experience and can express their sexuality. Even though sex is very personal and intimate, it is also very social at the same time, because many different aspects of our sexual lives are governed by laws, policies, and more informal social norms. Even something as simple as how and where we can talk about sex is influenced greatly by social policies and norms.

The conservative pro-family movement has recently had a strong influence on this public debate about sexuality. By insisting that very restrictive policies govern sexuality and that the conservative social norms guide sexual behavior, they take a position directly opposite the liberal agenda set in the sexual revolution of the late 1960s, which calls for a "live and let live" approach to social norms, and argues for reductions in governmental restrictions on people's sexuality. In the United States, we have become increasingly polarized between two ends of the political spectrum when it comes to sexuality.

In other countries, which have less social movement activity on these issues, policy debates about sexuality tend toward compromise. As a result, more moderate policy outcomes are common, and we see a slow but steady liberalization of sexual policies in Canada, Australia, and much of Europe. In the United States, as a direct result of the pro-family movement, there is more controversy and less compromise on issues of sexual politics. So, the US is not following the same pattern as other nations. In fact, there is not much of a pattern at all, but more of a patchwork of court decisions, legislation, and executive orders that sometimes favor the pro-family movement, and at other times do not. The final outcome of the "culture war" in the United States remains to be seen, but the strength of both the pro-family movement and their political opponents seems to be increasing over time. This means that more Americans are taking up one side of these issues or the other, and as time goes on, the chances that we will reach a middle ground on sexual policy in the United States is shrinking.

68

Politics of sex education

Interview with Janice M. Irvine

UNIVERSITY OF MASSACHUSETTS, AMHERST

Janice M. Irvine is Professor of Sociology at the University of Massachusetts. She is the Director of the Five College Women's Studies Research Center. She is the author of *Talk About Sex: The Battles over Sex Education in the United States* and *Disorders of Desire: Sex and Gender in Modern American Sexology*.

In your first book you wrote a historical analysis of twentieth-century sexology, and recently you published a book on the history of sex education controversies. Is there a theme that ties together this research?

As a sociologist, I approach sexuality as a domain that is profoundly social rather than thinking of it as a purely biological and instinctive part of life. In my research, I have tended to study different types of sexual discourse, by which I mean the specific webs of meaning that shape how we think, talk, and feel about sexuality. In my first book, *Disorders of Desire: Sex and Gender in Modern American Sexology*, I examined the history of sex research in the twentieth century. The book explores how sexology – the scientific study of sexuality – invented medical categories, languages, and norms regarding sexuality and gender, and at the same time played a role in turning sex into a marketable commodity in the form of advice and therapy.

I have always been interested in relations of power and the production of sexual knowledge. This led me to study the controversies over sexuality education in the United States. Since the 1960s, we have been fighting over what forms of sexual knowledge we will impart to our young people in the public school system. Basically these are political battles, because they involve disagreements about what types of sexualities are valued and therefore teachable and what forms of sexuality are so devalued that we cannot speak about them. Sex education is an important sexual discourse because it influences how young people become social and sexual actors.

Another theme that links these two books is the stigma that both sex researchers and sex educators have historically endured. Even today, sexology can be rendered suspicious and sex researchers themselves can be stigmatized with little difficulty. Sexology remains marginal or even ignored in the academy. Sex research has been consistently unfunded, under-funded, or de-funded after attacks by legislators, conservative groups, or the media. Sex educators have been under attack as well. The stigmatization of anyone who works in the area of sexuality is one indication of the deep cultural anxieties about sex in the United States.

How long has sex education been part of the curriculum in public schools?

The first calls for school sex education came in the early twentieth century from moral reformers interested in what was then called "sex hygiene." These included groups as different as suffragists, clergy, temperance workers, and physicians, all of whom wanted to eliminate venereal disease. As early as 1919, mainstream organizations such as the US Public Health Service endorsed formal sex education programs, believing that the schools would be the most effective sites for instruction of young people. In the first half of the twentieth century, many schools implemented sex education programs, such as in Chicago, Washington, DC, and Toms River, New Jersey. Still, many educators were uneasy about discussion of sexual health in the classroom, and sex education's progress was slow and sometimes controversial.

In 1964, a small group of professionals, led by Mary Calderone, a staid Quaker physician who had been the medical director of Planned Parenthood Federation of America, founded the Sex Information and Education Council of the United States (SIECUS). Calderone spearheaded a crusade to normalize the topic of sexuality by emphasizing the public health dimension rather than the morality of it. She sought to include sex education in curricula from kindergarten through graduate training, in particular medical schools. Even today, SIECUS remains the most visible organization calling for comprehensive sexuality education.

What kind of sex education do we find in public schools now?

Generally there are two types of programs taught in public schools today: comprehensive sexuality education, and what is variously known as abstinence-only or abstinence-only-until-marriage education.

SIECUS pioneered a model for comprehensive sexuality education in which young people would receive, from kindergarten through high school, age-appropriate information on a range of topics such as human reproduction, anatomy, physiology, and sexually transmitted infections, as well as issues such as masturbation, contraception, and abortion. Comprehensive sexuality education offers young people the opportunity to discuss sexual values and attitudes in the classroom. Advocates of comprehensive sex education endorse what they consider to be the health benefits of frank sexual discussion in the classroom. They believe that silence has fostered ignorance, shame, and social problems like teenage pregnancy. Supporters of comprehensive sexuality education view sexuality as positive and healthy, and they typically support gender equality and acceptance of sexual diversity. Comprehensive sexuality education stresses abstinence for youth, and it also provides information on topics such as contraception and abortion.

Advocates of abstinence-only education believe that the best approach to sexual health is to teach young people to abstain from all sexual behavior until they are married. All sexual behavior, in their opinion, should be confined to marriage. Controlling or eliminating sexual discussion best allows for the protection of young people and preservation of sexual morality. Discussion about topics such as contraception, in their view, has led to high levels of adolescent sexual activity, teenage pregnancy, and sexually transmitted diseases. They believe, therefore, that if we talk to young people about sexuality it should be controlled so as not to lead to destructive and immoral thoughts and behavior. They generally favor restrictions on other forms of sexual expression, such as masturbation or homosexuality, and they often oppose feminism and the gay rights movement.

Is there any research comparing the effectiveness of comprehensive sexuality education compared to abstinence-only curricula? Basically, which programs work?

The question of effectiveness is a very important one, especially since the United States government has been generously funding abstinence-only programs since 1982. In fact, this level of funding has drastically increased under the administration of George W. Bush. Abstinence-only sex education will receive $170 million in fiscal year 2005, more than double the funding it received in fiscal year 2001.

Unfortunately, despite all this federal funding, there is mounting evidence that these programs simply do not work. In 1996, when the welfare reform law was enacted which funds so many of these programs, an independent review concluded that there were no solid data to demonstrate the effectiveness of abstinence-only curricula. Evaluations of three prominent abstinence-only curricula – Sex Respect, Teen-Aid, and Values and Choices – did not support advocates' claims that the programs delayed sexual initiation among young people.

An independent research institute, Mathematica Policy Research Inc., has been conducting evaluation research on abstinence-only programs funded through the 1996 law. An interim report issued in June 2005 shows that, while young people who have attended these programs report positive attitudes about abstinence, the programs have little or no impact otherwise. They did not affect youth's intentions to abstain and had no impact on important decision-making factors such as self-esteem and open communication with parents. In addition, a report issued by Democrat Congressman Henry Waxman evaluated the content of the abstinence-only programs funded by the federal government. It found that over 80 percent of such curricula contained false, misleading, or distorted information about reproductive health.

On the other hand, there is some evidence that comprehensive sexuality education is effective on a number of levels. Independent researcher Douglas Kirby found that several curricula are effective in preventing teen pregnancy. Significantly, he found that curricula that teach about contraception and safer sex do not hasten the onset, or increase the frequency of, sex among young people, as many critics of comprehensive programs allege. Also, a study commissioned by the Joint United Programme on HIV/AIDS (UNAIDS) found that a number of good comprehensive programs are successful in delaying the onset of sexual behavior, reducing the number of partners, or reducing unplanned pregnancy and rates of sexually transmitted diseases.

Which approach to sex education in the schools do most people in the US support?

Repeatedly, most people tell pollsters they broadly support comprehensive sex education. Public opinion polls since the 1960s have consistently shown widespread support for sex education. A 2000 poll sponsored by the Kaiser Family Foundation indicated that, by a large majority, parents want their children to have *more* classroom hours of sex education that covers more "sensitive topics" than such programs currently do. A 1998 national poll found that 87 percent of Americans supported sexuality education in the public schools and a poll commissioned by SIECUS and Advocates for Youth found that 89 percent believe that, along with abstinence, young people should also have information about contraception and STD prevention.

So what do most public schools teach? Comprehensive or abstinence-only programs?

As I show in my book, *Talk About Sex: The Battles Over Sex Education in the United States*, the scope of sex education is narrow in the public schools. Although most public schools offer some form of sex education, very few students receive the type of comprehensive sexuality education advocated by SIECUS. Some students might have a semester-long course, while some hear only one or two sessions from an outside group like Planned Parenthood. Most students undergo a few class periods of instruction sometime between the seventh and twelfth grades. However, since the growth of abstinence-only education, many students only hear abstinence messages in those few classes they might have received. While in 1988 only 2 percent of teachers taught abstinence as the *sole* means of pregnancy and disease prevention, 23 percent did so in 1999. A poll of schools in September 2003 indicated a sharp increase to 30 percent among instructors who taught abstinence only and did not provide information about condoms and other contraceptives.

A study of public schools revealed that, among all districts in the US, 10 percent had a comprehensive sexuality education policy, 34 percent promoted abstinence as the preferred option for teenagers but allowed for discussion of contraception, and 23 percent required the sole promotion of abstinence. Thirty-three percent of districts had no policy on sexuality education. The abstinence-only-until-marriage districts either completely prohibited any instruction in contraception or required that teachers only emphasize its failures. The researchers concluded that of all US students who attended a public school including grades six and higher, only 9 percent were in districts with a comprehensive sexuality education policy.

Why is comprehensive sex education shrinking, given popular support for it?

Sex education has been a central issue in the culture wars that have flared in the United States since the 1970s. Since the 1960s, religious conservatives have viewed sex education as a powerful vehicle by which to agitate parents, recruit constituents, raise money, and ultimately consolidate political power through election to school boards and other political positions. Social conservatives believe that, like abortion, sexuality in the media, and gay rights, comprehensive sexuality is dangerous and immoral. Conservative national organizations and political movements have been actively involved with shaping sexual values in this country, and they have taken on sex education as one of their most important political issues. Therefore, by the end of the twentieth century, more than 700 communities had experienced intense controversies over sex education in their local schools. Often cast as spontaneous eruptions of grassroots outrage, sex education conflicts actually constitute one flank of this self-described initiative by national religious right groups. Moreover, these conservative groups were able to dominate the public conversation about sex education.

What does it mean that conservatives dominate the public conversation about sex education? How have they been able to do this?

Conservative national religious organizations, for example Concerned Women for America, and Focus on the Family, captured the terms of debate about sex education through the strategic use of emotionally powerful rhetoric used both nationally and locally at school board sessions and town meetings. Provocative and stigmatizing sexual rhetoric has played an important role in igniting community battles. One common tactic has been the use of highly charged sexual language in community debates. This includes, for example, calling a curriculum a "sodomy curriculum" or describing it as "pornographic." They also use provocative language to stigmatize sex educators themselves, calling them perverts or pedophiles.

Conservatives have also distorted and misrepresented comprehensive programs, for example claiming that if students learn about condom use or birth control they will go out and have sex. Studies indicate otherwise, but that does not stop conservatives from making the claim.

Finally, conservative critics employ what I call depravity narratives, which are tales about sexual groups or issues that rely on distortion, hyperbole, or outright fabrication. Many depravity narratives spread during controversies in the late 1960s. One recounted that a sex education teacher had had intercourse in front of the class as a pedagogical strategy. Other tales circulated to the effect that children were being encouraged to fondle each other, sexual intercourse would be taught in kindergarten, schools would install coed bathrooms with no partitions between stalls, and youth were being told about bestiality with donkeys and sheep. Depravity narratives are designed to shock people and to exploit popular anxieties about the destructive power of unleashed sexuality.

All of these strategies have been incredibly effective because of America's culture of sexual fear and shame. Regardless of whether these allegations about comprehensive sex education were actually believed, by either the activists themselves or their audience, they could mobilize sexual fears for political purposes. Stigmatizing accusations are difficult to refute, and they cast suspicion upon local programs and sex educators themselves. Highly charged sexual language and graphic symbols could scare and outrage people, turning a local debate into a civic brawl.

Has there been organized support for comprehensive sexuality education?

Comprehensive sexuality education is supported by a wide range of religious and public health agencies. Over 140 national organizations comprise the National Coalition to Support Sexuality Education. These include the American Medical Association, the American Public Health Association, the American Academy of Pediatrics, and the United Church Board for Homeland Ministries. They are committed to medically-accurate, age-appropriate comprehensive sexuality education. In addition, a new wing of advocacy emerged in the late 1990s. Prompted by the funding of abstinence-only programs in the 1996 welfare law, the National Coalition Against Censorship, along with other free-speech activists, took up sex education as a First Amendment issue. In broad public education campaigns, NCAC argued that federal funding of abstinence-only education represented censorship, in that it is state restriction on what teachers can or cannot teach about sex.

You have written a great deal about the intense emotions involved in sex education debates. What do you mean by this, and why are emotions important?

Early in my research, I saw how discussions about sexuality education became highly impassioned public arguments across the US. Community meetings erupted in shouting matches and even physical violence. I heard neighbors scream at each other and saw angry shoving outside of public meeting halls. School board members told me about receiving hate mail and death threats. Town meetings went from sleepy affairs to late-night shouting matches involving hundreds of residents. After a sex education foe collapsed from an anxiety attack while addressing an especially rancorous meeting, the tense minutes in the hushed school auditorium as he was carried out rank among the most dramatic in my research career.

Whereas early on I had thought volatile emotions were inconsequential compared to the rational terms of political debate, gradually I understood that the furious public displays of feeling were significant and required analysis and theorization. I began to recognize community battles as the outcome of political strategy such as the highly charged rhetoric I described earlier.

Emotions are significant for several reasons during local sex education conflicts. On the simplest level, they heat up the climate and draw attention to the issue. Intense emotions can mobilize followers, at least in the short term. Media coverage often intensifies when town meetings explode. In turn, headlines and articles that emphasize these outbursts of feeling not only sell newspapers but they coach citizens in the emotional expectations of town meetings. Even more important was the emotional climate of danger and shame that was reinforced by the rhetoric used during these conflicts, even if an audience was skeptical of some of the more outrageous claims. The intense feelings displayed in sex education controversies can teach us that emotion is not simply an instinctive reaction that is beyond the reach of social influences but that emotions have their own social and cultural logic. In turn, this means they are important in the political arena. In the end, I discovered that emotions are central in sex education politics, which seems to bring me full circle to my interests in power and knowledge.

69

Gender and sexual politics

American gay rights and feminist movements

Megan Murphy

STATE UNIVERSITY OF NEW YORK AT ALBANY

In recent years the political aspects of sexuality have increasingly become visible on the front pages of newspapers around the globe. Headlines include stories on abortion rights, same-sex marriage, hate crimes committed against gays and lesbians, anti-discrimination laws, and access to contraception. Sexuality consistently rears its head in popular cultural and political debates. This is largely the result of a growing number of social movements dealing with sexuality. The past few decades in the United States alone have witnessed a wave of movements, such as the gay and lesbian, transgender, S/M, feminist, and prostitutes' rights movements, which have tackled issues of sexuality head-on.

Less transparent in the headlines are the difficulties these movements face in their attempts to challenge dominant ideas about sexuality. These difficulties largely stem from the consequences of sexuality being a social construct. Conflicts over sexuality are always in part also conflicts over gender, family, social values, law, and religion. This strong tie between sexuality and society becomes evident in the ways that gender shapes sexuality and sexual politics. Scholars such as Judith Lorber (1993) argue that gender provides the acceptable patterns of sexual desires and behaviors for men and women. Similarly, Adrienne Rich (1980) argues that a system of "compulsory heterosexuality" places expectations on individuals to be heterosexual and to conform to traditional gender roles. A brief glance at any one social movement dealing with sexuality quickly reveals an inextricable connection between sexuality and gender.

In this chapter, I will discuss some of the ways movements addressing sexuality are challenged by the links between sexuality and gender. Specifically, I will look at the way the gay rights and feminist movements struggled to link gender and sexuality. I will then discuss contemporary shifts in the politics of gender and sexuality.

The gay rights movement

The gay rights movement – by which I mean the movement for gay, lesbian, bisexual, and transgender (GLBT) rights – in the United States developed largely for the purpose of gaining social acceptance for homosexuals. Outcast as "sexual deviants," GLBT people sought to prove that they were ordinary or "normal" people. Today the movement continues its fight for full social and economic equality. GLBT people are fighting to end the everyday discrimination and violence.

They are challenging the institution of compulsory heterosexuality, which asserts that heterosexuality is the only normal, acceptable sexual identity by rewarding heterosexuals and punishing homosexuals.

Throughout the years, the movement has made great strides toward achieving its goals. American culture appears to be growing increasingly tolerant and accepting of gays and lesbians. There has been a growing visibility of gay and lesbian characters on television and, at the time of writing, same-sex marriage is legal in the state of Massachusetts. Many other states have passed anti-discrimination laws and established marriage-like partnerships for same-sex couples. However, despite this progress, the movement has been somewhat limited, in my view, by not always addressing the role of gender in gay politics.

As homosexuals, gays and lesbians are not only breaking the rules of acceptable sexual behavior, but they are also breaking with traditional gender norms. Part of displaying one's gender category successfully is to display appropriate (hetero-) sexual attraction. Traditional gender conventions (which, I would argue, still hold strong) assert that to be fully masculine or feminine – in other words, to be a true man or true woman – one must display a sexual desire for the opposite sex. In failing to do so, men are often viewed as "sissies" or "fairies," while women are seen as "butch" or "man-hating." Having to contend with the consequences of breaking both gender norms and accepted sexual behaviors, the gay rights movement has always had to fight two simultaneous battles. GLBT people lose respect not only because they are not heterosexual but because either the public stereotypes them as gender-deviant or they have chosen to challenge gender norms. Until gender norms change so that sexual desires are no longer intrinsic to them, this will remain a problem for the gay rights movement.

The place of transgendered people and issues in the gay movement has also exposed the gender problem in this movement. In general, the term "transgender" refers to people who are gender-variant; that is, individuals who do not conform to the expected gender norms for women and men. Despite an initial period during the 1970s and 1980s, when there was considerable backlash against transgendered people and issues, trans issues have been included at the forefront of the gay rights movement since the 1990s. In spite of the movement advocating free gender identity and expression, transgender people often find they have unique experiences that, although linked, are not effortlessly combined with gay and lesbian goals. Transgendered people are not protected by gay rights laws which cover sexual orientation; transgendered activists struggle for gender orientation or gender identity rights, which are often not central to the gay movement. Similarly, in recent years, the gay rights movement has made same-sex marriage into its core concern. However, this fight largely centers on gays and lesbians, not transgender rights and concerns.

A queer movement in the 1990s was one attempt to link gender and sexual politics. Queers sought to challenge the way all of us are classified and controlled by binaries such as male/female, feminine/masculine, heterosexual/homosexual; the queer movement sought to weaken or erase the boundaries between these groups. The label "queer" was an attempt to make the gay and lesbian movement more inclusive, to successfully include transgender and bisexual individuals, and it emphasized the need to focus on and celebrate diversity within the GLBT community. However, in reality, the movement had very limited success. Queer Nation, the movement's main organization, lasted only two years before internal disputes caused its disintegration. However, the movement did help to launch the field of queer studies in academia, contributing significantly to a sophisticated analysis of the intersections between sex and gender.

The feminist movement

The American feminist movement has similarly encountered challenges in its efforts to reconcile sexuality and gender politics. Emerging in the 1960s, second-wave feminism addressed a host of gender-related issues, including sexuality. In their fight to end gender inequality and discrimination, feminists sought to change patriarchal values so that an egalitarian, oppression-free society could emerge. Feminists fought for the right to access safe and legal abortion and contraceptive services. They demanded equal educational and career opportunities. Furthermore, women insisted that they no longer be viewed as sexual objects. Women wanted to be respected for their intellect or leadership skills. However, at the same time, women were demanding sexual autonomy and freedom. When the first dialogue on the clitoral orgasm emerged, heterosexuality suddenly became less inevitable, as women were now potentially able to receive sexual pleasure from both men and women.

The success of the feminist movement in the United States has been immense. Through a widely dispersed network of feminist organizations and consciousness-raising techniques, feminist concerns slowly penetrated wider society. Gender roles were greatly expanded for women, beginning in the late 1960s and 1970s; for example, women became able to focus on careers, instead of family, if they chose to do so. Non-discrimination laws were passed throughout the country to prevent gender inequality in a range of settings. However, despite this progress, the feminist movement remains engaged in the fight today for full gender equality. Economic discrepancies between men and women remain a problem, while violence continues to threaten women throughout the world. In fact, much work remains for the current feminist movement in the United States.

The early years of the feminist movement were plagued by problems surrounding sexual politics. Despite the commitment of lesbians to feminist goals, they were largely excluded from the movement during its formative years. Some straight feminists viewed lesbians as sexual deviants. The presence of lesbians in the movement was considered damaging, because early feminists did not want to be linked with a deviant sexual group. Lesbians and their issues were purged from mainstream feminist organizations in the late 1960s and early 1970s.

The problem with lesbian inclusion was most salient in the largest American feminist organization, the National Organization for Women (NOW). NOW's first president, Betty Friedan, claimed that lesbian issues were not central to feminist concerns and that lesbians would put the movement in jeopardy by coupling feminists with sexual deviants. Many lesbians were removed from the organization, while other lesbians voluntarily withdrew from NOW membership. Lesbians developed their own feminist organizations, with lesbian concerns central to their goals. Gradually, lesbians and lesbian rights became accepted as part of key feminist goals, within NOW and elsewhere, but not until the women's movement had suffered considerable division and setbacks as a result of the controversy.

Early feminists were not mistaken in their thinking that including lesbians would impact the feminist movement. However, they did not realize that an analysis of lesbian issues would be essential for developing a broader understanding of the ways patriarchal, heterosexist society operated. Whether or not lesbians were included in the feminist movement, the sexuality of feminists would have none the less been called in question. Similar to gays and lesbians breaking traditional gender roles by displaying same-sex desire, the sexuality of feminists was called into question (whether in reality they were heterosexual, homosexual, or somewhere in between) because they challenged traditional gender dynamics. As a result, some in the mainstream feminist movement often conceded to the dominant gendered sexual expectations in the hope of appearing more credible. Some feminist leaders worked to maintain traditional displays of "femininity," including embracing heterosexual relationships and families, so that they could gain respect from the wider society.

In the 1970s and 1980s, lesbian feminism was a direct attempt to forge a movement that brought together sexual and gender politics. Lesbian feminists viewed lesbianism as a political, rather than a sexual identity. They claimed that to be a lesbian was to consciously step out of social, political, and economic dependence on men. Women whose core attachments were with other women could successfully live their lives outside of patriarchal systems of oppression where men are dominant, while women are oppressed. This view holds that gender and sexuality, as well as the forces of homophobia and sexism, are inextricably linked. As a result, lesbian feminist scholars such as Suzanne Pharr (1997) argue that homophobia is a "weapon of sexism" and that sexism cannot be eliminated until homophobia is eradicated. Though the movement of lesbian separatism itself was largely unsuccessful, fading relatively quickly in the 1980s, the theory generated from the movement has provided useful perspectives for analyzing gender and sexual oppression.

What the future holds

There appear to be symptoms of movements today which address sexuality and gender in innovative ways. One example of such a movement is that of GLBT youth. Informed by the theories generated from lesbian feminism and queer politics, GLBT youth appear to be comfortable with a politics that brings together gender and sexuality. In my experience of listening to and observing youth at a GLBT youth drop-in center, I have learned that these individuals are increasingly willing to address connections between sexuality and gender, despite the resistance from their peers and the wider society. For example, these particular youth experimented on a day-to-day basis with the ways their individual sexual and gender identities interact, challenging traditional conceptions and expectations. Many youth choose to be referred to by gender-neutral pronouns such as "ze." Furthermore, they experiment with gender, sometimes displaying highly feminine, masculine, or androgynous characteristics, depending on how they feel at that particular moment. They understand and value their sexual identities as highly fluid and ever-changing. Most youth that I met identify as "queer" and recognize the importance and necessity of diversity. In doing such things, they are directly addressing the types of issues which have caused a great deal of dissent over the years in the American feminist and gay rights movements.

This development among youth is increasingly being expressed politically. A group of queer youth at the drop-in center were trained in leading workshops to educate the wider community, students, and teachers about the issues facing lesbian, gay, bisexual, transgender, and queer youth. Furthermore, the Gender Public Advocacy Coalition (GenderPAC), a national organization working to end discrimination and violence based on gender stereotypes, has started a Gender-YOUTH program advocating gender rights on college campuses throughout the USA. Student activists engage in peer mentoring, community education, and grassroots organizing in order to promote an understanding of the connections between gender, sexuality, race, age, and class. In 2004, GenderYOUTH activists in eighteen states held a "Drop the Labels" campaign, focusing on educating the public about the consequences of gender-based bullying. These youth activists offer great promise for a future politics which successfully links gender and sexuality.

References

Lorber, J. 1993. *Paradoxes of Gender*. New Haven, CT: Yale University Press.
Pharr, S. 1997. *Homophobia: A Weapon of Sexism*. Berkeley, CA: Chardon Press.
Rich, A. 1980. "Compulsory Heterosexuality and Lesbian Existence," in A. Snitow, C. Stansell, and S. Thompson (eds), *Powers of Desire*. New York: Monthly Review Press.

70

A post-identity culture of sexual resistance

The case of Lebanese nonheterosexuals

Steven Seidman

STATE UNIVERSITY OF NEW YORK AT ALBANY

Lebanon is a marriage-and-family centered nation. Individuals are understood as extensions of their families, and marriage is at once a social duty and a condition of self fulfillment. Intimate norms are especially rigid for women, requiring exclusive heterosexuality, sexual modesty, virginal marriage, and a procreative imperative. A double standard gives men more latitude in intimate matters. This intimate code produces an abundance of stigmatized, outsider sexualities – the unmarried, loose, promiscuous women, barren men and women, cohabiting men and women, childless marriages, but, above all, nonheterosexuality. So unequivocally is heterosexuality understood to be the basis and the elementary fact of intimate behavior that this norm hardly needs to be spoken, much less defended or explained; it is simply the only way to claim a normal sexuality and gender. In this chapter, I consider how nonheterosexuals in Beirut negotiate an urban world that leaves no legitimate option beyond heterosexuality. How is compulsory heterosexuality resisted?

Needless to say, the world of nonheterosexuals in Beirut contrasts sharply with the gay, lesbian, bi, trans worlds of US or UK cities. The tight association of desire and sexual identity, and the formation of identity-based sexual communities, so salient in American and British cities, cannot be assumed in Beirut. I found that most individuals approach same-sex attraction as a desire or behavior. A language of sexual identity was exceptional. When individuals did use a vocabulary of identity e.g. typically using the English terms gay or lesbian or queer since the Arab terms (*shaadh, luti, khanit*) are denigrating, they mostly did so as a shorthand way to refer to a sexual preference, not as revealing a core, true identity. I did though at times encounter individuals who deployed a language of social identity that sounded like their American and British counterparts.

Lebanese confront a social world in which same-sex sexuality is publicly disrespected and, in the case of behavior, criminalized. Although state prosecutions are rare (data are not available), periodic police harassment and sexual violence, the shutting down of public spaces friendly to nonheterosexuals, and public scandal, remind us that in Beirut only heterosexuality grants full rights and respect. Lebanese hardly need such reminders since their kin, sect, and peers permit no legitimate alternative to heterosexuality.

For Lebanese whose desire falls outside of heterosexuality, they are not necessarily destined to lonely and isolated lives. Informal networks have formed and at times serve as the basis of a sexual dissident community. Through the internet or friends, or the few public spaces (clubs, bars, cafés, and organizations) that exist in Beirut, nonheterosexuals find each other, become sex partners, friends, lovers, or long term partners. A web of contacts and connections at times gives rise to social networks. These networks are often porous around the edges and exhibit varying degrees of social density and duration depending on the types of relationships between its members, their age, career status, mobility, and so on. They serve, though, as safe spaces for nonheterosexuals, as spaces of belonging similar to networks in the United States and Europe.

Between Beirut and Manhattan or London there is then some affinity. This is not entirely unexpected since many Lebanese, especially among the middle and upper classes, have been exposed to American and British gay, lesbian, and queer life through popular culture, academia, the internet, travel, or living abroad. A striking example of Anglo-European influence is the recent formation of a clandestine group of nonheterosexual women called "Meem." Composed of mostly young, educated middle-class women, this collective has published a remarkable book of personal narratives (Bareed Mista3Jil 2009). Noteworthy not only for its frankness and publicness, but also because its stories are organized around themes familiar to Anglo-Europeans such as the struggle with isolation and shame, coming out, affirming a lesbian, gay, bi, trans or queer identity, the migration to cities, the formation of networks, and so on.

Yet, even as some sexual dissidents create loose communities of belonging, these are different from their counterparts in the United States or the UK in one important way: Sexual dissidents in Beirut have not coalesced, *whether purposefully or not*, into identity-based public cultures, which would include businesses, social and political organizations, institutionalized cultural production (e.g. newspapers, magazines, fiction, scholarship, art, theater, music), and territorial enclaves. In Hamra, a 'middle class' dymanic neighbourhood, there is one publicly marked nonheterosexual space, a bar (Wolf) housed in a little-trafficked, dimly lit side street. And in Beirut, a city of well over a million residents, there is just one club (Acid) and one or two pubs where nonheterosexuals gather. Citywide, there is one public political organization, Helem, which is a non-governmental organization. Helem advocates for "gay and lesbian rights," promotes AIDS prevention, and offers social support services. It might be tempting to argue that the absence of a public sexual culture in Beirut is a product of a closeted sexual world; if, so the argument goes, social controls were to be relaxed, sexual identities and public cultures would likely emerge. Perhaps. It is, though, telling that Meem, which has a grassroots social base, seems intent on circumventing Helem's identity-political strategy. Meem describes itself as a "grassroots movement where women are empowered" and prefers the post-identity term "queer" to describe its standpoint and politics (Bareed Mista3Jil 2009: 2, 28). Arguably, the absence of a public sexual culture, as we know it in the Anglo-European world, speaks less to the "underdevelopment" of the gay Lebanese than to a non-Western approach to questions of sexual desire, identity, and publicness. This is the theme I want to further pursue.

Walking the streets of Beirut between 1997–2009, I've been struck, as a gay man, by my inability to identify nonheterosexuals. Over time I've come to think that there does not exist in Beirut what in Anglo-European societies we might call a gay/lesbian or queer sign system, or a symbolic code for signaling nonheterosexuality. This refers to public practices that are understood by the agent and the public at large to signify a nonheterosexual status. Such sexual signifiers are invented by nonheterosexuals in order to recognize one another and perhaps to claim a public status; they also allow heterosexuals to identify nonheterosexuals and to project a public heterosexual status by avoiding these signifying practices. In the United States, gender play has often served as a gay/lesbian or queer signifier. In Beirut, nonheterosexual men seem to embrace conventional masculine styles. Gender bending does not signal sexual status. Neither a hyper masculine nor a non–stereotypical man will be publicly understood as anything other than heterosexual, unless accompanied by an exaggerated femininity or in the company of suspected nonheterosexuals. It was hardly surprising then that in my almost two years in Beirut I could confidently identify no more than two or three individuals whose public behavior signaled a nonheterosexual status. In a startling contrast to urban cultures in the United States or Britain, Beirut's public life presents a virtual seamless culture of heterosexuality. As one young man remarked, "Really, you just don't see openly gay people." Once again, it's possible to read this absence as evidence of a closet drama, but this reading gets shaky when we consider the link between sexual and social dissidence.

I made a point of attending a wide range of cultural and political events, and talked with many cultural producers and consumers in Beirut. I've come to believe that social dissent is expressed in ideological, not identity terms. There is, in fact, a very public style for displaying dissent. An oppositional culture is prominent among bohemians, artists, leftists, secularists, and intellectuals. In a neighborhood in Beirut called Hamra, a dissident public culture has formed around its varied cultural venues (cafés, theaters, galleries, performance spaces). This culture champions, broadly speaking, an ideological agenda that is anti-consumerist, anti-sectarian, leftist, and challenges the rigid sexual, gender and class coding of bodies and self-presentations. Some nonheterosexuals and gender dissidents express their sexual difference *as part of this dissident public culture*. Again, Meem's statement of purpose captures this non-identitarian spirit: "We are the non–conforming sexual community of Lebanon: the lesbians, the bisexuals, the queer, the questioning women, the transgendered and transsexual men and women, the Muslims, the Christians, the Druze, the atheists and agnostics." The blending of sexual dissidence into a culture of social dissidence suggests that the absence of sexual identity communities is in no small measure an expression of a *resistance to identity-based models of self and politics*. This is hardly surprising in a nation in which kin and sect stake out enveloping and inflexible identities for the self.

To further explore this theme, I considered the sexual organization of public space in Hamra. As we've seen, there are very few exclusively gay/lesbian or nonheterosexual spaces. The heterosexualization of public space, reinforced by rigid binary gender norms, seems almost seamless. But, in fact, sexual dissidents use and occupy Hamra's public space. They are regulars in cafés *known* to be spaces where intellectuals, artists, musicians, activists, and nonheterosexuals gather. In these "counter-spaces" (Lefebvre 1991), freed from the surveillance and regulation of kin, sect, and state, multiple differences and a robust culture of tolerance provide a space of belonging for all sorts of dissidents who might elsewhere be less welcomed.

The owners and managers of these cafés often boast of their space as a haven for dissidents, including nonheterosexuals. With considerable pride, they have announced that sexual dissidents will be tolerated, indeed welcomed, so long as they avoid public affection (this also holds for heterosexuals) and remain a thread in the social mosaic of their clientele. No owner wanted their café to become known as a homosexual place. As one café owner confided:

> Gay couples sometimes frequent the café. I don't mind but I do not want this café to be known as their regular hangout. … [Also], I don't mind if they furtively display slight affection but I make sure that it doesn't go beyond that. If this escalates, I might ask them to stop or leave. … I have no judgment against them. However, I need to ensure that all my customers are comfortable and at ease.

Does this anxiety about their café becoming known as a homosexual hangout betray a homophobic sentiment? Probably, though it also speaks to a reality in which perceived homosexual businesses are periodically shut down. However, I also think that this anxiety expresses an unease this owner feels, *as a cosmopolitan*, with an identitarian social logic, or with the notion of an exclusively identity-based space.

This cosmopolitan unease surfaced in conversations with two owners of a café (a male couple) that is known as welcoming to sexual dissidents. They too were put off by the idea of their café being known as an exclusively gay or lesbian or sexually identified space. They preferred a cosmopolitan framing of their café as one that values ambiguity, diversity, and social mixing. "I want this to be a place," said one of the owners, "where no one judges you and where everyone feels comfortable to be themselves. Look around, this is a place that welcomes many different kinds of people. That's what we wanted." The desire for a space that values ambiguity and fluidity seems also to be what draws some patrons to this café. A heterosexual woman confided, "I guess there are a lot of gay and lesbians here but it's not noticeable. … No one shows public affection and nobody wants to offend anyone else. I guess no one really cares. I don't." While a culture that trades on the ambiguity and fluidity of identity provides "cover" for sexual dissidents, this does not mean that it is a closeted accommodation to a regime of compulsory heterosexuality. This would likely be true in Chicago or London or Sydney, but I don't think it's the case in Beirut. In a confessionally based nation, in which sectarianism serves as a master identity embedding selves in a thick regulatory order, the resistance to identity and the appeal to cosmopolitan fluidity and ambiguity is a compelling act signaling authenticity and transgression.

The status of nonheterosexual desire, and the public status of sexual dissidence, is far from settled in Beirut. There is an uneasy ambivalence I detected among Lebanese, even cosmopolitans, regarding the relation between desire, identity, and public life. In part this ambivalence is rooted in the continued moral and social authority of kin and sect which stigmatizes nonheterosexuality. Even in Hamra, it is only in a very few public spaces that nonheterosexuality crosses the line into moral legitimacy. And Lebanese, even nonheterosexuals, seem to believe that at present they have little choice but to present themselves as gender-conventional and to organize an intimate life that *publicly* admits only opposite-gendered desires and partners.

I did, however, meet individuals who chose to publicly defy this sexual and gender regime. They were open about their sexually dissident status to family members (typically female siblings or their mothers, almost never to their fathers), friends, and some coworkers. They acknowledged the grave risks and costs of their choices (estrangement from family and friends, threat of violence and public shame) but, as they gained a footing in informal networks, their lives took on an integrity and sense of empowerment. Often enough, a sense of crisis loomed as these young men and women reached their 30s; there is enormous pressure from kin, sect, and peers to marry and form a family. A graduate student and activist informed me that women who live as lesbians in their 20s often expect to be married by their 30s, or else they leave the country. A student researcher found that *all* of the 15 young women she interviewed conceded that "in the end they would … marry the opposite sex." For those who have not joined the 14 million or so in the diaspora, the compulsory status of heterosexuality often leaves sexual dissidents with a stark choice: to live a double life or to live a dissenting life that is often squeezed outside of a moral order of respectability and honor.

References

Bareed Mista3Jil. 2009. *[Mail in a Hurry]: True Stories*. Beirut, Lebanon.

Lefebvre, Henri. 1991. *The Production of Space*. Oxford: Blackwell.

Massad, Joseph. 2007. *Desiring Arabs*. Chicago, IL: University of Chicago Press.

McCormick, Jared. 2006. "Transition Beirut: Gay Identities, Lived Realities." In S. Khalaf and J. Gagnon, eds., *Sexuality in the Arab World*. London: Saqi.

Moussawi, Ghassan. 2008. "On the Shaming of Gender: Compulsory Heterosexuality and the Construction of Non-heterosexual Masculinities in Beirut." Master's thesis, American University, Beirut.

71

War and the politics of sexual violence

Margarita Palacios and Silvia Posocco

BIRKBECK COLLEGE, UNIVERSITY OF LONDON

When one hears the words "sexual violence," one normally thinks about domestic sexual abuse (from one family member to another one), sexual harassment in the work place, sexual abuse of children, and different sorts of sexual assault, including rape. In regular peace time, these are indeed the most frequent sexual crimes that take place in our society. There is, however, a second context of sexual violence. Sadly, there are numerous examples of warfare situations where not only soldiers, but civilians, have been the target of violence. Sexual violence during war takes place either through sexual slavery (i.e. the establishment of brothels for the military), gang rape of women right after a military conquest or victory, and through different forms of sexual torture of war prisoners. Some of the most striking examples of this type of sexual violence during the twentieth century include the sexual enslavement of Korean women by the Japanese army (between 1910 and 1944) and the mass rape of women during the partition of the Punjab region between India and Pakistan in 1947. Most recent examples include the rape camps established by the Serbs in the middle of Europe in the early 1990s to the mass rape of Bosnian-Muslim women, and the mass rape, sexual torture and killing of Tutsi women by Hutu militia during the Rwandan genocide in 1994.

There is yet another fairly current example of sexual violence in the context of warfare. Although not comparable with the previous ones – neither in terms of direct state intervention in its planning and execution, nor in terms of sheer number and death rates – the case of sexual torture of prisoners by US military personnel in Abu Ghraib Prison in Iraq, shook the world when pictures of naked prisoners simulating sexual acts were made public through the media.

Although there are evident differences between civilian sexual violence and warfare-related sexual violence, it is still possible to establish a line of continuity between them. Indeed, feminist research has attempted to move beyond this division between what could be called "private" versus "public" sexual violence. Feminists have argued that both types of sexual violence are indeed political insofar as they respond to prevailing social constructions of femininity and masculinity, and to the unequal relation of power between the genders. This perspective opposes "essentialist" ideas about genders and sexuality, and particularly challenges the notion of sexual violence as being the expression of otherwise irrepressible male sexual desire. From our cultural perspective, we argue that gender relations have to be understood as connected to other aspects of our identity, such as our nationality, class, ethnicity and race. Furthermore, gender and sexual dynamics are intimately linked to processes of nation-state formation and to the exercise of state power, in particular, the way the state regulates our bodies and intimate lives.

In order to develop this argument, we have divided this chapter in three parts. In the first part we present our analytical framework where we discuss a range of approaches to the understanding of sexual violence. In the second section we analyze the case of two war-torn societies, namely the former Yugoslavia and Rwanda, where mass rape aimed at ethnic cleansing took place. In the third and last section, we discuss the images of sexualized torture in the contemporary War on Terror and aim to relate these images to contemporary expressions of sexual violence. We finish with a short reflection about what can be called "structural violence" – a set of larger processes of economic exploitation, social marginality, and political exclusion – and how it can shed light on the understanding of the current mass killings of women particularly in Ciudad Juárez, Mexico.

Building an analytical framework

In public discourse, sexual violence is often portrayed in "essentialist" gendered terms; men are always portrayed as perpetrators and women as victims. From this perspective, sexual violence is understood as the expression of a masculine predisposition towards sexual aggression and violence. There are several problems associated with this sort of approach. First, in a paradoxical way this framing provides both a justification for the occurrence of sexual violence (suggesting its inevitability), and a "double victimization" of the targets of sexual violence, as victims of rape are often blamed for the violence they have suffered. Second, we object to the view that always understands women as victims and men as perpetrators. On the one hand this gender stereotype jeopardizes the possibility of male victims of sexual torture to come out to the public and to seek help and justice for what has happened to them. The concealment of violence against men reduces public awareness of sexual violence as a common war strategy. On the other hand, a women-only victim approach ignores the available research which shows how race impacts gender and sexual dynamics, including violence. As we will see, countering essentialism in the analysis of sexual violence therefore means not only understanding relations between men and women, but also relations between masculinized and feminized positions and how these may be marked by histories of racism, irrespective of the gender or ethnic identification of the persons involved.

One of the most compelling illustrations of this latter dynamic is the analysis of the "myth of the Black rapist." In the American South, for example, this myth played out in the wave of lynchings of Black men that would routinely follow episodes of the sexual assault of White women; the myth provided a justification for lynchings. More recently, the "myth of the Black rapist" has resulted in the automatic treatment of men of color as suspects and the indiscriminate use of rape charges, punitive procedures, and carceral regimes against them. In this context it has been argued that even today the politics of rape accusations against Black men cannot be disconnected from an analysis of the history of slavery and its legacy, and the way it has helped to create a public discourse as well as specific legal procedures which continue to foster forms of social exclusion and criminalization.

Moreover, anti-sexual violence initiatives focusing exclusively on male violence against women miss the way violence has profoundly different consequences for differently racialized and gendered subjects. Rather than leading to relevant forms of activist mobilization or examples of benign state protection for the vulnerable, state intervention may result in the unjust criminalization of gendered and racialized populations – men of color, in this specific instance – and the proliferation and consolidation of racist discourses. As stated previously, a non-essentialist analysis of sexual violence requires opening up the categories of men and women into notions of feminine and masculine positions. Only then is it possible to see how women are not exempted from, but may be deeply implicated in, such masculine logics and their effects.

The third problematic aspect of a view of sexual violence based on male-biological instincts is its inability to link sexual violence with broader political aspects of our identity, such as those related to our ethnicity or nationality. According to our view, in order to understand sexual violence one needs to consider the broader political context, in particular the role of the state. From this perspective, sexual violence functions as a sort of "identity technology," which aims to consolidate or annihilate certain specific (gendered/sexual/racial/national) identities. In other words, sexual violence can be viewed as an intervention in the world which *produces* identities and social relations. As we demonstrate in the case studies that follow, sexual violence can be used as a social technology through which notions of nation, ethnic identity and belonging are fabricated, or indeed, destroyed. The connection between sexual violence and projects of nation-building is in part due to the way the body of women, as in the figure of the archetypal mother and reproducer, is often made to stand for the nation in a range of contexts. Women represent the future, in both cultural and biological terms. Culturally, because women are seen as embodying the main values of the community and as the bearers of the identity and honor of the group. Biologically speaking, women represent the future because it is assumed that through reproduction a certain "pure genetic pool" is passed from generation to generation. Men, on the contrary (and through masculine-militaristic ideologies), are often presented as the guardians and saviors of those identity boundaries. As we will see in the case studies that follow, one of the main ideas behind nationalist ideologies has to do with the "myth of origin," which means that one can only join the collectivity if born into it. Sexual violence in this context is often the result of attempts at "purifying" the nation from perceived threats or forms of cultural pollution.

Bosnia, Rwanda, and Abu Ghraib Prison

As stated above, sexual violence, and particularly rape, is often connected to myths about an irrepressible male sexual drive. However, sexual violence cannot be explained simply as a result of a pre-social sexual instinct; rather it is related to racial and complex gender-social processes. As a form of power, sexual violence either contributes to the reinforcement of existing power relations (between different members of a community or between different communities), or it aims to re-establish structures of power that are being challenged. Now, although rape is an instrument of violence which attempts to degrade, dehumanize and humiliate the victim, it would be misleading to assume there is nothing "sexual" about it. Indeed, one of the most complex issues to understand is precisely the interplay of power and sexual desire, or more specifically, the way power operates through the sexualization of racialized bodies.

Let's look at the following three case studies of Bosnia, Rwanda, and Abu Ghraib Prison in Iraq.

Bosnia

The demise of the Soviet Union was followed by declarations of independence by Slovenia and Croatia during 1991, and a year later was followed by the declaration of independence by Bosnia-Herzegovina, which led to a civil war between Serbs, Croats and Muslims. This war lasted several years and resulted in more than 100,000 deaths, the displacement of millions, and the rape of thousands of women and girls. In year 2000, 16 women survivors of the war in Bosnia testified in the "Foca Rape Trial" before the International Criminal Tribunal for the former Yugoslavia in what was the first international trial focusing on rape as war crime. Its verdict was that sexual enslavement and rape are crimes against humanity. In Bosnia, as well as in Rwanda, the aim of mass rape was to destroy a particular culture or ethnic group, and both cases were described by the court as experiences of "rape as genocide or ethnic cleansing."

As it has now been documented, Serbian attempts at building a "Greater Serbia" faced, among other challenges, low birth rates which led to government and the Serbian Orthodox Church policies that encouraged Serbian women to be "faithful to the nation" and become mothers. The Serbian low birth rate was lower than that of other ethnic groups (such as Albanians, Muslims and Romanians), and this trend was perceived as a threat to the purity of the Serbian nation. Thus, in the context of the war between the Croats and the Muslims of Bosnia-Herzegovina the idea of women as having a duty to produce more children became a policy of forced impregnation or forced maternity of Bosnian-Muslim women.

Although sexual violence occurred at different moments and with different purposes (as part of lootings and intimidation in order to terrorize the local residents; as forms of sexual torture of male and female prisoners; and as sexual slavery), the most striking form of sexual violence was aimed at reproducing the Serbian people and the consequent elimination of the Bosnian-Muslim community. The Serbs established mass-rape camps in public places such as hospitals, schools, hotels, etc., where women were raped repeatedly in order to increase the Serb population. Women who became pregnant received special attention and were denied the right to abort. Considering the fact that those children would grow up not with Serbian but Bosnian families, it is interesting to note here that this policy of forced impregnation assumed that the identity of those children would still be Serbian and not Muslim. This assumption shows how not only the "biological contribution" of the mother is denied, but also the cultural upbringing of those children.

Since female purity is a central value within Muslim culture, it has been argued that rape was also intended to "pollute" women, to debase them and in doing so destroy the basic pillars upon which Muslim families and communities were built. Indeed much debate has arisen regarding the double victimization of these women who, after rape, became outcasts in their own communities.

Rwanda

In the case of Rwanda, it has been argued that land disputes and economic hardship due to the civil war that started in 1990 helped radicalize Hutu militias and allowed them to recruit large number of unemployed boys and young men in order to fight the Tutsi. Certainly, the economic hardship suffered by the Hutu while Tutsi elites enjoyed a privileged social position during the era of Belgian colonial power bred ethnic resentment. In fact, tensions between the two ethnic groups go back to the period of Rwandan independence. After independence in 1961, the Hutu rose to power and pursued a social revolution which attempted to free the country from both colonialists and Tutsi (indeed, Tutsi went into exile during the 1950s and 1960s).

Within this already very tense social context, the murder of two consecutive Hutu presidents (1993 and 1994) by Tutsi rebels triggered the violence that in three months killed 75 percent of Tutsi people. Some 800,000 Tutsi died and an estimate of 250,000 to 500,000 women and girls were raped. Since Tutsi and Hutu lived side by side (as family, friends, neighbors), these killings were not only political but very personal. Hutu were forced to show loyalty, and if one was Tutsi one was often killed along with one's family, friends and neighbors.

As in the case of Bosnia, ethnic cleansing had a clear gender component. Although Tutsi men were blamed for social problems such as unemployment, anti-Tutsi propaganda was very much directed against women. The negative and threatening features of their alleged "promiscuity,"

503

arrogance and "sexual adventures" with foreigners helped to position them at the "outer" boundary of the Hutu nation.

Once violence started, men and boys were the first ones to be killed. Women, however, before being killed, were the target of atrocious sexual violence and torture. There were mass rapes, their breasts were cut off, their pubic hair burnt, and their genitals cut wide open with spikes and machetes. These brutal acts of violence against women show the way women's bodies come to symbolize a nation and their mutilation serves to intimidate and debase the enemy.

Abu Ghraib

In 2004, photographs of Iraqi prisoners being subjected to a range of sexualized acts at the hands of United States military personnel were made public and circulated among news media globally. The images portray the explicit sexual abuse of prisoners. In one image, for example, a young woman, the US soldier Lynndie England, holds a distressed prisoner on a leash against the background of the Abu Ghraib detention facility which is located near the Iraqi capital, Baghdad. In another image, Iraqi prisoners are made to pile up on top of each other simulating sodomy, as two US soldiers, Lynndie England and Charles Graner, smile and give the camera the thumbs up (Figure 71.1).

When these photos were first published, the images provoked outrage and anger. They seemed to expose practices of abuse and torture which contradicted the official American rhetoric which portrayed the military invasion of Iraq and the War on Terror as liberating. As these photos provoked a public outcry, the official response from the American military and government was to isolate the case, call it an exception, and prosecute the individuals responsible for the crime. From our perspective, we question whether this practice was an exception. We also wonder what sort of conditions allowed for this kind of abuse of power? And we ask: What racialized and sexualized image of the Muslim subject is conveyed in these practices?

As both an offensive weapon and an instrument of torture, these dehumanizing images implying male Muslims engaging in sodomy have a double effect. First, they project the Muslim subject as both sexually deviant and potentially homosexual. From the Islamophobic *and*

Figure 71.1a

Figure 71.1b

homophobic perspective that informs the perpetrators' actions – which considers the Muslim subject as inherently sexually conservative and socially illiberal – this appears as a cruel irony particularly tailored to offend the prisoners. The role of women as agents of torture brings yet a second symbolic layer worth analyzing here: it is *precisely* women who, in the gendered logic of the torturers, can inflict particular harm, as they can further feminize, emasculate, and therefore humiliate, the anonymous male Muslim subjects. This is an example of the dynamics which we have described previously as the feminization of the victim of sexual violence and the masculinizing of the perpetrator – regardless of the gender identification of the persons involved.

In the context of Abu Ghraib, sexual violence clearly functions as an "identity technology" which *produces* racialized, sexually deviant Muslim bodies alongside neo-colonial White female masculinity specifically deployed to humiliate the enemy. Sexual torture therefore functions through the racial prejudice, cultural stereotyping, gendered and homophobic imaginary of the perpetrators, the US military.

Structural violence during peace time

The cases discussed above suggest that sexual violence is often a deliberate weapon of war and have confronted us with the complex dynamic of the social construction of the enemy target. As we have shown, sexual violence during warfare functions as a form of technology which produces or annihilates certain types of gendered/sexualized/racialized identities. Although difficult to grasp, we have also attempted to stress the ambiguous relation between aggression and desire, or between violence and sexuality.

In this last section we would like to introduce the notion of structural violence. This idea speaks to the way violence is connected to broader social processes of economic exploitation, social marginality, and political exclusion. Also, structural violence is related to the way that certain bodies are deemed dispensable, not only during war, but also in peace times.

For example, the murders of women in the US–Mexican border region – notably in the Mexican town of Ciudad Juárez, in the border state of Chihuahua – have struck a chord in both popular and academic discourse. The systematic occurrence of hundreds of violent murders since the early 1990s has been deemed a *feminicidio*, that is, a form of systematic gender violence against women. The neologism *feminicidio*, or "femicide," reflects feminist activists' deliberate effort to highlight the importance of gender in violence, including genocide. This

505

case also underscores a key point: sexual violence extends well beyond the domain of war and conflict. As other scholars have documented, in a global economy there are certain populations, often women or poor laborers and migrants, who are construed as sources of exploitable and disposable labor. The labor regime of border regions in towns such as Juárez, in the context of a neo-liberal model of capitalism, determines whose lives are viable and whose lives are wholly dispensable. The rationale for the brutal sexually motivated murders of women in Juárez, therefore, is clearly sustained by this specific extractive industrial model but also by the wider symbolic frameworks which construct women as disposable. The "disposability" of the women working in the Juarez factories extends from the factory (where they constitute a flexible resource which can be done away with and easily replaced depending on market demands), to the street and into the home – all spaces where they can be assaulted and murdered with impunity.

The notion of structural violence also stresses the fact that violence is a dimension of social life, and as such, it is best studied and approached not as an aberration or anomaly of violent "individuals," but rather as something which occurs in routine social processes. In summary, several issues emerged in this chapter. The first one refers to the coupling of power and sexuality. Questions that emerge here, for example, are about "bio-power" or how our identities (bodies, desires and subjectivities) are linked to the operations of state power, and through which processes these bodies come to embody either the "honor of the nation" or an enemy. A second theme refers to the social consequences of sexual violence: how do societies rebuild themselves after episodes of sexual violence? How do victims of sexual violence reintegrate into their communities? As we have seen, this has been a difficult experience not only for the raped women but also for their children born with the stigma of war.

Finally, the notion of structural violence has also confronted us with questions of justice. As discussed above, new developments in the law have allowed us to recognize sexual violence as constitutive of warfare, and have provided new frameworks for understanding the possibilities for justice and reparation. However, as the examples discussed above also suggest, legal instruments are themselves the crystallization of cultural and historical processes. As such, they are often the expression of specific exclusionary and punitive logics – as illustrated in the analysis of the "myth of the black rapist" – and therefore they fall short in the realization of justice. The understanding of sexual violence as structural – and not exceptional – allows us therefore to acknowledge the most fundamental and problematic space of difference between the *socially situated law* and the always deferred *and yet to come in the realm of ethics*. It is this space of difference that sustains our critical approach to the study of sexual violence.

Bibliography

Davis, Angela. 1983. *Women, Race and Class*. London: Women's Press.
Puar, Jasbir K. 2007. *Terrorist Assemblages: Homonationalism in Queer Times*, Durham, NC and London: Duke University Press.
Yuval-Davis, Nira. 1997. *Gender and Nation*. London: Sage Publications.

Part 11
Global and transnational sexualities

Introduction

When commentators use the term "globalization," they are often referring to the idea that the world seems as though it is getting smaller. There are a number of ways in which the world is, at least figuratively speaking, getting smaller. For example, air travel (and fairly broad economic access to being able to use it) has made flying the distance between Washington, D.C. and London roughly the same as getting in a car and driving from Washington to Boston. Moreover, e-mail, Skype, and constantly updated websites mean that the world is getting smaller in terms of the time it takes information to travel – one goes on a trip to Japan and posts photos via Facebook before one's friends back home have even gotten out of bed for the day. Thus, two key aspects of globalization involve space and time compression – technologies make vast distances seems shorter and shape our expectations to send and receive information almost instantaneously.

Globalization as a concept also encompasses changes in the world's economic system that have accelerated since the 1980s. Japan, North America, the United Kingdom and Europe have largely shifted manufacturing jobs to other regions such as Southeast Asia or Latin America. These economic powers now have post-industrial economies that primarily employ workers in the service sector – jobs in retail, cleaning services, secretarial work, financial planning, health services, security services, food services, etc. This means that workers are on one of two economic tiers – upper-tier jobs that require higher education, pay reasonably well and provide benefits, while the lower-tier jobs feature part-time (or temporary) minimum-wage jobs with no benefits. The world economic system is tiered as well, with workers from poorer countries providing the cheap labor for the manufacture of consumer goods or the cheap labor of the hotel, restaurant and other service industries that cater to tourists.

Globalization is linked to the concept "transnational," which means extending beyond the boundaries of the nation. Transnational carries the connotation of movement across borders. To the degree that the world has become smaller through globalization, a higher proportion of peoples' lives are now transnational in some way than 30 years ago, meaning that they travel across borders to work, play, and live, and they have responsibilities to more than one nation.

Globalization and the transnational movement of people affect sexuality in a number of ways. As media/internet sources more widely circulate particular versions of Western heterosexual ideals, globalization has a homogenizing influence on cultural ideals such as the norms of masculinity or standards of beauty and what it means to be sexually desirable. Sometimes it is partially for sexual reasons that people move transnationally – tourists seeking adventure, others immigrating because they believe they will find more sexual freedom and acceptance in a new country. Or, sexual labor may be the means by which (primarily) women are able to finance transnational movement. Sexual labor may also be a means for migrating women to support themselves in a new country or supplement the low wages associated with post-industrial service work. Additionally, sexual stereotypes of "foreigners" have been a consistent part of the immigrant and migrant worker experiences, where they may be interpreted as more sexually promiscuous or sexually prude than the native population. These stereotypes greatly impact the experiences of transnationals.

It's difficult to predict where globalization and transnational movement will ultimately lead. While globalization is associated with having a homogenizing influence on sexual norms, there are also those who actively resist homogenization; this can happen in quite opposite ways. One type of response to globalization has been moral leaders who have created sexual revisionist national histories that claim that sexual openness to things like same-sex intimacy is merely part of Western cultural imperialism. Another type of response has been for sexual subcultures within countries to reject rigid sexual and gender binaries and rethink sex and gendered norms and practices in more diverse, boundary-breaking ways.

72

Condoms in the global economy

Peter Chua

SAN JOSÉ STATE UNIVERSITY, CALIFORNIA

Many of us think of condoms in terms of personal use. We may think about condoms as preventing disease and pregnancy, especially in the age of AIDS and high rates of teenage pregnancy. We may also think of condoms in terms of how they will affect our sexual experience. Will using condoms reduce pleasure? Will condoms interfere with the romance of sex?

Many sociologists and social researchers also study condom use. They have focused on condom use among different groups. In particular, researchers have been interested in condom use among groups at risk, such as young women and gay men. Researchers have also sought to understand the social factors that prevent condom use. For example, there are studies of the role of education and public information in rates of condom use among different groups. Much of this research is intended to be used by public and private agencies, often public health agencies, to minimize unwanted pregnancies and disease.

Studies of condom use have also been central to organizations that promote antipoverty programs. Since the 1970s, national and global organizations have linked overpopulation with increased poverty and have called for state-led population reduction programs. By 2000, many First World governments, international NGOs, and for-profit corporations have provided experts and financial resources to many Third World governments. These organizations promote programs encouraging condom use and modern birth control options – ranging from "natural" methods to contraceptive and permanent surgical procedures.

Whatever their successes, birth control campaigns and programs have also functioned to control women's sexuality by shaping how they think about and approach sexuality (see Russell, Sobo, and Thompson 2000). For example, Third World feminists argue that modern contraceptives have actually limited Third World women's autonomy (see Briggs 2002; Kluasen 2004). Many poor women of color in the Third World such as indigenous Peruvian women experience family planning as coercive and not helpful. Instead of gaining greater personal and household autonomy, these women have understood birth control policies as government attempts to affect their sexual thinking and family planning practices. Government programs have intimidated them through contraceptive use campaigns in the media that *promote one type of family (small, heterosexual)* and stigmatize other family arrangements. Moreover, medical procedures such as unsafe abortions and sterilizations have been imposed without their consent, and often having unhealthy consequences.

While the study of condom use is important, the study of condoms as commodities has been neglected. Condoms are a commodity or a good produced by corporations for profit. In this chapter, I want to look at this hidden side of condoms – the economic, global production of condoms as commodities.

Capitalism and condoms

The story of condoms begins in the late nineteenth century. With the greater availability of latex extracted from Third World rubber plantations in the 1880s and the development of mechanical assembly lines, the making of male condoms became industrialized. It was only until World War II that condoms were mass-produced, initially for soldiers and later for post-war middle-class consumers in many First World areas. With population control programs starting in the late 1950s and HIV prevention in the late 1980s, condom manufacturing grew rapidly to meet demands from governments, target groups, and new consumers.

For example, during the 1980s and 1990s, the southern Christian city of Dothan, Alabama, was the global condom-making capital. The area had two of the largest condom corporations: Ansell – makers of the Lifestyles brand – and London International Group – makers of the Durex brand. In these and other condom factories, the corporations made assembly-line employees work with chemically unsafe materials. They relied on improved machineries to produce more condoms and to check their quality, while intensifying and speeding up the employees' work without increasing wages. In these ways, the assembly-line employees worked harder and earned the same pay, while more condoms were mass produced and the corporations obtained greater profits.

Work tasks in the Dothan plants were highly segregated along racial and gender lines. Such segregation often makes sexual harassment and intimidation possible. For instance, white men and white women held top executive and management positions. Working-class white men typically operated dipping machines that extrude latex or synthetic condoms. They received extensive technical training to operate these huge machines. Black men operated machines that mixed chemicals and other materials. They received lower wages and less training opportunities, which limited their chance to operate extruding machines. Many working-class white women and women of color were concentrated in quality-testing positions. As low-skilled, less-desired, and lower-pay positions than machine operators, quality-testing required employees to pay detailed attention and to conduct testing accurately and fast. The lowest pay was reserved for hand packers, who were typically working-class women of color.

The drive for greater profits reduced labor costs. Eventually, sporadic global competition caused condom-producing corporations to close factory plants (as they did in Dothan and many parts of western Europe) and shift operations to new plants in Thailand, India, and other Third World areas.

Leading condom manufacturers have relied on contracts from governments for business, growth opportunities, and global distribution. For instance, the United States through its Agency for International Development (USAID) provided 10.4 billion US-made condoms as part of international development projects in 114 countries from 1969 to 2000. It gave out these condoms at no or subsidized costs for population assistance, reproductive health, and HIV/AIDS projects. As a result, US corporations and project contractors such as Macro International and John Snow Inc. benefited financially at the economic expense of poor and marginalized people. While the US government provided millions of dollars to reduce fertility and increase HIV/AIDS prevention in the Third World, most of the money actually stayed within the US, employing thousands of US residents over the years. In contrast, poor Third World people who were expected to gain a large share of the US development money and to have their lives improve dramatically simply got US-produced health media messages and US-made condoms.

My research shows that condom distribution as part of First World aid to Third World countries actually makes them more economically dependent on the First World and free-market solutions (Chua 2001, 2003). The continual dependency on condoms made in the First World, and on First World reproductive health experts, hampers many local Third World solutions aimed at reducing poverty. As such, many First World countries benefit from these trade, economic, and political arrangements, increasing inequalities between the First and Third Worlds.

Further, the marketing of condoms and other contraceptives in Third World nations is accompanied by certain ideas about gender and lifestyle. In particular, First World corporations and governments and agencies promote an ideology that associates "Western" lifestyles and values with progress and freedom. In other words, it is not just condoms that are marketed but modern Western ideals of personal and social life.

Governments and corporations – by themselves – are not able to create new condom markets. They have had to rely on global project contractors, national health and welfare organizations, and local groups to promote condoms aggressively in the media and targeted outlets, and to change local understandings of health, sexuality, and gender relations. Reduced visibility of state–corporate programs seeking to change the sexual behavior of "risk" groups would then occur when health and women's organizations (such as the global Family Health International and a Senegalese group, Agency for the Development of Social Marketing) aggressively promote a free market economy.

While often seen as small and local, these groups extend the interests of governments and condom-producing companies. Consequently, they restructure and infuse free-market solutions such as the privatization and commercialization of public health promotion. These solutions amplify local inequalities by unevenly allotting large amounts of financial support, training, and material resources, including the public distribution of condoms.

While the promotional materials produced by these organizations perpetuate static and idealistic images of family, class, and gendered sexuality, they evoke particular desires and identities among their targeted groups. In rural India, US-funded Population Services International (PSI) has promoted the popular *Masti* brand of condoms – *masti* meaning pleasure in Hindi. Executive Director for PSI-India Cindy Squires informed me during our interview that PSI redesigned the brand to promote the "new positive image of Indian men," which is connoted by a black silhouette stallion logo. PSI wanted something more subtle than the earlier *Masti* branding of a "classic macho man who takes charge," than other condom brands with more family-caring or erotically suggestive images. In particular, PSI wanted to make rural men – the brand's market niche – identify less as traditionally macho (as characterized by PSI) and to exude low-key sexual energy as the new ideal gender and sexual identity.

Still, some individuals and groups produce more unconventional readings of these condom images, materials, and promotions, generating racial, gender, sexual, regional, and economic identities in ways that are often unexpected. Take for instance the promotion of the US-sponsored TRUST Premiere condom brand during a car show in the Philippines sponsored by DKT International. While generating greater public awareness and media attention about condoms, the swimsuit winner of the car-show beauty pageant Liezl Pecson highlighted the gender contradictions of the event. She said: "This [to be pageant contestants] is one way of showing what we can do as women. … Beauty is not enough. We need a thinking mind and a compassionate heart to be able to exceed society's common notion that women are second class to men, and even to their cars." While DKT International expected to use cars and the objectification of young Filipinas to promote condoms to urban poor Filipino men and, in the long run empower women, Pecson made a point to acknowledge the contestants' sexualized experiences at the same time attempting to address gender subordination in her remarks.

Protesting condom use

Supporters of condom use continue to face challenges from at least two dissimilar positions. The first involves social morality. Often, social and religious conservatives take this position, arguing that condoms encourage immoral sexual activities. Some contend that condoms act as a barrier to the procreation of children in nuclear families. Thus, they argue condoms undermine the naturally ordained idea of a heterosexual family structure.

This position is most frequently directed at unmarried men and women (particularly the young), as it asserts that condoms encourage heterosexual sexual promiscuity by having sex outside marriage and with multiple partners. The position suggests young people would practice sexual abstinence if government programs and others would not make condoms available. Hence, condoms should be prohibited.

Many – including contenders of Neo-Malthusianism and the Modernist position – fault social moralists for their support of heterosexism and women's inequality, and their opposition to diverse and consenting sexualities.

In contrast, the second position protesting against condom use places stronger emphasis on social justice globally. This position highlights that social justice and social equity lessen when corporations and governments advocate condom use. It shows how the ongoing political and economic interests of corporations and governments have led to the lessening of free clinics, free condom distribution, and public campaigns on reproductive health and HIV/AIDS prevention in the Third World.

While Third World public health withers from privatization, corporations and non-profit agencies supported by First World governments increasingly strengthen private-sector infrastructures and make them responsible for providing reproductive health services and promoting healthy practices. The few who manage these infrastructures gain monetarily through long-term government contracts, and also through the excessive fees they charge their clients (who are often poor women). The higher fees for reproductive health services and contraceptives reflect greater commercialization of government programs, thereby reducing the proportion who can afford to get these services and commodities.

Even while privatization and commercialization of public health programs restrict poorer groups from participation, corporations and governments remain highly interested in scientifically studying and regulating the sexual attitudes and behavior of poor and other "risk" groups. The corporations and governments support this social scientific research on sexuality that intrudes in women's sexual lives with the goal of making them conform to expected norms about how they should think and act sexually. This treats women as malleable objects for research. Consequently, greater privatization, commercialization, and scientific surveillance widen the economic gap and power imbalances among various social groups, further disadvantaging women, the poor, and people of color.

Protest has emerged from the Third World, principally from groups who have different ideas about personal and community health. For instance, dissident healthcare groups in the Philippines criticize their government for encouraging private enterprise "at the expense of the Filipino people." Or, the Council for Health and Development, which serves rural Third World populations, argues that condoms and similar First World modern products are luxuries, often inaccessible to the rural poor. In general, Third World critics contend that the privatizing and commercializing of reproductive healthcare may actually limit access to contraceptives, increase corporate and expert control over people's lives, and reduce women's participation in healthcare decision-making.

References

Briggs, Laura. 2002. *Reproducing Empire: Race, Sex, Science, and U.S. Imperialism in Puerto Rico*. Berkeley: University of California Press.

Chua, Peter. 2001. "Condom Matters and Social Inequalities: Inquiries into Condom Production, Exchange, and Advocacy Practices." PhD dissertation, Department of Sociology, University of California, Santa Barbara, CA.

——2003. "Condoms and Pedagogy: Changing Global Knowledge Practices", in Kum Kum Bhavnani, John Foran, and Priya Kurian (eds). *Feminist Futures: Re-Imagining Women, Culture, and Development*. London: Zed Books.

Ginsburg, Faye D. and Rayna Rapp. 1995. *Conceiving the New World Order: The Global Politics of Reproduction*. Berkeley: University of California Press.

Hartmann, Betsy. 1995. *Reproductive Rights and Wrongs*, revised edn. Boston, MA: South End Press.

Kluasen, Susanne M. 2004. *Race, Maternity, and the Politics of Birth Control in South Africa*. Basingstoke: Palgrave.

Russell, Andrew, Elisa J. Sobo, and Mary S. Thompson (eds). 2000. *Contraception across Cultures: Technologies, Choices, Constraints*. London: Berg.

73

Sexual tourism

Interview with Julia O'Connell Davidson

UNIVERSITY OF NOTTINGHAM, UNITED KINGDOM

Julia O'Connell Davidson is Professor of Sociology at the University of Nottingham. She has spent more than a decade researching sex commerce in the affluent and developing world, and has written extensively on prostitution, child prostitution, sexual tourism, and "trafficking." Her most recent book is *Children in the Global Sex Trade* (2005, Cambridge: Polity), and she is currently involved in research on migrant domestic and sex workers in Britain and Spain.

What do you mean by sexual tourism?

In the 1970s, the governments of both Thailand and the Philippines began to pursue economic policies that placed tourism at the center of their plans for economic development. Both countries already had large-scale sex industries that were put in place to serve United States military personnel. By the 1980s, a visible segment of the tourism markets in Thailand and the Philippines consisted of men from the affluent, economically developed world (Western Europe, North America, Australia and Japan) who were attracted by the cheap commercial sexual opportunities available in these much poorer countries. In tourist-sending countries, there was a proliferation of small companies that offered "sex tours" as well as guide books that promoted travel to consume commercial sexual services. Destinations like Bangkok in Thailand and Manila in the Philippines were marketed as a sexual "paradise" for single men.

From the late 1970s through the mid-1990s the term "sexual tourism" was largely used to refer this form of tourism to Southeast Asia, a form of tourism that relied upon and reproduced racist and sexist fantasies, as well as economic and political inequalities. However, it is now widely recognized that other regions also attract tourists in search of plentiful and affordable sexual opportunities with exoticized Others (Latin America and the Caribbean, Africa, and the Indian subcontinent), and that sexual tourism is not always linked to a large-scale, formally organized sex industry. The further we move from the stereotypical view of "sexual tourists" as men who take organized sex tours to Southeast Asia, the more difficult it becomes to draw a clear boundary between "sexual tourism" and other forms of tourism, because tourism and sex are so often entwined. There have historically been strong associations between travel and sex, and today, in the age of mass tourism, sex is widely understood to be part of the tourist experience. Whether with their own spouse or partner, with other tourists, or with sex workers, many people expect to have more sex whilst on vacation.

How widespread is sexual tourism? Are there certain countries that are centers of sexual tourism, and why is it tolerated in these countries?

It is impossible to say how widespread sexual tourism is. Even when you can get good data on the sex sector in any given country or region, it's very difficult to determine what proportion of the sector owes its existence to tourism, as opposed to local demand, or demand from domestic or foreign military. Also, even when reliable data on tourism is available, it's hard to say what percentage of tourists engage in sexual-economic exchanges with locals. Additionally, the world of sexual tourism is fluid and changing. For instance, Thailand's popularity amongst men who travel with the purpose of buying sex dwindled fast in the 1990s, while Cambodia and Vietnam started to attract more of this type of sexual tourist; in the mid-1990s, Varadero was *the* hot sexual tourism resort in Cuba, but by the turn of the century it was losing this reputation, and sexual tourists were advising each other to go to other parts of Cuba in search of cheap sex. And because the development of sexual tourism is linked to broader political and economic factors (in particular the pursuit of neo-liberal economic policies in poor and developing countries), new sites continually emerge. Prague in the Czech Republic was not on the "sexual tourism" map in the 1980s, but by the mid-1990s it had gained a reputation as a city where tourists can readily buy sex; also since the mid-1990s, sites of sexual tourism serving demand from domestic tourists have been emerging in China in towns along the borders with Vietnam and Myanmar.

Why is sexual tourism tolerated? Economics is an important part of the answer. Often governments will turn a blind eye to a sex trade that is intimately linked to a flourishing tourist industry. In the 1980s and early 1990s, some governments viewed a close relationship between prostitution and tourism as inevitable. But today, after extensive campaigning against sexual tourism by various groups and a great deal of negative publicity for countries deemed to have a problem with sexual tourism, there are few government officials in any country who would still openly condone direct links between tourism and prostitution. But here's where the more general association between tourism and sex becomes a serious problem for developing nations that rely on tourism as their main foreign-exchange-earning industry.

These countries are now under pressure to suppress sexual tourism, but as they have been marketed in affluent tourist-sending countries as "sensual" and "exotic," and tourists often want sex, as much as sun, sea and sand, and as local and migrant people in tourist areas earn so little from other forms of work in the tourist industry, this is a tall order. To effectively prevent all forms of tourist sexual exchange from taking place would not only be extremely costly but would also require such draconian actions on the part of the authorities that it would almost certainly have a negative impact on the overall tourist trade. Thus, most governments in developing countries where sexual tourism takes place approach the problem with one eye open, the other eye shut. There are sporadic police clampdowns on the most visible forms of prostitution in specific resorts or towns (often at the end of the tourist high season, or following bad publicity about sexual tourism in that location), but then the authorities allow its re-emergence in another resort or town.

Is there sexual tourism in Great Britain and the United States? Does sexual tourism in these nations differ from that in poorer nations?

I think we can safely say that neither Britain nor the United States has ever been explicitly marketed as a dream destination for amorous heterosexual male tourists in search of gorgeous, willing women. But then we can also safely say that some tourists – both international and domestic tourists – buy commercial sexual services whilst vacationing in Britain and the United States, and for some, the consumption of commercial sex may be an integral part of the planned "tourist experience." For example, tourists are amongst those who use Nevada's thirty-five licensed brothels, and given the fact that Nevada is the only state in the US in which brothels can be legally operated, it seems probable that some tourists travel there specifically in order to consume both the spectacle of the "Wild West" brothel and the services of a sex worker.

Soho in London also attracts British and overseas visitors who wish to consume the spectacle of its red-light area, and there are heterosexual male tourists whose itinerary for a trip to London includes a visit to one of Soho's famous "walk-up" brothels. Some gay travellers, especially men, are attracted to destinations in Britain (London, Brighton, and Manchester in particular) and in the US (New York, Los Angeles, San Francisco, Miami Beach, to name a few) that have strong associations with gay history and/or identity and that also offer extensive opportunities for both commercial and non-commercial sexual experience. Male sex workers and sex club managers in such cities report that tourists (domestic travellers as well as visitors from Europe, Japan, Australia and elsewhere) represent a significant portion of demand for commercial sexual services.

But having said this, neither Britain nor the United States experiences the large-scale, highly focused forms of sexual tourism that are found in cities and resorts in economically developing countries. One obvious reason for this is that it would cost a great deal more to stay in London or Las Vegas for two weeks and pay for commercial sexual services every day than it would to do the same thing in Hanoi or Recife. Another important difference between sites of sexual tourism in developing and affluent countries is that, in poorer countries, tourism is often associated with what has been termed "open-ended prostitution." Rather than entering into brief cash-for-sex exchanges, sex workers will often provide anything from two hours to two weeks of full access to their persons, performing non-sexual labour for the tourist (shopping, tidying, washing, translation, and so on) as well as sexual labour. Also, in tourist destinations in poorer countries, there are individuals who do not identify as "sex workers," but who seek sexual relationships with tourists either in the hope of receiving gifts that will supplement their very low income, or because they wish to migrate to a richer country and hope to find a sponsor or marriage partner who will facilitate their migration.

This means that tourists can have sex with local or migrant people without necessarily thinking of themselves as paying for it. For example, a tourist might pick up a woman in an ordinary tourist bar, wine and dine her, take her back to his hotel for a night of passion, and when in the morning she asks for $15 for her taxi fare home, he can give her the money, and perhaps a little extra (because he knows these people are poor and he's a generous guy), without seeing this as payment for sexual services. It follows that sexual tourism in poorer countries can appeal to a much wider range of people – to those who are happy to contract for the sexual services of someone they know to be a sex worker, and also to those men and women who would not dream of having sex with someone they considered "a prostitute." The same opportunities for self-delusion are not available in Britain and the US, partly because sex workers who are willing to spend twenty-four hours with a client simulating a romantic adventure charge a great deal more, and partly because the tourist cannot draw on exoticizing racisms to shore up his or her fantasies of mutuality with regard to individuals who are so obviously much poorer and more vulnerable. An ordinary, middle-aged, white American woman on vacation in London is unlikely to start flirting with a homeless black teenage boy sitting on the pavements begging for spare change, then invite him out for dinner and back to her hotel for sex – his poverty would be too obvious for her to read his sexual acquiescence as motivated by anything other than material need, and his place in the social order too familiar for her to eroticize him as an "exotic" Other. But in Jamaica, many ordinary middle-aged white women from Europe and the US are perfectly willing to embark on "holiday romances" with impoverished local men and boys who flirt with them on the beach.

Can you tell us something about the people who are involved in selling and buying sex?

This is a difficult question to answer because, whether you're talking about affluent countries or developing countries, the sex sector is extremely diverse and also stratified in terms of earnings, working conditions, and the motivations of workers. So you get many different people selling sex – male, female, and transsexual, old and young, straight and gay, people from ethnic or racial majority and minority groups. You also get some highly educated and socially privileged people selling sex, and although many people trade sex because they're forced into it either by economic desperation or other factors, in both affluent and poor countries there are some people who elect to sell sex for more positive reasons. But I think it would be true to say that, for most people in developing nations, the decision to enter into sexual-economic exchanges with tourists is linked to material need and the absence of other opportunities for earnings or attaining personal goals such as migration or starting a business.

In most of the countries where sexual tourism is widespread, governments have had little choice but to enter into a variety of International Monetary Fund agreements and World Bank structural adjustment loans, sector adjustment loans and program loans over the past three decades, and the policy packages associated with these loans have had a devastating impact on the poor. Structural adjustment processes are widely reported to have undermined traditional forms of subsistence economies, led to high levels of unemployment, redirected subsidies away from social spending and basic commodities towards debt servicing, encouraged massive currency depreciations, and driven down wages of those in work. This helps to explain the rapid growth of the informal economic sector in the countries affected, as ordinary people desperately seek ways in which to earn a living, or supplement impossibly low-waged employment. For those who live in, or have migrated to, tourist areas, prostitution and other forms of sexual-economic exchange often have much greater earning potential than other forms of informal tourist-related economic activity, such as hair-braiding or selling fruit, sweets or souvenirs. And for those people who manage to find employment in hotels or tourist bars or restaurants, sexual relationships with tourists can be a way to supplement wages that are inadequate to live on.

The tourists who enter into sexual-economic exchanges with locals and migrants are also a diverse group. They can be men or women, straight or gay, seventeen or seventy years old, middle-class professionals or working-class budget tourists, single or married, and from any ethnic or racial group. They also vary in terms of their sexual practices and attitudes towards sexual life, because, as I've said, sexual-economic relationships in tourist areas in poorer countries can be organized in ways that tourists from affluent countries don't recognize as "prostitution," which means that even people (both straight and gay) who strongly disapprove of, or are sexually turned off by the idea of, commercial sex can get involved in sexual tourism.

Having said this, there is a distinct and sizeable subgroup of what I would describe as "hard core" sexual tourists. These are people for whom the desire for particular kinds of sexual experience (generally those which are expensive, scarce, or risky at home, such as sex with multiples of prostitute women or men, and/or with children, or transsexuals) is a chief part of the motivation to travel. Some hard-core sex tourists find the pleasures associated with a particular destination so great that they eventually decide to settle permanently in their chosen "sexual paradise." Such expatriates (or "sexpatriates") often play an active role in promoting sex tourism and organizing tourist-related prostitution in a given destination. Predominantly male, white, and heterosexual, the worldview of this type of sexual tourist is often aggressively racist, sexist, and homophobic.

What is the role of children in the sex tourism industry?

The United Nations' Convention on the Rights of the Child defines children as persons under the age of eighteen. A sizeable minority of those who enter into sexual-economic transactions with tourists in developing countries are children. Most are aged between fifteen and eighteen, though there are younger ones as well. Although these younger children are but a tiny fraction of the people involved in the general phenomenon of sexual tourism, they have been significant for the development of sexual tourism in some places. In particular, there are resorts or towns in a number of countries that do attract pedophile tourists and others with a focused interest in sex with children. Young children's presence in the tourist-related sex trade has also been the focus of intense interest and concern from non-governmental organizations (NGOs), journalists, and national and international policymakers, to the extent that many people now have the mistaken impression that sites of sexual tourism are largely peopled by pedophiles, small children, and their pimps.

Campaigns against child prostitution in general, and "child sex tourism" in particular, have assumed that there is a firm line of demarcation between adult and child prostitution. However, this does not reflect the realities of sex commerce. Those aged above and below eighteen typically work alongside each other, in the same conditions, serving the same clients. With the exception of a limited number of cases in which a small "niche market," catering to demand from pedophile tourists, has emerged, the role of children in sexual tourism is pretty much identical to the role played by their adult counterparts.

How does a child become involved in international sex tourism and sex trade?

Children who become involved in the sex trade are usually members of impoverished communities, and/or groups that are socially, economically, and politically disadvantaged on grounds of race, ethnicity, or caste, or groups that are forgotten, feared or despised by the wider community (homeless, gay, slum-dwellers, drug users). Poverty (alongside racism and other forms of discrimination and the social devaluation of women and girls) very often also plays a key role in the phenomenon of forced, debt-bonded, or indentured child prostitution, for children are vulnerable to this type of exploitation, when they and/or their parents or other adult carers do not enjoy basic economic and social rights.

Can you tell us something about the adults who participate in child prostitution?

"Pedophile tourism" is a reality, and numerous cases have been documented in which Western and Japanese men travel as tourists, or take up permanent or temporary residence in poor and developing countries in order to gain sexual access to local children. The countries targeted include Sri Lanka, Cambodia, Thailand, the Philippines, the Dominican Republic, Costa Rica, and Brazil. These men know that it is easier, cheaper and safer to obtain sexual access to a child in poor and developing countries than it is back home. Also, racism plays an important part, as does the illusion of sexual and emotional mutuality that is more easily sustained when relationships are not explicitly constructed as "prostitution." Many pedophiles claim they want affectionate, non-coercive, and reciprocal sexual relationships with children. In poor countries, tourists' relatively much greater economic power allows them to draw children into more open-ended and longer-term sexually abusive relationships, within which the economic basis of the relationship can be disguised as sympathetic "help" (food, clothes, school fees) or indulgence of childish fancies (toys, excursions). The adult can more easily tell himself that he is genuinely loved and wanted by the children who visit him and acquiesce to sex.

Still, pedophiles are a minority amongst sexual tourists. The majority of children trading sex are aged between fifteen and eighteen. They are often too physically mature to be of interest to pedophiles. In most societies, older teenagers' participation in sexual and economic life is considered in a different light from that of younger children. The age of sexual consent is set below eighteen in many countries, and a great deal of sexual and esthetic value is placed on youth, so that a 16- or 17-year-old is not necessarily perceived as childlike or sexually immature.

Sexual tourists generally rely on popular ideas about childhood and sexuality, and their own personal sexual preferences and moral values, to make choices between potential sexual partners of different ages. So, while some tourists may be at pains to avoid younger sexual partners, others do not care very much whether the local person they pick up is fifteen or twenty, providing they fancy the way the partner looks. I have interviewed many sexual tourists (aged anywhere between seventeen and seventy) who like "fit" young sexual partners – they are not necessarily seeking out someone under the age of eighteen, but how are they to tell the exact age of the locals who proposition them, especially given that many are drunk by the time they "pull"?

What are international agencies and national governments doing to combat sexual tourism and especially child prostitution? What success have they had?

The national governments of countries that send large numbers of tourists to the developing world appear to be doing absolutely nothing to combat sexual tourism. They have, however, responded to a campaign against "child sex tourism" – a campaign largely orchestrated by one NGO, End Child Prostitution, Pornography and Trafficking in Children for Sexual Purposes (ECPAT). A key objective of ECPAT's campaign has been to shift the perception that sex with children in poorer countries is a low-risk crime by encouraging laws and policies in both receiving and sending countries that will make the prosecution of foreigners who commit sexual offences against children abroad easier and more likely. ECPAT lobbied hard and with a good deal of success for tourist-sending countries to introduce extraterritorial criminal laws that would allow states to prosecute their nationals for sexual crimes perpetrated against children in other countries. By 1998, twenty countries had introduced extraterritorial laws pertaining to child sex offences committed abroad, but in many of these countries no court cases had yet been initiated. Germany, the country where most cases had been pursued, had only prosecuted thirty-seven people under these laws, and only six of these cases led to conviction. Campaigners also lobbied for action against those who organized "child sex tours," again with some success. The Australian government enacted legislation in 1994 designed to strengthen action against tour operators who promoted "child sex tourism," and Britain introduced a similar law in 1996. But again, there have been few prosecutions under such laws.

In 1996, a World Congress Against the Commercial Sexual Exploitation of Children was held in Stockholm, and the governments of 122 nations signed the Congress Declaration and agreed to implement an Agenda for Action focusing on national and international cooperation with regard to policing "child sex tourism," and measures for prevention, protection, and the recovery and reintegration of children affected. Some national governments in developing countries have subsequently introduced changes to laws that bring their legislation on child prostitution into line with Article 34 of the Convention of the Rights of the Child (which states that all those under the age of eighteen should be provided with protection against all forms of sexual exploitation and abuse); some have worked more closely with children's rights NGOs in relation to prevention and recovery and reintegration issues; a few have run or supported campaigns to inform tourists that sex with minors will not be tolerated in their country. However, for obvious reasons it is very difficult for governments of poorer countries to implement the kind of measures that would be necessary to provide children with meaningful economic alternatives to sex work, and, without this, everything else looks very much like window-dressing.

I am increasingly cynical about campaigns against "child sex tourism." First, although NGOs involved in campaigns against "child sex tourism" have been keen to work with the tourist industry to combat the problem, because they focus attention on the minority of "deviant" tourists who travel in pursuit of sex with young children, they actually ask very little of that industry. Hugely profitable multinational corporations are applauded for assisting with the distribution of baggage tags emblazoned with the logo "No to child sex tourism!", for agreeing to monitor accredited members of travel agents' associations to ensure they are not advertising "child sex tours," for being willing to show in-flight videos telling people that it is illegal and wrong to have sex with 6-year-olds. But the industry is not being similarly pressured to address questions about the derisory wages paid to hotel workers, or to think about how this might connect to the phenomenon of sexual tourism, including that involving children. Nor have campaigns focused public attention on the social and environmental costs of tourism as an industry, or the fact that profits from tourism are largely repatriated to affluent tourist-sending countries and so will never "trickle down" to those who pick up tourists' litter, clean their toilets, make their beds, serve their food, and fulfill their sexual fantasies.

Second, campaigns against "child sex tourism" have emphasized that this is an international problem because those who exploit children cross national borders to do so, and this has encouraged a tendency to imagine that all we need are stronger laws and stricter law enforcement to "smoke out and hunt down" the bad guys. But "child sex tourism" is also an international problem in the sense that it is directly linked to the neo-liberal policies forced on developing countries by the IMF and the World Bank, policies that have encouraged economic dependence on tourism whilst simultaneously slashing public expenditure on services such as health and education, increasing unemployment, and reducing the already low living standards of the poor. In other words, these policies have created a situation in which large numbers of people willing and able to pay for sexual services are brought together with large numbers of people – adult and child – for whom selling sex is the best or only means of subsisting. For this reason, I would argue that sexual tourism is a problem of global justice, as much or more than of criminal justice, a point that often gets lost in campaigns against "child sex tourism."

Third, those who campaign against "child sex tourism" insist that children should not be stigmatized for their involvement in the commercial sex trade. But they generally remain silent about the stigmatization and criminalization of adult women in prostitution for fear of alienating potential allies, especially religious and other morally conservative thinkers. Similarly, although homophobia is often a factor precipitating teenage boys' entry into the sex trade, campaigners against "child sex tourism" have seldom sought to develop links with those who campaign for lesbian and gay rights. I don't believe it is possible to leave intact profoundly conservative gender and sexual ideologies that allow for the routine and systematic violation of the human rights of sex workers and homosexuals, and yet secure some kind of "stay of execution" for those aged under eighteen. It's therefore no surprise to find that governments of poorer countries have often responded to campaigns against "child sex tourism" by engaging in extremely brutal clampdowns on female sex workers in tourist areas, and that the numbers of women and teenagers who have ended up deported, or behind bars, or in "re-education," "rehabilitation," or whatever euphemism is preferred, as a result of international concern about "child sex tourism" far outstrips the number of Western pedophiles or "sex tour" operators who have been similarly treated.

74

Migrant sex work and trafficking

Sorting them out

Laura Agustín

INDEPENDENT SCHOLAR. BLOG: BORDER THINKING ON MIGRATION, TRAFFICKING AND COMMERCIAL SEX,
WWW.NODO50.ORG/LAURA_AGUSTIN/

When trafficking is mentioned in the media these days it's usually linked seamlessly with sexual abuse, exploitation, pimps, slavery and ruined lives. Although some hold that we live in a postfeminist world, everyone seems predisposed to assume the worst about women who sell sex – especially how helpless and sexually vulnerable they are, just because they were born female. My research over the past 15 years has broken the many suppositions behind such clichés into manageable pieces, not to say everything is hunky-dory but to get closer to the actual problems rather than the sensationalist, sexist fantasies. The fact that the problems have little to do with sex itself is illustrated in the following description.

A few years ago I met five women in Thailand and Australia, at the request of local NGOs who wanted a Spanish-speaker to visit them. In Sydney I was introduced to the owner of a legal brothel and two of her workers; in Bangkok I visited two undocumented migrants in a detention centre. The women came from Peru, Colombia and Venezuela and were mostly middle-class, although one had little formal education. But their travel stories were diverse.

The brothel owner was a permanent resident in Australia. Her migrant workers had come on visas to study English that gave them the right to work, but they had been required to pay for the entire eight-month course in advance and were in debt. The madam treated them well but kept them close, living in her house and travelling with her to the brothel.

One of the women in the detention centre had been caught with a fraudulent visa at Tokyo airport and deported back to her last stop, Bangkok. Originally invited to join her sister in Japan, she spent a year jail before being sent to the detention centre. The other detainee had been caught during a robbery carried out by her travelling companions in Bangkok (one stop on their travels around Southeast Asia). She spent three years in jail before being sent to the centre (and, by the way, all her papers were false, including a change of nationality). Both women were in the centre because they had no money to pay their plane fare home, and, so far, no one was offering to pay it for them, since both were complicit in the plans for their non-legal travel and work – disqualifying them as victims of trafficking.

The two recently arrived migrants in Sydney seemed to accept doing sex work, but they didn't have much choice of jobs, given the cost of the language course and their inability to speak English. The migrant to Japan said she believed she had not been destined to sell sex even though her sister had, but she felt guilty because her own family had been involved in getting her false papers. The woman caught in the robbery had sold sex informally during her travels, and seemed satisfied she'd be able to make money that way. The numerous people involved in these arrangements were said to be Pakistani, Turkish and Mexican.

Complex, ambiguous stories like these are often described and denounced as sex trafficking. Much of the outcry revolves around an abstract point – whether prostitution can ever be seen as a "real" job. This question is less relevant to undocumented migrants who have no visas allowing them to work in *any* legal job. Travels that involve selling sex are often talked of as though they were inherently different from all other kinds of travel to work, mostly because migration in general is little understood. In this chapter I'll examine generalisations that erase individual experiences and lead to non-productive debates. I'll look at ideas about migration, job markets, the informal economy, the sex industry, trafficking – and the idea of good sex itself.

Why do people leave home?

> You work, work, work and then they don't pay you, because there's no money … I worked in an ashtray factory, and when there was no money to pay me they said "take ashtrays," 100 ashtrays. So? Can you eat ashtrays?
>
> *(Ukrainian woman in Spain: Agustín 2005)*

> There wasn't any work and I wanted to be independent. I have a big family, but I didn't get along with them. I wanted to be on my own. I saw the neighbours who are doing okay, who have money because there's someone in Italy.
>
> *(Nigerian woman in Italy: Danna 2004)*

Both these migrants were selling sex when researchers spoke to them. Scholars explaining why people move to another country to work cite many causes: international structural conditions and globalisation of markets; national immigration policies; the feminisation of poverty; wage differentials between countries. They talk about loss of land, recruitment by foreign employers, the desire to join family abroad, flight from violence, persecution and natural disasters. Any single person may have multiple reasons to consider migrating, but no single condition guarantees that he or she *will* migrate. None of the theories accounts for the desires and aspirations that poorer people feel, just as richer ones do (to see the world, to get ahead, to escape limited lives), or for personality traits that make a migration seem plausible to some people and not to others (willingness to take risks, ability to tolerate uncertainty).

Working in informal economies

Legal jobs (in what's known as the formal sector) are regulated and tracked in government accounting. Legal migrant workers possess a work permit and visa; if they work in the informal economy, where no permits can be had, they are not working legally. This fact does not discourage many people from travelling or migrating, however, since they know that jobs in informal economies are plentiful all over the world. That is, they know that if they get across the border, someone will hire them, because there are jobs open. That migration policies don't mention these flourishing markets is confusing, since many of the jobs available are fairly ordinary, if non-prestigious, and can serve to bring in incomes significant to migrants and enhancing social life: manual labour on construction sites, farm labour, live-in domestic service and caring for children and the elderly in private homes, factory labour, restaurant kitchen employment, cleaning, home piecework and a wide variety of jobs in the sex industry. To take advantage of such jobs, migrants must first arrive.

Legal status is limited to entering as a tourist, student or temporary business traveller with the appropriate visa, or to enter with a job offer and formal working papers in hand. Obtaining a tourist visa can be next to impossible for citizens of many countries, or may require years of waiting because of country quotas. Or the potential tourist/migrant may be able to get a visa but not have the money to buy tickets and survive while looking for work. The imbalance between jobs available to migrants and visas offered to them creates a niche for those able to provide services to undocumented migrants. Many who want to travel search actively for help getting around the rules at home, while others search for them, to sell them trips and jobs. These vendors in the informal economy are known by a variety of names, from businessmen and travel agents to coyotes on the Mexican border and snakeheads in China. They are often relatives or friends, and they may be tourist acquaintances met during vacations who bring friends over to visit or work. Marriage may be part of the deal. Intermediaries may play a minimal part in the migration project or offer a package which links them closely to migrants every step of the way.

Without access to a charge account or formal bank loan, the would-be migrant probably goes into debt to pay for services that may include the provision of passports, visas, changes of identity, work permits and other documents, as well as advice on how to dress and handle interviews with immigration officials or police, the loan of money to show upon entrance with a tourist visa, pick-up service at the airport, land transport to another country or to pre-arranged lodgings, and names of potential employers. These services are not difficult to find in countries where out-travel has become common, and, in certain countries, formal-sector travel agents offer them under the table. Furthermore, for unauthorised migrants, no matter what job they get, under-the-table services continue to be needed after borders are crossed.

Migrating involves a series of risky judgements and decisions. Each step of the way, migrants must weigh information they're given against what they have heard from returned migrants, friends and family living abroad and news reports. Whether migrants buy a full package from a single entrepreneur or make a succession of smaller decisions, only one link in the chain needs to be weak for things to go wrong. Moreover, people who are over-eager to travel may do little research to test information given them and connive in situations that later make them vulnerable. The relationships are further complicated when intermediaries are migrants themselves. Institutions in countries of origin, including embassies and consulates granting visas, know that people are migrating quasi-legally or illegally. These countries have come to rely on money sent back by migrants. It is no wonder that migrants fail to view themselves as really "illegal," much less criminal. Intermediaries, many friends and families of migrants, are also not all criminal exploiters. Such networks have always existed, but only with heightened attention to the sex industry has this varied group been attacked en masse as unequivocally violent and cruel. Travel that results in selling sex is often positioned, in the mass media and amongst social crusaders, as different from all others.

Travelling to work in the sex industry

Selling sex may make travel possible, providing the money to buy tickets. It may be the way people from the countryside or small towns can begin to make a living in cities while they look for other jobs. Or it may be the most lucrative job available once people have arrived at their destination. All kinds of vendors, including domestic and sexual, follow soldiers on campaigns, pilgrims and seasonal and itinerant workers such as miners, seamen and farm workers. Mobility has been associated with selling sex throughout history; some Europeans migrating to the Americas and Australia sold sex to finance their voyages in the eighteenth and nineteenth centuries. These migrations were sometimes called "white slavery," to distinguish the migrants from formerly enslaved Africans. Avidly covered by the press, the idea that white women were forcibly prostituted created an international movement dedicated to its eradication. Research has shown that many or most of these women migrants (like today), simply saw a chance for new lives in other lands and were willing, at least temporarily, to sell sex to get a chance at them. Between the last upsurge of trafficking discourse and now, *the way* people migrated was not considered of great interest – in dramatic contrast to the present. Now the slavery idea is back in full force.

The sex industry, largely unregulated and outside official government accounting, operates through informal networks; to gain access, newcomers must meet an insider. The haphazard nature of this information economy is illustrated by a Ukrainian woman's story:

> Once I was talking with a friend and she asked if I wanted to go to Spain. I knew why, so I said: "Ah, do you want to … ?" and I don't know where she met this guy, he got the papers for us, made the passport, everything, the money and we left … This guy went to look for work, where are the best places to work, where there are men … He talked first with the boss … said he was looking for work for us.
>
> *(Agustín 2001)*

Many who work in the sex industry knew that their jobs abroad would have a sexual dimension, but they probably did not understand how they would feel or what working conditions would be. The commercial sex they knew about at home may have little in common with the options they have now: standing almost nude in a window or by the side of a highway for many hours, or doing hand jobs in a massage parlour all day, with little other social contact with clients. When part of the migration package included signing a contract without understanding what it meant, the value of foreign money or the language in which the contract was written, problems can obviously become severe. But, even when migrants say that they were deceived, it's not the sex work per se they want to get out of; often they would like to remain in the industry, but in less exploitative conditions.

> A friend proposed that I come, she knew a girl who could bring me … You sign a note for seven million pesos [€4,207] and they tell you that you can pay it back working for a month. You know what you're going to be doing. Anyone who says she didn't know, it's a lie, a married lady with children, how can she not know what she's going to be doing here? When you arrive, you crash, because the work is bad and it's a lie that the debt can be paid in a month. You talk with the other girls and see that the debt is more than it cost the girl to bring you. [But] I want to pay her, because she takes a risk, too, to bring you over …
>
> *(Oso 2003)*

Paying off debts in the shortest amount of time is nearly every migrant's primary goal, so the focus is on the future, not on past abuses. While the most tragic situations so often cited by the media and nongovernmental organisations come to light precisely because the police have become involved, reporters and activists seeking victims do not meet migrants who have *not* sought help, and some of them don't want to be found and rescued. In many cases, family or friends have collaborated in deceiving or misleading migrants. Sometimes, recently arrived and disoriented migrants feel psychologically dependent on intermediaries, who then can exercise too much control or influence. In the worst cases, migrants are threatened and held against their will, their personal documents are withheld and they are forced to have and sell sex.

> As soon as I was brought to Turin I understood that I had ended up in a blind alley: I found myself with a madam who ordered me onto the sidewalk and wanted 50 million [lire] [€25,800]. It was a real nightmare, I cried all the tears I had.
>
> *(Kennedy and Nicotri 1999)*

> Every girl that worked for Cindy knew which day she was going to be there and that she had to give her the money or deposit it in her account. Later Cindy would stay a while in each place where she had left girls ... at the same time she was maintaining control over what happened to them.
>
> *(Likiniano 2003)*

These kinds of situations have prompted not only appropriate concern but also a moral panic that drastically generalises *all* cases as dire and excludes more complicated stories like those at the beginning of this chapter. The words *force* and *exploitation* are bundled into a monolith that sweeps away individual migrants' degrees of knowledge, will and desire. Some women, for example, *feel forced* who could physically escape; others start out doing domestic work but *feel obligated* to sell sex because of the differential in pay, in order to send more money home or pay off debts faster.

The difficulty is that the fundamental terms of the argument attempt to pin down enigmatic issues of will, consent, understanding and choice – the extent to which people travelling with false papers understood the possible consequences of using them, whether they felt love for someone facilitating their journey, whether they knew what a contract meant, how their parents' participation in a deal affected their judgement, if they realised the consequences of being in debt. Such epistemological questions are often unfathomable when involving people secure in their homes, but they become even more so when those involved have left their homes behind to face cultural disorientation on a grand scale through migration. It is also patronising to assume people don't understand that all projects to change one's life involve risks. Women selling sex in Nairobi were asked if they realised it could be dangerous, to which they replied that they were not selling sex in order to live safely but to earn money and be independent (Pheterson 1996).

The purpose of showing the many forms a migration can take is not to deny that some forms are dangerous and unfair but rather to avoid homogenising hundreds of thousands of women's experiences and reducing all to a single supposedly universal truth. It is, of course, harder to deal with multiple, confusing levels of innocence and guilt, criminality and victimhood. But if we try to do that, we find that sex itself is not the centre of most stories.

The sex in sex work

> I don't understand what is bad about selling love for money ... With this job I have made it possible for all my brothers to study and I have supported my mother, so I am proud of being a prostitute.
>
> *(Nigerian woman in Italy: Kennedy and Nicotri 1999)*

Is it hard to believe that some people prefer selling sex rather than washing dishes, babysitting, or picking fruit? Consider that migrants, who come in all sizes, shapes and colours, and from infinitely varying backgrounds, need to be flexible and adaptable to succeed. They often do not know beforehand how they will be living, and they may not know the language. They may fear the police and feel enormous pressure to pay back debts. Their past work experience and diplomas, whether white-collar or blue, are usually worthless. Migrant schoolteachers, engineers, nurses, hairdressers and a range of others find only low-status, low-paying jobs open to them. Many of them, from everywhere on the social spectrum and of every gender identity, prefer to work at least temporarily in the sex industry, in one or another of a variety of jobs.

Bars, restaurants, cabarets, private clubs, brothels, discotheques, saunas, massage parlors, sex shops, peep shows, hotel rooms, homes, bookshops, strip and lap-dance venues, dungeons, webcam sites, beauty parlors, clubhouses, cinemas, public toilets, phone lines, shipboard festivities, as well as modelling, swinging, stag and fetish parties: sex is sold practically everywhere. Where these businesses operate without licenses, undocumented workers with nothing to lose can easily be employed: this is a paradox of prohibition. Already working illegally, migrants may consider these jobs no riskier than others and even advantageous.

> One day I met a friend of mine while I was walking in the town centre … I learned that she was a prostitute so her children could live in a decent way. This work has the advantage of financial ease and freedom to work schedules that allow spending more time with the children.
>
> *(French woman of Algerian parents in France: Cabiria 2002)*

On the other hand, selling sex is definitely not for everybody, and some migrants will take on worse-paid or riskier jobs to avoid it: many live-in maids in the first case, "mules" transporting drugs inside their bodies in the second.

What is it that outrages people about women who sell sex? Why are some sexual jobs considered worse than others? Why do some people think better-educated women with more job opportunities *can* choose to sell sex while poorer women cannot? What's going on when people in privileged countries set out to rescue women in the Third World from the sex industry?

The idea of good, and equal, sex

In this day and age, many people believe that sex should express love and that "good sex" must be loving. It is assumed that feelings of love intensify pleasure and that the resulting passion is meaningful and should lead to long-term, emotionally committed relationships. Departing from this supposition, other kinds of sexual relations appear to be inferior: anonymous, public, promiscuous, uncommitted, non-monogamous and commercial.

In the case of commercial sex – all the many varieties – convention would have it that the presence of money means a sexual relationship cannot be good because the parties are not equal. But what does *equal* mean here? One idea holds that sexual intimacy and money must be kept separate, because the person with money has the power to command and control what the other does. But that's not how people talk about buyers of other intimate services like psychotherapy, or services involving physical contact like chiropractics, acupuncture, manicure or therapeutic massage. Does anyone think these professionals' clients have all the control? The reply says that using the body isn't the problem per se but that when sexual organs are involved, everything is different, because sex is key to our innermost selves and when we have sex without love we alienate our deep personal identities. This makes sense to you or it doesn't, but cannot be proved. On such grounds all sexual jobs are decreed soulless, mechanical and damaging activities *when the person providing the sex is a woman*: this idea forms part of a larger theory about violence against women that sees women as particularly sexually vulnerable to men who are prone to violence and invasion and who will, given the opportunity of paying for sex, behave violently or demeaningly. This set of ideas about women's sexual vulnerability must be situated in time and culture: not that long ago, vaginas were imagined to be dangerous and devouring and prostitutes to be aggressive, violent women who mugged and robbed potential customers.

The demand that sexual relationships be equal plays a central role in framing migrant sex workers as victims of trafficking. If it's assumed that women from other cultures, because they are economically poorer, are backward, passive, vulnerable objects existing only to be exploited by men with money, then all sexual exchanges between them can be condemned as inequitable. This only works, however, if no other conditions are taken into account: the possibility of strong, controlling sex workers and unassertive clients; migrants' hard-headed determination to get ahead; many people's ability to separate their sexual experiences into meaningful and non-meaningful or into work and play; many workers' affectionate or conventional relationships with clients.

Everyone does not feel the same way about sex: that's the pure and simple of it. Everyone does not think sex is utterly different from all other human activity, or feel their personal identity is linked to it, or think that enjoyable sex must always lead to monogamy or means they are in love. Or that money changes or ruins sex. The suspicion that non-loving, non-committed-partner sex is amoral is recurring at the same time that forms of commercial sex are proliferating. So although we tell a powerful story about sex and love belonging together, we also understand that people want other kinds of sex, and, in fact that present-day searches for personal identity often encourage sexual experimentation. Only the sketchiest data can be gathered when businesses operate outside the law, as sex businesses do in many societies, so we cannot revert to a body of facts that tell us how much exploitation and unhappiness exist relative to how much empowerment and wellbeing. We hear about people who buy and sell sex from our friends, acquaintances, the media, and sometimes through reporting on migration – which is where sex trafficking comes in.

To understand why headlines and social commentators scream that all migrant women who sell sex are victims of trafficking, we need to go back to the still hegemonic idea that the proper place for sex is at home between committed lovers and family. This idea is particularly applied, for not the best of reasons, to people from poorer and non-Western cultures, so that it's imagined that people uprooted from there are particularly sad cases, with women who sell sex abroad imagined to be saddest of all. That notion requires us to reduce migrants to pawns on a global economic chessboard where they have no will or agency at all. Even those who concede that poorer migrants may want to leave home and even prefer to sell sex often insist that they are not *really* choosing anything because capitalism's structural conditions make them into victims by definition. Add that analysis to an emotional antipathy to selling sex and you see why headlines scream.

Positioning most of the world's women as pathetic sexual victims does serve to make their rescuers feel important, and there's no doubt that some people are helped and saved by campaigners. But the neocolonialism required to ignore what so many migrants say about themselves – their experiences, feelings, desires – is a backward step for women's movements that originally hoped to de-link women and sex as an inevitable couplet. It fails to respect different cultures and imposes values *currently* considered the best, rather than looking at the personal or local.

Many migrants reject being defined as sexually vulnerable and in need of rescue and protection.

> When you work a lot in one place then you ... you get tired of the clients ... Even
> though it will be the same, you imagine another place with other people, and then you

come to life inside … I go to another country, another city. Lately I live between Mallorca and Barcelona … In summer I always go to Mallorca to spend a little time with my son.

(Latin American woman in Spain: Cuanter 1998)

Sometimes I enjoy working; I can travel and see beautiful places. I can go to nice restaurants. I enjoy that the Turkish men view us as desirable.

(Ukrainian woman in Turkey: Gülçür and İlkkaracan 2002)

Granting migrating individuals the capacity to make decisions does not mean denying the vast structural changes that push and pull them. On the other hand, it does not mean making them over-responsible for situations largely not of their own making, as global, national and local conditions, as well as luck, intervene in individuals' decisions. As far as the sex goes, it takes too many forms, in a huge proliferation of venues and cultural contexts, for any generalisation to be made (Agustín 2007). If you are interested in complexity and challenge, this subject area is for you!

References

Agustín, Laura. 2007. *Sex at the Margins: Migration, labour markets and the rescue industry.* London: Zed Books.

——. 2005. "Migrants in the mistress's house: Other voices in the 'trafficking' debate." *Social Politics: International Studies in Gender, State and Society,* 12(1):99.

——. 2001. "Mujeres inmigrantes ocupadas en servicios sexuales." In *Mujer, inmigración y trabajo,* ed. Colectivo Ioé, 647–716. Madrid: IMSERSO.

Cabiria. 2002, 2004. *Rapport de synthèse.* Lyon, France: Le Dragon Lune.

Cuanter. 1998. "Las notas características de la prostitución y su acceso a los Servicios Sociales." Madrid: Instituto de la Mujer.

Danna, Daniela. 2004. *Donne di Mondo: Commercio del sesso e controllo statale.* Milan: Eleuthera.

Gülçür, Leyla and İlkkaracan, Pinar. 2002. "The 'Natasha' experience: Migrant sex workers from the former Soviet Union and Eastern Europe in Turkey." *Women's Studies International Forum,* 25(4): 411–21.

Kennedy, Iyamu and Nicotri, Pino. 1999. *Lucciole Nere. Le prostitute nigeriane si raccontano.* Milan: Kaos.

Likiniano. 2003. *Tráfico y Prostitución: Experiencias de mujeres africanas.* Bilbao, Spain: Likiniano Elkartea.

Oso, Laura. 2003. 'Estrategias migratorias de las mujeres ecuatorianas y colombianas en situación irregular.' *Mugak,* 23:25–37.

Pheterson, Gail. 1996. *The Prostitution Prism.* Amsterdam: Amsterdam University Press.

75

The public and hidden sexualities of Filipina women in Lebanon

Hayeon Lee

INDEPENDENT SCHOLAR, LEBANON

There are about 200,000 migrant women domestic workers – the majority from Sri Lanka, Ethiopia and the Philippines – in Lebanon, which has a population of about 4 million. Although the Philippine government officially banned citizens from coming to Lebanon following the July War in 2006, an estimated 40,000 Filipinos, mostly female domestic workers, still live and work in Lebanon. Since 1975, migrant women have gradually replaced Lebanese and other Arab women from poor backgrounds, who once made up the dominant domestic labor force (Jureidini 2009). In recent years, the human rights situation of domestic workers has been of public interest due to widespread media coverage of the abuse of these women, as this appears to have led to several suicides. However, the mechanisms of power behind these abuses are often overlooked, as are the complex ways in which Filipina women negotiate within these power structures in order to shape their lives in Lebanon.

Based on 37 interviews with Filipina women, 14 in-depth interviews with Lebanese employers, two interviews with recruitment agencies, and participant-observation mostly carried out in Beirut in 2007, this essay explores the sexuality of Filipina women. (All names have been changed for privacy.) The perceived sexuality of Filipina women – along with all the negative stereotypes – is often used as a means to control these women. Yet, I will argue that Filipina women do not surrender their sexual agency; they actively negotiate the challenges of living in an alien and sometimes hostile social environment, and this includes their sexuality.

Binit (girl) and *sharmuta* (whore)

The most common advice given to all madames[1] in Lebanon is to not let the live-in maid outside of the house alone. One recruiting agent named Ahmad always tells his customers, "Don't let her [the live-in maid] out by herself." He explains,

> My daughter [who is in her early teens], where she go out? She go to the school, she come back home, and if she goes out, she goes out with me or her mother. She's young. I don't let her go out alone. The housemaid, she comes to Lebanon. They are coming to work. She goes out with madame everyday ... You go to Hamra? You see the man? All the man in Beirut take girl. Go sleep with her. Give her money ... and she come back. She come

back good, [or] she come back pregnant. Or make love for one, two, three [men] for money … But the girl, she didn't know this man. Where he comes from, is he working or not. He sleep with her … He don't have AIDS or syphilis, you don't know … I prefer to don't let her out because I know the girl [who goes] out. They are free visa. They don't have license.

Ahmad makes several points. First, he likens the live-in maid to his own young daughter. It is not surprising that many Lebanese refer to the migrant domestic worker as a *binit* – or girl, with an undertone of virginity – sometimes even for women well into their forties. Since the keeping of a daughter's chastity is seen as crucial to upholding family honor in a patriarchal society like Lebanon's, the live-in maid, who works and lives at the employer's home and literally carries the employer's name on her residence card and work permit, is under the same rules as the daughter. However, when daughters are married, they receive recognition as adult women. As for the maid, she might never be treated as an adult – even when she arrives in Lebanon married and with children. As a naïve and gullible *binit*, the Filipina woman who comes back to her madame's house without AIDS or syphilis the first time she goes out is considered lucky; employers think, however, that it is only a matter of time that she will come back pregnant or diseased.

Sometimes, the fact that a *binit* is working in the private home without kin protection in a foreign country is translated as her being sexually available for male members of that home. While most interviewees have only heard of cases of rape, there were some who experienced sexual harassment. For example, the male employer of Lorna, a Filipina woman in her thirties, would from time to time hug her from behind, peek into her room while she was napping in minimal clothing, and make sexual comments. One time, when no one else was home, Lorna was terrified and ran to her room when her male employer showed up naked in front of her. Another time, he said that if she let him touch her breasts, he would pay her. "I don't need your money! Keep your money," Lorna shouted. Leonilda, a Filipina woman in her twenties, switched employers after first arriving in Lebanon, when the male employer of the family kept harassing her. "Sometimes he was taking a shower, but he will call you to give him something, like that. It's insult for you, *yanni* [I mean]. Especially me, I don't have a husband! [Laughs]. That's why I said, *la'* [no], I don't want," she said.

Second, Beirut is portrayed as full of dangerous men and temptations. This perception is strengthened by the widespread harassment Filipina women receive on the streets, more so than Lebanese women, who are also often treated as sexual objects. Many madames add that it is unsafe for the live-in maid to go out alone. They believe there are many bad men and women, who are often viewed as a *sharmuta*, or whore, and who are waiting to corrupt innocent live-in maids. For example, Nisrine, a Lebanese madame in her thirties, does not want the live-in maid to meet others "for her own sake and for ours … because I have a special relationship with her. I really like to keep it like this. [If I allow her to go out,] I will lose her I think." In addition, she believes Lebanon is unsafe for the maid. "Talk[ing] to strangers is very dangerous here in Lebanon. Security, *ma fi* [there isn't any]. One time, she was going to throw garbage very near, and after, I didn't let her. There was no electricity in the evening after ten o'clock, and then, someone stopped the car and he say, 'Come, come.' She was very scared, and I told her, 'You will not go, especially when there is no light on the road. Me or [my husband] will throw the garbage.'"

Third, there is no acknowledgement that domestic workers' sexual desires are natural. It is assumed that she is only here to work and it is common practice to bar her from socializing outside unless supervised, especially in the first few years of employment. For example, although Cynthia, a Lebanese woman in her thirties working for an international organization, is conscientious in terms of the Filipina live-in maid's treatment and workload, she does not allow the maid to have a day-off outside the house. She tells any Filipina live-in maid who works in her home, "The minute you decide that this is not your priority – working and making money for your family – and your priority is finding somebody, you tell me, you [must] leave."

It is convenient and economic for recruitment agencies to discourage madames to allow live-in maids to have a day-off outside the house: There is a three-month guarantee period for the customers, and if anything goes wrong, it is the agency that pays. And many madames, who pay up to US$2,700 to hire a woman from the Philippines to work in their home, are not willing to risk losing their "investment" after hearing stories of Filipina women sleeping with men, getting pregnant, running away, and bringing disease to their home. Furthermore, the *kafala* (sponsorship) system, along with domestic workers' exclusion from the labor law, ties workers to their Lebanese employer, creating a legal dependency of the former on the latter. Such an arrangement delegates near-absolute power to the employer to dictate her relationship with the live-in maid (Longva 1997:91–94). The negative sexual stereotypes of Filipina women often legitimize this control.

The stereotypes of Filipina women (and other migrant domestic workers) as naïve girls or whores are further reinforced by gossip, rumors, advice from family and friends, and horror stories. As James Scott points out, rumors tend not to only reflect a real event but speak to the desires and fears of those who spread it (1990:145). They are used to justify and regulate the behaviors of those who are subject to them. Madames themselves have commented on how, often times, conversations at tea parties, children's birthday parties, and other casual gatherings among women are devoted to problems stemming from their relationship with the live-in maid. Advice is exchanged, assessments given, and stereotypes confirmed. Cynthia justifies her refusal to give a day-off outside to the live-in maid, explaining, "I hear so many stories … The dirty kind about girls running away, girls meeting Egyptian workers, girls meeting Syrian workers on Sundays. … I don't want to get involved in that."

Even if one hates gossiping about the maid – as most of my Lebanese interviewees asserted – the norms set by such gossip and the warnings from recruitment agencies make up the same gauge Lebanese employers use to assess their own level of generosity toward the live-in maid. For example, Muhammad, an employer in his forties, believes his family is exceptional for letting the Filipina live-in maid keep her own passport, which he gave back to her after obtaining her residence permit. Such cases are rare. One study estimates that 91 percent of Lebanese employers believe it is their right to hold the maid's passport and legal papers (Caritas 2005). And after the first few weeks, Muhammad always gives the newly arrived live-in maid a day-off and allows her to go outside of the home. This is also not common. He says that many people warned him that this is not a good idea, but Muhammad says his family is "crazy." But what Muhammad has come to see as a difference of *values*, is, according to international human rights standards, one of *rights*, since it is a worker's right to keep her passport and to exercise her freedom of movement. In other words, employers who go against "harsh" norms regarding the maid, but are actually respecting the maid's basic human rights, may feel especially generous in relation to other Lebanese employers. And if something goes "wrong," everybody knows who to blame: the generous madame or mister.

Hence, the pretext of Filipina women's uncontrollable sexuality is used to justify exercising tight control over these women and refusing their freedom of movement. Such control often breeds isolation and loneliness, which could be related to the high suicide rate among this demographic.

Racial hierarchy

There is a clear division in terms of how Filipina women are viewed compared to Ethiopian or Sri Lankan women in Lebanon. According to Lena, who previously hired a Sri Lankan, two Ethiopians, and currently employs a live-in Filipina, the best maid to hire is the Filipina: "If you want an idiot, take a Sri Lankan … But from the moment you take a Filipina, you say to yourself, look, there's a certain respect of the person and the right of the person." Maha, a Lebanese madame in her forties, said the following about Sri Lankan and Ethiopian live-in maids: "I don't like them at all … They have bad character … They are very stubborn, the Ethiopians … They have a special character. I don't like them. Even the Sri Lankans, I don't like. They're really idiots. The best are the Filipinas."

Racial stereotypes and a hierarchy of foreign live-in maids and domestic workers, who dominate the domestic service sector, permeate Lebanese society. While many madames believe that it depends on the individual, rather than their nationality, many also believe that Filipina women are probably smarter, more educated, and more professional than, for example, Ethiopian, Sri Lankan or Bangladeshi women.

In addition, Cynthia, a Lebanese madame, says Filipina women are more "presentable," reflecting the Lebanese preference for the fairer (and thus more attractive) appearance of Filipina women. "There are people who prefer a white girl … and the children aren't afraid of them," says Ahmad, the previously mentioned owner of a recruitment agency in Beirut. And because Filipina women are known as the most expensive, Nepalis, who only demand $100 per month as salary, have become popular in recent years. "Nepalis are pretty and white like Filipinas. When everyone is taking $100 salary, no one will want Filipinas if they take $200," says Muhammad. (In fact, this is how Muhammad justifies lowering the Filipina women's salary to $150 upon arrival to Lebanon, when most of these women believe they will be receiving $200. The arbitrary lowering of salary for live-in maids of all nationalities upon arrival is common-place among recruitment agencies.) Ibrahim, another recruiting agent, thinks it is absurd that some madames look for white and "good-looking" girls. "It's racism … when you ask about color," he says. "The [customer is] stupid because when she asks … 'good-looking,' … Something strange, because she has husband, she has boys staying at home," he says. He has heard of many things that happen within the homes to these so-called "good-looking" domestic workers. According to one researcher, "So the sexual relations with the domestic maid can be viewed … as a threat to the honour and integrity of the family and … as providing assistance in the validations of one's heterosexual masculinity" (Jureidini 2006:142).

The view that Filipina women are "whiter" and more beautiful has also influenced their perception of their own sexuality. Many Filipina women are aware that, unlike their Sri Lankan or Ethiopian counterparts, Lebanese see them as more beautiful. Mercedita, a Filipina domestic worker, says, "Make-up, not even just powder, was *mamnu'* [forbidden]. Madames are too jealous, because they know Filipina, when they put make-up, some Filipina beautiful, you know? Not the same as Sri Lanka, Ethiopia. They are [also] beautiful … but black … Some [Lebanese] don't like. Not the same [as] Filipina, they are clean," says Mercedita. Muhammad, a Lebanese employer, confirms a tendency to sexualize Filipinos. "In Lebanon, they say they [Filipinas] are [sexually] easy." Jessica says some men in Lebanon prefer Filipina women over other nationalities. She says, "Egyptians like Filipinas, because they say Filipinas … are *clean*, they smell *good*, like that. *Loving*, like that."

Nevertheless, Filipina women are seen as secondary choices as spouses or even girlfriends, and Lebanese men who fall in love with Filipina women are stigmatized and seen as "losers," who could not make a Lebanese woman fall in love with them. In a dramatic case, Beatrice, who had been together with her Lebanese boyfriend for more than five years, was forced to tip-toe around her boyfriend's house in the dark, lest his mother see Beatrice's shadow from the balcony, which is across from the boyfriend's balcony. This was because the mother of Beatrice's boyfriend, who had met with Beatrice on several occasions, had implored him to stop seeing her, and he promised to do so. She says, "It's humiliating. They are very superficial and act nice in front of you, but inside, they think Filipinas are all just maids." So while Filipina women might be seen as superior to maids of other nationalities, this superiority is only among maids, who occupy a socially inferior status. In other words, Filipina women are simply viewed as a better fit for domestic service and sexual adventures, compared to domestic workers of other nationalities.

From an invisible to a public self

Filipina women are often seen by Lebanese as naïve, sexually desirable, and promiscuous. To what extent are these perceptions correct? While Filipina women are hyper-sexualized and exoticized within Lebanese society, and this image is used to legitimize the tight control madames have over the live-in Filipina maids, the same image gives Filipina women space to explore and enjoy their sexuality. This space is also due to Filipina women's specific living and working conditions in Beirut, especially for those who have a day-off or have left their employers to work as illegal freelancers.

Marissa believes she has changed in terms of how she views her own sexuality after she came to Lebanon. She had never been one to frequent night clubs, but here, she goes to clubs from time to time with her Filipina friends. When asked about what she thinks of how Filipina women dress here, especially on their day-off (usually Sunday), she says, "Sexy clothes ... Big earrings ... Of course in your own country, you cannot ... We're just adapting the culture of the Lebanese now. They'll think you're *sharmuta* [whore] in the Philippines." While Lebanese point to Filipina women as *sharmuta*, Marissa believes it is Lebanese society's standards of sexuality that affect Filipina women. Pointing to her medium-size hoop earrings, she adds, "I never wore big earrings like this in the Philippines. This is already big for me. But now I have a bigger one."

Twenty-nine-year-old Gladys has four children in the Philippines, and when I met her on a Sunday she was wearing extremely tight clothes, along with long, bleached, flowing hair and blue contact lenses. At the time, she was dating four boys. When I asked how she could see all of them when she only has Sundays off, she said, "I have time ... Two hours of [each of] them. [We both laugh.] I have one Egyptian, I have one Syrian, I have one Armenian, and I have one Lebanese." I ask who she thinks is the best. "The Syrian. What do you mean 'best?' In the bed?" We laugh again, and I clarify, "In everything." She answers again, "Syrian." Ironically, Gladys's designation of her boyfriend solely by their nationality mimics the simplification and stereotyping of migrant domestic workers by color and nationality.

I met Lara, a Filipina in her late forties who has been working in Lebanon for over 10 years, on a Sunday afternoon on a public bus in Beirut. At the time, Lara was showing her friend graphic photos of herself with her boyfriend, either French-kissing or in other sexual poses. Everyone in the bus was observing these ostentatious acts. Lara, who sat next to the aisle, was not showing her pictures in the middle of her seat toward her friend, but toward the aisle so that even I, who was sitting two seats behind them, could see the pictures. It felt as if she was trying to show off her young, cute Kurdish boyfriend in his mid-twenties (Lara was 47 years old at the time), boasting of her sensuality and sexual "achievements" before the Lebanese on the bus.

Curious, I spoke to Lara; she invited me to go to two birthday parties and then clubbing at Jazira – the most popular among several nightclubs in Beirut that specifically cater for Filipina women on Sunday afternoons. In the conversation before the birthday parties, Lara told me she has five children and that they have all grown up. For this reason, her children understand that her mother wants to be "happy" and don't mind that she parties with her young boyfriend in Lebanon. One of her friends, Nerissa, however, made fun of Lara for the way she dances. And despite all the claims Lara made to me regarding how much she loves partying and how there is no need for communication with her boyfriend except "I love you" and "I miss you," Lara seemed somewhat out-of-place at Jazira. After supporting her children for so long as the mother, she was clearly in the process of experimenting with her sexuality. She enjoys the attention she gets from men, telling me that she hopes her boyfriend is not at the club because she would like to dance with other men.

Lara crafts her relatively new sexuality specifically in the context of her acceptable absence from the Philippines, where she would be under the tighter control of her family. The fact that Filipina women are stereotypically seen as attractive – in the racial hierarchy of domestic workers – and sexually available has given Lara the chance to date someone 20 or more years younger than herself. Lara's sexual expression reinforces the stereotype of Filipina women as promiscuous, since she is married with children. But her investment in this self allows her to be "happy," as she puts it, on one of the seven days when she is not taking care of two children, cleaning a huge home, and serving the Lebanese family that employs her. Furthermore, Lara demonstrates how Filipina women use the stereotype directed against them as a resource for cultivating a "sexual self." This is a self which is not available to them back home and is an alternative to the self as the invisible maid.

To continue with the day I spent with Lara, we met the first birthday girl Nerissa at a tiny flat near Bourj Hammoud that belongs to a mutual friend. When we arrived, Nerissa was cooking for 15 people, almost naked in her pink tank top and underwear, with blasting music that could be heard a hundred meters away. Neighbors were peeking out of their windows to see what was happening. Because the kitchen had no ventilation, Nerissa was sweating and her eyeliner was dripping, but her long hair remained down, while she took a break from time to time, coming out to the living room to dance with her friends.

Nerissa is sexy and glamorous, and prides herself on how most Lebanese think that she is in her twenties by her hair, make-up, and the way she dresses, although she is in her forties. When we all went to Jazira, she quickly disappeared to dance with her several boyfriends. The second time I saw her at Jazira, I interviewed her. Like many other Filipina women, Nerissa has been working in Lebanon for the past 11 years to support her children and husband, who barely makes any money. She says she spends only $50 a month on herself and sends the rest to her family in the Philippines. She is professional at the workplace. Nerissa says that she is an excellent cook, but her "glamorous self" is equally important to her. She cultivates this sexual self and shows off, even if it's only for herself. When the madame is not home, she says she dresses the way she would when she goes clubbing and dances to the music while she cleans. At one point, her madame told Nerissa not to put on make-up when she is working. "*Ma fi* [no] make-up please," she told Nerissa. But the children and the male employer do not mind. According to some Filipina interviewees, Lebanese madames often see the Filipina woman in their home as a sexual threat.

Nerissa, like Lara, invests in her sexy, glamorous self in the specific context of being a Filipina woman in Lebanon. Perhaps the expectation and constraint of having to be the invisible and asexual maid makes this self even more important for Nerissa in Lebanon than in the Philippines. This is because the self as glamorous woman gives her a way to diversify her identity, rather than being stuck with that of a Filipina maid. And by investing in the sexy, glamorous self, at least once a week, Nerissa is the protagonist and attention-getter of everyone around her.

"Life outside" and "going with the flow"

For Marissa, who is in her early thirties and married in the Philippines, having a boyfriend in Beirut was not just an option, but a necessity. She says,

> I'm not proud what's happening here. I am happily married! Everybody will kill me ... But it's common outside and you go with the flow [i.e. having a boyfriend]. It's the life outside ... You need somebody to help you ... because [the boyfriends] are the ones supporting you for the food, clothes, the house, and your money is for the Philippines only.

In a sense, Filipina women implicitly exchange sexual favors or romance for some form of financial security from local or migrant men. Mercedita, like Marissa, who ran away from her employer and works two waitressing jobs at a five-star hotel in Beirut, has a Lebanese boyfriend. He pays for her rent, buys her clothes, and pays for her cell phone. "He tells me, 'Mercedita, save your money so that we can make your [legal] papers,' because I don't have papers," she says.

Marissa worked for two years as a nanny for a rich Lebanese family before she was tempted and "brainwashed," as she puts it, into believing that there is a better life "outside." Although Marissa was tightly controlled, often yelled at by her madame, and felt emotionally and verbally abused, she regrets her decision to leave her madame three years ago. She met her current boyfriend through her Filipina friend's Lebanese fiancée, and has been living with him for most of the time since she left her employer's home. She has a strong bond with her boyfriend. He "learned to love me," and is, she says, committed to her.

The constant stress and fear of living illegally in Beirut is exacerbated by Marissa's concern that someone back home will find out about her extramarital relationship. "I don't want to fight with other Filipina friends. I don't want ... them [to] ... tell my family that I'm living with a Lebanese man." And as there is much gossip, Marissa is always careful.

Marissa has a group of friends who are also Filipina freelancers (usually illegal), who get together regularly at someone's house to enjoy a generous Philippine feast, often joined by Egyptian, Kurdish, Lebanese, or Syrian boyfriends. Despite the fact that many of these women were married with children back home, it was rather uncommon to see a Filipina freelancer without a boyfriend at these gatherings. If a woman is single, her Filipina friends will try to find a boyfriend for her.

Even when a Filipina woman is a live-in maid, if she has a regular day-off and is permitted to leave the house, she will likely have a boyfriend. Out of the 25 Filipina I interviewed, whether working as freelancers or as live in maids who have Sunday off, more than half had a boyfriend. Furthermore, nearly half of these women were married back home. Indeed, certain Filipina women act as matchmakers. For example, Nida, a woman in her thirties working for a retired and divorced man, is separated from her husband but has two sons. After two years, she was allowed to go out alone on Sundays. Nida found herself in the midst of a community of Filipina women who pressured her to date. In fact, Nida related that one time a man, who her Filipina friends nagged her to go out with, called her employer's home during the day. Luckily, Nida answered the phone, but she was furious that her employer's private number was given without her permission. Nida distanced herself from this circle of women and now confides with only a few Filipina friends.

In many cases, it is mutual attraction and loneliness that drives many Filipina women to date and have boyfriends, typically with migrant men, who are also working in the country alone. When I commented at a Filipina friend's house party that many Filipina boyfriends seem to be migrant laborers, Leonilda explained that they are all like family because "we are all strangers in Lebanon."

Although Leonilda is sometimes embarrassed by the explicit sexual displays of Filipina women in Beirut's nightclubs, she is not critical. Commenting on the fact that many married Filipina women sleep with local men, she says:

> As they say, we are going to face the modern world. When you taste it, you always want it. [Laughs]. In the Philippines, it's different. [Women are not promiscuous]. But sexual life, it changes … Here, you are independent. You are alone … You don't have family. You have to start on your own … If you have a problem, if somebody helps you … they expect something from you …

Janet came to Lebanon in order to forget her last lover in the Philippines, who was married. She did not want to break apart the family. At the time of the interview, she was in a relationship with a married Egyptian man. She met him through the boyfriend of her sister, who was also working in Lebanon. She observed that many married Filipina women have boyfriends, because they want to be happy. They want "companionship" since many women work from Monday to Saturday; on Sunday, they want to be happy. "I am confused. I make [a] relationship … Am I happy because he is with me or [because he] loves [me] or what?"

The good woman and the whore

Several Filipina women I spoke with, particularly those who were religious and conservative, believe that the bad reputation Filipina women have in Lebanon is deserved because many of them seem to exhibit stereotypical behavior. These women believe that the only way to improve the image of the Filipina is to be a chaste, trustworthy person or avoid sex altogether. "We are here to work, not to have fun," some say. While most Filipina live-in maids believe that it is their right to have fun on Sundays, many believe that it is the responsibility of each Filipina to avoid giving Filipina women a bad name in Lebanon. For example, Pia is a domestic worker turned professional beautician who married a Lebanese. She laments how some Filipina women seem obsessed with gaining men's attention and end up with more than one boyfriend. While single Filipina women have a right to have a serious relationship, she thinks it is wrong for them to have many boyfriends and especially when they are married back in the Philippines. "I hate Filipinas who are *sharmuta*. They ruin the reputation of all Filipinas in Lebanon," she says.

Women like Pia are trying, in effect, to claim a status as "honorable" women by differentiating themselves from others who are *sharmuta*. It is also a form of censorship or social control when Filipina women who sleep around are stigmatized. But Filipina women like Pia often overlook the fact that the same kind of behavior by Lebanese women, and even more so for that of men, is not necessarily stigmatized. And the symbolic gain of "honorable" women is at the expense of reinforcing a stereotype that legitimizes the control of Filipina women's bodies and persons. Moreover, the focus on Filipina women's promiscuity drives the discussion far away from the real issue, which is that it is difficult for Filipina women to have a personal life outside of "work" and that they are not allowed to bring their partners and families to Lebanon. Even recent legislation enacted by the Ministry of Labor in January 2009 to improve the situation of domestic workers in Lebanon requires that all foreign maids work for three years without family reunification and still does not guarantee a weekly day-off outside the house.

Conclusion

The perceived sexuality of Filipina women in Lebanon is double-sided: on the one hand, the Filipina live-in maid is seen as an asexual *binit* (girl) who must be protected in order to guard the family honor; on the other hand, she is seen as a threatening *sharmuta* (whore). The *binit* can become a *sharmuta* at any moment and bring chaos to the home if the madame's control over the live-in Filipina maid is lessened and the latter gets corrupted by the outside world. For this reason, many Lebanese madames are reluctant to let Filipina maids outside of the home alone. In many cases, a domestic worker's sexual desires are assumed unnatural and inappropriate. The negative stereotypes associated with Filipina women's sexuality are spread through warnings and stories told by recruitment agencies, and rumors. Filipina women, compared to their Ethiopian and Sri Lankan counterparts, are seen as fairer, sexually more attractive, and promiscuous. These images of Filipina women legitimate employers' tight control of their bodies and persons.

For Filipina women, their assumed sexual promiscuity and attractiveness sometimes give them opportunities for exploring and experimenting with their own sexuality. For those who are allowed a day-off outside the house or who freelance illegally, some might start dressing and acting in a sexually assertive manner. They might go clubbing, have much younger boyfriends, or have multiple sexual partners. Among Filipina women, there is both acceptance and ambivalence towards their sexual conduct. Some resent them for perpetuating the bad reputation that Filipina women have acquired in Lebanon.

Ironically, then, while negative sexual stereotypes might legitimate control over Filipina women in Lebanon, these same stereotypes might also permit these women to exercise more choice in how they express their sexuality.

Note

1 This is the most common way people refer to female Lebanese employers, so the word "madame" will be used interchangeably with "employer" hereafter.

References

Caritas. 2005. "Summary of the Caritas Survey, 'Female Migrant Domestic Workers in Lebanon.'" In *Report of the Awareness Raising Workshop on the Situation of Women Migrant Domestic Workers in Lebanon*. Beirut: Caritas, June.

Jureidini, Ray. 2009. "In the Shadows of Family Life: Toward a History of Domestic Service in Lebanon." *Journal of Middle East Women's Studies*, 5(3): 74–101.

——. 2006. "Sexuality and the Servant: An Exploration of Arab Images of the Sexuality of Domestic Maids in the Household." In Samir Khalaf and John Gagnon (Eds), *Sexuality in the Arab World*, pp. 130–51. London: Saqi Books.

Kondo, Dorinne K. 1990. *Crafting Selves: Power, Gender, and Discourses of Identity in a Japanese Workplace*. Chicago, IL: University of Chicago Press.

Longva, Anh Nga. 1997. *Walls Built on Sand: Migration, Exclusion, and Society in Kuwait*. Boulder, CO: Westview Press.

Scott, James. 1990. "Voices under Domination: The Arts of Political Disguise." In *Domination and the Arts of Resistance: Hidden Transcripts*. New Haven, CT: Yale University Press.

76

Mexican immigrants, heterosexual sex and loving relationships in the United States

Interview with Gloria González-López

THE UNIVERSITY OF TEXAS AT AUSTIN

First, tell us about yourself.

I was born and educated through my undergraduate years in Monterrey, Mexico before I migrated to the United States in the mid-1980s. I eventually mastered my (still accented) English and have lived for almost 25 years in Texas and California. Prior to becoming a researcher, I was trained as a couple and family therapist in Los Angeles, and I have worked with Latin American immigrant families and women at community-based agencies located in Houston and Los Angeles. I received a Ph.D. in sociology from the University of Southern California in 2000. I have conducted sexuality research with Mexican and Mexican immigrant populations, and I currently teach graduate and undergraduate courses on sexuality, gender and society, and qualitative methods and sexuality research at the University of Texas at Austin. I am the author of *Erotic Journeys: Mexican Immigrants and Their Sex Lives* (University of California Press, 2005) and co-editor of an anthology titled *Bridging: How Gloria Anzaldúúa's Life and Work Transformed Our Own* (in press). I am currently conducting sociological research on the sexual, romantic, and life experiences of adult women and men with histories of incestuous relationships and who currently live in four of the largest urbanized areas in Mexico.

In the book Erotic Journeys, *you study gender and sexuality from a relational perspective. Could you explain what it means to study gender and sexuality this way?*

By relational I mean at least two specific things. First, theoretically, "relational" means that I have a special interest in learning about and closely examining individuals' sex lives not in isolation but within the context of their relationships with other human beings including but limited to partners, families, friends, and other personal relationships within specific situations. As a sociologist, I think that sexual expression is best understood in the context of relationships with others, that is, relational sexuality, rather than individual sexuality.

And second, methodologically speaking, "relational" means that I am studying the sex lives of my informants within the context of the two-way professional relationship that emerges during the research process; that is, the relationship I develop with them and the relationship they develop with me. For example, I gather my data by establishing a relationship with another human being who is willing to open up, share, and explore in depth her/his sex life through a relationship with me which involves dialogue, deep listening, and storytelling within a context of mutually respectful and honest interaction, while making sure that other ethical issues and concerns are taken into account including but not limited to confidentiality, anonymity, and a sense of safety, in the broadest sense of the word.

Women's virginity can have multiple meanings in different cultures. You coined the term capital femenino *to refer to virginity as a type of social endowment. Could you explain this, as well as the different meanings of virginity that you found in your research?*

First, I would like to share why virginity has been a social enigma for me for a long time and in some way the driving force sustaining my sexuality research project with Mexican immigrant women. In 1997 I started to conduct interviews with the immigrant women who eventually gave life to my book *Erotic Journeys*. As a researcher and as a Mexican woman, I was driven by my special interest and curiosity in understanding virginity within the context of Mexican society and culture.

My curiosity had its roots in the 1970s, back in the Northeast region of Mexico. I must have been 13 years old or so and I recall being terribly shy with regard to sexually related matters. I remember experiencing both curiosity and fear when I heard about a physician who advertised her services (mainly on TV and in newspapers) of "repairing women's virginity" in her small town which was located close to my hometown of Monterrey. I remember not being able to understand an interview with this woman physician, who was identified as "controversial." I also recall listening to people who would jokingly talk about "the buses loaded with women" who would go to her small town to supposedly have their virginity repaired. As a shy adolescent, I witnessed these dialogues in silence. Back then I did not even know what the word "virginity" meant, but I kept thinking about why people would be constructing narratives of scandal around these topics.

As I grew older, I kept remembering the controversial doctor who had been performing hymen reconstruction on bodies of women (women who could have been my sister or a close friend). Twenty years later, and as I was ready to defend my doctoral dissertation examining the sex lives of immigrant women, I looked for this woman physician. I was fortunate to find her. I talked to her about my project and requested an interview, which I later conducted in her small town in 1998.

"When and why did you start repairing a woman's virginity?" was among many of the questions that I asked during our conversation. She explained to me that back in the late 1960s she used to work as a doctor in small towns in the region and one day a group of mothers came to her crying. She learned that these mothers were in pain because their daughters had been raped. But besides the act of violence exercised against a young daughter's body, their main concern was that their daughters would not be able to find a good man who would eventually accepted them "as is" (that is, non-virgins) and would be willing to marry them. In other words, these mothers were deeply concerned about their daughters being rejected by a future boyfriend and potential husband because they were no longer virgins. The doctor thought that repairing a woman's virginity through hymen reconstruction (while making sure the vagina would bleed after being re-ruptured) would be a way to protect women from this kind of potential rejection from a man. Since the late 1960s to the day I interviewed this doctor in 1998, she had been conducting hymen reconstruction on countless women, usually free of cost or for a modest fee or donation, according to the financial situation of the woman. She explained to me that this service has never been for profit but as a way to protect women from sexism.

Although we could engage in a debate and argue that this doctor could be in fact reinforcing sexism by validating a woman's need to prove her virginity to a man, the contradictions, tensions and paradoxes that emerged in my head during the interview helped me understand what I was only beginning to understand through my research with Mexican immigrant women. So as I was analyzing the long in-depth interviews my 40 women informants so generously offered to me, I was about to learn an important sociological lesson with regard to women, virginity and gender inequality in Mexico: a woman who is a virgin (and presumably has an intact hymen symbolizing moral integrity) can actually exchange her virginity (i.e. virginal vagina) for the possibility of having a financially stable life via marriage. As I discovered this and engaged in previous published research on sexuality and sociological theory, the idea of *capital femenino* became the ideal concept to capture and examine the ways in which virginity may acquire a higher or lower "value" depending on very specific socioeconomic contexts and circumstances shaping the economic opportunities for women educated in a patriarchal society.

While my interview with this doctor helped me tremendously to understand what my informants were telling me through these in-depth interviews I conducted in Los Angeles, I was also becoming aware of the many socially constructed meanings that virginity may acquire within some patriarchal cultures. From the women and men that I interviewed, I learned that virginity may represent, symbolize, and/or mean many things including (but not limited to) decency, moral integrity, moral responsibility, and respect for oneself and for the family (especially the parents). For some women and men, virginity may symbolize a "little treasure," a "gold medal," or "a gift." Beyond the white dress, which may symbolize many things besides the "purity of the bride," blood stains on the honeymoon bed sheet may become proof and a reason to celebrate the virginity of a newly wed woman, or blood stains on a modest piece of cloth that a newly married woman might have used to clean herself after the sex act may become a memento to keep in a special place as she reminds herself and her husband of the moral integrity she possessed when they married.

While both women and men may construct the multiple meanings of virginity through countless expressions and in specific contexts and circumstances, we should remember that these meanings are vulnerable to future social constructions as both Mexican society and Mexican-American and other US-Latino immigrant communities reinvent their sexual moralities and social realities, in an increasingly connected and wired world, which goes hand-in-hand with the consequences of globalization.

A central point of Erotic Journeys is about how Mexican immigrants' sexual lives are transformed by the experience of migration. Could you explain some of the ways their sexual lives changed after migration?

As I conducted my fieldwork, these immigrant women and men taught me that their sex lives are fluid, unstable processes; they are always in flux, evolving. I learned that it would be practically impossible to establish a rigid "before-and-after" migration examination of their sex lives. After coming to this country and settling within their receiving communities (in Los Angeles in this particular case), these informants reinvented their sex lives in very specific ways and within very specific migration- and settlement-related contexts, situations, and circumstances.

First, immigrant women and men migrate to this country with a set of pre-established ideologies and practices, which upon migration and settlement are unpacked and revisited. I learned, for instance, that mothers who teach a new generation of Mexican-American girls may renegotiate the ways in which they educate their daughters with regard to sexuality. With regard to virginity, for instance, I learned that some mothers perceived the United States as a country where men "do not care about virginity" and therefore a daughter who has premarital sex might not be at risk of being stigmatized for not being a virgin at marriage. Interestingly, from this perspective, women still depend on their perceptions of men's opinions about women and sexuality. In other words, on either side of the border, gender inequality is redefined by women's perceptions of what men expect of them as women. In this regard, some of the men who were fathers raising daughters told me that virginity was no longer "a tradition." Instead, a new concern for them was to make sure a daughter would not get pregnant and drop out of high school and thus decrease her chances of going to college. For them, the dream-come-true of a daughter attending college would not only make them feel honored as parents (who might not have had these opportunities while growing up), but would also compensate for their hard work as immigrants now raising a new generation of Mexican-American children.

Second, I learned that a sense of anonymity and geographical relocation and physical distance from parents and other family authorities may give some young immigrant women an opportunity to reclaim their sex lives, especially now that they are not under the close moral surveillance of a parent or authority figure. For example, I interviewed a woman who told me that after she migrated she finally had the opportunity to have sex for the first time and eventually established a cohabitation relationship with a man. Being far away from her parents allowed her to have sex and "to live with a man" without being married, something unthinkable had she stayed in her small town in Jalisco. However, distance did not necessarily soften the emotions associated with being "morally disobedient" as a woman. For example, this same woman told me that she still felt shame and guilt for behaving in that way, even without her parents knowing about her sexual behavior.

Third, I also learned that immigrants migrate to the United States with a socially constructed image of the United States. However, upon settlement in these marginalized inner city barrios, they feel a deep sense of disillusionment. The United States is not the country they have constructed in their fantasies before migrating. Drug and gang activity, poverty, racism, a fast-paced life, segregation, the presence of homeless people, their everyday struggles to attain employment and survive, among other dimensions of their social realities, transformed the "American dream" into an "immigrant nightmare" for informants who settled into marginalized sectors of the country. The United States became a sexually dangerous place and a morally decadent nation characterized by lack of moral restraint, or *libertinaje*, an expression used by these informants as they described this country.

Fourth, women and men develop social networks with others who live within their immigrant communities. Conversations (formal and informal, individual or collective) evolved upon settlement and these interactions between immigrants may become a source of information for them (most notably women in this study) as they explore potential answers to their sex-related concerns, for example, with regard to HIV/AIDS, sex education of children, and sexual and romantic relationships with their partners, among other themes.

And fifth, men who work as day laborers (or *jornaleros* as they are known in some Mexican immigrant communities) may be exposed to sexual harassment from a potential (white, male, presumably "gay") employer as they look for work in the busy corners of the city of Los Angeles. This finding actually made me redefine my earlier radical approaches to gender studies and taught me an important sociological lesson: men who might have enjoyed some patriarchal privileges before migrating may experience the vulnerability of these same privileges as their lives are now shaped by complex race and class relations (among other factors) which place them in positions of disadvantage in the new social contexts shaping their everyday lives and survival journeys.

Building on that, how is the experience of immigration different for Mexican women who come to the United States versus Mexican men in regards to sex?

For the women and men that I interviewed, patriarchy might have been challenged as part of the immigration and settlement processes within some of the complexities I identified above, but patriarchy did not disappear. For example, the women I interviewed, more frequently than the men, reported "sexual gains" as part of the immigration journey. I would like to outline these gains for the women (as I discuss in page 218 in *Erotic Journeys*): (a) Paid employment and control over their paycheck may help women redefine their relationships with their heterosexual partners and in turn develop some kind of sexual autonomy and/or empowerment as women; (b) women may experience "woman-to-woman networking" (for example, social interactions with other immigrant women) as having a positive impact on the quality of their sex lives; (c) none of the women that I interviewed reported any kind of involvement in commercial sex (which may become extremely dangerous and exploitative for Mexican immigrant women); (d) none of the women reported exposure to drug, alcohol or gang activity and none of them had been homeless (for some of the men it was the opposite); (e) geographical distance from parents resulted in a weaker family control which allowed some of the women in the study to experience their sex lives with an enhanced sense of freedom.

In my interviews, it was not unusual to learn that some men may perceive that Mexican women "change" after they migrate (e.g. becoming assertive as a woman and calling 911 in the event of domestic violence) as men themselves are deciphering racial, class, citizenship status uncertainties, and linguistic challenges, among other forms of discrimination. These complexities invite us to look at how both women and men decipher patriarchy in both nations, especially within a changing Mexican society and in increasingly complex Latino barrios in the United States.

You found that your interviewees sometimes brought up machista or machismo during their interviews. What does machismo mean, or rather, how might it have multiple meanings?

Machismo has become a popular concept in Mexican society to refer to in order to explain different expressions of gender inequality. For example, it is not uncommon to hear people who would say that *machismo* is responsible for violence against women. In other words, *machismo* has become some kind of cultural translation or equivalent for sexism. Accordingly, my informants would use the concept of *machismo* to explain different forms of sexism in our interviews. Other concepts related to *machismo* include *machista* (which could be translated as "sexist"), or *macho*, which is also used to identify as "sexist man." The concept of *macho*, however, may have many nuanced meanings that may not necessarily have a negative connotation. For example, "being a macho" for men who belong to a particular generation may mean being a man who is a good, hard-working father. It may also have a special connotation associated with pride of being a man, or manhood. However, in my study, none of my informants used, and/or associated the concept of "macho" with any kind of positive connotation.

One recurring theme in Erotic Journeys *is that there are often differences in the sexual beliefs, practices and experiences of individuals who grew up in rural areas versus those who grew up in urban areas. In what ways do rural and urban sexualities differ?*

This is a good question because Mexico is becoming an increasingly urbanized. However, the women and men I interviewed who were from rural areas were born and raised in locations that were still far from being urbanized. So based on these in-depth interviews, I learned that for women educated in rural areas – where exposure to education and paid employment opportunities was limited or non-existent – virginity was highly valued. As *capital femenino*, virginity became a form of social endowment these women could exchange for marriage opportunities and a stable financial future. As part of this process, women and men may construct specific ideologies that may associate a desirable moral integrity with lack of premarital sexual activity in a woman, and women who do not comply with these moral expectations may become stigmatized and rejected. In this way, socioeconomics and ideologies seem to go hand-in-hand as some specific expressions of (desirable and undesirable) womanhood (i.e. being a woman or "femininity") are established. It is important to mention that this is relational; that is, it happens in the context of relationships with men and their families.

Moreover, I learned that in rural towns, some ideologies promote the sexual initiation of young men with a sex worker as part of a ritual initiation into manhood. These experiences were coercive and emotionally challenging for the men I interviewed. Interestingly, although these rural ideologies and practices with regard to sexuality may selectively affect both women and men, they are fluid and nuanced and not necessarily uniform for all those raised in rural contexts.

At the same time, being raised in urban contexts does not automatically mean that women and men will become "more progressive" in terms of sexual morality. Some of the women and men from Mexico City explained that they have been exposed to some versions of these ideologies and practices. Interestingly, I learned that more exposure to paid employment and education along with ideals of "modernity" may offer alternative, fluid, discourse-changing beliefs and practices in regard to sexuality and sexual morality. For example, the presence of women's groups advocating for gender equality and the presence of activists advocating gay and lesbian rights, are examples of the social forces that go hand-in-hand with the fluid and changing ideologies and practices with regard to sexuality that may allow for a possibility to embrace more gender equality and respect and acceptance within and beyond heterosexual relationships.

Many of your interviewees were Catholic. To what degree did you see Catholicism shaping sexuality?

This is a great question. As a woman who was raised in the Catholic faith, I was especially curious and interested in this aspect of my informants' sex lives. As I asked them questions about sexual morality, the church, and their own sex lives, the most important lesson that I learned was the following: the values and ideologies traditionally promoted by the church with regard to sexuality and relationships were neither the only direct cause nor the most influential social force controlling the sexual desires, behaviors, or beliefs of my informants. I also learned that when Catholic morality became an important force of social control in their sex lives, this was identified as influential more frequently *a posteriori* rather than *a priori*. What do I mean by this? After engaging in the sex act, for example, a woman may experience religious guilt and shame *after* the fact, but not necessarily *before* she had sex. I also learned that although the church has historically established in *theory* these moral ideologies and values with regard to sexuality in Mexico, it is the family as a social institution that puts these beliefs into *practice*. For example, this is exemplified by women who said that they did not have premarital sex because they were afraid of god but because they were afraid of an unexpected pregnancy and the risk of their parents forcing them to marry a partner who was not desirable as a husband. I remember the illustrative case of a woman who told me that her fear arose while engaging in premarital sex with her boyfriend: "No, I was not afraid of god, I was afraid of my mother!"

In my research I also learned that the Catholic faith had a more influential role on the sex lives of women and less significant (or limited) influence on the sex lives of men. In a book chapter called "Confesiones de mujer: The Catholic church and sacred morality in the sex lives of Mexican immigrant women," in *Sexual Inequalities and Social Justice* (Teunis and Herdt 2007), I talk about the complex ways women reconcile their Catholic faith, practices, and behaviors closely related to their sex lives, especially with regard to contraceptive use, condom use, and abortion, among other related issues.

Sexual story-telling frequently contains themes of pleasure and danger. Were there typical ways that you saw these themes in the sexual stories immigrants told you?

Yes, definitely. The point of intersection between both danger and pleasure was revealed to me: engaging in something "prohibited" increased the meaning of something being perceived as "forbidden" and thus the sensation of excitement and anticipation would increase. Some of my informant women, for example, told me that even though sex was "prohibited" and they would have to conceal a relationship with a boyfriend, that the "dangerous" situation in itself became a source of "pleasure." Engaging in romantic and sexualized activities thus became a process that is both pleasurable and dangerous. For example, I learned that men may go out to bars in increasingly vibrant and visible social spaces, and they may drink and engage in unprotected sex with people they do not know, which may similarly expose them to the same dynamics involving pleasure and danger. Although this is not necessarily exclusive to immigrants (this may happen in any town on earth and with "local" people), it is relevant in the context of immigration because of the larger social contexts and structures shaping their lives. For example, for men living in conditions of crowded housing where emotional isolation, poverty, and alcohol and drug use (among other factors) are part of the immigration experience, these exciting sexualized interactions may unleash conditions of vulnerability to sexually transmitted diseases, HIV/AIDS in particular.

You conducted three-hour in-depth interviews with Mexican immigrant women and men about their sexual lives. What are the challenges and rewards of employing in-depth interviews in sexuality research?

I have experienced more rewards than challenges while conducting sexuality research with Mexican women and men. I think the biggest reward is that it is always both an honor and a privilege (as a human being and a researcher) to have the opportunity to engage in such a deep and meaningful personal dialogue with another human being who is willing to share so much – so generously and so unconditionally – about the most intimate aspects of his or her personal life, sex in this case.

Second, each in-depth interview becomes a lesson for me as a researcher: I am always reminded of how little I know about sexuality and society. For example, conducting in-depth interviews on sexuality has allowed me to explore the ways in which I can stretch out, the ways in which I can continuously grow and develop intellectually and professionally, methodologically and theoretically. Each individual dialogue with a research participant keeps me humble as a scholar who is curious about understanding the intimate interconnections between sexuality, society and culture. An in-depth interview allows me to give my hand (metaphorically speaking) to another human being and invite her/him to teach me about the many complexities and nuances of sexuality within the context of social and cultural forces.

Third, in-depth interviews allow me to identify and learn more about the tensions, contradictions, and paradoxes with regard to how a human being may recall, interpret, and articulate their sex life as part of their own personal growth and development. In that regard, it is always invaluable to see how people may develop some kind of awareness as they immerse themselves in their own personal histories and stories. It is always a gift to be interviewing someone who may experience an "aha!" moment during the interview, someone who may learn more about their own personal and family life through the interview process. The interview may help provide answers to questions that they might have never asked themselves. It is always a reward for me as a researcher to recognize the ways in which our interview could be potentially and immediately beneficial for the informant.

And finally, one of the biggest rewards of conducting in-depth interviews is that this kind of methodology allows me to capture people's actual voices. I find this process to be very political and potentially self-empowering for an interviewee in the sense that this methodology allows people to articulate their own life histories and stories.

Some of the challenges that I have experienced include the following. First, I have learned that being alert and self-monitoring during the interview process may become an emotionally and intellectually exhausting process. This has become evident when I am driven to go on, but then the interview may become longer and equally exhausting for an informant. I learned about this in the beginning of my career and am now more aware of this situation; I think it is happening less and less.

Second, in-depth interviews involve dialogue that becomes very personal and intimate, which brings a sense of trust that may stimulate curiosity in an informant, who may in turn want to interview the researcher. When I conducted the interviews for my book *Erotic Journeys*, I was frequently asked about my own personal life during or after the interview. When this was the case, I always explained the methodological rigor I needed to follow but accepted that I would answer any question after the interview was completed. However, I realized by the end of the interview, an informant was ready to be done and she/he was not interested in asking any questions and/or had completely forgotten about it. Relatedly, I always had a list of professionals in various fields in case an informant had a question, or when histories of abuse were revealed during the interview and there was the need to refer them to a professional.

These are the rewards and challenges that come to mind at this moment and especially as I think of the research project that resulted in the book *Erotic Journeys*.

Do you have any concluding thoughts on immigration and sexuality?

In my study I felt like I was barely touching the surface of the sex lives of my informants, especially with regard to heterosexual relationships. I think there is an urgent need to do more sociological research on the sex lives of women and men in non-heterosexual relationship arrangements, especially for Mexican immigrant women who are in these romantic arrangements and who are practically invisible in the social science literature on gender and sexuality.

References

González-López, Gloria. 2007. "Confesiones de mujer." in *Sexual Inequalities and Social Justice*, ed. Niels F. Teunis and Gilbert Herdt, pp. 148–73. Berkeley: University of California Press.
——. 2005. *Erotic Journeys: Mexican Immigrants and their Sex Lives*. Berkeley: University of California Press.
Teunis, Niels F. and Gilbert Herdt (Eds). 2007. *Sexual Inequalities and Social Justice*. Berkeley: University of California Press.

77

Gender, sexuality, and the Lebanese diaspora

Global identities and transnational practices

Dalia Abdelhady

SOUTHERN METHODIST UNIVERSITY

Many scholars acknowledge that peoples, countries and their economic, political and cultural institutions are more interconnected than in the past. Increased interconnectedness is understood as a product of global processes brought about by actors such as multinational corporations (Nike and Microsoft), international financial organizations (the International Monetary Fund and the World Bank), global political bodies (the United Nations and the World Trade Organization), and cultural institutions (MTV and CNN). Globalization is a topic that is often met with mixed feelings and contradictory attitudes. On the one hand, globalization is understood as increasing interconnectedness between peoples and cultures and is associated with the spread of democratic values, individual freedoms, material wealth and global identities. On the other hand, globalization is also understood as increasing economic inequality, ethnic and social conflicts. In this chapter, I address the ways globalization shapes sexual boundaries and identities. Identifying diasporic immigrant communities as an important aspect of global processes, I use the experiences of Lebanese immigrants to show that ethnic differences and immigration status produce distinct identities, and at the same time generate creative forms of belonging and global attachments. Lebanese immigrants are spread around different parts of the world. I use diaspora to refer to their awareness of other immigrants in various countries and their ongoing connections to Lebanon and their new society. Specifically, I focus on the experiences of gay and lesbian Lebanese immigrants in New York. I aim to show the ways they move beyond traditional attachments based on their national background or sexual orientation, and choose to identify with more global social and political issues instead.

Ethnic difference

Lebanese immigrants have a strong sense of being Lebanese, which, for many of them, means different things. Stressing a wide range of factors from a delicious cuisine, strong family values, an appreciation of music and dance, and an entrepreneurial spirit to an experience of collective trauma induced by two civil wars, corrupt governments and economic dependency, all the individuals I interviewed had an answer to the meaning of being Lebanese. Clearly, none of these attributes are unique to the Lebanese or Arabs more generally. Experiences with discrimination also played an important role in strengthening their sense of ethnic difference. These experiences, however, were gendered, especially as they emphasized the construction of Lebanese/Arab men as terrorists and women as docile.

Roy illustrated the ways gendered interactions strengthened his ethnic identification. Roy was a 34-year-old graduate student who moved from Beirut to New York City in 1989. His initial reaction to being in a foreign environment was to affirm his Arab and Lebanese identity. Roy described how, during the first few years after leaving Lebanon, affirming his ethnic Lebanese identity was his response to the rejection he encountered in the new setting:

> It's a normal reaction I think, when you are in a strange country, and you feel alienated from the society at large, the normal reaction is to get back to your identity as the past beckons. In Lebanon, I never cared that I was Lebanese. The idea didn't mean anything to me. I didn't care I was an Arab. It didn't mean anything as well. It's only in the time I came to the US, when people started describing me as such, in a pejorative manner. As a reaction, there was a period when I was very involved in affirming my identity. I am not like that anymore. I think the whole idea [of identity], the whole notion is silly.

In Roy's experience, affirming his ethnic identity was an outcome of experiences of prejudice and discrimination and his way of distancing himself from the host society. When I asked if he could relate specific encounters, he commented:

> There are two instances that stick in my mind. During the [first] Iraq war, I was working out at a gym. I left one of the weights lying about. And the attendant came and asked me to remove the weights. Then, he turned his back and said, "Those fucking Arabs." So I went to the reception, wrote a complaint, voided my membership, and got my money back. After September 11, I was walking in the mall, about two hours after the planes struck. And some guy who was walking by looked at me, and started screaming at me: "Bastards, these bastards are gonna win." I didn't beat the crap out of him, which I could have done easily. I let it go. But it struck me. You feel accused in certain instances, accused without doing anything, accused in a transcendental manner; your state of being is one of being accused.

Both incidents are specifically gendered. In Roy's view, the gym is a masculine space. The attendant's comment was meant to assault not only his ethnic origins but his masculine identification as well. Roy further explains that, while the mall is a gender-neutral space, the person who harassed him was able to identify him as Arab because of his gender. Roy believes that unless an Arab woman is veiled, and is thus marked as Muslim, she is less likely to be identified as Arab. For men, however, given the constant media portrayal of Arab/Muslim male terrorists, men like Roy with dark hair and an olive complexion were more frequently targeted as well as feared. Roy's remark that he could have physically attacked his accuser at the mall was one that asserted his superiority is a specifically masculine way.

Similar to Roy, Abeer did not initially identify with American society. She came from Lebanon in 1994 to pursue a degree in medicine. She lived in Boston for two years and then moved to New York. Abeer explains that her foreign accent did not allow her to be part of American society:

> From what I saw from whites dealing with me as a foreigner, I felt very ostracized. Just because I speak with an accent, people would shout at me, hang the phone on me or not answer me. They would make believe that they don't understand what I'm saying.

Unlike Roy who experienced direct verbal confrontation, Abeer was faced with exclusion in more passive ways such as people hanging up on her during a phone conversation. Since people did not necessarily identify her as Lebanese or Arab, she was not confronted with Arab slurs or ethnic based harassment. She was, though, viewed as an immigrant. Abeer's sense of alienation in the United States was further strengthened as she sought relationships with American women when she first moved from Lebanon. In her experiences, the American-born women she had encountered could only accept her if she had denounced her Arab culture which they perceived as totally negative. Abeer could not relate to the simplistic understandings of her cultural background and moved on to forming relationships with other immigrant women who face similar predicaments in American society. As Abeer expressed, experiences of prejudice and exclusion were taken to mark immigrants' distance from the host society and strengthen their sense of belonging to a minority group that is negatively stereotyped. The inability to conform to the expectations of American-born women led Abeer to seek relationships with Arab and Southeast Asian women who get stereotyped in similar ways in American culture.

Immigrant status

Lack of belonging to the host society was also coupled with a sense of alienation from the homeland that the immigrants left behind. These immigrants' sense of difference in their homeland resulted from the way they got labeled as "foreign" by people in Lebanon. For example, Abeer referred to the way people in Lebanon remark on her foreign accent when speaking Arabic, which is compounded in her case, since people in the United States made similar comments about her foreign accent when speaking English. Referring to the consequences of her first and only visit to Lebanon, Abeer illustrated her ambiguous state of not belonging to either society:

> People thought that I'm very Americanized in my gestures, my values, the way I dress, the way I behaved myself and the way I started speaking. For them, I speak Arabic with an accent, which I cannot see but they see it, so I don't know why. But for them, I'm like their American friend. When I'm here, they know I'm a foreigner, and when I go there, they know I'm a foreigner. So that's a very silly state.

Abeer's experience shows that her lack of compliance with gender norms in Lebanon, in the ways she spoke or carried herself, led to her exclusion from her Lebanese circles as people considered her foreign and Americanized. Lack of belonging to either a homeland or a host society leads to an ambivalent position, or as Abeer stressed, a silly state. The "silly" state Abeer and others found themselves in could be considered temporary given her decision to stay in the United States and stop pondering a return to Lebanon. However, Abeer asserted that her lack of belonging to Lebanese society did not and would not translate into her belonging to American society. For Abeer, the initial sense of alienation from both Lebanese and American societies was based on her ethnicity but also her sexual orientation. She held that Lebanese society was not accepting of homosexuality in general. Still, in her experience, a gay community in New York was not accepting of her Arab heritage either:

> Among Arabs, I am not accepted since I am a lesbian. And among lesbians, I am not accepted since I am Arab, and proud of it. Arabs want me to give up my lesbian identity. I tried. I used to dress and act like the girl they want me to be, especially among family members. I did not do a good job at it so I stopped. Among lesbians, they don't like the fact that I am proud to be Arab. They emphasize that Arab culture is oppressive to women and queers. They are right, but they do not understand that I am proud of this part of my identity. I am both lesbian and Arab, yet, I am not accepted in either group.

As a result, Abeer found that the community she could best relate to was that of gay Arabs, but even within this group, gender differences led to the separation between gay men and lesbians. The separation of the two groups did not affect the way Abeer related to the community in general:

> To me it is very important be able to relate to other gay Arabs, because I share more common grounds with them than other gays and other Arabs. It joins two identities for me that were practically incompatible before. I think the community has to know that there are gay Arabs. It is also important to provide support to people who are very afraid of coming out or afraid of recognizing their own sexuality.

Abeer's lack of belonging in Lebanon, New York and the gay community in New York led her to get involved with the particular social issues that she was concerned about more than affirming her Lebanese ethnic identity. Specifically, Abeer was mostly concerned with homophobia in the Arab world and ethnocentrism in American society; she sought relationships with Arab gays and lesbians that would help her construct a positive understanding of her sexuality in either society.

Existing literature on diaspora communities emphasizes immigrants' sense of difference in relationship to those who never left the homeland and members of their host societies. Despite the sense of alienation in their homeland, most of the Lebanese immigrants I interviewed believe that their membership in the diaspora can allow them to be very effective in addressing problems in Lebanon, whether politically or socially. In fact, belonging to the diaspora, or existing outside the homeland, was seen as an added advantage for bringing about desired changes in Lebanon. Fareed is a graphic artist in his thirties. He lived in New York and, similar to Abeer, was active in its Arab gay community. He explained that being in New York allows him to challenge American society to be more accepting of Arabs; he wanted to be a "positive role model" for Arabs living in the United States. At the same time, he realized that his immigrant status also allowed him to contest Lebanese norms that rigidly enforce heterosexuality and condemn same-sex sexualities.

> That's one area that I'm happy with, which is the area of affecting change from here as Americans. I think that I have no problem getting involved with and I do, and I think all of us should do it. A, it's much safer. B, it's effective, it works, and we've seen it work. We had a letter-writing campaign because we had a raid by the Lebanese police against an Internet provider who was accused of posting up a gay Lebanese website. And even though the owners of the service have no clue what – they can't really control what happens on the server – some of them actually were thrown in jail, and it was a whole mess … I mean, this is all just to say that we as Lebanese and Arab Americans in general can be much more effective than we ever even think about, working from here to effect change there. I think our countries, especially the countries that have good relations with the US,

are more likely to listen to pressure or to complaints from the US than anything internal. I mean, internally, you can jump up and down and nobody gives a shit, they'll throw you in jail. But you get a letter of complaint from the US State Department or a US organization, and you get a couple of write-ups in *Time* magazine or whatever, and suddenly they'll take action because it's like: "Oh my God! We're being exposed."

Unlike Roy and Abeer, Fareed did not experience direct discrimination in American society. He believed that it was important to identify as American in order to be effective in bringing about change in this society. At the same time, Fareed illustrated how being outside of Lebanon granted more power in affecting change in the homeland. He realized that being in the United States gave him more clout given the American influence in the region. So, while he had no official status in Lebanon, he believed that a letter from an American organization could be more effective in challenging Lebanese state sexual oppression than political activism inside Lebanon. He also illustrated ways in which a traditionally taboo issue, homosexuality in this case, could be contested. His interest in participating in both American and Lebanese societies highlights the transnational attachments that some immigrants exhibit, which are today made possible through electronic information technology.

Creative identification

The Lebanese immigrants I interviewed were aware that their experiences of living in multiple societies mark them as different. While some stressed belonging to multiple nations, they all believed that they had no place where they fully belong. This lack of national belonging was in part a result of their frequent movement between different societies. Instead of seeking belonging to communities based on ethnicity and nationality, they carved out unique identities that bring together ideas, values and social practices from the different societies they belong to. These identities are informed by multiple cultures and therefore contest traditional national forms of identification. For example, Khaled described that, after advancing to candidacy in his Ph.D. program in a small town in upstate New York, he moved to New York City where he felt more at home. Describing the changes he went through after moving to New York City, Khaled revealed that:

I am more comfortable with myself now. And I am less interested in rejecting or accepting American culture, I am beyond that point right now. I think slowly now. I found some sort of balance between living in America and being from Lebanon. I bring the two together.

At one level, Khaled accepted his belonging to American society. After all, his partner of five years was Anglo-American and he considered himself part of the white majority; also, he was in the process of finishing his Ph.D., and had a teaching position at a high-ranking university in New York City. Realizing that his class background, social status, and skin color facilitated his tolerance in American society, Khaled refused to think of his experience as one of Americanization. In his view, Americanization did not describe his identity, as he does not see himself as fully assimilated to American society. Even when he tried to integrate into a gay community in New York (by going to gay clubs and participating in gay community organizations), he realized that he did not identify with the American gay subculture either. Khaled complained that he was commonly perceived as "an exotic other" by many gay men that he met at clubs or community organizations. Emphasizing his olive complexion, green eyes and foreign accent, the men Khaled encountered ignored his knowledge of both American and Arab cultures (and given his French education before he left Lebanon he is also knowledgeable of French culture) and reduced him to being merely "ethnic" in the United States. For Khaled, the gay community in New York City, and the mainstream society in general, was parochial and lacked an understanding of complex forms of identification as his belonging to multiple societies was ignored and his unique identity could only be understood in ethnic terms.

Instead of seeking membership in the gay community in New York, Khaled stressed that sharing similar class and cultural backgrounds were important elements in defining his social relationships. Most of Khaled's friends were French-speakers in New York and he confessed that he had more in common with friends who were interested in world literature – the topic of his research – and that his interests were based more on his class and cultural background. While refusing to be labeled Americanized, Khaled also refused to be defined as "Other" within American society. For Khaled, the "Other" implied identifying with something that is opposite to "America" or the "West" which he saw as fictitious since both East and West had always been intertwined historically and culturally. In his case, he realized that, given his Western-style education (both in Lebanon and the United States), his understanding of his identity as an Arab and Lebanese was achieved within a Western cultural tradition: "Even my understanding of Arabic culture and my position within it goes through certain European texts and frameworks."

Khaled was 28 years old when I met him at the Lincoln Center for the Performing Arts after watching a Lebanese movie that was part of the Human Rights Watch Film Festival in the summer of 2001. He had moved to the United States in 1994, but despite his seven-year stay, Khaled did not identify with American society. He also stressed that he did not feel fully integrated in Lebanese society either. For him, having to narrow his cultural repertoire to only one culture where he would fully belong was a form of social and cultural death:

> For instance, I go to Lebanon every year for three months, because I need to feel that I'm connected there. I am one of those people who feel like I don't belong here, I don't belong there. I am kind of in between, and that's exactly what I am. I don't feel I am fully Lebanese; I will die if I completely abide by all the social rules of that culture, and I will also die if I abide by all the social rules of this culture.

Khaled's ambivalent relation to the United States and Lebanon illustrates that, for him, this lack of full national belonging was mostly a desirable position as it allowed him to mix different aspects of these national cultures. Many of the Lebanese immigrants I interviewed believed that cultural mixture or hybridization encouraged a cosmopolitan outlook and was central to their sense of social identity. The ability to move between and beyond specific national cultures also allows my respondents to escape forms of exclusion that they face based on their ethnicity and sexual orientation.

While enriching to the lives of many respondents, the unique process of cultural mixing did not always result in a sense of harmonious identities and social positions. Mixing different identities and lifestyles in his daily experience, Fareed realized the ambivalence associated with forging an incomplete sense of belonging. During our conversation, Fareed shared his experience with living in Tennessee and Washington DC before he moved to New York. Living in three cities after leaving Beirut, Fareed realized that he did not completely fit in any of the three settings. Yet, such ambivalence about his social position motivated Fareed to seek coherence in his experience through involvement in volunteer activities and New York City politics. Indicating that for him identity meant a collection of experiences that left a mark in his life, Fareed noted that the many labels he wore varied from "American," "New Yorker," "White," "Arab,"

"Muslim," "Atheist," "Lebanese," "Gay," "Immigrant," and "Professional." At the same time, he stressed the need to move beyond unitary identities as defining his experience; these multiple identities could be used, though, as a pivot to bring about desirable social changes:

> It is so confusing, but I'm not totally that concerned about that. I think that your humanity has to precede all of these labels. I mean, if anything, I really use those labels just as tools to push the right buttons. But I'm not really that hung up on it. I think that growing in the world today, with borders falling left and right, because of technology and communication, the whole concept of labels and nationalism is becoming rather tired; unless you want to use it for your political motive, you know what I mean?

Fareed's emphasis on the declining importance of national identification as a result of global processes described his understanding of identities as transitory and strategic. While Fareed acknowledged that some of the multiple identities that he articulated are contradictory, his ability to draw on them strategically and creatively was more important than the pseudo sense of coherence that is traditionally sought after. Similar to Fareed, Roy also rejected the form of social coherence offered by traditional identities. In his explanation, Roy believed that all identities were problematic:

> I have an issue with identity right now. I tend to consider it more and more as a very bad idea; as something that's always causing trouble and without any validity. So, what constitutes my identity? [pause] I tend to abandon the idea of identity as such. I don't like it anymore, I don't enjoy it. It doesn't give me the same glow it used to.

In Roy's account, the rejection of all forms of identity was an active choice that some immigrants make in response to the conditions of their migration and displacement. As expressed by Roy, a sense of not belonging added to his feeling of ambivalence but also this "liminality" could be a comfortable location when there were common issues that might temporarily unite people. For Roy, participating in anti-war campaigns and labor-related activities allowed him to forge a feeling of commonality with others that he did not feel through traditional forms of identification.

Like Roy, Lebanese immigrants' awareness of their precarious situation motivated most of them to challenge traditional forms of belonging and identity. Key to contesting flat, unitary identities was an ability to engage in practices of social change that occur at the global level. The ways Lebanese immigrants challenged rigid forms of ethnic and national identification illustrate their cosmopolitan positioning in the world. Facing exclusion in the United States and Lebanon, they were motivated to be effective in changing the different societies they are members of. The kinds of social changes they were interested in are global in nature as they realize the broad forms of inequality and exclusion that they faced. Since global problems call for global efforts, Lebanese immigrants understand their positions as cosmopolitan citizens who are interested in global social change. These changes, however, can only be realized in specific societies and at the local level. Lebanese immigrants' attachment to their homeland and host societies was expressed in their interest in challenging social norms and engaging in activities that aimed at social change in both contexts. Issues of sectarian divisions, class inequalities, gay visibility, corruption, and illiberal ideas (economic and political) were among the topics that Lebanese immigrants engaged with in their homeland. In their host societies, they took on similar concerns for more equality, desegregation and multiculturalism. Such interests were global in nature, and many Lebanese immigrants emphasized their experience with migration as informing their understanding of the world as an interconnected place. For example, Fareed explained that as he grew up in Lebanon during the civil war and then moved to the United States where he could not fully belong, he became more sensitive to global issues of justice and freedom:

> But I think what bothers me more [than the situation in Lebanon] is just seeing a lot of social injustice out there, and I guess growing up in Beirut and growing up in a very political environment, you tend to be a bit more aware of these things ... I know what exclusion and segregation feel like and would want others to escape such feelings if possible.

Like Fareed, many Lebanese immigrants stressed their desire to move beyond their personal experience to alleviate forms of injustice and inequality in the lives of others. Abeer engaged with issues relating to gay visibility and homophobia; Roy chose workers' rights and anti-war protests; Khaled focused on cross-cultural education and immigrants' rights; and Fareed took on gay politics and civil rights. These cosmopolitan immigrants sought identification and engagement with universal causes as they framed their personal experiences within global narratives. Emphasizing the globe as a single place, cosmopolitan Lebanese immigrants understood experiences of fragmentation, homelessness, injustice and displacement as universal conditions that only strengthened their ability to avail themselves to several identities, and social and political causes.

Conclusion

New analyses of globalization emphasize the ways immigration has helped erode traditional boundaries based on language, ethnicity, and nationality. In this regard, the experiences of Lebanese immigrants illustrate the way an immigrant group forges plural forms of cultural and social organizations that move beyond national and ethnic boundaries. Given the emphasis on not belonging fully to more than one society, the majority of Lebanese immigrants understand their diasporic position as interconnected with multiple social and cultural spheres. Mixing cultural repertoires in daily experience marked their difference from others in their homeland and host societies. Such a difference, however, is continuously transcended as the same immigrants sought commonalities with others and emphasized their belonging to various groups. As Lebanese immigrants discard ethnicity as the basis for their identification and social positions, they emphasize non-traditional attachments that speak to global identities and cosmopolitan forms of belonging.

Index